# Higher Psychology

Morag Williamson • Mike Cardwell • Cara Flanagan

Nelson Thornes

Published in 2007 by:
Nelson Thornes Ltd
Delta Place
27 Bath Road
CHELTENHAM
GL53 7TH
United Kingdom

08 09 10 11 / 10 9 8 7 6 5 4 3 2

A catalogue record for this book is available from the British Library

ISBN 978 0 7487 8418 9

Cover photograph/illustration by
Illustrations by Beehive Illustration and Harry Venning
Page make-up by GreenGate Publishing Services, Tonbridge, Kent

Printed and bound in Slovenia by Korotan-Ljubljana

# Contents

# Acknowledgements

Action Plus Sports Images (p.62); akg images Ltd. (p.150); © Alamy/Ace Stock Limited (p.185); Albert Bandura (p.174 [both]); Albert Ellis Institute (p.267); © AM Corporation/Alamy (p.21); Andrew Milligan/PA/Empics (p.152); © Archives of the History of American Psychology, The University of Akron (p.256); Bridgeman Art Library (p.284); Buccina/Photodisc 63 (NT) (p.227); CartoonStock www.cartoonstock.com (pp.59, 306); © Content Mine International/Alamy (p.239); Corbis/Bettman (pp.55, 156); © Corbis/Layne Kennedy (p.158); Corbis Royalty Free (p.136, 222); Corel 283 (NT) (p.46); Corel 449 (NT) (p.61); Corel 639 (NT) (p.129); © Ego Id Super-Ego 1996 oil and tempura mixed method on wood 14.17 x 18.11, Luigi La Speranza (p.248); Frank Trapper/Corbis (p.216); © Gary Crabbe/Alamy (p.48); Getty Images (p.104); © Getty/Serge Krouglikoff (p.279); Harlow Primate Laboratory, University of Wisconsin, Madison, USA (p.4); Image 100 GC (NT) (p.261); Ingram ILG V2 CD4 (NT) (p.283); Janis Christie/Photodisc 54 (NT) (p.278); John Birdsall Photo Library (p.10); © John Woodrow Kelley www.johnwoodrowkelley.com (p.167); Kobal Collection (pp.18, 180); © Martin Jenkinson/Alamy (p.208); Mary Evans Picture Library (pp.272, 273 [top]); Monica Lau/Photodisc 79 (NT) (p.23); © Morgan Motor Company (p143); Nick D. Kim (p.272 [bottom]); NON SEQUITUR, © 2001 Wiley Miller. Distributed by Universal Press Syndicate. Reprinted with permission. All rights reserved (p.204); Obedience © 1965 by Stanley Milgram, courtesy of Alexandra Milgram (pp.198, 201); © Peter Arnold, Inc./Alamy (p.5 [bottom]); Philip Zimbardo, Psychology Department, Stanford University (p.194); © POPPERFOTO/Alamy (pp.148, 196); © Report Digital / Nick Hall (p.162); Rex Features (p.171); © Richard Bowlby (p.5 [left]); Robertson Films (p.13); Ronald Grant Archive/Warner Brothers (p.183); Ryan McVay/Photodisc 73 (NT) (p.72); Science Photo Library/Will McIntyre (p.267); © Steve Allen/Alamy, (p.156); The Far Side ® by Gary Larsen © 1984 Far Works Inc, All Rights Reserved (pp.107, 192); © The Mary D. Ainsworth Child-Parent Attachment Clinic (p.5 [right]); Time Life Pictures/Getty Images (pp.7, 150, 230); © United States Holocaust Memorial Museum (p.206); © Visual&Written SL/Alamy (p.291); Wellcome Trust Medical Photographic Library (p.67); Wellcome Trust Medical Photographic Library/Anthes Sieveking (p.71).

*Dedicated to the memory of Alexander (Jock) Sinclair, a proud Scot and a remarkable human being (MCC)*

*and to Laurie and Greg, with love (MHW)*

*and to Lucky (CLF).*

# Introduction

You have set yourself an ambitious goal – to achieve, probably within less than a year, a Higher in a subject that may well be new to you: psychology. This book is intended to provide you with all the information and guidance that you need.

## Layout of this book

You will see that this book is organised so that it follows precisely the structure of the Scottish Qualifications Authority (SQA) Higher Psychology Course. Since the SQA **Unit** Specifications are divided into **Topics**, each chapter in this book covers one Topic. There is no need to worry if your teacher or lecturer (or flexible learning materials) covers the Topics in a different order from the order of the chapters, as each chapter is self-contained so that any chapter can be your starting point.

You should also be aware that the Topics are drawn from particular **Domains** of Psychology. The six Domains covered in the course are: Developmental Psychology, Cognitive Psychology, Physiological Psychology, Social Psychology, Psychology of Individual Differences, and Research Methods.

Each Topic is further divided into three or four **Aspects**, following the bullet points in the 'Content and context' sections in the Arrangements.

The layout of content is similar in all chapters. An introductory page gives you a breakdown of the specification content for the Topic into its Aspects and a 'Comment' box that provides a little more information on what each Aspect is about. Each chapter contains helpful features such as

- **Key Terms.** Important psychological terms are defined. Some exam questions specifically ask for such definitions.
- **Star Studies.** Questions (in NABs and the exam) often ask for a single research study that is relevant to one Aspect of a Topic, so in most chapters you will find at least one Star Study per Aspect. Star Studies are set out in a standard format showing aim, method and procedure, results, conclusions, and evaluation.
- **Explanations.** Concepts and processes are explained, often according to one or more theories or models.
- **Research Evidence.** Evidence is highlighted in relation to concepts and theories.
- **Evaluation.** Concepts, theories, research evidence, and applications are not just explained, but evaluated.
- **Assessment Issues.** These provide guidance on the NABs and the exam and flag up specific ways of gaining marks and common pitfalls to avoid in assessments.
- **Sample exam questions.** At the end of each chapter you will find a series of exam questions and students' answers, accompanied by comments from a Higher Psychology examiner on the strengths and weaknesses of the answers, plus the marks that would be awarded.

## Assessment of the course

Your work is assessed in two ways:

### Internal UNIT assessment (NABs)
The SQA requires that, in order to receive the Higher course award, you must pass all the NABs (with a 60% pass mark). The NAB questions are very similar to exam questions, but there are some important differences (see below).

### External COURSE assessment (Exam plus Research Investigation (RI) report)
The **Exam** is worth 100 marks, your mark comes from 5 x 20-mark questions: two mandatory questions chosen in section A (corresponding to Unit 1), one mandatory question in section B (corresponding to Unit 2), and two questions chosen from section C (corresponding to Unit 3).

The **RI** is worth 25 marks (the raw mark of 50 is divided by 2).

The total is 125 marks.

Successful Higher candidates receive certification of (1) the three **UNIT assessments** and (2) the **COURSE** assessment. The Higher award and grade are based only on the COURSE assessment (i.e. exam + RI).

The table below shows, at a glance, how NABs and exam papers are constructed in relation to the three Units.

| Domains | Internal UNIT assessment (NABs) | External COURSE assessment (one 2½ hour exam) |
|---|---|---|
| **Unit 1  Understanding the Individual** | | |
| Cognitive, Developmental, Physiological | One 1-hour NAB test, comprising two mandatory 20-mark questions on two of the three Topics (Memory, Early Socialisation, Stress)*. Worth 100% of marks for the UNIT assessment. | **Section A** of exam: Two mandatory 20-mark questions on two of the three Topics (Memory, Early Socialisation, Stress)*. Worth 40% of the EXAM marks (32% of marks for the COURSE assessment). |
| **Unit 2  Investigating Behaviour** | | |
| Methods, issues and data analysis in research | One 30-minute NAB test, comprising one 20-mark question. Worth 50% of marks for the UNIT assessment. | **Section B** of exam: One 20-mark question. Worth 20% of the EXAM marks (16% of marks for the COURSE assessment). |
| Research skills | Research project plan and log Worth 50% of mark for the UNIT assessment. | **Research Investigation report** (RI) ** Worth 20% of marks for the COURSE assessment. |
| **Unit 3  The Individual in the Social Context** | | |
| Social Psychology, Individual Differences | One 1-hour NAB test: students choose two 20-mark questions – one from the four Social Psychology Topics, and one from the three Individual Differences Topics. *** Worth 100% of mark for the UNIT assessment. | **Section C** of exam: Two 20-mark questions – one chosen from the four Social Psychology Topics and one from the three Individual Differences Topics. *** Worth 40% of the EXAM marks (32% of marks for the COURSE assessment). |

* The two Topics that appear, in both NABs and exam, are not known in advance; therefore students must study all three Topics.
** If you are doing this unit, but not the whole course, you need to complete the Research project plan and log (practical portfolio) but do not have to submit a Research Investigation report (RI).
*** Although there are seven questions, the two questions you choose will be from the three specific Topics you will have actually studied.

## Construction of exam questions

Exam questions are set from the specification. If you look closely at the words that are used in the specification content for each Topic (the middle column of the table on the opening page of each chapter) and then look at the questions in past exam papers, you'll see that the wording of questions is based on the words used in the specification content. For example, the specification content for the Topic 'Memory' includes:

'Theories of forgetting, including trace decay, displacement, interference, cue-dependent forgetting, repression and motivated forgetting' (see p. 29).
The 2006 exam paper asked: 'Discuss **two** theories of forgetting, referring to research evidence in your answer.'

The question matches the specification. Furthermore, it should be clear that a suitable answer would focus on any of the two theories listed in the specification: it wouldn't be sensible to write about models of memory, or brain damage, or mnemonics, when the question specifies 'theories of forgetting'. If you familiarise yourself carefully with the specification content for every Topic, then you will never get a nasty surprise in the NABs and exam questions, and you will be clear about what the exam questions refer to.

In this book we have tried to assist you by mapping the book contents exactly onto the specification. Each chapter is broken down into Aspects and sections following the specification – compare the chapter contents (left-hand column of the table on the opening page of each chapter) with the specification content (middle column) – they match! Furthermore, within each section we have presented material which exactly matches the exam requirements for that specification area.

## Types of questions
Another way of giving yourself a head start in assessment is to make sure that you know the types of questions on NABs and exam question papers. When you take a close look at past exam papers and marking information, you'll see that:

(a)  There are questions on different types of content. Some questions ask you for a **definition** or short description of a concept or term, others ask for more detailed **explanations** of psychological concepts, processes or theories. Sometimes, a question will ask you to describe or discuss a **single research study** (or an element of it), and some questions will focus on an **applied aspect** of the Topic (e.g. stress-reduction strategies). In research methods questions (second Unit), a research **scenario** is provided, which you must interpret in order to answer the questions. Plenty of examples of these various question types are given in the **Assessment Issues** boxes.

(b)  All questions are worth **20 marks** in the exam and the NABs. There are broadly three types of exam questions used in sections A and C: Single essay question, two-part essay question, and structured question containing 3–5 parts. In section B (Research methods) there is one structured question of up to 8 parts. Similar question types appear in the NABs, except that single essay questions for Units 1 and 3 are worth 15 marks, not 20, and the remaining 5 marks can be made up of 1–3 short questions.

## How answers are marked
Marks are divided into **knowledge and understanding (*ku*)** and **analysis and evaluation (*ae*)**. These are two of the three Course Assessment Objectives of Higher Psychology (the third one is practical research skills examined in Unit 2 and the RI).

- *ku* skills are demonstrating your knowledge and providing evidence of your understanding of that knowledge.

- *ae* skills include explaining components of a behaviour, interpreting research findings in relation to relevant theory, comparing evidence from different cultural contexts, integrating knowledge from different psychological areas, identifying common underlying themes, weighing up strengths and weaknesses, and comparing and contrasting theories.

Throughout this book, in the sections on **Assessment Issues**, we have given tips on effective *ku* and *ae*.

In the NABs, *ku* is represented by 'Outcome 1' and *ae* by 'Outcome 2'. The main difference between NABs and exam questions lies in the *weightings* of *ku* and *ae*. In the NABs *ku* (Outcome 1) accounts for 75–80% of marks and *ae* (Outcome 2) accounts for 20–25%. In the exam, *ku* accounts for 60% and *ae* for 40%. The **weightings** of these marks are shown for every question, and they are also reflected in the **command** words of each question.

*Command words commonly used in NABs and exam questions\**
Name, State, Identify, Define /give a definition of …, Describe, What is …?, What is meant by …?, Explain, How …?, Give an example of …, Suggest    **All demand *ku* skills**

Evaluate, Assess, State a strength/weakness of …, Give/explain criticism(s) of …, Analyse    **All demand *ae* skills**

Consider, Discuss, Compare and contrast    **All demand both *ku* and *ae* skills**

\*This is not a definitive list of all possible command words.

The greater demand for *ae* skills in the exam means that, by the end of the course, you are expected to be able to demonstrate more sophisticated skills than at the end of each Unit. This is what is meant by **added value**: the value of the Higher exam is greater than the sum of its parts (the three Units). The 'added value' of the course assessment is seen mainly in the requirement for more advanced *ae* skills in the exam, the ability to respond to questions from across the whole course at a single sitting, to show integration of that knowledge across different parts of the course, and also in the application of research skills in the RI. This last element accounts for the third Course Assessment Objective, 'practical research skills'.

## SQA Website

There are numerous useful documents available from the SQA Psychology homepage (go to www.sqa.org.uk, then select your subject 'Psychology'), including:

Morag

Mike

Cara

- **Arrangements Documents.** Contains the National Course and National Unit Specifications, and is the key document for Higher Psychology, containing all the essential information on Aims, Course content, Course Assessment Objectives, Unit information, etc.

- **Marking Instructions** and questions for the most recent exam paper, comprising both 'specific content requirements' and 'generic requirements'.

- **Research investigation.** Includes the **RI Brief**, and **RI Guidelines**. The *RI Brief* is a set of research project outlines from which your teacher/lecturer will choose the particular RI research project you will carry out. The set of projects changes from year to year. The *RI Guidelines* is a comprehensive guide to tackling the RI. It contains a summary of important ethical guidelines.

- **Specimen Question Papers** (showing what the real exam looks like) and accompanying **Marking Instructions** (MI). You can also find here the **Course Assessment Specification** (CAS) which provides exact details of the structure of the exam paper, the number of questions and their mark value, the types of questions in the different sections, etc. It also gives the breakdown of marks for the RI.

Important note: the **Marking Instructions** are divided into **Generic Requirements** (describing the levels of *skills* expected in exam answers in order to achieve the various Higher grades) and **Specific Content Requirements** (indicating *what* is expected in exam answers). The specific content requirements, perhaps surprisingly, are not particularly useful for students as they are designed for use by markers and merely provide an outline summary of possible content. In contrast, the generic requirements are extremely useful for students, both as a guide for how to answer questions and as a yardstick to judge your own efforts when you practise answering exam questions.

## Studying

There is no doubt that the Higher Psychology course contains a large amount of content to be learned; therefore you need to be prepared to commit substantial study time every week. If you are following a school/college course, you are likely to spend about 9–11 weeks on each Unit. For the first and third Units you will study three Topics each, and will therefore spend about three weeks on each Topic. The second Unit is divided into Research Methods and Research Skills, each requiring four or five weeks of study. As a rough guide, we suggest that you plan your time so as to devote approximately five to eight hours' reading/learning to each chapter, although this will vary greatly depending on individual work rate.

Much of this introduction has focused on assessment because we're sure that you want to do really well and achieve a good Higher grade in Psychology. Don't forget to apply psychology to your *learning* of psychology: for example, use *memory techniques* in revision. Try some of the *stress-reduction strategies* to prevent exam stress interfering with your revision and performance. Adopt the hints and strategies that we suggest, and enjoy your learning – we hope you'll find this subject as fascinating as we do!

Morag Williamson, Mike Cardwell and Cara Flanagan

# 1 Domain: DEVELOPMENTAL PSYCHOLOGY
# Topic: Early socialisation

Developmental psychology is concerned with how children and adults change as they get older; it looks at various influences on development, such as the influences of parents, peers and other people around you. These are all environmental influences (called 'nurture'). Changes also happen as a consequence of nature. 'Nature' refers to biological factors such as genes, physiological functions and maturation.

Socialisation involves learning about one's culture in order to be able to interact with other people. An individual learns the customs, norms and behaviours that are characteristic of their culture. Early socialisation refers to the first few years of a child's life during which attachments to parents and significant others develop.

| Chapter contents | Unit content for the topic 'Early Socialisation' | Comment |
|---|---|---|
| **Aspect 1: Attachment** | | |
| The nature of attachment<br>        page 2<br>The Bowlby–Ainsworth paradigm<br>        page 5<br>Types and stages of attachment<br>        page 7<br>Different kinds of attachment<br>        page 10 | The nature of attachment and its role in early socialization, including:<br>● behaviourist and psychoanalytic explanations of attachment<br>● the Bowlby–Ainsworth paradigm<br>● stages and types of attachment<br>● multiple attachments<br>● father attachment<br>● cultural differences in attachment | *You should be able to define what psychologists mean by **attachment** and describe its importance for a young child, in the context of their earliest experiences of getting along with others. There are various explanations of how attachment develops: **behaviourist and psychoanalytic** explanations are sometimes called 'cupboard love' theories; but the main emphasis of this Aspect is on the work of **Bowlby** and **Ainsworth**. **Stages of attachment** have been proposed, by, amongst others, Ainsworth, who also established a classification of types of attachment (A, B, C), based on the 'Strange Situation' study. You will study different kinds of attachment: **multiple attachment** occurs where an infant is attached to more than one person; babies are often attached to their father; in different **cultures** children show different patterns of attachment behaviour.* |
| **Aspect 2: Deprivation** | | |
| Separation and deprivation<br>        page 12<br>Privation<br>        page 15<br>Long-term implications of privation<br>        page 17 | The nature of separation, deprivation and privation, including:<br>● evidence from studies with animals and humans, including institutionalised children and case studies of severe deprivation/neglect<br>● long-term implications for adjustment and mental health | *Unfortunately, the attachment process is sometimes disrupted for various reasons: in this Topic Aspect you will study research on **separation**, **deprivation** and **privation**; you will need to be able to distinguish between these three concepts. Psychologists are particularly concerned about whether these early experiences are harmful to the developing child, and you should be familiar with various types of research which has been conducted for this purpose: **animal studies** and **human studies**, including studies of children who have spent time in an orphanage or children's home (examples of **institutional** care) and the rare cases of **severe deprivation**, **privation** or isolation. You will study evidence of long-term ill-effects of early experience.* |
| **Aspect 3: Parenting** | | |
| Child-rearing styles<br>        page 20<br>The development of parenting skills<br>        page 23 | Child-rearing styles and their impact on development, including:<br>● cultural differences<br>● development of parenting skills in caregivers | *Parents vary greatly in the ways they treat their children, so, in this Aspect, you will study psychologists' attempts to classify **child-rearing (parental) behaviours** and research aimed at discovering links between the child-rearing style experienced by the child and their later development. Researchers have also compared child-rearing styles in different cultures, often by means of meta-analysis. You should be able to describe development of **parenting skills** in caregivers, on the basis of theoretical explanations and evidence from research with families.* |

# Aspect 1: Attachment

## The nature of attachment
### What is attachment?

'An affectional tie that one person or animal forms between himself and another specific one – a tie that binds them together in space and endures over time. The behavioural hallmark of attachment is seeking to gain and to maintain a certain degree of proximity to the object of attachment. Attachment behaviours aim to maintain proximity or contact e.g. following, clinging and signalling behaviours such as smiling, crying and calling.' (Ainsworth and Bell, 1970, p. 50)

This definition, written by the famous **attachment** researcher Mary Ainsworth, captures the essence of what attachment is really all about. Ainsworth describes attachment as an *'affectional'* tie that a person or animal forms between himself and another. What is an *'affectional'* tie? It is a tie that is based on emotions or *feelings* rather than any other need (such as bodily needs). The way that a mother and young child cling to each other tells us that this is a bond that must be based on some pretty strong emotions. This tie *'binds them together in space and endures over time'*. As we shall see, young children seek the company of their mother (or caregiver) and are disturbed when they are separated from them, even for short periods of time. This is not a one-way process, as any parent of a newborn baby will tell you!

> ## KEY TERMS
>
> **Attachment:** An emotional bond between two people. It is a two-way process that endures over time. It leads to certain behaviours such as clinging and proximity-seeking, and serves the function of protecting an infant.

## star**STUDY**
## Investigating attachment: Infants in Glasgow
### (SCHAFFER AND EMERSON, 1964)

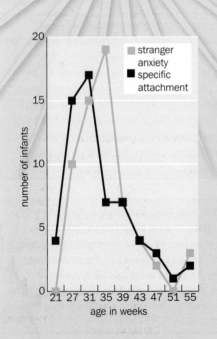

### Aims
To obtain a record of infant attachment behaviour.

### Method and procedure
Sixty infants from mainly working-class homes in Glasgow were observed every 4 weeks until they were 1 year old and then again at 18 months. At the start of the investigation the infants ranged from 5 to 23 weeks of age. Attachment was measured in terms of **separation protest** in seven everyday situations (e.g. infant was left alone in a room, or left in their cot at night). At every visit, the mothers reported the infants' typical responses to each of these situations. Mothers were also asked to whom these protests were directed. Schaffer and Emerson measured **stranger anxiety** by approaching the infant and noting at what point the infant started to whimper.

### Results
Most infants first showed signs of separation protest and stranger anxiety at about seven months, at about the same time as they showed specific attachments to one caregiver (see graph). Within 1 month of first becoming attached 29% of the infants had multiple attachments to the other parent, to grandparents, siblings, other relatives, friends and/or neighbours. Within 6 months this had risen to 78%.

Despite forming multiple attachments, most infants maintained one *principal* object of attachment. This was most often the infant's mother, although it was not infrequently the infant's father. The **primary attachment figure** was not always the person who fed or bathed the infant (the **primary caregiver**). In fact, Schaffer and Emerson reported that there was little relationship between time spent together and attachment.

Responsiveness appeared to be the key to attachment. Schaffer and Emerson observed that intensely attached infants had mothers who responded quickly to their demands and who offered the child the most interaction. Infants who were weakly attached had mothers who failed to interact.

### Conclusion
The findings suggest that attachment is *not* related to filling physiological needs. Instead, attachment could be best understood in terms of the various relationships that an infant forms with those who stimulate and respond to him/her.

## Evaluation

*Unreliable data*

The data collected may be unreliable because some of it was based on mothers' reports of their infants. Some mothers might have been less sensitive to their infants' protests when left alone.

*Biased sample*

The sample was biased (working class, from the 1960s). The conclusions may not apply to other families.

---

## explanation

*Behaviourists assume that all behaviour is learned. You are born like a blank slate (so they say) and are conditioned to learn new responses.*

### Behaviourist approach – learning theory

Behaviourists suggest that attachment is learned either through classical or operant conditioning.

**Classical conditioning** can explain attachment. Food (an unconditioned stimulus, UCS) produces a sense of pleasure (an unconditioned response, UCR). The person who feeds the infant becomes *associated* with the food. The 'feeder' eventually produces the conditioned response (pleasure) and thus becomes the conditioned stimulus (CS). This association between an individual and a sense of pleasure is the attachment bond.

Dollard and Miller (1950) offered a more complex explanation, based on **operant conditioning**. They suggested that a hungry infant feels uncomfortable and this creates a drive to reduce the discomfort. When the infant is fed, the drive is reduced and this produces a sense of pleasure (a reward). This is an example of **negative reinforcement**. Food becomes a *primary reinforcer* because it 'stamps in' (*reinforces*) the behaviour in order to avoid discomfort. The person who supplies the food is associated with avoiding discomfort and becomes a *secondary reinforcer*, and a source of reward in their own right. This rewardingness is attachment.

## evaluation

*Strength*

Learning theory can explain attachment. Infants do learn through association and reinforcement. However, food may not be the main reinforcer. Attention and responsiveness from a caregiver are also rewarding.

*Limitation*

Behaviourist theory is often criticised for oversimplifying human behaviour because it ignores emotional and cognitive (thinking) aspects of behaviour.

---

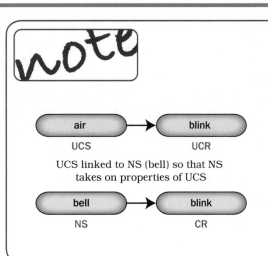

note

air (UCS) → blink (UCR)

UCS linked to NS (bell) so that NS takes on properties of UCS

bell (NS) → blink (CR)

### Classical conditioning

We are born with certain unconditioned reflexes such as blinking when a puff of air is blown at the eye. The air is an unconditioned stimulus (UCS) and the blink is an unconditioned response (UCR). If you ring a bell (a neutral stimulus, NS) at the same time as the puff of air is blown, the two become associated so that the NS takes on the properties of the UCS and will produce the eye blink even without the puff of air. The NS has now become a conditioned stimulus (CS) and the UCR is now called a conditioned response (CR) to the bell.

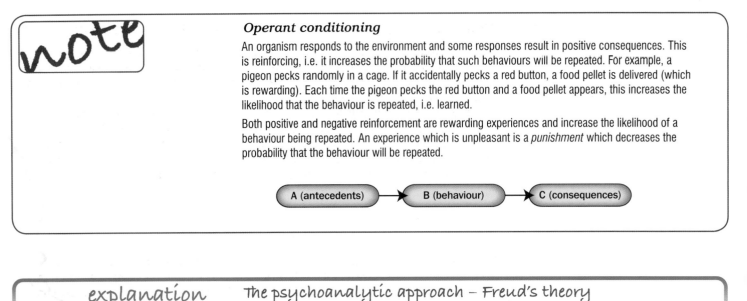

**note**

*Operant conditioning*

An organism responds to the environment and some responses result in positive consequences. This is reinforcing, i.e. it increases the probability that such behaviours will be repeated. For example, a pigeon pecks randomly in a cage. If it accidentally pecks a red button, a food pellet is delivered (which is rewarding). Each time the pigeon pecks the red button and a food pellet appears, this increases the likelihood that the behaviour is repeated, i.e. learned.

Both positive and negative reinforcement are rewarding experiences and increase the likelihood of a behaviour being repeated. An experience which is unpleasant is a *punishment* which decreases the probability that the behaviour will be repeated.

A (antecedents) → B (behaviour) → C (consequences)

## explanation

*The psychoanalytic approach emphasises the dynamics of behaviour, i.e. what drives us to behave in particular ways – biological factors and early experiences combine to produce the adult personality.*

## The psychoanalytic approach – Freud's theory

Sigmund Freud developed a theory of personality – an explanation of how each individual's personality develops. This theory can be used to explain many aspects of behaviour including attachment. He suggested that, at different stages of development, certain body parts are especially sensitive to physical stimulation and the child's libido (psychic energy) is attached to these parts. From 0–18 months, the body part is the mouth (the *oral stage* of development).

Freud also suggested that behaviour is motivated by different forces at different ages. He claimed that infants are born with an innate drive to seek pleasure; called the *pleasure principle*. He suggested that one 'structure of the personality' (the **id**) was motivated by this principle. The id is the primitive, instinctive part of our personality that demands immediate satisfaction. In infancy, the id demands oral satisfaction. The person providing this satisfaction becomes the love object, and an attachment is formed.

## evaluation

*Strength*
This theory explains both *why* infants become attached (because of the pleasure principle) and *who* they become attached to (the person who feeds them).

*Limitation*
Freud's theory is difficult to *falsify* – to prove that it is wrong.

You can read more about Freud's theory on pages 247–248.

## Cupboard love theories

Orphan monkeys spent most time with the 'cloth-covered mother', visiting the 'mother' with the feeding bottle for food. This suggests that attachment is related to comfort and not food.

Both explanations have been called *cupboard love* theories of attachment because they suggest that the infant becomes attached because they are fed and they become attached to the person who feeds them.

The study by Schaffer and Emerson (on page 2) challenges the 'cupboard love' view, as does a classic study by Harlow (1959). Harlow's study concerned rhesus monkeys that were raised on their own by two 'wire mothers'. One wire mother had a feeding bottle attached and the other was wrapped in soft cloth but offered no food. According to 'cupboard love' theories, the young monkeys should have become attached to the 'mother' associated with food and offering drive reduction. In fact, the monkeys spent most time with the cloth-covered mother and would cling to it especially when they were frightened (a proximity-seeking behaviour which is characteristic of attachment).

These studies suggest that 'cupboard love' is not likely to be the explanation for attachment, although we must remember that this research concerned monkeys and it may not be wholly appropriate to generalise the findings to human behaviour.

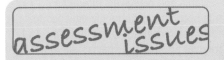

**What is meant by 'attachment', in early socialisation?** *(ku 2 ae 0)*

The words 'What is meant by …?' tell you that you should provide a definition or brief description of the concept of attachment. This kind of question would usually be worth no more than two marks, so the amount you write should be in line with that number of marks; in other words, don't write a long, detailed essay!

In both NABs and the exam you have, on average, 30 minutes per 20-mark question, so for a definition-style question like this one you would aim to spend around 3 minutes. This is rather crude arithmetic and we are not suggesting that you take a stopwatch into the exam! However, it may help to time yourself when practising with old exam questions for homework – you know from your own experience of past exams if you habitually tend to write too much or too little!

## The Bowlby–Ainsworth paradigm

John Bowlby worked as a psychiatrist in London, treating emotionally disturbed children. This work led him to produce theories about attachment and deprivation (see page 14). Bowlby's thinking was influenced by many psychologists including Mary Ainsworth, an American who worked with Bowlby as a research assistant for a short time. After that Ainsworth spent time in Uganda and then in America (Baltimore) observing mother–infant interactions. These studies provided Bowlby with important empirical evidence. Ainsworth recognised that, in order to study attachment systematically, a systematic method was needed – so she developed the Strange Situation which is described on page 8.

Although Bowlby and Ainsworth came from very different backgrounds, one a child psychiatrist and the other an empirical researcher, both agreed on the importance of attachment as a *secure base* from which an infant can explore the world. However, while Bowlby saw attachment as *adaptive* and emphasised its universality, Ainsworth focused on individual differences in attachment, believing that these had their origins in different types of *maternal sensitivity*.

*The evolutionary approach seeks to explain all behaviour in terms of* adaptiveness – *certain genetic characteristics enhance an individual's reproductive success and are thus 'adaptive'. Such inherited and adaptive characteristics are in turn passed on to offspring.*

John Bowlby (1907–1990)

Mary Ainsworth (1913–1999)

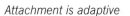

*explanation*

### The evolutionary approach – Bowlby's theory

*Attachment is adaptive*
Bowlby (1969) proposed that infants become attached to a caregiver because attachment is *adaptive*. Infants who do not become attached are less likely to survive and reproduce. Thus the attachment 'gene' is perpetuated and infants are born with an innate drive to become attached. There are two reasons why attachment is good for survival and reproduction:

The cute face of a baby acts as a social releaser – it elicits caregiving. It is no accident that all young animals have 'cute' faces: big eyes, small nose and chin, high forehead.

- It means the infant is more likely to be well cared for when young and defenceless.
- Attachments form the basis for later social relationships. They provide a template for how to have relationships with other people and this promotes survival and reproduction.

*Infants elicit caregiving*
What specific behaviours promote attachment in infants? Infants are born with **social releasers**. The obvious example of a social releaser is when a baby smiles or when it cries. Such behaviours *elicit caregiving* from others nearby. If a baby didn't have these innate social releasers, potential caregivers would happily go about their business, ignoring the baby.

*Adults respond to social releasers*
But social releasers alone don't explain why the infant becomes attached to certain people rather than others. As we have seen, such attachments don't simply form because individuals

**Social releasers:** Characteristics or social behaviours which elicit a caregiving reaction.

**Monotropy:** The innate tendency for a child to become attached especially to one figure. This attachment is qualitatively different to other attachments and is important in emotional development.

**Internal working model:** A mental model (*schema*) of the world which enables individuals to predict and control their environment; in particular a model of relationships.

*evaluation*

**Continuity hypothesis:** The view that there is a link between early attachment experiences and later social and emotional behaviour; for example individuals who were securely attached as infants are more likely to go on to be popular in school and more likely to be securely attached to their partners as adults.

**Secure attachment:** This is a strong and contented attachment of an infant to its caregiver, which develops as a result of sensitive responding by the caregiver to the infant's needs. Secure attachment is related to healthy cognitive and emotional development.

**Temperament hypothesis:** The view that a child's temperament is responsible for the quality of attachment between the child and their caregiver.

**Critical period:** A biologically determined period of time during which an animal is *exclusively* receptive to certain experiences.

**Sensitive period:** A biologically determined period of time during which an animal is *most* likely to acquire certain behaviours; such behaviours may be acquired at any time but less easily.

spend a lot of time together. Attachments form because infants and caregivers *interact*. Infants form one special relationship (**monotropy**). Infants become most strongly attached to the person who interacts best – the person who responds *most sensitively* to the infant's social releasers. This person becomes the infant's **primary caregiver** and plays a special role in the infant's emotional development. This concept is called monotropy – focused on one person.

*Internal working model*
The infant's relationship with their primary caregiver has a special significance. It is important for emotional and social development because it has emotional intensity. Bowlby suggested that the infant develops an **internal working model** of relationships based on this special emotional relationship with their primary caregiver. The internal working model is like a **schema**. It is a cluster of concepts about relationships – expectations about whether relationships involve consistent or inconsistent love, whether others make you feel good or anxious, and so on. The primary caregiver's behaviour is a model for what the infant will expect from others. The infant *internalises* this model.

*Strengths*
There is empirical support for many aspects of Bowlby's theory (see page 7). Further support comes from studies related to the **continuity hypothesis** – the idea that emotionally secure infants go on to be emotionally secure, trusting and socially confident adults. Bowlby's theory would predict such continuity.

One study that supported this hypothesis was conducted by Hazan and Shaver (1987). They printed a 'Love Quiz' in a newspaper, seeking to find out about adults' early attachment experiences and about their later attitudes and experiences in love. They found a link between Ainsworth's attachment types (described on page 7) and adult attitudes/experiences. **Secure attachment** types had happy, lasting and trusting love relationships. **Insecure-ambivalent** types worried that their partners didn't really love them. **Insecure-avoidant** lovers typically feared intimacy. This appears to support Bowlby's theory although the data are correlational which means we can't be certain that early attachment experiences caused later attachment types.

The Minnesota longitudinal study (Sroufe *et al.*, 1999) assessed attachment in a group of infants and re-assessed the same participants as they went through childhood. The study found that individuals who had been assessed as securely attached were later the highest rated for social competence, were less isolated and more popular. This again demonstrates continuity.

*Limitation*
However, such continuity in development can be explained without using Bowlby's theory. An innately trusting and friendly personality could be the prime factor in secure attachments and the prime factor in forming close adult relationships. This is called the **temperament hypothesis** (Kagan, 1984) – certain personality or temperamental characteristics of the infant shape a mother's responsiveness rather than vice versa.

Evidence that the infant's temperament may be important was reported by Belsky and Rovine (1987). Some newborns show signs of behavioural instability (e.g. tremors or shaking); they are 'difficult' babies. Such children are less likely to become securely attached to their mother than are newborns who are not 'difficult'.

## Research related to Bowlby's theory

### Adaptiveness: imprinting
Newborn animals, such as geese, imprint on their parents. They appear to form an indelible picture of their parent(s) within hours of birth and this helps them stick closely to this important source of protection and food. A young animal who wanders away from its parent would have to find its own food and is likely to be eaten rather quickly.

Since imprinting is innate there is likely to be a limited window of development – a **critical** or **sensitive period**. Bowlby applied the concept of a sensitive period to attachment. He suggested that infants are most sensitive to becoming attached during the middle of the first year (around six months); as the months pass, difficulties in forming attachments increase if there has been no available attachment figure.

## Monotropy

Schaffer and Emerson (see page 2) found that most infants were specially attached to one primary caregiver but many children had two or more equivalent attachments. Tronick *et al.*'s study of the Efe from Zaire (see page 11) found that infants aged six months had one primary attachment despite having many caregivers. Such research suggests some kind of hierarchy for attachments with the primary caregiver at the top. Lamb (1981), on the other hand, believes that different attachments simply serve different purposes rather than there being a hierarchy.

Nobel-winning ethologist Konrad Lorenz demonstrated imprinting in geese. When these goslings hatched Lorenz was the first thing they saw, and they then followed him everywhere.

## Sensitivity

Harlow's monkeys (see page 4) preferred the cloth mother but had no responsive care. The monkeys all became quite maladjusted in adulthood – they had difficulties in reproductive relationships and were poor parents. This underlines the importance of *interaction* in attachment.

The importance of sensitivity was expressed by Ainsworth in the **caregiver sensitivity hypothesis**. In her study of mothers and infants in Uganda, Ainsworth (1967) rated some mothers as more 'sensitive' because they provided spontaneous and plentiful details about their infants; she noted that these mothers tended to have 'securely attached' infants who cried little and seemed content to explore in the presence of mother. Ainsworth found further confirmation for the sensitivity hypothesis in her Strange Situation study, described on page 8.

### assessment issues

#### Common themes: nature and nurture

In many areas of study, including early **socialisation**, psychologists have proposed explanations which emphasise either '**nature**' or '**nurture**': the former refers to the ways in which our behaviour is influenced by our genes and biology; the latter concerns the ways that we are influenced by our environment, often focusing on our experiences with other people (e.g. parents, friends, media).

In his evolutionary approach to early socialisation, Bowlby emphasised the adaptiveness of the infant's innate behaviours in promoting attachment – the influence of nature. On the other hand, as we shall soon see, Ainsworth claimed attachment was influenced by the caregiver's behaviour (nurture). Most psychologists agree that both nature and nurture interact in influencing any particular behaviour, and that you can't have one without the other.

Don't forget that, in assessments, you can sometimes gain *ae* marks for 'analysis', when you interpret information according to the 'nature–nurture' dimension, a common theme in psychology.

## Types and stages of attachment
### How does attachment develop?

We have already referred to secure and **insecure attachment**. These are particular types or *styles* of attachment that may be established between any two individuals (usually the mother and infant). Ainsworth developed a technique called the Strange Situation to 'measure' these styles of attachment which is described in the Star Study below.

star**STUDY**

# Investigating attachment: The Strange Situation

(AINSWORTH *ET AL.*, 1978)

## Aims

In order to study the nature of attachment, Ainsworth *et al.* devised a method of controlled observation called the Strange Situation. The intention was to create conditions of mild stress to observe **separation anxiety** and **stranger anxiety** – both behaviours that are related to attachment. The intention was also to place an infant in a novel situation to observe willingness to explore in order to test the *secure base* concept.

## Method and procedure

In total, 106 middle-class infants were observed in the Strange Situation. The experimental room is a *novel environment*, a 9 x 9 foot square marked off into 16 squares to help record the infant's movements. The procedure consisted of eight episodes, each designed to highlight certain behaviours as shown in the table below.

Episodes of the Strange Situation test

|   | Episodes (about 3 minutes duration) | Behaviour assessed |
|---|---|---|
| 1 | Parent and infant play. | |
| 2 | Parent sits while infant plays | Use of parent as secure base |
| 3 | Stranger (experimenter) enters and talks to parent | Stranger anxiety |
| 4 | Parent leaves; infant plays; stranger offers comfort if needed | Separation anxiety |
| 5 | Parent returns, greets infant, offers comfort if needed; stranger leaves | Reunion behaviour |
| 6 | Parent leaves; infant alone | Separation anxiety |
| 7 | Stranger enters and offers comfort | Stranger anxiety |
| 8 | Parent returns, greets infant, offers comfort | Reunion behaviour |

Data were collected by a group of observers who recorded what the infant was doing every 15 seconds. The observer noted down which of the following behaviours was being displayed: (1) proximity and contact-seeking behaviours, (2) contact-maintaining behaviours, (3) proximity and interaction-avoiding behaviours, (4) contact and interaction-resisting behaviours, and (5) search behaviours. The behaviour was also scored for intensity on a scale of 1 to 7.

## Results

In some ways infant behaviours were *similar*. For example, exploratory behaviours declined in all infants from episode 2 onwards, whereas the amount of crying increased. Proximity-seeking and contact-maintaining behaviours intensified in all infants during separation and when the stranger appeared.

In terms of *differences*, there were three main clusters of behaviour (as shown in the table below), representing three attachment types.

Classification of behaviour in the Strange Situation

|  | Secure attachment (Type B) | Insecure attachment | |
|---|---|---|---|
|  |  | Avoidant (Type A) | Resistant (Type C) |
| Use of parent as safe base/ willingness to explore | High | High | Low |
| Stranger anxiety | High | Low | High |
| Separation anxiety | Some, easy to soothe | Indifferent | Distressed |
| Behaviour at reunion with caregiver | Enthusiastic | Avoid contact | Seeks and rejects |
| Caregiver's behaviour | Sensitive | May ignore infant | Ambivalent |
| Percentage of infants in this category | 66% | 22% | 12% |

## Conclusion

The Strange Situation highlights important behaviours related to attachment: willingness to explore, stranger and separation anxiety, and behaviour at reunion. Infants vary in the way they behave, showing individual differences which may be related to the behaviour of their caregiver. This suggests that an innate tendency (attachment) is affected by life experiences (caregiver's behaviours).

## Evaluation

### Has proved to be very useful

The Strange Situation procedure has been used widely in attachment research with infants and has been adapted for studies of children and even adults and puppies! Many of the studies reported in this chapter have used the Strange Situation procedure. This is a strength of both the technique and the classification system pioneered in this study.

### Is the classification valid?

**Validity** concerns the extent to which something is true. What does the Strange Situation actually measure? Does it measure something about the infant (that this child is a secure or insecure type) or does it measure the strength of one particular relationship? If infants are tested in the Strange Situation with other caregivers, they respond differently. For example, Main and Weston (1981) found that children behaved differently depending on which parent they were with, which suggests that it is the relationship which determines the response in the Strange Situation rather than the child's attachment type.

On the other hand, if you agree with the concept of monotropy, then the fact that an infant responds differently with someone other than their primary caregiver tells us something about that relationship but the attachment *type* is related to the one special relationship.

## The development of attachments

Research shows that infants pass through typical phases as they develop their relationships with others:

1. *Pre-attachment* (approximately 0–2 months) – newborn infants show *indiscriminate social responsiveness*. They are equally happy being picked up and comforted by familiar or unfamiliar people.
2. *Attachment-in-the-making* (approximately 2–7 months) – increasing ability to *recognise familiar people* and be comforted by them.
3. *Specific attachments* (from approximately 7 months) – appearance of separation protest and stranger anxiety.
4. *Multiple attachments* (from approximately 8 months) – initially, infants show attachments to one primary caregiver (as demonstrated by separation protest), but very soon most infants also show attachments to other people.
5. *Reciprocal relationships* (from about 8–24 months) – the infant learns to predict and consciously influence the responses of others. This is the beginning of real relationships.

> *Attachments are not formed by a congenital glue held in limited supply: They are welded in the heat of interactions.*
>
> *(Maurer and Maurer, 1989)*

*One weakness in any stage account of development is that it suggests a fixed pattern of development. It is the* sequence *that is important; the actual ages are approximate.*

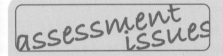
*assessment issues*

**Describe *one* research study that has investigated the attachment process in human babies. (*ku 6 ae 0*)**

This is an example of a question (NAB or exam) on a single research study. Look out for the 'command' word(s): in this case, you are asked to 'describe'. This means that you should give a number of elements: the name(s) of the researcher(s) and date, the aim and what was being studied, method, procedure and results. In other words: Who? When? What was done? With what results? If the question asked you to 'discuss', or 'describe and evaluate', you should include conclusions and evaluate the study: What did the results mean? Did they support or challenge a concept/theory? Was the methodology sound, in terms of sampling, control, validity? Was the research ethical?

In the sample question above, Ainsworth *et al.* (1978) would be a good choice. However, the procedure in this study is quite complex, and there is a risk that you will spend too much time describing this and too little time on the other elements of the study. You must provide details of *all* key elements of the study, which means that you need to summarise the procedure concisely.

Schaffer and Emerson (1964) found that 29% of infants found attachments to grandparents, siblings, other relatives, friends and/or neighbours in addition to their primary attachments.

> *[Fathers are] a biological necessity, but a social accident.*
>
> (Mead, 1949)

# Different kinds of attachment

Bowlby recognised the importance of multiple attachments, but considered that there was one special relationship – the mother–infant relationship. What then is the role of other attachment figures, especially a child's father? We will now look at fathers as attachment figures as well as the question of multiple attachments versus monotropy.

## Multiple attachments

Infants and children do form multiple attachments. The question is about the equivalence of these relationships. Schaffer and Emerson's evidence, on page 2, suggested that, despite forming multiple attachments, infants maintain one primary attachment figure (monotropy).

However, this evidence of monotropy may be related to how attachment is defined and measured. If it is defined/measured in terms of distress shown on separation (as is the case in the Strange Situation) then inevitably the most intense emotional relationship emerges as the primary attachment bond. However, attachment is related to social as well as emotional development, and therefore other attachments may be equally important (as Lamb suggests – see page 7). The research on infant–father attachment, for example, suggests a key role for fathers in social development. Relationships with siblings are also important for learning how to negotiate with peers.

## Father attachment

Bowlby emphasised the role of the female parent. He felt that the father's main role was that of support, both financial and emotional, for the mother, who could thus devote herself fully to child care (Bowlby, 1951). However, Schaffer and Emerson (1964) found that, for some infants, their father was the main attachment figure. At 6 months, 5% of infants had their father as the sole attachment figure compared with 17% who were solely attached to mother.

### Accessibility

Fathers usually spend less time with their infants and thus have fewer opportunities to engage in attachment-relevant situations, and this might explain why fathers are not primary attachment figures. However, as we have seen, there is evidence that *quantity* of time spent is not significant in terms of the development of attachment (Schaffer and Emerson, 1964). Lamb (1997) also reports that studies have shown a minimal relation between father accessibility (quantity of time) and infant–father attachment. In addition, studies have looked at families where men are the *primary caregiver* (which may or may not occur because the men are 'stay-at-home' dads). In such situations women are still found to devote more time to important caregiving activities than 'equivalent' men (i.e. men who are not the primary caregiver). Thus lack of attachment cannot be explained in terms of accessibility.

### Are male parenting behaviours social or biological?

The answer is that both social and biological factors are most probably important. In terms of cultural expectations, there continue to be sex-stereotypes that affect male behaviour, such as it being rather feminine to be sensitive to the needs of others. In terms of biology, there is evidence that men are less sensitive to infant cues than are mothers (e.g. Heermann *et al.*, 1994) although Frodi *et al.* (1978) showed videotapes of infants crying and found no differences in the *physiological* responses of men and women.

In the absence of a mother, men can form secure attachments with their children, as is the case in single-parent families. Research has found that, in families where the father is the primary caregiver, both parents often share the role of primary attachment figure (Frank *et al.*, 2005). So, men *can* be primary attachment figures.

### A different kind of attachment figure

Research has consistently highlighted the fact that fathers are more playful, physically active and generally better at providing challenging situations for their children. A father is an exciting playmate whereas mothers are more conventional, tend to read stories to their children, are soothing and better at providing a secure base (Geiger, 1996). It may be that *lack* of sensitivity/ responsiveness from fathers can be seen as positive, fostering problem-solving by making greater communicative and cognitive demands on children (White and Woollett, 1992).

Grossmann and Grossmann (1991) conducted a longitudinal study of families in Germany. Children whose fathers had scored low on social and interactive play and who did not feel secure with *their* mothers scored low on social functioning at age 22. This suggests that mothers and fathers have important but different roles to play in their children's development.

### A mutual interaction

We should not forget that attachment is a mutual process. Studies have shown that fathers who have early contact with their child have a stronger attachment with them in the months following the birth. This may work both ways – early contact may make fathers more interested/involved with their infants and infants more involved with their fathers.

## Cultural variations in attachment

Bowlby proposed that attachment is an innate process, which would imply that we should find similar patters of attachment worldwide. We can look at studies of attachment in other **cultures** to test this view. Studying the attachment process in other cultures (or subcultures) is important to our understanding of the nature of attachment. On the one hand, as child-rearing methods in different cultures represent the ways in which children are socialised, we might expect such methods to be different too. On the other hand, we have already seen that the mechanisms presumed to underlie attachment are *universal*, that is they should not be related to any cultural differences in childhood.

### Cultural similarities

Van IJzendoorn and Kroonenberg (1988) reviewed data from 32 studies using the Strange Situation conducted in 8 different countries. The results are shown in the graph. Secure attachment was the most common classification in every country; insecure-avoidant attachment was the next most common in every country except Israel and Japan. The results support the idea that secure attachment is 'best' for healthy social and emotional development because it is the most common form of attachment.

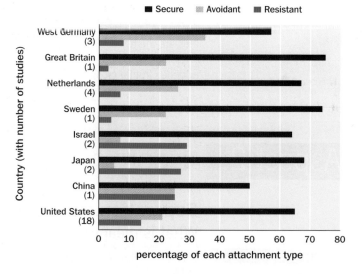

Tronick *et al.* (1992) studied an African tribe, the Efe, from Zaire who live in extended family groups. The infants were looked after and even breastfed by different women but usually slept with their own mother at night. Despite such differences in child-rearing practices the infants, at six months, still showed one primary attachment.

Fox (1977) studied infants raised on Israeli kibbutzim who spent most of their time being cared for in a communal children's home by a *metapelet*. They were nevertheless most closely attached to their mothers.

### Cultural differences

Grossmann and Grossmann (1991) found that German infants tended to be classified as insecurely attached. This may be due to different child-rearing practices. German culture requires keeping some interpersonal distance between parents and children, so infants do not engage in proximity-seeking behaviours in the Strange Situation and thus *appear* to be insecurely attached.

Takahashi (1990) reports that Japanese infants rarely experience separation from their mothers which could make them *appear* to be more distressed in the Strange Situation than their American counterparts.

*evaluation*

## Cultural variations

There are many limitations of studies of cultural differences. For example, researchers may use tests or procedures that have been developed in one culture and are not valid in another culture. This may make the individuals in the other culture appear 'abnormal' or inferior. The term that is used to describe this is an **imposed etic** – using a technique in one culture when it has been designed for use in another culture. The Strange Situation may be especially fearful for Japanese infants who never leave their mothers' side whereas some American infants are used to being cared for by strangers so the Strange Situation would not be especially strange.

A second limitation is that the term 'culture' doesn't necessarily equate to the term 'country', as many different groups, each with their own rules and customs, may co-exist within a country, as in the UK. So, when representing a set of data from, for example Japan, we may be mixing together many different cultural groups.

*assessment issues*

**Common themes: cross-cultural research in psychology**

Why are psychologists interested in studying people from different cultures? **Cross-cultural studies** have been carried out not just in early socialisation, but in obedience research, stress, atypical behaviour, etc. The underlying rationale is this: if people in different cultures tend to show rather different behaviours (e.g. in attachment style), we may conclude that these differences are a result of cultural differences in their environments. Where similar behaviours are found, we may conclude that these behaviours are universal in the human species, and thus are the result of innate factors.

Don't forget that, in assessments, you can gain *ae* marks for 'analysis', when you interpret evidence from a cross-cultural perspective, a common theme in psychology.

# Aspect 2:   Deprivation and privation

## Separation and deprivation

### What is meant by separation and deprivation?

**KEY TERMS**

**Separation:** This refers to the physical disruption of the caregiver–child bond. If suitable replacement care is available, and this meets the emotional needs of the child, then separation need not have any adverse consequences.

**Deprivation:** To be deprived is to lose something. In the context of child development, deprivation refers to the loss of emotional care that is normally provided by a primary caregiver.

It is clear that for most young children, *physical* **separation** from their primary caregiver is distressing. However, in many cases, some degree of physical separation is unavoidable, as children must spend time in hospital, in day care or even be left with a babysitter. For most children, physical separation from the primary caregiver has no lasting ill effects, *provided* that suitable substitute emotional care is available during that separation. In the absence of this (or where the separation is particularly prolonged), **deprivation** may ensue. As with separation, the child's attachment bond is disrupted, but the absence of suitable emotional care during the separation period my have more serious consequences.

There is a difference between separation and deprivation. When a child is separated this may result in deprivation if no substitute emotional care is offered: deprivation, therefore, is not the same as separation, but *may* accompany physical separation in certain circumstances.

### Research on separation and deprivation

#### Early research

In the 1930s and 40s, a number of psychologists studied children who had experienced prolonged separations from their families amounting to deprivation of emotional care. Such children were often profoundly disturbed. For example, Spitz and Wolf (1946) observed that 100 'normal' children who were placed in an institution became severely depressed within a few months. These effects were quite a surprise because at that time no one really thought about the effects of separation on infants and children. It was assumed that a good standard of physical care was all that would be required when infants and children were separated from caregivers.

### The 44 thieves study

Bowlby (1944) conducted his own research on the effects of deprivation. He recorded the details of two groups of adolescents who attended the Child Guidance Clinic in London where he worked. One group were juvenile 'thieves'; these children were found to lack a sense of responsibility and understanding for the feelings of others. The other group acted as a control group – they were emotionally maladjusted but not lacking in empathy or responsibility. In addition, Bowlby diagnosed 14 of the thieves as *affectionless psychopaths*, individuals who particularly lacked emotional sensitivity.

The children and their parents were interviewed about their early life experiences, with especial attention paid to early separations. It was found that the affectionless thieves had experienced frequent early separations from their mothers (see table below). More of the thieves experienced frequent separations than the control participants (39% compared with 4%). This effect was most marked in the group of affectionless thieves (86% of whom had had frequent separations). These data suggest that lack of continuous care may well cause emotional maladjustment.

|  | Separations from mother before the age of 2 | | |
|---|---|---|---|
|  | **Frequent** | **None** | **Total** |
| **Affectionless thieves** | 12 (86%) | 2 (14%) | 14 |
| **Other thieves** | 5 (17%) | 25 (83%) | 30 |
| **All thieves** | 17 (39%) | 27 (61%) | 44 |
| **Control participants** | 2 (4%) | 42 (96%) | 44 |

### The Robertsons' case studies

James Robertson and his wife Joyce produced a series of films in the 1960s (released between 1967–1973) showing the behaviour of young children who were separated from their families while their mothers were in hospital. Four of the children (Jane, Lucy, Thomas and Kate) were given foster care by the Robertsons in their own home; another child (John) was placed in a residential nursery for nine days. The children were all under three years of age (Robertson and Robertson, 1967–1973).

The children fostered by the Robertsons showed some upset. For example, Thomas rejected attempts to cuddle him and Kate expressed her feelings of anger at being left with her foster parents when playing with dolls. In general, though, the children seemed to adjust well and did not show signs of the PDD cycle. They slept well and did not reject their mothers when reunited. To help the children the Robertsons kept food and routines similar to those at home and fathers visited regularly to maintain emotional links with home. They received comfort from the foster mother, who was always available to them.

John's experiences were quite different. The film of John is so distressing that many viewers say they can't bear to watch it again. During the first two days in the nursery, John behaves much as normal but he becomes increasingly bewildered and confused. He makes determined efforts to get attention from the nurses but cannot compete with the other, more assertive children. The nurses are always friendly but always busy.

When John fails to find anyone who will respond to him, he seeks comfort from an oversized teddy bear, but this isn't enough. Over the next few days, he gradually breaks down and refuses food and drink, stops playing, cries a great deal, and gives up trying to get the nurses' attention.

John's father visits occasionally. In the first week, John greets his father enthusiastically but soon he rejects these visits. For long periods of the day, he lies with thumb in mouth, cuddling his large teddy bear. On the ninth day, when his mother comes to take him home, John screams and struggles to get away from her. For many months afterwards he continued to have outbursts of anger towards his mother.

John getting contact comfort from an oversized teddy bear – but no reciprocal attachment

The key difference between the case study of John and the others is that John was deprived of emotional care during separation whereas Jane, Lucy, Thomas and Kate all had substitute care. As long as children are given continuing emotional support they appear to cope with separation. When they have nothing but a teddy bear's affection they become despairing and detached – the PDD cycle.

### The PDD cycle

Robertson and Bowlby (1952) noted that young children tended to respond to separation in certain typical ways:

1. *Protest.* The first response from a child is acute distress. The child's behaviours are directed towards trying to get that person to come back – the child cries loudly and/or looks hopefully at any sound that might signal the caregiver's return.
2. *Despair.* The child may still look for the caregiver's return but shows signs of increasing hopelessness. The fact that the child now appears quiet is often interpreted as a sign that the initial distress on separation has been overcome, whereas, in reality, the child has given up hope.
3. *Detachment.* The final phase also suggests that recovery has taken place. The child now may welcome the attentions of others, and may even smile and be sociable. However, this is only an apparent state of well-being as, if the child's mother returns, the child does not show a normal greeting.

## explanation    Maternal deprivation hypothesis

The studies conducted in the 1930s and 40s, as well as Bowlby's own research described above, led Bowlby to formulate the *maternal deprivation hypothesis*. Bowlby believed that emotional care was as important for development as physical care. He famously said that 'mother-love in infancy and childhood is as important for mental health as are vitamins and proteins for physical health' (Bowlby, 1953, p. 240).

Bowlby believed that it wasn't enough to make sure that a child was well fed and kept safe and warm. He believed that infants and children needed a mother's emotional care to ensure continuing normal *mental* health. 'An infant and young child should experience a warm, intimate and continuous relationship with his mother' (Bowlby, 1953, p. 13). Bowlby believed that a child who is denied such care because of frequent and/or prolonged separations will become emotionally disturbed *if* this happens before the age of *about* two and a half years, and *if* there is no substitute mother-person available (Bowlby, 1953, p. 33). Bowlby also felt that there was a continuing risk up until the age of five.

Bowlby used the words 'mother/maternal' and 'deprivation'. 'Maternal' referred to a child's natural mother or 'permanent mother-substitute – one person who steadily "mothers" him' (Bowlby, 1953, p. 13). 'Deprivation' referred to the effects of *prolonged* separation. He believed that separation need not necessarily result in deprivation.

## evaluation

*Positive influences*
This hypothesis had an enormous impact on postwar thinking about child rearing and also on how children were looked after in hospitals. Before the research by Bowlby (and Robertson), children were separated from parents when they spent time in hospital or if their mother was in hospital. Visiting was discouraged or even forbidden. Robertson's film '*A Two-year-old Goes to Hospital*' and his campaign, coupled with the publication of Bowlby's maternal deprivation hypothesis, gradually changed all that.

*The critical period*
Bowlby claimed that the years up until about two and a half were critical in the child's development. This is called a **critical period hypothesis**. Bowlby claimed that, if a child was denied emotional care during this time, then permanent harm was fairly inevitable. His study of 44 thieves was used to support this view; however, other research has challenged his claim. For example, some studies of isolated children (described on pages 15–16) demonstrate good

In a study by Skeels and Dye (1939) it was found that IQ deficits typical of institutionalised children disappeared when some of the children were transferred to a home for mentally retarded adults. Could it be that the retarded adults provided the missing emotional care? To test this, Skodak and Skeels (1949) arranged for some other institutional infants to be placed in a home for the mentally retarded while a control group remained in the orphanage. They found, 1½ years later, that the IQs of the control group had, on average, fallen from 87 to 61 points whereas the transferred group's IQ rose from 64 to 92 points.

**Recent studies**

Rutter *et al.* (1998) studied a group of 111 Romanian orphans, who spent their early months and years in extreme physical and emotional privation in institutions. These children were adopted by British families before the age of two. By the age of four, the children had apparently recovered. This shows that recovery from extreme privation can be achieved given adequate care. However, it is important to note that the age of adoption is within the period that Bowlby regarded as critical, i.e. less than two and a half years of age.

*evaluation*

One of the main difficulties with all of this research is that we don't know whether or not the children were attached to someone during their sensitive years, and what the quality of that attachment was.

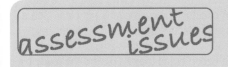

**Describe and evaluate evidence from research with institutionalised children. (*ku 4 ae 4*)**

The study by Hodges and Tizard (described on page 18) may also be used when answering questions about institutionalised children. However, in a question such as the one above you must avoid the temptation to focus solely on one study. Notice that the question asks for 'evidence from research' not just one study. The question is worth only eight marks, so write concisely about evidence from a number of studies, and don't get bogged down in excessive detail about any one study.

## Long-term implications of privation

Bowlby's maternal deprivation hypothesis predicted that deprivation would have serious long-term consequences for mental health. The studies we have reviewed on the last few pages indicate various other consequences of deprivation and/or privation. These are summarised in the table below along with some further consequences to be considered in the next few pages.

Long-term effects: research studies

| Long-term effect | Research study |
|---|---|
| Intellectual underfunctioning | Genie <br> Skeels and Dye (orphans) |
| Social / emotional maladjustment | Genie <br> Goldfarb (institutionalised children) |
| Poor parenting | Harlow (monkeys) <br> Quinton *et al.* (ex-institutional mothers) |
| Relationship difficulties | Hazan and Shaver (Love Quiz) |
| Mental disorder | Affectionless psychopathy (Bowlby) <br> Reactive attachment disorder |
| Physical underdevelopment | Genie |
| Little long-term effect | Czech twins <br> Triseliotis (adopted children) <br> Rutter *et al.* (Romanian orphans) <br> Bowlby *et al.* (individual differences) |

In the film *Good Will Hunting*, psychiatrist Sean McGuire (Robin Williams) tries to get through to Will Hunting (Matt Damon) who has been diagnosed with reactive attachment disorder.

The main question is about inevitability. How inevitable is it that children who experience early deprivation or privation will experience these long-term effects? The evidence is not clear. Some studies show that children do not recover, as in the case of reactive attachment disorder (below) and the evidence from Hodges and Tizard (Star Study below). Other studies suggest that the effects are reversible, for example the case study of the Czech twins (page 16) and the study by Triseliotis (page 16).

## Reactive attachment disorder

Reactive attachment disorder is a recognised mental illness. Individuals show a complete lack of ability to be affectionate with others or to form loving and lasting intimate relationships. They may lack a sense of a conscience.

Children with reactive attachment disorder have learned that the world is unsafe and not to depend on adult caregivers. They develop a protective emotional 'shell', which isolates them from the pain of their attachment failure. These shells become very difficult to remove, as children depend on them as their sole means of coping with the world. Anyone who tries to remove this shell is seen as a threat and so they turn against the very people who want to help them the most – their caregivers.

Attachment failure may be caused when a mother abandons her baby but may also occur even when mother and child remain together. Jones *et al.* (1987) describe such 'primary rejectors' as women who may have successful relationships with other children but, because of problems such as a difficult or premature birth, the early relationship with this particular child is difficult and never recovers.

See members.tripod.com/~radclass for a PowerPoint presentation on reactive attachment disorder.

## starSTUDY

# Investigating deprivation: Long-term effects

**(HODGES AND TIZARD, 1989)**

### Aims

Jill Hodges and Barbara Tizard undertook a longitudinal study following a group of institutionalised children from early life to adolescence to see (1) if children returned to their natural homes did better than those who were adopted (Bowlby claimed that home was best), and (2) what long-term effects were apparent from early deprivation/privation (early years spent in an institution).

### Method and procedure

The study focused on a group of 65 children who had been placed in an institution when they were less than 4 months old. At this age, children have not yet formed attachments. There was an explicit policy in the institution against the 'caretakers' forming attachments with the children and there was also a high turnover of staff. This meant that the children had little opportunity to form a close, continuous relationship with an adult.

By the age of 4, 24 of the institutionalised children had been adopted; 15 had returned to their natural homes and the rest remained in the institution. The children were assessed at the age of 4, 8 (51 children remained) and 16 (39 children). At each assessment, the children, their parents, and teachers were interviewed and asked to fill in questionnaires. At all ages, comparison was made with a control group of children raised in a 'normal' home environment.

## Results

The graph below shows that there were significant differences between the adopted and restored children in terms of attachment. The restored group got on particularly poorly with their siblings at both age 8 and 16 (as reported by the children themselves and their mothers).

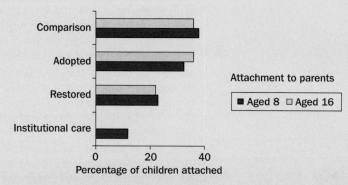

At age 16, there were no significant differences between the restored and adopted children but there were significant differences between the ex-institution children and their matched comparisons. For example, overall the teachers rated the ex-institution children as less popular with peers than average, and the ex-institution children were rated as more quarrelsome and more likely to bully and less likely to have a close friend.

## Conclusion

The findings relating to family relationships suggest that recovery from early privation is possible when there is sufficient care. The restored children returned to homes where their parents were often ambivalent about having their child back and had other children and material difficulties which competed for their attention, whereas the adopted children went to families who very much wanted a child and put a lot of time and energy into building up a relationship.

The findings relating to peer relationships tell a different story. There were major differences between the ex-institution group and their comparisons, rather than differences *within* the ex-institution group (i.e. the restored and adopted children). This suggests, in contrast to the family findings, that early attachment *does* have a special importance in social development.

## Evaluation

### Sample bias

It is also possible that the adopted and restored groups were different because the children first selected for adoption might have been the ones who were easier to get on with. This could explain why the adopted children got on better at home (because they were 'easier' children) and developed closer attachments but doesn't explain why they had more difficulties with peers.

### Alternative explanations for the findings

Hodges and Tizard suggest that the findings, at age 16, might be explained in other ways. For example, it could be that the ex-institution children suffered from poor self-esteem stemming from being adopted, which would explain their problems outside the home. Another explanation could be that the ex-institution children lag behind their peers in emotional development and this would explain their poor peer relationships – they are simply not yet ready to cope.

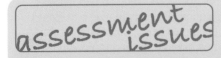

**"Some developmental psychologists claim that separation, deprivation and/or privation in early childhood have long-term implications for adjustment and mental health."**
**Assess research evidence in relation to this claim. (ku 12 ae 8)**

The focus of this essay question is on research evidence, but before you charge in and start writing *everything* from the last few pages, hang on a minute and think 'selectivity'. Each of the studies on the previous pages represents just one part of the overall picture regarding the effects of deprivation/privation on subsequent development. In your answer, you should select which studies to use and just provide a *summary* of the main findings and/or conclusions of each study.

In 'assessing' the claim in the quotation, remember that research that suggests a *lack* of long-term effects is as relevant as research that shows that they do exist. By constructing an argument in this way, you will attract *ae* marks.

Another important way to achieve *ae* marks in this question is to evaluate the evidence that you refer to. For example, you might consider the issue that much of the research depends on records (or lack of them!) of events from many years ago, so you should urge caution in interpreting such findings. On the other hand, don't be afraid to give *positive* evaluation points too: for example, one overall strength of the evidence is that it comes from a variety of methodologies.

As well as summarising the evaluative points from specific research studies (which *limit* their value in the debate concerning long-term effects), other more general limitations can be pointed out, such as the tendency to ignore fathers as attachment figures, the difficulty in demonstrating a causal link, and the fact that the development of children is susceptible to many influences, of which the presence or absence of the primary caregiver is only one, albeit an important one.

# Aspect 3: Parenting

## Child-rearing styles
### What is meant by child-rearing style?

**KEY TERMS**

**Parents:** All those who provide significant care for children in a home or family context, including biological parents, step-parents, foster parents, adoptive parents, grandparents or other relatives.

**Child-rearing style:** The term 'child-rearing style' (or 'parenting style') is used to describe the normal variations in parents' attempts to control and socialise their children.

**Authoritative style:** Parents are firm and clear in their demands but are also flexible and willing to explain decisions.

**Authoritarian style:** Parents value unquestioning obedience and control their children's behaviour.

Parenting is a highly varied activity that undoubtedly influences developmental outcomes for children. Some psychologists believe that specific parenting practices (e.g. the use of physical punishment) are less important in determining these outcomes than the general approach to child rearing adopted by **parents**. Different **child-rearing styles** can be distinguished by the degree to which the parents are *demanding* of the child (e.g. setting high standards and demanding obedience to parental authority) and/or *responsive* to the rights and needs of the child. Child-rearing styles also differ in the extent to which they are characterised by *psychological* control, i.e. the use of parenting practices such as guilt or love withdrawal. In Baumrind's typology of child-rearing styles (Baumrind, 1991, discussed below), parents who adopt **authoritative** and **authoritarian styles** are equally high in *behavioural control*, but whereas authoritative parents tend to be low in *psychological control*, authoritarian parents tend to be high.

### Different child-rearing styles

#### Authoritarian

Authoritarian parents usually *tell* children how to behave rather than providing them with options. They set strict standards of conduct for their children and require obedience to their imposed rules. They tend to focus more on bad behaviour than on good behaviour and are frequently critical of children for not meeting their standards.

Authoritarian parents usually do not explain *why* they want a child to behave in a certain way, nor do their decisions reflect any input from the child. As a result, children with authoritarian parents tend not to learn how to think for themselves nor understand why they must behave in a specific way.

### Authoritative

Authoritative parents also believe in firm enforcement of important rules but, unlike authoritarian parents, usually give their children the reasoning behind their decisions. Although they take notice of the child's views, the final decision belongs to the parents.

Authoritative parents encourage children to think about the consequences of their behaviour and so be responsible for themselves. They monitor their children's behaviour to ensure that they are behaving in an appropriate manner. This is usually done in a warm and supportive way, focusing more on positive behaviours than on negative 'rule-breaking' behaviours.

### Permissive

Parents who adopt a **permissive style** give up most control to their children. They make few, if any, rules, and those they do make tend not to be consistently enforced. Permissive parents do not set clear boundaries for their children's behaviour, tending instead to let their children make their own decisions, even if the child is not capable of making suitable choices how to behave.

Permissive parents tend to accept a child's behaviour, regardless of whether it is good or bad. They may feel unable to change inappropriate behaviour in their children, or may simply choose not to get involved.

## Cultural differences in child-rearing styles

Small (1998) studied child rearing in three very different cultures – that of the !Kung San of Botswana, the Japanese, and the Americans. The !Kung San are some of the few remaining hunter-gatherer groups in the world. There is no concept of personal ownership among the San, food is shared, and there is no concern for privacy. Babies stay with their mothers at all times, and, as they grow, they are never alone. The parental goals of the San are therefore social integration, mobility (to match the San lifestyle) and sharing.

Among Japanese children, the need for obedience is clearly understood so that corrective discipline is rarely needed. In fact, pressure to be good often comes from peers. In addition, teachers emphasise qualities such as empathy and pride in the group, and it is rare to find children who do not want to participate in group activities. As a consequence, children do not need to be taught to share; they tend to experience sharing behaviour as a social norm from an early age.

In the United States, the main parental goal is the child's eventual independence. Physical contact with infants is minimal compared with other societies. Although babies may cry a lot, parents do not always feel it necessary to respond right away. Many parents see themselves as teachers as much as protectors and place great importance on stimulating their children.

Parents in different countries, such as Japan and America, behave in general quite differently towards their children. For example, American parents emphasise independence, whereas Japanese parents foster interdependence.

Small concludes that beliefs about raising children in the West are vastly different from those elsewhere in the world. However, there is now a growing movement in the West toward what she calls 'attachment parenting', based on responsiveness to children's needs. This form of child-rearing style more closely mimics the practice of 'primitive' societies and appears to contradict contemporary Western ideas of the importance of fostering independence in children.

## Consequences of child-rearing styles

We might expect that children brought up by authoritarian parents might turn out differently from those whose parents are more indulgent, but is this the case?

### Effects on a child's emotional development

In her study of child-rearing styles, Baumrind (1991) found few differences between children of authoritarian parents and children of permissive parents. Children of both groups were less motivated to achieve and less independent than the children of authoritative parents. In contrast, the children of authoritative parents were responsible, assertive, self-reliant, and friendly.

Chamberlin (1978) investigated the hypothesis that authoritarian styles of child rearing led to more problems at home and in school than did more 'accommodative' styles (authoritative and permissive). Over 100 children were followed up from age 2 into their first year at school. Follow-up observations showed no significant differences in terms of their malfunctional behaviour. However, the home behaviour of boys being raised in the more accommodative styles was described in more positive terms by their mothers than was the behaviour of those raised with authoritarian styles. Girls raised with more accommodative styles were described in more positive terms by their teachers. Chamberlin found no evidence that the permissive style of child rearing produced 'spoiled brats', nor that authoritarian styles produced overly aggressive or inhibited children.

### Effects on a child's social development

Weiss and Schwarz (1996) found that children and adolescents from authoritarian families tend to show relatively poor social skills, low self-esteem, and higher levels of depression. Children and adolescents from indulgent homes, on the other hand, have higher self-esteem, better social skills, and lower levels of depression.

Hoffman (1970) looked at the relationship between child-rearing style and moral development in a review of correlational studies. 'Induction' parenting, which is similar to permissive parenting, was related to the most mature moral development while 'power assertion' (like authoritarian parenting) was related to the lowest moral development. Hoffman concluded that induction parenting allows children to develop their own moral reasoning rather than to obey instructions mindlessly.

### Effects on a child's cognitive development

The study by Weiss and Schwarz (1996) also found that children from authoritarian families tended to perform moderately well in school and be uninvolved in problem behaviour; the opposite was true of children from indulgent homes.

Research into prejudiced behaviour has found a link with authoritarian-style child rearing. Adorno *et al.* (1950) found that children who tended to be prejudiced also had a rigid cognitive style and had parents who used strict discipline and punishment and expected unquestioning loyalty. They called this the 'authoritarian personality' (see page 150). Such individuals seek simplistic solutions which ignore inconsistent information.

---

## evaluation | Child-rearing styles

### Lack of evidence

Rowe (1990) claims that, despite many years of research, there is little convincing support for the 'common sense' proposition that child-rearing styles have a significant formative influence on children's development. Rowe argues that non-intellectual traits (such as personality or activity level) are determined more by genetic influences or by relatively specific environmental influences, which are not linked to family or parental treatments. Rowe claims that as a result of this lack of consistent evidence, parents should be given less credit for children who turn out well and should take less blame for children who turn out poorly. However, more recent research suggests greater agreement that parenting does significantly affect a range of child outcomes, from school attainment to child abuse and criminality (Sutton *et al.*, 2004).

### A Westernised world

Although research has suggested important cultural differences in child-rearing styles, it is also evident that many of these differences are disappearing owing to 'creeping Westernisation' in other cultures. Power *et al.* (1992), in a comparative study of American and Japanese child-rearing styles, found that less than five per cent of US mothers showed a 'Japanese' child-rearing style, whereas nearly one-quarter of Japanese mothers had adopted a 'US' style – generally either permissive or authoritative.

### The value of permissive parenting

Although many studies have found less ideal outcomes for children raised with permissive parenting, this is actually the ideal parenting style for shy, withdrawn children. Such children need love and encouragement without the constraints of too much structure, so they can begin to form relationships (Reeve, 2006).

### Mothers versus fathers

Results from an ongoing longitudinal study in Finland (Aunola *et al.*, 1999) suggest that both mothers' *and* fathers' parenting styles impact on their children's development. However, in later childhood, mothers' and fathers' parenting styles affect different aspects of the child's development. Fathers are primarily important in guiding their children's relationships with the outer world (e.g. in searching for a job), whereas mothers are more influential in shaping the 'inner' world of their children.

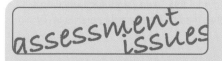

**(a) What is meant by 'child-rearing style'? Give *two* examples. (*ku* 4 *ae* 0)**

**(b) With reference to research evidence, consider the ways that caregivers may develop parenting skills. (*ku* 8 *ae* 8)**

You will have noticed that each of the sample questions given in this chapter gives the marks available divided into *ku* and *ae*: 'knowledge and understanding' and 'analysis and evaluation'. For *ku* marks you need to name, state, define, or describe something (a concept, theory, research study, application); for *ae* marks, you should analyse factors, influences, components of a theory, interpret evidence in relation to a theory or concept, and/or evaluate theory or findings, methodology, ethics, etc. Where a question requires *ae*, you will see 'command' words like 'analyse', 'discuss', 'consider', 'assess', 'evaluate'; these require higher-order thinking skills.

For the question above, part (a) requires only *ku*, but part (b) requires an equal mixture of *ku* and *ae*. Often, the required *ku* content is clear and straightforward (as long as you know your stuff!), but, for *ae* content, you need to think carefully: in part (b) of this question, you can gain *ae* marks for giving different theoretical explanations (e.g. evolutionary view, social learning theory and family-as-system theory – covered in the next few pages), and interpreting relevant research evidence.

## The development of parenting skills
## What is meant by parenting skills?

In this chapter, you have been studying the processes involved in parenting and caregiving. Currently, there is a great deal of interest in parenting, as seen in TV programmes like *Supernanny* and also in government policies. For example, in November 2004, Tony Blair stated that 'one of the most pressing new challenges is to support parents as they bring up young families'. It is claimed that many social problems, such as low achievement at school, poor self-esteem, mental ill health, crime and anti-social behaviour, can be reduced through better parenting, as a form of prevention. Initiatives such as SureStart, Parentline (a telephone helpline) and parenting courses have been put in place to support parents in what most people agree is a difficult task – raising children.

Although many people believe that parenting comes naturally, one survey found that 70% of parents felt that parenting was something that had to be learned (National Family and Parenting Institute, 2001). Psychological theories can be used to shed light on the innate versus learned (**nature–nurture**) question. We will first consider such theories and then look at intervention programmes for developing **parenting skills**.

## explanation          Explaining the development of parenting skills in caregivers

*The evolutionary view*
In the natural world, we see animals ranging from wild tigers to domestic cats tending to their offspring without instruction. One argument is that such behaviours are genetically programmed because they are adaptive – they maximise the survival and reproduction of an animal's offspring and thus the survival of one's own genes. So time, energy and effort spent in providing care are regarded as **parental investment** (Trivers, 1972).

Bowlby (see page 5) suggested that parenting behaviour is acquired through the process of attachment, another adaptive behaviour. An infant learns about relationships through the close emotional relationship with one's primary caregiver. Such knowledge is stored in an internal working model which generates expectations about what adult relationships will be like and how to behave with your children.

*Learning and social learning theory*
The reason animals naturally act as good parents could also be explained in terms of learning and social learning theory. Learning theory would suggest that parenting skills are acquired through reinforcement (e.g. picking up a crying baby usually leads to the crying stopping – this is an example of *negative reinforcement*). Social learning theory would claim that parenting behaviours are learned through observation and imitation of role models. Young animals,

Are parenting skills innate or learned through experience? Or do they need to be taught especially?

including humans, observe what their parents do and model their own parenting behaviours on this. Humans also acquire parenting skills through the media; for example parents in TV programmes act as role models.

*Family-as-system theory*
A rather different view of parenting is taken by the 'family-as-system' approach which emphasises family processes as a set of subsystems which are strongly inter-related and dynamic (it changes over time). For example, although it is tempting to assume that parental influences shape children's behaviour, influence also flows in the opposite direction (circularity of influence), as in the case of child temperament affecting parenting behaviour (see the temperament hypothesis on page 6). In the systems approach, parenting behaviour does not happen in isolation; it is just one component of a more complex set of processes.

Belsky (1984) adopted the family-as-system model of parenting skills in his *process model of parenting*. According to this model, three main influences affect the quality of parental functioning:

- *characteristics of the parent,* which includes the mental health of the parent and their own development history
- *characteristics of the child*, in particular easy or difficult temperament
- *contextual sources of support*, such as support from partner, relatives and friends as well as job conditions and financial circumstances.

These three influences are said to interact in a complex way to give rise to parenting behaviour.

*evaluation*

There is research evidence to support each of the explanations.

*The evolutionary view*
Research has shown that one's own attachment experience is related to later parenting skills. Quinton *et al.* (1985) studied women who had spent much of their early lives in institutions. They observed how these women interacted with their own children and concluded that they were less sensitive, less supportive and less warm than a group of non-institutionalised women. This result reminds us of Harlow's work with monkeys (see page 4) where the maladjusted monkeys were later poor parents.

*Social learning theory*
The evidence from Quinton *et al.* and from Harlow could equally be used to support social learning theory. We can also use the success of intervention programmes (see below) to support learning/social learning explanations.

*Family-as-system theory*
This is the fullest account of the development of parenting skills, which can incorporate the other two explanations as part of the characteristics of the parent. The model is helpful in considering how families can be helped through family and parenting intervention programmes. Many such programmes have focused on parent behaviours only, whereas greater success might be achieved by working on all three influences.

## Intervention programmes to enhance the development of parenting skills

### Policy interventions
Public policy approaches to supporting parenting have arisen partly as a result of Human Rights treaties. Under the UN Convention on the Rights of the Child 1989, it was agreed that children have a range of rights, including healthy development, not to be separated from parents wherever possible, and having their opinion sought in decisions affecting their care. The primary responsibility for fulfilling these rights lies, in most cases, with parents and therefore assistance/guidance to *parents* is established as a right of the *child*. In the UK, the government has set up the National Family and Parenting Institute (NFPI), and a number of other initiatives such as Parentline, Home-Start and SureStart which are aimed at directly supporting families.

www.parentlineplus.org
Parentline Plus which works for and with parents because 'instructions aren't included'

**Parenting programmes**

Many parenting programmes exist that have the common aim of producing better developmental outcomes for children by enhancing parenting skills, such as the one described in the Star Study below, the Webster-Stratton course. Such programmes usually focus on emotional and disciplinary issues. Another example is the STAR parenting programme (see www.starparent.com): their philosophy is that parenting is a problem-solving process: STAR stands for Stop, Think, Ask, and Respond; the final stage includes positive parenting (providing warmth and nurturing) and discipline – like an authoritative child-rearing style.

Although such interventions have in the past focused mainly on remedying parenting problems, the emphasis in research and policy in the UK seems to be shifting towards promoting and supporting parenting in all families.

*evaluation*

## Intervention programmes

*Cultural relativism*
As we have seen, child-rearing patterns vary between and within cultures, and appear to be adaptive, relative to the child's own culture – **cultural relativism**.

*Effectiveness*
Scarr (1992) argued that the main thing that parents can provide is a warm, supportive environment to enable their children to develop their innate potential (you can read about 'unconditional positive regard' on page 273.) Recent intervention studies have provided evidence of how these programmes can improve such aspects of parenting. For example, a study by Brenner et al. (1999) used a programme based on the STAR approach with a diverse group of American families. After 10 sessions, parents reported an increase in their positive nurturing behaviour as well as a decrease in their levels of verbal and corporal punishment and a decrease in child behaviour problems.

On the other hand, critics regard some interventions as patronising and ineffective (Lewis, 2002). There has been disagreement over whether programmes should be applied universally, as a preventative approach, or target only high-risk families, as a remedial approach, although Hutchings and Lane (2005) assert that these two approaches (preventative and remedial) are not incompatible. Some programmes have also been criticised for being ineffective; for example, the hugely expensive SureStart project has been criticised for producing little change in child outcomes (Melhuish et al., 2005).

## starSTUDY

# Investigating parenting: A study of parents' perceptions of a parenting programme
(PATTERSON ET AL., 2005)

### Aims
To provide a qualitative evaluation of a parenting intervention programme, in terms of parents' perceptions of its usefulness.

### Method and procedure
Groups of parents in an English city followed a 10-week Webster-Stratton Parenting Programme (two hours per week). This course is video based and includes guidance for parents on playing with their children, using rewards and dealing with misbehaviour. Groups of about 10 parents were led by health visitors. Activities included discussion of problem scenarios, role-play, and home practice of parenting techniques.

Parents of children aged two–eight years from three GP practices were invited to take part. 31 parents (one father; all others were mothers) completed the programme. The majority of the parents had children whose behaviour was in the 'normal' range. Parents were interviewed 2–12 weeks after the end of the course, and completed open-ended questionnaires at 6 and 12 months afterwards. The group sessions were also tape-recorded.

## Results

All data were **qualitative**. Interview and questionnaire responses, as well as the recorded sessions, were analysed and coded according to the recurring themes that appeared to be meaningful to the respondents. The main themes that emerged included:

- Parents felt that the techniques were helpful in building better quality relationships (closer and less authoritarian) with their children.
- Owing to learning specific skills (e.g. clear commands, rewards, time-out), parents found that they could get their children to cooperate, with less shouting and smacking. Parents reported a reduction in problem behaviours and an increase in positive behaviours.
- Parents had gained confidence in their own parenting skills and coping strategies.
- They were reassured at finding that other parents were struggling to cope, and found the groups supportive.

## Conclusion

Researchers concluded that participants had benefited in three main ways:

1. They had a less controlling and more rewarding relationship with their children, achieved by means of play and praise.
2. Parenting competence was enhanced, through development of practical skills and coping strategies.
3. There was increased support from group leaders and other participants, during and in some cases after the course.

Overall, it was claimed that parents' needs in these areas had been met by the programme, and that the programme could have a beneficial effect on the mental health of parents and children not in high-risk groups.

## Evaluation

### Strengths

Data were collected using three different methods, which led to similar conclusions. The study was unusual in that it discovered that parents in 'normal' families, not just those in high-risk groups, experienced problems that interfered with family relationships and threatened parents' mental health.

### Weaknesses

The benefits may be short lived; follow-up sessions would be needed to ensure long-term effectiveness. Additionally, sampling may have been biased because the parents who took part were those who were willing to take on a major commitment; they already had a strong interest in parenting. There was also substantial attrition (i.e. drop out) of participants. Therefore, any generalisation to the population should be treated with caution. Finally, the measures focused on parental satisfaction but did not objectively assess outcomes for the *children*, a major shortcoming in many parenting interventions (Scott, 2006).

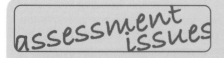

### Common themes: applications of psychology in everyday life

Psychological knowledge can illuminate virtually everything we do in life and is therefore often applied in everyday situations, with the aim of improving our life experiences and general well-being. When answering a question about how psychology is put into practice (and every Aspect in Unit 1 includes such content), you can gain marks if you refer to examples from 'real life' – but do make sure that your examples are relevant to the question asked! For example, the following answer would get few if any marks: 'My sister was happy at nursery school because she was securely attached to my mother'. Your examples should *add to* your explanation of the psychological process(es) involved.

## Exam questions and answers

*In this section we show you student answers to possible exam questions plus examiner's comments on these answers. Remember that in the actual exam (and NABs) your questions for this Topic will always add up to 20 marks. The question may be one essay worth 20 marks or a number of smaller questions (such as those shown below) which add up to 20 marks.*

### Question 1    What is meant by the term "deprivation" in early socialisation? (*ku 2 ae 0*)

| Tom | Alice |
|---|---|
| Deprivation refers to when a child is deprived of his or her mother's love. | To be deprived of something means it has been taken away from you, 'deprivation' in early socialisation refers to situations where a child has had a close relationship with his/her mother (or other caregiver) and is separated from the caregiver for a prolonged period so the child is lacking the care that it once had. Such separations may not cause any long-term emotional damage if the child has adequate substitute care. Otherwise there may be long-term damage such as Bowlby found in his study of the 44 thieves where some children had become affectionless psychopaths. |

**Examiner's comments**    Tom's answer to this question commits the classic 'crime' often found in definition-type answers: he uses the term of the question ('deprivation') in his answer ('deprived'); so, anyone reading this and hoping to find out what 'deprivation' is, will be disappointed! The rest of this answer simply doesn't provide enough information, either. Therefore, **0 marks** for Tom here.

Alice clearly demonstrates a full understanding of the concept of deprivation and therefore gains the full two marks. Actually, she has written more than is necessary; for a two-mark question, you would not normally be expected to refer to research evidence, therefore Alice would gain **2 out of 2 marks** even without the last sentence.

### Question 2    What have psychologists discovered about father attachment? (*ku 4 ae 0*)

| Tom | Alice |
|---|---|
| Father attachment is different to mother attachment because fathers are more likely to play with their children and they are more into rough-and-tumble play. This means that children have a different kind of attachment with their father. There's also the question that many fathers are not at home so children are not likely to form attachments. | There are social and biological reasons why fathers are different attachment figures. Social reasons are that male stereotypes discourage men from being nurturing, though this is changing. Boys and men used to feel it was not manly to be interested in babies but nowadays more men spend time looking after their babies and changing nappies, and you even get male nannies.<br><br>Biologically it has been suggested that men are innately less sensitive than women to an infant's cues (Heerman et al). However not all psychologists agree with this. One study found no differences in how men and women responded to infants. This study was by Frodi. They showed videotapes of children crying to men and women and measured their physiological responses. |

Examiner's comments    Although Tom briefly mentions one or two sound points, none of these are developed in any detail; for example, he could have referred to secure and insecure attachment to describe the 'different kind of attachment', and made it clear that he was making a comparison with attachment to the primary caregiver. Indeed, he seems to have assumed that the primary caregiver is always the mother, instead of pointing out that fathers can be primary caregivers; the question wording 'What have psychologists discovered …?' is a clue that results from research will be relevant in the answer, but unfortunately Tom has not spotted this. His answer is really only 'common sense'. So **1 out of 4 marks**.

Alice's answer is quite well-organised, as she looks systematically at both biological and social aspects, shows awareness of the relevance of the question to real-life issues, and draws on research evidence. However, the evidence she has chosen to refer to is not well targeted to the question, as it illustrates only simple physiological responses in women and men; she should, instead, have focused on evidence of the (more complex) processes and types of attachment in father–infant studies. So, although Alice clearly has a degree of knowledge and understanding of this topic area (and the question requires only *ku*), she would get **2 out of 4 marks** for this answer.

**Question 3**   Describe and evaluate Ainsworth's categorisation of types of attachment, and discuss evidence of cultural differences in these types of attachment. (*ku* 12 *ae* 8)

## Tom

Ainsworth found that infants could be categorised into 3 types: secure, insecure-resistant and insecure-avoidant. The key features are that securely attached infants are happier about being left by their mothers whereas insecure children are not. When the mothers returned the secure children greeted their mothers whereas insecure children ignored their mothers. The secure children were relatively OK with the stranger.

This study was very useful because it has meant that other researchers could do research on attachment because they had a way to classify the infants. However, one criticism is that the infants were quite distressed in the study – in fact they were deliberately distressed which shouldn't have happened.

Another criticism is that there are cultural differences in attachment and this method of classification may not apply to all infants. It depends on what their normal experiences are. For example a Japanese infant is not used to being away from its mother so in the Strange Situation the infant is likely to be more distressed than a child who is used to frequent separations, and therefore this child may seem insecurely attached when it isn't really.

Cross-cultural research by a Dutchman found that types of attachment were similar in many different countries. The majority of infants were securely attached. This suggests that attachment styles are universal. This is one of the strengths of cross-cultural research – you can investigate whether behaviours are innate because if they are they should be universal, otherwise they must be learned through cultural practices.

**Examiner's comments**   One strength of Tom's answer is that he has followed the three 'commands' of the question faithfully: he has described Ainsworth's categorisation, then evaluated it, then discussed cultural differences. (Sometimes students don't notice they may have to do more than one thing in the same question!) Tom makes a number of sensible points; however, each point is dealt with rather sketchily, and sometimes over-simplified, for example 'the secure children were relatively OK with the stranger'. He evidently has knowledge of the 'Strange Situation' procedure, on which Ainsworth based her categorisation, but does not give an outline of the technique at the start, which would have been helpful. Overall, *ku* skills are under-developed, in terms of lack of descriptive detail and lack of accuracy in knowledge of research. The section on cultural differences shows some *ae* skills, although more in-depth interpretation of the cross-cultural evidence is needed. This essay would be awarded **9 out of 20** (*ku* 5/12 *ae* 4/8).

## Alice

Ainsworth categorised types of attachment using the Strange Situation. The first type is secure. Infants who are securely attached (66%) use their caregiver as a secure base, are willing to explore, display a lot of stranger anxiety, but little separation anxiety (easily soothed) and greet their caregiver enthusiastically on reunion. The second type is insecure-avoidant. These infants are also willing to explore but show little stranger anxiety, are indifferent when separated and avoid contact with caregiver on return. The third type is insecure-resistant who are not very willing to explore, show high stranger anxiety and high separation anxiety, on reunion they seek and reject their caregiver.

This typology has proved very useful in attachment research, for example studies that look at long term effects of attachment types (e.g. Hazan and Shaver, 1969) show that early attachment styles are related to later romantic experiences.

The typology has been criticised because children show different types of attachment with different caregivers which suggests that any infant is not 'secure' or 'insecure' but some relationships are secure or insecure.

It was further criticised because there is a fourth category, disorganised attachment (Main and Weston, 1981).

Some research has found that there are not many cultural differences, in fact there are more differences within a culture than between cultures (Van Izjendoorn and Kroonenberg, 1988). However, when comparing attachments in different cultures (as was done in this study) one assumes that the Strange Situation is appropriate but it is based on the practices in one culture (American) and does not have the same meaning in other cultures. In addition the study assumes that countries are equivalent to cultures whereas there may be many different cultures, both individualist and collectivist, in one country.

Nevertheless some studies have shown that there are cultural similarities despite different child-care practices. Tronick et al. (1992) studied children raised in a collectivist African community who still showed one primary attachment despite multiple caregivers which supports Bowlby's theory of monotropy.

**Examiner's comments**   Alice's answer is also well organised in terms of dealing with every 'command' in turn, but she shows greater accuracy of knowledge and understanding, for example clear descriptions of attachment types. She has supported her argument with several references to appropriate research evidence and clearly signposts where she is 'evaluating' and 'discussing', gaining *ae* marks. On the other hand, there is a little repetition on the point of 'differences within'/'differences between' cultures. Also, although she rightly points out similarities between cultures, there is a lack of discussion of the differences that were found between cultures in the insecure categories. As far as quality of expression is concerned, Alice has to some extent described issues such as 'validity', and 'bias', but should actually use that terminology. Overall, this is a competent essay, with only a few omissions and relatively minor weaknesses. It would gain **16 out of 20** (*ku* 10/12 *ae* 6/8).

# 2 Topic: Memory

Cognitive psychology is concerned with mental processes. Cognitive psychologists believe that human behaviour can be best explained if we first understand the mental processes that underlie behaviour. Cognitive psychology is, therefore, the study of how people learn, structure, store and use knowledge – essentially how people think about the world around them.

Memory is an example of cognitive psychology. In some ways, memory is equivalent to learning. It is the process by which we retain information about events that have happened in the past.

| Chapter contents | Specification content for the Topic 'Memory' | Comment |
|---|---|---|
| **Aspect 1: The nature of memory** | | |
| Short-term and long-term memory<br>　　page 30<br>Research on encoding, duration and capacity<br>　　page 32 | The nature of memory, including:<br>● stages<br>● capacity<br>● duration<br>● encoding | *You should be able to define what psychologists mean by 'memory', and describe the three **stages** of the activity of remembering. One view of memory is that there are two main kinds of memory store, short-term memory and long-term memory, and these differ from each other in terms of how much information they can hold (**capacity**), how long they last (**duration**), and in what form the information is stored (**encoding**).* |
| **Aspect 2: Models of memory** | | |
| The multi-store model of memory<br>　　page 34<br>The working memory model of memory<br>　　page 36 | Models of memory, including:<br>● the multi-store model<br>● working memory | *A number of '**models**', or explanations, of memory have been put forward by cognitive psychologists over the years; you are expected to learn two of these, the **multi-store model** and the **working memory** model, including the research evidence which supports or challenges them.* |
| **Aspect 3: Theories of forgetting** | | |
| Forgetting in STM<br>　　page 40<br>Forgetting in LTM<br>　　page 42<br>Repression and motivated forgetting<br>　　page 44 | Theories of forgetting, including:<br>● trace decay<br>● displacement<br>● interference<br>● cue-dependent forgetting<br>● repression<br>● motivated forgetting | *Forgetting things is a common experience for all of us, and psychological **theories of forgetting** are many and varied. You will learn about six types of forgetting, including how these relate to short-term and long-term memory.* |
| **Aspect 4: Application of memory research** | | |
| Mnemonics<br>　　page 46<br>Visual imagery<br>　　page 48<br>Spider diagrams and pictorial notes<br>　　page 49<br>Context and state dependency<br>　　page 50<br>Elaborative rehearsal<br>　　page 50 | Application of memory improvement techniques to study and exam skills, for example:<br>● mnemonics<br>● visual imagery<br>● spider diagrams/pictorial notes, etc.<br>● context and state dependency<br>● elaborative rehearsal | *Findings from memory research can be very useful when applied in our everyday lives; as a student, improving your memory is a key factor in developing effective **study skills** and improving **exam performance**. Here, you will study a range of **memory improvement techniques** and the psychological processes involved. And, as well as learning about these various techniques, you will be able to put them to practical use in your own study and exam activities.* |

# Aspect 1: The nature of memory

## Short-term and long-term memory

The term **memory** has a number of meanings in psychology, as we shall see in this chapter, but the essential definition is that it refers to the process by which we *retain information about events that have happened in the past*. Note that 'the past' does not simply refer to things that happened *years* ago, but things in our immediate past. If you can recall anything about the start of this paragraph, you must be using your memory. Your memory for events in the present or immediate past (e.g. trying to remember an order of drinks at the bar) is referred to as your **short-term memory** (or STM for short). Your memory for events that have happened in the more distant past (such as remembering this distinction between STM and LTM in an exam) is referred to as your **long-term memory** (or LTM for short).

LTM refers to memories that last anywhere from 2 minutes to 100 years plus, i.e. anything that isn't short term. LTM is a bit like having a library with virtually unlimited storage capacity. We might think about STM as being like a note pad where we mentally scribble down things that we need to remember for just a very short period of time. The trouble with this 'notepad' is that it can't hold very much information and the 'ink' fades very quickly. An example of STM in action would be trying to remember a seven-digit phone number that you have just been given. This is maintained in STM by repetition until the number is dialled, and then fades.

The process of memory has three stages: **encoding**, storage and retrieval.

| | |
|---|---|
| **Encoding** | This stage is where we actually *create* a memory trace, i.e. a representation of an event in our memory. |
| **Storage** | Once encoded, we need to store the memory trace somewhere within the memory system. |
| **Retrieval** | Storing a memory isn't enough; we also need to be able to *recall* or *remember* it. |

| | |
|---|---|
| **Duration** | STM has a very limited duration (a memory in STM doesn't last long), whereas LTM has potentially unlimited duration. A memory in LTM could, theoretically, last for the whole of a person's life. |
| **Capacity** | This is a measure of how much can be held in memory. STM has a very limited capacity (7 plus or minus 2 'chunks' of information) whereas LTM has potentially unlimited capacity. |
| **Encoding** | Information in STM tends to be encoded acoustically (i.e. information is represented as sounds), whereas information in LTM is encoded semantically (i.e. information is represented by its meaning). |

# starSTUDY

# Investigating the nature of memory: Duration of STM

(PETERSON AND PETERSON, 1959)

## Aims

Have you ever had the experience of being introduced to someone and then, a short while later, realising that you can't recall their name? Some people who suffer from poor memories develop ways of improving their memory. One way to improve your memory is to repeat something over and over again. One way to improve your memory is to repeat something over and over again (that was a joke). This is called *verbal rehearsal*. The result of such rehearsal is that short-term memories are held in the short-term memory store and eventually become long term; i.e. you will remember the item.

What happens if you don't rehearse something? How long does that memory remain in your short-term store before it disappears in a puff of smoke?

Lloyd and Margaret Peterson set out to study systematically the length of time that information is retained in memory when there is no verbal rehearsal. In other words, they had three aims: to conduct a systematic and controlled study; to look at the duration of immediate or short-term memory; and to do this when verbal rehearsal is prevented.

## Method and procedure

Peterson and Peterson enlisted the help of 24 students. Recall was tested as follows: the experimenter said a *nonsense trigram* to the participant (e.g. WRT), and then said a three-digit number. The participant had to count backwards from this number in threes or fours until told to stop. Then the participant was asked to recall the nonsense trigram. Each participant was given two practice trials followed by eight trials. On each trial the *retention interval* (time spent counting backwards) was different: 3, 6, 9, 12, 15, or 18 seconds.

## Results

Participants remembered about 90% of the trigrams when there was only a 3-second interval and about 2% when there was an 18-second interval. The results are shown in the graph.

## Conclusion

We can conclude from this study that information remains in STM for less than 18 seconds if verbal rehearsal is prevented; most information has disappeared within a few seconds. This shows that the duration of STM is very short when rehearsal is prevented.

## Evaluation

*What does this study actually tell us about real life?*

Using nonsense trigrams is not much like what we do in real life. What was the last thing that you had to memorise? It probably wasn't a string of consonants but might have been something related to school work or might have been something like a new skill (e.g. riding a bicycle – that involves memory too). So an important criticism of memory research is that it relates to one special aspect of memory and may not apply to all memory.

*Students are not like everyone else*

A great deal of research in psychology is based on the behaviour of students. This is not surprising since most research is conducted in universities where students can (and are) required to be participants as a course requirement. It is quite likely that people aged 18–21 have rather different memories compared with people of other age groups, and students are probably (possibly) more than averagely intelligent! It is also likely that psychology students have a go at guessing what the experiment is about and this may affect their behaviour (and the results of the study).

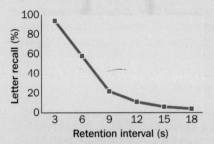

Examine the graph showing the results from Peterson and Peterson's study. How would you describe these results? What conclusions might you draw?

*Why was it necessary to count backwards during the retention interval in the Peterson and Peterson study?*

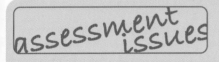

**Describe the *three* stages of the memory process. (ku 3 ae 0)**

It's not just *what* you know; it's *how* you tell it. An important element of learning psychology, which exam markers are always on the lookout for, is skill in expressing concepts and explanations. For Higher, you are expected to 'communicate psychological knowledge effectively', and this includes using relevant *terminology*. In the above example, naturally you would write about *encoding*, *storage* and *retrieval*, but in explaining these you could, for example, refer to 'creating a memory trace', 'mental representation', 'information processing', 'recall', etc. In general, try to 'write like a psychologist'!

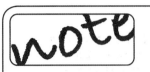

### What is stored in the brain?

The basic unit of memory (the *memory trace*) is thought to be *biochemical* in nature. The precise mechanisms of memory are not fully understood, but most psychologists believe that a memory results from changes in the connections or connection strengths between neurons in the brain. For example, if two *neurons* are frequently active together, the connection between them will be strengthened. Over time, this means that activity in one neuron will tend to produce activity in the other neuron.

Cover up the picture above. How many dots were there? The capacity of STM is probably fewer than 9 items, which would predict that you wouldn't get the answer right because there were 12 dots; if there were 5 dots, you should have coped.

# Research on encoding, duration and capacity

In the first section of this chapter you examined one experiment on memory in detail. In this next section, we will look at various other studies related to encoding, duration and capacity. Such research supports the view that short- and long-term memory are different.

## Research into the nature of STM

### Encoding in STM

When we try to keep information active in STM we repeat it over and over to ourselves; in other words, we maintain an *acoustic* memory trace. Any errors we make at recall tend to involve words that *sound* the same (see study by Baddeley, 1966). Even if the initial stimulus is visual, our representation of it in STM tends to be acoustic although visual codes are also used in STM. Brandimote *et al.* (1992) found that participants used visual encoding in STM if they were given a *visual* task (pictures) and prevented from doing any *verbal* rehearsal (they had to say 'la, la, la') in the retention interval before performing a *visual* recall task. Normally we 'translate' visual images into verbal codes in STM but since verbal rehearsal was prevented they did use visual codes.

### Duration of STM

The study by Peterson and Peterson (on page 33) demonstrated that STM has a very short duration when data is not rehearsed. This is supported in a study by Sebrechts *et al.* (1989) who tested the duration of STM by showing participants three words. The participants were then asked to recall the words (they didn't expect this and therefore shouldn't have been rehearsing them). They did quite well if they were tested immediately, but if the researcher waited even four seconds, recall was almost zero.

### Capacity of STM

A very old study by Jacobs (1887) demonstrated the capacity of STM using the serial digit span technique. A participant is presented with a sequence of digits and required to repeat them back in the original order. They are first given one digit to repeat and this is gradually increased adding one digit at a time to the sequence. The point at which a participant's recall is correct 50% of the time is said to be their digit span. Jacobs found that the average span for digits was 9.3 items and 7.3 for letters. This span increased steadily with age.

Why does it increase with age? This may be because people learn the technique of *chunking* – items are chunked together into bigger units. Chunking makes it possible to, for example, remember phone numbers – it is easier to remember 3 chunks (0771 032 3542) than 11 separate digits (07710323542).

*Seven plus or minus two*

George Miller (1956) wrote a memorable article called 'The magic number seven plus or minus two'. Why do so many things come in sevens? There are seven notes on the musical scale, seven days of the week, seven deadly sins, and so on. Could it be that we cope rather well with registering seven things at once (the span of immediate memory)? A number of studies have investigated this. People can cope reasonably well with counting seven dots flashed onto a screen but not many more than this. The same is true if you are asked to recall musical notes, digits, letters and even words.

It also seems to be true that people can recall five *letters* as well as they can recall five *words* – we chunk things together and then can remember more. Miller concluded that chunking is a vital activity to reduce the load on memory and enable you to remember more things at one time.

*The size of the chunk*

Simon (1974) demonstrated that the number of chunks did have some effect on memory. People had a shorter span for larger chunks, such as eight-word phrases, than smaller chunks, such as one-syllable words.

### Study on encoding (Baddeley, 1966)

Baddeley gave participants one of the four lists shown below. If asked to recall the words immediately (testing STM), those with List A (acoustic similarity) did worst. If participants were asked to recall the list after a 20-minute retention interval (testing LTM) during which they performed another task, those participants with List C (semantic similarity) did worst.

| List A | man, cab, can, cad, cap, mad, max, mat, map | *acoustically similar* |
|---|---|---|
| List B | pit, few, cow, pen, sup, bar, day, hot, rig, bun | *acoustically dissimilar* |
| List C | great, large, big, huge, broad, long, tall, fat, wide, high | *semantically similar* |
| List D | good, huge, hot, safe, thin, deep, strong, foul, old, late | *semantically dissimilar* |

This shows that words in STM tend to be remembered in terms of their sounds (*acoustically*), whereas words in LTM tend to be coded in terms of meaning (*semantically*).

## Research into the nature of LTM

### Encoding in LTM

LTM involves semantic coding (see study by Baddeley, 1966). That is, we encode information according to the *meaning* of words, rather than the way they sound. Encoding of information in LTM can also be visual (a good thing to know if you tend to revise from diagrams) or even acoustic.

### Duration of LTM

Experimental research on memory often suggests that people have rather poor long-term memories. Perhaps the problem is that experiments require participants to remember things that are not very interesting. To overcome this, Bahrick *et al.* (1975) set out to study very long-term memories in a natural context. They arranged for nearly 400 participants (aged 17 to 74) to see how many high school classmates' names they could recall and whether they could put names to faces in their high school yearbook. Participants who were tested within 15 years of graduation were about 90% accurate in identifying faces and names (i.e. visual and verbal recognition). After 48 years, this declined to about 80% for name recognition and 70% for photo recognition.

Waganaar and Groeneweg (1990) interviewed people who had been imprisoned in concentration camps during the Second World War. Thirty years on, their recall was still good for certain details, such as the name of the camp commandant, but they had forgotten many other details. This supports the idea that some long-term memories are enduring. The question is why are some memories enduring while others aren't? Later in this chapter we will look at why we *forget* some things and not others, which is really the same as asking why we remember some things and not others. It may be that we do remember a lot of things but just can't *recall* them. Or it may be that some information never entered memory in the first place.

### Capacity of LTM

LTM is said to have an unlimited capacity. Some people don't think so because they forget so many things. LTM may *appear* to be *limited* but this is because we simply can't access all the information stored there. What evidence is there for this unlimited capacity? One could argue that unlimited *duration* means there must also be unlimited capacity, and therefore studies of the duration of LTM are also relevant to the capacity of LTM.

Another approach is to think of the human brain as being like a computer. We measure computer capacity in terms of megabytes (or gigabytes or terabytes). Can we do the same with the human brain? Merkle (1988) has tried to do this. If you use the number of synapses (connections between neurons) in the brain then the capacity of memory may be in the range $10^{13}$–$10^{15}$, or between one thousand and one million gigabytes. This may sound small when compared with most computers, but it appears that the secret is *organisation*. The human brain has evolved a highly complex system of organisation. Computers may have capacity but, as yet, cannot rival the organisation of the brain.

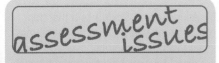

**Briefly describe *three* types of encoding that are used in short-term memory (STM) and long-term memory (LTM). (ku 6 ae 0)**

It may seem an obvious thing to say but, before answering any question in an assessment, you first need to decide what the question is *about*. The people who write the exam papers do try to make the questions as clear as possible – they are not intent on 'tripping you up'! In this case, all you need for a good answer could be found in the previous pages. Later in this chapter, you will find out about other aspects of memory and might be tempted to include such material in your answer to a question like this. However, it would not be creditworthy as the focus of the question is simply on *encoding*.

# Aspect 2:    Models of memory

## The multi-store model of memory

A 'model' of something should never be taken as an exact copy of the thing being described, but rather as a representation of it. A map of the London Underground, for example, is a representation of the Underground layout that helps us appreciate how it works and where it goes. A model of memory is also a representation. Based on the evidence available, a model provides us with what is essentially an analogy of how memory works. Describing memory in terms of 'stores' or 'levels' or 'loops' makes our understanding more concrete. In this Aspect we will be looking at two models, each offering a slightly different perspective on the organisation of memory. We will start with the multi-store model.

### *explanation*    The multi-store model

The multi-store model (MSM) was first described by Atkinson and Shiffrin in 1968. It is illustrated in the diagram. You should by now be quite familiar with the idea of a *short-term store* (STM) and a *long-term store* (LTM).

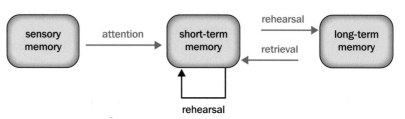

### KEY TERMS

**Sensory memory:** This is the information at the senses – information collected by your eyes, ears, nose, fingers, and so on.

There is a third store in this model. This is the *sensory store* or **sensory memory**. The sensory stores are constantly receiving information but most of this receives no attention. These incoming data remain in the sensory store for a very brief period. If a person's *attention* is focused on the sensory store (for whatever reason), the data are then transferred to STM. This explains the first step in remembering something – attention.

The second step is moving information from STM to LTM. Atkinson and Shiffrin said that this happens through *rehearsal*. This may well be familiar to you. When you try to remember things for a test, what do you do? Possibly you repeat the things you want to remember over and over again – verbal rehearsal! Atkinson and Shiffrin proposed a direct relationship between rehearsal in STM and the strength of the long-term memory – the more the information is rehearsed, the better it is remembered.

So the multi-store model is what it says, a description of how memory works in terms of three 'stores': your senses (sensory memory or SM), STM (limited capacity, short duration) and then LTM (potentially unlimited capacity and duration). Attention and rehearsal explain how data are transferred. Sounds good, or does it?

### *evaluation*

*It's right*
Many research studies show that there are three distinctly different memory stores. We have looked at some of these studies and seen how they show differences in terms of duration, capacity and encoding. These differences are further supported by the studies described below. Therefore the model makes good sense. The idea of STM and LTM continues to provide a framework that psychologists find useful for describing and understanding memory.

*It's wrong*
The multi-store model is probably an oversimplification of memory processes. The model just proposes one long-term store rather than separate stores for the different kinds of long-term memory. We actually have lots of different kinds of memory: memory for words (*semantic memory*), memory for what you did yesterday or a film you saw last week (*episodic memory*), and memory for riding a bicycle (*procedural memory*). Most memory experiments are concerned with semantic memory and the results don't necessarily apply to other kinds of memory.

This model also proposes just one *short-term* store and, as the working memory model suggests, there are probably more of these.

Finally, the multi-store model proposes one mechanism for how data are stored in long-term memory – rehearsal. Yet there are many situations when we remember things without having rehearsed the information. Depth of processing is an important alternative. The *levels of processing approach* (Craik and Lockhart, 1972) suggests that enduring memories are created by *processing* rather than rehearsal. By 'processing', Craik and Lockhart meant that it is what you do with the material which makes it memorable not just rehearsing it. The more you have to think about the meaning of a thing, the more you will remember it (quality rather than quantity). This was demonstrated in an experiment by Craik and Tulving (1975) where participants were given a list of words and asked questions about each word – whether it was in capitals or whether it rhymed with another word or what the word meant. When later asked to recall the words, participants recalled more of the words that were processed for meaning, i.e. semantically (see page 51 for more detail).

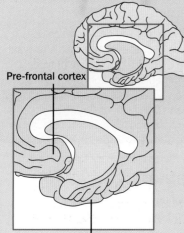

Pre-frontal cortex

Hippocampus

## starSTUDY

# Investigating the multi-store model of memory: A case study of HM

(SCOVILLE AND MILNER, 1957)

### Aims
To study the effects of brain damage on behaviour.

### Method and procedure
In 1953, a man referred to as HM had epilepsy of such severity that it couldn't be controlled by drugs. As a final measure, surgeons removed the hippocampus from both sides of his brain. This case study recorded his subsequent behaviour.

### Results
HM's personality and intellect remained intact but his memory was affected. More precisely, he had lost much of his memory for the 10 years prior to the operation (*anterograde amnesia*), and even more damagingly, he had lost the ability to store new information (*retrograde amnesia*). He had about a 90-second memory span, so he was effectively waking up every 90 seconds not knowing where he was or to whom he was talking. He could still talk and recall all the skills that he knew previously (*semantic and procedural memory*), but his memory did not incorporate new experiences. For many years, HM reported that his age was 27 and the year was 1953. After a while, he realised this was absurd and tried guessing the answer. He watched the news every night yet had no recall for major events. He happily reread magazines with no loss of interest. He couldn't memorise lists of words or recall faces of people he met.

### Conclusion
In short, HM's short-term memory was intact but he could not form new long-term memories. The hippocampus may be a specific location for the formation of long-term memory. He could still use his existing long-term memory. This study provides physiological support for the multi-store model – identifying a physical location for LTM transfer.

### Evaluation

*What caused his memory loss?*
HM's epilepsy may have caused general brain damage and this could explain his abnormal behaviour. We also don't know whether the trauma of the operation may have been responsible for subsequent behaviour rather than the loss of a part of the brain.

*Ethics*
HM's identity was protected but he can't have given his **informed consent**. Is this ground breaking science or cruel exploitation of a man whose life has been ruined by experimental brain surgery?

*Generalising from a study of one*

It is not reasonable to generalise from a sample of one unique individual. However, other studies have supported the importance of the hippocampus. For example, Baddeley (1990) described the same symptoms in a man, Clive Wearing, whose hippocampus was damaged by a viral infection. He too has no ability to form new memories and little recollection of the past although he does remember that he loves his wife Deborah. See also 'Areas of the brain associated with STM and LTM' below.

There are two videos you can watch about Clive Wearing at www.learner. org/resources/series150.html#

## KEY TERMS

**Decay:** This means a gradual deterioration or fading away. When used in connection with memory, there is an assumption that a memory trace in our brain disintegrates over time and so is lost.

## Further research that supports the multi-store model

### The sensory store

Evidence to indicate the duration of the sensory store was collected in a study by Sperling (1960). Participants saw a grid of digits and letters (as in the illustration below) for 50 milliseconds (a blink of an eye). Either they were asked to write down all 12 items *or* they were told that they would hear a tone immediately after the exposure and they should just write down the row that was indicated. When asked to report the whole thing, participants' recall was poorer (5 items recalled, about 42%) than when asked to give one row only (3 items recalled, 75%). This shows that information **decays** rapidly in the sensory store.

| Stimulus material used by Sperling | | | | |
|---|---|---|---|---|
| 7 | 1 | v | f | high tone |
| X | L | 5 | 3 | medium tone |
| B | 4 | W | 7 | low tone |

### The serial position effect

Glanzer and Cunitz (1966) showed that, if you give participants a list of about 20 words, presented one at a time and then ask them to recall any words they can remember, you can observe an interesting effect. They tend to remember the words from the start of the list (a *primacy effect*) and from the end of the list (a *recency effect*) but are less good at recalling words in the middle. The primacy effect occurs because the first words are best rehearsed and transferred to LTM. The recency effect occurs because these words are in STM when you start recalling the list.

### Areas of the brain associated with STM and LTM

One way to demonstrate the existence of separate stores in memory is to link STM and LTM to specific areas of the brain. Modern techniques of scanning the brain can be used (such as PET scans and fMRI which are used to detect brain tumours). These take images of the active brain and enable us to see what region is active when a person is doing particular tasks. Research has found that the prefrontal cortex is active when individuals are working on a task in immediate memory (Beardsley, 1997) whereas the hippocampus is active when long-term memory is engaged (Squire *et al.*, 1992).

*assessment issues*

**With reference to research evidence, describe and evaluate the multi-store model of memory. (ku 5 ae 5)**

Questions often ask you to refer to research evidence, so how should you decide *which* research studies and findings to use? First, make sure that you choose evidence that is relevant to the particular topic of the question. It is also useful to give examples of a *variety* of types of research. For this question, you could write about an experimental laboratory study using memory tasks, such as Glanzer and Cunitz (1966), as well as a case study of a brain-damaged patient, such as Scoville and Milner (1957), and a brain-scan study such as Squire *et al*. (1992).

## The working memory model of memory

The second model of memory that we will examine is the working memory model. Essentially this focuses on one aspect of the multi-store model – the short-term memory store, renaming it 'working memory'.

*explanation*

## The working memory model

Baddeley and Hitch (1974) proposed an alternative model to explain short-term memory. They felt that STM was not just one store but a number of different stores. Why did they think this?

- If you do two things at the same time and they are both visual tasks, you perform them less well than if you do them separately.

- If you do two things at the same time and one is visual whereas the other involves sound, then there is no interference. You do them as well simultaneously as you would do them separately.

This suggests that there is one store for visual processing and one store for processing sounds, which is shown in the diagram of the model.

Baddeley and Hitch used the term 'working memory' to refer to that bit of memory that you are using when you are working on something. For example, if you are calculating some sums, reading a sentence, or playing chess, there is part of your mind that is holding the information that you are currently engaged with – your working memory.

The working memory model

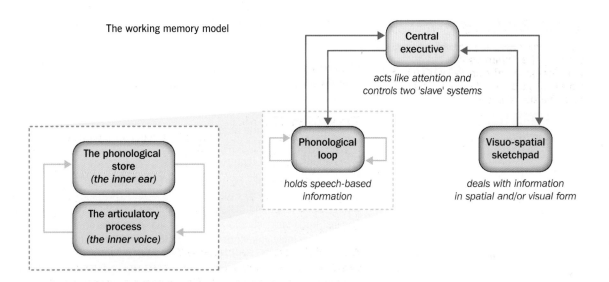

The details of the three components of working memory are:

- **Central executive**. When you pay attention to something, you focus your resources on it. The central executive acts like attention and draws on the phonological loop or the visuo-spatial sketchpad as 'slave systems'. The central executive has a very limited capacity; in other words, it can't attend to too many things at once.

- **Phonological loop**. This too has a limited capacity. 'Phonological' relates to sound ('phono' is like phone – a telephone carries sound). The phonological loop deals with auditory information and preserves the *order* of information. It is called a loop because information goes round and round in a loop. Baddeley (1966) further subdivided this loop into the *phonological store* and an *articulatory process*. The phonological store simply holds the words you hear. It is like an inner ear. The articulatory process is used for words that are heard or seen. These words are silently repeated (looped). It is like an inner voice. It appears that the phonological *loop* is used when learning new words. The phonological *store* 'simply' holds auditory data.

- **Visuo-spatial sketchpad**. Visual and/or spatial information is temporarily stored here. Visual information is what things look like. Spatial information is the relationship between things. The visuo-spatial sketchpad is used when you have to plan a spatial task (like getting from one room to another, or hammering a nail into the wall). It is also used if you are engaged in a visual task, such as working out how many windows there are in your house. To do this, most people create a visual image of their house in working memory and this enables them to 'count' the windows.

*evaluation*

*On the positive side*

The model explains many observations. For example, it is easier to do two tasks that are different (verbal and visual) than doing two tasks that are similar (and use the same slave system). The model also explains the **word-length effect** (see research below). Such support means that the model may accurately describe what is going on in your head.

*On the negative side*

There is some concern about the central executive. What exactly is it? The working memory model does little more than say that the central executive allocates resources and is essentially the same as 'attention'. Some psychologists feel that this is too vague and doesn't really *explain* anything. Other psychologists believe that the notion of a single central executive is wrong and that there are probably several components. In summary, the account offered of the central executive is unsatisfactory.

### KEY TERMS

**Word-length effect:** People cope better with short words than long words in working memory (STM).

## starSTUDY

# Investigating the working memory model: Dual task performance

(HITCH AND BADDELEY, 1976)

### Aims

To test the predictions of the working memory model: i.e. that performing two tasks that involve the same component of working memory should result in reduced performance speed when compared with performing two tasks that involve different components.

### Method and procedure

Twelve students were given two tasks to do simultaneously.

Task 1 was a verbal reasoning task that occupied the central executive. For example participants were given a statement 'B is followed by A'; they were then shown two letters (AB) and required to say true or false.

Task 2 was one of the following:
- no additional task (control condition)
- repetition of a single word (saying 'the, the, the' repeatedly)
- counting numbers in sequence (1, 2, 3, 4, 5, etc.)
- digit-span repetition (listening to and then repeating six random digits).

The last three tasks should all place similar demands on the phonological loop, but the tasks place increasingly greater demands on the central executive.

### Results

The more that Task 2 involved the central executive, the slower participants were at Task 1 (the verbal reasoning task), as shown in the table.

|  | Involvement of central executive | Mean time taken to solve verbal reasoning task |
|---|---|---|
| **control** | None | 2.79 |
| **'the, the, the'** | Very little | 3.13 |
| **'1, 2, 3'** | Some | 3.22 |
| **Random six-digit number** | The most | 4.27 |

### Conclusion

These results support the predictions of the working memory model because doing two tasks that both involve concurrent loads on the central executive causes difficulty.

### Evaluation

*Supports the model*

These results could not be explained by the multi-store model because that model does not consider the effect of task complexity on STM capacity. This suggests that the working memory model is a useful addition.

*Biased sample*
Students were used as participants and do not represent 'typical' memory abilities – their memories are likely to be better than average because they are (a) intelligent and (b) young. It is possible, therefore, that these results do not apply to all people.

## Further research that supports the working memory model

### The phonological loop and articulatory process

The phonological loop explains the word-length effect. It seems that the phonological loop holds the amount of information that you can say in two seconds (Baddeley *et al.*, 1975a). This makes it harder to remember a list of long words such as 'association' and 'representative' than it is to remember shorter words like 'harm' and 'twice' because the longer words can't be rehearsed on the phonological loop because they don't fit.

*However*, the word length effect disappears if a person is given an *articulatory suppression task*: for example, if you are asked to say 'the, the, the …' while reading the words. This repetitive task ties up the articulatory process and means that you can't rehearse the shorter words more quickly than the longer ones and the word length effect disappears. This is evidence of the articulatory process.

### The visuo-spatial sketchpad

Baddeley *et al.* (1975b) demonstrated the existence of the visuo-spatial sketchpad. Participants were given a visual tracking task (they had to track a moving light with a pointer). At the same time they were given one of two other tasks: task 1 was to describe all the angles on the letter F (a visual task); task 2 was to perform a verbal task. Task 1 was very difficult but not task 2: presumably because task 1 involved the same components of working memory whereas task 2 involved two different components.

### Evidence from studies of brain-damaged patients

Studies of individuals with brain damage also support the working memory model. SC had generally good learning abilities with the exception of being unable to learn word pairs that were presented out loud, which suggests damage to the phonological loop (Trojano and Grossi, 1995). Another patient, LH, who had been involved in a road accident, performed better on spatial tasks than on those involving visual imagery (Farah *et al.*, 1988). This suggests separate visual and spatial systems.

*Try reading something while saying 'the, the, the …' silently to yourself. Does this disrupt your reading? The working memory model suggests that the phonological loop is important when reading new material. If you read something you know well, is 'the, the, the …' less disruptive?*

*assessment issues*

**With reference to research evidence, describe and evaluate the working memory model. (ku 5 ae 5)**

Referring to research is usually a great way of showing *ae*: whenever you explain that so-and-so's findings support (or challenge) a theory, or when you evaluate a study, you can get those elusive *ae* marks! Even in lower-mark questions, with no *ae* marks, you can often get *ku* marks for referring to evidence.

And don't forget that you can gain credit this way – whether the question asks for it (as in the question above) or not!

| Comparison of the multi-store and working memory models | |
|---|---|
| **Similarities** | **Differences** |
| Research evidence often doesn't reflect everyday use of memory (i.e. lacks *ecological validity*), though some more recent research has used diaries to investigate everyday memory as distinct from the rather contrived memory tasks in lab studies. | Each model focuses on a different aspect of memory – the working memory (WM) model is concerned with STM alone. |
| Both are information-processing models, based on how computers handle information and may suggest that memory can be represented in a rather simple way although this is an oversimplification. | WM suggests more varied processes with STM whereas the multi-store model (MSM) suggests that STM is homogenous. |
| Both models ignore the influence of emotion on memory (consider repression on page 44). | Whereas the MSM focuses on the structure and the links between different memory stores, the WM model explains ongoing processes with the stores, i.e. how your memory actually works. |

# Aspect 3: Forgetting

To *forget* something has a number of meanings in psychology, but generally is taken to refer to a person's loss of the ability to recall or recognise something that they have previously learned. **Forgetting** from short-term memory (STM) is usually explained in terms of the information simply being lost from a limited-capacity and limited-duration store. But what about forgetting from long-term memory? Earlier in this chapter you read that the capacity and duration of long-term memory (LTM) is effectively unlimited, so why do we appear to lose information once we have submitted it to LTM? Not being able to retrieve information from LTM may be due to its no longer being *available* (i.e. it is no longer there) or because over time it has become *inaccessible* (for whatever reason). Forgetting, therefore, has a simple definition, but its explanation may be a little bit more complicated.

## Forgetting in STM

### explanation

### Explanation 1: decay theory

One way to think about memory is in terms of a *memory trace* (or engram). This refers to the physical representation of information in the brain. It is suggested that this trace simply disappears or *decays* if it is not rehearsed (remember what we said earlier about connections forming between neurons, see page 32). This would explain the results from the Peterson and Peterson experiment (1959). No rehearsal was permitted and the information had disappeared from STM after 18 seconds at the most.

### evaluation

There is a key problem with this explanation. How can we be sure that decay took place? It could be that the first information was simply pushed out or overwritten (as proposed by the **displacement** theory, described below). In the case of the experiment by Peterson and Peterson the digits that the participants were counting might have *displaced* the original nonsense trigrams. It is difficult to prevent rehearsal without introducing information that will overwrite the original information. So the numbers could have replaced the trigrams.

To be fair, there is some support for decay theory. Reitman (1974) tried to overcome this problem of overwriting by giving participants a different task in the retention interval. She asked participants to listen for a tone. This meant that their attention was diverted elsewhere, which should prevent rehearsal of data but they weren't actually dealing with any new information. In a 15-second interval participants' recall for 5 words dropped by 24%, which is evidence for decay ... except that we can't be *entirely* certain that new information had not entered STM; they might have been thinking about something else while listening to the tone.

### explanation

### Explanation 2: displacement theory

The second, obvious explanation for forgetting in STM is that a new set of information physically overwrites the older set of information. This happens because STM is a limited-capacity store. When it is full and more information is presented then all that can happen is displacement – by overwriting.

### evaluation

Waugh and Norman (1965) demonstrated that forgetting in STM is mostly due to displacement and not decay – read the Star Study on the oppositie page.

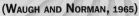

## starSTUDY

# Investigating theories of forgetting: Decay versus displacement

(WAUGH AND NORMAN, 1965)

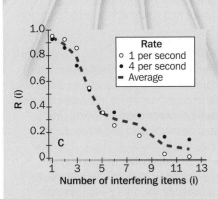

Graph axes: R (i) on the vertical axis from 0 to 1.0; Number of interfering items (i) on the horizontal axis from 1 to 13.

**Rate**
- ○ 1 per second
- ● 4 per second
- ■ Average

## Aims

We forget things which are not rehearsed very quickly. Is this because the memory trace decays within a brief interval or is it 'written over' (displaced) by the items that follow? This research aims to see which explanation was correct.

## Method and procedure

The participants were four students. Nancy Waugh and Donald Norman used the *serial probe technique* to investigate forgetting in STM. This involves reading out a series of single digits to a participant. For example the following 16 digits were read out: 3, 5, 4, 8, 2, 5, 9, 6, 3, 1, 7, 9, 4, 8, 6, 1. The probe is the last number in the series; in this case the probe is 1. Participants have to recall (or guess) the number that came after the first occurrence of the probe in the list. The correct answer here would be 7. The probe is placed early or late in the list to see the effects on memory.

Each participant listened to 90 lists read at a fast or slow rate. The fast rate meant that the digits were read out at 4 digits per second (which takes 4 seconds in total); the slow rate was 1 digit per second (and takes 16 seconds in total). When the list is read at a slow rate, there is more time between the first and last digits than when the list is read at the fast rate. If decay is the correct explanation, we would expect participants to find it harder to recall earlier digits in the slow condition. If displacement is the correct explanation, then the speed of reading the lists shouldn't matter.

## Results

The effect of the rate of presentation was relatively small compared with the effect of position. *Position:* participants recalled items nearer the end of the list much better (about 80%) than at the start of the list (about 20%). This would be the case for both decay and displacement. *Rate of presentation:* When the probe was late, recall was slightly better for the fast list (four digits per second) than the slow list. This difference was small but significant as you can see from the graph below (the more interfering items there were, the later the probe).

## Conclusion

This shows (1) that most forgetting in STM can be explained by displacement and (2) some forgetting in STM is due to decay.

## Evaluation

*Research support*
Shallice (1967) also found a small effect for rate of presentation but a larger effect for the position of the probe (i.e. the number of subsequent items), supporting the initial results.

*Mundane realism*
There is the question of how much this task represents everyday experience (i.e. may lack **mundane realism**). The results may not tell us much about forgetting in the 'real world'.

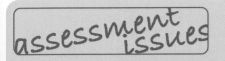

## Discuss theories of forgetting, with reference to research evidence. (ku 12 ae 8)

This is a straightforward one-part, 20-mark essay question. In the exam, two of the five questions you will have to answer are 20-mark essay questions; each of these may be either presented in one part, like this example, or subdivided into two related parts. You will also have to write one essay-style answer in the NAB, for 15 marks. Let's focus on the one-part essay question, like the example above, as it is in this kind of question that you have most freedom to answer in the way you wish, and therefore you need to put in the most effort in planning it!

Get into the habit of drawing up an essay plan every time you write an essay. You can *think* much, much faster than you can write, so, whether you list bullet points, or draw a 'mind map' (see page 48), your plan is your 'recipe' – and all you have to do is follow it.

In the example above, it would make sense to *introduce* the topic by defining 'forgetting', perhaps relating it to the three memory stages, the different types of memory stores, and/or the issue of availability versus accessibility.

In the *main argument*, decide whether to discuss a small number of theories (e.g. two or three) in depth, or a greater number (e.g. four or five) in less detail (there are more theories of forgetting on pages 42 and 43). Don't neglect your *conclusion* – summarise your main argument and relate this back to the title (don't just list all the points that you have already made).

*Throughout* your plan indicate your *ae* points and the research studies you're referring to.

# Forgetting in LTM

We now move from short-term to long-term memory. Explanations for forgetting in LTM are different from those for STM because LTM has unlimited capacity and duration; therefore insufficient space is not an issue.

*explanation*

## Explanation 1: decay theory

Do we forget things from years ago because the memory trace simply disappears, as in STM? Individuals who suffer brain damage where parts of their brain no longer function experience forgetting. In this case it is the loss of a memory trace that causes forgetting.

Lashley (1931) conducted some famous experiments on rats. He trained them to learn mazes and then removed sections of their brains. He found that there was a relationship between the amount of material removed and the amount of forgetting that happened. This again suggests that LTM forgetting may be related to physical decay.

*evaluation*

*If decay was the major explanation of forgetting then why do we have so many long-term memories? There is evidence that memories can be very long-lasting (e.g. evidence from Bahrick et al. on page 33). This means that decay is an unlikely explanation for most long-term forgetting because otherwise why would some memories remain intact and not others? It could be that regular usage prevents decay.*

*Decay or interference?*
If you recall, it was hard to distinguish between the effects of decay and displacement in STM. The same problem occurs with decay and interference in LTM. If something disappears from memory, has it decayed or has displacement/interference from other information been the cause? Baddeley and Hitch (1977) conducted a **natural experiment** to investigate this, testing recall of rugby fixtures played over a season. Some players played in all of the games in the season whereas others missed some games because of injury. The time interval from start to end of the season was the same for all players but the number of intervening games was different for each player. If decay theory is correct, then all players should recall a similar percentage of the games played because the time period was the same. If interference theory is correct, then those players who played most games should forget proportionately more because of interference. Baddeley and Hitch found that the more games the players had played, the more they forgot (proportionately). This supports interference theory.

*explanation*

## Explanation 2: interference theory

**Interference:** This occurs when something gets in the way of something else. When used in the study of forgetting, it refers to the tendency for one memory to 'interfere with' the accurate retrieval of another (similar) memory.

**Proactive interference (PI):** This is when past learning interferes with current attempts to learn something.

**Retroactive interference (RI):** This is when current attempts to learn something interfere with past learning.

In the 1950s, **interference** theory was *the* theory. Consider the following: you are used to opening a particular drawer to get a knife. Your mother decides to re-organise the kitchen and puts the knives in a different drawer. However, every time you go to get a knife you go to the old drawer. An old memory is continuing to *interfere* with new learning. After many months, you have got used to the new arrangement. Your mother decides it was a bad idea and changes back to the original scheme. Now what happens? You continue to go to the second location. The newer memory interferes with past learning.

Psychologists have found evidence of both **proactive** and **retroactive interference**. A typical study on interference (e.g. Underwood, 1957) involves learning lists of word pairs, such as cat–tree and candle–whale from lists A and B (on page 43). A participant is then required to learn a second list which interferes with the first list, such as: cat–stone, and candle–cloth from lists A and C. Finally, the participant is given the first word of the pair and asked to recall the word from List C (proactive interference) or List B (retroactive interference). A control condition is included to see what recall will occur when there is no interference.

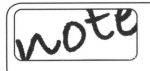

| List A | List B | List C |
|--------|--------|--------|
| Cat | Tree | Stone |
| Candle | Whale | Cloth |
| Book | Fork | Jail |
| Plant | Tank | Claw |
| Water | Market | Gold |
| Track | Lemon | Kettle |
| Dish | Cane | Swamp |
| Flask | Picture | Mast |
| Cigar | Jelly | Nail |
| Animal | Nurse | Pencil |

**To demonstrate proactive interference**

**Group 1 (experimental group)**

- Learns A–B, then A–C
- Test by giving list A words and ask to recall list C words

**Group 2 (control group)**

- Learns another list of word pairs, then A–C
- Same test as above

**To demonstrate retroactive interference**

**Group 3**

- Learns A–B, then A–C
- Test by giving list A words and ask to recall list B words
- Compare performance with experimental group 1

## evaluation

*Interference effects require special conditions*
Interference does cause forgetting but only when the same stimulus is paired with two different responses. These conditions are rare in everyday life and therefore interference only explains a limited range of forgetting.

*It is possible to recover from interference*
The study by Tulving and Psotka (1971) shows that retroactive interference does occur; however, when suitable cues are supplied the effect disappears (see 'Interference or lack of cues?' on page 44).

## note

### Availability and accessibility

The decay and interference theories suggest that forgetting happens because a memory trace is no longer there. It is no longer *available*. Therefore, this is *trace-dependent forgetting*. *Cue-dependent forgetting* means that the memory trace is there, only you can't *access* it. Forgetting, in this case, is due to retrieval failure.

## explanation

## Explanation 3: cue-dependent forgetting

Forgetting in LTM is mainly due to retrieval failure (lack of accessibility rather than availability). This is the failure to find an item of information because you have insufficient clues or cues. If someone gave you a hint, then the memory might pop into your head but, in the meantime, you are faced with a blank. It is possible that you have a vast store of memories and could access them – if only someone could provide the right cues.

There are several different kinds of cue. The context where initial learning takes place or the mood you were in may act as a cue later.

### External cues: context-dependent learning (or forgetting)
Abernethy (1940) arranged for a group of students to be tested before a certain course began. They were then tested each week. Some students were tested in their teaching room by their usual instructor. Some were tested there by a different instructor. Others were tested in a different room either by their usual instructor or by a different one. Those tested by the same instructor in the same room performed best. Presumably, familiar things (room and instructor) acted as memory cues. Look at the wall in front of you. Does anything there trigger a memory? If so, it is acting as a cue.

### Internal cues: state-dependent learning (or forgetting)
Goodwin *et al*. (1969) found that people who drank a lot often forgot where they had put things when they were sober but recalled the locations when they were drunk again! Miles and Hardman (1998) found that people who learned a list of words while exercising on a static bicycle remembered the words better when exercising again than they did while at rest.

**KEY TERMS**

**Cue-dependent forgetting:** This occurs when information may be stored in memory but may be inaccessible unless there is a specific cue to help retrieve it (e.g. a smell may trigger a memory from childhood).

*evaluation*

*This is a powerful explanation for forgetting*
Some psychologists believe that all forgetting is cue-dependent forgetting. Michael Eysenck (1998) said, 'It is probable that this is the main reason for forgetting in LTM.' There is a considerable amount of research to show the importance of cues and how they trigger memory (e.g. Tulving and Psotka, 1971). As we have seen, retrieval is best when conditions during recall match those during original learning. The *encoding specificity principle* further states that a cue doesn't have to be exactly right but the closer the cue is to the thing you're looking for, the more useful it will be.

*Everyday memory and procedural memory*
Many of the studies used to support cue-dependent forgetting are laboratory based and not very like everyday memory. Therefore, cue-dependent recall may not apply to some aspects of everyday memory. For example, procedural knowledge (knowing how) is not related to cue-dependent recall. Examples of this kind of memory include remembering how to play ping-pong or how to play the recorder. Such memories are rather resistant to forgetting, but not totally immune. If you haven't played ping-pong in years, there is some relearning to do but, even so, cues don't really explain this.

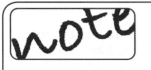

### Interference or lack of cues?

Tulving and Psotka (1971) conducted an experiment on forgetting. Participants were given 6 different word lists to learn each with 24 words. Each list was divided into 6 different categories (so over the 6 lists there were 36 categories, such as kinds of tree and names of precious stones). After each list was presented, participants were asked to write down as many words as they could remember (*free recall*). After all the lists were presented, there was a final free-recall test and then the participants were given the category names and again asked to recall all the words from all the lists (*cued recall*).

Some participants only learned one list; others learned two lists and so on. According to interference theory, the more lists a participant had to learn, the worse their performance would become. This was what Tulving and Psotka found. Those who were given only one or two lists remembered a higher percentage of their words than those given more lists. This is evidence of *retroactive interference*.

But when participants were given cued recall the *effects of interference disappeared*. With cued recall, participants remembered about 70% of the words regardless of how many lists they had been given. This shows that interference effects may mask what is actually in memory. The information is there (*available*) but cannot be retrieved. This is called *cue-dependent forgetting*. This means that forgetting happens at the retrieval stage (i.e. retrieval failure) rather than during initial encoding.

*Repression and motivated forgetting are also explanations for long-term forgetting.*

## Repression and motivated forgetting

Sometimes forgetting is purposeful; i.e. it is done deliberately. **Motivated forgetting** is when a person *wants* to forget something. There are two kinds of motivated forgetting: suppression and repression. Suppression is when you consciously try to forget a memory. For example, you might 'forget' to do your homework because you didn't want to do it so you simply pushed it out of your mind.

**Repression** is when you unconsciously try to forget something. The idea of repression was proposed by Sigmund Freud over a century ago. In his theory of personality (which is described on page 246), Freud used the term 'repression' to describe one method by which the **ego** protects itself from emotional conflicts. Traumatic events cause anxiety and, to reduce this, the memory of the event is banished. A repressed memory, therefore, is the memory of a traumatic event placed beyond conscious awareness – into the *unconscious mind*. This displacement makes one feel better, at least temporarily.

Freud further theorised that these repressed memories continue to affect conscious thought, desire, and action even though there is no conscious memory of the traumatic event.

Most psychologists accept as fact that it is quite common to *consciously* repress unpleasant experiences, even sexual abuse, and then later to spontaneously remember such events. However, most of the controversy centres on recovered memories – recovered during repressed memory therapy (RMT). Critics of RMT maintain that many therapists are not helping patients recover repressed memories, but are (often unwittingly) suggesting and planting 'false memories' of sexual abuse, alien abduction or even satanic rituals.

## Research on repression

### Response to emotionally charged words

One way to investigate repression has been to study participants' reactions to emotionally charged words. For example, Bradley and Baddeley (1990) read out a list of words. Participants were asked to respond by saying any word that came into their head (a *word association* task). Some of the trigger words were neutral (e.g. 'tree' or 'cow') whereas others were negative and emotional (e.g. 'angry' and 'fear'). Later, participants were given the trigger word and asked to recall their own response. They had more difficulty recalling those associated with the emotionally charged words. However, the results were different if there was a longer delay before testing. Some participants were tested after 28 days, and they remembered the emotional associations better than those tested quite soon after initial learning. It is possible that anxiety and arousal depress short-term recall but enhance long-term recall. Alternatively, it may be that anxiety or arousal initially causes repression but this disappears over time.

### Response to unhappy childhood events

Myers and Brewin (1994) conducted a *natural experiment* comparing 'repressors' with other emotional types. A 'repressor' is someone who deals with anxiety by being defensive. How do you know if someone is a repressor? You give them a personality test and if they score low on anxiety and high on defensiveness they are classed as a repressor. Myers and Brewin interviewed 27 female undergraduates, asking them to recall childhood memories and also to discuss their relationships with their parents. The repressors took twice as long to recall their unhappy memories, and the age of the first negative memory was older than for the non-repressors. In addition, the repressors were more likely to report difficult relationships with their fathers. This means that they had more anxiety-provoking memories and appeared to repress these; however, this may be 'inhibited recall' rather than true repression.

Williams (1994) also conducted a natural experiment to find out if memories are repressed. The study used the records kept at a city hospital emergency room detailing all cases of sexual assaults on children in the period April 1973 to June 1975. In this period, 206 girls had been admitted. Many years later, 129 of these girls (now women) were re-interviewed, aged 18 to 31. The women were asked to participate in a follow-up study of the lives and health of women who had received medical care from the city hospital during childhood (i.e. they were deceived). Over one third (38%) did not show any recall for the earlier sexual abuse. Of those who did recall the abuse, 16% reported that they had, at one time, not been able to recall these incidents but had 'recovered' the memory. The results suggest that having no memory of child sexual abuse is relatively common, which supports the idea that recovery of memories is possible – because some individuals have forgotten real incidents. Furthermore, that some individuals said that they had recovered their early memories shows that recovery occurs. Both results support the notion of repression in relation to painful memories.

### Case studies

There are also case studies of individuals who claim to have *event-specific amnesia*. For example, the man who killed Robert Kennedy, Sirhan Sirhan, claimed to have no recall of these events (Bower, 1981). Karon and Widener (1997) studied hundreds of cases of Second World War veterans who experienced battlefield trauma and repressed these memories. The result was many years of mental illness finally alleviated when the traumas were remembered in therapy. This provides evidence of repressed memories and the effects they have.

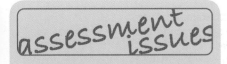

### Common themes: alternative approaches in psychology

You may have noticed by now that there is rarely a single 'correct' answer to any of the big questions about human behaviour! Although the Topic of memory is firmly located in the *cognitive* domain, psychologists also propose alternative explanations: for example, some aspects of memory are studied in terms of *physiological* processes (e.g. trace decay, role of emotion). As you can see in the preceding pages, one explanation of forgetting – repression – comes from the *psychoanalytic* perspective of Sigmund Freud, in stark contrast to the other – cognitive – explanations.

Have you noticed explanations from different perspectives in any other Topics of the course? It would be a good idea to highlight these, especially in your revision notes because, in NABs and in the exam, you can demonstrate *analytical* thinking by discussing the contributions of different approaches.

# Aspect 4:  Application of memory research

In this final Aspect of Memory we will be covering some very useful issues – applying research on memory to improving your memory, specifically to improve your study and exam skills. We start with a number of familiar mnemonic techniques, some of which you have used since you first started to learn. For example, everyone learns the alphabet by singing it – a mnemonic technique. The term 'mnemonics' can actually be applied to all of the techniques in this Aspect because they are all ways of helping people to remember and recall information; however, the specification identifies some specific kinds of mnemonic technique such as visual imagery and elaborative rehearsal. So we will start with a general look at some mnemonic techniques and then consider the specific ones.

## Mnemonics

### What is it?

A mnemonic is any structured technique used to help people remember and recall information. They are most commonly employed in areas when individuals are required to recall large amounts of unfamiliar information or to make associations between two or more units of information.

There are many such techniques, some of which will be familiar to you:

| Types of mnemonic | | |
|---|---|---|
| **Mnemonic** | **What is it?** | **An example** |
| **Acronyms** | A word or sentence formed from the initial letters of other words | ROYGBIV: colours of the rainbow: red, orange, yellow, green, blue, indigo, violet |
| **Acrostics** | A poem or sentence where the first letter in each line or word forms the to-be-remembered item | Every Good Boy Deserves Favour: the order of G-clef notes – E, G, B, D, F |
| **Rhymes** | A group of words with an identity and rhythm | 30 days hath September, April, June, and November. All the rest have 31 save February alone, which has 28 days clear and 29 each leap year |
| **Method of loci** | Used by the ancient Greeks. Loci literally means 'places' and the method requires the learner to associate parts of the to-be-recalled material with different places (usually, rooms in a familiar building or sites along an often-travelled road) in the order that they are to be recalled | You imagine a journey through a familiar landscape or location, such as the house where you live: Imagine walking through your front door and then walking through the house visiting every room in turn, just as if you were really doing it. In each room or special location in the room (a sofa, the fridge, etc.), place a piece of information – trying to create a memorable link. For example, place the phonological loop on the CD player. Then, in the exam, you imagine yourself walking around the house, and you will recall the different pieces of information. Have fun during revision making up imaginary journeys! |
| **Pegwords** | Pegwords are short words that sound like numbers and are easy to picture. This method is used when the order of information is important or when the to-be-recalled information involves numbers | See illustration on facing page |
| **Keyword/ linkword** | Used when trying to associate two pieces of information. Each piece of information is represented by a concrete image – the image is an approximation, for example 'broke' for 'Baroque music'. 'Broke' is the keyword. You then imagine a picture where the keywords are linked | To remember that Bach was a Baroque musician, you imagine a broken man sitting in a box – 'box' is a keyword for Bach (see Star Study) |

One way to remember things is the method of loci. Take a 'mental' walk around a familiar room, taking note of the different loci there. When you have to memorise material, you form visual images for ideas and find a way of associating them with the different loci in the room. When recalling this material, take the same 'mental walk'.

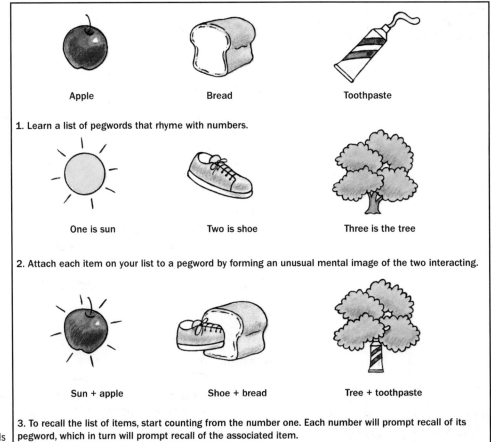

1. Learn a list of pegwords that rhyme with numbers.

2. Attach each item on your list to a pegword by forming an unusual mental image of the two interacting.

3. To recall the list of items, start counting from the number one. Each number will prompt recall of its pegword, which in turn will prompt recall of the associated item.

Using pegwords

## What is the psychology?

All the techniques above offer some way of organising the material to be remembered. By organising data, we establish links that help recall.

A further benefit of these mnemonic techniques is creating meaning; we find it easier to remember things that mean something.

## Research evidence

The benefit of organisation and links was shown in a study by Bower *et al.* (1969). Participants were given 112 words to learn. If the words were organised into conceptual hierarchies, recall was two to three times better than if the words were presented in a random order. An example of the conceptual hierarchies presented in this study is shown below.

| Minerals | | | | |
|---|---|---|---|---|
| Metals | | | Stones | |
| Rare | Common | Alloys | Precious | Masonry |
| Platinum | Aluminum | Bronze | Sapphire | Limestone |
| Silver | Copper | Steel | Emerald | Granite |
| Gold | Lead | Brass | Diamond | Marble |

Conceptual hierarchy used in research by Bower *et al.* (1969)

## Evidence from an applied study

Rummel *et al.* (2003) asked students to read a historical passage on aspects of human intelligence. They were randomly assigned to two different instructional conditions to process the passage: *mnemonic*, where keywords for intelligence theorists' surnames and line drawings linking the theorists and their contributions were provided, and *free study*, where participants were given summary paragraphs and were instructed to use their own preferred study methods. Participants given mnemonics remembered more names and contributions than did the participants in the free study condition.

Stalder (2005) found that acronym use consistently predicted higher performance on acronym-related exam items. Students rated acronyms as helpful in multiple ways, including increasing motivation to begin studying.

Snowman *et al.* (1980) trained 72 students over a period of 14 weeks in the use of various mnemonic techniques: mental imagery, method of loci, and prose analysis. The aim was to increase their ability to identify, encode, and retrieve information from prose. In comparison with a similar group that received traditional instruction (e.g. note taking, identification of main idea, word meaning analysis), the learning strategy group recalled twice as much information when tested.

## starSTUDY
# Investigating applications of memory research: Keywords
### (ATKINSON AND RAUGH, 1975)

Example of the keyword technique: the Russian word for 'building' is *zdánie*, which is pronounced somewhat like 'zdawn-yeh' with the emphasis on the first syllable. Using 'dawn' as the keyword, one could imagine the pink light of dawn set against the backdrop of a large building.

## Aims
To assess the keyword method for language teaching.

In this study, a foreign word is first linked with an English word which sounds like it, or like part of it (acoustic link) – this is the *keyword*. Then a visual image is created linking the keyword with the meaning of the word. When the language learner needs to use the foreign word, they recall the visual image.

## Method and procedure
English-speaking undergraduates (who had no prior knowledge of Russian) were given 120 Russian words and their English equivalents. Participants had been trained in the keyword method, but while some were provided with ready-made keywords to use, other participants had to make up their own. A control group was given no training in the keyword method.

## Results
The researchers found that both groups using the keyword method showed much better recall for the Russian words, both shortly afterwards and six weeks later. Memory was improved by almost 50% over the short term and almost 75% over the long term. In addition, those learners who had been provided with keywords showed better recall than those who had had to provide their own.

## Conclusion
This study shows that the keyword system improves recall of foreign vocabulary in language learners. It also demonstrates the effectiveness of visual imagery and multiple encoding (in this case, visual cues added to auditory and verbal information), in relation to memory effectiveness.

Furthermore, it supports the value of elaborative rehearsal as the participants had to spend time thinking about the links and thus elaborated the meaning.

## Evaluation

### Limited usefulness
Gu (2003) claimed that rigorous experimentation over two and a half decades points to a single conclusion: the keyword method is superior to almost all other methods tested for learning languages. However, while the technique is clearly effective, it is only effective for one aspect of language acquisition – acquiring a vocabulary. There are other, more complex aspects of language learning, such as abstract nouns, verb tenses, word order, etc.

### Different kinds of vocabulary learning
Ellis and Beaton (1993) pointed out that the study only involved one kind of vocabulary learning – receptive rather than productive vocabulary learning (being able to translate Russian to English rather than being able to produce a Russian word). The researchers conducted a further study and found that the keyword method is better for receptive vocabulary learning.

# Visual imagery
## What is it?
Constructing a visual image of something we wish to remember allows us to make full use of visual encoding. A simple example might be the way that books, and teachers, use pictures and diagrams to illustrate topics (even quite abstract material which is not usually regarded as 'visual').

### How can you use it?
Images that lead to the most effective recall are often vivid, distinctive or novel – for example it would be better to visualise a cat carrying a brick on its back, or building a brick wall, rather than a cat sitting on a brick. Visual imagery features in a number of mnemonic techniques, such as the method of loci and the numeric pegword system (described on page 47), and spider diagrams/pictorial notes (see below).

### What is the psychology?
Paivio (1971) proposed that words and images are processed separately, on the basis of his studies of patients who had damage to their temporal lobes and could not process images. According to Paivio, concrete words, which can be made into images, are double encoded in memory. They are coded once in verbal symbols and once as image-based symbols. This double coding increases the likelihood that they will be remembered. Paivio called this the *dual coding hypothesis*. This can be linked to the phonological loop in the working memory model of Baddeley and Hitch (see page 37).

Visual imagery also serves to organise information, and information that is organised is recalled better, as we saw in the study by Bower *et al.* (see page 47).

### Research evidence
In one experiment, participants were given 100 different cards, one at a time; each card had two unrelated words, for example 'cat' and 'brick'. Participants in one group had to produce a mental image linking the two. The other group were just asked to memorise the words. When given a cued recall test (i.e. given the first of each pair of words), the imagers recalled 80% of words, compared with the non-imagers' 45% (Bower, 1972).

## Spider diagrams and pictorial notes
### What are they?
These involve making notes of information in the form of a drawing, usually a branching pattern, with the main topic in the centre and component elements/ideas radiating outwards. Small sketches can be added, as well as colours (using highlighters or felt-tips). Each page of notes, therefore, has a unique, distinctive visual appearance (whereas pages of ordinary, linear notes all look very similar). This process, which adds a range of visual cues to the verbal material, has also been called mind mapping (Buzan, 1993).

Some advantages are that additional material can easily be inserted later, in any position (hard to do in linear notes), and links between two separate 'branches' can be readily indicated; this may facilitate *semantic processing* (and therefore effective storage).

**Make your notes distinctive**

*Some students re-write their revision notes. This may be useful if you are going to organise them better and/or elaborate them or make them more distinctive. All of these (organisation, elaboration and distinctiveness) are forms of processing which enhance memory.*

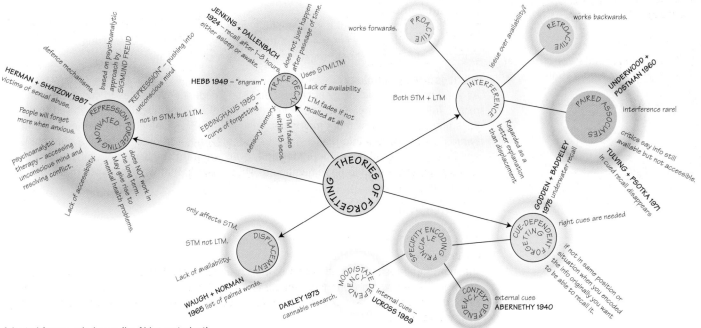

Adapted from a mind map (by Abby, a student)

### How can you use them?

Pictorial notes can be useful for summarising and memorising material when learning, or revising, or when drawing up an essay structure.

### What is the psychology?

When you draw a diagram, you have to think about how things are linked and this creates an enduring memory, according to the levels of processing approach (see page 35).

### Research evidence

One study that demonstrates this was conducted by Mandler (1967). He asked participants to sort a pack of 52 word cards into up to 7 piles, based on any system of categories. When each participant had finished, the cards were collected up and the participant was asked to repeat the task. This continued until the participant was 95% consistent in their sort (which took about 6 sorts). Recall was best for those who had used the most categories. This suggests that the act of organising information makes it memorable without any conscious effort.

### Evidence from an applied study

Farrand *et al.* (2002) compared the effectiveness of using the mind map study technique with self-selected study methods for recall of factual material (a 600-word text). The students using mind mapping had significantly better recall over a period of one week but were less motivated – possibly because using mind maps was unfamiliar to them and they were therefore less motivated to use it than a more familiar method.

## Context and state dependency

### What is it?

The retrieval of newly acquired information when the person is in the same context, place, state, mood, etc. as when the information was first learned. You should remember that one of the explanations for forgetting in long-term memory is cue-dependent forgetting – which is also cue-dependent remembering! We often have memories stored in our heads and they pop into mind given the right cue. There are two kinds of cue:

- *Context dependent*. Our memories are triggered by cues from the context in which learning took place. For example, you may be sitting in your classroom as you read this and look up at a particular poster. If you look at the poster again in a few weeks it may well jog your memory for this piece of information.

- *State dependent*. Have you ever had the experience that every time you are in a sad mood a certain song comes into your head? That song is linked to that mood; the recall of the song is mood dependent.

### How can you use it?

An important application of this is reducing your notes to bullet points, each containing one or two words which are cues. You just need to memorise the cue (using, for example, acrostics) and then it should trigger a whole string of information.

### What is the psychology?

As you know, the psychology of context and state dependency relates to cue-dependent recall. Tulving and Psotka (see page 44) carried out an experiment which showed that cues allow us to access more memories. Tulving (1968) explained this: elementary units (words) are organised into higher-order units (categories). In order to recall a nominal unit one first has to recall the higher-order unit, even when this higher-order unit was not part of the original material to be remembered. This suggests that we access our memories in a hierarchical manner.

### Research evidence

There is much evidence to support the effect of contextual cues on recall. For example, Thomson and Tulving (1970) gave participants word pairs to learn such as 'train–black' or 'white–black'. In some instances, the cue word (e.g. 'white') was strongly associated with the word to be recalled; in other cases, there was very little link (e.g. 'train'). Participants' recall was better when given the stronger cue. This demonstrated the *encoding specificity principle* (see page 44).

> " *Our recollections are largely at the mercy of our elaborations.* "
>
> *(Neuroscientist Daniel Schachter, 1996, p. 56)*

# Elaborative rehearsal

### What is it?

Elaborative rehearsal is a particular kind of rehearsal. In the multi-store model (see page 34), information is transferred from STM to LTM as a consequence of rehearsal. However some theorists assert that there are different types of rehearsal (Craik and Watkins 1973):

- *maintenance rehearsal,* where material is simply repeated to oneself in the same way as it was presented, i.e. rote repetition

- *elaborative rehearsal,* where material is expanded and manipulated, linking it with knowledge we already have so that it becomes more meaningful, i.e. a form of *semantic* processing.

We all think like this spontaneously much of the time, and we can exploit this ability to improve our studying, by getting into the habit of deliberately elaborating on new information that we wish to learn and retain. It may seem hard to believe that increasing the amount of material can *improve* memory, but that is exactly what elaborative rehearsal allows us to do, by increasing its *meaningfulness*. It is a process of *adding extra cues* to new information at the time when we encode it ('multiple encoding'), so that we have multiple pathways to the information at the time when we need to retrieve (recall) it.

### What is the psychology?

Craik and Lockhart (1972) proposed that enduring memories are created not through maintenance rehearsal but through *semantic processing* (elaborative rehearsal). So, it is not the *amount*, but the *nature* of rehearsal that matters. For example, suppose you hear a news item about an outbreak of Legionnaire's Disease in a local town. You might ask yourself questions such as: 'How is that disease caused? What are the symptoms? How serious is it? Have I been in that town recently?' and so on. In adding that kind of information from our own knowledge, we are *elaborating* on the original material, and are therefore much more likely to recall it later.

### Research evidence

Craik and Tulving (1975) presented participants with sentences that had the final word missing, along with a possible final word. They were asked whether this word would make sense if it was inserted into the sentence. There were two kinds of sentences: some were quite simple, such as 'She cooked the ...', and others were more complex, such as 'The great bird swooped down and carried off the struggling ...'. Later, when the participants were given a cued recall test (i.e. they were given the incomplete sentences again and had to recall the final word) recall was much better for those words that had completed the complex, rather than the simple, sentences. Although both types of sentence demanded semantic processing, the complex type required more elaborative processing.

*Revise with a friend – working with a partner can be an effective revision strategy, as long as you are both committed to working and not gossiping! Working with a partner means that you can discuss things and elaborate the concepts. You can set each other questions and mark each other's work – more discussion and more processing.*

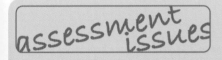

**With reference to research evidence, describe and evaluate memory improvement techniques and their application to study and exam skills. (*ku 12 ae 8*)**

You may enjoy learning about ways that psychology is applied in real life, because you may well have experienced for yourself the kind of situations studied. What could be more relevant to your own experience right now than techniques for improving your memory in relation to study/exam skills? Still, when answering exam questions on this Aspect, you should show objective, analytical thinking. Exam questions such as the one above contain a series of specific demands, so make sure that you address every part of the question; a 'shopping list' of techniques (or, worse, a description of your own favourite technique) will not do! Note that you must not just describe the techniques themselves, but also how they are applied; and you need to *evaluate* the techniques too, including how effective they are as study and exam skills. And don't forget to support your points throughout with research evidence.

You can demonstrate the skill of analysis by explaining how the applied techniques are related to theoretical concepts – as we have done in the 'What is the psychology?' subsections in this Aspect. Keep this principle in mind, whenever you study applied Aspects of any Topic in psychology.

*In this section we show you student answers to possible exam questions plus examiner's comments on these answers. Remember that in the actual exam (and NABs) your questions for this Topic will always add up to 20 marks. The question may be one essay worth 20 marks or a number of smaller questions (such as those shown below) which add up to 20 marks.*

**Question 1**    Describe both the multi-store model of memory and the working memory model, and compare strengths and weaknesses of the two models. Refer to research evidence in your answer. *(ku 12  ae 8)*

## Tom

*The multi-store model*
The multi-store mode, as its name suggests, says that memory consists of several stores. The first store is sensory memory where data from the senses (eyes, ears etc.) is held. The second store is short-term memory which is a limited capacity store (it holds 9 items or fewer, though these may be chunks rather than just single digits according to Miller) and is also limited in terms of duration (it only holds items for less than 18 seconds, which was shown by Peterson and Peterson). The final store is long-term memory which is potentially limitless in terms of capacity and duration.

An important part of this model is an explanation of how information is passed between the stores. Data is transferred from SM to STM by paying attention to sensory data and then passed to LTM if adequately rehearsed.

The distinction between the stores has been supported by research evidence. Baddeley found that the two stores encoded data differently. He gave participants four different word lists: acoustically similar, acoustically dissimilar, semantically similar, and semantically dissimilar. Those participants who had to recall words immediately had most difficulty with the acoustically similar word list. Those participants who had to recall words after 20 minutes had most difficulty with the semantically similar word list.

*The working memory model*
This model focuses on short-term memory alone because Baddeley and Hitch proposed that there was evidence of several different stores within STM or 'working memory'. The different stores are: the central executive which controls everything, the phonological loop which deals with sound and has limited capacity, and the visuo-spatial sketchpad which deals with visual information.

This model was supported by a study which showed that when people have to do a task that involves separate components they cope well whereas if the same component is involved they slow down. This shows that these components exist.

*Strengths and weaknesses*
Both models have good research support so that is a strength.

One weakness of the multi-store model is that it oversimplifies things. For example it doesn't separate STM into the separate stores that have been shown to exist by Baddeley and Hitch. The same problem is true for LTM where there are different kinds of memory (e.g. episodic and procedural). Furthermore the model suggests that information passes from STM to LTM as a consequence of rehearsal whereas Craik and Lockhart have shown that elaborative processing is just as important.

The working memory model has been criticised because some of the components are rather vague and don't really explain anything.

Even though the multi-store model has its weaknesses it still continues to be a good framework for viewing memory and certainly is supported by research studies.

**Examiner's comments**    At first sight, Tom's answer appears well-organised because of the arrangement of content under subheadings. However, it is good practice to provide both an introduction and a conclusion in an essay; there is a conclusion of sorts in the last two sentences, but it is rather weak.

Much of Tom's content is sound, but sometimes the emphasis is misplaced: instead of devoting a substantial paragraph to Baddeley's encoding research, it would have been more efficient and effective to give greater attention to the supporting evidence in the 'strengths and weaknesses' section. The answer fails to specify the 'strengths' here, and evidence of 'comparison' is also thin on the ground. Tom evidently has a degree of understanding of these theories, but his knowledge is somewhat patchy. Sometimes his English expression lapses into informality, e.g. '... don't really explain anything'. He gains **12 out of 20** *(ku 8/12  ae 4/8)*.

## Alice

Diagram of the multi-store model

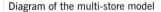

The diagram shows that there are 3 stores and shows how information is passed between the stores.

There is a lot of research evidence to support the view that there are 3 distinctly different stores. First of all Sperling (1960) showed evidence of a separate sensory store. He flashed rows of letters and digits. If participants were asked to recall one row their percentage recall was much higher than if they had to recall all the numbers/digits. This shows that information disappeared quickly from sensory store.

Evidence for a distinction between STM and LTM comes from studies where the duration of STM has been shown to be very limited. If rehearsal is prevented Peterson and Peterson found that people would have forgotten most nonsense syllables within a few seconds. This shows that STM is a limited duration store. It is also limited in capacity as shown by a study by Jacobs. Participants were given a serial digit span task and could only remember a maximum of 9 items. Miller called this effect 7 ± 2.

Other evidence comes from the study of people with brain damage, such as HM and Clive Wearing. Both of these individuals had damage to one area of their brain (the hippocampus) and lost their ability to form new memories. They retained some long-term memories from before the brain damage. This is supported by studies using brain scans which show that some areas of the brain are active while STM is used, whereas other areas are active when LTM is used.

The strengths of this model are also weaknesses. It is a simple model which is good and has generated lots of empirical research because it is easy to test. However it may oversimplify what is actually taking place in memory. The model assumes that rehearsal is all that is required to turn short into long-term memories, however the levels of processing approach suggests that it is depth of processing rather than any amount of superficial rehearsal. This was supported by a study done by Craig and Tulving who found people remembered things better the more deeply (semantically) they had to process them.

Another weakness of the model is that it assumes STM is all the same and LTM is all the same whereas there is evidence that each store consists of many different kinds of store. LTM can be divided into semantic, episodic and procedural memory and the working memory model has divided working memory into separate stores:

1. The central executive manages the system and has a very limited capacity.
2. The phonological loop deals with auditory information and preserves the order of information. It is subdivided into the phonological store and an articulatory process. The phonological store holds the words you hear. The articulatory process is used for words that are heard or seen. It is like an inner voice.
3. Visuo-spatial sketchpad: Visual and spatial information is temporarily stored here. Visual information is what things look like.

The proof of this model is that people are slower when they have to do tasks that involve the same component e.g. two tasks involving the central executive, but if they do two tasks that involve different components (e.g. central executive and the articulatory process) then they are no slower than when doing a task which involves just one of them.

The strength of this model, as for the multi-store model, is that it produces testable hypotheses that can be investigated to show that the model is correct. This model has also been supported by evidence from brain-damaged patients, such as SC whose memory was fine except for being unable to learn word pairs presented out loud, which suggests damage to his phonological loop.

The model has been criticised for vagueness. It is not precisely clear how the central executive functions and it probably is not just one unit but consists of several components.

**Examiner's comments**    Alice's diagram of the multi-store model (MSM), although not essential, gives the marker some evidence of her understanding; however, her explanation in words is rather sketchy, so she should be aware that a diagram or any visual representation given in an exam should *support rather than replace* the written content. For the sake of balance of content, the answer should address both models fairly equally – it would be better to provide a diagram of the working memory model too. It is also better to actually start the answer with words, putting the diagram after the first few introductory sentences. In fact, like Tom, Alice has neglected an introduction and conclusion.

Another imbalance in her treatment of the two models is the less substantial content on working memory – basically less in the way of supporting evidence. One clever evaluation strategy that Alice *has* used is to compare the multi-store model with a different theory of memory (levels of processing) in order to highlight a weakness in the concept of rehearsal (this is, incidentally, a strategy that can be used for many topics). However, the strengths and weaknesses of the MSM would have been better positioned near the end, so as to address the comparison with working memory, as required in the question.

Alice occasionally uses inappropriate expression, such as 'The proof of this model …', and '… to show that the model is correct'. There are also some inaccuracies and omissions in Alice's knowledge, and her content is not well organised. However, on the whole, Alice demonstrates a good, detailed understanding of the topic. She achieves **15 out of 20** (*ku* 9/12 *ae* 6/8).

**Question 2**    Describe a visual imagery technique to improve memory, and explain how students might use visual imagery techniques in study and exam skills. (*ku 4  ae 0*)

## Tom

One technique is mnemonics such as acronyms which you might use to help you remember something like the different components of the working memory model which are central executive, phonological loop, phonological store, articulatory process and visuo-spatial sketchpad: so you take all of the first letters and get CEPPSAPVSS and try to remember it as if it was a word.

## Alice

Mind mapping is a visual imagery technique where you start from a central point and link topics in a kind of hierarchy. You might use this to draw a diagram of the research on memory so you have STM and LTM and these branch out to encoding, duration and capacity and you put the studies in an appropriate place. This helps you remember things because you can visualise the mind map in the exam. You can also use them usefully when you are studying rather than just for revision because they help you think about the links between things and understand a topic better.

**Examiner's comments**    Tom appears to have seized on the words 'technique to improve memory', and (ironically!) has not seen the term 'visual imagery' in the question. Although his answer deals with a memory improvement technique, it is not one that uses visual imagery. Unfortunately, there is nothing in his answer that can gain any credit, so **0 out of 4 marks**.

Alice's answer provides a reasonably full description of mind-mapping as a visual imagery technique, as required in the question. It is slightly sketchy – for example, it would be useful to give a comparison with traditional linear notes, or reference to supporting evidence. However, it gives a clear description of construction of a mind-map, including an example, and specifies different uses in both study skills and exam skills. Although quite brief, it is concise, providing a fair amount of relevant information in a short paragraph, gaining **4 out of 4 marks**.

Physiological psychology seeks to explain behaviour in terms of the systems that operate in our bodies – such as the action of blood, hormones, nerves and the brain. Physiological psychology is part of the wider area of biological psychology which additionally looks at the influence of genetic factors on behaviour and the origins of adaptive behaviours in the evolutionary development of species. Such explanations emphasise 'nature' rather than 'nurture'. However, the way you think and feel has important influences on these physiological systems, as is illustrated by the study of stress.

Stress is what we experience when the perceived demands of a situation are greater than our perceived ability to cope. Such experience is produced by physical or psychological circumstances, and produces both physical and psychological effects.

| Chapter contents | Unit content for the topic 'Stress' | Comment |
|---|---|---|
| **Aspect 1: Biological processes in stress** | | |
| Stress and stressors page 55<br>Stress and the ANS page 58 | Biological processes in stress, including:<br>• General Adaptation Syndrome<br>• sympathetic/parasympathetic arousal of the autonomic nervous system<br>• fight-or-flight syndrome | *'Stress' has become an everyday word, and is something that most of us have experienced. In this first Aspect of the Topic, you will be able to define exactly what stress is, and describe the **biological processes** that take place when we are 'stressed'. The **General Adaptation Syndrome** describes three stages of the body's response to a stressor. The bodily systems that are mainly involved in stress are the nervous system and endocrine system, as you will see when you learn about **sympathetic and parasympathetic** arousal of the **autonomic nervous system**, and the **fight-or-flight syndrome**. Although we often regard stress as unpleasant and harmful, you will see that stress may be important for our survival.* |
| **Aspect 2: Origins and health effects of stress** | | |
| Origins of stress page 61<br>Individual differences in stress susceptibility page 63<br>Health effects of stress page 67 | Origins of stress:<br>• transactional nature of stress<br>• environmental, social and occupational sources of stress<br>Individual differences in stress susceptibility<br>Health effects of stress:<br>• short and long-term effects on physical and mental health | *In this Aspect you will learn both about the **origins** of stress and its **effects on health**. Firstly, you should grasp the idea that stress is **transactional**: whether we suffer stress or not depends on how we perceive the situation. **Environmental sources of stress** will be considered, such as overcrowding and noise, and you'll see that stress may also be associated with a person's **social** circumstances. **Occupational sources of stress** include workload and level of control.*<br>*In contrast to these 'external' sources of stress, you will learn how **individual differences**, such as gender, culture and personality, affect our **susceptibility to stress**.*<br>*Finally, we look at evidence of how stress can affect our **physical and mental health**, in the short and long term.* |
| **Aspect 3: Stress-reduction strategies and their effectiveness** | | |
| Physiological techniques page 70<br>Psychological strategies page 72<br>Social strategies page 75 | Stress-reduction strategies include:<br>• physical exercise and relaxation techniques<br>• cognitive strategies<br>• individual coping strategies and defence mechanisms<br>• social strategies and social support<br>• organisational stress-reduction strategies | *This Aspect takes a critical look at several of the **strategies** for **stress reduction** that are used by individuals and organisations. You should be able to distinguish between **effective stress-reduction strategies** and coping strategies that are 'maladaptive'. It is useful to envisage stress-reduction strategies at different levels, from physiological (e.g. **physical exercise** and **relaxation techniques**), through psychological (e.g. **cognitive**), to **social** measures. As well as being able to explain how these strategies work, and evaluating their effectiveness, you may also find them personally useful in tackling stress due to study – exams in particular – or other aspects of your everyday life.* |

# Aspect 1: Biological processes in stress

Hans Selye 1907–1982

## KEY TERMS

**Stress:** Although this term may be used interchangeably with 'stressor' and 'stress response', it may also be seen as the subjective experience of a lack of fit between a person and their environment (i.e. where the perceived demands of a situation are greater than a person's perceived ability to cope).

**Stressor:** This refers to any event that causes a stress reaction in the body. Stressors include environmental stressors (such as the workplace) and life events (such as illness or divorce).

*Remember that 'physiological' means 'of the body'; whenever you see the word 'physiology', just say 'of the body' quietly to yourself.*

## Stress and stressors

### What is meant by stress?

Much of our understanding of the nature of **stress** can be traced back to the pioneering work of Hans Selye in the 1930s (see, for example, the Star Study below). He conducted research with rats, subjecting them to different unpleasant stimuli (injections, extreme cold, severe pain) and realised that it didn't matter what the stimulus was, the physiological response was always the same. Selye described this physiological reaction as stress, and the unpleasant event that led to this response as a **stressor**.

The stress response is important to the survival of an animal because the physiological changes associated with stress are essential in the fight-or-flight response (i.e. attacking or running away). It is somewhat surprising, then, to find that the stress response is *adaptive*, and an essential part of our survival.

There is a difference between stress and a stressor: when the terms 'stress' and 'stressor' are used together, the former term (stress) might be used to refer to the way the body reacts to a stressful situation (e.g. 'I feel really stressed' is a little like saying 'I feel really ill'). The latter term (stressor) would then be used to refer to whatever event led to this physiological reaction (e.g. a stressful job).

An adaptive behaviour is one that enhances survival and reproduction. Individuals who possess the genes for an adaptive behaviour are more likely to reproduce successfully and then pass on the genes for these adaptive behaviours to their offspring. Genes for non-adaptive behaviours are not passed on because reproduction is less successful.

## starSTUDY

# Investigating biological processes in stress

**(SELYE, 1936)**

## KEY TERMS

**Hormones:** Chemical substances that circulate in your blood; small amounts have a large effect on target organs.

**Lymph system:** A network of organs, lymph nodes, lymph ducts, and lymph vessels that produce and transport lymph from tissues to the bloodstream. Lymph consists mainly of white blood cells (including lymphocytes) which attack bacteria.

### Aims

During his training as a doctor, Selye noticed that all hospital patients shared a common set of complaints such as diffuse aches and pains, loss of appetite and a coated tongue. Later, when conducting research on the effects of **hormones** using rats, he discovered that injections of many different substances caused all the rats to produce a similar response. He surmised that animals' response to external 'noxious' agents was somehow general, that there was one internal mechanism for dealing with 'noxious agents' – which he called 'stressors'. The aim of this study was to test this hypothesis.

### Method and procedure

Rats were exposed to various noxious agents: cold, surgical injury, production of spinal shock (cutting the spinal cord), excessive muscular exercise, or intoxications with sublethal doses of diverse drugs (adrenaline, atropine, morphine, formaldehyde, etc.). Their physiological responses were noted.

### Results

A typical syndrome was observed, the symptoms of which were independent of the nature of the damaging agent or the type of drug administered. This syndrome developed in three stages:
1. During the first stage (first 6–48 hours) all stimuli produced the same *physiological triad*: enlargement of the adrenal glands, ulcers (open wounds) in the digestive system (stomach, intestines) and shrinkage of the **lymph system**.
2. If the treatment was continued, the appearance and function of the internal organs returned practically to normal.

3. With continued treatment, after one to three months (depending on the severity of the damaging agent) the animals lost their resistance and displayed the symptoms of the physiological triad seen in the first stage.

## Conclusion

The results support the 'doctrine of non-specificity' that there is a non-specific response of the body to any demand made upon it. Selye suggested that the responses observed in rats to noxious agents might be similar to general defence reactions to illness.

## Evaluation

See evaluation of the General Adaptation Syndrome below.

---

**explanation**

## The General Adaptation Syndrome (GAS)

Selye's (1936, 1950) research led him to conclude that, when animals are exposed to different unpleasant stimuli they react in the *same way*. He described this universal response to stressors as the General Adaptation Syndrome (GAS):

- 'general' because it was the same response to all agents
- 'adaptation' because it was adaptive – the healthiest way to cope with extreme stress
- 'syndrome' because there were several *symptoms* in the stress response.

He further proposed that this model can explain the link between stress and illness, because stress results in a depletion of physiological resources and this lowers the organisms' resistance to infection.

*Adrenaline is a hormone which is described further on page 59.*

*Stage 1 Alarm reaction*
The threat or stressor is recognised and a response made to the alarm. *Adrenaline* is produced, leading to 'fight-or-flight' activity. There is some activation of the *HPA axis* (explained on page 59), producing **cortisol**.

### KEY TERMS

**Cortisol:** This hormone maintains a steady supply of blood sugar for continued energy. This enables the body to cope with the stressor, as distinct from the burst of energy needed for 'fight-or-flight' activity.

**Immune system:** Designed to defend the body against millions of antigens (i.e. bacteria, viruses, toxins and parasites) that would otherwise invade it.

*Stage 2 Resistance*
If the stress continues then it is necessary to find some means of coping. The body is adapting to the demands of the environment, but at the same time resources are gradually being depleted. The body appears to be coping whereas, in reality (physiologically speaking), things are deteriorating.

*Stage 3 Exhaustion*
Eventually the body's systems can no longer maintain normal functioning. At this point, the initial symptoms may reappear (sweating, raised heart rate, etc.). The adrenal gland may be damaged from previous over-activity, and the **immune system** may not be able to cope because production of necessary proteins (e.g. cortisol) has been slowed in favour of other needs. The result may be seen in stress-related illnesses such as ulcers, depression, cardiovascular problems, and other mental and physical illnesses.

---

**evaluation**

*Support from research*
The GAS model has had an important influence on our understanding of the relationship between stress and illness. It led to a vast amount of research, some of which is described later. This research supports the view that stress may lead to illness.

*Is it an appropriate model for explaining human stress responses?*
The fact that the GAS model is derived from research with non-human animals may explain why the model emphasises *physiological* factors. Humans are capable of thinking about their situation, which is certainly less true of non-human animals. This ability to think may mean that humans have the potential to control the extent to which an experience is stressful.

On the other hand, individuals who have no adrenal glands need to be given additional amounts of certain hormones in order to respond to stressors, otherwise they may die. This shows that part of the human stress response *can* be explained in terms of physiological systems.

*What actually causes stress-related illnesses?*
The GAS model proposes that resources become depleted so that the body can no longer fight infections. However, more recent research has shown that many 'resources' do not become depleted even under extreme stress. The current view is that the exhaustion phase is associated with increased hormone activity, such as cortisol, and it is this rather than depletion of resources that leads to stress-related illness (Sheridan and Radmacher, 1992).

## Research on stress and illness

Brady (1958) used pairs of monkeys. One monkey (the 'executive') was given the task of controlling electric shocks that were administered to itself and to another monkey (the 'yoked control'). As long as the 'executive' monkey pressed a lever every 20 seconds neither monkey received the shocks. The executive monkey died within a few weeks owing to a perforated ulcer. This suggests that stress not electric shocks causes ulcers – both monkeys received shocks but only the executive was presumed to experience high levels of stress.

Subsequent research has shown that ulcers are not always stress-related (many are caused by the virus *helicobacter pylori*) but the basic finding that stress is related to physical illness has been repeatedly demonstrated. For example, Cohen *et al.* (1993) used the 'viral-challenge technique' to study the effects of stress on over 400 volunteers. Individuals were exposed to the common cold virus and also given a questionnaire to assess their levels of perceived stress. Cohen *et al.* found a positive correlation between levels of stress and the likelihood of catching a cold. Friedman and Rosenman (1974) conducted a study linking coronary heart disease (CHD) to high stress. This study is described on page 66 as an example of individual differences.

## Research on stress and the immune system

### Stress depresses the immune system

Riley (1981) experimented with mice, inducing stress by placing the mice on a rotating turntable. Within five hours this led to a lowered lymphocyte count. Some mice were implanted with cancer cells. After 3 days of 10 minutes of rotation per hour mice were more likely to develop tumours than control mice given no stress. This shows that stress reduced immune activity (lymphocyte count) and was related to illness (more tumours).

Kiecolt-Glaser *et al.* (1984) looked at *T-cell activity* (an indicator of immune system activity) in the blood of students taking exams. Levels of T-cells were higher in the month before the students took exams, and dropped during the examination period itself.

### Stress *enhances* the immune system

Evans *et al.* (1994) looked at the activity of one particular antibody sIgA which coats the mucous surfaces of the mouth, lungs and stomach, and helps protect against infection. Evans *et al.* (1994) arranged for students to give talks to other students (mild stress). These students showed an increase in sIgA, whereas levels of sIgA decreased during examination periods which stretched over several weeks. Evans *et al.* (1997) propose that stress appears to have two effects on the immune system: up-regulation for very short-term stress (acute stress) and down-regulation for long-term stress (chronic stress). This fits with the essence of the GAS model and the SAM/HPA distinction (explained on page 60).

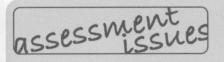
assessment issues

**Describe the findings of *one* research study into the biological processes of stress. (ku 5  ae 0)**

Clearly this is an example of a question on a single research study. But – did you spot the word 'findings' in the question? When you're under pressure in a NAB or exam, it's easy to miss crucial information through skim-reading questions. In this case, you are asked only about the findings, so beware going into 'automatic pilot' mode and trotting out *all* the details of your chosen study. You will get marks *only* for what you write about findings. Similarly, a research study question may ask only about the procedure, or conclusions etc.

## Stress and the ANS
### The adaptive nature of stress

When someone says 'I feel stressed', we feel for them assuming that it is a bad thing (People don't go round saying, 'Wow, it's great I'm feeling so stressed!'). However, we have already pointed out that stress is an adaptive response, or at least it sometimes is. Back in the *EEA* (*environment of evolutionary adaptation*, see Note) quick responses would have been a matter of life or death. Stress responses have evolved to provide animals with this ready responsiveness in times of danger, called 'fight or flight'. An animal that does not respond in this way is less likely to survive and reproduce.

What does this stress response feel like? We all know it well. Imagine you are sitting in a car about to take your driving test – you see the examiner walking towards you. Your hands feel clammy; your heart is racing; your rate of breathing speeds up; and you feel slightly flushed. These are all signs of the stress response. They occur because of activity in the **autonomic nervous system (ANS)**.

Some stress experiences are a flash in the pan – a stressor appears and the body responds. This is an *acute* stress response. Other stressful experiences last for a long time, such as worrying about your Higher exams for months beforehand! These are *chronic* stressors. As we have seen the body responds differently to these two types of stress.

**The EEA (environment of evolutionary adaptation)**

This is the environment that existed at a time in the past which our ancestors had to adapt to: i.e. those people who had certain physical and behavioural characteristics were more likely to survive and reproduce than those who didn't have such *adaptive* characteristics. This is generally regarded as the time, between approximately 10,000 and 2 million years ago, when our ancestors were hunter-gatherers on the African savannah.

*explanation* The autonomic nervous system (ANS)

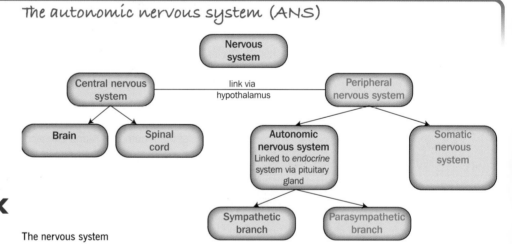

The nervous system

### KEY TERMS

**Autonomic nervous system (ANS):** The part of the nervous system that governs bodily functions related to survival and which is automatic – if it wasn't automatic, you might stop breathing when distracted!

**Endocrine system:** This is a system of glands throughout the body which secrete hormones; examples are the pituitary gland (in your brain) and adrenal glands (above your kidneys).

**Parasympathetic system:** The branch of the ANS that is related to relaxation and 'normal' physiological activity.

**Sympathetic system:** The branch of the ANS that is related to arousal and 'fight or flight'.

The autonomic nervous system is one part of the nervous system. It is called 'autonomic' because it governs itself (automatic). The actions of the autonomic nervous system are largely involuntary. This system is necessary because some bodily functions, such as your heartbeat, might not work very well if you had to think about them.

*The endocrine system and hormones*
The ANS governs the release of hormones from the **endocrine system**. Hormones are released in small amounts which are very short-lasting and only affect target organs, but their effects are very powerful. Hormones are similar to *pheromones*. You may have seen certain 'smelly' products for sale in shops that claim to increase your sex appeal – these are pheromones, chemical substances that can have a powerful effect on our behaviour. Pheromones work from person to person, whereas hormones circulate within the body but have equally powerful effects.

"It was the classic fight or flight response. Next time, try flight."

*Sympathetic and parasympathetic arousal*
The ANS is divided into two subsystems: the sympathetic and parasympathetic branches or systems. In emergency situations, the **sympathetic system** is aroused by the nervous system which sends messages to the *adrenal medulla*, and *adrenaline* is released. The effect is to increase breathing rate, heartbeat and blood pressure; shunt blood away from the skin and viscera to the skeletal muscles, brain, and heart; stimulate the conversion of liver glycogen into glucose; inhibit digestion and activity in the bladder and rectum; and reduce clotting time of blood; in addition, the pupils of the eye dilate, and hairs on the skin stand on end.

In short, stimulation of the sympathetic branch of the ANS prepares the body for emergencies: for 'fight or flight' (face the threat or flee).

The **parasympathetic system** returns the body functions to normal after they have been altered by sympathetic stimulation – heart and breathing rate return to normal, digestion takes place and sugar (glycogen) is stored. In times of danger, the sympathetic system prepares the body for violent activity. The parasympathetic system reverses these changes when the danger is over.

### evaluation

Gender differences in stress responses (see page 63) raise questions about the universal nature of the 'fight-or-flight' response. Most laboratory studies of physiological reactions to stress have been carried out on males; and, even when these studies have been carried out on animals, there has been a preponderance of male rats! Males, in the EEA, would be required to respond to emergencies with 'fight or flight', but women would 'tend and befriend' because their most adaptive response would be to look after their children and seek the protective company of other females.

### explanation

### Stress response 1: short-term (acute) effects

*SAM system (acute stress) Sympathetic–adrenal medulla*
Immediate (*acute*) stressors arouse the *sympathetic branch* of the ANS which causes the hormone adrenaline to be released by the *adrenal medulla* in the *adrenal glands*. You may have heard the phrase 'adrenaline-rush' meaning the physiological sensation that accompanies being scared or thrilled, i.e. being '*aroused*' (in a physiological sense). Adrenaline creates all those sensations that you commonly experience as stress, such as sweatiness and increased heart and breathing rate. It also stops you wanting to pee and slows down digestion (to conserve resources for fight or flight). This is the 'fight-or-flight' response.

### explanation

### Stress response 2: long-term (chronic) effects

*HPA axis (chronic stress) Pituitary–adrenal cortex*
If stress continues (becomes *chronic*) then the hypothalamic–pituitary–adrenal (HPA) axis is increasingly activated. This 'axis' may sound complicated but isn't. An important part of the brain – the hypothalamus – stimulates another important part of the brain – the pituitary – to secrete a hormone called adrenocorticotropic hormone (ACTH) – which in turn stimulates the adrenal cortex to produce *cortisol*.

**Hypothalamus**

**Pituitary gland**
(master gland, resistance to stress and disease, bodily growth)

**Adrenal gland**
(adrenal medulla and adrenal cortex)

*The word 'chronic' may suggest to you that it is 'bad' (e.g. 'that was a chronic film') but here it means 'persisting for a long time'.*

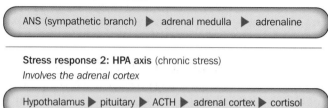

**Stress response 1: SAM system** (acute stress)
*Involves the adrenal medulla*

> ANS (sympathetic branch) ▶ adrenal medulla ▶ adrenaline

**Stress response 2: HPA axis** (chronic stress)
*Involves the adrenal cortex*

> Hypothalamus ▶ pituitary ▶ ACTH ▶ adrenal cortex ▶ cortisol

**note**

### The ANS and yoga

The autonomic nervous system is considered to be involuntary, but this is not entirely true. Practitioners of yoga and Zen Buddhism have demonstrated that a certain amount of conscious control can be exerted over the ANS. During periods of meditation, these people are able to alter a number of autonomic functions including heart rate and the rate of oxygen consumption. These changes are not simply a reflection of decreased physical activity because they exceed the amount of change that occurs during sleep or hypnosis.

**note**

### The adrenal glands, adrenaline and noradrenaline

The adrenal glands are two small structures situated one atop each kidney. They consist of two distinct regions:

1. The *adrenal cortex* which secretes a variety of steroid hormones, such as glucocorticoids (e.g. cortisol) and androgens (e.g. testosterone).
2. The *adrenal medulla* consists of masses of neurons that are part of the sympathetic branch of the ANS. When the neurons are stimulated they release mainly adrenaline but small amounts of noradrenaline as well (the Americans use the terms 'epinephrine' and 'norepinephrine'). These hormones are released into the blood and cause all the effects of sympathetic arousal.

*A note for the terminologically-challenged – if the phrase 'hypothalamic–pituitary–adrenal axis' stresses you, then don't worry. You will not lose marks if you cannot use such terms or phrases – just describe the system and forget the fancy words. Understanding is far more important.*

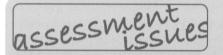

### Describe and evaluate the General Adaptation Syndrome (GAS), as an explanation of stress processes. (*ku 8  ae 2*)

A classic way that students lose marks is by overlooking that command 'evaluate'. Like some other command words, it signals that *ae* skills are required. It is terribly easy to ignore it, especially when you have a lot of well-learned *descriptive* knowledge (*ku*) at your fingertips – which is often the case with the GAS, the topic of the question above. Another danger is that you may well pass the NABs, and even get quite high marks, without paying too much attention to those irritating *ae* demands (termed Outcome 2 in NABs).

But beware – the exam is a whole new ball game! Whereas the percentage of Outcome 2 (or *ae*) marks in NABs questions is around 22% on average, in the exam the *ae* marks are much more important – they account for 40% of the total. So, in any 20-mark NAB question, only about *3–5 marks* are for Outcome 2, whilst in all 20-mark exam questions there are *8 marks* for *ae*.

When it comes to the crunch, with an actual NAB or exam paper in front of you, read the *mark allocations* just as carefully as the questions themselves, so that you know exactly what skills, and how much, you have to show.

There is plenty of advice throughout this book about developing your *ae* skills during the course; one very useful step is to thoroughly check the *feedback* you get from your teacher, whenever you have completed a NAB or class test, so that you can see exactly where you have (or have not!) gained marks for *ae*. Then, make sure you tackle those aspects, in preparation for the next NAB, and the exam!

# Aspect 2: Origins and health effects of stress

## Origins of stress

### Transactional nature of stress

Selye's model suggested that stress was the same regardless of the stressor. Cox (1978) called this the *physiological model* of stress, a model primarily concerned with what occurs *inside* an organism. Cox described two other models of stress: one is the *engineering model* which focuses on external sources of stress, such as environmental, social and work sources of stress. It is called the engineering model because when engineers work out the stress on, for example, a bridge, they are concerned with external stressors.

Bridges experience stress when external fractures, such as heavy lorries or high winds, create pressure on the structures.

The third model is the *transactional model*. The essence of this model is that stress occurs as a result of a transaction or interaction between two things: perceived demands from the environment and the individual's perceived ability to cope. The transactional model emphasises that it is an individual's *perception* of the stressor which is most significant in their ability to cope. This explains why some people feel very stressed about some situations (e.g. exams or bungee jumping) whereas others don't. If you do not perceive something as a threat, then the ANS is not activated. An individual's perceived ability to cope may be related to individual differences (personality, gender and culture), which are explored on pages 63–65.

We will first examine this transactional model in some more detail and then look at the three aspects of the engineering model: environmental, social and work sources of stress.

## Transactional model

Lazarus and Folkman (1984) developed the transactional model, realising that *cognitive appraisal* was the key – *perceived* demands and *perceived* ability. The emphasis is on what the individuals *thinks* (i.e. cognitive). Cognitive appraisal (mental evaluation) is a two-part process:

1. *Primary appraisal* determines whether the event is stressful. Is there a threat?
2. *Secondary appraisal* deals with one's ability and resources to cope with an event judged to be stressful. Can I cope with the threat?

### Research evidence

Lazarus (1999) presented evidence that cognitive activity determined whether or not the physiological stress response was activated, rather than just being affected by the presence of a stressor. Postmortem examination of patients showed that those who had been unconscious prior to death had normal levels of cortisol while the opposite was true of those who had remained conscious. This suggests that their stress response was not simply physiological but was related to cognitive appraisal.

## Environmental sources of stress

### Overcrowding

Overcrowding and crowding have been shown to create stress which produces aggressive and other disturbed behaviour. In a classic study, Calhoun (1962) placed an expanding rat population in a small area and observed that the rats soon set about killing, sexually assaulting and, eventually, cannibalising one another.

Some studies have reported similar effects in humans. For example, Schmitt (1967) found that as the density of the population in Honolulu increased, so the crime rate, death rate, and mental-disorder rate also increased.

Macintyre and Homel (1997) studied the effects of crowding (defined here as the number of unintended low-level physical contacts between club-goers) in six Australian nightclubs. The level of crowding observed in each nightclub was positively correlated with the number of observed aggressive incidents, even when controls were introduced for levels of male drunkenness and staff interactions with club-goers.

### Noise

The effects of unpredictable noise were demonstrated in a study by Glass *et al.* (1969). Sixty undergraduates completed various cognitive tasks in one of five conditions: loud or soft noise that was either random (unpredictable) or played at fixed intervals (predictable); there was also a no noise condition. Stress (ANS arousal) was measured using the *galvanic skin response* (GSR). After the task, participants were asked to complete four puzzles, two of which couldn't be solved – in order to create frustration. Participants showed greatest stress in the random noise condition (highest GSR and lowest task persistence indicating frustration). Participants in the predictable noise condition showed more stress than those in the no noise condition. Overall this shows that noise creates stress, especially when it is unpredictable. Glass *et al.* suggested that random noise is particularly difficult because we can 'tune out' constant stimuli, but unpredictable stimuli require continued attention, and this reduces our ability to cope with stress.

> ### note
>
> ### *The galvanic skin response (GSR)*
> When the ANS is active one of the effects is increased sweating. This increase in moisture on the skin can be detected if electrodes are placed on the skin because water conducts electricity and, when a person is sweating, the electrodes detect greater electrical conductivity in the skin. Thus GSR is used to measure increased stress (ANS activity $\rightarrow$ sweating $\rightarrow$ increased electrical conductivity).

**evaluation** | ### Environmental sources of stress

Environmental stress appears to produce negative effects – but not always. At a rock concert or in a football crowd, noise and crowding can enhance your positive feelings. Thus we can conclude that the effect of such stressors is to enhance existing feelings rather than simply having a negative effect; i.e. it has a transactional effect.

The research on noise also supports the transactional view of stress because it is the lack of control that was critical; noise alone was not necessarily stressful.

## Social sources of stress

### Lack of friends
Kamarck *et al.* (1990) demonstrated the importance of friendship in reducing stress. They recruited 39 female psychology student volunteers to perform a difficult mental task (stressful) while their physiological reactions were monitored. Each participant attended the lab session alone or they were asked to bring a close same-sex friend who was told to touch the participant on the wrist throughout the mental task. In general, the participants who were with a friend showed lower physiological reactions than those who were alone.

Brown and Harris (1978) interviewed 400 women living in Camberwell, London. Some of them had experienced a stressful event in the preceding year, yet not all developed any serious psychological problems such as depression. Those who did develop such problems shared one important factor, the absence of a close, supportive relationship.

### Life events
Major social events, such as marriage and divorce are stressful, even the positive ones. Holmes and Rahe (1967) suggested that this is because such events involve change, and change requires psychic energy to be expended: i.e. it is stressful and this affects health. Holmes and Rahe developed the Social Readjustment Rating Scale (SRRS) to test their idea (see page 68).

## Occupational sources of stress

Stress at work may be caused by both environmental and social factors, described above.

What things are stressful? Some people get a thrill from the sort of activities that others would find highly distressing.

### Job strain
Marmot *et al.* (1997) sought to test the job-strain model. This model proposes that the workplace creates stress and illness in two ways: (1) high demand and (2) low control. Marmot *et al.* assessed civil service employees assuming that the higher-grade employees would experience high job demand, and lower grades would experience low job control. A total of 7372 people agreed to answer a questionnaire and be checked for signs of cardiovascular disease (e.g. heart attack, stroke). About five years later, each participant was re-assessed and the following information was recorded: signs of cardiovascular disease (e.g. chest pains), presence of coronary risk factors (e.g.

smoking), employment grade (a measure of the amount of job demand an individual experienced), and sense of job control and amount of social support (both measured using a questionnaire).

Higher-grade civil servants had developed the fewest cardiovascular problems. Participants in the lower grades expressed a weaker sense of job control and also had poorest social support. The main conclusion is that low control appears to be linked to higher stress and also to cardiovascular disease, whereas high job demand is not linked to stress and illness. This does not fully support the job strain model.

### Work load

The study by Marmot *et al.* found that job demand was not a factor in stress. However, other studies have examined different aspects of 'demand' or 'work load'. For example, Johansson *et al.* (1978) found that a job that required continuous attention and responsibility but was quite repetitive (being a sawyer at a Swedish sawmill) was more stressful than less monotonous jobs with more flexibility (maintenance workers). The high-risk group was found to have higher illness rates and also have higher levels of adrenaline in their urine. This is evidence of a link between job demand, stress hormones and illness. This study also suggests that a sense of control *increases* stress, in contrast with the study by Marmot *et al.* but in line with Brady's results (see page 57).

### Individual differences

The study by Marmot *et al.* (above) suggested that lack of control was a source of stress in the workplace. However, there may be individual differences. Schaubroeck *et al.* (2001) found that some workers respond differently to lack of control – they are *less* stressed by having no control or responsibility. In this study, Schaubroeck *et al.* measured saliva and could assess immune system functioning directly from the saliva. They found that some people had higher immune responses in low-control situations. Some people view negative work outcomes as being their fault. For these employees, control can actually exacerbate the unhealthy effects of stress.

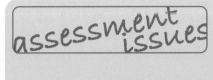

**With reference to research evidence, discuss one environmental, social or occupational source of stress. (ku 4  ae 4)**

Whichever 'source' you choose, make sure that it is one that you can write about in an analytical and evaluative way, as half of the marks for this question are for *ae*. Much of this *ae* should feature in your interpretation of the evidence you present, such as the studies described in this section. 'Joined-up' thinking can help here, especially for exam revision. When you have studied research methods (Chapter 4), you will be able to criticise evidence in terms of the research methods used. In other words, you will be *integrating* your knowledge across domains – this is one of the 'added value' skills expected in high-grade exam performance*. In fact, detailed descriptions of what is expected in a grade A performance can be found in the 'Generic Requirements' of the Marking Instructions (for Specimen paper and the most recent exam) on the Psychology pages of the SQA website (www.sqa.org.uk). Make yourself familiar with these and, when revising, check to see how your own efforts match up.
*For the NABs, this kind of integration of knowledge is *not* expected.

## Individual differences in stress susceptibility
## What is meant by individual differences?

There are important differences in the way that people react to stress. Some people appear to be able to face horrendously stressful living conditions and still remain relatively healthy, whereas others buckle at the slightest bit of pressure. Gender, culture and personality are all individual differences that may affect the way an individual perceives and responds to stressors.

## Gender differences

Psychologists have increasingly argued for the existence of gender differences in stress reactivity. Some of these differences may be physiological, with females showing less arousal of the sympathetic nervous system in stressful situations, and some behavioural, with females tending to engage in different *types* of coping behaviour.

### A biological explanation

Earlier in this chapter we suggested that, in the EEA, it would be adaptive for men to respond to emergencies with 'fight or flight' but women would 'tend and befriend' because their most adaptive response would be to look after their children. Taylor *et al.* (2000) suggest that women may be biologically programmed to be less affected by stress, because of the action of the hormone oxytocin. Individuals with high levels of oxytocin are calmer, more relaxed, more social and less anxious. In several animal species, oxytocin has been shown to lead to maternal behaviour and to affiliation. This might explain why, under stressful situations, women seek the support of others, which further serves to reduce their stress levels. Men also secrete oxytocin, but its effects appear to be reduced by male hormones, so oxytocin may have reduced effects on men's physiology and behaviour under stress.

Hastrup *et al.* (1980) found that women showed lowered stress responses when their cardiovascular reactions were tested during the time of their menstrual cycle. At this time their oestrogen levels were highest, and therefore it would seem that oestrogen might be reducing the stress – another biological explanation for why women are less stressed.

### Social explanations

Various social factors can explain why men are more prone to stress-related disorders (such as CHD) than are women. For example, males have less social support; women are more likely to have confidantes and friends than men, and women report making use of social support networks more than men (Carroll, 1992).

In general, women engage in fewer unhealthy behaviours than men, or at least they used to. Men smoked more and imbibed more alcohol, and this might have explained their higher rates of CHD. However, such habits are changing – women are smoking and drinking more, and their CHD rates have risen, whereas men are smoking and drinking less. This would lead us to expect a narrowing of the gender gap in CHD mortality rates, and Carroll (1992) reports that this has been happening.

Men experience more occupational stress; as women enter the workforce they become more stressed. Frankenhauser (1983) found that females in non-traditional female roles (e.g. lawyers, bus drivers, engineers) had higher *neuroendocrine* levels than women in traditional roles. This suggests that male stress may be a consequence of the activities they engage in.

## Cultural differences

### Social support

Researchers have typically found strong cultural differences in the degree to which members of different cultures rely on family or other close relationships for social support. It is assumed, for example, that members of **collectivist** cultures (as opposed to **individualist** cultures) may be less vulnerable to the negative effects of stress because of the greater emphasis on interdependence (and hence social support) among group members. However, it is often hard to disentangle the effects of stress and stress management from other factors that may prolong or shorten life. For example, research by Weg (1983) among the Abkarsian people of Georgia found that their longevity could be explained by a combination of factors, including genetic inheritance, physically active lifestyles, no alcohol or smoking, as well as high levels of social support.

However, Kim and McKenry (1998) found that African-Americans had more extensive family social support networks than white Americans, which would suggest that they would have *lower* stress, whereas in fact they experience higher blood pressure and CHD, which suggests higher stress.

### Stress from prejudice and discrimination

Racism makes life more stressful for Africans in the West. Discrimination and negativity are bound to be chronic stressors for individuals in target groups. The effects of such stress can be seen in the fact that, in the UK, African-Caribbean immigrants are seven times more likely to become diagnosed as schizophrenic than whites (Cochrane, 1977). One might think that this could be explained in terms of biological/genetic differences – except for the fact that similar rates are not found in their country of origin. Again, it is more likely that differences are due to greater stress as well as biases in clinical diagnoses (see page 260). Stress may arise from prejudice, poorer living conditions, and/or 'acculturative stress' – the stress of learning to live in a foreign and possibly hostile culture.

**KEY TERMS**

**Collectivist culture:** Any culture which places more value on the 'collective' rather than the individual, and on interdependence rather than independence. The opposite is true of an **individualist culture**.

*evaluation*

## Evaluation of cultural differences

Being able to fully understand how cultural *diversity* affects the experience of stress is problematic because very little research is carried out that examines the impact of stress on ethnic minorities. In addition, stress scales (such as the SRRS) are based on mainstream stressors, which *exclude* specific undesirable situations, such as economic marginality, unemployment and discrimination, that affect some groups more than others. This position is complicated by the fact that *inter-relations* between gender, ethnic group and socioeconomic status have largely been ignored in stress research.

## Personality differences

### Type C for cancer

Some people are classed as Type As or Type Bs: people who experience more or less stress, respectively (see Friedman and Rosenman's study on page 66). Type Cs suppress emotions, particularly negative ones, and are unassertive, likeable people who rarely get into arguments. Temoshok (1987) suggests that such individuals cope with stress in a way that ignores their own needs, even physical ones, in order to please others, and this has negative physiological consequences. All stresses are suppressed but eventually such stresses take their toll.

The link between repressed emotion (Type C) and cancer was demonstrated in a study by Morris *et al.* (1981). Women attending a clinic to investigate breast lumps were interviewed to assess their typical patterns of emotional behaviour. Those women whose breast lumps were found to be cancerous had reported that they both experienced and expressed far less anger than those women whose lumps were found to be non-cancerous. This supports the idea of a link between cancer and the suppression of anger.

Why is Type C associated with cancer rather than cardiovascular disorder? Temoshok suggests that this is because some stressors activate the ANS and endocrine system (acute stress) and this is related to CHD. More chronic stressors affect the immune system and increase the risk for cancer.

### The Hardy personality type

Kobasa (1979) suggested that some people are more psychologically 'hardy' than others. Hardiness enables people to cope better with stress. Kobasa proposed that hardiness can be taught and used as a stress-reduction technique. Hardiness is discussed in the section on stress-reduction techniques (see page 76).

### Internal or external locus of control

Rotter (1966) proposed that people with an internal locus of control experience less stress. Locus of control is about where you place the responsibility (or blame) for things that happen to you. People with an internal locus of control believe that they are responsible for the things that happen to them. They control their world – for good or bad. If you are experiencing something unpleasant and know you can stop it (perceived control), this reduces your sense of distress.

People with an external locus of control blame someone or something else when things go wrong. This means that when they are experiencing something unpleasant they feel that they have no control, and this may increase their sense of distress.

Kim *et al.* (1997) found that children with an internal locus of control showed fewer signs of stress when parents divorced. This shows that locus of control acts as a stress moderator.

star**STUDY**

## starSTUDY

# Investigating the origins of stress: Individual differences

(FRIEDMAN AND ROSENMAN, 1974)

## Aims

Friedman and Rosenman proposed that some individuals (Type A) are typically impatient, competitive, time pressured, and hostile. Type B individuals lack these characteristics and are generally more relaxed. Friedman and Rosenman predicted that Type As would be less able to cope with stress and therefore more likely to experience CHD.

## Method and procedure

The study recruited 3154 healthy men aged between 39 and 59, living around San Francisco. This was a longitudinal study. The men were first interviewed in 1960, using a set of 25 questions to assess the way that a person typically responds to everyday pressures that would create feelings of impatience, competitiveness or hostility. For example, the participants were asked how they would cope with having to wait in a long queue or working with a slow partner. The interview was conducted in a provocative manner to try to elicit Type A behaviour. For example, the interviewer might speak slowly and hesitantly, so that a Type A person would want to interrupt.

The researchers recorded the participants' answers and the way that the participants' responded. Participants were then classed as A1 (Type A), A2 (not fully Type A), X (equal amounts of Type A and B), and B.

## Results

1. Eight and a half years later, 257 of the total sample had developed CHD: 178 of these had been assessed as Type A (69%), whereas half as many were Type B (31%).
2. Twenty-two years later, 214 men had died from CHD: 119 were Type A and 95 Type B, a rather less impressive difference (Friedman, 1996).

## Conclusion

This offers strong support for the idea that aspects of a person's temperament are associated with CHD. The key factor may be stress. The results from the follow-up study 22 years later suggest that personality type may not be as important as originally suggested. However, it might be that some of the men took preventative measures after being diagnosed with CHD and that this altered the death rates later recorded.

## Evaluation

*Is it stress or hostility?*
Hostility rather than stress may explain the results. Matthews *et al*. (1977) suggested that high levels of hostility produce increased activity within the sympathetic nervous system.

*Application*
The results have been applied to improving health. Friedman *et al*. (1986) conducted the Recurrent Coronary Prevention Project and found that, after five years, those CHD patients who had been taught how to modify their stress response had fewer second heart attacks than those who received counselling or no treatment.

assessment issues

**Describe *two* types of individual differences that may affect susceptibility to stress. (*ku* 6 *ae* 0)**

The first thing to notice about this question is extremely obvious – it asks for *two* things, so we're sure you'll agree it would be daft to write about one thing, or three, or nine, or whatever!

Having got that clear, let's focus on what this question is *about*. If you have looked at the Higher Psychology Specimen Paper (on the SQA website), you'll have noticed that the words used in questions are usually very similar to the words used in the Unit *specification content* (which can be found on the opening page of every chapter in this book, as well as on the SQA website). The question above closely reflects the words of the specification content which says 'individual differences in stress susceptibility'. If you organise your revision notes using the words of the specification content as headings and subheadings, you should instantly recognise what each question is about and bring the relevant knowledge to mind.

# Health effects of stress

Selye's GAS model predicts that prolonged (chronic) stress will result in ill health because resources are depleted. As we have seen, recent research suggests that the link between stress and illness may be due to direct effects on the immune system rather than depletion of resources. We are going to consider some of the short- and long-term health effects of stress, remembering that such effects are the result of a complex relationship between stressors, cognitive appraisal and individual differences.

## Effects of stress on physical health

### Short-term effects

The short-term effects of stress on physical health are described on page 56 – it makes you physiologically aroused (the first stage of the GAS model) and reduces the functioning of the immune system.

### Long-term effects

In this chapter we have described various studies that demonstrate the long-term effects of stress on physical illness: ulcers (Brady), CHD (Friedman and Rosenman), cold virus (Cohen *et al*.), reduced functioning of the immune system (Kiecolt-Glaser *et al*.), and cancer (Morris *et al*.). Stress may be a *direct* cause of physical illness (as described by the GAS model) or stress may *indirectly* cause illness because stressed individuals are more likely to smoke and drink and these habits lead to physical illness.

*Stress and cardiovascular disorders*
Among the main physical disorders linked to stress are cardiovascular disorders. Russek and Zohman (1958) looked at heart disease in medical professionals. One group of doctors was designated as high stress (GPs and anaesthetists) while others were classed as low stress (pathologists and dermatologists). Russek found heart disease was greatest among GPs (11.9% of the sample) and lowest in dermatologists (3.2% of the sample). However, such findings may be due to direct or indirect effects, or both.

## Effects of stress on mental health

### Short-term effects

The short-term effects of stress on mental health are the subjective experience of anxiety which *may* depress performance – moderate amounts of stress actually enhance performance as described by the Yerkes-Dodson law (see figure).

### Long-term effects

Many explanations of mental illness are based on the **diathesis-stress model** (see page 000). There is a considerable body of research that suggests that mental illness is caused by inherited genes; however, not all individuals with such genes develop a mental disorder. This suggests that genes *predispose* an individual to developing a mental disorder (*diathesis*); the disorder only develops if the individual is exposed to *stressful* life conditions.

*Stress, life events and schizophrenia*
Brown and Birley (1968) reported that life events (which are stressors) play an important role in precipitating episodes of schizophrenia. They found that approximately 50% of people experience a major life event in the 3 weeks prior to a schizophrenic episode while only 12% reported a major life event in the 9 weeks prior to that. A control sample on the other hand reported a low and unchanging level of life events over the same period, suggesting that it was the life events that triggered the relapse.

*Stress, life events and depression*
Kendler *et al*. (1995) reported that the highest levels of depression were found in women who were exposed to recent negative life events (such as an assault or serious marital problems) *and* were most genetically at risk for depression (i.e. identical co-twin of a woman diagnosed with depression).

*Stress and eating disorders*
Mumford *et al*. (1991) studied Asian girls living in the UK, finding that girls who scored highest on a questionnaire about eating disorders were the ones most traditional in their dress and outlook. One explanation may be that stress was highest in this group because more-traditional Asian girls experienced a greater culture clash. This supports the diathesis-stress model – vulnerable individuals would be more likely to show symptoms of eating disorders when exposed to stressors.

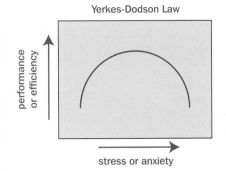

Yerkes-Dodson Law

performance or efficiency

stress or anxiety

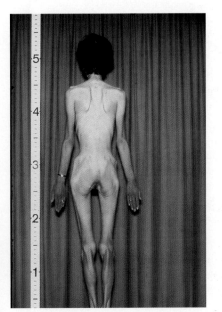

The picture shows the emaciated body of a woman suffering from anorexia. The diathesis-stress model proposes that such mental illnesses develop when an individual who has certain genes (such as those related to obsessive behaviour) is exposed to stressful life conditions (such as parental conflict). This is the diathesis-stress model.

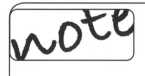

**Stress, separation and healthy physical and mental development**

An interesting link can be made between maternal separation and the effects of stress. Studies of rats have shown that taking a young rat away from its mother for 24 hours leads to excess production of stress hormones. These hormones may reduce the ability of the brain to perform other important functions associated with physical and mental growth. As a result, they can be damaging over time. Human babies who suffer stress because of neglect tend to be physically smaller and mentally slower than their peers. Studies of Romanian children have shown that they had higher levels of a human stress hormone (cortisol) on weekdays when they were in a badly run day care centre, than on weekends when they were home with their parents (Carlson *et al.*, 1995).

## starSTUDY
# Investigating the health effects of stress
**(RAHE *ET AL.*, 1970)**

## Aims

Rahe *et al.* used the SRRS (see below) to test Holmes and Rahe's hypothesis that the number of life events a person experienced would be positively correlated with illness. Rahe *et al.* aimed in particular to study a 'normal' population as distinct from the populations previously studied – individuals who were already ill in hospital.

### The Social Readjustment Rating Scale (SRRS)

| Rank | Life event | LCU |
|---|---|---|
| 1 | Death of a spouse | 100 |
| 2 | Divorce | 73 |
| 3 | Marital separation | 65 |
| 4 | Jail term | 63 |
| 5 | Death of a close family member | 63 |
| 6 | Personal injury or illness | 60 |
| 7 | Marriage | 53 |
| 8 | Fired at work | 47 |
| 9 | Marital reconciliation | 45 |
| 10 | Retirement | 45 |
| 11 | Change in the health of family member | 44 |
| 12 | Pregnancy | 40 |
| 13 | Sex difficulties | 39 |
| 14 | Gain new family member | 39 |
| 15 | Business readjustment | 39 |
| 16 | Change in financial state | 38 |
| 17 | Death of a close friend | 37 |
| 18 | Change to a different line of work | 36 |
| 19 | Change in number of arguments with spouse | 35 |
| 20 | Mortgage over $10,000 | 31 |
| 21 | Foreclosure on mortgage or loan | 30 |
| 22 | Change in responsibilities at work | 29 |
| 23 | Son or daughter leaving home | 29 |
| 24 | Trouble with in-laws | 29 |
| 25 | Outstanding personal achievement | 28 |
| 26 | Wife begins or stops work | 26 |
| 27 | Begin or end school | 26 |
| 28 | Change living conditions | 25 |
| 29 | Revision of personal habits | 24 |
| 30 | Trouble with boss | 23 |
| 31 | Change in work hours/conditions | 20 |
| 32 | Change in residence | 20 |
| 33 | Change in schools | 20 |
| 34 | Change in recreation | 19 |
| 35 | Change in church activities | 19 |
| 36 | Change in social activities | 18 |
| 37 | Mortgage or loan less than $10,000 | 17 |
| 38 | Change in sleeping habits | 16 |
| 39 | Change in number of family get-togethers | 15 |
| 40 | Change in eating habits | 15 |
| 41 | Holiday | 13 |
| 42 | Christmas | 12 |
| 43 | Minor violations of the law | 11 |

LCU stands for 'life change units', a measure of the amount of stress associated with each life event.

## Method and procedure

A military version of the SRRS was given to all the men aboard three US Navy cruisers, a total of over 2700 men. The men completed the questionnaire just before a tour of duty, noting all the life events experienced over the previous six months.

An illness score was calculated on the basis of the number, type and severity of all illnesses recorded during the tour of duty (about seven months). Rahe *et al.* didn't include sick bay visits that appeared to be due to a desire to get out of work (because the individual wasn't actually ill).

## Results

An LCU score and an illness score was calculated for each man. Rahe *et al.* found a significant **positive correlation** between these scores of +0.118. A positive correlation is one where both **co-variables** increase together. This relationship is illustrated in the **scattergram** left.

## Conclusion

The results support the **hypothesis** of a link or positive correlation between life changes/events and physical illness. It is possible that the link is stress: Life changes cause stress, and we know that stress causes illness. Therefore life changes are sources of stress. Both positive and negative events are included in the SRRS, so we see that it is change rather than negativity that is important. It is the overall amount of 'psychic energy' required to deal with an event that creates stress.

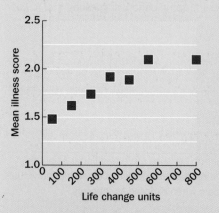

## Evaluation

### *Unreliable data*

The LCUs were calculated by asking the men to recall life changes over the previous months. It is possible that they didn't remember these events accurately. For example, a man might repress the memory of an event that was a negative experience or might not recall exactly when it took place.

### *Is the SRRS a valid measure?*

The SRRS was a landmark development in stress research; however, many psychologists have suggested that it is not a valid measure of stress. The main complaints that have been made are that the scale focuses on acute life events rather than ongoing (chronic) stressors; it does not distinguish between desirable and undesirable events, and does not take social resources into account which may moderate the effects of stress. This means that the checklist is a rather crude measure of stress, which could explain why such a weak (though significant) correlation was found in the study by Rahe *et al.*

Other measures of life changes have been developed, such as the 'Hassles and Uplifts Scale' (DeLongis *et al.*, 1982) which assesses ongoing (chronic) strains of daily living such as worries about money, current affairs, your job, your friends, sex, the weather, looking after your home, losing things, and so on. DeLongis *et al.* (1988) studied stress in 75 married couples and found a significant positive correlation of +0.59 between hassles and next-day health problems, such as flu, sore throats, headaches and backaches.

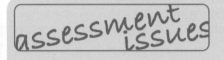

**Referring to research evidence, discuss the possible effects of stress on a person's physical and mental health. (*ku 12 ae 8*)**

As well as doing 'exactly what it says on the tin' for this question, be alert to the possible relevance of material from other areas you have studied; the more psychology you study, the more links you will spot between different Topics. This is one way of showing 'added value' by means of *integration* of your knowledge.

In the above question, the 'mental health' aspect provides an opportunity to draw links. For example, as we have seen in this section, stress has been linked to maternal separation and deprivation, studied in the Early Socialisation Topic. Also, those who study Atypical Behaviour (Chapters 10 and 11) will learn about the role of stress in psychological disorder. Don't overdo it, though; use your knowledge of other Topics to support your answer, but don't forget that the question is still about *stress*.

# Aspect 3: Stress-reduction strategies

**PHYSIOLOGICAL LEVEL**
Physical exercise, relaxation techniques, drugs

**COGNITIVE LEVEL**
Psychological and psychosocial
Cognitive strategies

**EMOTIONAL LEVEL**
Individual coping strategies,
defence mechanisms

**SOCIAL LEVEL**
Social strategies, social support

**ORGANISATIONAL LEVEL**
Organisational stress-reduction
strategies

In the first two Aspects of this chapter we looked at *sources* of stress. Now we turn to considering how stress can be reduced. For many people, the key way to deal with stress is simply to distract themselves by watching more television. In fact, watching television has been shown to be a good stress buster (Palmer and Strickland, 1995). Other common methods include excessive drinking, using prescription drugs or even just having a bath. Such methods are means of *coping* by dealing with the symptoms of stress but may not be that helpful in long-term reduction of stress.

In contrast, stress-*reduction* strategies aim to reduce the stressor itself as well as increase a person's ability to cope. Stress-reduction strategies can be related to the transactional model (see page 61) which emphasises that stress is the result of an individual's *perception* of the stressor; successful reduction strategies aim to alter or manage an individual's perception of the stressor and/or their own abilities to cope.

Stress can be reduced at different levels, as shown in the diagram on the left. We will look at these different levels on the next few pages, starting with the physiological level.

# Physiological techniques of stress reduction

Physiological techniques focus on alleviating the *physiological* symptoms associated with the stressful situation, even if the situation itself cannot be changed. They may achieve this in a number of ways including the use of relaxation to control some aspects of the body's stress reaction.

## Physical exercise

Going to the gym and jogging are increasingly popular pastimes which may improve your health and reduce stress. Early research found that London bus conductors suffered fewer cardiovascular problems than bus drivers (Morris *et al.*, 1953), suggesting that people who were more active (conductors) had less stress and thus fewer cardiovascular problems.

Various explanations have been put forward as to why physical exercise may reduce stress:

- Physical exercise may de-activate sympathetic arousal because vigorous physical activity may send a message to the brain that a threat, or demand, has been dealt with so the 'fight-or-flight' response (sympathetic arousal) can now be 'switched off'.

- Sonstroem (1984) found that regular physical exercise increased feelings of self-esteem and reduced depression. This may be due to increased feelings of control.

- Fleshner (2000) suggests that physical activity may prevent stress-induced suppression of the immune system. Fleshner and her co-workers studied rats. Stressed rats that had been regularly running on a wheel and then infected showed an increase in bacteria-attacking white blood cells migrating to the infection site, causing the healing time to speed up by three to four days compared with a group of rats who had no wheel (and thus no physical activity). This suggests that the same might be happening in humans – physical activity has a beneficial effect on the working of the immune system.

*evaluation*

## using drugs

Physical exercise is a cheap and natural way to reduce stress. A less natural way to reduce stress is to use drugs that specifically target stress. For example, the group of drugs most commonly used to treat anxiety is *benzodiazepines* (BZs). They are sold under various trade names such as Librium, Valium, Halcion and Xanax. BZs slow down the activity of the central nervous system.

*Beta-blockers*, on the other hand, reduce the activity of the autonomic nervous system rather than the brain. As we saw earlier (page 58), stress leads to arousal of the sympathetic nervous system and this creates increased blood pressure, heart rate, elevated levels of cortisol, and so on. Beta-blockers are often used by sportsmen and women to reduce arousal because ANS arousal may have a negative effect on performance.

## Relaxation techniques

The physiological symptoms of stress, such as raised blood pressure and increased muscle tension, are *involuntary*. We are unable to control them consciously because they are governed (for a good reason) by our autonomic nervous system (ANS). If these systems were controlled consciously then we would spend our time thinking about nothing else! However, we can learn some voluntary control through relaxation techniques. By breathing more slowly, thinking about being safe and so on (the activities outlined on the facing page), you can reduce activity of the sympathetic nervous system and activate the parasympathetic nervous system. The result should be a reduction in all symptoms associated with stress, for example reduced heart rate and blood pressure.

### Meditation and yoga

There are many forms of meditation. Most trace their ancestry from ancient yoga and Zen Buddhism. Some forms use a secret *mantra* (sound) which is repeated over and over with eyes closed. In other forms of meditation a *mandala* is use – a visualisation of some object such as a thousand-petal lotus. Regardless of their origin, all the meditative techniques have at least two phases. The first is to quiet the body, and the second is to quiet the mind.

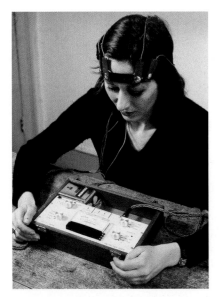

A patient wired up for biofeedback. A machine provides a patient with specific visual or auditory information about bodily functions which are not usually observed, for example blood pressure. This enables the individual to learn some way to control these involuntary behaviours.

Meditation is often considered the process of trying to eliminate the constant 'chatter' of the mind. As arousal is reduced, so is anxiety. Self-transcendence, or an altered state, is then achieved. Most people who meditate find that they feel creative, positive, calm and energetic after meditation.

**Biofeedback**

Biofeedback involves four processes:

1. *Feedback*. The patient is attached to various machines which provide information (feedback) about ANS activity. For example, the patient can hear their heart beat or is given a signal (light or tone) to show higher or lower blood pressure.
2. *Relaxation*. The patient is taught techniques of relaxation.
3. *Operant conditioning*. Relaxation leads to a target behaviour; for example heart rate is decreased or muscle tension is relaxed. This is rewarding, which increases the likelihood of the same behaviour being repeated. Such learning (conditioning) takes place without any conscious thought. The reward leads to an unconscious 'stamping in' of the behaviour.
4. *Transfer*. The patient then needs to transfer the skills learned to the real world.

A good way to illustrate this is to consider a classic study on feedback by Miller and DiCara (1967). They used curare to paralyse 24 rats, keeping the rats alive using artificial respiration. Half of the rats were rewarded whenever their heart rates slowed down, and the others were rewarded when their heart rates speeded up. The reward was 'a sense of pleasure' – this was achieved by electrically stimulating a part of the brain known as the pleasure centre. The result was that the heart rates of the rats in the 'fast' group speeded up and the heart rates of the rats in the slow group slowed down. Two things are important. First, the learning that took place was entirely involuntary, as the rats were paralysed. It was the automatic ANS responses (heart rate) that were conditioned. Secondly, the learning was the result of operant conditioning – behaviour stamped in because it was rewarded.

*evaluation*

Conditioning is a behaviourist explanation for how behaviour is learned. See page 3 for a more detailed explanation.

*Relaxation*
Relaxation does not treat the source of stress, such as workplace tension. However, it does provide the patient with a potentially long-lasting means of dealing with stress symptoms – by applying relaxation techniques.

*Meditation and Yoga*
A study by Malathi and Damodaran (1999) showed the beneficial effects of yoga on the exam performance of 50 medical students. Those students who practised yoga had lower anxiety scores and did better in their exams than a control group. Schell *et al.* (1994) further showed that people practising yoga were able to change the activity of their autonomic nervous system – participants in a yoga group had a significantly lower heart rate during yoga practice.

*Biofeedback*
Biofeedback has been found to be successful in treating a wide assortment of behaviours (e.g. heart rate, blood pressure, skin temperature and brain waves) and disorders (e.g. curvature of the spine, migraine headaches, asthma, and Raynaud's disease (where there is restricted blood flow to fingers and toes).

However, the technique requires specialist equipment which means that it is expensive and can only be undertaken with specialist supervision. It may be that the success of biofeedback is simply due to the relaxation element, although Bradley (1995) found that biofeedback was more effective than relaxation on its own to control muscle-tension headaches. Alternatively, it may be that the method offers patients a sense of increased control and this produces beneficial effects.

Relaxation is more than just taking it easy. First of all, you should tighten all your muscles and then carefully relax them starting from your head and working downwards. Secondly, you should imagine yourself in a location that you find especially relaxing, safe, and comfortable. You should spend 5–10 minutes on each activity.

Check out some websites on relaxation techniques: www.isma.org.uk/exams.htm and www.shpm.com/articles/stress/stress3.html

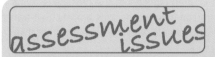

**Describe the use of physical exercise and relaxation techniques in stress reduction. (*ku 6  ae 0*)**

It's probably true that more exam marks are lost because students do not answer the question set than for any other reason. One reason for this may be misjudgement under pressure in the exam room, combined with our tendency to plump quickly for the first course of action that comes to mind rather than calmly considering the question in order to arrive at the *best* course of action. Sometimes, a single word in a question acts like a 'trigger'. In the case of the above question, a candidate may spot the word 'stress', and proceed to write 'everything I know about stress', with disastrous results. However, as you can see, the question is not about physiological processes of stress, nor about origins, nor effects on health; it's not even about stress reduction in general – it asks for details of two specific types of stress-reduction techniques.

Another reason for not answering the question set may be the belief that you can use whole pre-prepared answers, based on past papers and memorised in advance – this just doesn't work!

Someone who is experiencing stress may cope with the stressor in many different ways. Psychological strategies target the source of the problem rather than just dealing with the symptoms of stress.

# Psychological strategies of stress reduction

The second approach to stress reduction involves the use of strategies that help the person to cope with the situation itself rather than just dealing with the symptoms of their stress. A person can focus on the specific problem or situation that has arisen, trying to find some way of changing it or avoiding it in the future, or may learn specific stress-management techniques that minimise the negative effects of stressful situations. This second approach is known as the *psychological* approach to stress reduction.

## Emotional strategies

### Individual coping strategies

There are consistent individual differences in the coping strategies that people use to handle stressful situations.

Lazarus and Folkman (1984) distinguished between *problem-focused* and *emotion-focused* styles of coping using the *Ways of Coping Scale*. Stress can be managed by tackling the problem itself (problem-focused) but often this is not possible and so a more realistic approach is to reduce the stress response (emotion-focused). Emotion-focused coping is most useful as a short-term strategy. It can help reduce one's arousal level before engaging in problem-solving and taking action, and it can help people deal with stressful situations in which there are few problem-focused coping options such as situations when people feel the stressor is something to be endured.

Subsequent research has shown that there are more than just two coping styles. For example, Endler and Parker (1990) devised the *Multidimensional Coping Inventory* which identified a third strategy: *avoidance-oriented*. This involves denying or minimising the seriousness of the situation, similar to Freud's ego defence mechanisms but at a more conscious level.

Endler and Parker found that people who experience high levels of anxiety tend to use the emotion-oriented and avoidance-oriented strategies rather than the (problem focused) task-oriented strategy. The situation is very different in those with the Type A behaviour pattern. They have a strong tendency to use the task-oriented strategy, even when it is not appropriate (Eysenck, 1994).

### Freud's defence mechanisms

Freud (1910) suggested that we unconsciously deal with anxiety by means of ego defence mechanisms, such as:

- *Projection* – unknowingly displacing one's own unacceptable feelings onto someone else. For instance, you might suspect others of cheating in an exam because that is what you did.

- *Denial* – simply denying the existence of something which is threatening. However, denying the existence of the thing does not make it go away. An example of this would be an Elvis

Presley fan who believes that Elvis didn't really die, but that there is a conspiracy behind reports of his death.

- *Displacement* – unconsciously redirecting an emotion from the person who has caused it onto a third party; for example, kicking your sister when your father shouts at you.

- *Repression* – placing uncomfortable thoughts in the unconscious; for example, you might forget that a favourite pet had died because you failed to feed it.

*evaluation*

*Individual coping strategies*
Individuals may have preferred coping styles, but their response in any particular situation will also be determined by what is possible. For example, problem focus is not an available option in a terrorist attack.

*Ego defence mechanisms*
These can be effective in protecting the individual from overwhelming anxiety in the short term, but in the long term may cause various psychological disorders or may result in disturbed sleep because of vivid dreams. One study found that the use of denial following an HIV diagnosis was associated with more rapid disease progression in HIV-seropositive gay men (Ironson *et al*. 1994).

## Cognitive strategies

All cognitive strategies focus on the way a person *thinks* about the stressful situation (or other problem). They are based on the assumption that stress or other problems are due to faulty thinking, and that the problem can be dealt with by replacing negative, irrational thoughts with positive, rational ones.

There is one cognitive therapy that was specifically developed to deal with stress, stress inoculation therapy, which is examined below. Two other cognitive therapies are used as well:

- Cognitive restructuring therapy was introduced by Aaron Beck (1976) who focused on depression but his techniques can be applied to all sorts of undesirable behaviours. This therapy is described on page 251.

- Rational-emotive behaviour therapy (REBT) was developed by Albert Ellis (1957). This therapy is described on page 268.

### Stress inoculation therapy (SIT)

Donald Meichenbaum (1985) developed a form of cognitive therapy specifically to deal with stress. It is different from other stress treatments because an individual should develop a form of coping *before* the problem arises. Meichenbaum suggested that you should *inoculate* yourself against the disease of stress in the same way that you receive inoculations against infectious diseases. He proposed three main phases to this process:

1. *Conceptualisation phase*. The client is educated about the nature and impact of stress. For example, the client is taught to view perceived threats as problems to be solved and to break down global stressors into specific components that can be coped with. This enables the client to reconceptualise their problem.
2. *Skills acquisition phase (and rehearsal)*. Coping skills are taught and practised primarily in the clinic and then gradually rehearsed in real life. A variety of skills are taught, such as positive thinking, relaxation, social skills, methods of attention diversion, using social support systems, and time management.
3. *Application phase (and follow through)*. Clients are given opportunities to apply the newly learned coping skills in different situations, which become increasingly stressful. Various techniques may be used, such as imagery (imagining how to deal with stressful situations), modelling (watching someone else cope with stressors and then imitating this behaviour), and role-playing (acting out scenes involving stressors). Booster sessions (follow-through) are offered later on.

*evaluation*

*Deals with causes not symptoms*
The focus on skills acquisition provides long-lasting effectiveness. Skills are taught, practised and followed through. They are tailored to the needs of the individual.

*Limitations*
Cognitive therapies require a lot of time and effort, motivation and money. The strengths of SIT are also its limitations – it is effective because it involves learning and practising many new skills, but this complexity makes it a lengthy therapy which would suit only a limited range of determined individuals. It may be that the effectiveness of SIT is due to only certain elements of the training. For example, it might be equally effective to just learn to talk more positively and relax more.

## starSTUDY
## Investigating stress-reduction techniques: SIT
**(MEICHENBAUM, 1977)**

### Aims
Meichenbaum conducted this study to demonstrate the effectiveness of his method of stress inoculation therapy (SIT) in treating phobias. He compared SIT with systematic desensitisation (SD) which has proved highly effective as a form of treatment for phobias. SD involves presenting clients with a hierarchy of fearful stimuli, starting with the least fearful. When a client can relax and cope with the least fearful stimulus, the therapist introduces the next most fearful situation (see page 270).

### Method and procedure
The participants in the study were individuals who were phobic about snakes *and* rats. The patients were divided into four groups:
1. Snake phobia treated with SIT.
2. Snake phobia treated with SD.
3. Rat phobia treated with SIT.
4. Rat phobia treated with SD.

### Results
Meichenbaum found that both forms of therapy reduced the target phobia. However, most importantly, those patients who received SIT showed a reduction in the second, non-treated phobia.

### Conclusion
This shows that SIT can inoculate against other stressful situations, unlike other forms of treatment which are specific only to the target situation.

### Evaluation

*Generalisability*
This study shows the effectiveness of SIT in treating specific phobias, but it may not be as effective with more generalised stress or more severe stress.

*Individual differences*
The outcome wasn't the same for all participants, so this means that there are individual differences in the response to the therapy.

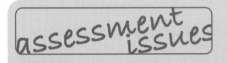

**Briefly describe *one* strategy for reducing stress. (ku 2   ae 0)**

This is an uncomplicated question with no *ae* required. Even so, questions like this on applied Aspects should be approached with care. Some processes, like stress, are very familiar to us through our own experience and therefore we may inadvertently slip into 'common sense' mode: for the above question, 'make yourself a cup of tea and put your feet up' will not do! And beware of producing a list of bullet points of advice – you are not being asked to produce a health promotion leaflet. So, although it's worth only two marks, these marks still have to be earned, by means of sound *psychological content*.

## Social strategies of stress reduction
### What are social strategies?

The third broad category of stress-reduction techniques are social ones – relying on others to assist you in reducing your stress. This includes the importance of having friends (and a social life) as well as stress reduction and management programmes within the workplace (including schools!) to help workers reduce stress.

### Social support

There is considerable research evidence that demonstrates the importance of social support in the reduction of stress. Previously in this chapter, we described research that demonstrates this: for example, Brown and Harris's study of depressed women (page 62), Kamarck *et al.*'s study of participants taking part in a stressful task with or without a friend (page 62), and Kiecolt-Glaser *et al.*'s study of students taking exams (page 57).

A wealth of other research confirms the importance of social support. For example, Nuckolls *et al.* (1972) studied 170 pregnant women: the women with high life stress and low social support had more early pregnancy complications than those with high life stress and high social support (91% compared with 33%).

Tache *et al.* (1979) found that cancer was more common among adults who were divorced, widowed, or separated, than among those who were married (see page 67 for similar studies on the effects of relationships on health). Presumably, this was because of a lack of close social support.

*evaluation*

There are several points to consider. First of all, some of the research is correlational and we can't be certain that lack of social support *caused* the ill-health. There may be intervening factors such as poor social skills which might lead to a lack of friends and induce higher stress levels.

A further point is the fact that social support isn't always positive. Schaefer *et al.* (1981) suggested that *perceived support* (i.e. the quality of support) is positively related to well-being whereas the *social network* (the quantity of available support) may actually have a negative effect because the wider your social network the more demands there are placed on you.

Kilpatrick (2005) also argues that some social support is detrimental. For example, some social networks may be unhealthy because they reinforce behaviours that are, in themselves, harmful. Drug and alcohol abusers who are in recovery need to stay away from these networks if they want to stay away from temptation.

*note*

### Pets and stress reduction

Having a pet may be good for your health. Research has shown that when dog or cat owners are asked to perform a stressful arithmetic task, they show less stress in the company of their pets than in the company of a friend. This may be because a pet companion will not be critical of your performance and such 'unconditional positive regard' is good for you. Other studies have found a variety of benefits associated with owning a pet – it relieves depression, reduces blood pressure, lowers anxiety levels and may improve survival after a heart attack (Skarnulis, 2004).

An unstressed author with her pet cat Lucky

## Organisational techniques

Stress inoculation therapy, described on page 73, is a form of training that is at both the organisational as well as the psychological level. Some other forms of training and organisational strategies are considered here.

### Hardiness

Suzanne Kobasa identified a personality type that was especially resistant to stress – the Hardy personality. Kobasa argued that if some people were naturally resistant to stress (because they were Hardy) then perhaps it would be possible to teach others how to become more Hardy, and thus manage stress better. Hardy individuals demonstrate three characteristics – the three Cs:

- *Control.* Hardy people attribute control to themselves rather than external factors that are beyond their control.
- *Commitment.* Hardy people are involved with the world around them, and have a strong sense of purpose.
- *Challenge.* Hardy people see life changes as challenges to be overcome rather than as threats or stressors.

The point is that all three of these characteristics will result in a reduced physiological arousal to potential stressors. Kobasa suggested the following ways to train 'Hardiness':

- *Focusing.* The client is taught how to recognise signs of stress, such as muscle tension, and also to identify the sources of this stress.
- *Reliving stress encounters.* The client relives and analyses stress situations to understand current stressors and current coping strategies.
- *Self-improvement.* The insights gained are used to learn new techniques. In particular, the client is taught to focus on seeing stressors as challenges and learns to take control.

### Employee assistance programmes (EAPs)

Strictly speaking, these are not stress-reduction strategies as they are not preventative; they aim merely to provide support, such as counselling, where individual employees are already suffering stress. In a study of UK Post Office employees, Cooper *et al.* (1992) found evidence that an EAP can alleviate stress.

### Organisational measures

Cox (1993) suggests that US managers tend to regard stress as an individual problem, whereas in Scandinavian countries stress is seen as arising from organisational factors. In Scandinavia, responsibility for working conditions, including stress levels, tends to be seen as shared between management and labour groups (e.g. trade unions), so organisational measures are more common there. Cox (1993) proposed various organisational measures:

- *Organisational change.* When changes take place they should aim to minimise stress.
- *Organisational culture.* There should be commitment to stress reduction, as a health and safety issue, from the top and throughout all levels.
- *Job design* to take stress into account, e.g. increasing employee's sense of control. The study by Marmot *et al.* (1997, see page 62) showed the importance of control in relation to stress.
- *Work schedules* should be flexible and family friendly.

*evaluation*

*Research support for Hardiness*
Wiebe (1991) assessed male and female undergraduates for Hardiness and then gave them a task to do under stressful conditions. The Hardy individuals displayed greater tolerance, reported that they found the task less threatening and the men showed less increase in heart rate during the task.

Maddi (1987) devised a stress management program based on Hardiness training. A group of managers who took part reported more job satisfaction and spoke of tremendous improvements in their work and personal relationships. Their levels of anxiety, depression and obsessiveness dropped quite noticeably, as did some physical symptoms of mental strain such as headaches and loss of sleep. None of these changes occurred in a comparison group of managers who did not take the course.

However, the technique did not work for everyone. A few of the trainees showed little improvement in their Hardiness scores and in the other measures; they tended to be the ones who missed a number of the sessions and were reluctant participants in the sessions that they did attend.

*Research on organisational measures*
A number of research investigations have been carried out in employment organisations. However, findings are mixed: employee stress levels may be reduced, but it is not clear whether organisational benefits can be achieved (Parks and Sparkes, 1998).

Estimates of the cost of stress and stress-related illness range from £5 billion (TUC) to £12 billion (CBI) each year (that's around £500 each year for every working adult). Sickness among staff cost the NHS more than £300 million in 1997 in England alone (*Daily Telegraph*, 25 March 1998).

Figures like these remind us how serious a problem stress is in all of our lives. They paint a gloomy picture, yet there are positive steps that we can all take to minimise the negative impact of stress. We have looked at many very different stress-reduction techniques. The jargon of these techniques, however, can sometimes blind us to the fact that there are very real and helpful things that we can all do to lower our stress levels. Presumably, you are reading this because you are anticipating taking an exam in the near future, so stress reduction is a vital consideration for you too.

assessment issues

### Common themes: psychology and you

Every Topic in the Higher (except the second unit) contains an applied Aspect, which highlights the relevance of psychology to our everyday lives. Indeed, the course is intended to promote skills to 'enhance … understanding of issues of personal relevance' (SQA Course Arrangements, p. 5). More specifically, certain applied Aspects are designed to help your 'development of effective study skills and learning strategies, revision and examination techniques' (SQA Course Arrangements, p. 15). Stress-reduction strategies, featured on the previous pages, and memory-improvement techniques (pages 46–51) are directly applicable to your own study activity. Note that the stress-reduction techniques for exam performance (above) are not just 'teacherly advice'; as a budding psychologist, you'll recognise that these tips are based on objective research evidence.

*In this section we show you student answers to possible exam questions plus examiner's comments on these answers. Remember that in the actual exam (and NABs) your questions for this Topic will always add up to 20 marks. The question may be one essay worth 20 marks or a number of smaller questions (such as those shown below) which add up to 20 marks.*

**Question 1**    Describe the processes of sympathetic *and* parasympathetic arousal in the stress response. (*ku* 6 *ae* 0)

| Tom | Alice |
|---|---|
| *Sympathetic arousal happens when an animal experiences a threat. This causes the ANS to become aroused and the adrenal gland releases adrenaline. The effect of adrenaline is to create physiological arousal, for example pupils are dilated and blood pressure increases. The animal is in a state of readiness for fight or flight.*<br><br>*When the threat is over, the parasympathetic system takes over and returns the body to its normal resting state where digestion is resumed and you can pee and defecate.* | *The sympathetic and parasympathetic systems are two branches of the autonomic nervous system. They are activated automatically to help us deal with emergency situations where our well-being is threatened. In other words, they are our stress response.*<br><br>*If a threat is perceived by the central nervous system (brain), this activates the autonomic nervous system which sends messages to the adrenal medulla (a part of the adrenal gland located above the kidneys). The adrenal medulla releases adrenaline and noradrenaline. These hormones have an intense physiological effect which arouses the body to fight or flee. The specific changes are that breathing rate, heartbeat and blood pressure are increased; blood is moved from the skin and viscera to the skeletal muscles, brain, and heart; digestion is inhibited and liver glycogen is converted into glucose for quick energy; and activity in the bladder and rectum is reduced. There are other changes as well which we commonly associate with feeling stressed such as sweating and hairs on the skin stand on end.*<br><br>*The task of the parasympathetic system is to return the body functions to normal after they have been aroused by sympathetic arousal – heart and breathing rate are normal, digestion takes place and sugar (glycogen) is stored.* |

**Examiner's comments**    Although Tom evidently has a basic grasp of these processes and the points he makes are fairly accurate, there is simply not enough detail, so he gains **2 out of 6 marks**.

Alice provides a thorough explanation of sympathetic arousal in the first paragraph, although she has not made it clear that what she is describing is sympathetic arousal. The answer also lacks balance, in that parasympathetic processes are treated rather sketchily, compared with the full details on sympathetic processes; wherever a question asks for two elements, as in this case, it is sensible to assume that the marks will be divided equally or roughly equally between the elements. Alice gains **4 out of 6 marks**.

**Question 2**    Evaluate the claim that there are individual differences in susceptibility to stress. (*ku* 2 *ae* 6)

| Tom | |
|---|---|
| *There are individual differences in people's susceptibility to stress. This means that people respond differently on account of a different personality, gender or culture.*<br><br>*An example of a personality difference is Type A personality. Friedman and Rosenman (1974) did a study which showed that Type A personalities were more likely to develop heart disease than Type Bs. This study took place over 8 years. It just concerned men so it may be gender-biased. There is other research on personality differences. There is a type C personality which is prone to cancer because they keep their emotions bottled-up. Kobasa proposed that there is a 'Hardy' personality which is a person who copes better in stressful situations. Some people have an internal locus of control (Rutter) which means they can cope better with stress than people with an external locus of control.* | *Men suffer more from heart disease which suggests they experience more stress which may be due to various things. It may be that they experience more stress e.g. because they have stressful jobs. This is supported by the fact that women who were doing jobs more like men had higher stress levels. Men also smoke and drink more which would increase their heart disease, and they have poorer friendship networks than women. Finally, it may be that women have evolved so they can cope better with stress because they respond to threat with a 'tend and befriend' response rather than 'fight or flight'.*<br><br>*People from different cultural groups respond differently to stress. This may be because some groups have more social support than others, which would reduce stress. Some cultural groups may experience more stress because of prejudice which may, for example, lead to more mental illness.* |

**Examiner's comments**    Tom's knowledge of this topic is quite thorough: he has selected relevant material for his answer and has addressed a range of individual differences in relation to stress so he easily gains the two *ku* marks. His explanations are quite analytical, often proposing reasons for links that have been found between individual differences and stress, so he gains some *ae* credit. However, the command of the question is to 'evaluate', and this is reflected in the six ae marks out of the total of eight; the main weakness of Tom's answer is his neglect of evaluation, which could have been achieved by, for example, reference to research findings, including criticisms of methodology and difficulty drawing cause-and-effect conclusions. He would have been wiser to focus on a smaller number of individual differences and evaluate each in more depth. He gains **5 out of 8 marks** (*ku* 2/2 *ae* 3/6).

## Alice

Some models of stress propose that there is a universal stress reaction. For example, the 'fight or flight' model proposes that all organisms (animals and humans) respond to a threat by automatic activation of the sympathetic ANS. This leads to the release of adrenaline and physiological arousal.

However, more recently researchers realised that this is more of a male response because participants tested have always been males. Evolutionary psychologists propose that it would have been adaptive in the EEA for males to respond in this way but females would have been protective towards their children – a 'tend and befriend' response. This is supported by the fact the female hormone oxytocin is secreted in women as a response to stress (Taylor et al. 2000). Individuals with high levels of oxytocin are calmer, more relaxed, more social and less anxious, and the hormone contributes to maternal behaviour and to affiliation. This might explain why, in stressful situations, women seek the support of others, which further serves to reduce their stress levels (because social support reduces stress). Men also secrete oxytocin when stressed, but its effects appear to be reduced by male hormones.

This finding has been supported by Hastrup et al. (1980) who found that women showed lowered stress responses during their menstrual cycle which is a time when their oxytocin levels would be highest.

The idea of a universal stress response is also challenged by research on personality which shows that different people respond to stress differently. The classic study by Friedman and Rosenman (1974) showed that some people respond to stressful situations by being impatient, competitive, and hostile. They termed these Type As whereas Type Bs were those who were relaxed in stressful situations. The individuals who were Type As were found, 8 years later, to be much more likely to develop heart disease.

**Examiner's comments**    Alice's answer is an answer of 'two halves'. She has decided to focus on just two types of individual differences and this should have allowed her to discuss each in some depth. However, her account of gender differences is rather too detailed, leaving inadequate time to deal with personality differences. She has made good use of research evidence in considering gender, less so in relation to personality. She shows analysis and evaluation in her discussion of gender in relation to stress, but her account of personality differences (as well as being too brief) contains little material worthy of *ae* marks. Alice is awarded **6 out of 8 marks** (*ku* 2/2  *ae* 4/6).

## Question 3    Discuss *one* research study into the effects of stress on physical *and/or* mental health.
(*ku* 6  *ae* 2)

## Tom

One study into the effects of stress on physical health was the study by Friedman and Rosenman. In this study there were over 250 men who were asked questions about how they would respond to everyday pressures. The questions were asked in a provocative manner to make people become annoyed. Type As were the impatient, hostile ones in a stressful situation. Type Bs were more relaxed.

They then checked the men again 8 years later to see how healthy they were. They were all healthy and had no heart problems at the start. More than twice as many of the Type As had heart attacks. The same was true when they checked the men 24 years later though the difference was smaller.

The conclusion is that stress leads to higher coronary disease, though we can't presume that stress is the cause because this was a natural experiment.

One criticism of this study is that it was all men and men respond to stress differently than women, so the results can't be generalised to all people.

**Examiner's comments**    Tom's answer contains a number of inaccuracies: the results are expressed in an unclear manner and the size of the sample is wrong by a factor of 10. In addition, no date is provided. However, method, procedure and conclusion are essentially sound. The evaluation points are also sound, although it would be worthwhile explaining why one cannot draw a cause-and-effect conclusion. Tom gets **6 out of 8 marks** (*ku* 4/6  *ae* 2/2).

## Alice

Rahe et al. studied the link between life events (which are stressors) and physical illness. The aim of this study was to look at people from a 'normal' population rather than patients who had sought medical care.

The participants were the men aboard three US Navy cruisers, about 3000 men. They filled in a version of the SRRS just before a tour of duty and then their health was monitored during their 7 month tour of duty. An illness score was calculated based on how often they were ill and how severe it was.

They found a significant positive correlation between life change units and illness score. The correlation was +0.118 which is low but significant.

Conclusion: this suggests that stress does cause illness though it doesn't actually demonstrate that it causes illness because the study was a correlation.

To evaluate the study we might consider whether the SRRS is a valid measure of stress. For a start you have to be able to accurately recall what events have happened over the last 6 months. For example people might repress unpleasant events. Another issue about validity is that some people think that life events aren't the most important stressors in our lives and that, for example, daily hassles are more stressful. A study by DeLongis et al. found a higher correlation between daily hassles and illness.

**Examiner's comments**    Alice provides a very good answer, with only minor inaccuracies or omissions, for example a slightly fuller explanation of the SRRS/LCUs variable would be helpful. Alice also does not give the date of the research. However, overall Alice demonstrates adequate understanding of limitations of the study. In spite of these imperfections, Alice gains the **full 8 marks**.

# 4 Topic: Methods, issues and data analysis in research

R esearch methods are systematic approaches to discovering things about the world. Psychologists use a wide range of different methods to obtain and analyse data about people's behaviour and experience. If we are to fully understand, and evaluate, psychological theories and concepts, we must understand the research methods and procedures that have provided the evidence for these theories.

| Chapter contents | Unit content for the topic 'Methods, issues and data analysis in research | Comment |
|---|---|---|
| **Aspect 1: The experimental method** | | |
| Experiments and variables page 81<br>Hypotheses and operationalisation page 82<br>Experimental design page 85<br>Experimental control page 87<br>Different types of experiment page 90 | *Cyclical nature of the research process*: Stages are: theory about human behaviour – hypothesis – design/conduct research and collect data – support/reject hypothesis + confirm/adjust theory – new hypothesis, etc. (page 125)<br>The experimental method<br>● *Types of experiment*: laboratory, field, natural/quasi-experiments (page 90)<br>● *Features of the experiment*: allows cause-and-effect conclusions, replicability (page 96)<br>● *Strengths and weaknesses* of experimental methods (page 94)<br>● *Operationalisation of variables*: independent variable and its conditions; dependent variable (page 81), control of extraneous and confounding variables (page 87)<br>● *Experimental designs*: independent measures/groups, repeated measures, matched pairs; comparative advantages and disadvantages of each (page 86) | *Notice that the **Unit content** for this chapter (and Chapter 5) is different in some ways from that of other chapters. For a start, it looks much greater in quantity. Don't be put off; this is simply because the information is broken down into much smaller 'chunks'. You'll also find that, in studying research methods, your learning will be of a different kind from that required in the other Units. The emphasis here is on how these methods work in practice, rather than on theoretical concepts (although, as with the content of other Units, you still need to be able to analyse and evaluate). To help you learn, this chapter contains **Activities** (in orange boxes) and **Questions** (in yellow boxes). Suggested answers to the questions can be found on the **website** www.nelsonthornes.com/researchmethods* |
| **Aspect 2: Research issues** | | |
| Ecological validity and realism page 95<br>Descriptive statistics page 98<br>Quantitative and qualitative data page 102<br>Sampling page 103<br>Ethical issues page 105<br>How to deal with ethical issues page 107 | Non-experimental methods<br>● Survey, including questionnaires and interviews, questionnaire/interview construction (page 110)<br>● *Observation*: naturalistic, participant/non-participant, use of observation schedule (page 118)<br>● *Case study* (page 122)<br>● *Strengths and weaknesses* of non-experimental methods (pages 111,116,120,123)<br>● *Comparative strengths and weaknesses* of experimental and non-experimental methods (pages 111,116,119,120,123)<br>● *Multi-method approaches in practice*, including case studies involving several methods (page 125) and use of observation in experiments (page 118)<br>Research issues common to all methods<br>● *Hypotheses*: experimental/alternative hypothesis and null hypothesis, one- and two-tailed hypotheses (pages 82–84)<br>● *Realism/ecological validity* (95–98)<br>● *Sampling*: definitions of sample and population; features of a good sample – sample size, representativeness, avoidance of bias, generalisability; principles and practice of random sampling; opportunity/convenience sampling; self-selecting sampling (pages 103–104) | *Finally, you'll see that the order of material in the chapter (see first column) is different from the order given in the second column (which is the order given in the Unit specification). This has been done because it makes sense to introduce the concepts in a different order from the specification. We suggest you go through the chapter as it stands; the page numbers are provided for each concept so that you can easily find these when revising or referring to concepts in the chapter.* |
| **Aspect 3: Non-experimental methods** | | |
| Surveys page 110<br>Correlational design and analysis page 114<br>Observation page 118 | Data analysis<br>● *Definitions and distinctions between quantitative and qualitative data* (page 102)<br>● *Descriptive statistics*: measures of central tendency (mean, median, mode), measures of dispersion (range), bar charts, percentages and pie charts (page 100), scattergrams (page 115) | |

| Chapter contents | Unit content for the topic 'Methods, issues and data analysis in research | Comment |
|---|---|---|
| | • *Correlational design and analysis*: correlational hypotheses, use and interpretation of scattergrams, positive and negative correlations, interpretation of strength of correlation, limitations of correlation (page 114)<br>Knowledge of inferential statistics is not required<br>Ethical issues in research<br>• *Ethical issues in research*: ethical principles in psychological research with humans, including the role of studies, such as those by Milgram and Piliavin, in the development of ethical codes (page 107) | |

# Aspect 1: The experimental method

*You actually know all about experiments – you conduct them without thinking. For example, when you start a new class with a new teacher you see how they respond to your behaviour – you might make a joke or hand your homework in late (both IVs) to see how the teacher responds (the DV). You are experimenting with cause and effect.*

*A variable is just a 'thing' – something that can change. For example, noise is a variable; it can be soft, comfortable or loud. Age is a variable; people can be old, middle-aged, young or very young. These would be* **'conditions' of the independent variable***.*

### KEY TERMS ◀

**Experiment:** A *research method* that involves the direct manipulation of an *independent variable (IV)* in order to test its possible causal effect on a *dependent variable*.

**Dependent variable (DV):** A measurable outcome of the action of the *IV* in an experiment.

**Independent variable (IV):** Some event that is directly manipulated by an experimenter into two or more levels/conditions in order to test its effect on another variable (the *DV*).

**Conditions of the independent variable:** There may be two or more conditions of the independent variable. For example, in the experiment by Baddeley (see page 33) there were four conditions or *levels* of the IV: acoustically similar, acoustically dissimilar, semantically similar and semantically dissimilar.

## Experiments and variables
### What is an experiment?
An **experiment** is a way of conducting research where:

- One *variable* is made to change (by the experimenter)
  - This is called the **independent variable** or IV.
- The effects of the IV on another variable are observed or measured
  - This is called the **dependent variable** or DV.

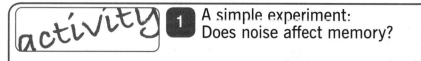

**activity**    **1**    A simple experiment: Does noise affect memory?

The variable we are going to change (the IV) is noise.

The variable we are going to measure (the DV) is performance on a memory task.

- You will need a radio and two lists of 20 words each. (You can use the right-hand word list on page 101. There are 40 words in the list.)
- Divide your class into two groups: Group N (noise) and Group S (silent).
- Group N should have the radio playing very loudly when they are shown the list of words. They have one minute to try to remember them and then one minute to write them down.
- Group S should do the same task in silence with the second list of words.

Which group remembered most words?

### And another experiment: Drunken goldfish
Many early psychology experiments focused on learning in animals. The learning usually involved simple mazes where the animal was rewarded if it turned in the desired direction at the end of a maze shaped like a Y.

In one experiment goldfish were trained in a maze and afterwards some were placed in a water solution high in alcohol (some 'keeled' over!).

When the goldfish were retested a week later those goldfish who had not been exposed to alcohol could remember the maze task perfectly but those who keeled over in the alcohol solution had no memory for the task. This demonstrates the severe effects of alcohol on learning (Ryback, 1969).

### And another experiment: Is performance affected by expectation?
If you want people to perform better does it help to lie to them about the quality of the materials they are using? Do people perform better if they think the materials they are using are better?

*Many things that are called experiments are actually investigations. An experiment must have an IV and a DV.*

A study by Weick *et al.* (1973) tested this by telling two jazz bands (Band A and Band B) that the piece of music they were rehearsing was either (a) by a composer whose work was well respected or (b) by a composer whose work had been negatively reviewed. Weick *et al.* found that people did perform better if they thought that they were playing a well-respected work. Participants also remembered the piece better and liked it better.

However, this finding might be because Band A was actually a better band than Band B. To overcome this problem the experiment was designed so that both bands played music by both composers and played two musical pieces: Piece 1 and Piece 2.

Band A was told that Piece 1 was by the superior composer and Piece 2 was by the inferior composer.

Band B was told that Piece 1 was by the inferior composer and Piece 2 was by the superior composer.

*Suggested answers to all the questions in this chapter can be found on the website www.nelsonthornes.com/higherpsych*

1. Think of some other variables, and for each say how they can vary (i.e. levels of the variable).
2. Does noise affect memory?
   a. What was the IV?
   b. What was the DV?
   c. What was the aim of this experiment?
3. Drunken goldfish
   a. What was the IV?
   b. What was the DV?
4. Is performance affected by expectation?
   a. What was the IV?
   b. What was the DV?
   c. What was the aim of this experiment?

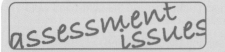

**Research methods questions are different.**

In the Unit NABs and the exam section on research methods, you will find a different kind of question from those in the other two Units/sections. For a start, there are more of them, although with lower marks each (so they still make up 20 marks, like the other questions). There is an example of a research methods question at the end of this chapter.

The main feature of the question is that you are given a description of some research – a *scenario* – which you must *interpret* in order to answer the questions. The scenario could give an example of a research study like those you have been reading about – drunken goldfish, jazz musicians, and noise effects on memory. And, as in the practice questions on these examples, you must *read every word in the scenario very carefully indeed* to glean the information you need. Sometimes, the correct answer lies in one key word in the scenario. A table or graph of results may be provided; again, inspect this kind of material closely. Think of yourself as a detective, looking for clues – you have the advantage of knowing that the clues are definitely there, waiting to be found!

# Hypotheses and operationalisation
## What is meant by a hypothesis?

A **hypothesis** states what you believe to be true. It is a precise and testable statement of the relationship between two variables.

A hypothesis for the noise and memory experiment would be:

*People who do homework without the TV on get higher marks than those who do homework with the TV on.*

*A hypothesis is not the same as the aims of a study.*

The hypothesis is sometimes called the *experimental hypothesis* ($H_1$) if it relates to an experiment or the *alternative hypothesis* (alternative to the **null hypothesis**, $H_0$) for either experimental or non-experimental research.

### One-tailed and two-tailed hypotheses

A **one-tailed hypothesis** states the direction of difference between two conditions or two groups of participants.

A **two-tailed hypothesis** predicts simply that there will be a difference between two conditions or two groups of participants.

For example:

One-tailed    People who do homework without the TV on get *higher* marks than those who do homework with the TV on.

Two-tailed    People who do homework with the TV on get *different* marks from those who do homework with no TV on.

When you look at a one-tailed cat you know which way it is going. A two-tailed cat could be going either way.

**KEY TERMS**

**One-tailed hypothesis:** This states the direction of the predicted difference between two conditions or two groups of participants.

**Two-tailed hypothesis:** This predicts that there will be a *difference* between two conditions or two groups of participants, without stating the *direction* of the difference.

*note*

### Why have one- and two-tailed hypotheses?

Psychologists use a one-tailed hypothesis when past research (theory or study) suggests that the results will go in a particular direction. A one-tailed hypothesis is sometimes called a *directional* hypothesis.

Psychologists use a two-tailed hypothesis when past research is equivocal, so they don't know which way to predict the results and just predict 'a difference' or 'a relationship'. A two-tailed hypothesis is sometimes called a *non-directional* hypothesis.

### The null hypothesis ($H_0$)

In some circumstances (e.g. for the purpose of statistical tests) there is a need to state a null hypothesis – this is a statement of *no difference or no relationship* between the variables.

For example:

- There is no difference between the quality of work done in noisy or silent conditions.
- There is no relationship between age and intelligence.

NB Some people add the phrase 'any difference must be due to chance factors'. You can do this but it is not necessary.

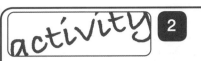

1. Write a hypothesis for the experiments on
   a. Goldfish and alcohol.
   b. Effect of expectations on performance.
2. State whether each hypothesis was one- or two-tailed and explain why you chose this kind of hypothesis.
3. For each of the following, decide whether it is a one- or two-tailed hypothesis.
   a. Boys' scores on aggressiveness tests differ from girls' scores.
   b. Students who have a computer at home do better in exams than those who don't.
   c. People remember the words that are early in a list better than the words that appear later.
   d. People given a list of emotionally charged words recall fewer than participants given a list of emotionally neutral words.
   e. Hamsters are better pets than budgies.
   f. Words presented in a written form are recalled differently from those presented in a pictorial form.
4. Now write your own. For each of the following experiments write a one- or two-tailed hypothesis and a null hypothesis.
   a. A study to find out whether girls watch more television than boys.
   b. A study to see whether teachers give more attractive students higher marks on essays than students who are less attractive.
   c. A study to investigate whether lack of sleep affects schoolwork.

## Operationalisation

A 'good' hypothesis should be written in a testable form i.e. a way that makes it clear how you are going to design an experiment to test the hypothesis.

Think back to the experiment on goldfish. This study sought to investigate the effect of alcohol on learning:

*Hypothesis*: Goldfish who are given alcohol are less likely to remember their way around a maze than those who are not given alcohol.

The concept of 'learning' (the DV) has been *operationalised* in order to produce a testable hypothesis ('learning' = 'remembering their way around a maze'). 'Give alcohol' (the IV) has been *operationalised* by adding a precise amount of alcohol to the water of half of the goldfish, but not to the water of the other goldfish.

'**Operationalisation**' means to specify a set of operations or behaviours that can be measured or manipulated. For example, 'social development' can be broken down into the following 'operations: the tendency to seek the company of others; to show enjoyment when with others; to have a number of friends; to display social skills such as negotiating with friends, etc.

Let's look at some other examples:

*Hypothesis:* People work better in quiet rather than noisy conditions.

What precisely do we mean by 'do better' and 'quiet' and 'noisy'? We need to define the operations:

- 'work better' = obtain a higher score on a memory test
- 'quiet' = no sound
- 'noisy' = radio playing.

*Operationalised hypothesis*: People obtain a higher score on a memory test when tested in quiet (no sounds) rather than noisy (radio playing) conditions.

*Hypothesis*: People are happier if they work.

- 'happier' = obtain a high score on a happiness questionnaire
- 'work' = have a full-time job (over 40 hours per week).

*Operationalised hypothesis*: People obtain a higher score on a happiness questionnaire if they work full-time (over 40 hours per week) than if they do not work.

*questions* **2**

1. Do older people sleep more or less than younger people?
   a. Identify the IV and DV in this question.
   b. How could you operationalise the IV?
   c. How could you operationalise the DV?
   d. Write a fully operationalised one-tailed hypothesis.
   e. Write a fully operationalised two-tailed hypothesis.

2. People rate food as looking more attractive when they are hungry. Answer questions a–e above.

3. A teacher wishes to find out whether one maths test is harder than another maths test. Answer questions a–e above.

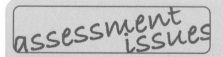
*assessment issues*

### In psychological research, what is meant by a 'dependent variable'? (*ku 2 ae 0*)

You may be asked, in NABs and exam questions, to give a *definition* or *brief description* of an independent variable or a dependent variable or a hypothesis. There may be only two or three marks for such questions, but these are easy marks (as long as you have learned your stuff!). The risk is that you may give too sketchy an answer, maybe because you know it so well that it seems 'obvious'. Do ensure that you give a *full and detailed description*.

# Experimental design

We are going to look now at **experimental design**.

## Independent groups and repeated measures

The experiment on noise and memory (on page 81) is an example of an **independent groups** design:

- Each participant was tested in only one condition.
- There were two separate (independent) groups of participants.

We could redesign this as a **repeated measures** design:

- Each participant would be tested in both conditions.
- They would be tested in the noise condition (with one memory test) and retested in the no noise condition (with a similar but different memory test).

**KEY TERMS**

**Experimental design:** A set of procedures used to control the influence of participant variables in an experiment.

**Independent measures/groups:** Participants are allocated to two (or more) groups, each representing different experimental conditions. Allocation is usually done using *random allocation*.

**Repeated measures:** Each participant takes part in every condition under test.

*Note that research design is different from a research method. This can be confusing. The term 'method' refers to a way of conducting research in a systematic manner (e.g. an experiment). 'Design' is the detailed plan used within a research method (such as repeated measures design).*

|  | Noise condition | | | No noise condition | | |
|---|---|---|---|---|---|---|
| **Independent groups** | Sara | Rob | Mike | Linda | Pip | Janet |
|  | Paul | Sue | Sam | Chris | Rosie | Jack |
| **Repeated measures** | Sara | Rob | Mike | Sara | Rob | Mike |
|  | Paul | Sue | Sam | Paul | Sue | Sam |

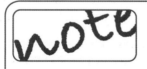

### Try this one

In a memory study there are two groups of participants:

- Group 1 did the learning task *with* the TV on, and then did a second learning task *without* the TV on.
- Group 2 did the learning task *without* the TV on and then did a second learning task *with* the TV on.

Varying the order of the tasks like this is called **counterbalancing** (see page 87) and is done to **control** for practice and fatigue (**order effects**, see page 88).

Is this now an independent groups design, or is it still repeated measures?

*It is still repeated measures because, even though there are two groups, the analysis will still involve comparing the same individual's score on one task with their score on the other task.*

**KEY TERMS**

**Matched pairs:** Pairs of participants are matched in terms of key variables, such as age and IQ. One member of each pair is placed in the *experimental group* and the other member in the *control group*.

**Participant variables:** Characteristics of individual participants (such as age, intelligence, etc.) that might influence the outcome of a study.

## Matched pairs design

**Matched pairs** is a third kind of experimental design. It involves the use of independent groups but each participant in Group A is paired with one in Group B. This is done by pairing participants on key **participant variables** (e.g. IQ, memory ability, gender or score on some pre-test – any characteristic that may affect the findings) and then placing one member of each pair in each group.

| Disadvantages | Dealing with problems created by design |
|---|---|
| **Repeated measures design** | |
| ➕ One of the memory tests may be more difficult than the other and this is why the participants do better in one condition (the noise condition) than the other (no noise condition). | You can make sure the tests are equivalent. Create a list of 40 words and **randomly allocate** these words to the two lists so both lists are equivalent. |
| ➖ When the participants do the second memory test they may guess the purpose of the experiment, which may affect their behaviour. For example, some participants may purposely do worse on the second test because they want it to seem as if they work better in noisy conditions. | You can lie to the participants about the purpose of the test to try to prevent them guessing what it is about. This is called a **single blind design** (the participant is blind to the aim of the study). |
| ➖ The order of the conditions may affect performance (an *order effect* – a potentially **confounding variable**). Participants may do better on the second test because of a practice effect OR participants may do worse on the second test because of being bored with doing a similar test again (*boredom* or *fatigue effect*). | You can use **counterbalancing** (see page 87). |
| **Independent groups design** | |
| ➕ No control of **participant variables** (i.e. the different abilities of each participant). For example participants in Group 1 might be more able than those in group 2. | *Randomly allocate* participants to conditions to ensure groups are equivalent. Match participants in each group on key variables (see matched pairs design). |
| ➖ You need twice as many participants because there are two groups. | |
| **Matched pairs design** | |
| ➖ It is very time-consuming to match participants. | Don't use matched pairs design. |
| ➖ May not control all participant variables. | |

## KEY TERMS

**Random allocation:** Allocating participants to experimental groups or conditions using *random techniques* (see page 104).

**Single blind design:** A type of *research design* in which the participant is not aware of the research aims or of which condition of the experiment they are receiving.

**Confounding variable:** An extraneous variable that has affected the DV and has thus confounded the findings of the study.

*You can work out the advantages of each design by looking at the disadvantages of the other designs and reversing them.*

## questions 3

Look back at the experiments on page 81.

*Noise and memory*
1. Write a suitable hypothesis for the new experiment using a repeated measures design.
2. Explain why you think that a repeated measures design would not be as good as the independent groups design.

*Alcohol and goldfish*
3. Was this an independent groups design or repeated measures design?

*Is performance affected by expectation?*
4. Was this an independent groups design or repeated measures design?
5. What do you think was the advantage of choosing this design?

*For each of the following experiments state whether it is a repeated measures or independent groups design. To do this, ask yourself, 'Would the findings be analysed by comparing the scores from the same person or by comparing the scores of two (or more) groups of people?' (Write down your answer.)*
6. Boys and girls are compared on their IQ test scores.
7. Hamsters are tested to see if one genetic strain is better at finding food in a maze compared with another group.
8. Reaction time is tested before and after a reaction time training activity to see if test scores improve after training.
9. Participants are tested on a memory task in the morning and in the afternoon.
10. Three groups of participants are given different words lists to remember to see whether nouns, verbs or adjectives are easier to recall.
11. Participants are asked to give ratings for attractive and unattractive photographs.

*Counterbalancing literally means to achieve balance by having an equal weight at both ends.*

**Counterbalancing:** An experimental technique designed to overcome *order effects* (or other *extraneous/confounding variables*). Counterbalancing ensures that each condition is tested first or second in equal amounts.

## Counterbalancing

**Counterbalancing** ensures that the order of different tasks does not affect the results. For example, if participants do memory test 1 with the TV on and then memory test 2 without the TV on, then the reason they do better without the TV may because they do this condition second and have got better at doing memory tests.

In order to counterbalance this, we can have two groups who do the conditions (with and without TV on) in reverse order:

Group 1   memory test 1 with TV on; memory test 2 without TV

Group 2   memory test 1 without TV; memory test 2 with TV on

This is still a repeated measures design because the final analysis will involve comparing two memory scores for each individual (with TV and without TV).

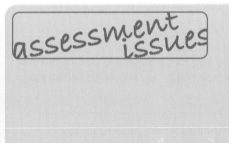

1. Look back to the experiment 'Is performance affected by expectation?' on page 81. Counterbalancing has been used here although not for order effects. Explain how counterbalancing has been used in this study and why it was used.

2. A psychologist conducted a study to see whether visual imagery helps memory. To do this there were two lists to be recalled – one had words only, the other had images instead of words.
   a. Describe how you could conduct this study using (i) repeated measures design, (ii) independent groups design and (iii) matched pairs design.
   b. Which design would be best? Explain your answer.
   c. For which kind of design would counterbalancing be necessary?
   d. Explain how you would design the counterbalancing.

*assessment issues*

**Name the experimental design used in this study. (*ku* 1 *ae* 0)**

The words used in relation to research methods have very precise meanings. These can present hidden traps, unless you make yourself very conscious of them. In this question, you are asked to state the 'design' used in an experimental study. You might be tempted to write 'lab' or 'field' or 'natural' or 'quasi' – but you would get *zero* marks, as these are *types* of experiment (which are described on page 90); they are not *designs*. The required answer here would be one of the following: independent groups, repeated measures or matched pairs (depending on the precise information given in the scenario about the experiment).

## Experimental control

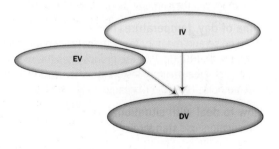

The experimenter 'controls' the independent variable (IV) in an experiment – making it change to see what happens to the dependent variable (DV). The experimenter also has to control other variables (extraneous variables, EVs) to make sure that they don't change, otherwise they may influence the DV and you cannot conclude that the IV was the cause of any change in the DV. Methods of experimental design aim to control EVs.

**Extraneous variable (EV):** In an experiment, this is any variable other than the *independent variable* that might potentially affect the *dependent variable*.

**Control:** This refers to the extent to which any variable is held constant or regulated by a researcher.

## There are DVs, IVs and then there are other variables

*Order effects* are an **extraneous variable** that may confound the results. For example, if we do the noise and memory experiment as a repeated measures design:

1. Participants do memory test with noise.

2. Participants do memory test without noise.

They do better on the second test.

- Is this because they do better when tested without noise? (Level of noise is the IV.)
- Or because they have *practised* doing the test? (Amount of practice has become an alternative and unintentional IV.)

*Amount of practice* is, in this case, an extraneous variable.

## Participant variables

Any *personal* variable might act as an extraneous variable – but only if an independent groups design is used. When a repeated measures design is used, *participant variables* are controlled because the same person participates in both conditions.

### Age, intelligence, motivation, experience
Participants in one condition may perform better because they share certain characteristics rather than because of the IV that they receive. In the noise and memory experiment, it might be that one group of participants were younger (and thus had better memories), or were more intelligent, more highly motivated or more experienced at doing memory tests.

### Irrelevant participant variables
When considering participant variables as EVs, we must only focus on those that are relevant to the task. Therefore, in the noise and memory task, liking of spicy food would not be an EV (or at least it would be hard to see why it would be).

## Situational variables

**Situational variables** are features of the research *situation* that may influence the participant's behaviour and thus can also be EVs.

### Order effects
If a participant did condition A first and then condition B, they might do better on condition B because they had an opportunity to practise. On the other hand, they might do worse because they have become tired or bored.

### Investigator effect
The way in which the investigator asks a question may *lead* the participant to give the answer that the investigator 'wants'. Or the way the investigator responds may encourage certain kinds of responses.

This is called an **investigator** or **experimenter effect**. For example, research has found that male experimenters are more pleasant, friendly and encouraging with female participants than they are with male participants (Rosenthal, 1966). An experimenter might also be more encouraging on one experimental task so this would explain why a participant does better on that task rather than on another task, meaning that the IV may not be responsible.

An investigator effect may be *direct* (a consequence of the investigator's interaction with the participant) or *indirect* (a consequence of the investigator's design of the study). Investigator effects are not the same as *participant effects*.

### Time of day, temperature, noise
If the noise and memory experiment was conducted using an independent groups design, it might be that Group 1 (noise group) does the memory test in the morning and Group 2 (no noise) does the memory test in the afternoon. If Group 2 does better it might be because there was no noise (the IV) or because they did the test in the afternoon – time of day may be an EV.

### How to deal with situational variables
Investigators use **standardised procedures** to ensure that all participants are tested under the same conditions. Standardised procedures are like a recipe – if different procedures are used then different outcomes may be due to the procedures and not the IV.

### How to deal with investigator effects
Investigators use **standardised instructions** to ensure as far as possible that communications with participants are similar and contain no hints about research aims or expectations.

Or they use a **double blind** design: in this case, neither the participant nor the person conducting the experiment (who has not always designed it) knows important details of the study, such as the research aims and hypothesis, and which experimental condition the participant is receiving, so the experimenter cannot affect the participants' performance.

**Participant effects:** A general term used to acknowledge the fact that participants react to cues in an experimental situation which may affect the validity of any conclusions drawn from the investigation.

**Participant reactivity:** The bias in responses that occurs because a participant knows they are being studied.

**Demand characteristics:** Features of an experiment that a participant unconsciously responds to when searching for clues about how to behave. These may act as a *confounding variable*.

**Experimental group:** In an independent groups design, a group of participants who receive the experimental treatment (the IV). There may be more than one experimental group, reflecting levels of the IV.

**Control group:** In an independent groups experiment, a group of participants who do not receive the experimental treatment. Their behaviour acts as a baseline against which the effect of the IV may be measured.

**Experimental condition:** In a repeated measures design, the condition containing the *independent variable*. There may be more than one experimental condition in an experiment, reflecting levels of the IV.

**Control condition:** In a repeated measures experiment, the condition that provides a baseline measure of behaviour without the experimental treatment (IV), so that the effect of the experimental treatment may be assessed.

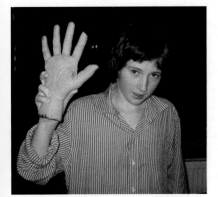

Participants want to offer a helping hand. This sometimes results in their being over-cooperative and behaving artificially. There is also the 'screw you' effect where a participant deliberately behaves in such a way as to spoil an experiment.

## Participant effects

In addition to investigator effects there are also **participant effects** which can be EVs. If participants know that they are taking part in an experiment this may alter their behaviour because they usually want to please the experimenter and be helpful; otherwise, why are they there? Participants may actively seek cues as to how they should behave (**participant reactivity**) because they want to help and also because they are unsure about what is expected. This leads to **demand characteristics** – cues that unconsciously suggest what is expected of participants. For example, in the study on noise and memory, participants who do the test in a noisy environment may have lower expectations of doing well on the memory test because the atmosphere is more 'casual' than when the test is conducted in silent conditions. Thus demand characteristics may act as an alternative IV (*confounding variable*) because they explain the change in the DV.

## A different kind of control

Sometimes you will see the phrases: **experimental group** and **control group**.

For example, a researcher might want to investigate the effects that rewards have on performance. To do this children are asked to collect rubbish from a playground and are offered a chocolate bar as a reward.

We cannot conclude anything about the effects of the reward because all the children were told that they would receive a reward. We need to have a control group who are offered no reward so that we can make a comparison.

We need two groups: an *experimental group* (offered a reward) and a *control group* (offered no reward). This allows us to compare the effects of the reward (IV) on collecting rubbish (the DV).

Or we need to have two conditions for the same participants: an **experimental condition** (children offered a reward on one occasion) and a **control condition** (same children offered no reward on another occasion).

In some experiments, there may be more than one experimental condition; for example, in a test of the effects of noise on learning, there might be two noise conditions, loud and soft.

### assessment issues

**Explain what is meant by an 'extraneous variable', in psychological research.**
(*ku 2 ae 0*)

**Identify a possible extraneous variable, in this study.**
(*ku 2 ae 0*)

Be on the alert for *two* types of research methods questions, as illustrated in the pair of questions above. One requires you to *apply* your knowledge of research methods to the specific situation of the *given research scenario*, and the other asks you to write about an aspect of research methods in a more *general* way. Which is which in the above pair? The questions contain words that make this clear: if you are asked about 'this study' or see the words 'in this research' or 'in the scenario described above', you need to apply your knowledge to the specific situation of the scenario. If the question states 'in psychological research' or makes no reference to the scenario, then you should simply show your knowledge of research methods in a more general way. Of course, it's possible that a question may ask you to do both, for example 'Describe the interview method of research and discuss *two* strengths of the use of interviews in this study'.

 **5**

1. Name *two* extraneous variables that might affect the study on noise and memory, if the study was:
   a. repeated measures.
   b. independent groups.

2. How could each of the extraneous variables described in question 1 be controlled?

3. In a study, participants' memory was tested in the morning and in the afternoon, to see if there was any difference in their ability to recall numbers.
   a. Give an example of *one* possible investigator effect in this study.
   b. Describe how you might deal with this investigator effect.
   c. Give an example of how participant reactivity might affect the findings of this experiment.
   d. Describe how you might deal with such participant reactivity.
   e. Give an example of a possible demand characteristic in this study.
   f. Describe how you might deal with this problem.

4. Participants were given a list of adjectives describing Mr. Smith. One group's list had positive adjectives first, followed by negative adjectives. The other group's list had the adjectives in reverse order. They were all then asked to describe Mr. Smith.
   a. Give an example of a possible demand characteristic in this study.
   b. Describe how you might deal with this problem.

## Different types of experiments

On page 81 we considered the question 'what is an experiment?' There are different types of experiments, all share one thing in common – they have an *independent variable* and a *dependent variable*:

- **Laboratory experiment.** This is an experiment conducted in a *special environment* where variables can be *carefully controlled*. Participants are *aware* that they are taking part in an experiment although they may not know the true aims of the study. In general, the participants go to the experimenter rather than the experimenter going to the participants.

- **Field experiment.** This type of experiment is conducted in a more *natural environment*, i.e. in 'the field'. As with the laboratory experiment, the independent variable is still *deliberately manipulated* by the researcher and causal relationships can therefore be demonstrated. Participants are often *unaware* that they are participating in an experiment, thus reducing *participant reactivity*. The experimenter generally goes to the participants. A field experiment is conducted in a more natural setting than a *lab experiment* and may therefore have greater **mundane realism**.

- **Natural experiment.** In some situations it is not possible (ethically or practically) to manipulate the IV and therefore researchers take advantage of IVs that have been naturally manipulated; for example, a school adopts a new teaching method (IV), and researchers test children's performance (DV) on both the old and new methods. The effects of the IV on the DV can be observed by the experimenter. Strictly speaking, an experiment involves the *deliberate* manipulation of an IV by an experimenter. Natural experiments are not, therefore, 'true experiments', because no one has *deliberately* changed the IV, and causal conclusions should not be drawn. Also, there may be bias from participant variables as participants are not randomly allocated to conditions.

Note that it is possible to do research in a laboratory which is not an experiment. For example, controlled observations are conducted in a laboratory (we will look at these in Aspect 3).

Note also that there are field *studies* as well as field *experiments*. Any study which is conducted in a natural environment is called a field study – it is only a field experiment if there is an IV that has been manipulated by the experimenter.

An experiment permits us to study cause *and* effect. It differs from non-experimental methods in that it involves the manipulation of one variable (the IV), while trying to keep all other variables constant. If the IV is the only thing that is changed, then it must be responsible for any change in the DV.

**Confederate:** An individual in a study who is not a real participant and has been instructed how to behave by the investigator/experimenter. A confederate may act as the *independent variable* but confederates are not always an IV, they may simply help guide the investigation.

## activity 3 A field experiment

A number of studies have investigated the effects of appearance on behaviour, for example:

- Bickman (1974) left a 10 cents coin (dime) in a telephone box. If a **confederate** was dressed in a suit he got the dime back 77% of the time, if he was wearing unkempt work clothes there was a 38% return rate.

- Bickman also found that New York pedestrians were more likely to obey someone dressed as a guard than someone in milkman's uniform or dressed casually. The confederates issued orders to passers-by: 'Pick up this bag for me', 'This fellow is overparked at the meter but doesn't have any change. Give him a dime', or 'Don't you know you have to stand on the other side of the pole?'

In these field experiments, the IV is appearance and the DV is helping behaviour.

You can try a similar experiment.

- Students should work in pairs. One member of the pair is the observer and the other is the confederate who wears one of two outfits:
  – smartly dressed
  – casual.

- The task is to ask people if they would be prepared to stop and answer some questions for a school project.

- If the passer-by says no, thank them.

- If the passer-by says yes, explain that this was an experiment for your school work and all you wished to know was whether they were prepared to help or not.

- The observer should record
  1. How many passers-by said yes or no for each condition (smart or casual)?
  2. Any other comments made by passers-by.

## questions 6

You can answer these questions even if you have not conducted the activity above.

1. What are the research aims of the experiment?
2. How do you know it is an experiment?
3. How do you know it is a field experiment?
4. Write a suitable hypothesis for this experiment.
5. Why should the same person dress in the two different outfits (instead of using two different people to play each part)?
6. What was the experimental design that was used?
7. Give *one* advantage and *one* disadvantage of using this experimental design in this study.
8. Present your results in a table like the one below.

|  | Smartly dressed | Casually dressed |
|---|---|---|
| **Passer-by said yes** |  |  |
| **Passer-by said no** |  |  |

9. What do you conclude?

## Lab versus field experiments

To help you to understand the difference between lab and field experiments, look at the examples below and answer the questions.

*Example A*

Helping behaviour was investigated in a study on the New York subway. A confederate collapsed on a subway train and investigators noted whether or not help was offered. The confederate was either holding a black cane or carrying a bottle of alcohol and smelling of alcohol (thus appearing drunk). Piliavin *et al.* (1969) found that when the victim carried a cane 95% of bystanders helped within 10 seconds, but if he appeared drunk help only came spontaneously (within 10 seconds) in 50% of the trials.

*Example B*

Participants were asked to wait in a room before the experiment began. There was a radio playing either good or bad news and a stranger was present. When they were asked to rate the stranger, the degree of liking was related to the kind of news they had been listening to, showing that people like others who are associated with positive experiences (Veitch and Griffitt, 1976).

*Example C*

The participants were children aged three to five years old. Each child was taken on their own to a special room where there were lots of toys including, in one corner, a five-foot inflatable Bobo doll and a mallet. The experimenter invited the 'model' to join them and then left the room for about 10 minutes. Half of the children watched the model playing aggressively with the Bobo doll while the others watched the model play non-aggressively with the doll. Later the children were given an opportunity to play with toys including the Bobo doll. The children who saw the aggressive behaviour were more likely to behave aggressively (Bandura *et al.*, 1961).

*Example D*

One group of school pupils were given information about how their peers had performed on a maths task. They were either told that their peers had done well or done poorly on the test. The children were later given a maths test in class. Those who expected to do well did better than those led to expect to do poorly (Schunk, 1983).

*Example E*

The Hawthorne Electric factory in Chicago asked researchers to study what factors led to increased worker productivity. The study found that increased lighting led to increased productivity – but then found that *decreased* lighting also led to increased activity (Roethlisberger and Dickson, 1939). The conclusion was that the participants knew that they were being studied and this interest in their work was what explained their increased output, masking the real IV. This has been called the **Hawthorne effect.**

*Example F*

Participants were tested in their teaching room; they were given nonsense trigrams (e.g. SXT) and were asked to count backwards until told to stop. Participants were then asked to recall the trigram they were given. The counting interval was used to prevent the trigram being rehearsed. When the counting interval was 3 seconds participants could recall most trigrams; when it was 18 seconds they couldn't recall many trigrams (Peterson and Peterson, 1959).

For each of the examples (A–F), answer the following questions:

1. Identify the IV and DV.

2. Was the task required of participants artificial/contrived?

3. Was the study conducted in a natural setting?

4. Was the setting high or low in mundane realism?

5. Did the participants know they were being studied?

6. Were the participants brought into a special (contrived) situation, or did the experimenter go to them?

7. What relevant variables might not have been controlled?

8. Do you think this was a lab or field experiment?

KEY TERMS

**Experimental realism:** The extent to which participants take an experiment seriously. If the simulated task environment is sufficiently engaging, the participants pay attention to the task and not to the fact that they are being observed, thus reducing *participant reactivity*.

# Lab experiments are artificial

Many people criticise lab experiments for being artificial or contrived.

- Participants know they are being studied and this is likely to affect their behaviour.

- The setting of lab experiments is not like real life. This is described as being low in *mundane realism*. (When a study is high in mundane realism, people behave more like they 'normally' do. However, this may be countered by **experimental realism**.)

- The IV or DV may be *operationalised* in such a way that it doesn't represent real-life experiences, for example using trigrams to test how memory works.

For all these reasons, participants in a lab experiment are less likely to behave as they would in real life.

### ... but field experiments pose problems too

- The same problems may also arise in field experiments, so that field experiments are not necessarily more like real life than lab experiments.

- In field experiments it is more difficult to control extraneous variables and therefore less certain that any change in the DV is due to the IV.

- There is also a major **ethical issue** – if participants don't know they are being studied, is it right to manipulate and record their behaviour?

# Natural experiments

We will now look at some examples of natural experiments. A naturalistic study is only a natural experiment if there is an IV and DV.

### An example of a natural experiment

A study was recently conducted on St Helena, to see whether the introduction of television would produce an increase in anti-social behaviour (Charlton *et al.*, 2000). The residents of this tiny island (47 square miles) received television for the first time in 1995 (see page 179 for details of the study). The vast majority of the measures used to assess pro- and anti-social behaviour showed no differences after the introduction of television.

### Another natural experiment

Physical underdevelopment occurs when children don't have sufficient food. But it also occurs when children are deprived of emotional care – a condition called 'deprivation dwarfism'. One study that demonstrated this was conducted by Widdowson (1951). He recorded the case of a group of apparently malnourished orphanage children. Despite being given dietary supplements they remained underdeveloped. However, when a new supervisor arrived who gave them better emotional care they began to improve. It is likely that the hormones produced by stress affect growth as well as physical health to produce this deprivation dwarfism.

### Generalisability of natural experiments

Drawing valid conclusions from natural experiments is problematic because:

- The IV has not been deliberately manipulated; therefore one can't claim that the IV was responsible for changes in the DV.

- Participants are not ***randomly allocated*** to conditions and this means that there may be biases in the different groups of participants. For example, in the study on music and IQ (on page 94) there are likely to have been other factors that differentiated between the 'music lesson' and 'non-music lesson' group. This would act as a ***confounding variable***.

- The sample studied may have unique characteristics. For example, in the St Helena study the people were part of a particularly pro-social community which means that the findings can't be generalised to other cultures.

*note*

### Results and conclusions

The results of a study are *facts*. They relate to the *participants'* behaviour.

The conclusions are an *interpretation* of the facts. They are a statement about *people*, a *generalisation* made on the basis of how the participants performed.

### Quasi-experiments

Some people consider that studies of gender differences are experiments. For example, comparing whether boys or girls have higher IQs, they would say that gender is the IV and IQ score is the DV. But no one has 'manipulated' gender. It is a *naturally occurring* variable. However, researchers do 'manipulate' to some extent, by selecting participants that fit each category (condition) of the IV. Such studies are called *quasi-experiments*.

**4**

## A quasi-experiment: Music lessons can boost IQ

A recent study looked at the effects of music lessons on IQ (Schellenberg, 2004). The participants (aged six years) had their IQs tested before the study began. They were allocated to one of four groups. Two groups had 36 weeks of extra-curricular music tuition: one had singing-based tuition, the other studied keyboard. A third group had extra drama lessons on top of normal school, and the control group simply attended school as usual. The children completed IQ and other tests at the end of the school year. Schellenberg found that the 'music' groups' IQ performance increased significantly more than the 'drama' and control groups'.

You can conduct similar research making use of existing data, thus conducting a natural experiment.

**IV:** Divide your class into those who have received extra music lessons and those who have not. You must operationalise this IV – i.e. decide what constitutes 'having music lessons'. Would one week of lessons count?

**DV:** For each member of your class, calculate a score based on their Standard Grade exams. One way to do this is to add all scores together and divide by the number of subjects taken. This gives you a final score for each student (a *low* score indicates *better* performance. You can use the table below to record your data.

| Participant | Standard grade marks | | | | | | | | | | Total score | Final score<br>Total score/<br>no. of<br>scores | Music<br>lessons<br>(Y/N) |
|---|---|---|---|---|---|---|---|---|---|---|---|---|---|
| | Exam 1 | Exam 2 | Exam 3 | Exam 4 | Exam 5 | Exam 6 | Exam 7 | Exam 8 | Exam 9 | Exam 10 | | | |
| 1 | | | | | | | | | | | | | |
| 2 | | | | | | | | | | | | | |
| Etc. | | | | | | | | | | | | | |

**Analysis:** Combine the data collected by your classmates. Calculate a mean score for all pupils with music lessons and without music lessons and draw a graph to illustrate this data. What can you conclude?

## Comparing lab, field and natural experiments

| Nature and use | Strengths | Weaknesses |
|---|---|---|
| **Laboratory experiment**<br>To investigate causal relationships under controlled conditions | ➕ Well controlled, confounding variables are minimised, thus we can be more certain that changes in the DV are due to the IV<br>➕ Can be easily replicated, confirming the original findings | ➖ Task and/or situation may lack mundane realism, thus participants' behaviour may not reflect 'real life'<br>➖ Participants are aware of being studied which may lead to demand characteristics (an extraneous variable)<br>➖ Experimenter may communicate expectations (investigator effects) |
| **Field experiment**<br>To investigate causal relationships in more natural surroundings | ➕ Less artificial, usually higher mundane realism because the situation is more natural<br>➕ Participants usually not aware of being studied which reduces participant reactivity (e.g. demand characteristics) | ➖ Less control of extraneous variables, therefore less certain that changes in the DV are due to the IV<br>➖ More time-consuming and thus more expensive |
| **Natural experiment**<br>To investigate causal relationships in situations where IV cannot be directly manipulated | ➕ Allows research where IV can't be manipulated by the experimenter for ethical or practical reasons, e.g. studies of deprivation<br>➕ Enables psychologists to study 'real' problems such as the effects of disaster on health (increased mundane realism) | ➖ Cannot demonstrate causal relationships because IV not directly manipulated<br>➖ Likely to be many confounding variables (e.g. lack of random allocation)<br>➖ Can only be used where conditions vary naturally<br>➖ Participants may be aware of being studied |

*questions* 8

1. Answer the following questions for the St Helena and orphanage studies:
   a. Identify the IV and DV.
   b. Write a suitable hypothesis for this experiment.
   c. What was the experimental design?
2. The following questions relate to the study by Schellenberg.
   a. This was not a natural experiment. What kind of experiment was it? Explain your answer.
   b. Write an alternative hypothesis for this study.
   c. Write a suitable null hypothesis.
3. Five studies are described below. Identify each study as a lab, field or natural experiment, and explain your decision:
   a. Two primary schools use different reading schemes. A psychological study compares the reading scores at the end of the year to see which scheme was more effective.
   b. Children take part in a trial to compare the success of a new Maths programme. The children are placed in one of two groups: the new Maths programme or the traditional one and taught in these groups for a term.
   c. The value of using computers rather than books is investigated by requiring children to learn word lists, either using a computer or with a book.
   d. The effect of advertisements on gender stereotypes is studied by showing children ads with women doing feminine tasks or doing neutral tasks and then asking them about gender stereotypes.
   e. A study investigated the anti-social effects of TV by seeing whether people who watch a lot of TV (more than five hours a day) are more aggressive than those who don't.

*assessment issues*

**Explain *two* weaknesses of the use of the experimental method in this study. (*ku 0 ae 4*)**

If, as shown in this question, you are asked for a weakness (or weaknesses, or more general evaluation) of the research 'scenario' in terms of the method used, it may be that some problem is immediately obvious to you. However, if not, don't panic. The thing to do is to go systematically through the various weaknesses that are often associated with the particular method, and see which apply to *this particular study*. Some of the commonest problems are to do with lack of control of variables, various types of bias (such as sampling bias), low ecological validity, lack of causal relationship in a correlational study, and of course *ethical issues* that may have arisen.

# Aspect 2: Research issues

## Ecological validity and realism

The aim of any study is to find out about how people behave in everyday life. We want to generalise from the results of the study to everyday life.

**Ecological validity** is the degree to which the behaviour observed in a study reflects the behaviour that occurs in *everyday* settings. It is associated with:

- *generalisability* – the extent to which findings can be generalised from a particular psychological study to the real world
- *representativeness* (mundane realism) – the extent to which a study mirrors conditions in the real world.

**KEY TERMS**

**Ecological validity:** Concerns the extent to which a research finding reflects behaviour that occurs in settings other than the specific setting in which the study took place.

## Studies with high or low ecological validity

Consider the studies described below. Do you think they have high or low ecological validity?

### Obedience to unjust authority (Milgram, 1963)

Forty male participants were told that the study was investigating how punishment affects learning. There was an experimenter and a 'learner' (a 47-year-old accountant). The participant drew lots with the learner (a confederate) and always ended up as the 'teacher'. He was told that he must administer increasingly strong electric shocks to the learner each time he got a question wrong. The machine was tested on the 'teacher' to show him that it worked.

After a while, the learner, sitting in another room, started to give wrong answers and received his (fake) shocks in silence until they reached 300 volts (very strong shock). At this point, he pounded on the wall and then gave no response to the next question.

In the baseline study, Milgram found that 65% of the participants were fully obedient, i.e. continued to obey up to the maximum voltage of 450 volts.

Milgram repeated this study in many different situations:

- The location was moved to a run-down office (48% obedience).
- The teacher was in same room as the learner (40% obedience).
- The teacher held learner's hand on the shock plate (30% obedience).

These **replications** show that the initial conclusion was correct: situational factors affect obedience to unjust authority.

### Obedience in the real world (Hofling *et al.*, 1966)

Hofling *et al.* conducted a study in a US hospital. Nurses were telephoned by a 'Dr. Smith' who asked that they give 20mg of a drug called Astroten to a patient. This order contravened hospital regulations in a number of ways:

- nurses were told not to accept instructions on the phone
- or from an unknown doctor
- or for a dose in excess of the safe amount (the dosage was twice that advised on the bottle)
- especially for an unknown drug.

Nevertheless, 21 out of 22 (95%) nurses did as requested. When the nurses involved in the study were interviewed afterwards they said, in their defence, that they had obeyed because that's what doctors expect nurses to do – they behaved as nurses do in real life, or did they?

### More nurses (Rank and Jacobsen, 1977)

In another study (this time in Australia) nurses were also asked to carry out an irregular order. This time 16 out of 18 (89%) *refused*. There were important differences:

- The drug was familiar (Valium).
- The nurses could consult with colleagues.

### Obedience in the Second World War

Mandel (1998) found evidence that, in a real-world setting, people behaved quite differently from Milgram's participants. In the Second World War, Major Trapp, the commander of Reserve Police Battalion 101, had orders to kill all the civilian Jews in a small Polish town – but Trapp told his men that if they didn't wish to obey orders he would assign them to other duties. Nevertheless, most of the men did obey – despite the fact that the task involved many of the factors that Milgram later found led to *reduced* obedience (face-to-face contact, some disobedient peers, absence of pressure from authority figure). (See page 206.)

### High or low?

You might think that the study of nurses by Hofling *et al.* had high mundane realism and high ecological validity. *It had low mundane realism.* Even though it was conducted in a natural setting, the task was quite artificial. Rank and Jacobsen's study used a task that was *more true to real life* – the nurses dealt with a familiar drug and were allowed to consult with each other.

Although Hofling *et al.*'s study was conducted in a more natural setting than Milgram's, this *doesn't automatically mean that it had higher ecological validity.* You must always explain *why* a study has high ecological validity. The *replications of Milgram's study* suggest that his findings *do* apply to other settings whereas the same is not true for the study by Hofling *et al*.

Furthermore, the doctor–nurse authority relationship is a special one and it is not therefore reasonable to generalise from this to all other kinds of obedience. It is part of a nurses' job to obey the orders of doctors, as the nurses in Hofling *et al*.'s study argued in their defence. Milgram's study concerned the *obedience of ordinary people to perceived authority*, so the results can be generalised to everyday life. Milgram used the experimenter–participant relationship as an example of an everyday obedience relationship so, in a sense, his study did have mundane realism – it did mirror the real world.

However, not all studies have confirmed Milgram's findings: for example the observations made by Mandel of a real-world obedience situation. These challenge our original conclusion because now it appears that Milgram's findings have not been replicated in other settings – but how much is this situation typical of everyday life? Can we generalise from the behaviour of German troops in the Second World War? Would they be more or less obedient than other people? Should we consider other factors? For example, their obedience up to this point may have made it more difficult for them to disobey.

**Think outside the box**

There are no simple answers.

Every study has some ecological validity – some are just more ecologically valid than others.

*Just because a study is conducted in a contrived, artificial lab doesn't mean it is low in ecological validity.*

*Just because a study is conducted in the real world doesn't make it high in ecological validity – it may still be contrived.*

*In field research, there is too little control to allow for definite conclusions, whereas, in laboratory research, there is too much control to allow for interesting conclusions.*

**Conclusion**

In virtually all studies there is a balance to be struck between experimental control and ecological validity/realism: the greater the control, the greater the danger of compromising the ecological validity.

Greatest control exists in the laboratory. However, when we study people in a laboratory their behaviour is clearly affected by the laboratory environment, and the tasks they are required to do are often very contrived.

If we study people in their daily life, the tasks/situations are more realistic but it is usually impossible to do this in a controlled way.

Some psychologists argue that we can only discover things about behaviour if we uncover cause-and-effect relationships in highly controlled experiments. Others argue that field studies are the only real option for psychologists who are interested in how life is actually lived.

 9

An area of study that has interested psychologists is massed versus distributed practice, i.e. whether learning is better if you practise something repeatedly in a short period of time (massed) or space your periods of practice (distributed). This topic has been studied in different settings.

- Study 1: participants were required to recall nonsense syllables on 12 occasions spread over 3 days or 12 days (Jost, 1897). Recall was higher over 12 days.
- Study 2: Post Office workers had to learn to type postcodes either using massed or distributed practice (Baddeley and Longman, 1978). Distributed practice was again found to be superior.

You should present arguments for why each of these studies could be viewed as having high and low ecological validity.

**assessment issues**

**Explain *one* weakness of the study described. (*ku 0   ae 2*)**

Compared with questions from other Units/sections, in research methods questions it is often the case that 'less is more'. This is because you can build up a high mark by gaining lots of little marks for very precise, small 'nuggets' of information. However, try to avoid the common pitfall of using terminology in a 'vacuum'. Let's assume that one suitable answer to the question above is 'poor ecological validity'. If you write just that, you *may* get some very small credit but exam markers are looking for evidence of your *understanding*, therefore you should also give an explanation of that term (and in any case, the question asks you to 'explain'). Of course, the opposite situation could arise, where you give an explanation of the problem but can't remember the terminology! Naturally, if you want full marks, make sure you give *both*.

## Descriptive statistics

There are three ways of *describing* the results of any study.

- *Measures of central tendency*: a descriptive statistic that provides information about a 'typical' response for a set of scores.
- *Measures of dispersion*: a descriptive statistic that provides information about how spread out a set of scores is.
- *Visual display* such as a bar chart.

*What are nominal, ordinal, interval and ratio data? (NOIR)*

*Nominal.* The data are in separate categories, such as grouping people according to their favourite football team (e.g. Aberdeen, Inverness Caledonian Thistle, etc.).

*Ordinal.* Data are ordered in some way, for example asking people to put a list of football teams in order of liking. Aberdeen might be 1st, followed by Inverness and so on. The 'difference' between each item is not the same, i.e. the individual may like the 1st item a lot more than the 2nd one but there might only be a small difference between the items ranked as 2nd and 3rd.

*Interval.* Data are measured using units of equal intervals, such as when counting correct answers or using any 'public' unit of measurement. Many psychological studies use *plastic interval scales* where the intervals are arbitrarily determined and we can't therefore actually know for certain that there are equal intervals between the numbers. However, for the purposes of analysis, such data may be accepted as interval.

*Ratio.* There is a true zero point, as in most measures of physical quantities.

# 1. Measures of central tendency

Measures of central tendency inform us about central (or middle) values for a set of data. They are 'averages' – ways of calculating a typical value for a set of data. An average can be calculated in different ways:

The **mean** is calculated by adding up all the numbers and dividing by the number of numbers. The mean:

➕ makes use of the values of all the data

➖ can be misrepresentative of the numbers if there are extreme values

➖ can only be used with **interval** or **ratio** data (see below).

The **median** is the *middle* value in an *ordered* list. The median:

➕ is not affected by extreme scores

➕ can be used with **ordinal data**

➖ is not as 'sensitive' as the mean because not all values are reflected in the median.

The **mode** is the value that is *most* common. The mode:

➕ is useful when the data are in categories (such as number of people who like pink) i.e. **nominal data**

➖ is not a useful way of describing data when there are several modes.

# 2. Measures of dispersion

A set of data can also be described in terms of how dispersed or spread out the numbers are.

The easiest way to do this is to use the **range**. The range is the difference between the highest and lowest number.

Consider the data sets below:

3, 5, 8, 8, 9, 10, 12, 12, 13, 15

mean = 9.5    range = 12 (3 to 15)

1, 5, 8, 8, 9, 10, 12, 12, 13, 17

mean = 9.5    range = 16 (1 to 17)

The two sets of numbers have the same mean but a different range, so the range is helpful as a further method of describing the data. If we just used the mean the data would appear to be the same.

There is a more precise method of expressing dispersion, called the **standard deviation**. This is a measure of the spread of the data around the mean. The standard deviation for the two sets of numbers above is 3.69 and 4.45 respectively. This can be calculated using a mathematical calculator.

**KEY TERMS**

**Mean:** The arithmetic average of a group of scores, calculated by dividing the sum of the scores by the number of scores. The mean takes the values of all the data into account (whereas the *mode* and *median* just take all the data into account – but not the values).

**Median:** The middle value in a set of scores when they are placed in rank order.

**Mode:** The most frequently occurring score in a set of data.

CENTRAL TENDENCY

MEAN
MEDIAN
MODE

**Special tip**

Many candidates find it hard to remember the link between 'measures of central tendency' and 'mean, median, mode'.

One way to help you remember links is to produce memorable pictures. The flag above is an attempt to illustrate the idea of a central tendency and link this to the three appropriate terms. Try to develop your own memorable picture for this and other concepts – the more outrageous, the better!

**KEY TERMS**

**Range:** A *measure of dispersion* that measures the difference between the highest and lowest score in a set of data.

**Standard deviation:** A *measure of dispersion* that shows the amount of variation in a set of scores. It assesses the spread of data around the mean.

| | Advantages | Disadvantages |
|---|---|---|
| **Range** | ➕ Provides you with direct information<br>➕ Easy to calculate | ➖ Affected by extreme values<br>➖ Doesn't take into account the number of observations in the data set |
| **Standard deviation** | ➕ More precise measure of dispersion because all values taken into account | ➖ May hide some of the characteristics of the data set (e.g. extreme values) |

## 3. Visual display

A picture is worth 1000 words! Graphs provide a means of 'eyeballing' your data and seeing the findings at a glance.

A **pie chart** consists of a circle that is divided into slices where the angle of the slice represents the frequency of each item. For example, if people were asked to name their favourite football team and 20% choose Rangers, 35% choose Hearts and 45% choose Celtic then you can calculate the angle of the slice by working out 20%, 35% and 45% of the 360 degrees in a circle:

20% of 360 = 20 x 360/100 = 72°
35% of 360 = 35 x 360/100 = 126°
45% of 360 = 45 x 360/100 = 162°

In a **bar chart** the height of the bar represents frequency. There is no true zero and data need not be in any order or continuous. This chart is suitable for *nominal* data as well as for numerical scores.

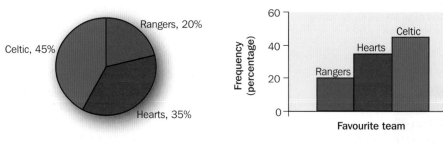

Pie chart showing favourite football teams          Bar chart showing favourite football teams

*A graph should be simple. It should clearly show the results of a study.*

*There should be a short title.*

*The x and y axes must be labelled. The x axis goes across the page; it is usually the IV. The y axis goes up vertically; it is usually the DV or 'frequency'.*

*Always use squared paper if you are hand-drawing graphs.*

Each of the following bar charts presents the data collected in an experiment on organisation and memory (see page 101). Only one of these graphs is useful, two of them are a 'waste of time' – which one is the useful one?

*Graph A: Individual participants' scores*
Participant number 1 in the organised word group is placed next to participant number 1 in the random word group. Students like to draw 'participant charts', BUT THEY ARE TOTALLY MEANINGLESS.

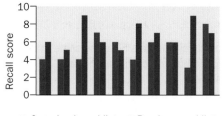

■ Organised word list   ■ Random word list

*Graph B: Grouped participants' scores*
The findings from each participant are shown in this graph. They are grouped together so that you can see all the scores from participants in the organised word group and all the scores from the participants in the random word group.

This is *slightly better* than Graph A because we can just about tell that the random word list led to better recall – but a glance at the means (as in Graph C) shows this effortlessly.

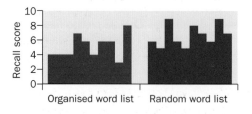

Organised word list      Random word list

10

1. What can you conclude from looking at Graph A?
2. What does Graph B show you?
3. Why is Graph C the best of the three graphs?
4. Why is Graph A meaningless?
5. Write a title that would be suitable for all three graphs.
6. Describe the *y* axis of all three graphs.

*Graph C: Means*
This graph shows the *mean scores* for each group. The findings are clear, which is the point of using a graph. It allows you to 'eyeball' the data.

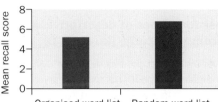

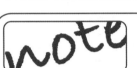

### Significance

In the analysis of research data, the kind of *descriptive* statistics we have shown on the previous pages constitute just the first stage. *Inferential* statistical testing is then used to discover whether any difference or relationship between variables is *significant*: in other words, whether the difference or relationship is unusual enough to be a real difference and has not just occurred by chance. In order to find out if a difference/ relationship is significant, researchers carry out a statistical test and then check the results of the statistical test against tables of significance which show whether the difference is big enough to be significant. Note that, in the exam, you won't be asked questions about 'significance', but you may find this concept helpful in understanding how psychologists handle research data.

**KEY TERMS**

**Pilot study:** A pilot study is a small-scale trial run of a research design before doing the real thing. It is done in order to find out if certain things don't work. For example, participants may not understand the instructions or they may guess what the experiment is about. They may get very bored because there are too many tasks or too many questions.

5 **Do It Yourself – Memory and organisation**

A favourite experiment for students is one that concerns organisation and memory. If words are presented to a participant in categories they are more easily memorised than if presented in a random order. You can try conducting this experiment yourself using the word lists provided. To help plan your experiment, work through the questions below.

1. Identify the IV and DV.
2. How should the IV be operationalised?
3. How should the DV be operationalised? (i.e. how will you measure it?)
4. Should you use repeated measures or independent groups? Write down the relative advantages/ disadvantages of each to help you decide.
5. Write a suitable hypothesis for your study.
6. How many participants will you need?
7. Are there any extraneous variables that need to be controlled? How will you control these?
8. Write your standardised procedure, including the standardised instructions.

*NOW conduct a* **pilot study** *and then make any alterations to the design that you feel are necessary.*

9. After you have conducted the study, record the findings for each participant in a table. If you do not have time to conduct this experiment yourself, invent an appropriate set of data.
10. Use the descriptive statistics outlined on pages 98–100 to *describe* the findings from your research on memory and organisation. Use one example of each: one measure of central tendency, one measure of dispersion and a graph.
11. What do you *conclude* from your findings?
12. Identify *one* problem you discovered when conducting this study.

| Organised list | Random list |
| --- | --- |
| **Dogs** | Pear |
| Labrador | Beagle |
| Beagle | Clarinet |
| Boxer | Hail |
| Spaniel | Rain |
| **Fruit** | Drinks |
| Apple | Rose |
| Pear | Squash |
| Plum | Hand |
| Orange | Boxer |
| **Weather** | Iron |
| Snow | Coke |
| Rain | Gold |
| Sleet | Harp |
| Hail | Piano |
| **Flowers** | Metal |
| Daffodil | Apple |
| Rose | Body |
| Pansy | Fruit |
| Tulip | Instruments |
| **Instruments** | Daffodil |
| Harp | Plum |
| Piano | Nose |
| Flute | Weather |
| Clarinet | Copper |
| **Drinks** | Labrador |
| Water | Water |
| Milk | Flowers |
| Squash | Brass |
| Coke | Foot |
| **Body** | Tulips |
| Nose | Pansy |
| Foot | Dogs |
| Toe | Sleet |
| Hand | Milk |
| **Metal** | Orange |
| Brass | Toe |
| Gold | Snow |
| Copper | Flute |
| Iron | Spaniel |

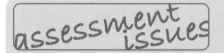

**Suggest *two* types of descriptive statistics that would be suitable for the data from this study. (*ku 2 ae* 0)**

To answer a question like this, first identify how much information is given in the scenario about the data obtained. This may be very obvious; for example a summary table of results may be provided. On the other hand, there may be no such giveaway, and you will have to work out for yourself what the scores would look like. For example, in the scenario you may be told that researchers 'recorded how many images the participants could see on the screen at any one time [by video-game players and by non-players]'*. So you need to decide first, whether the data are interval/ratio, ordinal or nominal, then select suitable descriptive statistics. A good rule of thumb would be to suggest *either* a measure of central tendency *or* a measure of dispersion, *plus* a suitable type of graph. For the example above, two good suggestions would be *mean scores* and a *bar chart* of mean scores. Don't forget that if the scenario describes a *correlational* study, the most appropriate graph to suggest will be a scattergram.
*Source: Question B1, Higher Specimen Paper, SQA website.

# Quantitative and qualitative data

A researcher may collect **quantitative** or **qualitative data**. People sometimes refer to research methods as being either qualitative or quantitative. This is misleading, however, because it implies that certain methods always produce certain kinds of data. For example, experiments are usually referred to as 'quantitative', and textual analysis is usually described as 'qualitative'. Experiments, however, can produce qualitative data as well as numbers. Milgram (see page 96) measured the extent to which participants were prepared to comply with the demands of the experimenter (quantitative data) but he also described the behaviour of his participants in some detail (qualitative data), as well as interviewing them after the study and recording their explanations for their behaviour and their reactions after the experiment.

### Quantitative data
Quantitative data are about 'quantities' of things. They are numbers, raw scores, percentages, means, etc. They are measurements of things, telling us how much of something there is. You can collect quantitative data about what people think by, for example, asking people to rate their feelings about a topic.

### Qualitative data
Qualitative data are about 'qualities' of things. They are descriptions, words, meanings, pictures, texts, and so forth. They are about what something is like, or how something is experienced. Studies which deal mainly with qualitative data are in the minority in this book and this reflects the dominance of quantitative data in psychological research.

|  | Strengths | Weaknesses |
|---|---|---|
| **Quantitative data** | ➕ Easier to analyse because data are numbers | ➖ Reduce information about people to oversimplified statistics (statistically significant but humanly insignificant) |
| **Qualitative data** | ➕ Represent the true complexities of human behaviour, and gain access to thoughts and feelings which cannot be assessed using other methods | ➖ More difficult to analyse, thus conclusions are more difficult to draw |

## KEY TERMS

**Target population:** The group of people in whom the researcher is interested; the group of people from whom a *sample* is drawn; the group of people about whom *generalisations* can be made.

**Generalisability:** The degree to which the findings of a particular study can be applied to the *target population*.

**Sample:** A selection of participants taken from the *target population* being studied and intended to be *representative* of that population.

**Representative sample:** A *sample* selected so that it accurately stands for or represents the *population* being studied.

**Bias:** A systematic distortion.

**Opportunity sampling:** Selecting people who are most easily available at the time of the study. This is also called *convenience* or *availability sampling*.

**Stratified sample:** Groups of participants are selected in proportion to their frequency in the population in order to obtain a *representative sample*. The aim is to identify sections of the population, or strata, that need to be represented in the study. Individuals from those strata are then selected for the study using a *random technique*.

**Quota sample:** Similar to *stratified sampling* but the selection of participants from each stratum is not necessarily random; it may be that you just take the first available participants from each stratum and stop when the required number (quota) has been reached.

**Volunteer sample:** A *sample* of participants produced by a *sampling technique* that relies solely on volunteers to make up the sample; this is also called a *self-selected* sample.

**Random technique:** Any technique in which there is no systematic attempt to influence the selection or distribution of the items or participants that form part of the investigation. *Random* means that each member of the population has an equal chance of being selected.

**Random sample:** A *sample* of participants produced by using a *random technique* such that every member of the *target population* being tested has an equal chance of being selected.

*A sampling method is about how participants are identified not about who eventually takes part. For example, some potential participants may refuse to be part of an* opportunity *or* random *sample. The remaining participants are 'volunteers'.*

# Sampling

When conducting any research study you need to find some participants!

Participants are drawn from the **target population**: the group of people that the researcher is interested in.

Researchers can make **generalisations** about the target population from the **sample** as long as the sample *is representative of the target population*.

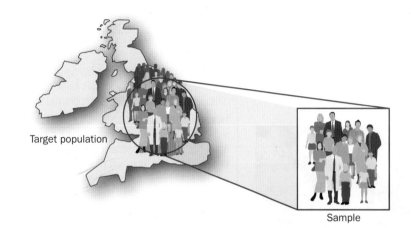

Target population

Sample

All sampling methods aim to produce a **representative sample** but inevitably introduce **bias**.

## Sampling techniques

### Opportunity (convenience) sample
How? Ask people walking by you in the street, i.e. select those who are available.

➕ **Opportunity sampling** is the easiest method because you just use the first participants you can find.

➖ It is inevitably biased because the sample is drawn from a small part of the target population; for example a sample selected from people walking around the centre of a town would be made up of people not at work, or not from rural areas.

### Stratified and quota sample
How? Subgroups (or strata) within a population are identified (e.g. boys and girls, or age groups: 10–12, 13–15, etc.). Participants are obtained from each stratum in proportion to their occurrence in the target population. Selection from each stratum is done randomly (**stratified sample**) or using another method (**quota sampling**).

➕ This is more representative than an opportunity sample because there is equal representation of subgroups.

➖ Although the sample represents subgroups, each quota taken may be biased in other ways (in the same way that all opportunity samples are biased).

### Volunteer (self-selecting) sample
How? Advertise in a newspaper or on a notice board.

➕ This offers access to a variety of keen participants.

➖ A volunteer sample is biased because participants are likely to be more highly motivated and/or with extra time on their hands (*volunteer bias*).

### Random sample
How? Obtain a complete list of the target population and select the required number of people using **random techniques** (see below).

➕ This is unbiased because all members of the target population have an equal chance of selection.

➖ In reality, it is often impossible to obtain a complete list of the target population.

*It is easy to mistake a **systematic sample** for a random sample. If you select the starting number using a random method and then you select every 10th person, this would actually be a random sample but just using every 10th person is not a random method.*

**Systematic sample:** A method of obtaining a representative sample by selecting, say, every 5th or 10th person. This can be random if the first person is selected using a random method.

The lottery is drawn randomly by pulling numbers 'out of a hat'. This method can be used to obtain a random sample when the target population is relatively small (a hat can only hold so many names!). Or it could be used for random allocation of participants: put all participants' names into a hat and draw out half of the names for group 1.

## Systematic sample

How? Selecting every nth person from a list of the target population, for example every 10th.

⊕ The sample is spread evenly across the population, avoiding bias.

⊖ The sample may still be biased (e.g. if every 10th person is sitting at the front of the class).

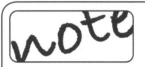

### Sample size

Studies are often criticised for having used a small sample. Such samples are more likely to be biased because, for example, if you have selected 5 people out of a group of 10 boys and 10 girls you could get all girls, whereas if you select 11 people you must have at least 1 boy and thus a more representative sample.

However, large samples also have drawbacks. They are costly to obtain and may obscure important individual differences. For example, we might study the effects of noise on performance. Let us assume that noise has no effect in general although it does happen to affect people with poor rather than good memory. In a small sample, you may observe no effect from noise on memory, but, with a sufficiently large sample, a small effect is seen because enough people with poor memory have been included, leading to the false conclusion that noise has an effect on all people's memory.

Coolican (1996) suggests that about 25–30 participants is adequate for a repeated measures design.

### Randomness

One way of obtaining a random sample is to use a source of random numbers (e.g. a table of random numbers, a computer or calculator) to select people. You start with a list of your target population (such as the telephone directory, electoral roll, school register, or other existing list or database of people) and select person 13, 21, 39, etc. (using the source of random numbers). You could also use the 'lottery method':

Random selection is used to obtain a *random sample* of participants (as described above) or for *random allocation* of participants to conditions when using an independent measures design (as described on page 85).

 11

1  A psychology experiment aims to investigate how preschool children differ from those already at school in terms of their ability to remember symbols that look like letters.
   a. If the experimenter wanted to obtain a random sample of each of the two age groups, how might this be done?
   b. Explain the purpose of using a random sample.
   c. Identify the experimental design in this study and give *one* advantage and *one* disadvantage of using this design.
   d. What would be a suitably sized sample for this study?
   e. What are the IV and the DV in the experiment?
   f. The children were shown 20 different symbols. Why was it better to use 20 symbols rather than just 2 symbols?
   g. Why might it be better to use 2 rather than 20 symbols?

2. A teacher organises a project to enable her psychology class to have a go at using matched pairs design. The class is divided into two groups, one will receive word list A (nouns) and the other word list B (verbs). They will be tested on recall.
   a. Suggest *two* participant variables that could be used to match classmates.
   b. Explain why each of the variables you chose would be important to control in this study.
   c. What are the two conditions in the experiment?
   d. Suggest *two* ways that participants could have been allocated to conditions if the teacher decided to use an independent measures design.
   e. All the words that the teacher used had two syllables and were of similar length. Give *one* reason why.
   f. The teacher decided to repeat the study using all the pupils in the school. She selected every 5th pupil in the register. What kind of sample is this?

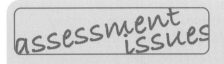

**How may the researchers have selected their random sample, in this study?** (*ku 2 ae 0*)

Students sometimes respond to a question like this by simply writing everything they know about random sampling. This question is *not* asking for a definition or for principles of random sampling, but about *how* the random sample may have been obtained *in the given study*. So, your answer should refer to the need for a *full list of the target population* (specify what kind of people they are according to the information in the scenario – e.g. adult male video-game players, infants aged four to eight weeks, etc.). You also need some *source of random numbers* (calculator, computer, or tables) to select the required number of individuals. Although the idea of 'drawing names out of a hat' is quite useful to illustrate the principle of chance in random sampling, it would be unlikely to gain credit here (because there are much more efficient methods and hats are not big enough for most target populations). Other possible questions on sampling may ask for features of a good sample, or *description* or *evaluation* of different types of sampling.

---

**KEY TERMS**

**Ethical issues:** These arise in research where there are conflicts between the research goals and the participant's rights.

# Ethical issues

An **ethical issue** is a conflict between the aims of the research and the rights of participants. Such conflicts are about what is *acceptable*. We will consider various ethical issues which arise in psychological research.

Ethical issues are like a see-saw

As you'll see in the following pages, ethical considerations are important in *all* psychological research, not just some high-profile studies where pain and distress have been inflicted on participants. Even a simple act like asking people in the street to complete a questionnaire has ethical implications. Concern over such issues has increased greatly in the last 20–30 years. Much of the early psychological research in this book would not be possible today, as research must now conform to an ethical code (in the UK, the BPS's *Ethical Principles* apply; these are summarised on page 107). Everyone conducting psychological research, including psychology students, is expected to be aware of their responsibility to ensure that participants are treated in an ethical manner.

### Deception
Is it acceptable to deceive a participant about the true aims of a study?

From the *researcher's* point of view, **deception** is sometimes necessary because otherwise the participant might alter their behaviour to fit the experimenter's expectations.

From the *participant's* point of view, deception is unethical – you should not deceive anyone without good cause. Perhaps more importantly deception prevents participants from being able to give **informed consent**. They may agree to participate without really knowing what they have let themselves in for and they might be quite distressed by the experience.

Deception also leads people to see psychologists as untrustworthy. It means that a participant may not want to take part in psychological research in the future.

### Informed consent
From the *researcher's* point of view, *informed consent* means that you have to reveal the true aims of a study – or at least you have to tell participants what is actually going to happen which may reveal the true aims and spoil the study.

From the *participant's* point of view, you should be told what you will be required to do in a study so that you can make an informed decision about whether or not you wish to participate. The details should include anything that might be important in making a decision about participating. This is a basic human right (established during the Nuremburg war crimes trials – Nazi doctors had conducted various experiments on prisoners without their consent).

**KEY TERMS**

**Deception:** An *ethical issue*, most usually where a participant is not told the true aims of a study (e.g. what participation will involve) and thus cannot give truly *informed consent*.

**Informed consent:** An *ethical issue* and an *ethical guideline* in psychological research whereby participants must be given comprehensive information concerning the nature and purpose of the research and their role in it, in order that they can make an informed decision about whether to participate.

*In Milgram's studies of obedience (see page 96 and in more detail on pages 198–199) participants thought they were delivering shocks to another participant. Do you think that the participant (the 'teacher') would be unduly distressed by the experience of thinking that he was causing such harm to another? Is this 'acceptable' psychological harm?*

*The participants in Milgram's study were told that it concerned the effect of punishment on learning. They were asked for their consent to take part and told that they would be paid $4.50 for taking part. Furthermore, they were told that they could withdraw from the experiment at any time and would still be paid for having taken part.*

*If a participant asked to stop during the experiment, the experimenter had been instructed to deliver a set of 'prods', such as saying, 'It is absolutely essential that you continue' or 'You have no other choice, you must go on'.*

### KEY TERMS

**Right to withdraw:** An *ethical issue* that participants should have the right to withdraw from participating in an experiment if they are uncomfortable with the study.

**Confidentiality:** An *ethical issue* concerned with a participant's right to have personal information protected.

**Privacy:** An *ethical issue* that refers to a zone of inaccessibility of mind or body and the trust that this will not be 'invaded'. Contrast with *confidentiality*.

## Protection from physical and psychological harm

From the *researcher's* point of view, some of the more important questions in psychology involve a degree of distress to participants.

From the *participant's* point of view, nothing should happen to you during an experiment that will make you have a negative experience. There are many ways you can cause harm to participants, some physical (e.g. getting them to drink coffee excessively) and some psychological (e.g. making them feel inadequate, have lower self-esteem, or feel embarrassed). 'Harm' might include positive feelings as well because participants should be in the same state as they were at the beginning of the study *unless they have given their informed consent*.

Aside from actual harm, research participants should be protected from undue *risk* during an investigation. The risk of harm must be no greater than in ordinary life.

## The right to withdraw

From the *researcher's* point of view, it may not be possible to offer participants the **right to withdraw**: for example when conducting a field experiment where participants are not aware that they are being studied.

From the *participant's* point of view, you ought to have the option to quit if you find that you don't like what is going on. This compensates for the fact that even with informed consent you may not fully understand what is involved.

## Confidentiality

From the *researcher's* point of view, it may be difficult to protect **confidentiality** because the researcher wishes to publish the findings. A researcher may guarantee *anonymity* (withholding your name) but even then it may be obvious who has been involved in a study. For example, knowing that a study was conducted on St Helena (see page 178) permits some people to be able to identify participants.

From the *participant's* point of view, the Data Protection Act makes confidentiality a legal right. It is acceptable for personal data to be recorded if the data are not made available in a form which identifies the participants (which is really confidentiality because of anonymity).

## Privacy

From the *researcher's* point of view, it may be difficult to avoid invasion of **privacy** in a field experiment.

From the *participant's* point of view, people do not expect to be observed by others in certain situations. We have a right to privacy.

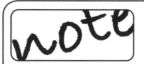

### Confidentiality and privacy – what's the difference?

The words 'confidentiality' and 'privacy' are sometimes used interchangeably, but there is a distinction between the two.

Confidentiality concerns the communication of personal information from one person to another and the trust that this information will then be protected.

Privacy refers to a zone of inaccessibility of mind or body and the trust that this will not be 'invaded'.

We have a right of privacy. If this is invaded, confidentiality should be respected.

In one study, psychologists investigated invasion of personal space by conducting a field experiment in a public urinal. There were three conditions: a confederate stood immediately next to a participant; one urinal away; or was absent. The experimenter recorded micturation times (how long participants took to pee) as an indication of how comfortable the participants felt (Middlemist *et al.*, 1976).

*Is it acceptable to observe people in such a place?*

In another study Piliavin *et al.* (1969) investigated the behaviour of bystanders in an emergency situation. A confederate collapsed on a New York subway train and the experimenters observed how long it took for anyone to offer help. Such field studies raise many ethical issues, such as having no opportunity for gaining informed consent, and there is also the question that such staged procedures may raise the suspiciousness of ordinary people when the same events occur naturally.

In this activity provide explanations for all your answers.

1. Do you think that participants in Milgram's study would have been unduly distressed by taking part?

2. If they were distressed, do you think that this is acceptable?

3. Do you think that it was acceptable for Milgram to deceive the participants in his study?

4. Did Milgram obtain *informed* consent from his participants?

5. Did Milgram give participants the right to withdraw from his experiment?

6. Do you think that it is unacceptable to observe people in a public urinal?

7. Do you think that it is acceptable to involve people in a psychological study without their knowledge?

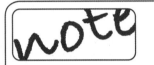

### Issues versus guidelines

Issues are not the same as guidelines even though informed consent is both an issue and a guideline. An issue is a conflict; a guideline is a means of resolving this conflict.

---

**► KEY TERMS ◄**

**Ethical guidelines:** These are a set of rules that help to guide conduct within psychology by establishing principles for standard practice.

**Protection from harm:** An *ethical issue*. During a research study, participants should not experience negative physical or psychological effects.

---

*THE FAR SIDE®  BY GARY LARSON*

## How to deal with ethical issues

There are many ways to deal with ethical issues. We will consider a few of them.

### Ethical guidelines

Psychologists are a group of professionals (like solicitors, doctors, etc.). They have a professional organisation consisting of fellow professionals that monitors their behaviour – in the UK it is the British Psychological Society (BPS); in the US it is the American Psychological Association (APA). This association draws up a set of **ethical guidelines** (also called *principles* or a *code of conduct*) that tells psychologists what behaviours are not acceptable and tells them how to deal with ethical dilemmas.

#### Limitations

Guidelines absolve the individual researcher of any responsibility; they can simply say, 'I followed what the guidelines say so it's not my problem'. Guidelines also close off discussions about what is right and wrong.

#### The BPS code of conduct

In 1978, the British Psychological Society (BPS) published its *Ethical Principles for Research on Human Subjects*. This document is regularly revised; the current version is the *Code of Ethics and Conduct (BPS, 2006)*. Some key points are given below:

- *On deception.* Intentional deception of the participants over the purpose and general nature of an investigation should be avoided whenever possible. Participants should never be deliberately misled without extremely strong scientific or medical justification. Even then there should be strict controls and the disinterested approval of independent advisors.

- *On informed consent.* Whenever possible, the investigator should inform all participants of the objectives of the investigation. The investigator should inform the participants of all aspects of the research or intervention that might reasonably be expected to influence their willingness to participate. The investigator should, normally, explain all other aspects of the research or intervention about which the participants enquire. Failure to make full disclosure prior to obtaining informed consent requires additional safeguards to protect the welfare and dignity of the participants.

- *Children.* Research with children or with participants who have impairments that limit understanding and/or communication such that they are unable to give their consent requires special safe-guarding procedures.

- *On* **protection from harm**. Investigators have a primary responsibility to protect participants from physical and mental harm during the investigation. Normally, the risk of harm must be no greater than in ordinary life: i.e. participants should not be exposed to risks greater than or additional to those encountered in their normal life styles. If harm, unusual discomfort, or other negative consequences for the individual's future life might occur, the investigator must obtain the disinterested approval of independent advisors, inform the participants, and obtain real, informed consent from each of them.

# note

## History of ethical guidelines

The first set of guidelines for conducting research with human participants was produced in the late 1940s as a consequence of the inhumane experiments conducted by Nazi physicians at concentration camps. The guidelines were called the Nuremburg Code and introduced the concept of informed consent and the right to withdraw. The American Psychological Association (APA) produced their first *Code of Conduct* soon afterwards. In 1964, the APA suspended Milgram's membership owing to questions about the ethics of his work. Many other research studies in the 1950s, 1960s and 1970s, such as those by Asch on conformity and by Piliavin and colleagues on bystander behaviour, raised similar ethical concerns. These eventually led, in 1974, to the creation in the US of the National Commission for Protection of Human Subjects of Biomedical and Behavioural Research to provide ethical guidance for researchers. The Commission published the *Belmont Report* (1978) which identified three basic principles: respect for persons (the consent process), beneficence (costs and benefits, principle of doing no harm), and justice.

Evaluation of methods used to deal with ethical issues

| Ethical issue | How to deal with it | Limitations |
|---|---|---|
| **Deception** | The need for deception should be approved by an **ethical committee**, weighing up benefits (of the study) against costs (to participants).<br>Participants should be fully *debriefed* after the study and offered the opportunity to withhold their data. | ● Cost–benefit decisions are flawed because both are subjective judgments, and the costs are not always apparent until after the study.<br>● **Debriefing** can't turn the clock back – a participant may still feel embarrassed or have lowered self-esteem. |
| **Informed consent** | Participants should be formally asked to indicate their agreement to participate and this should be based on comprehensive information concerning the nature and purpose of the research and their role in it.<br>An alternative is to gain **presumptive consent**, and/or offer the right to withdraw. | ● If a participant knows such information this may invalidate the purpose of the study.<br>● Even if researchers have sought and obtained informed consent, that does not guarantee that participants really do understand what they have let themselves in for.<br>● The problem with presumptive consent is that what people say they would or wouldn't mind is different from actually experiencing it. |
| **The right to withdraw** | Participants should be informed at the beginning of a study that they have the right to withdraw at any time with no penalty. | ● Once the study is underway, participants may feel that they shouldn't withdraw because it will spoil the study.<br>● In many studies participation is a requirement of an undergraduate psychology course, so students wouldn't feel they could withdraw. |
| **Protection from harm** | Researchers should avoid any situation that may cause a participant to experience psychological or physical damage. | ● Researchers are not always able to predict accurately the risks of taking part in a study. |
| **Confidentiality** | Researchers should not record the names of any participants; they should use numbers instead or use false names. | ● It is sometimes possible to work out who the participants were on the basis of the information that has been provided; for example if the geographical location of a school is included you can work out who the participants were. |
| **Privacy** | People should not be observed without their informed consent unless it is in a public place.<br>Participants may be asked to give their retrospective consent or allowed to withhold their data. | ● There is not universal agreement about what constitutes a public place.<br>● Not everyone may feel this is acceptable, for example lovers on a park bench. |

## KEY TERMS

**Debriefing:** A post-research interview designed to inform the participants of the true nature of the study and to restore them to the same state they were in at the start of the experiment. It may also be used to gain feedback about the procedures in the study.

**Ethical committee:** A group of people within a research institution that must approve a study before it begins (also called *institutional review board, IRB*).

**Presumptive consent:** A method of dealing with lack of *informed consent* or *deception*, by asking a group of people who are similar to the participants whether they would agree to take part in a study. If this group of people consent to the procedures in the proposed study, it is *presumed* that the real participants would agree as well.

 **13**

For each of the studies below answer the questions that follow:

*Study A*
In order to study the effects of sleep deprivation students are asked to limit their sleep to five hours for three nights and then sleep normally for the next three nights. Each day, the students' cognitive abilities are assessed using a memory test.

*Study B*
Participants volunteer to take part in a study. They are told that the study is about public speaking, but the real aim is to see how people respond to encouragement by others. Some participants speak in front of a group of people who smile at them, while others talk to a group who appear disinterested.

*Study C*
Marathon runners are assessed on how much sleep they have the night before and the night after a race to see the effects of extreme exercise on sleep.

*Study D*
A teacher is doing a psychology course and decides to try a little experiment with her class of eight-year-olds. She gives half the class a test in the morning, and half of them do the same test in the afternoon to see if time of day affects performance.

1. Identify the IV and DV.
2. How could you operationalise the DV?
3. What kind of experiment do you think this is? (Explain your answer.)
4. Identify at least *two* possible ethical issues.
5. Describe how you would deal with each ethical issue.
6. Describe *one* limitation for each of your methods of dealing with the ethical issues.

## assessment issues

**Outline the role of studies by Milgram or Piliavin, in the development of ethical codes for psychological research. (ku 2 ae 2)**

Research methods questions on ethics often ask you to identify or describe *specific* ethical concerns from the scenario information. However, the question above does *not* require you to interpret the scenario. It requires you to discuss the development of ethical codes with reference to two particular studies that are identified in the specification. The specification specifically says, 'Ethical issues in psychological research, including the role of studies by Milgram *or* Piliavin, in the development of ethical codes for psychological research' so you can see that the question has been lifted directly from the specification. You must use your own knowledge of these studies and relate this to how ethical codes developed – how the unpleasant treatment of participants in certain research studies provoked *concerns* and *debate* amongst psychology professionals about the ethical responsibilities of researchers, and that this ultimately gave rise to the establishment of ethical codes.

Other types of questions on ethical issues might focus on descriptions of specific principles, whether or not related to the scenario.

# Aspect 3: Non-experimental methods

## Surveys

### Questionnaires and interviews

One way to collect data about people is to *ask* them about their thoughts, attitudes and feelings. Such methods are collectively called *self-report techniques* or **surveys**, which include **questionnaires** and **interviews**.

A questionnaire is a set of questions. It is designed to collect information about a topic or even more than one topic.

The two great strengths of questionnaires are:

➕ You can collect the same information from a large number of people relatively easily (once you have designed the questionnaire, which is not so easy).

➕ You can access what people think. Other research methods rely on 'guessing' what people think and feel on the basis of how they behave. With a questionnaire, you can ask people – whether they can and do give you valid answers is another matter.

A questionnaire can be given in a written form or it can be delivered in real time (face to face or on the telephone) by an interviewer.

A **structured interview** has pre-determined questions; i.e. it is a questionnaire that is delivered face to face.

An **unstructured interview** has less structure! New questions are developed as you go along, similar to the way your GP might interview you. The GP starts with some predetermined questions but further questions are developed as a response to your answers. For this reason, the unstructured or semi-structured approach is sometimes called the *clinical interview*.

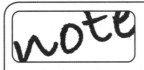

*A questionnaire can be a* research method *or a* research technique.

The aims of a study may be to find out about smoking habits in young people. The researcher would design a questionnaire to collect data about what people do and why. In this case, the questionnaire is the research method.

The aims of a study might be to see if the attitudes towards smoking of children who are exposed to an anti-smoking educational programme differ from those of children not exposed to such a programme. The researcher would use a questionnaire to collect data about attitudes, but the analysis would involve a comparison between the two groups of children – an experimental study using a questionnaire as a research technique (means of collecting data).

Surveys may collect *quantitative data*: numerical information about your age, how many hours you work in a week, how highly you rate different TV programmes.

Or they may collect *qualitative data*: a more complex account of what people think or feel. An unstructured interview is most likely to produce qualitative data because the questions that develop are likely to ask respondents to elaborate their answers (e.g. 'Why do you feel that?').

A comparison of questionnaires and interviews

| | Strengths | Weaknesses |
|---|---|---|
| **Questionnaires** Respondents record their own answers | ➕ Can easily be repeated so that data can be collected from large numbers of people relatively cheaply and quickly (once the questionnaire has been designed). ➕ Questionnaires do not require specialist administrators. ➕ Respondents may feel more willing to reveal personal/confidential information than in an interview. | ➖ Answers may not be truthful, for example because of **leading questions** and **social desirability bias**. A further problem is **response set** – some people prefer to give the answer 'yes' rather than 'no' (or vice versa). ➖ The sample may be biased because only certain kinds of people fill in questionnaires – literate individuals who are willing to spend time completing them. |
| **Structured interview** Questions predetermined | ➕ Can be easily repeated. ➕ Requires less skill than unstructured interviews. ➕ Easier to analyse than unstructured interviews because answers are more predictable. | ➖ The interviewer's expectations may influence the answers the interviewee gives (this is called **interviewer bias**). This may especially be true because people don't always know what they think. They may also want to present themselves in a 'good light' and therefore give 'socially desirable' answers (social desirability bias). ➖ In comparison with unstructured interviews, the data collected will be restricted by a predetermined set of questions. ➖ People may feel less comfortable about revealing personal information than in a questionnaire. |
| **Unstructured or semi-structured interviews** Interviewer develops questions in response to respondent's answers to elicit more detailed information | ➕ Generally more detailed information can be obtained from each respondent than in a structured interview. ➕ Can access information that may not be revealed by predetermined questions. | ➖ More affected by interviewer bias than structured interviews. ➖ Requires well-trained interviewers, which makes it more expensive to produce reliable interviews. ➖ Interviews may not be comparable because different interviewers ask different questions (low **inter-interviewer reliability**). **Reliability** may also be affected by the same interviewer behaving differently on different occasions. ➖ The answers from unstructured interviews are less easy to analyse because they are unpredictable. |

## KEY TERMS

**Leading question:** A question that is phrased in such a way (e.g. 'Don't you agree that …?') that it makes one response more likely than another. The form or content of the question suggests what answer is desired.

**Social desirability bias:** A tendency for respondents to answer questions in such a way that presents them in a better light.

**Response set:** A tendency for respondents to answer questions in the same way, regardless of context.

**Interviewer bias:** The effect of an interviewer's expectations, communicated unconsciously, on a respondent's behaviour.

**Inter-interviewer reliability:** The extent to which two interviewers produce the same outcome from an interview.

### Special tip

Often students write something like 'The advantage of a questionnaire is that you can collect lots of data'. The problem with this is that it is not clear what 'lots of data' means. Compared with what? You can collect a large amount of data in an experiment or an interview.

- You need to provide clear detail (What is 'lots of data'? Why is there 'lots of data'?).
- You need to offer a comparison (e.g. compared with an interview).
- A good answer would say, 'The advantage of a questionnaire is that you can collect data from more people than you would if using the interview method, which results in lots more data.'

### Ethical issues for questionnaires and interviews

- Deception may be necessary.
- Questions may be related to sensitive and personal issues.
- Confidentiality and privacy must be respected.

**Reliability:** A measure of consistency over time; for example if you gave the same questionnaire to a participant on two occasions you should get the same result. The reliability of an experiment can be determined through *replication*.

**Test–retest reliability:** A measure of external reliability, i.e. the consistency (reliability) of test scores across time. This is established by testing the same group of people with the same test on two occasions. A high correlation indicates that scores are consistent across time and thus reliable.

**Validity:** Refers to how true or legitimate something is, whether a questionnaire or experiment is testing what it intended to test. In the context of classification, for example of mental illness, it refers to the legitimacy of the assessment, the extent to which it is true and meaningful.

**Concurrent validity:** A means of showing that a test is valid by comparing its results with those from a currently existing test recognised as having *validity*. It aims to demonstrate the extent to which performance on a test correlates positively with other tests of the same attribute. If a test is a good one, we would expect a high *positive correlation*.

# Reliability and validity of surveys

## Reliability
**Reliability** refers to whether something is consistent.

If you use a ruler to measure a height of a chair today and do this again tomorrow, you expect the ruler to be reliable (consistent) and provide the same measurement. You would assume that any fluctuation was because the chair had changed.

Any tool used for taking measurements must be reliable (e.g. a psychological test assessing personality or an interview about drinking habits).

If the tool is reliable, it should produce the same result on every occasion. If we measure something twice using a reliable tool and find that the result is different on the second occasion, then we know the thing (chair or personality) has changed.

Using a reliable tool enables us to feel confident that any difference between objects/people is due to the objects and not to the measuring device.

If the same questionnaire or interview (or psychological test) is repeated twice it should produce the same outcome. One way to assess this is to check for **test–retest reliability**: for example, give participants a test and then give the *same participants* the same test a month later to see if the same result is obtained. The two scores can be compared by calculating a **correlation coefficient** (see page 115).

## Validity
The **validity** of a questionnaire or interview is related to the question of whether it really measures what you intended it to measure. If respondents' answers are affected by *social desirability bias* then the findings will lack validity.

Another issue is whether the questions are actually testing what the researcher intended to test. For example, if a questionnaire was about attitudes to paranormal experiences, the question 'What month were you born in?' would lack validity unless you could link it in some way to attitudes to paranormal experiences. One way to assess this is **concurrent validity**, which can be established by comparing the current test with a previously established test on the same topic. Participants take both tests and then you compare their scores on the two tests.

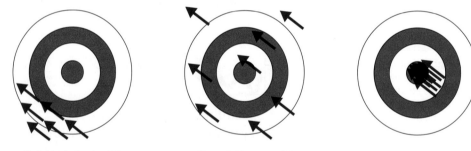

Reliable, but not valid          Not reliable, not valid          Reliable and valid

Different archers produce the patterns of arrows above. Being reliable is being consistent; being valid is being on target (related to what you are aiming to do).

---

*questions* 14

1. Explain the difference between a structured and an unstructured interview.
2. Explain the difference between a questionnaire and an interview.
3. If you wanted to find out about attitudes towards dieting, why would it be preferable to conduct an interview rather than a questionnaire?
4. Why might it be better to conduct a questionnaire than an interview?
5. How can 'leading questions' be a problem in interviews or questionnaires?
6. What is 'social desirability bias'?
7. Why is it important for questionnaires to be reliable and valid?
8. Explain how a researcher could check the reliability and validity of a questionnaire.

## Writing your own survey

### Writing good questions

When writing questions there are three guiding principles:

- *Clarity*. Questions need to be written so that the reader (respondent) understands what is being asked. One way to do this is to operationalise certain terms. There should be no ambiguity.

- *Bias*. Any bias in a question might lead the respondent to be more likely to give a particular answer (as in a leading question). The greatest problem is probably social desirability bias.

- *Analysis*. Questions need to be written so that the answers provided are easy to analyse. If you ask 'What kind of job do you do?' or 'What makes you feel stressed at work?' you may get 50 different answers from 50 people. These are called **open questions**. Alternatively one can ask **closed questions** where a limited range of answers are provided, such as listing 10 job categories or 10 sources of stress. Such closed questions are easier to analyse, as are **forced-choice questions**, where the participant is only offered a limited choice of responses.

### note

#### Open questions

*Qualitative* data typically come from asking open-ended questions, the answers to which are not limited by a set of choices or a scale.

Examples of open questions:

1. What factors contribute to making work stressful?
2. When do you feel most stressed?

#### Closed questions

Closed questions provide limited choices, are easy to analyse (*quantitative* data) but may not permit people to express their precise feelings.

Examples of closed questions:

1. Which of the following factors at work makes you feel stressed? (You may tick as many answers as you like.)

   [ ] Noise at work      [ ] Lack of control
   [ ] No job satisfaction  [ ] Workmates
   [ ] Too much to do

> Note that these questions do concern what people think and feel, but such questions would not produce qualitative data because respondents' choices have been limited.

2. How many hours a week do you work?

   [ ] 0 hours
   [ ] Less than 10 hours
   [ ] Between 10 and 20 hours
   [ ] Between 20 and 30 hours
   [ ] More than 30 hours

3. **Forced choice question**

   A. The worst social sin is to be rude
   B. The worst social sin is to be a bore

4. **Likert scale**

   Work is stressful.

   [ ] Strongly agree    [ ] Agree    [ ] Not sure
   [ ] Disagree    [ ] Strongly disagree

5. How much stress do you feel in the following situations?
   (Circle the number that best describes how you feel.)

   At work
   A lot of stress    5  4  3  2  1    No stress at all

   At home
   A lot of stress    5  4  3  2  1    No stress at all

   Travelling to work
   A lot of stress    5  4  3  2  1    No stress at all

6. **Semantic differential technique**
   (Place a tick to show your feelings.)

   People who are bosses are usually

   Hard _ _ _ _ _ _ _ Kind
   Passive _ _ _ _ _ _ Active
   Small _ _ _ _ _ _ _ Large
   Beautiful _ _ _ _ _ _ _ Ugly

### Designing good surveys

A good survey (questionnaire or interview) should contain good questions (obviously). Some other things to consider when designing a good survey are:

- *Filler questions*. It may help to include some irrelevant questions to mislead the respondent about the main purpose of the survey. This may reduce **demand characteristics**.

- *Sequence for the questions*. It is best to start with easy ones, saving difficult questions or questions that might make someone feel anxious or defensive until the respondent has relaxed.

- *Sampling technique*, i.e. how to select respondents as described on page 103.

- *Pilot study*. The questions can be tested on a small group of people. This means that you can refine the questions in response to any difficulties encountered.

---

*questions* 15

1. A psychology student designs a questionnaire about attitudes to eating. Below, (a)–(c) are some questions from this questionnaire:
   (a) Do you diet?    ALWAYS    SOMETIMES    NEVER (circle your answer)
   (b) Do you think that dieting is a bad idea?
   (c) Explain your answer to (b).

   For each of the above questions:
   a. State whether it is an open or closed question.
   b. State whether the question would produce quantitative or qualitative data.
   c. Give *one* criticism of the question.
   d. Suggest how you could improve the question in order to deal with your criticism.
   e. Suggest *one* strength of the question.

2. You have been asked to write a questionnaire about people's attitudes to ghosts and other paranormal phenomena.
   a. Write *one* closed question that would collect quantitative data.
   b. Write *one* open question that would collect qualitative data.
   c. Write an example of a leading question for this questionnaire.
   d. Explain how social desirability bias might affect the validity of the responses to your questionnaire.
   e. Describe *one* strength of using questionnaires to collect data in this study.
   f. Describe *one* weakness of using questionnaires to collect data in this study.

---

*assessment issues*

**Name the research method used in this study. (ku 1 ae 0)**

A deceptively simple question! We saw earlier (on page 81) that you need to be very careful and precise in the use of research methods terms (e.g. don't confuse 'types' of experiment with 'designs' of experiments). Beware of a similar confusion between 'method' and 'design' (see note on page 110). In the exam question above, you are asked for the *method* used, so make sure that you don't respond by describing the *design*. It is sensible to expand a little on the name of the method, especially if it is a *survey* – specify whether the study has used *questionnaires* or *interviews*.

---

**KEY TERMS**

**Correlation:** The extent of a relationship between two variables; usually a *linear correlation* is predicted, but the relationship can be *curvilinear*.

**Positive correlation:** As the value of one *co-variable* increases, this is accompanied by a corresponding increase in the other *co-variable*.

**Negative correlation:** A relationship between two *co-variables* such that as the value of one co-variable increases, that of the other decreases.

# Correlational design and analysis
## What is meant by a correlation?

A **correlation** is a relationship between two variables (**co-variables**).

Age and beauty co-vary. As people get older they become more beautiful. This is a **positive correlation** because the two variables *increase* together.

You may disagree and think that as people get older they become less attractive. You think age and beauty are correlated but it is a **negative correlation**. As one variable increases, the other one decreases.

**Co-variables:** The two measured variables in an investigation using correlational analysis.

**Zero correlation:** No relationship (*correlation*) between *co-variables*.

*A correlation is not a research method. Therefore, we don't talk about a correlational investigation but an investigation using a correlational analysis. Correlational analysis is mainly used with non-experimental research methods, where there is no manipulation of an IV, and usually little control of other variables.*

**Scattergram:** A graphical representation of the relationship (i.e. the *correlation*) between two sets of scores.

**Correlation coefficient:** A number between −1 and +1 that tells us how closely the *co-variables* in a correlational analysis are related.

Or you may simply feel that there is no relationship between age and beauty. This is called a **zero correlation**.

When conducting a study which uses a correlational analysis, the hypothesis states the expected relationship between co-variables. In the case of age and beauty the null hypothesis would be:

*There is no relationship between age and beauty.*

Possible alternative hypotheses:

*Age and beauty are positively correlated (one-tailed).*

*Age and beauty are negatively correlated (one-tailed).*

*As people get older they are rated as more beautiful (one-tailed).*

*Age and beauty are correlated (two-tailed).*

## Visual display: the scattergram

A correlation can be illustrated using a **scattergram**. Each individual has a pair of scores, one for each *co-variable* – in our case the co-variables are age and beauty. A dot is plotted on the graph for each individual – their age and their beauty rating. If the dots lie in a diagonal pattern from bottom left to top right the *direction* of the correlation between the co-variables is *positive*, whereas if they are arranged from bottom right to top left the direction is *negative*. The *strength* of correlation between the co-variables is indicated by how widely scattered the dots are: the closer the dots are to the 'diagonal line', the stronger the relationship. A statistical test can be used to calculate the **correlation coefficient**, a measure of the extent of correlation that exists between the co-variables. The test can also tell us whether the correlation is *significant* (see page 116). Correlation coefficients are never greater than 1 and are positive (for a positive correlation) or negative (for a negative correlation): +1 is a perfect positive correlation and −1 is a perfect negative correlation. However, in practice in psychological research you are very unlikely to find a perfect correlation. Strength of correlation can also be expressed in words: *weak, moderate,* or *strong*.

*note*

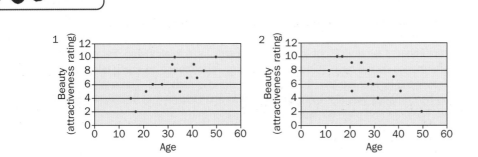
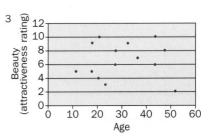

Graph 1 illustrates a positive correlation.
Graph 2 shows a negative correlation.
Graph 3 shows a zero correlation.

The correlation coefficients for all three graphs are:

(1) +0.76

(2) −0.76

(3) +0.002

The plus or minus sign shows whether the correlation is positive or negative. The coefficient (number) tells us how closely the co-variables are related. −0.76 is just as closely correlated as +0.76; it's just that −0.76 means that as one variable increases the other decreases (*negative correlation*), and +0.76 means that both variables increase together (*positive correlation*).

Evaluation of investigations using correlational analysis

|  | Strengths | Weaknesses |
|---|---|---|
| **Investigations using correlational analysis** | ➕ Can be used when it would be unethical or impractical to manipulate variables; may use pre-existing data.<br>➕ If the correlation is significant, further investigation is justified.<br>➕ If the correlation is not significant, you can rule out a causal relationship. | ➖ People often misinterpret correlations and assume that cause and effect have been found, whereas all we can conclude is that a relationship exists: it *may* be causal, one variable may affect the other in the way we predicted, *OR* there may be cause and effect but in the opposite direction (*cause and effect reversal*).<br>➖ There may be other, unknown (**intervening**) **variable**(s) that can explain why the *co-variables* being studied are linked. |

## Significance

Once we have calculated a correlation coefficient we need to know whether it is strong or weak. In order to do this, we use tables of significance which tell us how big the coefficient needs to be in order for the correlation to be significant (see note on significance, on page 101).

The table on the left gives an approximate idea of the values needed. The more pairs of scores you have, the smaller the coefficient can be – even coefficients as small as +0.02 (or less) can be significant if the number of pairs is very large (see results from Rahe *et al.* on page 68).

A coefficient of either −0.45 or +0.45 would be significant if there were 16 pairs of data but not if there were 14 pairs.

The *magnitude* of the number informs us about significance; the *sign* tells us which direction the correlation is in (positive or negative).

## A final word on correlation

The correlations we have looked at are all *linear* – in a graph of perfect positive correlation (+1), all the values would lie in a straight *line* from the bottom left to the top right.

However, there is a different kind of correlation – a *curvilinear correlation*. The relationship is not linear: it is curved, but there is still a predictable relationship. For example, stress and performance do not have a linear relationship. Performance on many tasks is depressed when stress is too high or too low; it is best when stress is moderate. The relationship between stress and performance was first identified by Yerkes and Dodson and thus called the Yerkes–Dodson law. The graph on page 67 illustrates this relationship.

**Significance table**

| N = | One-tailed test |
|---|---|
| 4 | 1.000 |
| 6 | 0.829 |
| 8 | 0.643 |
| 10 | 0.564 |
| 12 | 0.503 |
| 14 | 0.464 |
| 16 | 0.429 |
| 18 | 0.401 |
| 20 | 0.380 |
| 22 | 0.361 |
| 24 | 0.344 |
| 26 | 0.331 |
| 28 | 0.317 |
| 30 | 0.306 |

These values are for the statistical test called *Spearman's test of correlation*.

*Ethical issues for correlational analysis*

● If you are using pre-existing data, you should respect confidentiality and be aware of the possible social sensitivity of such data.
● The way the results are presented may erroneously suggest that a causal relationship has been demonstrated.

**questions** 16

1. Think of *two* variables that are likely to be positively correlated and *two* variables that are likely to be negatively correlated.
2. What does a correlation coefficient tell you about a set of data?
3. Give an example of a positive correlation coefficient and a negative correlation coefficient.
4. Explain what the following correlation coefficients mean:

| +1.00 | −1.00 | 0.00 |
|---|---|---|
| −0.60 | +0.40 | +0.10 |

5. Consider the number +0.36. Identify the magnitude and sign of this number.
6. If this value was obtained after testing 20 people, would it be significant? (Use the significance table on page 116.)
7. Sketch a scattergram to illustrate this correlation.
8. If you conducted a study with 30 participants, would a correlation of +0.30 be significant?
9. Would −0.40 be significant?
10. Guiseppe Gelato always liked statistics at school and now that he has his own ice cream business he keeps various records. To his surprise, he found an interesting correlation between his ice cream sales and aggressive crimes. He has started to worry that he may be irresponsible in selling ice cream because it appears to cause people to behave more aggressively. The table below shows his data.

| All data rounded to 1000s | Jan | Feb | Mar | Apr | May | Jun | Jul | Aug | Sep | Oct | Nov | Dec |
|---|---|---|---|---|---|---|---|---|---|---|---|---|
| Ice cream sales | 10 | 8 | 7 | 21 | 32 | 56 | 130 | 141 | 84 | 32 | 11 | 6 |
| Aggressive crimes | 21 | 32 | 29 | 35 | 44 | 55 | 111 | 129 | 99 | 36 | 22 | 25 |

a. Draw a scattergram to display Guiseppe's data.
b. What can you conclude from the data and the scattergram?
c. What intervening variable might explain the relationship between ice cream and aggression?
d. Describe how you would design a study to show Guiseppe that ice cream does (or does not) cause aggressive behaviour. (You need to operationalise your variables, decide on a suitable research design and sampling method, etc.)

**assessment issues**

**Give a suitable alternative hypothesis for this study. (ku 2 ae 0)**

How will you answer this question if the study in the scenario uses a correlational design? Such studies have an alternative and a null hypotheses and the alternative hypothesis may be one- or two-tailed (directional or non-directional) but these are worded differently from experimental hypotheses. To answer the question above, in respect of a correlational scenario, remember to use words like 'association' or 'relationship' or 'link'. Words like 'affects', 'improves', 'causes', 'has an effect on' – should be avoided like the plague because they apply to cause-and-effect relationships!

It may be worth noting that the scenario itself, and/or the questions, may not tell you explicitly that the study uses correlational analysis; if not you will have to work this out yourself from clues in the information. As soon as you realise that you're dealing with correlation, remind yourself that many of the elements of this type of research design are quite distinct, especially when compared with the experimental method: there are two variables, but they should be called 'co-variables', not IV and DV. The most suitable graph to display results is a scattergram (which suits only a correlational design), not a bar chart or pie chart. Be prepared, also, to answer questions on interpretation of direction and strength of a relationship from a given scattergram, as well as on conclusions as to the nature of the relationship (can you assume cause and effect?). You won't be asked questions about 'significance', but you may find this concept helpful in understanding correlation in general.

# Observation
## What is meant by observation?

The starting point for scientific enquiry is observation. We observe what is going on and then develop some research questions for further studies. For example, we might observe that some children have difficulty adapting to their new school when they move from primary to secondary. We observe this and then devise a research study to find out more about this.

The issue with collecting data through observation is to make it as objective as possible so that it is not just the personal view of the observer. Observational studies can vary in design on a number of dimensions, as considered below.

### Method and technique

All research involves making observations. In some research the overall method is observational where the emphasis is on observing a relatively unconstrained segment of a person's freely chosen behaviour. Observational methods may also be used in an experiment – in which case, 'observation' is a research *technique* instead of a research *method*.

### Ethical issues for observations

- Informed consent is often not possible.
- Participants' privacy must be respected. You should not observe people without their informed consent unless it is in a public place where people would normally expect to be observed by others; even then researchers should consider whether privacy is being invaded.

## Controlled and naturalistic observations

In both cases systematic methods are used to record observations. In a **controlled observation**, some variables are controlled by the researcher, reducing the 'naturalness' of behaviour being studied; for example the setting may be moved from the person's normal environment or some of the items in the environment may be deliberately chosen. Participants are likely to know that they are being studied and the study may be conducted in a laboratory.

In a **naturalistic observation**, behaviour is studied in a natural situation where *everything has been left as it is normally*. (Note that naturalistic observation is different from a natural experiment where the relationship between an IV and DV is observed).

### An example of a naturalistic observation

Do little boys criticise each other if they behave like girls? Do little boys 'reward' each other for sex-appropriate play? Is the same true for little girls?

One study observed boys and girls aged three to five years during their free-play periods at nursery school. The researchers classified activities as male, female or neutral and recorded how playmates responded. Praise and imitation constituted some of the positive responses; criticism and stopping play were some of the negative responses. The researchers found that children generally reinforced peers for sex-appropriate play and were quick to criticise sex-inappropriate play (Lamb and Roopnarine, 1979).

### An example of a controlled observation

The same research as described above could have been conducted by controlling some of the variables. For example, the researchers might have set up a special playroom in their laboratory with certain types of toys available (male, female and neutral). They could have observed the children through a *one-way mirror* so the children would be unaware of being observed.

# Other types of observation

## Observation in an experiment

In the 'Bobo doll study' described on pages 92 and 174 (Bandura *et al.*, 1961) the children's aggressiveness was observed at the end of the experiment to see if those exposed to the aggressive model behaved more aggressively. At the end of the experiment, each child was taken to a room which contained some aggressive toys (e.g. a mallet and a dart gun), some non-aggressive toys (e.g. dolls and farm animals) and a life-sized Bobo doll.

The experimenter stayed with the child while the child played for 20 minutes, during which time the child was observed through a one-way mirror. The observers recorded what the child was doing every five seconds, using a behaviour checklist (see page 121) with items such as specific aggressive acts imitated, specific aggressive phrases imitated, non-aggressive behaviour imitated, and so on.

## Indirect (content analysis)

In studies using **content analysis**, observations are made of data that have already been collected and are in the form of text. This includes published texts such as books or films or TV programmes, and personal texts such as diaries or drawings or even text messages. Such observations are 'indirect' because they are observations of the communications produced by people.

## Participant and non-participant

In **non-participant (overt) observation**, the observer is merely watching the behaviour of others and does not participate. In some studies, observers also participate, which may affect their objectivity and introduce bias. A classic example of a **participant observation** is described below.

## Disclosed and undisclosed

A drawback of **disclosed observation** is that, when participants know that their behaviour is being observed, this is likely to alter their behaviour. Observers often try to be as unobtrusive as possible. One-way mirrors are used to prevent participants being aware that they are being observed. This is called **undisclosed** (covert) **observation**.

## A participant, undisclosed observation

In the 1950s, the social psychologist Leon Festinger read a newspaper report about a religious cult that claimed to be receiving messages from outer space predicting that the end of the world would take place on a certain date in the form of a great flood. The cult members were going to be rescued by a flying saucer, so they all gathered with their leader, a Mrs. Marian Keech. Festinger was intrigued to know how the cult members would respond when they realised that their beliefs were unfounded, especially as many of them had made their beliefs very public. In order to observe this at first hand, Festinger and some co-workers posed as converts to the cause and were present on the eve of destruction. When it was apparent that there would be no flood, the group leader said that their prayers had saved the city. Some cult members didn't believe this and left the cult, whereas others took this as proof of the cult's power (Festinger *et al.*, 1956).

# Reliability and validity of observations

## Reliability

Observations should be consistent which means that ideally two observers should produce the same record. The extent to which two (or more) observers agree is called **inter-observer reliability**. This is measured by correlating the observations of two or more observers. A general rule is that if (Total agreements)/(Total observations) > +0.80, the data have inter-observer reliability. Low reliability can be dealt with by training observers.

## Validity

The *validity* of observations is affected by **observer bias** – what someone observes is influenced by their expectations. This reduces the objectivity of observations and can be dealt with by using more than one observer and averaging data across observers (this balances out any biases).

If participants know that they are being observed, they may alter their behaviour so that what is observed no longer represents 'real' behaviour.

Observations will not be valid (nor reliable) if the **coding system/*behaviour checklist*** (described on page 121) is flawed. For example, some observations may belong in more than one category, or some behaviours may not be codeable.

## questions 17

1. With reference to the study by Lamb and Roopnarine (an example of a naturalistic observation), give *one* advantage and *one* disadvantage for studying children in this way.

2. A psychologist decided to observe the non-verbal behaviours between two people having a conversation. (Non-verbal behaviours are those which don't involve language – such as smiling, touching, etc.).
   a. Explain why it would be desirable to conduct a pilot study.
   b. If this is to be a naturalistic observation, *where* should the student researchers make their observations?
   c. Each conversation is observed by two students. Identify *one* way in which you could ensure reliability among the different observers, and explain how you might put this into practice.
   d. Describe *two* features of the study that might threaten the validity of this study.
   e. Explain how you could deal with these two features that might threaten validity.
   f. Describe *one* way of ensuring that this study would be carried out in an ethically acceptable manner.

### Evaluation of observational studies

| | Strengths | Weaknesses |
|---|---|---|
| Observational studies | ➕ What people say they do is often different from what they actually do so observations may be more valid than questionnaires/interviews.<br>➕ Gives a more realistic picture of spontaneous behaviour. It is likely to have high **ecological validity**.<br>➕ A means of conducting preliminary investigations in a new area of research, to produce hypotheses for future investigations. | ➖ There can be little or no control of **extraneous variables**.<br>➖ The observer may 'see' what he/she expects to see. This is called **observer bias**. This bias may mean that different observers 'see' different things, which leads to low **inter-observer reliability**.<br>➖ If participants don't know they are being observed, there are ethical problems such as deception and invasion of privacy. If participants do know they are being observed, they may alter their behaviour. |

## activity 6

### Making observations

Work with a partner and take it in turns to observe each other. One of you will be Person A and the other will be Person B.

- Person A should have a difficult task to do (e.g. answering one of the exam questions at the end of this chapter).
- Person B should have a boring task to do (e.g. copying out the exam question).
- Each person should spend five minutes on the task.
- The person doing the observing should note down any aspect of their partner's behaviour.

*In controlled observations, it is the participant's environment that is controlled or structured – not the techniques used to obtain observational data. Structured techniques are used in both naturalistic and controlled observations.*

## Observational techniques

You might think that making observations is easy but, if you tried the activity above, you should now realise that it is difficult for two main reasons:

- ➖ It is difficult to work out what to record and what not to record.
- ➖ It is difficult to record everything that is happening even if you do work out what to record and what not to record.

Observational research, like all research, aims to be objective and rigorous. For this reason it is necessary to use observational *techniques*.

### Unstructured observations

The researcher records all relevant behaviour but has no system for making the recording (e.g. sampling procedures or an observation schedule). The behaviour to be studied is largely unpredictable.

One problem with **unstructured observations** is that the behaviours recorded will often be those which are most visible or eye-catching to the observer, but these may not necessarily be the most important or relevant behaviours.

### KEY TERMS

**Unstructured observations:** An observer records all relevant behaviour but has no system. The behaviour to be studied may be largely unpredictable.

**Behaviour checklist:** A list of the behaviours to be recorded during an observational study.

**Coding system:** A systematic method for recording observations in which individual behaviours are given a code for ease of recording.

**Structured observations:** The researcher uses various 'systems' to organise observations, such as a *sampling technique* and an *observation schedule*.

**Observation schedule:** A systematic method for recording observations in which categories of behaviour have been identified, such as a *behaviour checklist* or a *coding system*.

**Continuous observation:** Every instance of a behaviour is recorded in as much detail as possible. This is useful if the behaviours you are interested in do not occur very often.

**Event sampling:** An *observational technique* in which a count is kept of the number of times that a certain behaviour (event) occurs.

**Time sampling:** An *observational technique* in which the observer records behaviours in a given time frame (e.g. noting what a target individual is doing every 30 seconds). You may select categories from a checklist.

## Structured observations

In systematic or **structured observations**, the researcher uses various 'systems' to organise observations:

- **sampling procedures** – who you are observing and when.
- **observation schedule** – how to record the behaviour you are interested in.

*Sampling procedures*

In **continuous observation**, you record every instance of the behaviour you see in as much detail as possible. This is useful if the behaviours which interest you do not occur very often.

In many situations, continuous observation would not be possible because there would be too much data to record; therefore, there must be a systematic method of sampling observations:

- **Event sampling** is counting the number of times that a certain behaviour (event) occurs in a target individual or individuals.
- **Time sampling** involves recording behaviours in a given time frame. For example, noting what a target individual is doing every 30 seconds. You may select one or more categories from a *checklist*.

*Observation schedule*

One of the hardest aspects of making observations is deciding how different behaviours should be categorised. This is because our perception of behaviour is often seamless; when we watch somebody perform a particular action we see a continuous stream of action rather than a series of separate behavioural components.

In order to conduct structured observations, one needs to break this stream of behaviour up into different categories. An *observation schedule* (also called a *coding system* or *behaviour checklist*) is constructed when making preliminary observations. What is needed is *operationalisation* – breaking the behaviour being studied into a set of components. For example, when observing infant behaviour, have a list such as smiling, crying, sleeping, etc., or when observing facial expressions, have a list of different expressions as shown on page 122.

The coding system should:

- Be *objective*: the observer should not have to make inferences about the behaviour and should just have to record explicit actions.
- Cover *all possible component behaviours* and avoid a 'waste basket' category.
- Have categories that are *mutually exclusive*, meaning that you should not have to mark two categories at one time.

### The Facial Action Coding System (FACS)

Ekman and Friesen (1978) designed this coding system. It is used to investigate how people display and recognise emotion using non-verbal cues.

 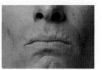

For illustrations, see www-2.cs.cmu.edu/afs/cs/project/face/www/facs.htm.

| Code | Description | Code | Description | Code | Description |
|---|---|---|---|---|---|
| 1 | Inner brow raiser | 17 | Chin raiser | 45 | Blink |
| 2 | Outer brow raiser | 18 | Lip puckerer | 46 | Wink |
| 4 | Brow lowerer | 20 | Lip stretcher | 51 | Head turn left |
| 5 | Upper lid raiser | 22 | Lip funneler | 52 | Head turn right |
| 6 | Cheek raiser | 23 | Lip tightener | 53 | Head up |
| 7 | Lid tightener | 24 | Lip pressor | 54 | Head down |
| 9 | Nose wrinkler | 25 | Lips part | 55 | Head tilt left |
| 10 | Upper lip raiser | 26 | Jaw Drop | 56 | Head tilt right |
| 11 | Nasolabial deepener | 27 | Mouth stretch | 57 | Head forward |
| 12 | Lip corner puller | 28 | Mouth stretch | 58 | Head back |
| 13 | Cheek puffer | 41 | Mouth stretch | 61 | Eyes turn left |
| 14 | Dimpler | 42 | Slit | 62 | Eyes turn right |
| 15 | Lip corner depressor | 43 | Eyes closed | 63 | Eyes up |
| 16 | Lower lip depressor | 44 | Squint | 64 | Eyes down |

 **18**

Imagine that you wished to investigate interpersonal deception to see if it was possible to use facial expressions to tell whether or not someone is lying.

1. Describe how you would design a study using observational techniques to investigate this. Record at least six design decisions, and describe each one carefully.
2. Would you describe your study as a naturalistic observation, a controlled observation or a natural, field or lab experiment? Explain why.
3. What would be the relative advantages of doing this study as (a) a naturalistic observation or (b) a lab experiment?

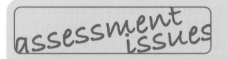

**Describe how *one* other research method could be used to investigate people's ability to identify emotions from facial expressions. (*ku 2 ae 0*)**

Let's assume that the research scenario in the question describes an *experimental* study of people's responses to facial expressions, where participants have to identify particular emotions from pictures of faces on a computer screen. As the example above shows, questions commonly ask for an *alternative research method* for studying the particular research question set out in the scenario. There is usually no single 'correct' answer to such a question. It's up to you to *select* a particular method and *make a case* for it, describing how that method could be used. Run mentally through all the research methods you know to identify one that would be suitable. But beware of the common human failing of *opting for the first reasonable solution* that occurs to you, rather than carefully looking at *all* alternatives and then selecting the best – the latter is precisely the strategy that is likely to get you the most marks. So, choose a research method which is suitable for the given research aim, but also one about which you can remember plenty of material! Which method *would* you choose here?

## Case studies

### What is meant by a case study?

A **case study** is a research investigation that involves the detailed study of a single individual, institution or event. Case studies usually involve a variety of different research methods/ techniques – questionnaires, psychological tests, interviews (with relatives and friends as well as the individual being studied), direct and indirect observation, and possibly even experiments. These findings are then selected and organised, for instance to represent the individual's thoughts and emotions.

Case studies are generally ***longitudinal***; in other words, they follow the individual or group over an extended period of time.

### Examples of case studies

#### Privation

We looked at an example of a classic case study in Chapter 1, the study of Genie (see page 15). The full story as told by Rymer (1993) included interviews with Genie's mother and with the psychologists who looked after Genie (examples of retrospective recall). The results of various psychological tests were used to gain insights into Genie's abilities, including brain scans and IQ tests. Rymer also used transcripts of the research done by Susan Curtiss on Genie's language development (an example of indirect observation). All in all, you can see that the 'case study' comprised a variety of different sources of evidence.

#### Memory and brain damage

In Chapter 2, we covered the Topic of memory and looked at two other classic case studies: HM (Scoville and Milner, 1957) and Clive Wearing (Blakemore, 1988) who both suffered brain damage which affected their memories (see page 35). In particular, the brain damage highlighted the distinction between STM and LTM.

In the study of HM, interviews were used as well as archival data. HM was given various learning and memory tasks that could be regarded as **experimental**. The study of Clive Wearing used **direct observation** and diaries **(indirect observation)**, as well as **interviews** with his wife.

Data from these case studies cannot be used as evidence of a causal relationship between specific behavioural or cognitive functions and brain areas because the damage is not a deliberate manipulation – this would be unethical. However, such cases do provide additional evidence to support existing experimental studies.

Evaluation of case studies

| | Strengths | Weaknesses |
|---|---|---|
| Case studies | ⊕ The method produces rich, in-depth data, so information that may be overlooked using other methods is likely to be identified. <br> ⊕ Can be used to investigate atypical instances that may be rare, so unusual information is accessible, for example in investigations of people with brain damage where it would not be ethical to conduct experiments. <br> ⊕ The complex interaction of many factors can be studied, in contrast to experiments where many variables are held constant. | ⊖ It is difficult to generalise from individual cases, as each one has unique characteristics. <br> ⊖ Reports of past events cannot be validated. <br> ⊖ The research may lack objectivity because the researchers become well acquainted with the individual and more subjective, or because of the researchers' theoretical bias which may lead them to overlook aspects of the findings thus reducing validity. <br> ⊖ There are important ethical issues such as confidentiality – many cases are easily identifiable because of their unique characteristics, even when real names are not given. |

## questions 19

1. Suggest *two* advantages of using case studies rather than experiments.
2. How might researcher bias affect the results of a case study?
3. In which of the following situations would you recommend conducting a case study and why?
   a. A researcher wants to know if patients who are receiving treatment to help them cope with severe anxiety had any traumatic events in their early lives that could account for their symptoms.
   b. A hospital is interested in finding out if two of their head injury patients who have recently shown improvements have especially good relationships with their family or were particularly mentally active prior to their accidents.
   c. A student is keen to conduct her coursework into the difference between males and females in terms of their prejudices towards people with mental health problems.

## assessment issues

### Division of marks in research methods questions: *ku* and *ae* marks.

Like questions in the other Units, marks for research methods questions are divided into *ku* and *ae* skills. In practice, questions that offer *ae* marks are often those which ask for *evaluation* (e.g. strengths/weaknesses, advantages/disadvantages, limitations) of a method or a design, or of types of sampling or types of descriptive statistics, etc. Alternatively, you may be asked to evaluate the given study itself. So, for every aspect of research methods that you have learned, make sure that you can *describe* its main features (for *ku* marks) *and evaluate* it (for *ae* marks). Other research methods questions featuring *ae* marks are often those asking you to address *ethical* issues raised by the given study. In addition, if you are asked to *interpret* findings and draw conclusions, for example from a graph or table, *ae* marks may be available for *analysis* (rather than for evaluation).

# A few other research techniques

This chapter only covers some of the research methods and designs that are used by psychologists. We will now very briefly mention some other methods and designs that you are likely to encounter when you read about research in psychology.

## Cross-cultural studies

Psychologists quite often compare behaviours in different cultures. A **cross-cultural study** is a way of seeing if cultural practices affect behaviour. It is a kind of *natural/quasi-experiment* where the IV is, for example, child-rearing techniques in different cultures and the DV is some behaviour, such as attachment. This enables researchers to see if the DV is due to child-rearing techniques; nurture rather than nature. There are many limitations with such studies:

- For example, researchers may use tests or procedures that have been developed in the US and are not valid in the other culture; this may make the individuals in the other culture appear 'abnormal' or inferior. The term that is used to describe this is an **imposed etic**.

- A second limitation is that the group of participants may not be representative of that culture and yet we make generalisations about the whole culture – or even the whole country.

## Longitudinal and cross-sectional design

When a study is conducted over a long period of time, it is said to have a **longitudinal design** (it's long!). Such studies enable researchers to observe long-term effects and make comparisons between the same individual at different ages.

An alternative way to do this (which takes much less time) is to use a **cross-sectional design**. In this design, a group of younger participants is compared with an older group of participants.

- The problem with a cross-sectional study is that the two groups of participants may be quite different. The *participant variables* in a cross-sectional design are not controlled in the same way that they are not controlled in an *independent groups design* (in fact, a cross-sectional study uses an independent groups design, and a longitudinal study uses a *repeated measures design*). This means that, in a cross-sectional design, differences between groups may be due to participant variables rather than to the independent variable.

### Role-play

In some investigations, participants are told to take on a certain role and then their behaviour can be observed as if it were real life. For example they might be asked to imagine that they are lying, or to pretend that they are a prison guard. **Role-play** is a form of *controlled observational study*.

- his enables researchers to control certain variables so real-life behaviour can be studied which might otherwise be impractical or unethical to observe.

- The question is whether people really do act as they would in real life. In Zimbardo's study (Zimbardo, 1973, see pages 193–194), the participants acting as guards may have been following what they *thought* was guard-like behaviour, as seen in films. If they were real-life guards, they may have acted more in accordance with personal principles rather than according to social norms.

# Overview
## Research in practice

In reality, very few studies simply use one method. In many experiments, the dependent variable is recorded using observation or survey techniques, and the study may include qualitative data such as comments made by participants when they are debriefed. Other studies reported in this book use the *multi-method approach* – combining all sorts of different techniques and methods to investigate the target behaviour. Some examples are given below.

### The scientific method

Throughout this book you have been studying explanations of behaviour and studies related to these explanations. This is the bedrock of psychology, and of every science.

The other day Cara's younger daughter Rosie said to her, 'So what is it psychologists do?' and Cara answered that psychologists try to explain why people do certain things. Rosie's next question was 'How do they do that?' The answer is that they do research studies to test their beliefs (theories) about why people do the things they do. This is the scientific method, a cyclical process as shown in the diagram below.

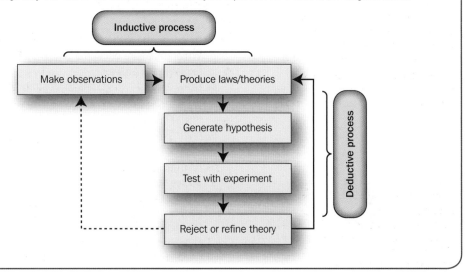

## The multi-method approach

### A study of infant attachment (Schaffer and Emerson, 1964)

We looked at this study in Chapter 1 (see page 2). This was basically a non-experimental study, using naturalistic observation, interviews and rating scales, but it also included an experimental element, when mothers were asked to record infants' responses (a DV) to seven everyday situations (an IV).

### Long-term effects of privation (Hodges and Tizard, 1989)

In this natural experiment (see page 18), data about family and peer relations were collected using interviews and psychological tests, producing qualitative and quantitative data respectively. The qualitative data were used to provide further insights into the children's development; for example one mother said of her son, 'I wouldn't be surprised if one day when he was a teenager we woke up and he was gone'.

### Individual differences in stress responses (Friedman and Rosenman, 1974)

This study (see page 66) demonstrated that Type As were more likely than Type Bs to develop heart disease; the Type A/B typology was initially developed as the result of a survey of lay executives and physicians, who were asked for their opinion of what causes heart disease.

### Research methods give you added value

It's likely that you will study this chapter (for the Unit 'Investigating Behaviour') after either 'Understanding the Individual' (Chapters 1–3) or 'The Individual in the Social Context' (Chapters 6–12). So, you will already be familiar with a large number of Star Studies from those Topics. Now that you are studying research methods in their own right, go back to these Star Studies and look at them in a new way. Ask yourself, 'What kind of research method was used?'; 'What was the hypothesis?'; 'What kind of sampling technique was used?'; 'How was the DV measured?'; 'What were the strengths and limitations of the method(s) used?', and so on. You should be able to analyse the methodology of these studies very thoroughly. This would be an example of *integration* of your understanding across different parts of the course.

It can also work as a *two-way benefit*: describing and analysing the methodology of Star Studies will increase your understanding of research methods and enable you to answer the exam question on research methods. The exam question is just like a Star Study with queries like those outlined above.

**questions** `20`

1. A psychology class conducts a study on memory. Each student does a memory test first thing in the morning and then again in the afternoon. The table below shows how many items they got correct each time.

| Student | 1 | 2 | 3 | 4 | 5 | 6 | 7 | 8 | 9 | 10 |
|---|---|---|---|---|---|---|---|---|---|---|
| Morning test | 18 | 20 | 17 | 16 | 19 | 22 | 21 | 19 | 15 | 13 |
| Afternoon test | 20 | 18 | 15 | 12 | 18 | 20 | 16 | 16 | 17 | 14 |

   a. Calculate the mean, median and mode for each data set.
   b. Which measure of central tendency would be most suitable to use to describe this data? Explain your answer.
   c. Draw at least two graphs to illustrate this data: you could do a bar chart showing the means for each condition (morning and afternoon test) or a scattergram showing the relationship between the scores for each participant.
   d. From studying your graphs, what conclusions could you draw from this data?

2. In each of the following, identify the research method and, where relevant, the research technique(s) or design.
   a. Scores from a questionnaire 'How good is your memory' are related to Standard Grade results.
   b. A male or female confederate stands by the roadside with a broken down car to see if people are more likely to help a male or female.
   c. Psychology Higher results from two classes are compared to see if teacher A's teaching style was better than that of teacher B.
   d. Children are shown two films: one that shows a child being helpful and another that shows a child not being helpful. They then are given free-play time to see if they are more helpful.
   e. Students are asked to explain what methods they find most successful for revision.
   f. Interactions between mothers and their newborn babies are observed and comparisons made between first-time mothers and those who have had two or more children.
   g. A study on gambling is based around the experiences of one individual.

**activity** `7`

### Review

1. Now that you have come to the end of the chapter, write down all the new words that you have learned (that you can remember) and then check through the KEY TERMS boxes in this chapter to see what words you had forgotten. You might work with a partner and when you have finished get another pair to check your list. See who in the class can correctly identify the most terms. You could even record the results in a bar chart!
2. Make your own KEY TERMS quiz. On a set of cards, write all the key terms – one on each card. Write their definitions on a separate set of cards: match terms and definitions, or test each other using them.
3. Look back through this chapter and decide which topic you have found the most challenging. To help you understand this topic better, create something memorable for you and your classmates. It could be a PowerPoint presentation, a mobile, a poster for your classroom, a cartoon strip, a poem or even a rap.

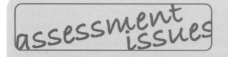

**assessment issues**

**The research topic described in the scenario used the method of naturalistic observation. Suggest how this research topic might be further investigated, using a multi-method approach. (ku 3 ae 0)**

Although the actual research topic described in the scenario can vary greatly in NABs and exam questions, the scenario always features a recognisable research method (or methods) that you have learned on your course, i.e. an experiment (lab, field, natural or quasi), a survey (questionnaire or interview), an observation, or a case study. But, as well as these straightforward *single* methods, the course content also covers '*multi-method approaches,* including case studies involving several methods and use of observation in experiments'. Make sure that you don't overlook these 'hybrid' methods, when revising.

## Chapter: Research methods

*In this section we show you student answers to a possible exam question on research methods plus examiner's comments on these answers. Remember that in the actual exam (and NABs) there will be a number of short-answer questions (such as those shown below) which will always add up to 20 marks.*

## Question 1

A psychologist studied the effects of physical appearance on people's compliance with a charitable request. She recruited a male student who normally wore two facial studs, one through his lower lip and the other through an eyebrow.

The male student asked passers-by to give a donation to a fictional charity on a Saturday morning in a busy shopping centre. He carried a collecting can and wore an 'official' badge. For the first hour he did not wear the studs and for the second hour he did. Each passer-by was subsequently stopped by the psychologist, who had been standing out of sight recording their behaviour.

She asked each person *why* they had given money or not. The results are shown below.

Quantitative data from study

|  | Student's appearance | |
| --- | --- | --- |
|  | With studs | Without studs |
| Gave money | 26 | 38 |
| Did not give money | 33 | 22 |

**(a)** Give a suitable experimental hypothesis for the research study described above, *and* state whether it is one-tailed or two-tailed. (*ku* 3 *ae* 0)

| Tom | Alice |
| --- | --- |
| *People give more money to someone not wearing a facial stud. This is one-tailed.* | *People are less likely to comply with a charitable request when someone is wearing a facial stud than when they aren't.* |

**Examiner's comments**   Of the 3 marks for this question, 2 are for the hypothesis and 1 for stating whether it's one-/two-tailed. Both students gain **2 out of 3 marks**, but in different ways. Tom is correct in stating that his hypothesis is one-tailed (1 out of 1 mark), but the hypothesis itself is sketchy and imprecise (1 out of 2 marks): it was not the *amount* of money that was measured, but whether people *gave* or *did not give*. He should also clarify the 'charity' setting, and the comparison between wearing and not wearing facial studs should be indicated.

Alice's hypothesis *does* express these elements precisely **(2 out of 2 marks)**; however, she has forgotten to say that it's one-tailed **(0 out of 1 mark)**.

**(b)** Describe the independent variable (IV) in this study. (*ku* 2 *ae* 0)

| Tom | Alice |
| --- | --- |
| *The IV is the variable that the experimenter has manipulated.* | *The IV is the person's appearance – wearing or not wearing a facial stud.* |

**Examiner's comments**   Although Tom does show some understanding of an IV, he has ignored three crucial words – '*in this study*', and therefore gains **0 out of 2 marks**. Research methods questions are *either* based on the specific scenario content – in which case they state 'in this study' (or similar), *or* they require you to show your knowledge of research methods in a more general way, for example just asking, 'What is meant by an "independent variable" in psychological research?'.

Alice gains the full **2 marks**; she has based her answer on information in the scenario and described the IV fully, including the two conditions or 'levels'.

**(c)** State *one* possible extraneous or confounding variable in this study, and explain how it could be controlled. (*ku* 1 *ae* 2)

| Tom | Alice |
| --- | --- |
| *One possible extraneous variable would be the time of day because it would be earlier in the day when the first condition was tested (not wearing a stud) and people might have been rushing to work and less likely to comply. You could deal with this by using counterbalancing – test people on two days: first day you test no stud, then with stud, and on second day, with stud and then no stud.* | *Participant variables can be extraneous variables so it might happen that the first group of people who were stopped just happened to be more charitable than the second group* |

**Examiner's comments**   This time, Tom *has* spotted the two parts of the question, and gets all **3 marks**.

Alice gets only **1 out of 3 marks** for identifying an appropriate extraneous variable; she has not explained how it could be controlled.

**(d)**  **Explain one ethical concern that arises in this study, and suggest how this might be overcome.** (*ku* 0  *ae* 4)

| Tom | Alice |
|---|---|
| Participants might be less likely to give money in the future because they were upset by being tricked by the psychologist. This could be dealt with by debriefing participants. | One issue is lack of informed consent before taking part. They were not told what the study was about; in fact they didn't even know they were taking part so they were observed without their consent. To overcome this problem the psychologist could offer them the chance to withhold their data as a form of retrospective consent. She could do this when she debriefed them after she had asked questions. Still, some people think retrospective consent isn't good enough. |

*Examiner's comments*   Although Tom's answer shows good understanding, it is too brief; it is a pity he did not further develop his points. He gains **2 out of 4 marks**. He might have pointed out the nature of the *deception* in this research, and that ethical codes state that researchers should avoid deception if at all possible. He could also have elaborated on how the debriefing would be done.
  Alice is awarded 4 out of 4 marks. Unlike Tom, she has not been afraid to 'state the obvious'.

**(e)**  **Give a definition of qualitative data, in psychological research.** (*ku* 2  *ae* 0)

| Tom | Alice |
|---|---|
| Qualitativet data provides information about feelings and thoughts. | Qualitative data is more complex than data in numbers. It would be words or descriptions about what something is like, or how something is experienced. You get qualitative data using open questions in a questionnaire or interview. |

*Examiner's comments*   Tom should know better than to write one very short sentence when there are 2 marks on offer! His definition of qualitative data, though not wrong, is limited, so he gets only **1 out of 2 marks.**
  In contrast, Alice's definition is accurate and her reference to sources of qualitative data indicates her understanding. Her answer is short but concise and worth the full **2 out of 2 marks**.

**(f)**  **(i)  Identify *one* example of quantitative data from the study described above.** (*ku* 1  *ae* 0)
    **(ii)  Identify *one* example of qualitative data from the study described above.** (*ku* 1  *ae* 0)

| Tom | Alice |
|---|---|
| (i) Amount of money they gave.<br>(ii) The reason they gave. | (i) Numbers of participants who gave money, e.g. 26 people gave money to the student with studs.<br>(ii) The reasons they gave to the researcher, e.g. 'I don't like to give money in public'. |

*Examiner's comments*   Tom loses marks through inaccurate reading of the scenario: for (i) he gets **0 out of 1 mark**. For (ii) he just scrapes **1 out of 1 mark**; he may have felt it was obvious that he was referring to the second part of the procedure where the researcher stopped the participant, but it is always wise to give a clear description.
  Alice's answers are clear and precise; therefore she gets **2 out of 2 marks**.

**(g)**  **The psychologist could have decided to use a non-experimental method, such as naturalistic observation. Briefly describe the method of naturalistic observation, and discuss *one* of its weaknesses.** (*ku* 2  *ae* 2)

| Tom | Alice |
|---|---|
| In a naturalistic observation an observer watches people as they go about their normal lives and they are probably not aware of being observed. One problem with this kind of study is an ethical one because you are really invading the person's privacy even if it is a public space. | Naturalistic observation is when you observe people in a natural environment like their home or at work or in the street and you have not changed any of the environmental variables. It is all as it normally is. You should have a clipboard with an observation schedule to tick the behaviours, or they can be filmed. One weakness of this method is that if you have more than one observer they may not agree on how to record behaviour, for example one may think someone is smiling but the other might think it's not a smile. They would have to have inter-observer reliability and they could do this by watching videos and agree what is a smile or a frown etc. |

*Examiner's comments*   Tom gains only 1 of the *ku* marks, as his description of the method is very sketchy, and only 1 *ae* mark, for the same reason. Total of **2 out of 4 marks** (1/2 *ku*  1/2 *ae*).
  Alice's answer provides a fairly clear and thorough response, and gets the **full 4 marks**. She has been particularly careful to 'discuss' the weakness rather than simply stating it.

Overall marks for the answer:
Tom has a total of **11 out of 20 marks**, an answer typical of a grade C exam performance.
Alice has an impressive **17 out of 20 marks**, a fairly assured Grade A.

Research methods are systematic approaches to discovering things about the world.

Psychologists test their theories and explanations by conducting research studies. If you are to fully understand, and evaluate, psychological studies, you need to plan, conduct and report your own research study.

| Chapter contents | Specification content for the topic 'Research Skill' | Comment |
|---|---|---|
| **Aspect 1 Where do you begin?** | | *The skills that are assessed through the RI are the skills needed to plan, conduct and report research.* |
| page 129 | The research skills for this unit involve:<br>• planning and implementing your own psychological Research Investigation (RI)<br>• a report of your research investigation | ***1. Planning skills***<br>*The planning skills will be shown in your practical portfolio, which will consist of the **research project plan and log** of your RI. This will resemble a real-life research proposal, which is always a researcher's first step. Completion of your plan and log makes the actual report writing considerably more straightforward. This log is assessed internally as part of the NABs (worth 50% of the marks for this* Unit*).* |
| **Aspect 2 The research project plan and project log** | | |
| Exemplar: a model research project plan and log with examiner's comments<br>    page 131 | In doing the RI students will develop the ability to:<br>• manage the various elements of a research project within a schedule<br>• devise ethical standard procedures<br>• obtain a sample of participants and collect data from them<br>• analyse the data<br>• draw conclusions and write a formal research report | ***2. Conducting skills***<br>*The RI is conducted in small groups of no more than four, but written up by each individual. The whole class may be doing the same study but working in small groups for data collection. Each stage of implementation is recorded in your log.*<br><br>***3. Reporting skills***<br>*The reporting skills will be shown in your research investigation report. This must be written up individually; no two reports will be the same because each candidate will express themselves differently. The RI is externally assessed and is worth 20% of the marks for the* Course*.* |
| **Aspect 3 The research investigation report** | | |
| Report presentation<br>    page 133<br>Report format and mark scheme<br>    page 134<br>Exemplar: a model report with examiner's comments<br>    page 135 | It is envisaged that students will spend 25–30 hours for preparation, including learning necessary research skills and how to write a report | |

## Aspect 1:  Where do you begin?

As part of the Higher course assessment you are required to conduct a research investigation as part of the Unit on Investigating Behaviour.

The Research Investigation (RI) is a gift from the SQA to you. The SQA is giving you some easily obtained marks – as long as you follow the instructions exactly.

Also on the SQA website, you'll find advice in *Your Coursework* and in *RI Guidelines*

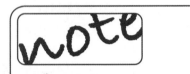

**Steps in the research process**
- Establish research question (aim) and variables
- Carry out background reading in appropriate areas
- Establish hypotheses
- Design research
- Plan schedule
- Collect data
- Analyse data
- Write draft, receive teacher feedback
- Write final report.

## 1. What should I study?

The SQA publishes a document called *Research Investigation Briefs* which specifies what projects are acceptable in any exam year. You *must* select a project from this brief (which can be found at www.sqa.org.uk; select Psychology and follow the link to material on the Research Investigation). The list of projects is drawn from the Topic areas of the specification. For each project, a brief is given which includes background information, aim of the study, experimental/alternative hypothesis, method, specific ethical considerations, results and references.

## 2. How should I plan my project?

The SQA supplies a *research project plan and log (practical portfolio)* to help you plan your project. A filled-in example is shown on pages 131–132.

This log is assessed internally and it is not handed in with the report itself. This means that some students regard it as just another hoop to jump through but it isn't. It is like a real-life research proposal and it ensures that you have carefully planned what you are going to do and have sought approval from your teacher/lecturer before starting the investigation. If you don't do this you may find that:

- Your project was ethically unacceptable.
- The design was poorly thought through and the data you collected were meaningless.
- You didn't leave enough time to complete the investigation and report.

The log gives your teacher/lecturer an opportunity to carefully monitor your progress and ensure that you do get maximum marks.

## 3. What do I have to hand in?

After you have planned your study and collected the data, you must write a *research investigation report.* This report must be your own work. You may have conducted the planning and data collection with a small group (four or fewer) but must write the report yourself. The report should be 1500–2000 words long (excluding the appendices) and is normally handed in before Easter. It is marked externally (not by your teacher/lecturer). It is the report that gets the mark but careful planning will ensure that you maximise what you can put into the report.

More details about how to write the report are on given on page 133, and there is a model exemplar on pages 135–139 with specific instructions about what goes in each section.

Once you have finished your RI, you must also hand in your completed *Plan and log*. This is marked by your teacher/lecturer, and constitutes half the NAB marks for the Unit.

**Ethical considerations**

**You are strongly advised to avoid anything that raises even the smallest ethical concern. In particular you should avoid:**
- **Under-age children as participants:** The SQA states that all participants must be 16 years of age or over, regardless of any parental consent gained.
- **Psychological and physical harm:** No one (participants, the general public or researchers) should be put in any situation which may cause alarm or potential danger, even if this has been done in previous psychological research.
- **Privacy:** Participants should not be questioned on aspects of their sexuality or their mental health, including eating disorders.
- **Confidentiality:** Appendices should not include names/addresses or any other means of identifying participants.
- **As far as possible, investigations should be kept 'in house':** If the public is used great care should be taken not to offend in any way.

(From SQA Ethics guidance)

*IF IN DOUBT, DON'T DO IT!*

# Aspect 2:  The research project plan and log

## Exemplar: a model research plan and project log with examiner's comments

Unit: Psychology - Investigating Behaviour (Higher)

## Part 1 – Research project plan and log (Practical portfolio).

——— *This portfolio accounts for 50% of assessment marks for the Unit.* ———

| | | | |
|---|---|---|---|
| **Candidate:** | *Rosie Setter* | **Teacher/lecturer:** | *Mr D. Sutherland* |
| **Centre/group:** | *01126* | **Date:** | *March 5th 2002* |

The project plan and log is in three parts. Over the duration of the research project, candidates should complete the following planning and log sheets:

*Section A: Planning - the research question*
*Section B: Planning – the research method and design*
*Section C: Log of progress – insert planned dates before you start, and tick/give dates when completed*

### Section A: Planning - the research question

| | |
|---|---|
| **Title of your study** | MEMORY and ORGANISATION |
| **Relevant area of Psychology** E.g. Social, Individual Differences, Cognitive, Developmental or Biological. | Cognitive psychology |
| **Specific concept/theory which study relates to** | Organisation in long-term memory, e.g. categories, conceptual hierarchies, semantic coding, effect on recall. |
| **Related research studies** Give researchers' names, and dates | Bousfield (1953), Bower and Springston (1970), Craik and Lockhart (1972), Mandler (1967). |
| **Aim of your study** | To discover whether organisation of information into a hierarchy leads to improved recall. |
| **Experimental/alternative hypothesis** | Participants remember more words from organised word lists than from random order word lists. |
| **Null hypothesis** | There is no difference in recall between the two conditions, organised and random word lists; any difference found must be the result of chance factors. |

### Section B: Planning – the research method and design

| | |
|---|---|
| **Method** Experimental or non-experimental; if non-experimental, state specific method | Experimental ('lab' experiment) |
| **Design** Independent measures, repeated measures, matched pairs, or correlation | Repeated measures |
| **Variables to be investigated** If experimental, give IV (conditions) and DV – say exactly how these are put into practice and measured. If non-experimental, state variables to be correlated | IV = Presentation of word lists. Condition A = words organised into hierarchy. Condition B = words in random order. DV = Number of words recalled |
| **Variables to be controlled** | Same (standardised) instructions to participants; same environment; similar materials across conditions; same procedure e.g. timings; level of difficulty of word lists; order effects (a confounding variable) controlled by counterbalancing: one group do condition A then B, the other group do condition B then A. |

**Examiner's comments**

This plan and log shows all the key points of the research project, in adequate detail. The student has completed sections A and B, and the 'planned completion dates' in section C, before starting her RI and has monitored her progress in section C, as she went along.

Having carefully set out all the key information in the planning sections, this student will find her RI much easier to write.

| Sample<br>Details on: number of participants, ages, sex, etc.<br>Sampling technique | 12 participants, all female, aged 16–18 years. All are students at the school, and none are psychology students, i.e. all naïve.<br><br>Opportunity sampling |
|---|---|
| Materials/apparatus required<br>Give a list of specific materials.<br>(Full text of brief, request for consent, standardised instructions, and debrief should be attached) | Brief for participants and consent form, debrief, standardised instructions, 2 word lists, pen and paper, timer. |
| Outline of procedure to be followed | Participants will be:<br>- invited to take part, briefed, asked to sign the consent form<br>- given standardised instructions<br>- tested in groups of 3: given one of the word lists to learn for 5 minutes<br>- asked to do an interference task<br>- write the words they can recall (3 minutes)<br>- asked to follow the same procedure with the second list<br>- finally, they will be thanked, debriefed, asked for any comments / questions. |
| Ethical issues to be addressed in this study<br>To include both the ethical aspects of standard procedure and issues specific to this study. | Obtain informed consent. Ps to be told that it will be confidential, and they will have the right to withdraw, and to see the results. In this study Ps might be distressed or embarrassed at their performance, so researchers will assure them it is not an intelligence test, and they must not worry if they get a low score. |
| Description of data analysis techniques to be used | Raw data tables; calculations and summary table of means, medians and ranges (in each condition and overall), bar graphs of means/medians. |

## Section C: Log of progress – insert planned dates before you start, and tick/give dates when completed

| Task | Planned completion date | Actual completion date | Comments<br>Did this go well? Were there any difficulties? How were these overcome? Was a change of plan necessary? |
|---|---|---|---|
| Form group/ share contact details/ plan data-gathering | 7th December | 7th December | Did this in class. Planned a time to meet once a week. No problems. |
| Write brief, standardised instructions, etc. | 10th December | 12th December | Took longer than we thought – had to work on it at home. |
| Prepare other materials | 15th December | 17th December | One group member off ill, so materials were completed a bit late. |
| Collect own data | 8th January | 8th January | Did this on time! |
| Collate group data | 9th January | 12th January | One member had not tested enough participants – had to wait till he found more. |
| Analyse data | 15th January | 20th January | Had to get teacher's help with this, but managed it only a few days behind schedule. |

**To submit your practical portfolio for assessment, hand in these completed planning and log sheets, with the following attachments:**

- actual materials used for collecting data, including participant responses (e.g. samples of completed questionnaires or task sheets) where applicable. ✔
- raw data tables ✔
- summary table(s) and graph(s) ✔
- calculations ✔

| Candidate Declaration: I certify that this Practical Portfolio is my own work. | Teacher/Lecturer Declaration: I certify that the production of this work has been supervised, and to the best of my knowledge it is the candidate's own work. |
|---|---|
| Signature: _____ Rosie Setler _____ | Signature: _____ A. Teacher _____ |
| Date: _____ March 5, 2002 _____ | Date: _____ March 18, 2002 _____ |

**Examiner's comments**
Although this log shows that the student completed the tasks a little later than her own deadline, she has set the planned completion dates to allow for 'slippage' (this is common practice in professional project management). In your log, you could add further steps, for example 'complete first draft of RI report', 'submit final version' (this final date will be set by your teacher/lecturer).

**Examiner's comments**
This student has treated the list of attachments as a checklist, ticking each one – this is a good idea. All of these attachments are materials already required for her RI. They are not shown here, but, for your own log, make sure that you have kept copies of these materials when you hand in your RI (it's best to keep your whole RI saved to disk, if possible).

# Aspect 3: The research investigation report

## Report presentation

Assessed on:

- quality of presentation (written or word processed)
- contents page
- pages numbered
- all sections in conventional format
- tables/graphs/appendices numbered and referenced in the text.

## Report style

Should comply with the following:

- title should be formal and appropriate to the actual study
- appropriate use of terminology
- formal style of expression, appropriate to the discipline; past tense used throughout (passive/impersonal voice)
- anonymity/confidentiality observed
- coherence of whole report.

### Tense

Scientific reports are usually written in the past tense because they are describing things that have already happened. There are some cases, however, where the present tense is appropriate – when a statement concerns something that remains applicable: for example, 'Flanagan found … which shows that … is more effective.

### Person and voice

Scientific reports are usually written in the third person; for example 'the researchers' instead of 'we', and in the passive voice, for example 'Participants were asked to …' instead of 'I asked them to …'.

### General points

- Check your spelling and punctuation.
- Write/print report on A4 on one side only.
- There is no need for fancy binders, a single staple is sufficient and means the report is easy to read.
- Keep a copy of your report, on disk and/or on paper. In particular, you will need copies of your materials, raw data tables, summary table(s), graph(s) and calculations, for your plan and log.

### Journal articles

It may help if you see what a real psychology report looks like. There are some published on the web, for example:

- Milgram's obedience study (www.radford.edu/~jaspelme/gradsoc/obedience/Migram_Obedience.pdf)
- an article on decay and interference (www.msu.edu/~ema/altmg02.pdf).

### What kind of help?

Your teacher/lecturer may offer you feedback on the first draft of your report. Such feedback is very valuable so make sure you do use it. What you must NOT use is material copied from a book or from the Internet *unless* you present it as a quotation and cite the reference and page number. Even if you rephrase the text, you must cite the reference and not present it as your own.

   Copying someone else's work is called *plagiarism*, and the SQA will award zero marks for your project and may also cancel your entry for *all* exam subjects in that year. It is a very serious business. (See SQA document *Your Coursework: a guide for candidates*).

# Report format and mark scheme

This information is taken from the SQA *Research Investigation Guidelines*.

| Section | Sub-sections | Marks available |
|---|---|---|
| **Abstract**<br>150–200 words | Short summary. | 5 |
| **Introduction**<br>*Why you did it*<br>500–650 words | Background research (*5 marks*)<br>Rationale/link to current study and aims (*2 marks*)<br>Experimental/alternative and null hypotheses (*3 marks*) | 10 |
| **Method**<br>*How you did it*<br>35–400 words | Enough detail so that this exact study could be replicated. Written in prose and not bullet lists.<br>Design (*4 marks*)<br>Sample, Materials, Procedure (*4 marks*) | 8 |
| **Results**<br>*What you found out*<br>100–150 words | To include descriptive statistics:<br>• Summary table of data (i.e. appropriate measures of central tendency and dispersion) with clear titles/explanation.<br>• Graphs. Label axes and provide legend for any abbreviations. Also include units of measurement.<br>Raw data and calculations to be placed in the Appendix.<br>NB You are not required to use inferential statistics (statistical tests). You should only use the word 'significant' if you have used inferential statistics. | 8 |
| **Discussion**<br>*What you think it means*<br>500–650 words | Statement and explanation of results (*4 marks*)<br>Evaluation of methodology and design (*5 marks*)<br>Implications of results and suggestions for future research (*3 marks*) | 12 |
| **References** | In the body of the report sources cited by name and date; page numbers given for any quotes used.<br>Details of all sources cited and bibliography of all sources used. | 3 |
| **Appendices** | Standardised instructions, questionnaires, observation schedules and any other materials used. In the case of questionnaires, ensure that the marking instructions are included.<br>Raw data, calculations. | No mark |
| **Presentation** | Use of appropriate format for a scientific report. | 1 |
| **Style** | Use of appropriate terminology, style of expression and coherence of overall report. | 3 |
| **Marks total** | | 50 |

# Exemplar: a model report with examiner's comments

## Candidate declaration

I confirm that the materials submitted within are my own work; I confirm that I have read the *Your Coursework* booklet and understand the consequences of submitting work that is not my own/has been plagiarised from another source.

Signature _____

Date _____

The booklet *Your Coursework* can be read at www.sqa.org.uk/files_ccc/ YourCoursework2006_ 101105.pdf

Title page

### An investigation into ORGANISATION in MEMORY
Psychology Higher RI report

By Rosie Setter, Brigadoon Royal Academy

**Title** *(no marks)*

This should be short but specific.

Avoid catchy titles, such as 'What do we know about memory?' The title should clearly convey the research question.

Page 1 of the report

## Abstract

The aim of this study was to investigate factors that may lead to improved recall. Previous research has found that words that are organised into conceptual hierarchies are easier to recall than randomly ordered words, and that people tend to automatically organise words into categories when recalling them.

The independent variable was kind of word list (organised or random) and the dependent variable was number of words recalled. The experimental hypothesis was 'participants remember more words from organised word lists than from random order word lists'.

The method used was a lab experiment with a repeated measures design. The opportunity sample of 12 girls, aged 16–18, were required to study and later recall (after 1 minute) two lists of words which were either hierarchically organised or random in order. The presentation of lists was counterbalanced to prevent order effects and to account for the two words lists being of different difficulty. Participants were given 3 minutes to recall each list.

The results of the study were that mean recall was higher for the organised word lists (21.8) than for the random lists (1.76) which suggests that using mnemonic techniques that involve organisation will be a successful revision strategy.

*This abstract is 200 words long.*

**Abstract** *(5 marks)*

The abstract is a short summary of the whole report. It might be a good idea to write this when you have finished writing the whole report but it is placed at the beginning so readers can get an overview of the study. It should be about 150–200 words long, and should include:

• Aim

• Short statement of issue being investigated (e.g. mention previous research on this topic)

• Identification of IV and DV, or co-variables

• Summary of the alternative (or experimental) hypothesis

• Method and design used

• Brief outline of procedure

• Sample size and method of selection

• Summary of main results

• Brief conclusion.

You only have a limited number of words so make each statement concise but clear.

Page 2 of the report

## Introduction

This study deals with the area of cognitive psychology and the topic of memory. An important aspect of any research is being able to apply it to the real world and one way to do this is to use memory research to help us improve our memories. There are many techniques to do this which are backed up by psychological research. For example the effectiveness of mnemonics such as acronyms or rhymes or method of loci can all be explained by the principle of organisation. One example, for remembering the planets, is "My Very Easy Method Just Speeds Up Naming Planets" (www.youramazingbrain.org.uk, 2006). Having topics organised in to meaningful segments improves our ability to recall them.

For example, research on chunking has shown that people have better recall when letters or digits can be chunked. One study of chunking was by Bower and Springston (1970). They showed participants a sequence of letters which was either random or organised so that some letters formed well-known groups, such as FBI or BBC. The participants who were given the 'chunked' list were able to recall many more letters.

Bousfield (1953) conducted a study that showed how organising material is related to memory. In this study words lists were organised by having four categories: names of people, names of animals, professions and vegetables. In each category there were 15 appropriate items. These 60 words were then jumbled up and given to participants to learn. When the participants were asked to freely recall the words they tended to cluster the words from particular categories together. This shows that people tend to organise material when they are recalling things.

Craik and Lockhart (1972) proposed that enduring memories are formed through 'deep' processing i.e. when we process material semantically; organisation is a form of semantic processing. This is supported by a study by Mandler (1967) who asked participants to sort 52 word cards into categories of their own choosing. They had to repeat this until they had two identical sorts and were then asked to recall the words. Despite not being asked to learn the words they could recall almost half of them. This shows that categorisation (or organisation) is related to memory.

Page 3 of the report

Bower did a study (Bower et al., 1969) which showed how organisation is not only related to memory but can improve memory. In this study participants were given 112 words to learn. Participants were shown words organised into conceptual hierarchies as shown below or given words in a random order. Recall was 2–3 times better for organised word hierarchies.

An example of a conceptual hierarchy

|  | Minerals | | | |
| --- | --- | --- | --- | --- |
| Metals | | | Stones | |
| Rare | Common | Alloys | Precious | Masonry |
| Platinum | Aluminum | Bronze | Sapphire | Limestone |
| Silver | Copper | Steel | Emerald | Granite |
| Gold | Lead | Brass | Diamond | Marble |

All of this research demonstrates the link between organisation and memory. In this current study the aim was to investigate the effect of categories and organisation on recall, by conducting a study similar to the study by Bower et al. and using organised word lists. In the research studies above it is arguable that it was long-term memory rather than short-term memory that was tested since recall was more than 30 seconds after learning, so long-term memory was tested as well.

The experimental hypothesis was that participants remember more words from organised word lists than from random order word lists. (This is a one-tailed hypothesis.)

The null hypothesis was that there is no difference in recall between the two conditions: organised and random word lists, and that any difference found is the result of chance factors.

*This introduction is 565 words long.*

---

### Introduction *(Total 10 marks)*

This section should provide the background to your study. It should start with general background information (related theories and studies) and should progress towards the specific aims and hypotheses for this particular study.

- In total the introduction should be 500–650 words long.
- For marking it is subdivided into three components (see below).

### 1. Background research *(5 marks)*

Use research (theories and/or studies) to introduce the area of the research question, including the domain of psychology within which it is 'located', relevant theory(ies) and concept(s) and related previous research.

All of this material must be related to your specific research question rather than be a general essay on the topic area.

If you are modifying an existing study, give details of the original study.

*Be focused, like a tornado*
Start with a broad statement of the research area.
Narrow down to the specific topic.
Leading logically to your experimental/alternative hypothesis.

### 2. Link to current study and aims *(2 marks)*

Make an explicit link between the research background and your hypotheses. You should state the aim(s) of your investigation.

It is advisable to have a single aim. There is no reward for conducting research with many aims/hypotheses and your report will just become more muddled – stick to one aim, one experimental/alternative hypothesis.

### 3. Hypotheses *(3 marks)*

State both the experimental/alternative and null hypotheses.

Make sure the variables are clearly expressed in the experimental/alternative hypothesis, and the conditions of the IV (where applicable) are indicated.

State clearly whether the experimental/alternative hypothesis is one- or two-tailed.

Page 4 of the report

## Method

### Design

This study was a laboratory experiment. This method was chosen because it means extraneous variables can be controlled and causal relationships can be demonstrated. Repeated measures design was chosen because participant variables can be controlled, which would otherwise be confounding.

In order to control for word difficulty two lists of words were used (A and B). Half the participants had word list A in organised form and word list B in a random order, and vice versa. This was done by giving the first 6 participants list A organised and the last 6 participants had list B organised.

Furthermore conditions were counterbalanced to avoid order effects so half of each group of 6 participants did the organised condition first and half did the random condition first.

The IV had 2 levels (conditions): organised or random order. The DV was number of words recalled.

All participants were given the same standardised instructions and were tested in a similar environment, without distractions. In both conditions, the timings were the same for the presentation of word lists (5 minutes), interference task (1 minute) and recall (3 minutes).

### Sample/Participants

Twelve participants were selected from the target population of the school, using opportunity sampling. They were all girls aged 16–18. All of the participants were naïve, they were not psychology students.

Page 5 of the report

### Materials

The materials were the word lists, and a pen and paper to record the words recalled. A timer, a brief including a request for consent, standardised instructions, and a debrief were also used.

There were two sets of 40 words, organised into a hierarchy in one condition (see Appendix 1).

### Procedure

• All participants were asked to sign an informed consent form (see Appendix 2). Ps were told that they would be given a test but it was not an intelligence test, and they must not worry if they get a low score (to avoid unduly distressing them). Ps were also told that the data collected would be confidential and that they would have the right to withdraw, and told they would see the results.

• Participants were tested in groups of 3.

• Each group was tested in a small office seated at separate tables. They were tested in the morning.

• Once sat down they were given the standardised instructions to read (see Appendix 3).

• They were then given one word list and told they had 5 minutes to learn the words.

• The words were taken away and after one minute the participants were asked to recall the words. During the interval the participants were given an 'interference task – they were asked to count backwards in 3s from 1000 to prevent rehearsal. Finally they were given 3 minutes to recall the words.

• Next they were given a second word list and the same procedure was repeated.

• At the end the participants were debriefed (see debriefing in Appendix 4), thanked for taking part and given a contact phone number if they had any queries.

This method section is 496 words long.

This is longer than the recommended length, which is only a rough guide and is balanced out by other sections of the RI which are shorter.

## Method (Total 8 marks)

The main criterion for awarding marks in this section is whether you have provided sufficient detail for your study to be replicated (repeated) by someone else.

The method is like writing a recipe for a cake. You need to provide every detail so that someone else could do the same thing; this is replication.

It is not just a matter of whether someone could do a *similar* study but whether they could do the exact same study. If one varies small details, such as kind of participants this may explain why the findings differ, so replication must be identical as far as possible in order to validate the original findings.

• 350–400 words is about right for the method section.

• For marking, it is subdivided into two components as described below:

### 1. Design (4 marks)

State whether an experimental or a non-experimental *method* was used, and identify the actual *method*.

• If experimental, identify the experimental design (e.g. repeated measures).

• Outline briefly why this method and design were chosen: for example, provide an advantage of the method/design that applies to this study.

• For experimental studies, state how participants were assigned to experimental/control groups and how many were in each group.

• Describe IV/DV or co-variables fully, including different conditions and the meaning of DV scores.

State any controls used (e.g. extraneous/ confounding variables, standardised instructions). This should be a *very* detailed account.

### 2. Other aspects of the method (4 marks)

**Sample and participants:** How many, how were they selected and from what target population? Include any other relevant details (e.g. were they 'naïve'; what age and sex?).

**Materials:** Much of this should be placed in the appendix but everything should be identified here, such as: informed consent, standardised instructions, debrief, test materials, questionnaires and marking scheme, observation schedule, diagrams/pictures of apparatus used and layout of research situation.

**Procedure:** this is a step-by-step explanation of what happened, including ethical procedures. If the study was experimental, make sure you explain the different variations of the IV. And make sure you do record all details, such as whether participants were tested alone or as a group, what time of day participants were tested/observed and so on.

Page 6 of the report

### Results

*The results are summarised in the table below. The mean and median are given as they are appropriate measures of central tendency for interval data, as is the case of memory recall scores. The mean is best because it takes all the values of the data into account but the median is also useful because it is not affected by extreme scores. The range gives a measure of how dispersed the scores were and thus gives a fuller description of the data sets.*

### Summary table

*The table shows the number of words recalled in each experimental condition. The raw data and calculations of the means, medians and ranges are shown in Appendix 5.*

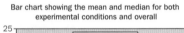

Number of words recalled

| | Organised condition | Random condition | All data |
|---|---|---|---|
| Mean | 21.8 | 17.6 | 19.3 |
| Median | 20.5 | 17 | 18.5 |
| Range | 22 | 18 | 24 |

### Graph

*This shows the results at a glance.*

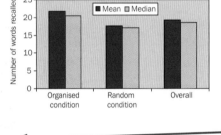

Bar chart showing the mean and median for both experimental conditions and overall

*The results do appear to support the experimental hypothesis that participants remember organised word lists better (mean = 21.8, median = 20.5) than random order word lists (mean =17.6, median =17) because the mean and median are higher for the organised condition than for the random condition. Recall is better when words are presented in an organised manner.*

> The results section is 179 words long.

> The main factors for gaining high marks for your discussion are to *discuss* the issues raised and to be thorough. It is more about *quality* (elaboration) than *quantity* (number of points made).

Page 7 of the report

### Discussion
#### Summary of results and relevance

*The results of this study show that organising information into categories leads to better recall rather than trying to learn an unorganised (random) word list, supporting the experimental hypothesis. The difference between the two conditions was quite large – in the organised condition participants remembered an average of about 3 more words than in the random condition. Some of the participants commented that it was much easier to learn the words when they were organised. This leads to the conclusion that long-term memory can be improved through organisation.*

*One interesting point to note is that sometimes participants 'recalled' words that were not in the list but did belong to one of the categories. This demonstrates semantic coding confusion.*

*All the results can be explained in terms of semantic processing, suggested by Craik and Lockhart (1972); participants remembered things better in organised hierarchies as it is more meaningful. Organisation may also reflect the way long-term memories are stored, as suggested by the study by Bousfield (1953) which showed that people actually recalled words in an organised fashion. Our memories may be organised in hierarchies.*

---

### Results *(8 marks)*

In this section you should use descriptive statistics to provide a summary of your results.

- 100–150 words is about right for the results section.
- Start with a *few sentences* explaining what descriptive statistics you have used and *why* in relation to the data and the research aims.
- Provide a *summary table* of data (appropriate measures of central tendency and dispersion) with clear titles/explanation. Raw data and calculations should be placed in the Appendix. (If the study was correlational, the full table of pairs of scores could be put here.)
- Use *graphs* to summarise your data, such as bar or pie charts, or a scattergram in the case of correlational analysis.
- End with a *statement* of the result and whether or not it supports the experimental/ alternative hypothesis.

Note in particular:

- There is no need to present lots of different graphs; one is often sufficient.
- Do not use participant-by-participant bar charts (see page 100) as these are meaningless.
- Make sure you support the graphs/charts with explanations in prose.
- Provide a title for all graphs/charts, label axes and include a legend for any abbreviations. Also include units of measurement.

**NB You should only use the word 'significant' if you have used inferential statistics (a statistical test), which are not required. If you do wish to use inferential statistics you can, but there are no extra marks. You can find easy instructions for inferential statistics in Cara Flanagan *Research Methods for AQA 'A' Psychology*. Nelson Thornes.**

---

### Discussion *(Total 12 marks)*

This section should provide a commentary and evaluation of the results, linking the results back to the original research and hypothesis, and forwards to future research.

- In total the discussion should be 500–650 words long.
- For marking it is subdivided into three components, as described below:

---

### Summary of results and relevance *(4 marks)*

State the results and conclude whether or not the experimental/alternative hypothesis has been supported.

*Explain* your results, for example discuss some examples.

Consider the relevance of your results for current theory/concept(s) and the implications for broader theoretical issues.

Page 8 of the report

## Evaluation of method and design

There were some limitations to the study. The sample was taken from a very limited target population – A level students. It is likely that the memory abilities of this particular group are not the same as the wider population since they are academic students and also young. This could be improved by selecting participants from a wider spectrum of abilities and age groups.

A second limitation is that using word lists to study memory only represents one kind of memory and it may not be reasonable to assume that the same factors apply to all aspects of memory. In order to study memory in general rather than just this kind of memory the study should test people on other things, like memory for pictures.

An important point is that the results might have been influenced by demand characteristics because the organised word lists looked different. The words in the organised word lists were in groups so it looked less daunting than the long list of random words. Therefore the random word lists should have been put into groups as well so both lists looked the same.

From an ethical viewpoint participants might have been distressed, a point that had been considered at the start but they still might have been distressed despite the fact they were told it wasn't an intelligence test. Getting a low score on the memory test might mean that some participants would have less confidence in themselves when studying for exams. In order to deal with this debriefing should have made everyone feel they had done quite well and/or that the reasons for poor performance on this test weren't related to intelligence.

## Implications and further research

The implications of this study could be applied to advice for exam revision. The results suggest that one way to improve your memory is to organise your material into categories and hierarchies. There are various revision techniques that use this idea such as mind maps and acronyms (Your amazing brain, 2006). Many students spend time organising their notes and this research suggests that categorising is an effective strategy to improve memory.

This research might be extended to look at the effects of visual images on recall so that different kinds of memory were studied rather than just word lists. For example participants might be given a set of images that were either in random order or grouped together in categories and see whether recall was better for the grouped items.

*Conclusion:* The experimental hypothesis was supported; participants recalled more words when they were presented in a hierarchically organised list (mean = 21.8) than when presented in a random order (mean = 17.6). This leads us to conclude that organisation is one way to improve memory.

This discussion is 644 words long.

Page 9 of the report

## References

Your amazing brain (2006) [[online]]. Bristol, At-Bristol. Available from: www.youramazingbrain.org.uk/yourmemory/mem_tricks.htm (accessed 10th March 2006).

Bousfield, W.A. (1953) The occurrence of clustering in the recall of randomly arranged associates. *Journal of General Psychology*, 49, 229–240

Bower, G.H., Clark, M., Lesgold, A., and Winzenz, D. (1969) Hierarchical retrieval schemes, in recall categorised word lists, *Journal of Verbal Learning and Verbal Behaviour*, 8, 323–43.

Bower, G.H. and Springston, F. (1970) Pauses as recording points in a letter series. *Journal of Experimental Psychology*, 83, 421–30.

Craik, F.I.M., and Lockhart, R.S. (1972) cited in Cardwell, M. and Flanagan, C. (2005) *Psychology AS: The complete companion.* Nelson Thornes.

Mandler, G. (1967) Organisation and memory. In Spence, K.W. and Spence, J.T. (Eds.) *The psychology of learning and motivation, Vol. I.* London: Academic Press.

Total marks
50/50

---

**Evaluation of method and design**
*(5 marks)*

Consider specific weaknesses of your study, including ethical ones. Do not simply say, 'The sample was too small and unrepresentative', because this is true of most studies – select specific problems.

Suggest remedies for the problems. Note that 'remedies' are not the same as 'suggestions for future research' – in the case of 'suggestions' you are likely to be testing a new hypothesis.

**Implications and further research**
*(3 marks)*

Briefly discuss implications of the findings, suggestions for new research arising from the results of this study, and/or 'real world' applications.

Conclude with a brief summary of the main statistical conclusion(s) in relation to hypotheses.

**References** *(Total 3 marks)*

Use the references on the left as a guide to the conventional format. Note that journal articles are recorded in a slightly different style to books.

Ensure that all sources are included in this list and referenced by name and date in the body of the report.

**Presentation and style**
*(1 + 3 marks)*

See notes on page 133.

The appendices have not been included in this book but would need to be present and correct to receive full marks.

On these pages there is a student report which would only get a mark of 25 out of 50, approximately equivalent to a Grade C for this component. Try putting yourself in the examiner's shoes: provide marks for each section of the report and comments about what could be improved. You can find a blank marksheet to help you do this, on the web **www.nelsonthornes.com/higher**, where there is also a marked version of this report, to compare with your marks. Then rewrite the report so it would get a perfect mark of 50.

### Research Investigation:
### Stress and Physical Illness

By Craig Lang
Bannock High School

**Abstract**

NB The material in this introduction is an example of plagiarism. You are not allowed to copy text from out of a book. (We have done it here because it is copied from our own book!)

---

**Page 2 of the report**

## Introduction

Much of our understanding of the nature of stress can be traced back to the pioneering work of Hans Selye. He conducted research with rats, subjecting them to different unpleasant stimuli (injections, extreme cold, severe pain) and realised that it didn't matter what the stimulus was, the physiological response was always the same. The stress response is important to the survival of an animal because the physiological changes associated with stress are essential in conditions of fight or flight, i.e. it is an adaptive response, an essential part of our survival.

The physiological changes Selye observed in his experimental rats were caused by prolonged exposure to a stressor, often in situations of low control. Despite the stress response being adaptive, there are obviously lots of occasions where, like Selye's rats, we are also exposed to prolonged stressful situations and feel powerless to escape. It is in these conditions that stress becomes more problematic, and may lead to ill health.

Selye explained the relationship between stress and ill heath in terms of the General Adaptation Syndrome:

Stage 1   Alarm reaction: Adrenaline is produced, leading to 'fight-or-flight' activity. There is some activation of the HPA axis, producing cortisol.

Stage 2   Resistance: If the stress continues then it is necessary to find some means of coping. The body is adapting to the demands of the environment, but at the same time resources are gradually being depleted.

---

**Page 3 of the report**

Stage 3   Exhaustion: Eventually the body's systems can no longer maintain normal functioning. At this point the initial symptoms may reappear (sweating, raised heart rate, etc.). The adrenal gland may be damaged from previous over-activity, and the immune system may not be able to cope because production of necessary proteins (e.g. cortisol) has been slowed in favour of other needs. The result may be seen in stress-related illnesses such as ulcers, depression, cardiovascular problems and other mental and physical illnesses.

There are many studies that support this model. For example, Brady (1958) used pairs of monkeys. One monkey (the 'executive') was given the task of controlling electric shocks that were administered to itself and another monkey (the 'yoked control'). The executive monkey died within a few weeks due to a perforated ulcer. Cohen et al. (1993) used the 'viral-challenge technique' to study the effects of stress on over 400 volunteers. Individuals were exposed to the common cold virus and also given a questionnaire to assess their levels of perceived stress. Cohen et al. found a positive correlation between levels of stress and the likelihood of catching a cold.

Major social events, such as marriage and divorce are stressful, even the positive ones. Holmes and Rahe (1967) suggested that this is because they involve change and change requires psychic energy to be expended i.e. it is stressful and this affects health. Holmes and Rahe developed the Social Readjustment Rating Scale (SRRS) which was used by Rahe et al. (1970) to test the idea. In this study nearly 3000 men from the Navy were studied for 6 months and a significant positive correlation was found between their LCU score on the SRRS and how often they had been ill in 6 months.

---

**Page 4 of the report**

This study was criticised by DeLongis et al. (1988) who said that, the reason the correlation wasn't that strong was because more stress is caused by daily hassles and uplifts than by life events. They produced a hassles and uplifts scale.

In this study the aim was to test the link between stress and physical illness using an adaptation of the daily hassles and uplifts scale.

The alternative hypothesis is that illness and daily hassles are positively correlated. The null hypothesis is that there is no correlation between stress and daily hassles.

(615 words)

## Method
### Design

This study is a correlational study, that is there are two co-variables: stress and hassles and we are looking at to what extent the two variables are correlated. There is no IV in this study but the co-variables were operationalised. The co-variable of stress was operationalised by the score a person got on the hassles scale. The co-variable of illness was operationalised by counting how often someone had been ill over one month.

The only controls used were to make sure that people did understand the instructions. In order to ensure truthfulness we used the school attendance register, with participants consent, to find out how often they had been absent.

## Page 5

### Sample/participants

There were 12 participants in the study. They were a sample of people the researchers knew at school so they were various ages and male and female. No one was under 16 years of age.

### Materials

The main materials were the Hassles questionnaire. This was based in part on the questionnaire designed by Delongis et al. but adapted so it was more relevant to today. The questionnaire is in the Appendix. For each Hassle a participant had to rate how often it was experienced with 5 being 'very often' and 0 being 'never'. There were no uplifts on the scale. There were 30 hassles that were listed.

An informed consent document and a set of standardised instructions and a debrief were also used.

### Procedure

The study was conducted as a group of 4 and we divided the questionnaires between us. Each group member had 3 questionnaires which were given out to friends (participants). Each participant was asked if they would mind helping with our Psychology Project. Then they were asked to read and sign the informed consent form. Next they were read the standardised instructions (see Appendix) and when they were ready they were given the Hassles scale and they had as much time as they wished to complete this. They returned the questionnaire when they had finished. When the questionnaires were handed back the participants were read the debrief and thanked for taking part.

(347 words)

## Page 6 of the report

### Results

Once all 12 questionnaires were returned, scores were calculated for each person and also their attendance score for the previous month. This meant we had two scores for each participant. Next the mean scores and the range for each co-variable were worked out as shown in the table below.

### Summary table

The table shows the mean scores and range. The raw data are in the appendix.

|  | Hassles score | Absences |
|---|---|---|
| Mean | 16.5 | 13.8 |
| Range | 18 | 15 |

### Graph

The most suitable graph to use is a scattergram.

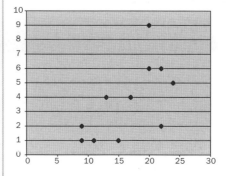

## Page 7 of the report

Results (continued)

You can see from the graph that there is a distinct positive correlation between the variables. So this suggests that the more hassles someone has the more illness they experience, a positive correlation.

(120 words)

### Discussion

The results of the study suggest that the alternative hypothesis can be accepted (that illness and hassles are positively correlated) and the null hypothesis can be rejected. This study therefore confirms the original theory and all of the earlier research that illness and stress are associated. We cannot, of course, conclude that stress causes illness because this is a correlational study. The results should be treated with caution because the sample used was restricted to adolescents who might be less affected by hassles than older people – but that would mean an even stronger correlation for older people.

As pointed out above one limitation of the design was the restricted sample that was used in terms of ages. This could be remedied by using people of different ages.

Another limitation was the small sample size. So by getting people of different ages there should also be more participants altogether.

The problem with looking at a wider sample in terms of age is that some of the hassles on the list might not be relevant, for example 'Having to study for exams' so a questionnaire would have to be devised that was suitable for people of different ages.

## Page 8 of the report

It might also have been better to get people to answer the questionnaires in a supervised classroom so they would not be tempted to discuss their answers with others.

Otherwise the design of this study was very straightforward and it was simple to collect the data and analyse it. There were no ethical problems and no one objected afterwards.

If the study was to be conducted in the future, as suggested it would be better to use more people to get a better sample. Also uplifts could be included in the scale and it could be revised it so it was suitable for people of all ages.

In conclusion it was found that daily hassles were positively correlated with days off school supporting the relationship proposed by Selye between stress and illness.

(332 words)

### References

Holmes, T.H., and Rahe, R.H. (1967) The social readjustment rating scale. Journal of Psychosomatic Research, 11, 213–218.

DeLongis, A., Folkman, S., & Lazarus, R.S. (1988). The impact of daily stress on health and mood: Psychological and social resources as mediators. Journal of Personality and Social Psychology, 54 (3), 486 –495.

Brady, J.V. (1958) Ulcers in executive monkeys. Scientific American, 199, 95–100.

# 6 Topic: Prejudice

Social psychology is the study of social behaviour, which occurs when two or more members of the same species interact. Social psychologists are concerned with how people influence each other's behaviour (social influence) and with how our thoughts influence our social behaviour (social cognition).

Prejudice is an example of social cognition; the way we think about particular groups of people may lead to prejudiced behaviour (discrimination).

| Chapter contents | Unit content for the topic 'Prejudice' | Comment |
|---|---|---|
| **Aspect 1: Nature of prejudice** | | |
| Stereotyping, prejudice and discrimination<br>     page 143<br>The consequences of prejudice: racism and sexism<br>     page 147 | Nature of prejudice including:<br>• stereotyping and discrimination<br>• cognitive, affective and behavioural aspects<br>• definitions and examples of racism and sexism<br>• harmful effects of stereotyping | *Prejudice has long been recognised as a major problem in many societies, and social psychologists have extensively researched this unpleasant side of human behaviour and experience. In this Aspect you will learn to define and distinguish the concepts of* **stereotyping**, **prejudice** *and* **discrimination**. *You will be able to explain how these are related to the psychological processes of* **cognition**, **affect** *(emotion), and* **behaviour**. *The* **harmful effects of stereotyping**, *and of prejudice in general, show why people are so concerned about prejudice. You will also take a closer look at two particular types of prejudice (***racism*** and ***sexism***) that give rise to such concern.* |
| **Aspect 2: Theories of prejudice** | | |
| Authoritarian personality<br>     page 150<br>Social identity theory<br>     page 152 | Theories of prejudice, including:<br>• authoritarian personality<br>• social identity theory | *A number of theories have been proposed to explain the origins of prejudice. Here, you will examine two of these –* **authoritarian personality** *and* **social identity theory**. *You should be able to describe the strengths and weaknesses of these explanations, including* **evidence** *that supports or challenges them.* |
| **Aspect 3: Reduction of prejudice** | | |
| Socialisation and education<br>     page 155<br>Increasing contact<br>     page 156<br>Institutional racism<br>     page 161 | Reduction of prejudice:<br>• education/socialisation, including Jane Elliott's strategy and Aronson's 'jigsaw technique'<br>• contact and equal-status contact<br>• superordinate goals<br>• reduction of institutional racism | *You won't be surprised to learn that many attempts have been made to discover effective ways of reducing prejudice and discrimination, in research and in the 'real world', often through* **socialisation** *and* **education** *processes. Through studying this Aspect you will be able to describe particular* **classroom strategies**: **Jane Elliott's** *'blue eyes–brown eyes' exercise, and* **Aronson's** *'jigsaw classroom'. You will also see that there are important common factors in prejudice reduction:* **contact/equal-status contact** *and* **superordinate goals**. *Attempts to* **reduce institutional racism**, *for example in the police, are also considered.* |

**164   Sample questions with students' answers and examiner's comments**

# Aspect 1:  The nature of prejudice

## Stereotyping, prejudice and discrimination
### What are stereotyping, prejudice and discrimination?

These three concepts are linked: **stereotyping** concerns what we *know* about the object of our prejudice; **prejudice** is our *attitude* towards or *feelings* about an individual or group; and **discrimination** is the *behaviour* that arises from prejudiced attitudes.

## Stereotyping

Stereotypes are fixed, and usually fairly simplistic, generalisations about a particular group or class of people. In general, most of us are 'cognitive misers' – we are unable or unwilling to process large amounts of information so we take shortcuts. Therefore, we tend to form stereotypes of those around us. This has the effect of making our social world more predictable, as we can make assumptions about how others are likely to behave. These stereotypes are often negative and unflattering and may underlie prejudice and discrimination, and so have negative consequences for the targets of our stereotyping. Typically, stereotypes have the following attributes:

- *simplification* – for example we may judge someone's promiscuous behaviour as evidence of their being a 'typical male'

- *exaggeration* or *distortion* – for example we may caricature men wearing flat hats as being very slow and ponderous in their driving habits

- *generalisation* – for example all members of a particular nationality are seen as sharing the same characteristics

- *cultural attributes are seen as 'natural'* – for example we see members of a particular cultural group as being 'naturally' warlike or peace loving.

Although stereotypes are usually simplistic in nature, they are not necessarily *false* assumptions about the target group, as they often contain a '*grain of truth*'. Stereotypes are often widely shared, therefore reinforcing the fact that some degree of accuracy may be evident in the stereotype. Although stereotypes can and do change over time, those who hold them are often reluctant to abandon them. Even in the face of disconfirming evidence, people cling to obviously inaccurate stereotypes. One reason may be that stereotypes cause us to be selective in our perception of certain individuals so that what we perceive merely confirms our existing stereotypes (called a *confirmatory bias*).

### Research on stereotyping
*Ageism*
A meta-analysis of studies of ageism found that attitudes toward older people are more negative than towards younger adults, although such stereotypes about the elderly tend to be mixed, with elderly people being stereotyped as warm (positive) but also as incompetent (negative) (e.g. Cuddy and Fiske, 2002). This stereotype is generally a product of the perceived social position of elderly people and predicts the kind of emotional prejudices that they are likely to face. Cuddy *et al.* (2005) found that such mixed stereotypes of the elderly are consistent across varied cultures, including **collectivist cultures** such as China and Japan.

*Heterosexism*
Various **outgroups** are frequently the focus of negative perceptions, for example homosexuals have long been considered to be deviants. In a public opinion survey in the 1960s, they were rated as the third most dangerous group of individuals in the United States, outranked only by communists and atheists (Aguero *et al.*, 1984). Even in the world of psychology, homosexuals have been perceived negatively; it was not until 1973 that the American Psychiatric Association removed homosexuality from its official list of mental disorders. Such heterosexist bias is also evident in the media. Cowan and Valentine (2006) monitored 168 hours of peak-time TV on BBC 1 and BBC 2 and found that, during that time, lesbian and gay people and their lives were realistically and positively portrayed for just 6 minutes.

Not all stereotypes are accurate – the late Peter Morgan, anything *but* ponderous when behind the wheel of his race-tuned Morgan car!

The full report of *Tuned Out* by Cowan and Valentine is available at: www.stonewall.org.uk/documents/tuned_out_pdf.pdf

## starSTUDY

# Investigating stereotypes: Confirmatory bias

(COHEN, 1981)

## Aims

This study aimed to investigate the effect of **schemas** (and stereotypes) on memory. We would expect people to remember information which is consistent with stereotypes better than that which is inconsistent because schemas organise incoming data.

## Method and procedure

*Experiment 1* Stereotypical behaviours for waitresses and librarians were selected by asking students to identify things they associated with each occupation. Using these behaviours, two 15-minute videotapes were made showing a man and a woman talking, first while eating dinner and then during an informal birthday celebration. Ninety-six undergraduates were shown one of the videotapes; they were told either that the woman was a waitress or that she was a librarian. Tape A contained nine librarian features and nine waitress features; tape B was the reverse (see table). Thus the two tapes depicted equal amounts of waitress-like and librarian-like behaviour; certain behaviours were consistent with a waitress stereotype and inconsistent with a librarian stereotype, and vice versa. Participants were told to form an impression as if it were a real-life situation. The experimenter casually mentioned the woman's occupation.

After watching the video, the participants were asked to rate the woman on a 37-item trait questionnaire and to recall features about the woman's appearance and behaviour, using the list of the 18 features.

Librarian and waitress features recorded on tapes A and B

| Tape A | | Tape B | |
|---|---|---|---|
| **Librarian features** | **Waitress features** | **Librarian features** | **Waitress features** |
| Roast beef | No salad | Salad | Burgers |
| Plays piano | Beer | Wine | Plays guitar |
| Fresh flowers | Informal table setting | Formal table setting | No fresh flowers |
| Wears glasses | Not travelled in Europe | Travelled in Europe | Does not wear glasses |
| Book-shelves | Television | No television | No book shelves |
| Angel food birthday cake | Spent day working | Spent day reading | Chocolate birthday cake |
| Golf clubs | No artwork | Artwork | Bowling ball |
| Classical music | Night-gown as gift | Best-seller as a gift | Pop music |
| Non-affectionate with husband | Romantic novel as gift | History book as gift | Affectionate with husband |

*Experiment 2*: This was the same as experiment 1, except on this occasion half of the 56 participants were told the woman's occupation before the videotape and half were given this information afterwards.

## Results

In experiment 1, Cohen found 78% accuracy for recall of consistent information compared with 71% recall of inconsistent information. The findings for experiment 2 are shown in the table below.

Timing of occupational information

| | Timing of occupational information | |
|---|---|---|
| **Prototype features:** | **Before the videotape** | **After the videotape** |
| **Consistent** | 74% | 68% |
| **Inconsistent** | 66% | 57% |

## Conclusion

Both experiments show that people remember consistent information better than inconsistent data, thus supporting the view that stereotypes affect our perception of the world. The second experiment demonstrated that schemas/stereotypes affect both encoding and retrieval processes. Stereotypes act as filters, screening out information which is inconsistent, resulting in a confirmation of existing stereotypes (a *confirmatory bias*).

## Evaluation

### Biased sample

This study, like so many psychological studies, relied on undergraduates as participants. Such individuals have unique characteristics in terms of, for example, intelligence and age. This means that we cannot generalise these findings to all people. It might be that older people are less affected by stereotypes because of having wider experience, or they may be *more* affected by stereotypes because of reduced cognitive capacity with increased age!

### Subsequent studies

Many other studies have demonstrated the effect of stereotypes/schema on how we process information. For example, one study (Abbey, 1982) looked at gender differences. Abbey arranged for a man and woman to talk for five minutes, observed by a hidden man and woman. The men, whether watching or conversing, rated the woman as more seductive than the women did the men. The men also were more sexually attracted to the opposite-sex actor than the females were. These results were interpreted as evidence that men are more likely to perceive the world in sexual terms. In other words, their stereotypes/schemas organise and filter information along sexually oriented lines.

# Prejudice

As the name suggests, prejudice involves the 'prejudging' of someone or something, without having direct evidence to support that judgement. Prejudice involves more than just having a preconceived idea about another person or group; it also involves forming an *evaluation* of them. Although it can be positive, prejudice is usually taken to mean a negative attitude towards that person or group.

Being prejudiced against a whole group of people (men, women, Muslims, Catholics, etc.) means that we have formed our judgement with reference to an existing bias that is most probably based on our social stereotypes. At its most extreme, a prejudiced attitude may result in our actively *discriminating* against members of a particular group, denying them opportunities that we would afford a more favoured group.

Because of a previous negative experience with one member of a particular group, an individual may develop the stereotype that all members of that group share the same characteristic. For example, someone who has a series of unfortunate relationships with members of the opposite sex may develop the view that 'all women are the same', and so they adopt a prejudiced view of *all* members of that sex (sexism).

### Research on prejudice

#### Ageism

Research suggests that older adults are rarely actively disliked, but instead are victims of a distinct form of emotional prejudice that is usually reserved for those of low status – pity. Fiske *et al*. (2002) found that pity was the emotion that college students were most likely to feel towards older people. Ageism, however, is thought to be a unique form of prejudice as, unlike gender or ethnic groups, membership of age groups is in constant transition over the lifespan.

#### Heterosexism

Hegarty (2002) provides an explanation for why some people express more tolerant attitudes towards lesbian and gay people – the reason lies in a belief in immutability (i.e. fixed and unchangeable). In his research, participants who believed that homosexuality was more a matter of biology than personal choice expressed more tolerant attitudes toward lesbians and gays, but only if they were more tolerant individuals to begin with. But how do such tolerant people feel when they experience heterosexism in others? Richman *et al.* (2004) asked men and women whether they had ever intervened when someone close to them had expressed a heterosexist prejudice. Only 7% of the men said they had intervened when the prejudice was based on sexual orientation, whereas 75% of women had intervened in similar circumstances. The major reason cited for the men's failure to intervene was indifference.

## Discrimination

Discrimination can occur at many levels, from simple avoidance to hostile attacks on members of the target group. Types of discrimination include **racism** (against members of another racial group), **sexism** (against members of another sex), *ageism* (against another age group) and *heterosexism* (against alternative forms of sexuality). Discriminatory behaviours may be linked to underlying prejudiced attitudes (e.g. an employer's prejudice against older people may lead them only to offer jobs to people below a certain age), or to the prevailing social climate. This latter type of discrimination was vividly portrayed in the 1988 film *Mississippi Burning*, which tells the story of the real-life murders of three civil rights workers in Mississippi in 1964. The prevailing social climate meant that a white Mississippi jury would never convict the murderers (members of the Ku Klux Klan), so the US government charged them under an 1870 law of conspiring to deprive the murdered men of their civil rights.

### Research on discrimination
*Ageism*
There is mounting evidence to suggest that older people are increasingly a stigmatised group in Western cultures. Research has shown that stereotypes of older people as 'incompetent' can lead to discrimination against them in the workplace and in other settings such as hospitals or nursing homes. A report published in 2006 by the Commission for Social Care Inspection (CSCI) found that there is explicit discrimination in the care of older people in the way that services are organised so that provision differs from that given to adults of working age. More subtle forms of ageism are evident in the finding that only 1.5% of characters on television are elderly people (Zebrowitz and Montepare, 2000) and in advertising, where older people tend to be either ignored or represented inappropriately.

*Heterosexism*
A number of research studies have established that experience of heterosexism is related to greater psychological distress for lesbian, gay and bisexual (LGB) individuals. These studies have shown that for LGB individuals, heterosexism, in the form of harassment, discrimination and violence, is related to adverse health and occupational outcomes (e.g. Mays and Cochran, 2001). Symanski (2005) found that heterosexism had a significant influence on lesbians' mental health, accounting for approximately one-third of the variance among this population for mental health.

## The components of prejudice

Prejudice assumes the existence of an underlying (and usually negative) attitude towards members of a category or group, but what do we mean by *attitude* in this context? Myers and Spencer (2003) define an attitude as 'a favourable or unfavourable evaluative reaction towards something or someone, exhibited in one's beliefs, feelings, or intended behaviour'. This suggests that prejudice, like many other attitudes, is predominantly an *evaluation* of the attitude object. But most attitudes, and this includes prejudice, are also characterised by *cognitions* about the attitude object, as well as *behavioural* tendencies (e.g. to approach or avoid the object in question). This view of prejudice emphasises the importance of three distinct components of a prejudiced attitude, as described below.

### The cognitive component
The *cognitive* component of prejudice is what we *know* about the object of our prejudice. This component is based primarily on our beliefs about the characteristics of a person or group. It is an extension of our tendency to categorise (i.e. stereotype) members of a group. If we dislike a particular group, then we are selective in our processing of evidence that supports our beliefs about members of this group (e.g. 'they're all lazy, untrustworthy, dirty, stupid'). When applied to racism, the cognitive component of a racial prejudice is likely to be characterised by sincere, though stereotyped, beliefs about race differences. People who hold such prejudices often believe that there is good evidence and convincing arguments to support their beliefs.

*What's the difference between ...*

**Stereotyping and prejudice**

Stereotypes are generalisations about a group of people, and as such represent our *knowledge* about the group. Prejudice, on the other hand implies an *evaluation* of the group that may or may not be based on an underlying sterotype.

**Prejudice and discrimination**

Prejudice involves an underlying *attitude* towards an individual because of their membership of a particular group. Discrimination may involve *acting* on this attitude, or simply conforming to current social norms of discrimination against members of that group.

**Stereotyping and discrimination**

Sterotypes are often negative and unflattering, and as such may justify discriminatory behaviour. However, they only represent a way of *thinking about* the world, whereas discrimination involves *acting towards* members of a target group in an unfair or biased way.

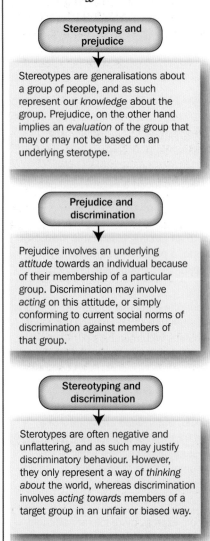

In 1999, Amadou Diallo, an unarmed black male, was shot dead by white police officers outside his New York apartment. Diallo had been stopped by the police, and when he reached into his jacket to retrieve his wallet for identification, police officers (believing his wallet to be a gun) immediately opened fire. Prompted by this incident, Payne (2001) tried to establish the psychological processes taking place when an individual is forced to make an automatic categorisation after exposure to a black face. In his study, Payne found that among white participants, exposure to a black face increased the likelihood of mistaking a tool for a gun. Why would this be the case? It is possible that this effect is primarily the consequence of cognitive beliefs (stereotypes) among the white population associating blacks and guns. However, cognitive beliefs are only one of a number of internal mechanisms that drive our actions. Affect (emotional feelings) is another component of prejudice that could influence participants' responses. It is possible that some participants were more likely to 'see' the gun after seeing a black face not because of stereotypes associating blacks and guns, but rather because they perceived the black face more negatively. This in turn made it more likely that the participant would make a negative or discriminatory response.

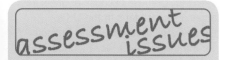

### The affective component

The *affective* component of prejudice is what we *feel* about the object of our prejudice. This arises as a result of the emotional reaction we experience whenever we come into contact with the object. When applied to racial prejudices, a person may have an aversion to people of another race for no very obvious reason. For example, there is a popular belief that Japanese people (who have very little body odour) do not like the way that Caucasian people smell, and so do not like to be with people who have Caucasian body odours. Another example is the way that many people react to immigrants with strong anger and resentment because of the belief that 'they take our jobs'.

### The behavioural component

The *behavioural* component of prejudice refers to a tendency to *act* in a particular way towards the object of our prejudice, usually arising from beliefs and feelings about them. In other words, the behavioural component is discrimination. Applied to racial prejudice, a person may act according to the affective and cognitive components of their prejudice; for example they may exchange racist jokes or use disparaging racist language about a particular ethnic group because they genuinely dislike the ethnic group (affective) and believe it is inferior (cognitive). It is possible for the intention to discriminate to exist on its own, without any affective or cognitive components. For example, an employer may act in a discriminatory manner (e.g. not employing women) to avoid unsettling the workforce.

## The consequences of prejudice: racism and sexism
### Racism

Racism is a way of thinking whereby an individual is judged and treated according to their membership of a perceived racial group rather than by their value as an individual. Racism can be based on ideas of biological inferiority or inferiority based on cultural deficiency or technological underdevelopment (Fontaine, 1998). A consequence of a racist ideology is the belief that social discrimination by race is justifiable.

### Forms of racism

Racism can be classified into three types (Fontaine, 1998):

- *Individual or direct* racism – individuals express racist views as part of their personal outlook on life. Such direct racism can be seen in the taunting of black footballers in the UK, or in hate crimes perpetrated by white youths against Asian residents.

- *Subconscious or indirect* racism – individuals hold negative attitudes towards racial minorities based on stereotypical assumptions, fear or ignorance. The case of Amadou Diallo (see above) is a classic example of the dangers of subconscious racism.

- *Institutional racism* – government agencies and organisations may limit opportunities on the basis of race. **Institutional racism** may be direct (e.g. Apartheid in South Africa) or indirect (e.g. claims of differential policing methods used against white and black youths in the UK). We will examine institutional racism further towards the end of this chapter.

Are you subconsciously racist? Find out by taking the Project Implicit test at: implicit. harvard.edu/implicit/research/

Racism in football – Barcelona forward Samuel Eto'o decided to take things into his own hands and left the pitch after sections of the Real Zaragoza crowd subjected him to racist chants.

See the 'Show Racism the Red Card' website, www.theredcardscotland. org/index.html

### Research on racism

*Discrimination and mental health*

In a recent UK study, Bhiu *et al.* (2005) found evidence that racial discrimination at work can have a notable impact on mental health. Researchers studied a representative sample of over 2000 working individuals to investigate the relationship between discrimination at work and the risk of developing common mental disorders such as anxiety and depression. Black Caribbean groups reported the most cases of unfair treatment at work and were nearly three times more likely to have developed a common mental disorder compared with white workers. Bangladeshi, Indian and Irish groups were also three times as likely to suffer from mental disorder as a result of discrimination at work. Overall, across all ethnic groups studied, the experience of racist insults and unfair treatment at work was associated with a twofold increase in the risk of a mental health disorder.

*Racism in sport*

In November 2004, as Spain played host to England in a friendly, thousands of Spanish fans hurled racist abuse at England's black players. Such examples of racism and xenophobia are more widespread than we would like to imagine. In many European countries, for example, the predominant form of racism is anti-Semitism (Merkel and Tokarski, 1996). In Italy, a Jewish player, Ronnie Rosenthal, was unable to play even one game for Udinese because of pressure from neo-fascist circles. Far-right political groups have targeted football fans in the UK for many years; in the 1970s, the National Front gave regular coverage in its magazine *Bulldog* to football and encouraged hooligan groups to compete for the title of 'most racist ground in Britain' (Garland and Rowe, 1996). However, Garland and Rowe also found evidence of a distinct trend in Britain which did not apply to other European countries. The British experience of racism within football has been met with a widespread (and successful) *anti-racist* response from supporters and other bodies.

## Sexism

Sexism refers to any form of discrimination or prejudice against people based purely on their sex. Although this is usually a form of discrimination by men against women, it can equally apply to discrimination by women against men, or to any other form of discrimination where the sex of the person rather than their individual characteristics is the determining factor defining treatment. In many patriarchal societies, women are viewed as the 'weaker' and less important sex. In the West, the feminist movement has attempted to stop sexism by addressing women's rights in education, employment, etc. Similarly, a corresponding 'masculinist' movement has begun to address issues that often discriminate against males, such as creating 'maternity' leave for men, and demanding equal access to children following divorce.

### Forms of sexism

Sexism comes in many different forms, including *blatant*, *covert*, and *subtle* sexism (Benokraitis and Feagin, 1999). *Blatant* (or overt) sexism refers to an obviously unequal treatment of women relative to men. Examples include sexual harassment, sexist jokes, or any other obvious forms of unequal treatment. *Covert* sexism refers to an unequal treatment of women that is hidden and very often difficult to document. This includes any form of action where the perpetrator consciously undermines one gender, for example imposing deadlines that are impossible to keep, with the object of 'keeping women in their place'. *Subtle* forms of sexism are actions that are visible but often not noticed because we have internalised such behaviours as normal or acceptable. This might include the use of sexist language (e.g. the use of expressions like 'young lady' or 'girl') that reinforces unequal sex differences between men and women, or the assumption that women might not be interested in a promotion because they have child-care commitments.

### Research on sexism

Swim *et al.* (2001) asked college men and women to keep a diary of incidents of everyday sexism in their lives and how these made them feel. Women experienced about one or two sexist incidents per week. These included experience of traditional gender role stereotypes and prejudice, demeaning comments and behaviours, and sexual objectification (i.e. being seen as a sex object). These incidents affected the women's psychological well-being by decreasing their comfort, increasing their feelings of anger and depression, and decreasing their self-esteem. Men reported similar changes in anger, depression and self-esteem, but they reported relatively fewer sexist incidents over the same period.

Jeavons and Sevastos (2003) investigated the common belief that a 'glass ceiling' (an invisible barrier that determines the level to which a woman can rise to in an organisation) exists for women in senior management positions. Controlling for factors such as job experience, education, age, etc., researchers found no significant difference in promotion opportunities for men and women. However, qualitative data showed that, compared with men, women tended to be employed at a level that was lower than their qualifications warranted. Therefore, despite equal rates of promotion, women tend not to progress as far as men. Women also continue to earn less than men probably because of the jobs they do. For example, in an analysis of younger workers the Equal Opportunities Commission (2006) found that jobs which are classified as 'women's work' tend to command lower wages than men's work even when they require similar qualification levels.

## The harmful effects of stereotyping

### Internalising negative stereotypes

Majority group characterisation of a minority group can be adopted by members of the minority group as well. According to *social identity theory* (see page 152), an individual's self-concept is partly shaped by their membership in social categories (e.g. female, Christian, Celtic supporter). Individuals may, therefore, internalise stereotypical negative traits as part of their self-concept simply because they are widely held to be true of their group. Research has tended to support the idea that negative stereotypes can have harmful self-fulfilling effects on group members. For example, Steele and Aronson (1995) found evidence that the emotional pressure of a negative racial stereotype concerning intellectual ability (given in the test instructions) lowered black performance on intelligence tests.

### Making associations

Stereotyping on the basis of an ethnic or religious category is destructive to relations between different groups in society. Such stereotypes can convey the impression to the majority that the negative actions of a few individuals represent the collective values of the whole minority community. For example, for many in the UK, to be a mugger is synonymous with being black, and to be Muslim is synonymous with terrorism. We come to accept our stereotypes as the norm, *despite* evidence which serves to challenge this view.

### Lowered expectations

Negative stereotypes about a particular group can have harmful consequences for the quality of life that they can expect. Take the elderly as an example. With increased health and longevity, many older adults are ageing well, but negative stereotyping may mean that society does not make the most of their valuable knowledge and experience. Negative stereotypes can also exacerbate poor performance in areas of functioning where decline is more evident. For example, beliefs that memory is bad in old age can reduce motivation to remember things.

## assessment issues

**Define 'sexism' and describe *one* example. (*ku* 4 *ae* 0)**

Whenever you are asked a definition-type question in relation to prejudice, remind yourself that there are some subtle differences between everyday use and psychologists' use of words like 'prejudice' and 'sexism'. So make sure you wear your 'psychologist's hat' when composing your answer. For example, people often assume that *sexism* is exclusively to do with unfair treatment of women. However, in answering this question, you should point out that it can mean unequal treatment of *either* sex, simply because of their sex. For this question you must also give an example, so choose one that you can describe fully as it is worth two of the four marks. A well-explained example of a concept (as opposed to just saying 'e.g. doctors') is always a sound way of showing your knowledge and understanding (*ku*), so it's good to get into the habit of providing examples, whether they are required by the question or not.

# Aspect 2: Theories of prejudice

**Authoritarian personality:** An individual who is intolerant of ambiguity and overly respectful of authority. Authoritarian individuals are likely to be prejudiced, conformist and obedient. It is possible that such characteristics are associated with a parenting style characterised by conditional love, strict discipline, and expecting unquestioning loyalty.

**Intergroup processes:** Interactions between ingroup and outgroup members.

**Ingroup:** Referring to any group of which we perceive ourselves to be a member as distinct from the **outgroup**.

In this Aspect we will look at two theories of the origin of prejudice: **authoritarian personality** and social identity theory. One explanation seeks to explain prejudiced behaviour in terms of the individual's personality – people are prejudiced because it is in their nature. The other seeks to explain prejudice in terms of **intergroup processes** – prejudice as an inevitable consequence of our tendency to classify ourselves in social groups, some of which are **ingroups** and others **outgroups**.

## The authoritarian personality

Following the horrors of the Second World War, particularly the rampant anti-Semitism observed in the Holocaust, several influential theorists came to regard such extreme prejudice as pathological and searched for personality syndromes that could explain it. The most prominent of these theorists was Theodor Adorno, who claimed that the key to prejudice lay in what he called an 'authoritarian personality'. Adorno believed that some people were more receptive to fascist ideas of supremacy, and so would be more likely to develop prejudiced attitudes toward target groups.

### The F-scale and other techniques

Adorno *et al.* (1950) published their findings in a book (all 1000 pages of it) filled with data, most notably the results of the 'F' (for fascism) scale. This scale identified nine key dimensions of a fascist personality, including conventionality, submissiveness, aggression and heightened concerns about sex (see example at the bottom of the page).

The F-scale was only one of the measures used by Adorno and his colleagues. They also measured ethnocentrism (a tendency to look at the world primarily from the perspective of one's own culture) and used clinical interviews that resembled psychoanalytic sessions. A feature of this massive undertaking, and a major source of later criticisms of the study, was the use of a highly biased sample. Because participation in the study was so demanding, researchers first used college students, a conveniently captive audience, and then persuaded the leaders of various organisations to survey their own groups – the groups included unions, prison inmates and psychology clinic patients.

#### The main findings

Probably the most interesting discovery from this study was that people with authoritarian leanings (i.e. those who scored high on the F-scale and other measures) identified with the 'strong' and were generally contemptuous of the 'weak'. They were very conscious of their own and others' status, showing excessive respect, deference and servility to those of higher status. Adorno *et al.* also reported a **positive correlation** between authoritarian personality and prejudice. People who scored high on authoritarianism tended to have a simplistic way of thinking about the world, characterising people and their actions into 'right' or 'wrong'. They displayed a cognitive style where there was little 'fuzziness' between categories of people, with fixed and distinctive stereotypes about other groups very much in evidence. The rest of the world was seen in black and white and anyone who wasn't an ingroup member was a target for hostility.

Theodor Adorno

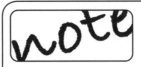

*Examples of F-scale questions*

In the F-scale, respondents were asked whether they agreed or disagreed with a range of questions, each responding to one of the key dimensions of fascism, for example:

● 'Obedience and respect for authority are the most important virtues children should learn' (Dimension: submissiveness)
● 'Homosexuality is a particularly rotten form of delinquency and ought to be severely punished' (Dimension: aggression and sex).

## explanation

## The authoritarian personality

Adorno *et al.* were the first to find a link between child rearing, character structure and personality. Someone who possessed the authoritarian personality syndrome was characterised as a dependent person who had grown up in very strict households where rules were followed to the letter and where there were very strict punishments for any rule breaking. Children raised under such harsh and punitive regimes harboured retaliatory urges toward their parents, although these urges were usually displaced onto substitute targets (scapegoats) instead. In this way the theory draws on Freudian (psychoanalytic) concepts, namely the **ego defence** mechanism of displacement as a means of dealing with conflict (see page 247).

As a result of this punitive early environment, these children grow up internalising the very strict moral beliefs of their parents and feeling insecure if they are unable to live up to them. In the world of the authoritarian personality, strength and power are good and everything else is a sign of weakness. As a result, these people view their own ingroup as being powerful and good, so therefore all other groups (particularly minority groups and any other socially 'devalued' group) are seen as weak and wrong. This attitude coupled with their simplistic thinking style (intolerant of ambiguity) would explain the link between authoritarian personality and prejudice against outgroups.

## evaluation

*Right, left or both?*
Shils (1954) challenged the view that authoritarianism could only be explained with reference to the political right. Shils pointed out that fascism (right wing) and Bolshevism (left wing) actually shared many important features. Both place high value on total power and look down on weakness.

*Methodological flaws*
Hyman and Sheatsley (1954) argued that the biggest flaws in Adorno *et al.*'s study were methodological. Representative sampling was nonexistent, as organisations were free to select their own respondents for study. The clinical interviews were analysed far too subjectively and what participants said about themselves could not be verified. The F-scale was vulnerable to response bias; therefore high F-scale scorers might not be genuine authoritarians but merely 'acquiescers' (i.e. tending to agree with statements).

*Support for the 'personality' explanation*
Following Adorno *et al.*'s initial work, there has been widespread support for the personality account of prejudice. The unifying theme in all this research is that there is a direct relationship between people's psychology as individuals and an understanding of prejudice (Reynolds *et al.*, 2001). Two characteristics of the authoritarian personality that have been extensively studied are right-wing authoritarianism (RWA – needing very little situational pressure to submit to authority) and social dominance orientation (SDO – a belief in the legitimacy of the social hierarchy). McFarland and Adelson (1996) assessed the extent to which RWA, SDO and other personality variables could account for prejudice and made the astonishing discovery that, between them, RWA and SDO could account for most of the variance observed *whatever* the prejudice. Altemeyer (1998) concluded that 'if you want to explain the many different kinds of prejudice … they are largely matters of personality.'

*An alternative explanation*
Reynolds *et al.* (2001) suggest that authoritarianism, rather than being considered a distinct personality trait, may actually be an expression of group-based beliefs and values. In their study, rather than authoritarianism correlating directly with prejudice, the relationship between the two depended on the self-categorisation of the perceiver (i.e. nationality, gender and age group).

assessment issues

**What do psychologists mean by the 'authoritarian personality'?**
**(ku 6 ae 0)**

The *authoritarian personality* is a big and complex concept. To answer this question you could use a wide range of material, including: findings from Adorno *et al.*'s research using the F-scale and other scales, especially their description of authoritarianism found in high-scorers on the F-scale and/or the correlation they found between child-rearing practices, authoritarian personality type, and prejudice. This is the kind of question where it makes good sense to describe some research evidence, even though this is not explicitly required in the question itself. It is also an opportunity to show your awareness of *links* with other areas of psychology, for example, Adorno's use of Freudian concepts like *displacement*, and the claim that early socialisation experiences can strongly influence later psychological development.

# Social identity theory (SIT)

We will now turn to the second explanation of prejudice. We have various means of reducing the complexity of our social world and one of these is to classify groups as 'us' and 'them' (ingroups and outgroups). We favour members of our ingroup even when we have nothing to gain personally. The effect of such prejudiced attitudes is discrimination towards outgroup members.

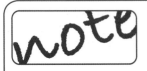
note

### SIT and the football terraces

Prejudice between fans of different football clubs can be explained using SIT. One feature of SIT is the finding that individuals will raise the significance of ingroup characteristics so that they increase their *relative status* compared with the outgroup. In Glasgow, one football club (Glasgow Celtic) historically represents the Irish Catholics; wearing green and white, waving the Irish tricolour and singing rebel songs from the Republic. The other (Glasgow Rangers) has come to represent British Protestants. Rangers fans are routinely criticised for their sectarian chants, reminding the Catholic half of the city that only they (Protestant Rangers fans) are born to walk the streets of Glasgow and that Catholic Celtic fans are not proper Scots and only here under sufferance.

Rangers and Celtic fans trade religious insults.

explanation    Social identity theory

SIT was developed by Tajfel and Turner (1979) in order to understand the psychological basis of intergroup discrimination. Of key importance in this theory is that apart from 'personal identity', an individual also has a number of 'social identities'. Because people divide their world into distinct social categories (age, gender, nationality, religion and even football affiliation), our *social* identity is based on perceived membership of these different social groups. Prejudice is the result of our need to boost our own self-esteem by distinguishing *our* group (the ingroup) from other groups (the outgroups). This process inevitably produces a comparison that enhances characteristics of our own group at the expense of the outgroup. Two biases are involved: perception of our own group as superior, leading to behaviours that favour our group (*ingroup favouritism*) and perception of other groups as inferior, leading to acts that discriminate against them (*outgroup discrimination*).

**Minimal group studies**

In research on *minimal groups* Tajfel and others attempted to identify the *minimal* conditions that would lead to ingroup favouritism and outgroup discrimination. This research emphasised that the mere act of categorising themselves as a member of one group rather than another was sufficient for them to discriminate against the outgroup (see Star Study on page 154).

*evaluation*

*The importance of self-esteem*

A number of studies have demonstrated that when groups have lowered self-esteem, they are more likely to show ingroup bias. However, this is not always the case; some studies have found that ingroup bias is higher in groups with enhanced status and levels of self-esteem. This suggests that, although the need to raise self-esteem is an important determinant of ingroup bias and intergroup discrimination, its role is not always clear.

*Does ingroup bias equal prejudice?*

Most of the studies of SIT have shown clear evidence of ingroup bias, but is this the same as prejudice, as defined earlier in this chapter? You may remember that we defined prejudice as 'An unjustified, usually negative, attitude towards an individual based solely on their membership of a particular category or group'. Research has tended to support the idea of ingroup favouritism but there is not such strong support for outgroup discrimination. Indeed, many studies have shown that both ingroup members *and* outgroup members are treated positively, although the former more so than the latter (Brewer, 1979). What would happen if individuals were given the opportunity to behave negatively against the outgroup? Mummendey *et al.* (1992) did just this. Instead of allocating rewards, participants were asked to distribute unpleasant high-pitched tones to ingroup and outgroup members; rather than discriminate against the latter, participants attempted to minimise the negative experience for *all* group members.

## Research related to social identity theory

### Intergroup comparison

Haeger (1993) asked participants from six European countries to write down whatever came to mind when they thought of their own country. Analysis of their responses showed that 20% had spontaneously drawn comparisons between their country and other countries, in a way that favoured their country (e.g. 'People are free to speak their mind here unlike in some other countries').

### Intergroup discrimination and self-esteem

Lemyre and Smith (1985) found that participants who were allowed to discriminate between ingroup and outgroup members when distributing rewards showed higher levels of subsequent self-esteem than control participants who were merely asked to distribute rewards between two ingroup members *or* two outgroup members. This suggests that people feel better when they discriminate against outgroups.

### Poor white racism

SIT can explain the finding that anti-black discrimination is higher among white people from poorer backgrounds than it is for those from middle-class backgrounds (Vollebergh, 1991). Such behaviour may be motivated by the desire to avoid comparisons with wealthier social classes and so preserve a positive self-esteem by drawing comparisons with a similarly deprived group.

# Investigating theories of prejudice: The minimal groups experiment

(TAJFEL, 1970)

## Aims

To investigate whether perceived group membership was sufficient for ingroup favouritism and outgroup discrimination to occur.

## Method and procedure

Participants were 64 schoolboys aged between 14 and 15 years. The boys already knew each other as they were members of the same year group in the same school in Bristol. They were told the experiment was investigating visual judgements and were shown 40 different dot clusters on a screen and asked to estimate the number of dots in each cluster.

The boys were then divided into groups of eight, supposedly on the basis of how they scored in the visual judgement test (but really they were divided randomly). They were either in an 'overestimator' group *or* an 'underestimator' group (based on whether they had consistently over or underestimated the number of dots).

Each boy was asked to choose a column from a matrix such as the one below where the numbers represented rewards (money) to be distributed to each boy. The matrices varied, so sometimes the top row was an ingroup member and the bottom row was an ingroup member (ingroup choice), or the top row was an ingroup member and the bottom row was an outgroup member (intergroup choice) or both rows were outgroup members (outgroup choice). There were 18 matrices in total.

Examples of an intergroup choice matrix

| Member no. 74 of overestimators group | 12 | 10 | 8 | 6 | 4 | 2 | 0 | 1 | 5 | 9 | 13 | 17 | 21 | 25 |
| Member no. 74 of underestimators group | 25 | 21 | 17 | 13 | 8 | 5 | 1 | 0 | 2 | 4 | 6 | 8 | 10 | 12 |

## Results

For intergroup choices, the large majority of participants gave more money to members of their ingroup than to members of the other group. They could have maximised profits for both groups but tended to simply maximise the profit for their own group.

In contrast, the results for the ingroup and outgroup choices were closely distributed around the point of fairness (i.e. each boy being given close to the same amount).

## Conclusion

This study demonstrates that the mere categorisation of people into groups (however meaningless) is sufficient to trigger ingroup bias and outgroup discrimination. By allocating more points to their own group, the boys were ensuring that they would be in the 'best' group, thus bolstering their own self-esteem in the process.

## Evaluation

*Valuable research*

The power of this study is in its demonstration that even categorisation into relatively meaningless social groups is enough to create ingroup bias. If this finding is projected onto groups that have far more established identities, we can see how easy it would be to slip into discriminative practices against outgroups.

*Demand characteristics*

In Tajfel's study, as with other studies using this method, it is possible that participants experienced **demand characteristics** and felt they had little choice but to discriminate against the other group. Participants may try to work out how the experimenter *really* wants them to behave. In this case they may have felt they had little choice but to discriminate against the other group.

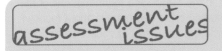

**Discuss *two* theories that attempt to explain the origins of prejudice. Refer to research evidence in your answer. (*ku* 12 *ae* 8)**

A good choice of theories for this essay question would be *authoritarian personality theory* and *social identity theory*. But you must also include research evidence from studies; when writing about research evidence there are several important strategies to follow, especially when there are *ae* marks available, as here. First, make sure that, wherever possible, you refer to *evidence that supports* and *evidence that challenges or contradicts*. Here, for example, in support of authoritarian personality theory, you might cite Adorno *et al.*'s classic research as well as the more contemporary McFarland and Adelson (1996). For social identity theory you might cite Tajfel's (1970) minimal group study, as well as the study by Mummendey *et al.* (1992) who challenged one element of Tajfel's conclusions. You could also refer to further studies, if you wish. Secondly, don't stop at simply describing results – do go on to make it clear exactly *how* these findings support (or contradict) the theory. These strategies will show your ability to analyse and evaluate, and therefore help you achieve the *ae* marks. Thirdly, you can *evaluate* your chosen studies in terms of their methodology. This not only adds to your evaluative content but also shows integration of your knowledge of research methods. Finally, whenever you use a 'Star Study' in a question like this (which asks you to 'refer to research evidence'), beware of the danger that you will end up giving a long, detailed description of the method and procedure – it's the findings, and your interpretation of them, that are important here.

# Aspect 3:  Reduction of prejudice

Because prejudice has such devastating consequences for society, its reduction is of key importance to psychologists. Prejudice reduction refers to a collection of techniques designed to break down the destructive stereotypes and attitudes that fuel discrimination. Most prejudice-reduction programmes take place on a relatively small scale, bringing together people from different groups to help them develop a better mutual understanding (e.g. the contact hypothesis). Sometimes, efforts are made to reduce prejudice within a whole population (e.g. desegregation). Perhaps the most effective way of reducing prejudice is through widespread educational reforms and changes in the way that we socialise our children.

## Socialisation and education

Children are not born with prejudiced attitudes. They learn these from their family, peers, teachers, the media, and others around them. If a child is to become a respected member of society, they must learn those characteristics deemed desirable within that society. If prejudice is learned in this way, then it should also be possible to reduce prejudice by changing the socialisation experiences of children, or by re-educating them into more tolerant attitudes.

### Socialisation

| KEY TERMS |

**Socialisation:** The process whereby an individual's values, attitudes, skills, etc. are shaped in a way considered desirable within a particular society.

Probably the most obvious explanation of the development of prejudice is that it is acquired through direct **socialisation** by parents or from other sources such as peer group influences and other forms of cultural transmission (Brown, 1995). We often assume that children move gradually from innocence to prejudice, picking up prejudiced attitudes along the way. However, research by Aboud and Doyle (1993) suggests that children are prejudiced at ages as young as five. They discovered that while very young children seem to have prejudiced attitudes, by the time they are eight or nine, these attitudes have started to decline as children focus more on individual characteristics of people rather than stereotyping them. Children's susceptibility towards prejudice thus seems to be linked to their cognitive development and not just to socialisation or blind imitation of parents' attitudes or peer pressure.

#### Reducing prejudice through socialisation

If parents *do* have a significant influence on the attitudes of their children (and this is by no means certain), then it follows that changing early socialisation experiences would affect what children learn. Parents who make an effort to model non-prejudiced attitudes and behaviours for their children, and who reward their children for expressing non-prejudiced attitudes, should produce children who are less likely to be prejudiced themselves. Rosenhan (1970) interviewed individuals who participated in US civil rights activities in the 1960s and found that one of the key factors in their involvement was having parents who had expressed outrage about moral issues *and* had acted on their principles; individuals' whose parents had not acted as models were less inclined to be active themselves.

Of course, peer socialisation is also an important force in the lives of children. Aboud and Doyle (1996) worked with children between 8 and 11 years of age. The children were placed in pairs such that they had different levels of prejudice as established on a pre-test. They were required to do a task which involved assigning positive or negative characteristics to whites, blacks and Chinese. More tolerant children tended to challenge their less tolerant partners and were much less likely to change their attitudes than the prejudiced children. High-prejudice children on the other hand, did show a significant decline in prejudice after the task.

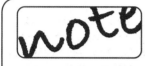

### One Scotland: no place for racism

'One Scotland' is the Scottish Executive's campaign to tackle racism in this country. It aims to raise awareness of racist attitudes and highlight its negative impact. Most Scots believe that they are not racists but racist incidents are still continuing to rise, currently standing at nearly 4000 a year (www.onescotland.com).

Despite a vigorous and expensive advertising programme, a survey conducted in 2005 found increases in prejudiced attitudes. For example, 9% believe that it is not racist to assault physically or use violence towards people from other ethnic backgrounds or their property, and 25% believe that people are justified in verbally attacking asylum seekers who get housing and benefits in Scotland (www.scotland.gov.uk/Publications/2005/06/2895508/55101).

Campaigns, such as One Scotland, aim to tackle racism in Scotland and celebrate its cultural diversity.

Desegregation was not popular with everyone – Elizabeth Eckford was one of nine black students who enrolled at a school in Little Rock, Arkansas. She turned up at school but was turned away by the white students, shouting, 'No nigger bitch is going to get into our school' (www.atimes.com/atimes/Front_Page/GC11Aa01.html).

### Reducing prejudice in the media

Certain groups such as ethnic groups, women, gays and lesbians, and disabled people have often been under-represented on television and in films, and portrayed in an adverse light. This has long been a source of concern, as it may perpetuate stereotypes and so contribute to maintenance of prejudice. In a study of ethnic group representation in popular TV programmes in the UK, Cumberbatch *et al.* (2001) found that Asian people were most under-represented ('almost invisible' at 0.9% of TV characters), and ethnic minority participants were far less likely to appear in major roles. One positive finding was that there was little evidence of overt examples of prejudice.

Some attempts at counter-stereotyping have been made; TV programmes have deliberately presented characters that counteract a stereotype, such as a woman or a disabled person acting an important and positive role. Greenfield (1984) reported that programmes such as *You and Me* (UK) and *Sesame Street* (US) did have positive effects on inter-racial attitudes, and Clifford *et al.* (1995) claimed similar positive effects in attitudes towards disabled people. However, any effects of the media will be moderated by other influences to which children are exposed, such as parents and peers (Himmelweit *et al.*, 1958).

## Desegregation

In 1954, the US Supreme Court ordered the desegregation of public schools in the southern states. The belief was that mixing children from different ethnic or religious groups together in the same school should result in more tolerant intergroup attitudes. However, research has tended to be quite pessimistic about the benefits of desegregated schools. Stephan (1978) reviewed the results of 18 studies in the US and found that in half of them desegregation actually *increased* prejudiced attitudes among children. On the other hand, some studies have

Find out more about the jigsaw technique at www.jigsaw.org/

looked at the possible benefits of cooperative learning groups within ethnically diverse schools. Such techniques, which emphasise the importance of each individual's contribution to the overall group product, have been far more successful. In a meta-analysis of 25 studies which compared the effects of a cooperative learning programme with 'normal' classroom interactions, the cooperative learning groups produced significantly higher levels of inter-ethnic attraction than the control groups (Miller and Davidson-Podgorny, 1987). Aronson *et al.* (1978) have developed this idea even further with their **'jigsaw technique'**.

## The 'jigsaw technique'

Stephan (1978) had not only found that desegregation had failed to live up to its promise to reduce prejudice but had also found a general *decrease* in the self-esteem of students from ethnic minorities following desegregation. Aronson *et al.* (1978) decided to change the atmosphere of the classroom so that contact between members of different ethnic groups was more positive and constructive. They developed the jigsaw classroom, a setting designed to reduce prejudice and raise children's self-esteem by placing them in small desegregated work groups. Each child would be dependent on the other children in the group in order to complete tasks, and to do well in the class. Because of the nature of the jigsaw classroom, each child has equal status; they work interdependently, and they work in pursuit of a common goal.

### The jigsaw classroom in action

- If the children in a jigsaw classroom were working on a project about Scotland, the class might be broken down into five groups of six children each. Each group would have a diverse mix of children from different ethnic groups.

- Within each group, different children would be given the responsibility of researching different aspects of the topic: one child might be given the task of finding out something about Scotland's history, another its physical geography, another its customs, and so on.

- Children from different groups who were working on the same aspect would compare notes and share information. Children would then return to their groups, and each present their 'piece of the jigsaw' to the other group members so that each group member had a thorough understanding of the whole topic and could, for example, pass a test on it.

- The teacher's role would be to defuse any tensions that arise and to remind group members about helping each other so that the group ultimately succeeds in its task.

*evaluation*  | Jigsaw technique

*Effective technique*
Aronson *et al.* claim that it is a remarkably efficient way to learn material. It encourages listening, engagement and empathy by giving each child an essential part to play in the group activity. Because each person depends on all the others, no one individual can succeed completely unless everyone works well together as a team. This not only encourages interaction among all children in a group, but also teaches them to value each other as contributors to their common task. Research in Japan (Araragi, 1983) and the US (Aronson and Bridgeman, 1979) has shown that children in jigsaw classrooms tend to perform better academically and show greater increases in self-esteem than those in traditional classrooms. Of equal importance, they show more evidence of real integration and less evidence of prejudice against other ethnic groups.

*Cooperation versus interdependence*
Walker and Crogan (1998) conducted a field study to see if the jigsaw technique would work in the social climate of Australia, with its overwhelmingly negative stereotype of Aborigines, and white Australian hostility to increases in Asian immigration. They found that racial prejudices were much reduced and in particular found that the key element of the jigsaw classroom was interdependence rather than cooperation; cooperation alone actually made existing intergroup prejudices worse.

Jane Elliott as she is today

## The work of Jane Elliott

In 1968, shortly after the assassination of black civil rights leader Martin Luther King, Jane Elliott, a third-grade teacher in a small all-white, all-Christian town in Iowa, USA, divided her class into two groups for a lesson in discrimination. Elliott believes that the best way to fight racism and sexism is to make people experience it themselves, even if only for a brief period in a highly controlled environment. She divided her class into brown- and blue-eyed participants. On the first day of the exercise, the brown-eyed children were made to feel superior while the blue-eyed children were ridiculed for no reason other than the fact that their eye colour was different. Blue-eyed children had to wear distinguishing coloured 'collars' around their necks (in the same way that Jews were forced to wear the Star of David during the European Holocaust) and were discriminated against in a variety of ways that affected their experiences in the classroom, such as not being given extra privileges. On the second day, the roles were reversed so that now it was the brown-eyed children who were ridiculed and discriminated against by the blue-eyed children. This exercise helped the children to experience at first hand what it felt like to be the object of discrimination, and how arbitrary such discrimination can be.

*evaluation*

For more on the film *Blue Eyed*, see www.newsreel.org/nav/title.asp?tc=CN0015

### Elliott's work

In 1985, 11 of the original children returned for a reunion and confirmed the positive influence that the experience had been on their lives. Elliott has also used her exercise with employees of the Iowa prison system, receiving a similar response from them; with college students from various racial and ethnic backgrounds; and with groups of Aborigines and white Australians (Elliott *et al.*, 2001, 2003). In one study, black students confirmed that this was the sort of treatment they lived with every day. In her Australian exercise, Aborigines revealed how they felt their culture was being destroyed by assimilation programmes, while the whites were genuinely surprised and shocked by the pain that they had inflicted. *Blue Eyed*, a film based on the original study, has allowed many white people to experience the feeling of being discriminated against in the same way that society often discriminates against women, people from different ethnic backgrounds, homosexuals and the disabled. The exercise has been shown to be effective in shocking people out of their complacency and ultimately reducing prejudice and discrimination in many different age groups and target populations.

### note

**Diversity training**

In the year 2000, nearly 60% of schools and universities in the US had instituted some sort of multicultural curriculum requirement. The aims of such diversity courses are to heighten students' awareness of the social problems confronting minorities and to promote a more open attitude towards them. Chang (2002) compared students who were nearing the end of a diversity course with students who were just beginning one. Students near the end of their course showed significantly lower prejudice scores than those just starting out. Similarly, Hogan and Mallott (2005) found that prejudice was lower in students who had completed a diversity course specifically addressing race and gender issues.

### assessment issues

**Describe the procedure of *one* research study that has investigated reduction of prejudice. (ku 4 ae 0)**

In this single research study question, check the 'command' word first – in this case it is 'describe'. You should see that this corresponds to the marks allocation. 'Describe' demands *ku* skills and so four *ku* marks are on offer; if you had been asked to 'discuss' or 'evaluate' there would also be *ae* marks available. It's also crucial to notice that in this question you are asked only about the *procedure*, whereas sometimes this type of question asks for an account of the whole study. So the sensible thing to do is to use a study about which you can recall lots of detail of the procedure (even if you can't remember too much about the findings, it won't matter here!). Aronson *et al.*'s (1978) 'jigsaw classroom' would be suitable or Sherif's Robbers' Cave study described on page 159. Resist the temptation to evaluate, as that may divert your attention from ensuring that you give enough descriptive information for the four *ku* marks.

## Increasing contact

According to the **contact hypothesis,** increasing social contact is the best way to reduce prejudice between different groups. This hypothesis does not just apply to members of different ethnic groups, as the positive effects of contact have been demonstrated in many different areas including attitudes toward the elderly, psychiatric patients, gays and children with disabilities (Hewstone, 2003).

**KEY TERMS**

**Contact hypothesis:** A belief that direct contact between members of hostile groups will reduce prejudice.

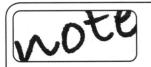

### The faith schools debate and the contact hypothesis

The current UK government encourages single-faith secondary schools, provoking heated debate, including claims that they help perpetuate prejudice and social division. However, in 2005, Trevor Phillips, Chair of the Commission for Racial Equality, stressed that the key issue was not about religion but about the reduced *ethnic mix* in schools. This is not just in some faith schools but in many ordinary state schools too. In other words, he claimed, contact between ethnic groups is decreasing: 'We are sleepwalking our way to segregation [which] destroys talent …,' he said. 'We are becoming strangers to each other.' See www.cre.gov.uk for full speech.

# The contact hypothesis

The contact hypothesis is the idea that merely bringing members of different groups into contact with each other will reduce prejudice. Deutsch and Collins (1951) had shown that white families who were moved to a racially integrated housing programme subsequently showed less prejudice towards blacks than white residents who had moved to a segregated housing programme. However, things did not work quite so smoothly in school desegregation as we have already seen, with more than half the studies of desegregation showing an increase rather than a decrease in prejudiced attitudes (Stephan, 1978). One possible reason is the lack of equal status between the relatively more privileged white children and the less well-off black students being bussed into their schools. Mere contact alone, it appears, does not work.

### Equal status contact

Research on the contact hypothesis has highlighted five important conditions under which contact between individuals is likely to have a favourable outcome. Members of different groups should be brought together under conditions of:

- equal status
- in situations where stereotypes are likely to be disconfirmed
- where there is intergroup cooperation
- where members of the two groups can get to know each other properly
- where wider social norms support equality between the two groups.

A meta-analysis of 516 studies by Pettigrew and Tropp (2000) revealed a highly significant *inverse* correlation between contact and prejudice: the more the contact, the lower the prejudice. The more that studies included the above conditions, the more successful they were at reducing prejudice.

### Why does it work?

Pettigrew (1998) proposed four potential mechanisms to explain *why* contact works: providing opportunities to learn about the outgroup; attitude change as a result of cooperation; ingroup reappraisal; and, probably most importantly, generating affective ties. Increased contact offers opportunities to form new friendships, and research has suggested that intimate contact is far more effective in reducing prejudice than the more superficial contact possible in work and in neighbourhoods (Pettigrew, 1997).

*evaluation*

## The (equal) contact hypothesis

*Applications*

The contact hypothesis has underpinned the main policy initiatives being pursued in Northern Ireland in an attempt to overcome segregation and improve relations between Catholics and Protestants (Cairns and Hewstone, 2002). A very recent study (Cairns *et al.*, 2006) analysed data from earlier surveys to test the contact hypothesis on intergroup attitudes of Catholics and Protestants in Northern Ireland. They found that contact was positively related to attitudes toward denominational mixing, trust and forgiveness, even amongst those most affected by sectarian violence.

*Limitations*

There are many other conflicts worldwide where even intimate contact between members has not led to a reduction in prejudice and hostility. For example, in the former Yugoslavia, 12% of all marriages were mixed (Serb/Muslim), yet the region still experienced civil war during the 1990s. Similarly, there is plentiful evidence that contact does not prevent people from slaughtering former friends and neighbours, as was the case between Hutu and Tutsi in Rwanda during the 1994 conflict. The conclusion, therefore, appears to be that, although increased contact can *reduce* prejudice, it does not guarantee immunity from it.

## Superordinate goals

Research suggests that re-categorising members of a different group so that they are seen as part of one's own ingroup can reduce intergroup conflict. Because the outgroup has effectively become part of the ingroup, negative intergroup attitudes and prejudices vanish. One way of

**Superordinate goals:** Having an aim which is equally important to members of all groups and which cannot be completed without the cooperation of all individuals.

achieving this re-categorisation is through the principle of **superordinate goals**. Although the contact hypothesis has achieved considerable success in reducing intergroup tensions and prejudices, there is a well-established principle which suggests that, if members of competing groups engage in a superordinate task, these individuals will come to like each other better (see the Star Study below).

Superordinate groups are often created in response to an external threat (e.g. the shortage of drinking water in the Star Study), but in real life the positive intergroup attitudes that such threats promote tend not to outlast the threat that created them. Superordinate goals and identities are not sufficient to reduce intergroup prejudice and conflict. In the real world, superordinate groups can quickly splinter again, with disastrous outcomes. For example, the alliance of the United States and the Soviet Union against Nazi Germany during the Second World War was immediately followed by many years of mistrust and hostility between the two nations during the Cold War. As psychologist J. Richard Hackman observed in a lecture in 1999: 'The best way to get peace on earth is an invasion from Mars' (cited in Pittinsky, 2006).

## starSTUDY

# Investigating the reduction of prejudice: The Robbers' Cave study

(SHERIF ET AL., 1954)

### Aims

One of the aims of this study was to see whether groups who are in conflict, and who are brought into contact under conditions involving superordinate goals, cooperate toward the common goals. It also investigated whether this cooperation would have the effect of reducing existing conflict between the groups.

### Method and procedure

Participants were 22 healthy, normal well-adjusted boys between the age of 11 and 12, who did not know one another prior to the study. The boys attended a summer camp in the Robbers' Cave State Park in Oklahoma, US. They were placed into two groups (the 'Eagles' and the 'Rattlers') and then took part in a variety of activities and encounters designed to increase competition and conflict between the groups. The situations were such that one group could achieve its goal (e.g. prizes) only at the expense of the other group.

Members of each group developed hostile attitudes and highly unfavourable stereotypes toward the other group. At the same time, there was an increase in ingroup solidarity and cooperation. In an attempt to reduce hostility between the groups (1) they were brought together in a number of 'get to know you' sessions, such as shooting firecrackers together or a joint picnic, and (2) a series of problem situations were introduced that involved superordinate goals, thus creating a state of interdependence between groups. These included combating a drinking-water shortage that affected all and securing a much desired film (*Treasure Island*) that could not be obtained by one group alone.

### Results

The 'get to know you' contact sessions did not lead to any appreciable decrease in hostility between the two groups, with some sessions actually ending in food fights.

After the introduction of superordinate goals, there was a sharp decrease in hostility and negative stereotyping towards the other group and its members. Ratings of the outgroup changed significantly from largely unfavourable ratings to largely favourable ratings. When asked who they would like to spend time with, choices of outgroup members grew from practically none, during the intergroup conflict phase, to 23% following the introduction of superordinate goals.

### Conclusion

The researchers concluded that *contact* between groups in the absence of superordinate goals does not produce any meaningful lessening of tensions. However, contact with superordinate goals effectively reduced intergroup hostility and prejudice *and* increased friendly associations and attitudes relating to outgroup members.

## Evaluation
*Real-world application*

Critics have suggested that this study could not be applied to real-world social conflicts because the short-term nature of the study does not address long-term intergroup conflicts; however, there have been replications with boys' camps in Lebanon (Diab, 1970) and in the Soviet Union (Andreeva, 1984).

*Research support*

Tyreman and Spencer (1983) failed to produce the same degree of intergroup conflict within a Scout group in the UK. They also found it relatively easy to increase cooperation between different Scout patrols, even in the absence of a superordinate goal. Tyreman and Spencer suggest that this might be explained by the fact that, unlike the boys in Sherif *et al.*'s study, the Scout movement in the UK already possesses a higher goal (e.g. the values of the Scout movement).

### assessment issues

**Analyse the role of superordinate goals in the reduction of prejudice. (ku 4 ae 4)**

A useful starting-point for this question – as is often the case – would be to define what is meant by the term 'superordinate goals'. Your definition would be likely to include a reference to the fact that superordinate goals can be an important factor in reducing prejudice and, if you can throw in an example, all the better. To show *analysis* (for the *ae* marks), you could then elaborate on how this process might work, for example by referring to concepts such as ingroups and outgroups, and intergroup competition versus cooperation, etc. Reference to supporting evidence could also gain credit, such as the Robbers' Cave study. Other analytical points might include interaction with factors such as intergroup contact and the question of whether superordinate goals are effective in the long-term in real-world settings.

# Institutional racism

The collective failure of an organisation to provide an appropriate and professional service to people because of their colour, culture or ethnic origin which can be seen or detected in processes; attitudes and behaviour which amount to discrimination through unwitting prejudice, ignorance, thoughtlessness and racist stereotyping which disadvantages minority ethnic people.

(Macpherson Report into Institutional Racism, 1999)

The 2000 report *Black and Excluded* published by the TUC's Stephen Lawrence Task Group revealed that racism is rife in the jobs market and had worsened during the 1990s, despite growing employment opportunities. Unemployment among black and Asian workers was at a massive 13%, compared with just 6% among their white counterparts (TUC, 2000a). Also published by the TUC, *Qualifying for Racism* (2000b), found that despite the fact that 21% of black and Asian employees are educated to degree level (compared with 16% of white employees) they are facing declining opportunities for career advancement. The report found evidence of a growing 'management and supervisory gap' between black and white workers.

## Institutional racism in the police

The BBC's *Secret Policeman* programme (see note on next page) undoubtedly raised public awareness of institutional racism in the police, and it is clear that this kind of investigative journalism can play a role in prejudice reduction. Following the programme, the Independent Police Complaints Commission (IPCC) considered the issues raised and made a number of recommendations concerning the training of police officers in the UK.

*note*

## *Institutional racism in the police:* **the Secret Policeman** *investigation*

'Secret policeman' Mark Daly

In 2003, BBC reporter Mark Daly spent several months working undercover as a policeman in Manchester. His mission was to discover whether racism in the police had been eradicated following the admission, in 1998, by the chief constable of Greater Manchester Police that his own force was institutionally racist. This startling admission had preceded the Macpherson Report which, in 1999 had branded London's Metropolitan Police institutionally racist. This report found that ethnic minorities in Britain felt under-protected as victims and over-policed as suspects. Daly's brief 'career' as a Manchester policeman produced some disturbing revelations about his fellow recruits. Racist abuse such as 'Paki' and 'Nigger' were commonplace, as was the idea that white and Asian members of the public should be treated differently because of their colour. This idea of discriminatory policing was not only acceptable for some, but preferable.

The IPCC recommendations are to:

- Speed up disciplinary procedures in cases of gross misconduct and dismiss officers in cases where there is compelling evidence.

- Develop national regulations for police trainees where officers only hold the office of constable after a prescribed period of training.

- Review the recruitment process to develop methods of identifying personality traits that are unacceptable in police officers.

- Carry out a national review of the delivery of race and diversity training and develop a method of evaluating the effectiveness of such training.

## Institutional racism in mental health care

David 'Rocky' Bennett, a 38-year-old Jamaican-born Rastafarian, died at a secure centre in Norwich in 1998 after being 'restrained' face down on the floor for nearly half an hour by mental health nurses. In response to investigations following his death, government ministers have decided that training the 40,000 strong mental health workforce in 'cultural competence' should be a priority for the service. The appointment of community development workers who will work with faith leaders and voluntary organisations will address the problem that young black males currently see psychiatric hospitals as centres of 'coercive and dangerous treatment' (*The Guardian*, 27 April 2004).

## Race Relations legislation

The UK Race Relations Act 1976 made racial discrimination unlawful in employment, education, housing, etc., and in the provision of goods and services. An amendment to the Act (2000) puts more emphasis on positively promoting racial equality in various ways. Under this legislation, all public authorities, including schools, colleges, health authorities, local government and other public services have a statutory *duty to promote race equality*. This means that institutions have an obligation to strive to eliminate racial discrimination and promote good relations between different racial groups.

Some key action points are:

- Produce a race equality policy.

- Produce an action plan, with targets.

The Commission for Racial Equality (CRE) provides plentiful guidance on how organisations should set about this task; see 193.113.211.175/duty/index.html

- Provide equal opportunities training.
- Monitor and review progress.
- Encourage applications from under-represented groups.

In the US, employers and universities are expected to adopt a policy of recruiting from ethnic minority groups and women, for example by targeting mainly black or female colleges and advertising in newspapers, magazines and radio and TV channels that are popular with minority groups. They must set percentage targets for recruitment of ethnic minorities and women. This is known as 'affirmative action', or 'positive action', and is aimed at redressing racial and gender disadvantage.

## evaluation | Evaluation of attempts to reduce institutional racism

Research in the UK, US and other countries has shown a dramatic decline in racist attitudes since the 1930s (e.g. Dovidio *et al.,* 1996). But many researchers are concerned that, although blatant racism is much less *expressed* (as it is illegal), this does not mean that it has gone away. Instead it has gone 'underground'. For example, people with racist attitudes may be careful enough to avoid saying unacceptable things in the workplace, but amongst like-minded friends such caution disappears (Hogg and Vaughan, 2002). A more fundamental problem is that racial prejudice may be so deep-seated – as a result of socialisation and prevalent social norms – that it is hard to detect at a conscious level (Devine, 1989); this makes it very difficult to evaluate prejudice-reduction initiatives.

Race equality legislation appears to be effective in making institutions more representative of ethnic groups in the UK, at least in the public sector. However, companies and businesses are not legally bound to collect ethnicity data on their employees, or to set diversity targets, and the duty to promote race equality applies only to public authorities. Therefore, some critics believe that racial equality is being held back in some areas of employment and legislation needs to be strengthened (*The Guardian*, 17 November 2005).

Affirmative action is not without controversy in the US, and in some countries (such as France) it is strongly opposed. In 2003, a white student who had been denied a place at the University of Michigan pursued a law suit claiming that its affirmative action policy on admissions was unconstitutional and was tantamount to racial discrimination against whites. In a landmark ruling the Supreme Court upheld the university's case, citing evidence of many benefits of affirmative action. In Britain, it has been argued that similar policies should be used to tackle the 'glass ceiling' on the careers of ethnic minority doctors (*The Lancet*, 5 July 2003).

## assessment issues

**Describe and evaluate strategies for reducing institutional racism.**
**(ku 4 ae 4)**

The twofold command 'Describe and evaluate' is very common in NABs and exam questions. Give some thought to how best to organise your material for this kind of question, especially where you have to describe and evaluate *more than one* thing – in this case, 'strategies'. Let's assume that you pick two strategies to write about (although you could use more and write about each in lesser depth). One way of structuring your answer would be: describe strategy no.1, then describe strategy no.2, then evaluate strategy no.1, then evaluate strategy no.2. However, it's probably more effective and 'natural', to describe and evaluate strategy no.1, then describe and evaluate strategy no.2. Either way, it's sensible to 'top and tail' your answer with a brief introductory sentence and brief conclusion. Although you may feel that such planning is only necessary for full essay questions, lower-mark questions can also be quite complex in their demands (like this one), so even here, planning pays.

## Chapter: Prejudice

### Exam questions and answers

*In this section we show you student answers to possible exam questions plus examiner's comments on these answers. Remember that in the actual exam (and NABs) your questions for this Topic will always add up to 20 marks. The question may be one essay worth 20 marks or a number of smaller questions (such as those shown below) which add up to 20 marks.*

**Question 1**    (a) Explain what is meant by 'stereotyping' and analyse some of the harmful effects of stereotyping. (*ku* 4 *ae* 2) (b) Describe and evaluate *two* types of strategies aimed at reducing prejudice, referring to research evidence in your answer. (*ku* 8 *ae* 6) [20]

### Tom

(a) The term 'stereotyping' refers to the fact that people have a fixed view of people or things. The harmful effects are that stereotypes can lead to prejudiced behaviour such as racism and sexism.

(b) One strategy that is used to reduce prejudice is the Jigsaw method. This is used in classrooms to try to get children to get to know members of outgroups better. The children are placed in groups each of about 5 children. The groups should be mixed in terms of children belonging to different ethnic groups. The whole class is studying a topic which is broken down into aspects and each child in the group is responsible for finding out about one aspect. The children may work with children from other groups who are investigating the same aspect. At the end the children report back to their own group about what they have found out so all members of the group can put together the pieces of the jigsaw and perhaps take a test on the topic.

Research studies e.g. by Aronson have found that this method works very well. Recent research has found that cooperation alone doesn't reduce intergroup discrimination as much as the interdependence that's part of the Jigsaw method.

A second strategy is to increase contact. However research has found that just putting rival groups together may actually make matters worse rather than better, for example attempts at desegregation in the US. So it is important to make 'contact' a positive experience by ensuring, for example, that the different groups have equal status. One way to do this is superordinate goals such as those used in the Robber's Cave study where boys were on a summer camp. The boys were put into groups and given tasks to make them strongly identify with their group. Then the researchers gave them some tasks to try to reduce their intergroup prejudice. Contact alone didn't work but when they had to do a task such as repairing a broken down water supply (a superordinate goal where everyone had to work together for their common good), then group hostility ceased and group members became quite friendly.

There is some question about whether this research can be applied to everyday life because it might only be a short-term solution – these studies weren't long-term. Also the studies involved children who may be more willing to change their attitudes especially when the attitudes were not deeply ingrained in other aspects of their personality.

**Examiner's comments**    In part (a) Tom appears not to have revised this area of the topic. He gains a total of 1 mark for the two undeveloped points he mentions. **1 out of 6 marks** (*ku* 1/4 *ae* 0/2).

His part (b) is much better. Tom gives detailed and mainly accurate descriptions of his two strategies (for the *ku* marks), and several evaluative and analytical points (for *ae* marks). However, the latter are mainly in relation to his second strategy, whereas his evaluation of the jigsaw classroom is sketchy. He has referred to evidence, as required in the question, but he should have given names (and dates) of all research he has mentioned. He gains **10 out of 14** marks (*ku* 6/8 *ae* 4/6).  Tom's total mark for this 2-part essay: **11 out of 20** (*ku* 7/12 *ae* 4/8)

### Alice

(a) Stereotypes are fixed, usually fairly simplistic generalisations about a particular group or class of people. People use stereotypes because they are 'cognitive misers' i.e. we take shortcuts in our thinking to save time and effort. Stereotypes also make our social world more predictable, as we can make assumptions about how others are likely to behave. Stereotypes are often negative and associated with prejudice.

Such negative effects may harm the prejudiced group in many ways. Obviously the prejudiced group may experience discrimination and also may experience lowered self-esteem because they themselves internalise the negative views that other people have of them. This can impact on their performance so the stereotypes become self-fulfilling. For example, Steele and Aronson (1995) found that black performance on IQ tests was lowered more than for white students if the instructions for the test included a negative stereotype of cognitive ability for the black students. This is to do

with expectations and you can also see this in research with old people which found their memory problems were not due to actual deterioration but were really due to loss of motivation to remember, because of their belief in the stereotype of poor memory in old age.

Negative stereotypes are also destructive to relations between different groups in society because they give a message to the community in general that the negative views are right. For example, the negative stereotype created by the Muslim bombers in London has led to a widespread stereotype that all Muslims are dangerous. Society in general also loses out because the talents of those in stereotyped groups are not used.

(b) There are many ways to try to reduce prejudice including legislation but perhaps the two best known psychological techniques are increasing contact (the contact hypothesis) and the Jigsaw technique.

In the US Deutsch and Collins (1951) developed the contact hypothesis which is that merely bringing members of different groups into contact should reduce prejudice. They did a study and found that white families who were moved to a racially integrated housing programme showed less prejudice towards blacks than white residents who had moved to a segregated housing programme. However, in school desegregation (following the 1954 ruling from the US Supreme Court) desegregation resulted in an increase in prejudiced attitudes (Stephan, 1978). It seems that contact decreases prejudice only under certain conditions such as equal status, where there is intergroup cooperation, and/or where members of the two groups can get to know each other properly. Pettigrew and Tropp (2000) found that the more the studies involved these factors, the more successful they were at reducing prejudice.

Pettigrew (1997) claims that increased contact offers opportunities to form new friendships, and the affection that grows with this intimate contact is far more effective in reducing prejudice than superficial contact.

Aronson and colleagues designed the Jigsaw technique to make contact between members of different ethnic groups in schools more positive and constructive. In the classroom, children engaged in group work where each child would be dependent on the other children in the group in order to complete tasks and do well in the class. Each child had equal status and they worked interdependently and in pursuit of a common goal.

Aronson et al. claimed that their technique was very successful both as a means of learning material generally and also decreasing prejudice. Aronson and Bridgeman (1979) found that children's school performance increased, their self-esteem increased and prejudice against other ethnic groups decreased. However, some critics claim that the reduced prejudice is not generalised to ethnic groups as a whole. The Jigsaw approach uses the concept of superordinate goals investigated by Sherif in his Robbers Cave Study. This study also found that contact alone was insufficient to change prejudiced behaviour but if a group had to work towards a shared goal where everyone had equal status and importance (e.g. repaired a broken water supply), then intergroup attitudes changed dramatically and people started to like each other.

**Examiner's comments** Alice's answer to part (a) is very thorough, for both requirements. In particular, her *analysis* is good: she distinguishes between harmful effects of stereotyping that impact upon the individual and those that affect society; and she explains the steps in the process of internalised negative views that lead to lowered self-esteem and lowered performance as a consequence. She also uses research evidence to show how this kind of process applies to different kinds of stereotyped groups (ethnic groups, elderly people). She has done more than enough to earn full marks, **6 out of 6 marks** (*ku* 4/4 *ae* 2/2).

In part (b), Alice has again produced a very competent answer. One particular strength is the way she has *interpreted* the research evidence that she offers, rather than just stating the findings (for example, her explanation of the somewhat unexpected findings of Stephan, 1978). Another strength is that in her last paragraph she has referred to research evidence which is relevant to both of her chosen strategies. This has gained her *ae* marks. A little more detail of the jigsaw procedure would be useful (for *ku* marks). Nonetheless, Alice gets **14 out of 14 marks** (*ku* 8/8 *ae* 6/6). Alice's total mark for this 2-part essay: **20 out of 20** (*ku* 12/12 *ae* 8/8)

## Question 2    What is meant by the concept of 'social identity'? (*ku* 3 *ae* 0)

| Tom | Alice |
|---|---|
| An individual's self-concept is partly shaped by their membership in social categories (e.g. being female, Christian, Celtic supporter etc). We each have a 'personal identity' but also have a 'social identity'. Because people divide their world into distinct social categories (age, gender, nationality, religion and even football affiliation), our social identity is based on perceived membership of these different social groups. One of the consequences of this social identity is that we favour our ingroup and discriminate against outgroup members. | Social identity is one aspect of your personal identity. We all have a sense of who we are which is in part defined by our personal characteristics (such as skin colour, personality etc) but is also determined by the social groups we belong to. |

**Examiner's comments** Tom has provided a good description of the concept of social identity, giving examples of categories, and also setting it in context by referring to personal identity. In addition he outlines the key related ideas of ingroup favouritism and negative outgroup bias. His answer is slightly repetitive and, instead of briefly mentioning the terms 'ingroup' and 'outgroup' in his last sentence, he could have linked these to his explanation of group membership. However, he has made good use of terminology and generally expressed ideas clearly. His answer is worth the **3 marks** (*ku* 3/3 *ae* 0/0).

Alice's answer includes some important points, but unfortunately, unlike Tom, she has not developed them to any extent and has given very limited examples. Her first sentence is also slightly inaccurate. She gains only **1 mark** (*ku* 1/3 *ae* 0/0).

S ocial psychology is the study of social behaviour, which occurs when two or more members of the same species interact. Social psychology is concerned with how people influence each other's behaviour (social influence) as well as how our thoughts influence our social behaviour (social cognition).

Antisocial behaviour refers to any behaviour that is considered harmful or disruptive within a group or society. Aggression is one type of antisocial behaviour; prejudice and discrimination (see Chapter 6) are also considered to be antisocial.

| Chapter contents | Unit content for the Topic 'Antisocial behaviour' | Comment |
|---|---|---|
| **Aspect 1: Theories of aggression** | | |
| Instinct theories<br>　　page 167<br>Bio-social theories<br>　　page 169<br>Learning theories<br>　　page 170<br>Gender differences<br>　　page 171 | Theories of aggression:<br>● Instinct theories:<br>　– psychoanalytic approach<br>　– ethological approach<br>● bio-social theories, including:<br>　– frustration-aggression hypothesis<br>　– excitation transfer theory<br>　– learning theory<br>　– social learning theory<br>　– influence of environmental cues<br>　– gender differences | *Biologists and social scientists have intensively researched* **aggression** *in non-human animals and humans. In this first Aspect of the Topic, after grappling with definitions, you will examine a range of major theoretical explanations that psychologists have proposed: those that emphasise* **'instinct'**, *i.e. the* **psychoanalytic** *view based on Freudian theory, as well as the* **ethological** *perspective;* **bio-social theories** *which recognise the interaction of biological and social factors. The role of experience, and environmental factors, are analysed in the discussion of* **learning theories** *and the effects of* **environmental cues**. **Gender differences** *in aggression are pronounced, and you will consider why this is the case.* |
| **Aspect 2: Aggression and the media** | | |
| Research studies relating to aggression and the media<br>　　page 177<br>Mediating factors<br>　　page 180 | Aggression and the media:<br>● research studies into effects of media violence<br>● mediating factors, including<br>　– desensitisation to violence<br>　– parental involvement in children's viewing | *Many people believe that* **violence in the media** *makes humans aggressive. Here you will consider to what extent* **research evidence** *supports or challenges this view. You will see that, if there is indeed a link, it is unlikely to be a simple, causal influence. You will see that various factors are involved in this complex process, such as the possibility that viewers may become* **desensitised** *to violence, and that children may or may not be influenced depending on whether their* **parents** *talk to them about what they see on TV.* |
| **Aspect 3: Control and reduction of aggression** | | |
| Individual processes<br>　　page 183<br>Using the antecedents of aggression<br>　　page 185 | Approaches to control and reduction of aggression:<br>● incompatible responses<br>● reducing frustration<br>● catharsis<br>● role-modelling<br>● anger-management interventions | *Various techniques are applied, in therapy, amongst offenders, and in the workplace, to reduce aggressive behaviour. You should be able to describe and evaluate several of these, including the use of* **incompatible responses** *such as humour, and avoiding the* **frustration** *that can often lead to aggression.* **Catharsis** *and* **role-modelling**, *based on psychoanalytic theory and learning theory respectively, are also considered. You will also study the practical application of* **anger-management interventions**, *which often combine a number of techniques.* |

# Aspect 1:   Theories of aggression

## Instinct theories

### What is antisocial behaviour and aggression?

'Antisocial acts are those that show a lack of feeling and concern for the welfare of others' (Baron and Richardson, 1994). There are many different forms of behaviour that would qualify as 'antisocial' under this definition, but aggressive behaviour against others is usually viewed as one of the most disturbing forms of **antisocial behaviour**. **Aggression** is difficult to define because many examples of harmful behaviour do not necessarily count as aggression, such as capital punishment or accidentally bumping into someone and injuring them. There are many different kinds of aggression, such as predatory aggression (killing other species for food), social aggression (unprovoked aggression with the purpose of establishing dominance), and defensive aggression (responding to attack by another). Gratuitous violence is aggression simply for the sake of aggression.

### Theories of aggression

Some psychologists believe that aggression is an important aspect of our evolutionary ancestry and is therefore best understood in that context. Such approaches are called *'instinct theories'* and are examined first. Other psychologists believe that aggression is largely a learned behaviour, like all other behaviour, or is triggered by environmental cues. These *learning theories* are discussed on pages 172–174. There is a third group of theories, *bio-social theories*, which incorporate innate and learned/social factors (see pages 169–172).

### How do instinct theories explain aggression?

**Instinct** theories suggest that aggression is an innate, inescapable drive and thus difficult to control unless the urges are channelled elsewhere. Instinct theories explain aggression in terms of biology – genetics, **hormones** and so on. In this section we will also look at evidence that suggests that aggression has a biological basis.

---

*explanation*

The struggle between Thanatos and Eros, death and life

### The psychoanalytic approach

Freud (1930) believed that two basic and opposing drives (instincts) motivate all our thoughts and behaviours – sex and aggression. He referred to these as *Eros* and *Thanatos*. *Eros* represents the life instinct, with sex being the major driving force in human nature leading to reproduction. The second drive, the death instinct, is the urge in all living things to return to a state of calm, or, ultimately, of non-existence. This manifests itself as a drive to self-destruction or death. These drives reside in the **id** (the instinctive part of our personality that contains our basic urges, see page 247). However, the **ego** (the rational part of the mind) can redirect this instinct so that it becomes a desire to destroy and be aggressive towards others: 'a portion of the [death] instinct is diverted towards the external world and comes to light as an instinct of aggressiveness and destructiveness' (Freud, 1930).

Originally Freud had only theorised about a life instinct but, after the First World War, he reluctantly accepted that there was also an instinct for aggression, because only this could explain the organised group violence he observed. However, he was optimistic and felt that an individual could bring Eros into play to counter aggressive urges. Freud claimed that nothing can end the tendency to aggression, but that it is possible for people to redirect their energies to remove the impetus to destruction. This process is called **catharsis**.

---

*evaluation*

The evidence for catharsis is poor (see page 183), and there is really almost no other empirical research evidence that could be used to assess this theory. It is more of a myth than a theory, and thus quite difficult to test. Lorenz's model, which is described next, lends some support as it generates similar predictions.

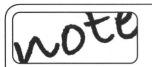

## explanation

### The ethological approach

Lorenz (1966) argued that the same laws applied to all animals because they are all governed by the same laws of natural selection. His observations of non-human animal behaviour led him to suggest that aggression is:

- *An innate tendency* – aggression is triggered by environmental signals, for example the male stickleback (a fish) will behave aggressively when it sees anything red, i.e. competitive males who have red markings (Tinbergen, 1951).
- *An adaptive response* – aggressive behaviour promotes survival and reproductive success because the strongest, most aggressive animal usually controls access to resources such as food, territory and mating.
- *Not naturally harmful* – in non-human animals, ritualised forms of aggression evolve to prevent actual harm taking place. For example, two male stags will circle each other, make threatening noises and put on displays of strength. The use of threat displays to deter competitors means that physical aggression is often not needed.

Lorenz proposed the **hydraulic model** of aggression. In essence, Freud's theory is also a hydraulic model because it too suggests that aggressive impulses build up until the pressure is too great and then they 'burst' out.

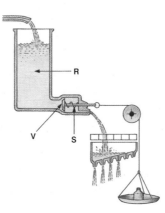

In Lorenz's hydraulic model, aggressive energies increase like water in a reservoir (R) until they are released by stimulus (S) or until the pressure becomes too great on the valve (V). The aggressive energy then floods out.

In particular, Lorenz pointed to:

1. The importance of an aggression-releasing stimulus; for example, in the case of the male stickleback, the colour red acts as a '*releaser*'.
2. The energy that was released; this is called *action specific energy*, i.e. energy that leads to certain behaviours. In the case of the male stickleback this would be to attack the red object.
3. The need for release, and thus the benefit of providing humans with acceptable means of 'emptying their reservoir' to avoid outbursts of harmful aggression i.e. catharsis.

### Ethology

Ethology is the biological study of behaviour. Ethologists study animal behaviour using naturalistic observation and focus on the importance of innate capacities and the adaptiveness of behaviour.

**Hydraulic model:** This model suggests that aggression builds up until it overflows and has to be expressed; if it can be dissipated before overflow then aggression will be prevented.

## evaluation

### Instinct theories

There are several criticisms of this approach. First, it is deterministic: it suggests that aggression is inevitable unless channelled elsewhere. This may be true of animal behaviour but humans are capable of thinking about the consequences of their actions and thus can control aggressive impulses.

Secondly, both instinct theories do not account for cultural differences in aggression (see evidence on page 173). Even in non-human animal behaviour, social factors have been shown to override biological ones. For example, when an area of the brain (called the *amygdala*) is electrically stimulated in monkeys, docile animals become aggressive but if the monkey is in the presence of more dominant monkeys, then the monkey doesn't behave aggressively (Aronson, 1999).

More modern instinct theories (sociobiological theories) incorporate an element of learning and are not quite so determinist. They do suggest that aggression is an *adaptive* behaviour; it is *partly* controlled by inherited mechanisms and *partly* by learning.

## The biology of aggression

Instinct theories rely on the idea that aggression has a biological basis, and there is evidence that demonstrates the importance of biological factors (while not necessarily excluding social factors).

First, certain parts of the brain (chiefly the *limbic system*) have been linked to aggressive behaviour in animals (Papez, 1937). This has been supported in studies of humans. In one notorious case of violent behaviour in 1966 in Texas, Charles Whitman killed his wife and mother and then used a rifle to shoot down 38 people, killing 14. An autopsy revealed a large tumour in the limbic system of his brain.

Secondly, certain hormones have been linked with aggressive behaviour. Testosterone may not *cause* aggression but levels are higher in people who behave aggressively (although it could be a cause or an effect). Lower levels of the hormone *serotonin* are also associated with aggression and so are high levels of *adrenaline* (the 'fight-or-flight' response described in Chapter 3).

Thirdly, we can look at genetic evidence. For example, Mednick *et al.* (1984) found that adopted children whose biological fathers were criminals were more likely to become criminals themselves than were adopted children whose adopted fathers were criminals. This suggests that a tendency to being criminal (and presumably more aggressive) is in your genes – however, not all criminals are aggressive. More impressive evidence comes from a recent study demonstrating a gene–violence link. Caspi *et al.* (2002) studied 442 New Zealand men and found that those who had low MAOA gene activity *and* had been abused in childhood were four times more likely to have been convicted of a violent crime by the age of 26. The MAOA gene is important in eliminating excess neurotransmitters, such as adrenaline and serotonin.

The genetic basis of aggression has also been demonstrated in selective breeding programmes. More (or less) aggressive breeds of dogs or bulls can be developed by selecting suitable males and females for breeding.

(See also 'Biological explanations of gender differences', page 175).

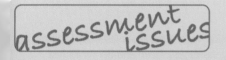

assessment issues

**With reference to research evidence, discuss the contributions of any *two* psychological approaches to our understanding of antisocial behaviour. (*ku 12 ae 8*)**

Psychologists of virtually every persuasion – social, behaviourist, ethological, psychoanalytic, biological – queue up to offer explanations of antisocial behaviour. Exam questions, like the one above, often require you to discuss *alternative explanations* (plenty of analysis and evaluation opportunities here!). Many other topics also involve a range of approaches. So, for example, when you study the psychoanalytic approach to aggression you can draw on your knowledge of psychoanalytic concepts (such as the *id* and the *ego*) from your study of the Topic of attachment. Examiners will give you credit if you can demonstrate this kind of 'joined-up thinking' (or *integration*).

## Bio-social theories
### How do bio-social theories explain aggression?

The term 'bio-social' obviously refers to a combination of biological and social elements. The theories considered over the next few pages explain aggression in terms of both factors but suggest that aggression has its *origins* in characteristics of the situation (social factors) rather than in biological factors. For example, frustration-aggression theory proposes that aggression is due to frustration triggered by external social factors which creates an internal state of physiological arousal leading to aggressive behaviour. Excitation-transfer theory also focuses on physiological arousal created by external social factors which is then transferred from one situation to another, where it is expressed as aggression.

In this section we also consider environmental cues as these are linked to the frustration-aggression hypothesis – environmental cues lead to frustration and increased physiological arousal.

*explanation*

## The frustration-aggression hypothesis

Dollard *et al*. (1939) suggested that frustration *always* leads to some form of aggression and *all* aggression is the result of frustration. Frustration is anything that blocks or delays us as we strive to achieve a goal. Aggression is triggered by external, social factors rather than internal, biological ones. Such social factors include people and any characteristics of the situation. These social factors create a state of frustration or physiological arousal, which motivates the organism to act.

This is a drive theory, similar to the instinct theories described earlier. We are born with a drive to be aggressive and, according to this theory, aggression activates that drive. If the drive is not satisfied it builds up.

Berkowitz (1978) reformulated the initial frustration-aggression hypothesis, proposing that frustration leads to negative feelings (e.g. anger or anxiety) rather than directly to aggression. This is called the *cognitive-neoassociation model*. Negative feelings may lead to aggression but can be controlled by higher cognitive functions (e.g. how you perceive the situation), so frustration doesn't automatically lead to aggression.

*evaluation*

There is some research support for the frustration-aggression hypothesis. For example, Kulik and Brown (1979) arranged for students to phone two strangers (**confederates**) to ask for charity donations. Both confederates refused to donate. There was a 'low provocation' condition (confederate said that the cause was worthy but just didn't have much money) and a 'high provocation' condition (confederate challenged the worthiness of the cause). Frustration was assessed by a device in the cradle of the phone which measured the force used by the participant to hang up the phone. Later the participants were asked to send out brochures about the charity including one of three covering letters. The letters varied in aggressiveness of tone and there was a **positive correlation** between levels of frustration and later aggressiveness.

However, there is a wealth of evidence that shows that frustration doesn't always lead to aggression, supporting Berkowitz's reformulation. Cognitive activity may eliminate aggression. For example, Burnstein and Worchel (1962) arranged for a confederate to disrupt a group's problem-solving task; this usually resulted in aggression directed toward the confederate but, if the confederate indicated that he had problems with a failing hearing aid, no aggression towards the confederate was observed.

On the other hand, cognitive factors may increase aggression; for example the presence of aggressive cues in a study by Geen and Berkowitz (1967) led to aggressiveness. Geen and Berkowitz first frustrated their participants and then showed them a film which had either aggressive or non-aggressive content. Aggression was later assessed through the level of electric shocks that the participants administered to a learner. If the participant had watched an aggressive film or there was an aggressive trigger present in the room, such as a gun, the level of shocks given was greater.

*explanation*

## Excitation-transfer

Loud noise, high temperatures, alcohol, physical exercise, and music have all been associated with aggression. This link can be explained by excitation-transfer theory (Zillmann, 1979). The environmental cues (which are discussed in detail below) create excitation, or physiological arousal which is then *transferred* to another situation.

Two conditions appear to be necessary for excitation transfer to take place: (1) the individual must be predisposed to behave aggressively and (2) the true cause of the arousal must not be obvious, otherwise the individual would be more likely to attribute arousal to the true cause.

*evaluation*

Zillmann (1971) provided research support in an experiment where participants were provoked by verbal abuse. They were then divided into two groups: one exercised on a cycling machine while the others watched some slides quietly. Those in the exercise group subsequently gave more electric shocks to a confederate who provoked them.

Some psychologists (e.g. Eysenck, 2001) claim that this theory has rather limited application because in real life we are often aware of why we are aroused and, therefore, are not affected by such arousal. However, as we shall see, the evidence related to temperature and noise suggests otherwise.

# Environmental cues

### Temperature

Heat was found to be linked to frustration in a field experiment by Kenrick and MacFarlane (1986). The number and duration of horn blasts from stationary drivers were recorded when the experimenter's car remained at a standstill at traffic lights that had turned green. Hooting was found to be positively related to outdoor temperature but only for drivers with windows open (those with windows closed were presumably using air conditioning and so stayed cool).

Heat has also been associated with violent crime (Anderson, 1987). Data on rates of murder, rape, assault, robbery, burglary, theft, and car theft were gathered from archival sources. The first three crimes were considered violent, the latter four as less violent. It was found that violent crimes were more common in the hotter quarters of the year and in hotter years. Furthermore, it was also found that this temperature–crime relation was stronger for violent than for non-violent crime.

The link between aggression and temperature may be indirect, as explained by *routine activity theory* (Cohen and Felson, 1979) which states that the opportunities for interpersonal aggression increase in the summer because people change their patterns of routine activity and are more likely to be out of doors and so come into contact with other people, which creates more opportunity for interpersonal aggression. Increases in alcohol consumption during hot weather may further compound this relationship.

A direct link between temperature and aggression can be explained by *negative affect escape theory*. Baron and Bell (1976) claim that negative affect (mood) increases as temperatures become uncomfortably hot. As negative affect increases, so do aggressive and escape motives. At high levels of negative affect, if escape from the heat *is* possible, escape behaviour is displayed and aggression is not. If escape is *not* a possibility, then aggressive behaviours are displayed.

### Noise

Geen and O'Neal (1969) found that high levels of noise increased aggressiveness. First, participants watched either an aggressive or a non-aggressive film; they were then given the opportunity to shock someone in another room during which time they were either exposed to no noise or to loud noise. Participants were more likely to shock the other person when they were in a noisy environment but only if they had seen the aggressive film.

Donnerstein and Wilson (1976) investigated whether aggression would be decreased by having a sense of control. Half the participants were first angered by a confederate (creating a state of frustration); the other half were not. Participants were then given the chance to shock someone in another room, during which:

- Condition 1 – they were exposed to a noise that they could turn off
- Condition 2 – they were exposed to a noise that they could *not* turn off
- Condition 3 – participants were not exposed to any noise.

Participants who were angered gave much higher levels of shock. If they had some control over the noise, levels of aggression were lower than in both the other conditions.

Evans *et al.* (1998) provided compelling evidence for the stressful effects of long-term exposure to uncontrolled noise. They looked at children aged seven to eight years in rural areas outside Munich, Germany, before and after the opening of a new airport. Approximately half the children lived in an area under the flight path of the airport, while the others lived in quiet areas. The children in the noise group experienced significant increases in blood pressure and in stress hormones (which may lead to higher levels of aggressive behaviour) while the children in the quiet areas experienced no significant changes.

In the film *Falling Down*, Michael Douglas is the uptight commuter stuck in an LA traffic jam. The heat and irritation of his surroundings finally become too much and he snaps, triggering off a chain of disastrous events.

*evaluation*  | Environmental cues

*Temperature*
Evidence for a direct link between aggression and temperature was shown in an experimental study by Baron and Bell (1976). They found that participants gave more electric shocks to a

confederate who provoked them when in a warm, stuffy room (mid-80s) but were less aggressive when the temperature rose above 90°F. This also supports negative affect escape theory.

However, laboratory experiments may elicit false responses. Participants know that they will escape the hot temperature as soon as the experiment is over, and this would make their behaviour different from how it would be in the real world. It is also possible that, when a laboratory gets very hot, participants realise what is being studied and this might lead them to react against the situation, resisting highly aggressive behaviour. This could explain the apparent curvilinear relationship found in experimental studies.

A different explanation of the aggression–temperature link is a biological one – the production of testosterone increases when you get hot. As we noted earlier (page 169), high levels of testosterone are linked to aggressive behaviour.

*Noise*
Noise may just be a cue or trigger for aggressiveness rather than a cause. For example, in the study by Geen and O'Neal (1969), noise and no prior cue to aggression (no frustration) did not result in aggressive behaviour. On the other hand, there is evidence that noise acts like any other **stressor**, increasing activity of the **autonomic nervous system**, leading for example to increased heart rate and hormone levels such as testosterone (Bronzaft, 1997). This is the premise of excitation-transfer theory (above).

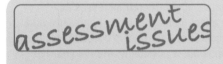

### assessment issues

**Describe and analyse *one* bio-social explanation of antisocial behaviour. (*ku 6 ae 2*)**

The 'describe' part of this question should present no problem: you should write about a bio-social theory such as *frustration-aggression* or *excitation-transfer*. The 'analyse' part (for the *ae* marks) asks you to delve more deeply. For example, you should explain how biological and social factors interact according to the bio-social approach. Indeed, this is an excellent chance to refer to the underlying **nature–nurture** theme which crops up in many areas of psychology. Also, by comparing the bio-social approach to other explanations with either a 'nature' or a 'nurture' emphasis, you could widen the scope of your *analysis*.

## Learning theories
## How do learning theories explain aggression?

In the first part of this chapter we looked at instinct theories which suggest that aggression is an innate and adaptive behaviour. Following this we looked at bio-social theories which combine nature and nurture – suggesting that a drive to be aggressive is innate but the drive is triggered by social (environmental) events. Now we turn to explanations focused on nurture – the view that aggressive behaviour is something we learn either directly or indirectly.

### explanation

### Learning theory

In Chapter 1 (see page 3), we used learning theory (the behaviourist approach) as a way of explaining attachment. Behaviourists believe that learning theory can explain *all* behaviour using the concepts of **classical** and **operant conditioning**.

*Operant conditioning*
The key to operant conditioning is the 'stamping in' of a behaviour through rewards. If you behave aggressively towards your mother when she asks you to clean your room and she backs down, you are rewarded for this behaviour. This increases the likelihood that you will repeat the same behaviour at other times and in other situations. Gradually you learn this new behaviour. Behaviourists say that the behaviour has been *reinforced*.

Operant conditioning also involves punishment. If your aggressive action towards your mother results in her becoming angrier this could discourage you from trying to behave like that in future. Your mother's angry response is a 'punisher' and reduces the probability of future, similar behaviours.

All of this takes place without any thought or conscious awareness.

*Classical conditioning*
Behaviourists also explain behaviour in terms of classical conditioning although, as far as aggressiveness goes, this is a less likely explanation. Classical conditioning occurs through the process of *association*. Initially an organism has various reflex responses to stimuli, for example being attacked by another animal (unconditioned stimulus) results in feelings of aggression (unconditioned response). If that animal has a certain smell, this smell (a neutral stimulus) becomes associated with the attack and takes on its properties (becomes a conditioned stimulus). The conditioned stimulus will now produce the response of aggression (conditioned stimulus produces a conditioned response).

*explanation*

## Social learning theory (Bandura, 1962)

Albert Bandura (1962) felt that traditional learning theory did not provide a complete explanation for aggressive behaviour; *direct* experience could not explain the acquisition of all new behaviours. Social learning theory (SLT) proposes that most learning takes place *indirectly*; we learn about the specifics of aggressive behaviour by observing others (e.g. the forms behaviour takes, how often it is enacted, the situations that produce it and the targets towards which it is directed). This is not to suggest that the role of direct factors is ignored (see below).

*The processes of social leaning*
We learn about aggressive responses through *observation*. We also observe and learn about the *consequences* of aggressive behaviour by watching others being successful in getting what they want. This is called indirect or **vicarious reinforcement**. Thus we learn the behaviours and then learn whether and when such behaviours are worth *imitating*.

Bandura (1986) claimed that in order for social learning to take place, the individual must form *mental representations* of events in their social environment. The individual must also represent possible rewards and punishments for their aggressive behaviour in terms of *expectancies* of future outcomes.

*Production of behaviour*
Behaviour is maintained through *direct* experience. If an individual models an observed behaviour and is rewarded (i.e. gets what he wants or is praised by others) for aggressive behaviour, they are likely to repeat the same action in similar situations in the future. This is *direct* reinforcement. This will influence the *value* of aggression for that individual.

In addition to forming expectancies of the likely outcomes of their aggression (from direct and indirect reinforcement), individuals also develop confidence in their ability to carry out the necessary aggressive actions. Individuals for whom aggressive behaviour has been particularly disastrous (e.g. they weren't very good at it) have less confidence (lower sense of **self-efficacy**) in their ability to use aggression successfully to resolve conflicts, and may therefore turn to other means.

| **KEY TERMS** |
| --- |

**Vicarious reinforcement:** Is indirect reinforcement. The probability of repeating a behaviour is increased if someone else is observed receiving a reward for that behaviour.

**Self-efficacy:** An individual's belief in their own ability to produce positive outcomes, i.e. belief in their own competence.

*evaluation*

*Strengths*
A key strength is that SLT can explain differences between and within individuals. Differences *between* individuals include cultural variations of which there is infinite diversity. There are societies that are highly violent, such as the US, and societies that manage to live in cooperative friendliness such as the Pygmies of Central Africa (Aronson, 1999). Such differences must be due to social learning because genetic variation between ethnic groups is not large enough to explain such differences.

Differences *within* individuals can be related to selective reinforcement and *context-dependent learning* (see page 49). People respond differently in different situations because they have observed that aggression is rewarded in one situation and not in another.

The studies on the next few pages provide strong support for SLT; however, they focus on children's behaviour. There are some studies that demonstrate adult imitation; for example Phillips (1986) found that daily homicide rates in the US almost always increased in the week following a major boxing match.

*Limitation*
SLT is not a complete explanation of aggression. It explains aggressive behaviour but not the impulse to be aggressive. Even if you have watched a model behave aggressively, you only will act if frustrated or aroused. Bandura did not deny the role of biological factors; he believed that a person's biological endowment creates a potential for aggression. SLT explains how aggressive behaviours are learned and also when they are displayed.

## starSTUDY

# Investigating theories of aggression: Imitation

(BANDURA *ET AL.*, 1961)

Adult model kicking bobo doll and child participant imitating this behaviour

## Aims
To investigate whether children will imitate a model's behaviour in a new setting when the model is no longer present.

## Method and procedure
Seventy-two boys and girls aged three to five years were divided into three groups. One group observed an aggressive model interacting with a life-sized inflatable Bobo doll; the second group observed models who were non-aggressive in their behaviour towards the doll, and the third group saw no model. In the aggressive condition, the model displayed some distinctive physically aggressive acts, such as striking the doll on the head with a mallet and kicking it about the room, accompanied by verbal aggression such as saying 'POW!'

After exposure to the model, children were frustrated by being shown attractive toys that they could not play with; they were then taken to a room where, among other toys, there was a Bobo doll. Their play behaviour was observed through a one-way mirror.

## Results
Children in the aggression condition reproduced a good deal of physical behaviour that resembled the behaviour of the model, whereas children in the other groups exhibited virtually no aggression toward the Bobo doll.

Approximately one-third of the children in the aggressive condition also repeated the model's aggressive verbal responses while none of the children in the other groups made such remarks. Boys reproduced more imitative physical (but not verbal) aggression than girls.

## Conclusion
This study shows that children do produce new behaviours that they have observed and generalise them to other situations, thus showing that learning occurs through indirect rather than just direct reinforcement.

One of the factors crucial in performance is motivation to act. In the Bobo doll studies, children were frustrated in order to evoke an aggressive response. This means that these studies also demonstrate the role of frustration in aggressive behaviour.

## Evaluation
*Ecological validity*
One criticism of this study was that it was a highly contrived situation lacking **ecological validity**. Ecological validity is further challenged because the children may well have been aware of what was expected of them (i.e. they displayed **demand characteristics**). In fact, Nobel (1975) reports that one child arriving at the laboratory for the experiment said, 'Look, Mummy, there's the doll we have to hit'.

Another, related issue is that the study only looks at aggression towards a doll rather than towards a real person (who tends to hit back). However, responding to this criticism, Bandura produced a film of a young woman beating up a live clown. When the children went into the other room, there was the live clown! They proceeded to punch and kick him.

*Short-term behaviour*
A second criticism is that the study only looked at short-term behaviour. It may not be reasonable to assume that the same principles would apply to behaviour reproduced weeks or even years later.

## Other Bobo studies

Bandura and Walters (1963) conducted a further study to demonstrate *why* a child would be motivated to repeat the model's behaviour. Three groups were shown a different ending to a film of an adult model behaving aggressively towards a Bobo doll: the model was either rewarded, punished or no consequences were shown. Those children who saw the model rewarded showed a high level of aggression in their own play, those who saw the model punished showed a low level of aggression, and those who saw no consequences were in between.

Bandura (1965) conducted a further study to demonstrate the difference between learning and imitation. Bandura offered rewards to all the children for performing the model's behaviour. In this case, all three groups performed a similar number of imitative acts. This shows that seeing the punishment didn't prevent learning, it just prevented imitation.

## Gender differences

We finish this Aspect with a brief look at gender differences in aggression. It is a common observation that males (humans and other animals) are more aggressive than females. Is this due to biological differences or is it because males are socialised to behave in this way?

explanation

### Biological explanations of gender differences

Since males and females are biologically different we might expect that the aggression differential is related to biological factors.

One explanation relates to the hormone *testosterone*. This hormone is found mainly in males and has been linked to higher levels of aggressiveness (see page 169). Research has found that castration (which reduces testosterone output) leads to lower aggression in male animals, and their aggression increases if given testosterone (Simpson, 2001).

There is also evidence that female aggressiveness is linked to hormone activity – from the female hormone *progesterone*. Floody (1968) reviewed research on pre-menstrual tension (PMT) and reported increases in irritability, hostility, and child abuse associated with this time when levels of progesterone are high.

In terms of chromosomal differences, a classic study by Jacobs *et al.* (1965) found a surprisingly high level of XYY men in prison populations for violent crimes (normal males have XY chromosomes; females are XX). This suggests that the Y chromosome is linked to aggression because when it is duplicated (in XYY individuals) aggression increases.

From an evolutionary standpoint, it can be argued that gender differences in aggression initially evolved in the EEA (see page 58) because men and women needed different strategies to ensure survival and reproductive success. For example, women cannot afford to engage in violent behaviour because their survival is crucial to the survival of their offspring, whereas male violence (to fight off rival males and to fight off predators) was an adaptive behaviour (Campbell, 2002).

evaluation

*Testosterone*
The evidence is largely based on animal studies which may oversimplify the link between testosterone and aggression. In any case, hormones generally moderate behaviour rather than *cause* it. In general, the effect of testosterone is to increase levels of aggressiveness once it has been triggered, but it is only one of many factors that affect aggressiveness (Simpson, 2001). This explains why many men exhibit no aggressiveness at all despite producing testosterone. Even in animals, testosterone only affects some kinds of aggression; for example it doesn't affect predatory aggression (Bermond *et al.*, 1982).

*Chromosomal differences*
The research described above on chromosomal differences was later discredited because it was found that there were similar mutations among men in the normal population. However, there is evidence that XYY individuals may be more aggressive; Theilgaard (1984) concluded that they were, in fact, more prone to aggression than normal XY males.

*explanation*

## Social explanations of gender differences

Gender differences may be rather more due to social than biological factors. Men may be more aggressive because they are socialised to behave this way. Parents and peers reinforce boys for behaving like boys and girls for behaving like girls. This is called differential reinforcement. Girls and boys are also indirectly reinforced by observing how role models behave (social learning theory).

One source of evidence for this view is **cross-cultural studies**, such as the classic study by Margaret Mead (1935) of men and women in Papua, New Guinea. In two tribes there were no gender differences in aggression, whereas in a third tribe, the *Tchambuli*, the women were more aggressive than the men. Cook (1992) also found that women are more aggressive in some cultures. Such differences can only be explained by cultural practices (i.e. nurture).

Support for the social view also comes from evidence that men and women *express* their aggression differently. Men are more likely to be physically aggressive whereas women use more indirect and verbal methods. Physical aggression may be less frequent in women because they are physically weaker but it is also likely that physical aggression is less socially acceptable for girls, a view supported by the finding that boys become less physically aggressive as they get older, presumably because they learn that it is not acceptable (Björkqvist *et al.*, 1992).

*evaluation*

*Are there gender differences?*

It may be that gender differences are an artefact of research methods because it all depends how you operationalise aggression – physical or verbal, direct or indirect, within and between groups, sex of opponent and so on. For example, men are more aggressive when unprovoked, but gender differences disappear in conditions of provoked aggression (Bettencourt and Miller, 1996).

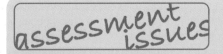

## assessment issues

**Describe and evaluate the contribution of social learning theory to our understanding of aggression. Refer to research evidence in your answer. (ku 6 ae 4)**

This is a straightforward question asking about a specified theory, the kind of question that could crop up in relation to various topics. The question also requires you to 'refer to research evidence' – just how many studies should you mention? There is no hard and fast rule. For this question no doubt you have many relevant studies at your fingertips! Beware of trying to describe too many (it's only a 10-mark question, not a full essay), but don't err on the side of too few either. Perhaps three or four studies would be about right, including a Bandura study. Don't get carried away with describing any particular study in great detail – this question does not focus on a single research study. Some lateral thinking might help too: is there some research evidence from the area of gender differences that could be relevant here, or any material from the area of aggression and media violence?

   Also, don't forget that whenever you refer to research evidence, and especially when there are *ae* marks up for grabs (as here), you can gain credit for *analysis*, by explaining how the research findings support or challenge the theory in question, and possibly *evaluation* marks for criticisms of the methodology (which, incidentally, would also show *integration* of your knowledge of research methods).

# Aspect 2: Aggression and the media

August 1987 BRITON KILLS 14 IN RAMPAGE **Some people claimed that Michael Ryan (above) acted as he did because he was copying Rambo (the heroic and aggressive star of the films with the same title), but Cumberbatch (2001) said that there is no actual evidence that he ever saw the film: 'People have been looking for something to blame and video has been a soft target'.**

## Research studies relating to aggression and the media

### Does media violence increase viewer aggression?

The effects of media violence have been the subject of intense research for at least the last 50 years: 'the media' refers to television, films, books, computer games, and so on. We will start by examining some of the research evidence, and then we will consider *how* the media may exert such an influence, i.e. the mediating factors, concluding with an attempt at answering the question, 'Does media violence increase viewer aggression?'

### Research on the effects of media violence

#### Experimental studies

Bandura *et al.* (1963) extended the original 'Bobo' research on aggression to include exposing children to filmed versions of a model behaving aggressively and found that up to 88% of children studied readily imitated the aggression they saw on the video film (Bandura, 1994). A number of field experiments have sought to demonstrate the causal link between media violence and aggressive behaviour. Such studies have the advantage of reducing demand characteristics. Gadow and Sprafkin (1989) reviewed 20 such studies and concluded that almost all studies showed an increase in participants' aggression after they viewed violent TV programmes.

#### Longitudinal studies

Eron and Huesmann studied over 800 American boys aged 8 and found that the children who watched violent television at home behaved more aggressively in school. They returned to study the same boys at age 30 and found that those participants who had watched more violent TV as 8-year-olds were more likely, as adults, to be convicted of serious crimes, to use violence to discipline their children, and to treat their spouses aggressively (Eron and Huesmann, 1986). A number of other longitudinal studies have produced similar results (e.g. Johnson *et al.*, 2002). Such research suggests that there is an association between watching violence on TV and violent behaviour.

#### Video games and aggression

Psychologists have only recently begun to study the effect of violence in video games. Dill and Dill (1998) reviewed the research evidence in this area and concluded that 'exposure to video game violence increases aggressive behaviour and other aggression-related phenomena'. A recent study by Gentile *et al.* (2004) surveyed 607 US students (mean age 14) and found that exposure to violent video games, while statistically significant, correlated only very weakly (+0.10) with having arguments with teachers and (+0.07) with having physical fights with other students.

#### Effect on susceptible individuals

Slater *et al.* (2003) proposed that people with certain dispositions would be more attracted to violent media and then this would reinforce their aggressive tendencies, a *'downward spiral model'*. They studied 2300 US school students and found that a sensation-seeking disposition correlated with both aggression and media violence exposure.

Other studies have looked at whether violent criminals are more likely to be affected by watching violent programmes. Browne and Pennell (2000) studied convicted offenders and found that almost two-thirds (64%) of the violent offenders preferred violent films compared with only 25% of the non-violent offenders and just 11% of a control group. Browne and Pennell suggested that preferences for violent videos will serve to reinforce distorted attitudes and values, making further violent offending more likely.

#### Meta-analysis of research

Paik and Comstock (1994) examined 217 studies of the relationship between media violence and aggressive behaviour, carried out between 1957 and 1990 (participants' ages ranged from 3 to 70 years of age). They found a highly significant relationship between watching television violence and aggressive behaviour. The greatest effect was evident in preschool children, and the effect for males was slightly higher than it was for females.

*evaluation*

## Research on the effects of media violence

*Experimental studies*

Fowles (1999) contrasts watching television in the laboratory with watching television at home. 'At home television viewing is an entirely voluntary activity: The child is in front of the set because the child has elected to do so and in most instances has elected the content … In the behavioral laboratory, the child is compelled to watch material not of the child's choosing and probably not of the child's liking.'

As regards field experiments Gadow and Sprafkin found that violence also increased simply in association with watching any TV programme, whether it was high or low in violence. For example, Coates *et al.* (1976) found that children who were shown pro-social children's TV programmes, such as *Sesame Street*, displayed an almost threefold increase in aggression. You should also consider the findings from the natural experiment described in the star study on the next page.

*Longitudinal studies*

Longitudinal studies demonstrate a relationship between media violence and aggressive behaviour but that doesn't mean that aggression is *caused* by watching media violence. It might be that more aggressive individuals choose to watch violence on TV and this explains the relationship. However, Huesmann *et al.* (2003) analysed data from a study of about 400 young men aged 21–23 (time 2) who had first been interviewed over a decade earlier when they were aged between 6 and 9 (time 1). The researchers found a significant positive correlation between watching violent TV at time 1 and later aggression at time 2, and argue that these results show that TV violence is causally related to later aggression because results from a reverse test, using early aggressive behaviour to predict later violence viewing, are less strong.

An alternative possibility is that the link between violent media and aggression can be explained in terms of social class. Past research has shown that people from lower social classes are more likely to watch violent TV programmes *and* to be more aggressive (Cumberbatch, 2001).

*Video games and aggression*

Some reviews have been less positive. Sacher (1993) found 7 studies linking violent video games to aggressive behaviour, whereas 19 found no such linkage. Most of the studies that *have* found a relationship have been correlational (which doesn't demonstrate a causal link between watching TV and aggressive behaviour). One issue is that studies of violent video games rarely distinguish between aggressive *play* and aggressive *behaviour.* Observations of children at play may confuse mock aggression (such as pretending to engage in martial arts) with real aggression (attempting to hurt someone).

*Paik and Comstock*

The actual correlation produced by Paik and Comstock (1994) was +0.19 which may seem low but is very significant when large samples are involved. However, this degree of correlation means that only about 4% of the variance in aggressive behaviour is explained by viewing television violence.

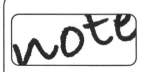

### *How much violence is there on TV?*

The National Television Violence Study (1994–1997) evaluated almost 10,000 hours of broadcast programming in the USA. Researchers found (in Year 3 of the study) that 61% of the programmes portrayed some interpersonal violence, much of it in an entertaining or glamorised manner. The highest proportion of violence was found in children's programmes, yet this was also the genre that was least likely to show the long-term negative consequences of violence. Researchers also identified those elements that increase the risk of children learning aggressive attitudes and behaviours. High-risk portrayals of violence were:

- an aggressive model who is attractive
- violence that appears justified
- violence that goes unpunished
- minimal consequences to the victim
- violence that appears realistic to the viewer.

## starSTUDY

# Investigating aggression and the media: The St Helena study

(CHARLTON ET AL., 2000)

ATLANTIC OCEAN

AFRICA

Ascension Island

St Helena

Tristao da Cunha

## Aims

To assess the effects of the introduction of television on the community of St Helena, a British Colony in the south Atlantic Ocean, which received television for the first time in 1995.

## Method and procedure

Before television arrived, Charlton and his team collected data about the residents of St Helena, through in-depth interviews with adults and children and by observing children in classrooms and school playgrounds. This provided base-line data for later comparison.

After television became available, most of the same measures were repeated annually over the next five years. In addition, a **content analysis** was done of the programmes watched by the children to assess how much violence they were watching.

## Results

The vast majority of the measures used to assess pro- and antisocial behaviour showed no differences in either after the introduction of television. Those measures that did show a difference were fairly equally split between positive and negative changes. Five of these showed decreases in pro-social behaviour in boys and girls, but two showed increases (boys only). There were only two significant changes in antisocial behaviour scores – both of which were lower after the introduction of television.

## Conclusion

The researchers concluded that very little changed following television's arrival. This may be because the social values of the islanders, which are strongly against antisocial behaviour, had a stronger influence on the children than those shown in TV programmes.

## Evaluation

### Conflicting research

In contrast, an earlier study by Williams (1986) found that the introduction of television to a small farming and timber-logging community in Canada led to increased levels of physical and verbal aggression in children (although this was based on data from just 16 children). The difference may lie, as suggested, in the existing social values of the community. According to social learning theory, children may *learn* new behaviours but they would only *reproduce* them in situations where existing social norms support such behaviour.

### Methodological weaknesses

In a **natural experiment**, such as Charlton and Williams above, researchers are not able to control other concurrent influences (e.g. social, cultural and historical factors) that may contribute to any observed changes in behaviour. Thus we cannot be sure that any changes were due to the independent variable (introduction of television).

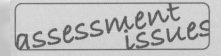

assessment issues

**Discuss the claim that media violence can affect viewers' level of aggression. (ku 12 ae 8)**

This is a clear-cut, one-part essay question, short and simple – but, in contrast, your answer will need to address a complexity of research evidence, conflicting findings, methodological issues, theoretical explanations, and mediating factors. You may well wonder, 'Where do I start?' The simple answer is to start by drafting an *essay plan*. You may have already practised this in NABs or homework, but if not you should try it as soon as possible. Your plan might be a *mind map*, or a list of *bullet points*. Students often think it's a waste of precious time in an exam, but it's actually a sound investment: once you have spent two or three minutes brainstorming your key points and putting them into some sort of logical order, all you have to do is write your essay by working through the points systematically. Using a plan means that you are less likely to have to add in little asterisks (*) to tell the marker you're sorry you forgot a bit and it's at the end. In revision, practise writing plans for essay questions (including those for two-part essay questions).

Some people are affected by media violence, but why does this happen?

# Mediating factors

A *mediating factor* is something which forms a connecting link between two other things, in this case between the media and aggressive behaviour. As we have seen, many studies have demonstrated an association between media violence and subsequent aggression. However, as yet, no clear-cut answers have emerged about *how* television exerts such an influence. We will examine a few of the possible explanations.

## Links to aggression

Huesmann and Moise (1996) suggest five ways that exposure to media violence might lead to aggression.

### Observational learning

Children observe the actions of media models and may later imitate these behaviours, especially when the child admires and identifies with the model. Television may also inform viewers of the positive and negative consequences of violent behaviour. Children can be expected to imitate violent behaviour that is successful in gaining the model's objectives. The more *real* that children perceive violent televised scenes to be and the more they believe that the characters are like them (identification), the more likely they will be to try out the behaviour that they have learned.

### Cognitive priming

This refers to the activation of existing aggressive thoughts and feelings, and explains why children observe one kind of aggression on television and commit another kind of aggressive act afterwards. Immediately after a violent programme, the viewer is primed to respond aggressively because a network of memories involving aggression is retrieved. Frequent exposure to scenes of violence may lead children to store scripts for aggressive behaviour in their memories, and these may be recalled in a later situation if any aspect of the original situation (even a superficial one) is present.

### Desensitisation

This argument assumes that under normal conditions, anxiety about violence inhibits its use. Media violence, however, may stimulate aggressive behaviour by *desensitising* children to the effects of violence. The more televised violence a child watches, the more acceptable aggressive behaviour becomes for that child. Frequent viewing of television violence may cause children to be less anxious about violence. Therefore someone who becomes desensitised to violence may perceive it as more 'normal' and be more likely to engage in violence themselves.

An example of this was shown in a study by Drabman and Thomas (1974) who showed child participants either an exciting sports film or a film containing aggression and then asked them to watch a TV monitor and 'supervise' the two younger children that they could see playing. The participants were led to believe that what they were seeing was live, but in fact it was a video recording in which the children became aggressive towards each other, fighting and destroying each other's toys. Participants who had earlier seen the film containing aggression took longer to seek adult help, suggesting that they had become desensitised, or apathetic, in the face of real-life violence.

### Lowered physiological arousal

In a related aspect of desensitisation, Huesmann and Moise (1996) report that boys who are heavy television watchers show lower than average physiological arousal in response to new scenes of violence. The arousal stimulated by viewing violence is unpleasant at first, but children who constantly watch violent television become used to it, and their emotional and physiological responses decline. As a result, they do not react in the same way to violent behaviour, and so are less inhibited in using it.

### Justification

Violent behaviours on television may provide a justification for a child's own violent behaviour. Children who behave aggressively watch violent television programmes to relieve their guilt and justify their own aggression. When violence is justified or left unpunished on television, the viewer's guilt or concern about consequences is also reduced. The child then feels less inhibited about showing aggression again. Viewing television violence may also produce attitude change and what is viewed may suggest that problems can be solved through aggressive behaviour.

**evaluation** | **Evaluation of links to aggression**

*Observational learning*

Bandura's research (see page 173) supports the view that children learn specific acts of aggression and also learn increased aggressiveness through imitating models even when such models are not real as in the case of cartoon characters. However, such imitation is actually quite rare outside of Bandura-style studies using specially prepared videos. There have been anecdotal claims of copycat acts of violence but no real evidence for this. For example, the two boys who murdered James Bulger were said to be inspired by the video *Child's Play*, but Cumberbatch (2001) reports that no known link was found.

*Cognitive priming*

The importance of cognitive priming was demonstrated in a study by Josephson (1987) where hockey players were deliberately frustrated and then shown a violent or non-violent film where an actor held a walkie-talkie. In a subsequent hockey game the participants (boys) behaved most aggressively if they had seen the violent film and the referee in their game was holding a walkie-talkie. Presumably the walkie-talkie acted as a cue.

*Desensitisation*

Cumberbatch (2001) argues that people might get 'used' to screen violence but that this does not mean that a person will also get used to violence in the real world; screen violence is more likely to make children 'frightened' than 'frightening'.

*Lowered physiological arousal*

It has also been claimed that watching violence leads to *increased* arousal and thus more aggression. The excitation-transfer model suggests that arousal creates a readiness to behave aggressively if there are appropriate circumstances (Zillmann, 1988). However, some theorists (see page 183) believe that watching violence has beneficial, cathartic effects – arousal allows one to release pent-up aggressive energies.

*Justification*

Many TV programmes have mixed pro- and antisocial messages, for example the 1980s television series *The A Team*, where the good guys behave violently. Liss and Reinhardt (1979) suggest that the negative effects of such programmes can be explained in terms of justification. The use of aggression by pro-social characters lends an aura of moral justification to their violence, with which children readily identify.

## Parental involvement in children's viewing

Parents play an important role in mediating the effects of media violence. Huesmann and Bachrach (1988) reviewed relevant evidence and concluded that 'Family attitudes and social class are stronger determinants of attitudes toward aggression than is the amount of exposure to TV, which is nevertheless a significant but weaker predictor'.

There are many ways that parents can mediate the effects of television, for example:

- *Limit the amount and type of television watched*. Particular attention might be paid to programmes which show violent behaviours that children might imitate. Children can also be encouraged to watch programmes with pro-social content rather than simply turning off programmes with violent content.

- *Discuss the contents of television programmes*. This is an appropriate strategy for older children where simple restriction of viewing might be difficult. Parents can encourage older children to analyse and question programme content to encourage them to become more critical viewers and less affected by what they watch. Huesmann *et al.* (1983) found that the effects of TV violence on children could be reduced by teaching them critical viewing skills. For example, children could be taught to evaluate TV content by reducing their belief in the reality of programmes and encouraging them to compare what they see on TV with information from other sources.

- *Change own behaviours*. Parents act as models and should therefore monitor their own viewing habits in order to set a good example. Parents can also spend time watching programmes with their children so that they can explain conflict situations or comment on violent behaviour.

### *Does media violence increase viewer aggression?*

Psychologists are divided about the overall conclusions that can be drawn from more than 50 years of research involving something like 3500 studies. In 1972 the US Surgeon General concluded that 'the overwhelming consensus is that such media violence is harmful', and Eron (1993, p. 14) said, 'There can no longer be any doubt that heavy exposure to televised violence is one of the causes of aggressive behavior, crime and violence in society'.

On the other hand Freedman (2002, p. 210) in his book *Media Violence and its Effect on Aggression: Assessing the Scientific Evidence* concludes by saying, 'Let me end by acknowledging again that to many people it seems self-evident that media violence causes aggression. I think I have shown in this comprehensive, detailed review that the scientific evidence does not support this view.'

The anti-effect lobby does not propose that the media have no effect, but just that studies have either been poorly done or fail to demonstrate a conclusive answer to the questions posed at the beginning of this section. Livingstone (2001) suggests that the challenge within media effects research is not to try to answer simple questions with simple answers, but to construct a more complex picture, drawing on existing findings and based on the differences, contradictions and parallels among diverse studies. In order to achieve this, suggests Livingstone, we must accept that there is considerable distance between the findings of psychological research and the 'simple conclusions' desired by policy makers and the public.

## Some general considerations

### Pro-social effects

The media can have pro-social as well as antisocial effects. In general, the effect sizes are larger for pro-social studies: if you expose participants to pro-social media and compare their behaviour with that of a control group the difference in behaviour between the two groups is greater than when you expose the experimental group to antisocial media (Hearold, 1986).

### What counts as violence?

Researchers fail to agree on what counts as violent behaviour. For example, some regard violent behaviour as the act (or threat) of injuring or killing someone, independent of the method used or the surrounding context, and thus include cartoon violence as an example of violent media. Others specifically exclude cartoon violence from their research because of its comical and unrealistic presentation.

### The anti-effects lobby

There is growing concern that the media are unreasonably the focus of blame for violent behaviour. First of all, the evidence does not clearly support the hypothesis that media violence leads to violent behaviour. For example, Belson (1978) conducted very detailed interviews with about 1500 adolescent boys and found that those boys who watched least television when they were younger were least aggressive in adolescence, *but* boys who watched most television were *less* aggressive (by about 50%) than boys who watched moderate amounts. This suggests that the link between watching television and aggression is unpredictable.

Gauntlett (1998) argues that there are serious flaws with the *'effects model'* – the expectation that we will find direct and reasonably predictable effects of the media on aggression. He argues that it is a 'backwards' approach because it starts with the media and tries to make links back to violence rather than starting with people who are violent and trying to see what media interaction they have had. One study that did this reported no effects – Hagell and Newburn (1994) interviewed 78 violent teenage offenders and found that they watched *less* television and video than their non-offending counterparts. It is possible that watching TV keeps people safely at home!

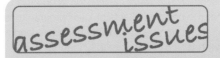

**Discuss *one* mediating factor that may be involved in the influence of media violence on the viewer. (*ku 4 ae 2*)**

Whenever NABs and exam questions give you a *choice*, make the most of it. You have a free hand to select whichever (relevant!) factor (or theory etc.) you like. That means that you can choose one that you know most about, in terms of what the question demands. For this question, ensure that you choose a factor that you can both describe (for four *ku* marks) *and* for which you can also provide material for the two *ae* marks. You should be able to *analyse/ evaluate* your chosen factor, and that evaluation could include *research evidence* that supports or challenges it. Remember that the use of relevant evidence is so important in the study of psychology that, apart from very low-mark questions, evidence can always attract marks regardless of whether the question explicitly asks for it.

## Aspect 3: Control and reduction of aggression

As well as explaining what *causes* aggression in human beings, social psychologists are also concerned with its control and reduction. Aggression is not an automatic response, and as such can be controlled or reduced. As with most other areas of psychology, however, there is little agreement about what is the most effective way of tackling this thorny issue. Some techniques focus on changing an individual's state directly, for example reducing aggressive impulses through substitute activities. We will start by looking at these 'individual processes'. Other techniques focus on changing the antecedent psychological conditions that give rise to aggression, which we will examine on page 185.

# Individual processes
## Incompatible responses

Baron (1976) suggested that stimuli that produce responses incompatible with anger or aggression might be highly effective in reducing the occurrence of such behaviour. They believed that when angry individuals experience empathy towards their victim, or when they are amused by them or even experience sexual arousal, these conditions lead to responses which are incompatible with aggressive feelings. A number of studies have produced findings that support such a hypothesis, the most direct support coming from Baron's own study. In this study, motorists were delayed for 15 seconds at traffic lights after they had turned green. Whilst the light was at red, experimental manipulations designed to elicit incompatible responses were implemented. In one condition, a female confederate wearing a clown's costume passed in front of the motorist (incompatible response – humour). In a second condition, a female confederate passed on crutches and with a bandaged leg (empathy). In a third, the female confederate was dressed in a brief and revealing outfit (mild sexual arousal). Compared with a control condition, where the same female confederate was conservatively dressed as she passed by, motorists in the other conditions were far less likely to honk their horns at the subsequent delay.

The *incompatible response hypothesis* would propose that humour – making someone laugh – would be an effective way of defusing tense and potentially aggressive situations. It is generally accepted that aggressive humour can indeed provide some form of tension release, and may lead to a reinterpretation of a given situation or event (Martin and Lefcourt, 1983). However, although humour provides a release for aggression it is uncertain whether aggression is *actually* reduced or increased by more overtly aggressive humour.

*evaluation* | **Incompatible responses**

*Incompatible or distracting?*
McDonald and Wooten (1988) provide an alternative explanation for Baron's findings. Based on a similar experimental setup to Baron's, they added a condition that was as equally *distracting* as Baron's clown or scantily clad assistant (i.e. two women arguing), but which would not yield responses incompatible with aggression. Their findings were that the extra 'argument' condition was as likely to delay horn honking as the other experimental conditions, and far more so than the control condition, even in the absence of incompatible responses. They concluded that any stimulus that serves to *distract* an individual from a precursor to aggression (e.g. frustration or anger) should reduce the magnitude of subsequent aggression.

# Catharsis

> *A psychiatrist tells his violent New York gangster client, 'You know what I do when I'm angry? I hit a pillow. Try that.' The client promptly pulls out a gun and fires several rounds into the pillow.' Feel better?' asks the psychiatrist. 'Yeah, I do,' responds the gangster.*

This scene, from the 1999 film *Analyze This*, starring Billy Crystal as the psychiatrist and Robert De Niro as his gangster client (in picture), demonstrates a belief that is widespread in our culture, that we should vent our anger by 'letting off steam'. By so doing, we are led to believe, we will feel better. Indeed, one explanation for the popularity of body-contact sports, such as boxing, rugby and martial arts, is that they offer a socially acceptable mechanism for the expression of what would otherwise be socially disruptive aggressive tendencies.

Robert De Niro and Billy Crystal in a scene from *Analyze This*.

According to catharsis theory, acting aggressively, or even just viewing aggression in others is an effective way to purge our own aggressive feelings. This idea, originally attributable to Breuer and Freud (1893) was that expressing anger was much better than bottling it up inside. The principle of catharsis is based on the hydraulic model of anger (see page 168), whereby frustration leads to anger, which builds up inside an individual until it is released in some way. Letting the anger out here and there in relatively harmless ways is seen as better than letting it build up to a dangerous 'explosion' of rage.

*evaluation*

## Catharsis

Almost as soon as researchers started studying this theory, it became clear that there was a problem. In a typical experiment, Hornberger (1959) found that participants who had hammered nails after being insulted by a confederate were subsequently *more* aggressive towards the confederate than participants who had not vented their anger in the same way. In an influential review of catharsis theory, Geen and Quanty (1977) concluded that venting anger does not reduce aggression; if anything, it makes people more aggressive afterwards. Other recent research (see Star Study below) has also reached the same conclusion. Geen and Quanty did concede that venting anger *can* reduce physiological arousal, but only when an individual expresses their anger directly against the person responsible for their frustration (and then only when they believe that they will not retaliate). Venting anger against substitute targets, or merely viewing aggressive behaviour in a third party does not, they concluded, reduce aggression.

### Who believes in catharsis?

Biaggio (1987) administered a questionnaire assessing endorsement of the *hostility catharsis hypothesis* to 102 undergraduate students and 131 American and Canadian psychologists (randomly selected from 4 divisions of the American Psychological Association). She found that students were more likely to endorse the catharsis hypothesis than were psychologists, females more so than males, and Freudian and humanistic psychologists more than behaviourists.

## star**STUDY**

### Investigating reduction of aggression: Catharsis

(BUSHMAN *ET AL.*, 1999)

### Aims

Although research has consistently shown it not to be the case, there exists a persistent notion that discharging anger harmlessly onto some inanimate object is a good way to dissipate aggressive impulses. Evidence actually suggests that *suppression* of anger is more likely to reduce aggressive impulses whereas expression of anger stimulates them. In this study, researchers were interested to see if this effect could be reversed if people believed that catharsis *did* work.

### Method and procedure

Over 300 undergraduates of both sexes were divided into 3 groups. One group read a supposedly scientific argument favouring the therapeutic effectiveness of catharsis; the second read an argument against its effectiveness, and the third read a passage unrelated to the subject. They were then asked to write an essay that, they were told, would be marked by another participant in the experiment. Half were then given their essays back with a good mark and many friendly comments, whereas the other half were given theirs back with a bad mark and many insulting comments. The students were then asked to place in rank order 10 activities that they might enjoy doing after the experiment, including reading, playing a computer game and hitting a punch bag.

### Results

Those students who received the bad grades/comments were more likely to be angry than those who received the more positive comments. In turn, angry students were more likely to choose outlets that gave them the opportunity for aggression (such as hitting the punch bag). Those students who had read the pro-catharsis argument *and* had been made angry were especially interested in hitting the punch bag.

### Conclusion

The results suggest that people are easily persuaded that the physical discharge of anger is an effective way of getting rid of aggression and will seek aggressive outlets because of this belief. In reality, anger actually dissipates more rapidly than we think. However, many people believe that whatever they do in the brief interval before calm returns is somehow responsible for the reduction of their aggressive feelings.

### Evaluation

*Demand characteristics*

The researchers attributed the greater desire among the angry students to hit the punch bag to their exposure to a message supporting the effectiveness of catharsis. It is possible, however, that the experimental set-up itself led the participants to behave in this aggressive way as, (being smart undergraduates) they may well have taken their cue from the condition they were in and acted accordingly.

*The power of propaganda*
This study provides an explanation for why so many people still believe in the power of hostile catharsis to relieve aggressive impulses. It is because we are bombarded with propaganda-like messages in the media and in popular culture that convince us that lashing out will somehow make us feel better.

## Role-modelling

Bandura's social learning theory claims that people learn behaviours and attitudes from role models whom they wish to emulate. In his famous Bobo doll studies (see pages 174 and 175), Bandura found that whether or not children acted aggressively depended on their observations of another person's rewards and punishments rather than their own personal experiences. According to this view, children learn to act aggressively when they imitate the violent acts of adults, especially family members and peer group members. One study of over 2000 adults explored the relationship between observed family aggression in childhood and severe marital aggression in the next generation. The results showed that observing physical aggression between parents was more strongly related to involvement in marital aggression than being hit as a teenager by one's parents (Kalmuss, 1984). The influence of the media in providing violent role models for children was demonstrated in a content analysis of 518 music videos which showed that attractive role models were aggressors in more than 80% of violence depicted in music videos (Rich *et al.*, 1998).

In order to control aggression, therefore, Bandura believed that family members and the mass media should provide positive role models for their children and the general public (Bandura and Ribes-Inesta, 1976). The *'Big Brothers, Big Sisters'* programme, for example, has found that positive relationships with non-parental adults reduced aggression and improved youth behaviour generally, and could compensate for poor family relationships. In the media, a genre of media violence that typically trivialises the consequences to the victim is the cartoon (fans of *Itchy and Scratchy* take note). Nathanson and Cantor (2000) showed that the aggression-promoting effect of violent cartoons could be reduced by increasing children's involvement with the victim. In this study, the researchers found that a violent cartoon could increase boys' endorsement of aggressive solutions to problems, but that asking children to think about the victim's feelings could intervene in this effect. As a side effect, this empathy-promoting intervention reduced the degree to which the children found the cartoon funny.

How can you reduce the influence of violent cartoon characters on the aggressive behaviour of children who watch?

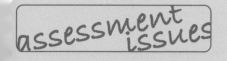

**Describe and evaluate *one* research study related to the control or reduction of aggression. (*ku* 4 *ae* 4)**

This is an example of a question on a *single research study*. You may find one or more of this type of question in the NABs and exam. The key features to look out for are, first, whether both *ku* and *ae* skills are required or just *ku*; check this by looking at the *commands* (e.g. 'describe' and 'evaluate') in the question, and the *mark allocations*. In this case, both are required and marks are equally split across the two. Secondly, should you write about the whole study or just a particular element of it (e.g. procedure or results)? Check the wording of the question. This one doesn't specify a particular aspect, so you should write about the whole study: give the name(s) and date (preferably), aim or what was studied, method/procedure, results (all for *ku* marks) and conclusions and evaluation (for *ae* marks).

A suitable choice here would be the Star Study on *catharsis*, by Bushman *et al.* (1999). As with any research study question that requires *ae* skills, make sure that you say how the findings support (or not) the concept being investigated.

## Using the antecedents of aggression

In the first section of this Aspect we looked at techniques to reduce aggression which focused on individual responses. A different approach is to look at possible sources (or antecedents) of aggression – such as frustration and anger – and try to control these.

## Reducing frustration

If frustration is linked to the development of anger and aggression, then it seems plausible that reducing frustration will result in a corresponding reduction in aggressive feelings. Research has suggested the potential of sport and martial arts to reduce aggression. There are also more formalised programmes used in schools, such as the PAThS (Promoting Alternative Thinking

Strategies) programme: children are taught how to identify and communicate their emotions, and to increase their frustration tolerance and self-control.

*evaluation*

### Reducing frustration

Many studies have shown that sport alone is often not a successful means of reducing aggression, whereas martial arts research has been more promising. Cox (1993) reviewed the literature on the martial arts, giving an overview of the personality traits of martial artists. He concluded that individuals involved in the martial arts are not more aggressive than the average person when they begin their training, and they become even less so as they continue their training. They may also become less anxious, more self-confident and have higher self-esteem as a result of their studies. Adler (2003) explored the relationship between the practice of martial arts and aggressive tendencies, concluding that for most martial arts, more intense training was associated with increased tolerance for frustration, and therefore decreased levels of aggressive behaviour.

The PAThS programme typically shows over 30% reduction in aggressive behaviour post-training, as well as a significant increase in an individual's ability to tolerate frustration.

## Anger-management interventions

One of the most powerful risk factors for violence is anger. People who have not learned to control their anger are particularly at risk for aggressive outbursts. The aim of anger-management programmes is to help individuals learn to control this potentially explosive emotion. Teaching people to understand and control their anger helps them to avoid the escalation of negative feelings and also to avoid conflict situations with others.

See www.colorado.edu/cspv/blueprints/ model/programs/PATHS.html

Most anger-management programmes use a combination of techniques. First, individuals develop their ability to understand the perspective of others (i.e. to put themselves in the shoes of another). Second, they are taught to recognise their emotional and physical states when angry and to be able to control these, perhaps through relaxation. Finally, they learn how to use a specific strategy to moderate their responses to potential conflicts. In order to achieve this, individuals are trained in problem-solving skills so they can identify the problem, generate alternative responses, and then consider the consequences of each before selecting an appropriate response.

*evaluation*

### Anger-management interventions

Anger-management training has been shown to decrease the aggressive behaviour of at risk teenagers. Feindler *et al.* (1984) found that students trained in anger-management skills decreased their aggressive behaviour at home and at school and displayed more self-control after training. In another programme, at risk aggressive teenagers were less likely to re-offend after 10 weeks of anger-management training (Larson, 1992). However, although many studies show clear short-term gains, the long-term effectiveness of anger-management interventions is less certain. In a three-year follow-up study of aggressive primary-school children, there was sustained improvement in self-esteem but there was no change in aggressive behaviour over the same period (Lochman, 1992). Other studies have tended to be relatively small scale, some with fewer than 50 participants, and many finding that observational measures of post-training changes in aggressive behaviour were not as significant as self-report measures.

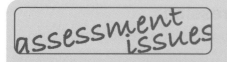

assessment issues

**Describe the use of role-modelling as a strategy for reducing aggression. (*ku 4 ae 0*)**

You'll have spotted that this question focuses on an *applied* Aspect of the psychology of aggression – the words 'use' and 'strategy' are the clues! So it would *not* be sensible to devote your whole answer to social learning *theory,* or *concepts* of observational learning, imitation, etc., or to a research *study.* All of these do have some relevance, and could be mentioned, but your answer should deal primarily with the way role-modelling can be *used* or *applied* as a deliberate strategy. One way of enhancing your answer would be to provide an *example* from everyday life, for example Nelson Mandela and Mahatma Gandhi are regarded as influential role-models of non-violent behaviour for political campaigners.

| Chapter: Antisocial behaviour | Exam questions and answers |

*In this section we show you student answers to possible exam questions plus examiner's comments on these answers. Remember that in the actual exam (and NABs) your questions for this Topic will always add up to 20 marks. The question may be one essay worth 20 marks or a number of smaller questions (such as those shown below) which add up to 20 marks.*

**Question 1**   Describe and evaluate strategies for the control *and/or* reduction of aggression, referring to research evidence in your answer. (*ku 8  ae 8*)

### Tom

There are five main ways that aggression may be controlled or reduced.

1. Incompatible responses. This view says that you can't feel angry if you are doing something that is not compatible such as laughing. So one way to reduce your anger is look at a humorous TV programme.

2. Catharsis. This way suggests that you can reduce aggression by diverting your energy somewhere else. This is linked to the instinct approach which says that aggression is an innate force which you can't avoid. One suggestion is to do some intense physical sport to channel the aggression somewhere else.

3. Role models. You can learn to control your aggression in the same way that people acquire aggressive behaviour – by observing role models such as parents and people on TV.

4. Reducing frustration. Some theories suggest that aggression arises because you feel frustrated, so in order to control aggression you should control frustration.

5. Anger management programmes. These are like therapies that have been devised to teach people how to manage their anger before it leads to aggressive behaviour.

Baron did a study with motorists who were delayed at traffic lights. If they saw someone wearing a clown's outfit or scantily clad they were less likely to honk their horns. This suggests that incompatible responses stop people behaving aggressively. However the aggression might have been stopped because the participants were distracted rather than having an incompatible response.

In Bandura's study with the Bobo doll some children were exposed to a model who acted aggressively towards the Bobo doll whereas other children watched a model who just played with the doll and other toys. Later the children who watched the aggressive model then behaved more aggressively than the others and also imitated specific acts of aggression that they had witnessed. This shows that people do imitate role models. It also shows the role of frustration in aggression.

**Examiner's comments**    Tom's answer starts in a very business-like way, giving an overview of five approaches before focusing on a smaller number in more detail. He clearly demonstrates knowledge and understanding of these. However, there is a major problem in his last paragraph: although he describes the influence of role-modelling in increasing aggressive behaviour and supports this with evidence, he fails to explain how this knowledge is used or applied to control/reduce aggression. This is a very common weakness of students' answers to questions on applied aspects, like this one. His answer could also be improved by giving the dates of research studies.

As far as style of writing is concerned, numbered or bulleted points are best avoided unless, as Tom has done, these are paragraphs rather than a few words for each point. In essay questions, you must elaborate your points to demonstrate understanding as well as knowledge.

Tom could have gained more ae marks by expanding evaluation of incompatible responses and role-modelling, and by relating these strategies to their theoretical basis, for example social learning theory and/or the frustration-aggression hypothesis. To allow himself time and space to do so he could have reduced the amount of detail he has given on the strategies that he has described at the start but which he has not focused on later (e.g. catharsis). Tom receives **8 out of 16 marks** (*ku 5/8  ae 3/8*).

### Alice

The instinct theory of aggression suggests that aggression is an important adaptive behaviour and it is inevitable. Freud observed behaviour in the First World War and concluded that you could only explain the violence of men in terms of an aggressive instinct. Freud believed that nothing can stop this instinct except if you try to channel such energies into productive things. This is what is meant by catharsis. The ethologists had a similar view of aggression and suggested it needed to be released before it built up and overflowed (the hydraulic model).

This idea sounds quite reasonable except research has found that the opposite happens! For example Hornberger (1959) arranged for participants to be insulted by a confederate to make them feel angry and aggressive. Some participants were then given a task of hammering nails which should have been a cathartic

experience but in fact these participants became more aggressive. Another study by Bushman et al. (1999) tried to see if catharsis worked if participants were encouraged to believe that it was a successful method of controlling aggression. Students were asked to write an essay which was then returned either with a good mark and friendly comments or a bad mark and insulting comments. All participants were then asked to rate various activities in terms of how enjoyable they were including 'hitting a punch bag'. The students who had read that catharsis was good for you and had been given a bad mark (and reported feeling angry) were more likely to select the punch bag than participants who didn't read about catharsis. However it is hard to know how realistic this study is and whether people would behave like that in real life.

In fact other research (Geen and Quanty) did find that catharsis can work if the anger is vented directly towards the person who made you angry. Just focusing your anger on a third party does not seem to have any effect.

The frustration-aggression theory suggests that aggression occurs because someone is frustrated. Dollard et al. suggested that frustration always leads to some form of aggression and all aggression is the result of frustration. Frustration occurs when you don't get what you want or don't get to do what you want to do.

Kulik and Brown frustrated some students who were making phone calls

to collect money for charity. The more frustrated they were the more verbal aggression they showed.

If frustration leads to aggression one should be able to reduce aggression by dealing with frustration. One programme that is used in schools is called PAThS, where children are taught how to identify and communicate their emotions, and to increase their frustration tolerance and self-control. The success rate of this programme in controlling aggression has been good.

**Examiner's comments**  Alice's answer is better organised than Tom's. Catharsis is given thorough attention, including evaluation. However, the answer lacks balance because frustration reduction is treated rather sketchily. It is a pity that she did not give further detail of the PAThS programme. A brief concluding sentence or two would have been helpful, and could have gained further ae marks. This answer would be awarded **13 out of 16 marks** (ku 7/8  ae 6/8).

**Question 2**  Describe and analyse gender differences in aggression. (ku 4  ae 4)

### Tom

Men are thought to be more aggressive than women. One explanation for this is their hormones make them more aggressive. There is evidence to support this view. In one study they castrated male animals which lowers their levels of testosterone. These animals behaved less aggressively. In fact testosterone is also present in women and may explain why they are also sometimes aggressive. But since women don't have as much testosterone this explains why women are less aggressive. Another hormone, progesterone, has been linked to aggressive behaviour in women but this hormone is only present in great amounts at certain times of the month. Floody reported that women can be more irritable and hostile before their periods (pre-menstrual tension).

In opposition to the biological view, the social view suggests that men behave more aggressively because they are socialised to behave this way. Men are expected to behave assertively or at least they are not criticised for behaving like this whereas women are. This aspect of gender differences can be considered not just in terms of whether men and women behave more aggressively but whether men and women express their aggression differently. Men are more physically aggressive whereas women use more indirect, verbal methods. This might develop because women are physically weaker so they learn to use verbal rather than physical aggression. Or it may be that they are also selectively reinforced for this behaviour in the same way that men and women are selectively reinforced for the way they behave. And they are also likely to see male and female models behaving in this way.

**Examiner's comments**  Tom's answer shows a degree of analysis as well as description, which are both required by the question. His explanation of the role of hormones is a little simplistic, and he should have clearly flagged up that he is referring to a biological perspective. To his credit he has offered supporting evidence. In his paragraph on social origins of gender differences, he makes some good points but in a rather muddled way. If he had related his points about reinforcement and role models to learning theory and social learning theory he would have gained more marks for analysis. Overall, he could have achieved further *ae* marks by referring to cultural differences and/or evaluating evidence for the different views. For this answer, Tom gains **6 out of 8 marks** (ku 4/4  ae 2/4).

### Alice

There are two ways to explain gender differences in aggression. It's either social or biological. Social explanations focus on social learning theory and stereotypes. Boys and girls learn about what behaviour is appropriate for their sex and they copy this. This means that aggression might vary in different cultures because individuals in different cultures are reinforced differently depending what the stereotypes are. There is a classic study by Margaret Mead where she observed various tribes in New Guinea. There

were three tribes and the gender differences in aggression varied from one tribe to another, for example in the Tchambuli the women were more aggressive but in other tribes there were no gender differences in aggression. Mead was a Westerner and she may have been biased in her observations.

The biological view suggests that men are more aggressive because it is in their nature. Evolutionary psychologists suggest that men have evolved to be more aggressive because it assists successful reproduction e.g. fighting off rivals, whereas women could not afford to engage in violent behaviour because their survival is crucial to the survival of their offspring.

**Examiner's comments**  Alice gives a sound explanation of social learning theory principles in relation to gender differences; however, it would be improved by giving *examples* of the different expectations of girls and boys in a specific culture (e.g. Western culture). Although she refers appropriately to cross-cultural research, she has not analysed the findings in relation to the question and has barely hinted at limitations of the research. Her consideration of biological factors is brief and lacks clarity. The evolutionary approach is sketchy, and hormones are barely mentioned (a different biological explanation). Had she elaborated on one or the other (and possibly linked the two areas) she would have obtained more marks. Alice is awarded **3 out of 8 marks** (ku 2/4  ae 1/4).

S ocial psychology is the study of social behaviour, which occurs when two or more members of the same species interact. Social psychology is concerned with how people influence each other's behaviour (social influence) as well as how our thoughts influence our social behaviour (social cognition).

Conformity and obedience are examples of social influence. 'Social influence' concerns 'how the thoughts, feelings and behaviour of individuals are influenced by the actual, imagined or implied presence of others' (Allport, 1968). In the case of conformity our behaviour is influenced by the views of others; obedience is a response to a direct request from someone, usually an authority figure.

| Chapter contents | Unit content for the topic 'Conformity and obedience'' | Comment |
|---|---|---|
| **Aspect 1: Nature of conformity** | | |
| Studies of conformity page 190 Explanations of conformity page 192 Minority influence page 195 | Nature of conformity: <br>• normative and informational social influence <br>• compliance and internalisation <br>• studies of conformity <br>• individual and situational factors in conformity <br>• minority influence | *Conformity is a form of **social influence**, that is, one of the many ways in which we influence, and are influenced by, others, in our daily lives. Here, you will learn to define and distinguish between different types of conformity: **normative** and **informational social influence**, **compliance** and **internalisation**. Research **studies** into conformity provide insights into why people conform, even when they know they are going against their own beliefs. You will identify particular **factors** that make conformity more or less likely. Most emphasis in research has been on conformity to a **majority**, but, perhaps surprisingly, **minority influence** also occurs in certain conditions.* |
| **Aspect 2: Nature of obedience** | | |
| Studies of obedience page 197 Explanations of obedience page 201 | Nature of obedience: <br>• obedience studies <br>• factors in obedience behaviour, including: <br>  – perceived legitimate authority <br>  – socialisation <br>  – autonomous and agentic levels of behaviour | *Obedience is another form of social influence. Research into obedience has become one of the most famous, or infamous, areas of psychology. In this Aspect you will study the procedures and findings of such **research studies**, and analyse the reasons why people tend to obey, even in situations where they may harm another person. You will be able to describe a range of **factors** that affect obedience, including the **perceived authority** of the person giving orders, **socialisation** processes that lead us to obey, and **autonomous** versus **agentic** behaviour.* |
| **Aspect 3: Resisting social pressure** | | |
| Intrapersonal processes page 203 Interpersonal processes page 205 | Strategies for resisting social pressure/coercion: <br>• responsibility for own actions <br>• moral reasoning and awareness of own values <br>• disobedient models <br>• questioning motives of advertisers, politicians, cults <br>• education | *Social influence research has often indicated that people are very willing to conform or obey; however, in this Aspect you will see that **social pressure** or even **coercion** can be effectively **resisted**. You will be able to describe various **strategies** that people adopt, either spontaneously, or through encouragement: awareness that we have to **take responsibility for our actions and their consequences**; ability to **reason and make moral judgments**; awareness of our own **values**. Resistance to pressure can also be promoted through observing **disobedient role models**, and **questioning the motives** of those who seek to persuade us, e.g. **advertisers**, **politicians**, **cults**. Finally, **education** is a key vehicle for helping people to resist.* |

# Aspect 1: Nature of conformity

## Studies of conformity
### What is meant by conformity?

**Conformity** is said to occur if an individual chooses a course of action that is favoured by the majority of other group members or is considered socially acceptable. Because the individual is clearly influenced by how the *majority* think or behave, this form of **social influence** is sometimes referred to as *majority influence*. Our social life is also characterised by *social norms*, which are generally accepted ways of thinking, feeling and behaving that are shared by the other members of our social group. We *should* act in a certain way in certain situations because otherwise we would be breaking an important social norm. When a social group has well-established norms that specify appropriate behaviour, pressures arise for individuals to maintain this norm (i.e. to conform). Deviants who go against social norms may experience considerable pressure to bring them back into line.

Majority influence is distinguished from **minority influence**, which is discussed on page 195 onwards. In the case of majority influence the views/behaviour of the majority affect *one or more persons*; in the case of minority influence the views/behaviour of a minority group affect *one or more persons*. Most majority influence is characterised by *public compliance* rather than *private acceptance*, whereas the opposite is true of minority influence.

star**STUDY**

## Investigating the nature of conformity

**(Asch, 1955)**

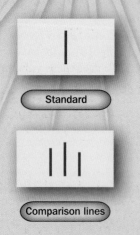

Standard

Comparison lines

### Aims
The aim of this study was to find out how people would behave when given an *un*ambiguous task. Would they be influenced by the behaviour of others, or would they stick firmly to what they knew to be right? How much conformity to majority influence would there be?

### Method and procedure
In total, 123 male American undergraduates were tested. Asch showed a series of lines (the 'standard' line and the possible answers as shown here) to participants seated around a table.

All but one of the participants was a **confederate** of the researcher. The confederates were instructed to give the same *incorrect* answer on 12 *critical* trials. In total there were 18 trials with each participant. The true participant was always the last or last but one to answer.

### Results
On the critical trials, 36.8% of the responses made by true participants were incorrect, i.e. conformed to the incorrect response given by the unanimous confederates. 25% of the participants never gave a wrong answer; thus 75% conformed at least once.

Just to confirm that the stimulus lines were unambiguous, Asch conducted a control trial with no confederates giving wrong answers. Asch found that people do make mistakes about 1% of the time.

### Conclusion
This shows a surprisingly strong tendency to conform to group pressures in a situation where the answer is clear. For Asch the important finding was that there was any conformity at all. However, Asch also saw the fact that on two-thirds of the trials his participants had remained independent as clear evidence of how people could *resist* the pressure to conform.

This study is represented in most social psychology textbooks as resounding evidence of people's tendency to conform when faced with a unanimous majority. It is also evidence of conditions under which people resist conformity.

### Evaluation
*What does this study actually tell us about real life?*
Asking people to judge the length of the lines is a rather insignificant task and one where they would probably be willing to conform to save face. On a more important task we would expect conformity levels to drop. The fact that the participants had to answer out loud and in a group of strangers means that there were special pressures on them to conform, such as not wanting to sound stupid and wanting to be accepted by the group. The findings only tell us about

conformity in special circumstances. For example, Williams and Sogon (1984) tested people who belonged to the same sports club and found that conformity may be even higher when with people you know.

*Is the study a 'child of its time'?*
It is possible that these findings are particular to one culture – the participants were all men, all American and the research was conducted in America in the 1950s, the era of McCarthyism – a highly conformist society. This was the claim made by Perrin and Spencer (1980) who tried to repeat Asch's study in England in the late 1970s. They found that out of 396 trials there was only one in which a student conformed. However, these were science students who may have felt more confident about their ability to estimate line length. There are studies (e.g. Larsen, 1974) which have found support for Asch; however, Lalancette and Standing (1990) found no conformity and concluded that the Asch effect appears to be an unpredictable phenomenon rather than a stable tendency of human behaviour.

Try the Asch experiment yourself: library.thinkquest.org/C007405/exp/online

## Research into conformity

### Ambiguous situations

Jenness (1932) asked students to guess how many beans there were in a jar. They were then given an opportunity to discuss their estimates and, finally, to give their individual estimates again. Jenness found that individual estimates tended to converge to a group norm. It seems reasonable that, in an *ambiguous* situation, one looks to others to get some ideas about a reasonable answer.

Sherif (1935) also investigated responses to an *ambiguous* stimulus, using the *autokinetic effect*. In the dark a stationary point of light appears to move. Sherif asked participants to estimate how far the light moved, then asked them to work with three others who had given quite different estimates of movement. After their discussion each was asked to provide individual answers again. These had become quite similar, demonstrating a tendency to establish and conform to group norms.

### Fear of ridicule

Asch suggested that fear of ridicule is one reason why participants conformed in his study. This was supported in a study by Schachter (1951) where participants tried to influence a 'deviant' confederate (a confederate who disagreed with them). They were told the case history of a juvenile delinquent (Johnny Rocco) and asked to decide whether his behaviour would improve if he was given more loving attention or more punishment. The case was presented in such a way that participants were likely to go for the loving attention approach. After this discussion the group was asked to select members to continue to participate in another task. If the confederate had disagreed and resisted attempts to change his view, the other group members rejected him for membership in a future group. Whereas, if the confederate had agreed, he was later included. This shows that lack of conformity does lead to group rejection.

### Individual differences

Asch (1956) suggested that people low in self-esteem are more likely to conform perhaps because they are more likely to fear rejection from the group. Burger and Cooper (1979) investigated another possible individual difference: the desire for personal control. Participants had to rate whether cartoons were funny or not in the presence of a confederate who was asked to do the same. Those participants who measured high on desire for personal control were less likely to rate cartoons in the same way as a confederate.

### Gender differences

Some studies have found that women are more conformist than men (Eagly and Carli, 1981). This may be explained in terms of the fact that women are more concerned with social relationships then men and this means that, in the experimental situation, they have different short-term goals. The result is that women *appear* to be more conformist than they are in the real world (Eagly, 1978).

*Apparent non-conformity may actually be a case of not conforming to one set of norms but conforming to another set – for example individuals who dress like Goths.*

THE FAR SIDE® By GARY LARSON

*The Far Side® by Gary Larson © 1984 FarWorks, Inc. All Rights Reserved. Used with permission.*

**Suddenly, Professor Liebowitz realizes he has come to the seminar without his duck.**

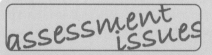

assessment issues

**Give a definition of "social influence". (ku 2 ae 0)**

It's a no-nonsense definition question, and it's worth only two marks, but they are two marks that could easily be lost. This Topic is full of specialist terminology, so you need to ensure that you can explain key terms like 'normative', 'informational', etc. But don't overlook the term 'social influence' itself. As a general rule, if a term is in the Unit content, you need to be able to define or explain it. The term 'social influence' is important here because you should be aware that conformity and obedience (as in the Topic title) are just two types of social influence, and there are several other types that are studied by psychologists.

## Explanations of conformity
### Why do people conform?

People conform for all sorts of reasons, ranging from complete acceptance of the majority viewpoint at one extreme to simply 'going along' with the crowd at the other. Fear of ridicule was one explanation that we have already examined.

---

### explanation

**KEY TERMS**

**Normative influence:** People conform in order to be liked and accepted as part of a group.

**Informational influence:** People conform because they believe the majority is right. This occurs especially in ambiguous situations and/or where the majority is known to have superior knowledge.

### Normative and informational social influence

Deutsch and Gerard (1955) proposed that there are two different reasons why people conform:

1. **Normative influence** – when we follow the crowd
   If we simply go along with the majority without really accepting their point of view, we are conforming in behaviour alone. Psychologists have called this type of conformity *compliance*. A majority may be able to control other group members by making it difficult for them to deviate against the majority point of view and thus exerting pressure on them to conform. Going against the majority isn't easy, as demonstrated in Asch's study, where participants clearly felt uncomfortable deviating from the majority position.
2. **Informational influence** – when we accept the majority's point of view
   In some cases individuals go along with the majority because they genuinely believe them to be right. As a result, we don't just comply in behaviour alone, but we also *change* our own point of view in line with the majority viewpoint. Because we are conforming both publicly *and* privately, this form of conformity is known as *acceptance* (which may simply be *identification* or could be *internalisation* – these terms are explained in the 'Note' below). In conditions of uncertainty we may turn to the majority for *information* about how to behave. The majority, therefore, has *informational influence* over group members when they are uncertain how to behave.

---

### note

#### Types of conformity

The fact that an individual goes along with the majority in *public*, does not indicate that they have changed their *private* attitudes or beliefs. Kelman (1958) proposed three different kinds of conformity depending on the extent to which private beliefs were changed:

- *Compliance*. This is conforming to majority opinions and behaviour in public but privately maintaining one's own attitudes.
- *Identification*. An individual takes on the majority beliefs and behaviours both publicly and privately but this may only be temporary and will not be maintained when the individual leaves the group.
- *Internalisation*. This occurs when an individual privately accepts the majority view. The new attitudes and behaviours become part of the individual's personal value system.

---

### explanation

### Individual versus situational factors

Normative and informational influences are social (situational) pressures. It might be that some people conform more than others because they are 'conforming types' – which is a dispositional

## KEY TERMS

**Individual factors:** An enduring aspect of an individual's behaviour – their disposition or personality such as self-esteem, confidence, intelligence, experience or gender.

**Situational factors:** Anything in the environment, including the behaviour of other people and social roles.

(individual) explanation. Look back to the studies on pages 190–191 and also at the Star Study below. Which of these studies found that **individual factors** were more important and which found that **situational factors** were more important?

Research on individual differences suggests that, for example, people who are low in self-esteem are more likely to conform. In Asch's study a number of participants did not conform. The situational factors were the same for all participants, therefore individual factors must account for the difference. Other individual factors might be gender, experience in previous situations or personality differences. Adorno *et al.* (1950) described the 'authoritarian personality' – people who are more likely to conform because of the way in which they were brought up (see page 150).

Situational factors were also at work in Asch's study. They explain the conformity that was observed; the behaviour of the confederates was a situational factor. Those who obeyed did so because of the strong agreement amongst the confederates. When agreement is reduced (presence of one dissenter) then conformity drops dramatically – to about 5%.

## evaluation | Factors which moderate the effects of majority influence

*Cultural factors*
Compared with individualist cultures such as the UK and USA, conformity appears to be higher in societies where group harmony is a priority. This is what Smith and Bond (1993) found in a review of 31 studies of conformity. Conformity may be seen as a *positive* feature in cultures where *interdependence* is more highly valued than *independence* (**individualist** rather than **collectivist** societies).

*Group cohesiveness*
In situations where a group of people know each other (unlike Asch's experiment) conformity may be even higher, as shown in the study by Williams and Sogon (see page 191).

*Importance of task*
In situations where people have a strong moral basis for their beliefs they are less easily swayed by the opinions of others. Hornsey *et al.* (2003) found that students who had strong beliefs about the recognition of gay couples in law were publicly and privately less likely to conform to majority opinion.

*Size of the majority*
Asch (1956) found that the size of the opposing majority did affect conformity – up to a point. He found that as the size of the majority grew, so did the percentage of trials in which the naïve participant conformed. There was a high percentage of conformity when a lone dissenter faced a unified majority of three people, but increasing the number of confederates beyond three did not raise conformity levels significantly.

## starSTUDY

# Investigating the nature of conformity: Individual versus situational factors

(ZIMBARDO *ET AL.*, 1973)

### Aims
This study explores how we conform to social roles. Each of us has a number of roles: sister, student, friend and so on. For each role in our society there is a set of norms that tell us how a sister or a student should behave and we tend to follow these.

Philip Zimbardo was concerned about the growing unrest in US prisons in the 1960s. This unrest led to some violent riots. Some people believed that the reason for such violence was that both prisoners and guards have personalities which make conflict inevitable. Prisoners lack respect for law and order, and guards are domineering and aggressive. This is an individual (dispositional) explanation – explaining behaviour because of the individual's personality or disposition.

The alternative explanation is that the behaviour of prisoners and guards is a product of the situation in which they are placed. Both of them behave as they do because of the social role expected in the prison situation. This is a situational explanation.

If you placed 'ordinary' people in a prison environment and designated some of them as guards and others as prisoners, how would they behave? If the guards and prisoners in this mock prison behaved in a non-aggressive manner, this would support the dispositional

hypothesis. On the other hand, if these ordinary people come to behave in the same way that we see in real prisons then we must conclude that the environment plays a major role in influencing behaviour, the situational explanation.

## Method and procedure

Participants were male students who volunteered for a psychological study of 'prison life' (they were to be paid $15 a day). The 24 men who were most stable (physically and mentally) were selected and randomly assigned to being a prisoner or a guard: 2 acted as reserves and 1 dropped out, finally leaving 10 prisoners and 11 guards.

The 'prisoners' were unexpectedly 'arrested' at home. On entry to 'prison' they were put through a delousing procedure, searched, given a prison uniform with ID number, nylon stocking caps (to make their hair look short), and a chain around their ankle. They were in prison 24 hours a day.

The guards only referred to the prisoners by number. The prisoners were allowed certain 'rights': three meals a day, three supervised toilet trips, two hours for reading or letter-writing, and two visiting periods and movies per week. They had to line up three times a day to be counted and tested on the prison rules.

The guards had uniforms, clubs, whistles, handcuffs and reflective sunglasses (to prevent eye contact). **Deindividuation** was an important part of the process, encouraged for example by the wearing of uniforms.

## Results

The guards grew increasingly tyrannical. They woke prisoners in the night, locked them in a closet and got them to clean the toilet with their bare hands. Some guards even volunteered to do extra hours without pay.

The participants appeared at times to forget that they were only acting. Even when they were unaware of being watched they still played their roles. When one prisoner had had enough he asked for parole – rather than saying that he wanted to stop being part of the experiment. Had he come to think that he was actually a prisoner?

Five prisoners had to be released early because of extreme depression (crying, rage and acute anxiety). These symptoms had started to appear within two days. In fact the whole experiment was ended after six days, despite the intention to continue for two weeks.

## Conclusion

This study demonstrates that both guards and prisoners conformed to their social roles. Participants' behaviour was the result of normative social influence. In terms of the original aims of the experiment, we can conclude that situational explanations of the behaviour of prison guards appear to be most important rather than dispositional ones, because 'ordinary' students all too easily became brutal prison guards when placed in the right setting.

## Evaluation

### Demand characteristics and ecological validity

A **demand characteristic** is a feature of an experiment that in some way 'invites' a participant to behave in a particular way. Participants in this study took on very specific role behaviours because that is what they were asked to do (a demand characteristic). In real life a prison guard (or prisoner) might be less likely to act as the social role dictates. Instead they would adapt the role to suit their personal beliefs and the requirements of the situation. Most of the guards later claimed that they had simply been acting. This means the experiment may tell us very little about people's behaviour in real life.

Alternatively, it could be argued that the participants were very much 'in role' and the same pressures may operate so that this 'prison in miniature' may illustrate how certain contextual factors (e.g. uniforms that create a sense of power and of dependency) exacerbate other factors. It is not the *same* as real prison but provides insights about how context may cause people to behave in certain unexpected ways.

### Usefulness

Savin (1973) believed that 'the ends did not justify the means' in this study. Although it is claimed that the study was influential in radically altering the way that American prisons are run, in truth the American prison system has become *more* impersonal rather than less impersonal in the days since Zimbardo's study.

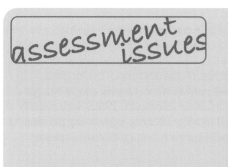

### How may conformity be affected by situational factors? (*ku* 5 *ae* 0)

Whenever you are asked to write about something in the plural (in this case *factors*), you need to decide whether to deal with *two* (minimum) or *more*. Sometimes this may be a hard choice to make, but your choice should be based on how much you know about each factor (or theory, or strategy, etc.), and on the number of marks available. You should EITHER write about *two* factors in a fair amount of *detail*, OR write about *more than two* factors in *limited* detail.

Other points to watch out for in this question: make sure that you write about *factors* (rather than, say, *types* of conformity); make sure that you write about *situational* (not *individual*) factors; make sure that you say how the factor *affects* conformity (don't just state the factor). In sum, every single word of the question is important!

*In a general sense, to 'conform' to something is to fit in with it or be moulded by it. This means that the term 'conformity' could be used in relation to majority or minority influence. However, technically psychologists have restricted the use of 'conformity' to situations of majority influence only. In your exams, however, 'conformity' is used to refer to both majority and minority influence.*

**Comparing majority and minority influence**

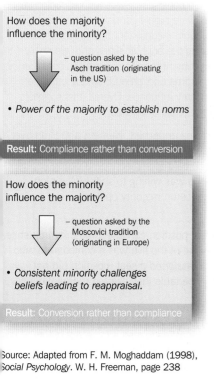

How does the majority influence the minority?

– question asked by the Asch tradition (originating in the US)

• *Power of the majority to establish norms*

**Result:** Compliance rather than conversion

How does the minority influence the majority?

– question asked by the Moscovici tradition (originating in Europe)

• *Consistent minority challenges beliefs leading to reappraisal.*

**Result:** Conversion rather than compliance

Source: Adapted from F. M. Moghaddam (1998), *Social Psychology*. W. H. Freeman, page 238

## Minority influence
### What is meant by minority influence?

So far, our discussion of social influence has focused on the power of the *majority*. Many European social psychologists have been critical of the American preoccupation with the power of the majority. Serge Moscovici, one of the foremost of such critics, claims that the idea of an all-powerful majority simply does not fit with historical reality. If the only form of social influence was majority influence, then we would all think and behave in the same way, and this would be unchanging from generation to generation.

History has shown us just how powerful minorities can be. For example, the suffragette movement of the 1920s gradually changed public and political opinion so that eventually women were given the vote. Minorities such as the suffragette movement tend not to have much power or status, and may even be dismissed as troublemakers, extremists or simply 'weirdoes'. How then, do they ever have any influence over the majority? Moscovici (1976) claims that the answer to this question lies in their *behavioural style*: i.e. the *way* that the minority get their point across. The crucial factor in the success of the suffragette movement was that the proponents of this position were *consistent* in their views, and this created a considerable degree of social influence. Minorities that are active and organised, who advocate and defend their position *consistently* can create social conflict, doubt and uncertainty among members of the majority, and ultimately this may lead to social change. Such change has often occurred because a minority has converted others to its point of view. Without the influence of minorities, we would have no innovation, no social change. Many of what we now regard as 'major' social movements (e.g. Christianity, trade unionism or feminism) were originally due to the influence of an outspoken minority.

### The difference between majority and minority influence
#### Numbers
Majority influence involves a number of real or imagined people affecting the attitudes and/or behaviour of an individual. Minority influence is exerted by a minority of one or more people. In other words the difference lies in the number of people (real or imagined) doing the influencing, not in the number of people being influenced.

#### Innovation or status quo?
Majority influence is typically seen as maintaining the current status quo; i.e. it is a form of social influence which is *resistant* to change. Majorities serve to promote uniformity among group members and exert pressure on those who deviate from group norms. Minority influence, on the other hand, is associated with change and innovation. The views of a deviant minority generate a social conflict with mainstream ideas, values and norms; the resolution may be a movement towards the minority position (i.e. social change).

#### Imitation or originality?
Because minorities must work harder to get their position across, their arguments are thought to produce more cognitive effort in the majority than is the case with majority influence. Nemeth (1995) suggests that majority influence leads to restricted 'convergent' thinking based simply on imitation, whereas minority influence leads to more 'divergent' and original thinking as alternatives are weighed up against each other in a search for the best solution.

## Compliance or conversion?

In order for minority influence to take place, there must be a **conversion** within individuals who were formerly part of the majority. This conversion involves a careful thinking through of the arguments of the minority and the gradual acceptance of their point of view. As a result, the process of minority influence is relatively slow to take place. Majority influence, on the other hand, is a far more passive process, as individuals comply with the majority position without a great deal of thought. This is referred to as the **dual-process model** of social influence (Moscovici, 1980), with majority influence representing the need for social approval, and minority influence representing the need for information about reality. Both lead to behavioural change but each through different processes.

## Research on minority influence

### Behavioural style

Moscovici *et al.* (1969) proposed that the minority must be consistent in their views and that this consistency will create conflict in others, leading them to question and possibly change their views even when the stimulus is explicit (unambiguous). To demonstrate this, the researchers arranged for 4 participants plus 2 confederates to name the colour of 36 slides. The slides were blue-coloured but both confederates consistently said that the slides were green. Overall, the participants agreed with the minority on 8.42% of the trials (i.e. they said that the slides were coloured green). Most impressively, 32% gave the same answer as the minority at least once.

When participants repeated the same task, in a second experiment, they were asked to write down their answer. This led to greater agreement with the confederates.

### Non-situational factors

Moscovici *et al.* suggested that consistency was the key characteristic of successful minority influence. In one variation of the experiment described above the confederates answered 'green' 24 times and 'blue' 12 times; i.e. they were not consistent. In this case, agreement with the minority was reduced to 1.25%.

Nemeth *et al.* (1974) suggested that confidence rather than consistency was the key factor. To test this they compared one condition where confederates were highly consistent (they said 'green' to every slide) with another condition where confederates were inconsistent but this inconsistency was related to a property of the stimulus (they said 'green' to the brighter slides and 'green-blue' to the dimmer slides). Such 'inconsistency' led to greater agreement than the unrealistic consistency of the former condition. If confederates said 'green' half the time and 'green-blue' the other half (i.e. inconsistent and random) then there was also no minority influence. Overall, this suggests that consistency only works when it is 'patterned' and not just blind repetition.

Flexibility rather than consistency has also been found to be important. Nemeth and Brilmayer (1987) found that a minority of one who refused to change his position (when arguing in a mock-jury situation for the amount of compensation to be paid to someone in a skiing accident) had no affect on others. However, a minority member who was willing to shift his opinion slightly in the direction of the majority did exert an influence on majority opinion.

### Situational factors

Moscovici and Nemeth (1974) demonstrated that *seating* position can affect minority influence. In this study five people sat around a rectangular table; one of the five was a confederate who expressed a minority opinion. When the confederate was *assigned* a seat, position did not matter; but if the confederate *chose* to sit at the head of the table they exerted more influence.

### Minority and majority influence

There is evidence that minority and majority influence may work together. Clark (1994) looked at social influence in a jury setting. Student participants were asked to read a transcript of the arguments presented in the film *Twelve Angry Men*. In the film, all but one member of a jury initially believed in the defendant's guilt in a murder trial. Slowly one juror (played by Henry Fonda) changes the minds of the others because of his consistent and unwavering conviction about the man's innocence. In the experiment, some participants were just given Henry Fonda's arguments to read whereas others were told how he gradually changed the minds of the other jury members. Social influence occurred in both groups but was stronger where the participants read the arguments (minority influence) and knew that others eventually conformed (majority influence).

Martin Luther King was an important leader of the Civil Rights movement in America. What characteristics was he likely to have possessed in order to exert his minority influence?

## explanation

### Minority influence

*Conflict rethinking*
Moscovici proposed that the confidence and consistency of a deviant minority challenges the way the majority thinks and causes them to rethink their position, thus bringing about internalised attitude change rather than superficial compliance.

*Social cryptoamnesia*
There is a point in any group where, after some members have started to agree with the minority, the minority then turns into a majority. Van Avermaet (1996) called this the *snowball effect*. However, we should remember that minority influence generally shows itself in private rather than public, so how does this snowball effect take place?

The answer may lie in *social cryptoamnesia*. It has been observed that major attitude changes (conversion) take place only when the spirit of the times (called the 'Zeitgeist') has changed. For example, at the start of the suffragette movement a few women (who were perceived as somewhat crazy) campaigned for a change in voting legislation – one threw herself in front of a horse race and was killed, and several chained themselves to the railings of 10 Downing Street. It was only some years later that popular (majority) opinion actually changed. Thus, opinion change was not the direct effect of minority influence. What probably happened was that the minority influence changed private attitudes and these views gradually became the 'spirit of the times'. When change occurred (women were given the vote) this was in accord with majority opinion. Perez *et al.* (1995) coined the phrase 'social cryptoamnesia' – by the time change occurs people have forgotten the original source of opinion change, but innovation was actually due to minority influence.

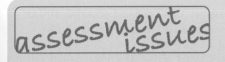

## assessment issues

**Explain and evaluate the concept of "minority influence". (ku 3 ae 3)**

Here you are being asked to put a concept 'under the microscope'. The question requires more than a definition, which would have been worth only two marks. To 'explain' something (for the *ku* marks) you need to do more than just 'define' it; you should add to it to demonstrate your understanding possibly by using an everyday example. How do you *evaluate* a *concept* (to gain the *ae* marks)? In psychology there is often debate and controversy over new ideas, and in this case the notion of 'minority' influence arose out of research *findings that could not be explained* by the well-established concept of majority influence. In addition, as ever, an important way of showing evaluation is by providing research evidence that supports or challenges, whether or not the question explicitly requires evidence.

# Aspect 2: Nature of obedience

**KEY TERMS**

**Obedience:** This refers to a type of social influence whereby somebody acts in response to a direct order from a figure with perceived authority. There is also the implication that the person receiving the order is made to respond in a way that they would not otherwise have done without the order.

Stanley Milgram and his research has had an astonishing influence, including a film (*Tenth Level* with William Shatner and John Travolta) and a song (*We Do What We're Told* by Peter Gabriel), see www.stanleymilgram.com

## Studies of obedience
### What is meant by obedience?

So far in this chapter we have looked at types of indirect social influence where people can choose whether or not they will yield to the perceived pressure of the majority or the minority. A more *direct* form of social influence where, it might be argued, the individual has less choice in whether they give way or not, is **obedience**. In this form of social influence, the individual is faced with the choice of whether to *comply* with a direct order from another person or whether to *defy* the order.

Much of the impetus for research in this area came from the need to understand the situational conditions under which people would suspend their own moral judgements in order to carry out an order from a malevolent authority figure. The underlying motivation for this, of course, was far more than idle curiosity; it was an attempt to explain the atrocities committed during the Holocaust and defended during the Nuremberg war trials as 'simply obeying orders'.

starSTUDY

## Investigating the nature of obedience: Obeying unjust authority

(MILGRAM, 1963)

### Aims

It makes sense to be obedient in some situations; obedience is a healthy and necessary social behaviour. But why do people obey when the action required is inhumane? Stanley Milgram set out to investigate whether ordinary people will obey a legitimate authority even when required to injure another person – i.e. show obedience to unjust authority.

### Method and procedure

Milgram recruited 40 male participants by advertising for volunteers for a study of how punishment affects learning, to take place at Yale University. Everyone was paid $4.50 and told that they would receive this even if they quit during the study.

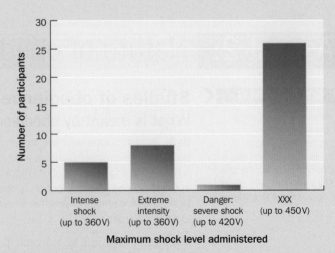

There were two confederates: an experimenter and a 'learner' (a 47-year-old accountant). The participant drew lots with the confederate but the draw was faked and the participant always ended up playing the role of 'teacher'. He was told that he must administer increasingly strong electric shocks to the learner each time the latter got a question wrong. The machine was tested on the participant to show him that it worked.

The learner, sitting in another room, gave mainly wrong answers and received his (fake) shocks in silence until they reached 300 volts (very strong shock). At this point, he pounded on the wall and then gave no response to the next question. He repeated this at 315 volts and from then on said and did nothing. If the 'teacher' asked to stop, the experimenter had a set of 'prods' to repeat, such as 'It is absolutely essential that you continue' or 'You have no other choice; you must go on'.

### Results

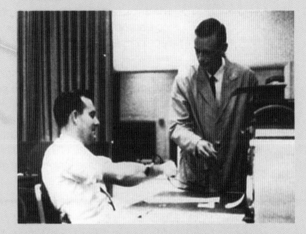

Maximum shock level administered

Prior to the actual study, Milgram asked psychology students to say how far they thought participants would go. They estimated that less than 3% would go to the maximum level. The main finding was that 65% of the participants continued to the maximum voltage, far beyond what was marked 'Danger: severe shock'. Only 5 participants (12.5%) stopped at 300 volts, the point when the learner first objected.

Some participants displayed signs of being very stressed; for example Milgram reported (1963, page 377), 'I observed a mature and initially poised businessman enter the laboratory smiling and confident. Within 20 minutes he was reduced to a twitching, stuttering wreck, who was rapidly approaching a point of nervous collapse. He constantly pulled on his earlobe, and twisted his hands. At one point he pushed his fist into his forehead and muttered "Oh God, let's stop it". And yet he continued to respond to every word of the experimenter, and obeyed to the end.'

## Conclusion

The results suggest that ordinary people are astonishingly obedient to authority when asked to behave in an inhumane manner. This suggests that it is not evil people who commit evil crimes but ordinary people who are just obeying orders. In other words, crimes against humanity may be the outcome of situational rather than dispositional factors. It appears that an individual's capacity for making independent decisions is suspended under certain situational constraints – namely being given an order by an authority figure.

## Evaluation

### Ecological validity

Many people feel that the research situation was artificial and contrived and therefore we cannot use the findings to explain atrocities in the real world. See pages 96–97 for arguments against this position.

### Individual differences

Interviews with participants after the experiment showed considerably different attitudes about what they were doing. Some of the participants showed no emotion and were 'happy' to go along with what they were told to do. Others showed clear signs of being very uncomfortable. Some participants stopped relatively early on, whereas, as we know, a number went all the way. When the experiment was repeated with different people, it was found that educated participants were less obedient and military participants were more obedient.

What all of this tells us is that the simple conclusion that situational factors cause obedience is wrong. Dispositional factors are important as well because not everyone obeys.

### Psychological harm

Baumrind (1964) attacked Milgram's study for the severe distress it created in participants. Milgram defended himself in several ways. First, he did not know, prior to the study, that such high levels of distress would be caused (this did not stop him carrying out various replications). Secondly, he asked participants afterwards if they had found the experience distressing and interviewed them again a year later: 84% felt glad to have participated, and 74% felt that they had learned something of personal importance. Thirdly, Milgram suggested that it may be the findings of his study rather than the methods used that have led to its being branded unethical.

note

### *Why was Milgram's research subjected to so much hostile criticism?*

Milgram's research changed the way in which we view the nature of destructive obedience. Prior to this research, it was traditional for social scientists to explain such behaviour as the Nazi war crimes in terms of the actions of deviant personalities. Milgram's research, however, suggested that destructive obedience may be evoked in the majority of people by purely situational factors. In other words, claimed Milgram, his research was criticised because of the *results* rather than the procedures used. Milgram's findings appeared all the more shocking because they challenged Western assumptions about freedom and personal responsibility. The capacity for moral decision making, it appeared, is suspended when an individual is embedded within a powerful social hierarchy. This has led some to comment on the 'ordinariness' of such evil acts rather than seeing them as the product of pathological personalities (Arendt, 1963). Milgram's research effectively 'opened our eyes' to the possibility that each of us is capable of performing in the same way as his research participants had done and, by implication, the same as SS guards in the Nazi death camps.

## Research on obedience
### Variations on Milgram's baseline experiment

*You might wonder why all studies explore the issue of obedience to 'unjust' authority. It is difficult to investigate 'just' authority (such as a lollipop lady telling you when to cross the road) because there would be no reason to disobey!*

Milgram (1974) conducted various follow-up studies, using the same basic procedure. The findings are shown in the graph below. They support the view that situational factors affect obedience – they may either increase obedience or increase resistance to obedience.

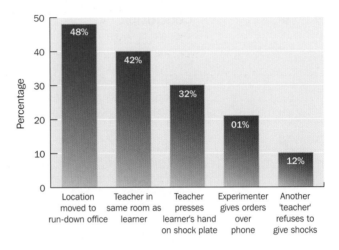

In another replication, Zimbardo (1969) found increased obedience if the 'learner' had to wear a name tag and hood (called *deindividuation* – removing the person's individual identity).

Smith and Bond (1993) reviewed a number of studies that replicated Milgram's baseline experiment in different countries. Rates of obedience varied from 85% in Germany to 16% for female Australians. However, one can't be sure how equivalent the studies are to each other; for example the conditions were often slightly different.

### Field studies of obedience to authority
Milgram's studies have overshadowed research into obedience but many other studies have contributed to our further understanding of obedience to unjust authority.

*In the street*
Bickman (1974) tested the effects of perceived authority on obedience in a more natural setting (described briefly on page 91). Confederates dressed in a sports jacket and tie, a milkman's uniform, or as a guard, and made requests to passers-by: for example, asking them to pick up some litter or to give someone a dime for his parking meter. Participants obeyed most when the confederate was dressed as a guard. This study shows what most of us know – we obey someone who looks like they have authority more than someone who does not.

*Doctors and nurses*
Hofling *et al*. (1966) conducted a study in a hospital (described on page 96). The order from an unknown doctor contravened hospital regulations yet 21 out of 22 (95%) nurses did as requested. As in Milgram's study, when nurses were asked beforehand whether nurses would obey under these circumstances, they all said that no nurse would. When the nurses involved in the study were interviewed afterwards they said in their defence that they had obeyed because that's what doctors expect nurses to do.

The study by Rank and Jacobsen (1977) also described on page 96 suggests that, if situational factors are different, nurses are not at all obedient. This supports Milgram's conclusion, i.e. that situational rather than individual factors explain obedience.

*The obedience alibi*
On pages 96 and 206 we review evidence from Mandel (1998) which suggests that, in real life (as opposed to contrived situations), people may be highly obedient despite the presence of situational factors that should *reduce* obedience (e.g. face-to-face contact, some disobedient peers, absence of pressure from authority figure). Mandel concluded that by trying to explain the behaviour of Holocaust perpetrators in terms of situational obedience, Milgram offered little more than an 'obedience alibi' for their actions. This explanation 'permits' people to say, 'I was only obeying orders' whereas there is more to the behaviour than that.

*Obedience or conformity or both?*

The study by Zimbardo *et al.* (see page 193) can be related to obedience as well as conformity because obedience is a form of conformity to social roles. People obey in the experimental situation and nurses obey doctors because that is what is regarded as 'normal' in those situations – this behaviour is an established social norm.

Were the nurses in Hofling *et al.*'s study obeying orders or were they complying (showing conformity) with a social norm (the norm of what is expected for nurses)? This illustrates the difficulties inherent in making distinctions between things – it doesn't always work in practice! If you wish to use Zimbardo *et al.*'s or Hofling *et al.*'s study to illustrate conformity or obedience, then make sure that you are explicit about why it does illustrate conformity or obedience.

## assessment issues

**Describe and analyse what psychologists have learned from research studies into obedience. (*ku* 6 *ae* 4)**

Whenever a question asks about obedience, examiners find that, as sure as night follows day, a number of students will write about Milgram's classic study – and nothing else! If you were to do that in response to this question you would get very few marks, and certainly no more than five marks, since you need to refer to at least two research studies. In any case, the focus here is clearly on *what psychologists have learned,* i.e. findings and interpretation/analysis of findings. You can show 'analysis' in various ways: what are the possible *reasons* for obedience, suggested by the findings? What factors produced more or less obedience (e.g. in Milgram's research)? And was it really obedience, or was it actually conformity to social roles or situational norms (e.g. Hofling *et al.*; Zimbardo *et al.*)? Are there variations in levels of obedience across cultures (e.g. Smith and Bond)? What do findings tell us about origins of 'evil' in humans? For a 10-mark question like this you would not need to address *all* of these points, but they may give you some ideas on how to set about 'analysing' a topic.

## Explanations of obedience
## Why do people obey?

The 'touch-proximity condition' in Milgram's experiment, where the 'teacher' holds the hand of the 'learner' on the shock plate. Some participants were still very obedient despite the close physical proximity: 30% still gave the maximum shock.

On the previous few pages we have examined evidence related to obedient behaviour, much of which suggests that situational factors may be responsible for obedience in humans. Now we will outline some of these situational factors as well as some possible individual factors. In addition to situational and individual factors as an explanation for obedience, we can also look at the psychological processes that affect when a person may choose to obey or disobey.

### explanation | Situational factors that affect levels of obedience

*Proximity of victim*
In Milgram's proximity study (1974), both teacher and learner stayed in the same room, and in the touch-proximity study teachers had to hold the learner's hand on a plate in order to deliver the shocks once the learner had refused to cooperate. Obedience rates dropped, suggesting that physical presence and contact made teachers empathise more strongly with the learner's suffering and made it harder to deny or ignore.

*Proximity of authority*
In another variation, the experimenter left the room before the 'learning' session and continued to give instructions by telephone. Here, only 9 out of 40 (23%) participants went to the maximum shock level, showing that the authority figure's direct surveillance is a crucial factor in determining obedience in this setting.

*Presence of allies*
A further study gave the responsibility for shock delivery to three supposed participants (two accomplices and the real participant) acting as a team. When the two bogus teachers had

expressed reservations and refused to carry on, almost all 'real' participants also withdrew their cooperation. Only 4 out of 40 (10%) proceeded to 450 volts. This finding suggests that it may be difficult to confront authority alone, but that the presence of other rebels may help the person to see resistance as legitimate and formulate strategies for disobedience (see also Gamson *et al*. on page 207).

*evaluation*

Each of the factors outlined above has arisen from Milgram's studies of obedience, outlined earlier (page 198). But do these factors apply *beyond* the laboratory? Mandel's evidence, reported on page 96, suggests that the same factors may not operate in the real world. However, it is possible that the behaviour of the German troops is also not typical. Goldhagen (1996) argues that it was not situational obedience that led to events in the Holocaust but the anti-Semitism that was rife in Germany at the time. Another possible explanation is that because they had been soldiers over a period of time, and therefore had previously obeyed many orders, this acted as 'gradual commitment', a psychological process described below.

*explanation*

## Individual factors that affect levels of obedience

### Experience
One participant in Milgram's study, Gretchen Brandt, stopped at 210 volts because of her own experiences as a young person in Nazi Germany, saying, 'Perhaps we have seen too much pain' (Milgram, 1974). An individual's past experiences will influence the degree to which they are willing to obey. Their sense of expertise will also influence willingness to obey. Another participant Jan Rensaleer, was an industrial engineer. He stopped at 225 volts, saying, 'I know what shocks do to you.' Karen Dontz, a nurse who administered the full 450 volts, said, 'In hospital I know what rights I have; here I didn't know'. In hospital she would have felt in a position to question authority because of the knowledge she had, but she didn't feel able to do it here.

### Gender
We have already seen that women may be more conformist than men (see page 191) and so we might expect gender to be a significant factor in obedience. On the other hand, women tend to be less aggressive than men (see page 174) and more empathetic, so we might expect less willingness to give shocks. Kilham and Mann (1974) did find a gender difference in an Australian replication of Milgram's study where 16% of women obeyed compared with 40% of men; however, Milgram (1974) did not find a difference when he repeated his study with women although he did find that women reported greater feelings of conflict than men.

*explanation*

## Psychological processes that explain why people obey

### Socialisation
**Socialisation** refers to the process by which an individual acquires the knowledge, values, social skills and sensitivity to others that enables them to become a part of society. We are taught from a young age that we should obey people who have *legitimate authority* such as policemen, teachers and even school crossing patrols. Such individuals fulfil given social roles which are invested with authority by society. This gives the authority figure the right to exert control over the behaviour of others. Bickman's study (see page 200) showed how people respond to people with perceived legitimate authority as demonstrated by the fact that they were wearing a uniform.

### Gradual commitment
In Milgram's study, all participants give lower-level shocks. In actuality, no shock level is ever 'administered' that is more than 15 volts from the previous level. Having committed themselves to a particular course of action (i.e. giving shocks), it became difficult for Milgram's participants subsequently to change their mind. This is similar to the *foot-in-the-door* method of persuasion which is a tactic designed to maximise the likelihood of compliance. A trivial initial request, once accepted, is followed by larger requests that the individual then feels obliged to agree to.

### Agentic and autonomous behaviour
Central to Milgram's explanation of obedience is what he termed the **agentic state**, by which he meant 'the condition a person is in when he sees himself as an agent for carrying out another

**KEY TERMS**

**Agentic state:** The state a person is in when they see themselves acting as an agent for another person and thus do not feel responsible for their own actions.

**KEY TERMS**

**Autonomous state:** The state a person is in when they see themselves acting alone and feel responsible for their own behaviour.

person's wishes' (Milgram, 1974). Milgram argued that people shift back and forth between an agentic state and an **autonomous state**, the latter referring to the state a person is in when he 'sees himself acting on his own'. Upon entering an authority system, Milgram claimed, the individual no longer views himself as acting out of his own purposes but rather comes to see himself as an agent for executing the wishes of another. Unlike autonomous behaviour, individuals in an agentic state see themselves as not responsible for their own actions (because someone else is). This is discussed further on page 204.

*The role of buffers*
In Milgram's original study, the teacher and learner were in different rooms, with the teacher protected (i.e. *buffered*) from having to see his 'victim', and also from the consequences of his electric shocks. When the learner was in the same room, this buffering effect was reduced, as was the tendency to obey the commands of the experimenter, and therefore the overall levels of obedience. This 'buffering' effect is similarly used to explain the apparent willingness of people to dispatch weapons of mass destruction. A cruise missile does not, after all, have the same immediacy of consequence as a rifle.

*assessment issues*

**Discuss factors affecting obedience behaviour. Evaluate relevant research evidence in your answer. (ku 12 ae 8)**

In this one-part essay question, the balance of *ku* and *ae* marks is 12 and 8, respectively (a ratio of 3:2 as always in any 20-mark question). To tackle this question, it is a good idea to check first what *skills* are required, and where the *ku* and *ae* marks come from. The command 'discuss' involves both types of skill, and 'evaluate' involves just *ae* skills. Secondly, how will you organise your *knowledge* in the essay? Should you 'discuss factors' first, then 'evaluate evidence' after that? In fact, that approach would probably not work very well, as you should link each factor to its relevant research study(ies). Although there is no single correct way to structure any essay, one possible way to organise 'factors' (or 'influences', or 'processes', or whatever) is to put them into *categories* – you may well have learned the factors in a categorised way, in any case. For this question, factors might be classed as individual or situational, and various psychological processes are relevant factors too. To incorporate these points into a good essay structure, you should first draft a *plan* – e.g. a mind map or list of headings and subheadings – then follow it. If you make yourself spend a few minutes thinking carefully about the best way to organise your knowledge, and fight off the impulse to just start writing immediately, you'll find that writing the essay itself is plain sailing.

# Aspect 3: Resisting social pressure

From the Daleks in *Doctor Who* ('Resistance is useless') to the Borg in *Star Trek* ('Resistance is futile'), we could be forgiven for believing that in the world of social influence, resistance really is pretty useless. Fortunately, this is not the case: psychologists have shown that, in the right situation, resistance *is* possible, and in many cases can be pretty effective as well. In this Aspect we examine how people can resist mindless compliance to inappropriate, unjust and even malevolent authority and social pressure. We will look at intrapersonal and interpersonal processes that help us to resist social pressure.

## Intrapersonal processes

In this section we are concerned with explanations for resistance to social pressure which focus on psychological processes *within* an individual, i.e. *intra*personal. As you will see, some explanations are related to Milgram's studies described in Aspect 2 of this chapter – we can explain resistance by using the very same research. In all of those studies some people obeyed but some people resisted and thus can provide us with insights into the reverse of conformity and obedience.

## Taking responsibility for one's own actions

### Moral control

Bierhoff (2002) interprets 'social responsibility' as involving both a concern for the welfare of others, and also a progression towards our own personal goals. The first part of this definition is related to empathy, and the second to guilt. We may feel a responsibility to help others in distress, but we may also anticipate feelings of guilt if we *don't* concern ourselves with the interests of others. These anticipated feelings of guilt result in a personal moral control that guides our interactions with other individuals.

### Agentic shift and the displacement of personal responsibility

As we have seen, Milgram (1974) suggested that when people obey they move to an agentic state where they no longer feel personal responsibility for their actions. Kelman (1973) also showed that personal agency is weakened in conditions where groups reach a decision such that no one person feels personally responsible for that decision. In both individual and group situations, people no longer see themselves as the agent for their actions, and therefore do not consider themselves personally accountable for either what a group does collectively or what they themselves do when instructed by someone in authority.

### Increasing personal responsibility

Kipper and Har-Even (1984) designed a study to see if participants would behave differently if they were given different roles in a shock experiment. One group of participants (the spontaneous group) was free to choose the level of shock administered to a learner; a second group was instructed to act like a teacher, focusing more on the task. The greater task focus of the second group would, it was predicted, lead to a denial of any feeling of personal responsibility for the learner. The spontaneous group, however, would be more concerned about the consequences of their actions on the learner and so more likely to choose lower shock levels. As predicted, the task-focused group escalated the level of shocks as the test proceeded, while the shocks administered by the spontaneous group remained at a moderate level. Furthermore, the task-focused group attributed responsibility for the shocks to the nature of the task, whereas the spontaneous group focused more on personal responsibility in determining their behaviour. This study shows that the role played by an individual can affect the degree to which they exercise their personal moral control in response to social influence. Taking personal responsibility for one's actions is also seen as a sign of psychological good health (and reduction of stress), with one of the aims of psychotherapy being to increase the patient's experience of responsibility for what they do (Shapiro, 2006).

## Moral reasoning and awareness of own values

### Kohlberg's theory of moral reasoning

On the basis of his research into morality, Harvard moral philosopher, Lawrence Kohlberg (1969) identified six stages of moral reasoning that he grouped into three major levels. Each of these three levels represented a fundamental shift in the moral perspective of the individual. In the *pre-conventional* level, people judge the morality of an action mostly by its direct consequences (e.g. 'Will I be punished for doing this?'). At the *conventional* level of reasoning, individuals have developed an understanding that norms and conventions are necessary in order to maintain the society in which they live. In the *post-conventional* level, individuals reason that some aspects of morality, such as regard for life and human welfare, should be upheld irrespective of convention or normative obligation.

As a result of interviews with Milgram's experimental participants, Kohlberg (1969) found that most of those who resisted the instruction to give increasingly severe electric shocks reasoned at higher stages of moral development. Why might this be so? One possible reason is that as people move through the three levels of moral development, the reasons for behaving morally become more internalised. Thus, the motive for more advanced moral thinkers to resist is more to do with acting in accordance with their self-accepted moral code than any desire to gain approval or avoid punishment. Perhaps this might explain the morally heroic actions of Kohlberg himself in the years following the end of the Second World War (see note on the next page).

### Resisting obedience in real-life conflicts

Although Kohlberg's theory offers a persuasive explanation for why some people resist destructive obedience and others do not, it is a theory based largely on the actions of individuals faced with situations that are either simplistic (e.g. children cheating in the

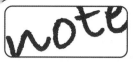

### Beds or bananas? Moral reasoning in action

At the end of the Second World War, Kohlberg volunteered to help smuggle Jewish survivors of the Nazi concentration camps out of Europe and into Palestine by sea. This was made all the more difficult by the fact that many Western countries still refused to accept these refugees, and Britain, who ruled Palestine at the time, prevented settlement by mounting a sea blockade. Kohlberg and his shipmates learned how to deceive port workers by telling them that the old freighter they were using to transport refugees was carrying only bananas. However, the banana crates were secretly beds and they were able to fool government inspectors who were part of the blockade. When his vessel was eventually intercepted by the British, Kohlberg returned to the US to begin his research on moral reasoning (from www. arches.uga.edu/~relong).

classroom) or abstract (e.g. whether to steal a drug to save a dying woman). Kohlberg's analysis of how people resist destructive obedience in situations that are more like real life was rather more limited. His only interview with an individual involved in a real-life conflict was with Michael Bernhardt, a soldier who refused to shoot innocent civilians in the My Lai massacre of 500 South Vietnamese civilians during the Vietnam War. Kohlberg praised his interviewee for his 'conscious decision to take responsibility for his own actions'. This, according to Kohlberg, reflected a high level of moral reasoning. Bernhardt had resisted the order to open fire on the civilians of My Lai, yet regardless of this resistance, the consequences were still the same – the victims were simply shot by the other members of his company (Linn, 2001).

However, Linn and Gilligan (1990) point out, Kohlberg disregarded the fact that Bernhardt had ignored other moral options, such as stopping other soldiers from shooting or attending to the wounded. This suggests a fundamental limitation of psychological theories of morality, in that they focus too heavily on the nature of moral *reasoning* to the neglect of moral *conduct*. Adopting a detached moral position, as Bernhardt had done at My Lai, does not necessarily represent maturity of moral conduct.

### Humanisation and dehumanisation

Individuals may employ a number of psychological 'manoeuvres' to disengage their internalised moral values, so allowing themselves to engage in what would normally be seen as immoral or inhumane conduct. In Milgram's obedience studies, for example, participants appeared more willing to obey the instructions of the experimenter when they were encouraged to do so by obedient confederates (*diffusion* of responsibility) or when the experimenter offered to take responsibility for any harm to the victim (*displacement* of responsibility). By altering their interpretation of events, participants were thus able to maintain positive self-regard despite their apparently immoral behaviour.

A consequence of this moral disengagement process is that individuals may no longer treat their victims as fellow humans. In essence, victims become 'dehumanised', i.e. stripped of human qualities and portrayed as subhuman objects. The process of dehumanisation is an important element in man's inhumanity to his fellow man. Levi (1989) asked a Nazi death camp commandant why his guards went to such lengths to degrade victims whom they were going to kill anyway. The commandant explained that this was necessary so that those who operated the gas chambers would not suffer moral distress because of their actions.

This chilling revelation confirms what Milgram had already discovered in his obedience studies, that it is difficult to mistreat *humanised* people without risking personal distress and self-condemnation. Most people refuse to behave cruelly (despite the presence of authoritarian commands) towards humanised others, when they are more directly aware of the suffering of their victim (Milgram, 1974). The implication of this finding is profound – that accepting a common humanity between individuals brings the best out in people (Bandura, 2002).

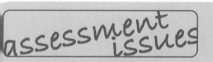

**Analyse the role of moral reasoning in people's resistance to social pressure or coercion. (ku 2 ae 2)**

This Aspect deals with *practical* strategies that people use to resist social pressure or coercion, but you also need to know the various *theoretical* explanations underlying these strategies, and some of these are the reverse of explanations of conformity and obedience (covered earlier in the chapter). In this case, you are asked about *moral reasoning*. Kohlberg's theory should spring to mind, and a brief description of this should gain you the *ku* marks. An example could also help gain credit here (from the text above, or one of your own). For the *ae* marks, make sure that you then explain *how* a higher level of moral reasoning might account for resistance: for example, acting in terms of an internalised moral code which overrides any desire for approval from others (which would tend to produce compliance to social norms). In this way, you would be using your knowledge of why people often *do* conform and obey, to analyse why they sometimes *resist*.

# Interpersonal processes

Interpersonal processes of resistance to social pressure focus on psychological processes *between* individuals i.e. *inter*personal.

# The role of disobedient models

## Modelling disobedience

In a variation to his base-line study, Milgram introduced two confederates who would share the task of teaching the learner. In this situation, the 'confederate' teachers (1 and 2) read the list of words and gave feedback to the learner, but it was up to the real participant (teacher 3) to administer the shock when required. Following instructions that were unknown to the real participant, teacher 1 refused to continue with his role after the 10th shock level. After the 14th shock level, teacher 2 also refused to continue, and teacher 3 was instructed to take over the role of the other two. At this point, the vast majority (90%) used the opportunity to extricate themselves from their role, and defied the experimenter. The successful disobedience of teachers 1 and 2 had made it easier for the real participant to defy the instructions of the experimenter.

## A contrasting example

The example of Reserve Police Battalion 101 (described on page 96) offers a contrast to the behaviour of participants in the study above. In this real-life incident during the Second World War in the Polish town of Józefów, Major Wilhelm Trapp, the battalion's commanding officer, announced that he had received orders for the mass killing of over 1500 Jews. Unlike Milgram's experimenter, however, Trapp gave his men a way out of this predicament by telling them that those who 'did not feel up to the task of killing Jews', could be assigned to other duties. This offer was repeated even after the killings had begun, yet only a handful of men chose to extricate themselves from the killings. Unlike the real participant in one of Milgram's studies, who used the successful defiance of the confederates to get out of giving any more shocks, the same did not happen at Józefów. Browning (1992) estimated that at least 80% of the men of Reserve Police Battalion 101 continued to kill until the job was done. Mandel (1998) argues that defiance is unlikely to occur 'if a subordinate does not strongly desire to extricate himself from the task to which he is assigned'.

## Disobedience or dissent?

It is important to distinguish between those who actively resist the commands of a destructive authority figure (and disobey), and those who merely express their dissent (yet continue to obey). In Milgram's experiment, many of the participants dissented, saying that they didn't want to continue giving shocks to the learner, but only a minority actually disobeyed the experimenter and stopped giving shocks. In Zimbardo's Stanford prison experiment (see page 193), there was also a great deal of dissent from prisoners and guards, but disobedience was rare. Even for the minority of individuals who *did* resist in these studies, such isolated acts failed to alter the situation itself as the majority felt unable to challenge the power of authority.

Members of Reserve Police Battalion 101 were ordered to kill Jewish civilians in Poland but were given the option to be assigned to other duties. About 80% obeyed despite the fact that there were some disobedient models.

## starSTUDY

# Investigating resistance to social pressure: Encounters with unjust authority

(GAMSON *ET AL.*, 1982)

## Aims

Gamson *et al.* (1982) set out to study obedience to unjust authority, like Milgram had, but this time they used groups of participants. Would groups, as opposed to individuals, be more likely to rebel against authority, because of the possibility of collective action, or would they also obey?

## Method and procedure

Participants were told that their task was to help a (fictitious) public relations company called MHRC to collect opinions on moral standards. Thirty-three groups of participants met in groups of nine at a motel, and were paid $10 for two hours' work. They were given a summary of a current legal case: Mr. C, whose franchise for running a service station had been ended because of his immoral behaviour, was suing the oil company. It also transpired that Mr. C. had spoken out on television against higher petrol prices.

The participants were asked to discuss their attitudes towards Mr. C's lifestyle while being videotaped. A coordinator switched off the cameras at various times and instructed individuals to argue as if they were offended by Mr. C's behaviour. Then he switched the cameras back on. The groups soon realised that they were being manipulated to produce a tape of evidence supporting the oil company's position.

## Results

In some of the groups, the participants threatened to confiscate the videotapes of the discussion, and to expose the oil company in the media. In all groups there was some rebellion although eight groups nevertheless signed the affidavit giving MHRC permission to use the video tape in a trial.

## Conclusion

This study supports the view that groups do behave differently from individuals. If one member in a group spontaneously rebelled, this minority opinion swayed most of the groups and ultimately led to group conformity. However, in some groups the majority of people did not have anti-authoritarian values. Therefore, despite the fact that some members had expressed rebellion, group opinion was not changed.

## Evaluation

*Ethical issues*

There are a number of ethical issues raised in this study. First, the participants reported that they found the experience quite distressing. One said that the experiment was 'the most stressful experience I've had in the past year'. The researchers did stop the study prematurely, having originally intended to run a total of 80 groups.

Second, Gamson *et al.* used an interesting method of gaining informed consent which some might regard as unethical because it really is a form of deception. The method is called 'prior general consent'. They contacted prospective participants and asked if they would be willing to take part in research on any of the following: brand recognition of commercial products; product safety; a study where you will be misled about the purpose until afterwards; research involving group standards. When participants agreed to all four they were then informed that only the latter kind of study was in progress. In fact this was a deception, *but* they had agreed to be deceived because the list included taking part in a study where they would be misled about its purpose. Such unethical behaviour does not challenge the findings of the study but it is important to the way that the public perceives psychologists.

*Ecological validity*

Experiments such as this always differ from the 'real world' in various different ways which means that we have to ask, 'How much does this tell us about everyday life?' In this study all the participants were strangers. We may behave differently with individuals or groups who know us and whom we know.

## Questioning motives

### Advertisers

'For long-term benefits, then, it seems more valuable to concentrate on helping children develop skills for making decisions than to teach them which specific decisions to make' (Austin and Johnson, 1997). This quotation emphasises the importance of developing media literacy among vulnerable consumer groups. There is a powerful lobby for demanding controls on advertising to adolescents and young people, and in some cases this has influenced legislation. In Sweden, there are strict laws and guidelines on television advertising of children's products which, it is argued, establishes a better 'balance of power' between consumers and producers.

However, there is little doubt that as children get older they become more aware of the consumer world and how it works. They move from credulous naivety through part understanding to adult knowledge and scepticism (Furnham, 2002). Studies that have attempted to increase the critical viewing of advertisements by children and adolescents have met with mixed results. In their study of alcohol-specific media-literacy training Austin and Johnson (1997) found that training increased children's understanding of the persuasive intent of advertisements, leading to the children in the study expressing a decreased expectation of positive consequences from drinking alcohol and a decreased likelihood of choosing an alcohol-related product. Austin and Johnson concluded that the real power of media-literacy training appears not to be its direct and immediate behavioural effects but in its long-term effects on the decision-making process itself.

### Politicians

Are politicians motivated by a desire to do the best for us? Or are their motives selfish?

We live in cynical times, particularly when it comes to the motives of politicians. In a *YouGov* poll published in 2002, only 1% of those surveyed thought that their local councillors were 'self-sacrificing'. Even during the Second World War only one-third of people believed that politicians were taking decisions in the best interests of the country (Healey *et al.*, 2005). Part of the reason why many people are 'turned off' politics and politicians is that they find the political system impenetrable owing to its specialist language and seemingly archaic procedures (MORI poll, 2005). Such findings suggest that many people feel 'alienated' from the political system and from politicians.

Such alienation, coupled with a distrust of whether politicians really *are* looking after the best interests of their constituents has led many to question the motives of the politicians whom they themselves elected. In 2005, 12% of the public claimed that they would voluntarily encourage others to vote for a specific political party, while 37% said that they would *discourage* others from voting for a specific party! The public continues to distrust politicians, with recent research by the Hansard Society (2005) suggesting that people's perception of MPs is of 'liars and hypocrites' who are 'out of touch' with common concerns. A complicating factor in this analysis is that surveys suggest that most people believe that their local MP is twice as trustworthy as 'MPs in general' (BMRB survey, 2004). Resistance is not always passive, as in many cultures it is traditional to take part in May Day demonstrations to give voice to grievances and concerns. For example, in May 2006, over two million Americans demonstrated in support of immigrant workers' rights.

### Cults and mind control

In recent years, religious and other cultic groups have generated considerable public criticism as a result of the harmful consequences of the techniques used to recruit, persuade, and control their members. Many of these techniques are highly, although often subtly, manipulative and deceptive. Cult influence tactics are powerful tools which, in the hands of an unscrupulous cult leader, can elicit extreme, and in some cases fatal, levels of compliance. Some techniques commonly used by cult members and strategies for resisting them are given below.

- *Black and white, simplistic reasoning.* Cult recruits are often encouraged to divide the world into 'good' and 'bad'. The shades of grey which we accept as being a part of our world are usually intolerable to a cult member. Andersen and Zimbardo (1984) suggest that this blinkered perspective can be overcome if people avoid making decisions when under stress, particularly in the presence of the person who has triggered the emotional reaction. It is also important to reject any 'us and them' dichotomy that cuts the cult member off from outsiders.

- *Dramatic shifts of values or beliefs.* Research has shown that beliefs and values are highly resistant to dramatic short-term change. Radical changes in thinking which are typical of cults require extreme situational influences such as those provided by skilled cult leaders. Andersen and Zimbardo believe that this form of influence can be resisted if an individual paraphrases other people's thoughts, to check that they understand the message clearly, and by seeking outside information and criticisms.

- *Disruption of family ties.* As family members pose a threat to the influence of the cult, many cults refuse to allow their members to attend family events. Andersen and Zimbardo stress the importance of maintaining links with family and friends rather than relying exclusively on other cult members as a means of resisting influence.

### The role of education

Most adolescents have exaggerated perceptions of what is normal among their peer group. For example, they may believe that drug use is more common and more generally accepted in the peer group than it actually is. Hansen and Graham (1991) examined two approaches to preventing alcohol and drug use among young adolescents. The first approach, *normative education*, was to establish beliefs in conventional norms among students. This programme taught students that substance use (i.e. alcohol, tobacco, marijuana) among their peers was lower than they might otherwise expect. It also taught students that substance use was generally not approved of by their peer group. In the second approach, *resistance skills training*, students were taught a variety of techniques that would help them to resist social pressure, for example being assertive in peer interactions. Results showed that resistance training alone was relatively ineffective, but when combined with normative education, the strongest results were obtained. As a result of this combination of approaches, when tested one year later, students were less likely to have engaged in substance use.

Are cults spiritual, positive, gentle, harmless, heretical, mind controlling, dangerous, homicidal … or all of the above? See www.religioustolerance.org/cultmenu.htm

*assessment issues*

**Describe strategies that may help people to resist social pressure or coercion by cult organisations. (ku 4 ae 0)**

You will have recognised that this is an 'applied Aspect' question. Students often lose marks on this type of question through lack of substance, i.e. 'waffle'! Two ways to avoid waffling are, first, to use appropriate psychological vocabulary in your answer (e.g. in this case, 'simplistic reasoning', 'awareness of your own values and beliefs', 'maintain family ties', etc.). Secondly, provide evidence wherever possible; here you could refer to Andersen and Zimbardo (1984). If the question specified 'advertisers' rather than 'cults', you could refer to Furnham (2002), and/or Austin and Johnson (1997). Another way of enhancing your answer to this question would be to give an example of a cult that exerts pressure or coercion on members.

*In this section we show you student answers to possible exam questions plus examiner's comments on these answers. Remember that in the actual exam (and NABs) your questions for this Topic will always add up to 20 marks. The question may be one essay worth 20 marks or a number of smaller questions (such as those shown below) which add up to 20 marks.*

**Question 1** (a) Explain *two* situational factors that may affect conformity. (*ku* 4 *ae* 0)
(b) Discuss strategies for resisting social pressure/coercion, referring to research evidence in your answer. (*ku* 8 *ae* 8)

### Tom

(a) Two situational factors that affect conformity are normative and informational influence. Normative influence is when you conform because you want others to like you and so you try to behave like the rest of the group. Informational influence is when you conform because the situation is ambiguous so you look to others to tell you what to do. Normative influence was shown in Asch's study where there was no doubt about the answer but people didn't want to look foolish so they followed the group to belong. Informational influence was shown in Sherif's study because the answer wasn't clear.

(b) There are many different strategies that people use for resisting social pressure. One example of this is when people are drawn to joining cults. First of all one of the features about people in cults is that they see everything in terms of black and white. In order to avoid this people are advised to avoid such extremes and to try to avoid making decisions when under stress because this leads to this kind of 'black and white' thinking. A second feature of cults is the leaders try to change your beliefs. This can be resisted if people put the messages into their own words and are aware of their own values and also compare the cult messages to information from the outside world. Third, cults gain their power by cutting people off from their families so in order to resist cult pressure people should keep in touch with their family. If you allow yourself to be cut off in this way you will stop thinking independently and are much more likely to be influenced by what the cult leaders and members say.

Advertising is another example of social influence where one group of people are trying to pressure you into behaving the way they want you to, and politicians also try to change our opinions, and it is important to question what they say and not be unduly influenced.

In all of the above cases of social influence and resistance the key may lie in education. People need to be educated about how to deal with persuasive messages. One programme of education tried to get adolescents to have more realistic attitudes about drug use. The researchers used two different approaches, 'normative' and 'resistance skills training'. The study found that just using resistance skills training on its own wasn't very effective but the two approaches combined were effective in changing attitudes and behaviour one year later.

**Examiner's comments** Question 1 is a two-part essay question. Tom has tackled part (a) in terms of *reasons* for conformity – normative and informational influences – and explains fairly well how these arise from the situational factor of *ambiguity* (or lack of it). He also enhances his answer by referring to evidence. Although it could be better organised (e.g. by explaining normative followed by informational influence, instead of skipping from one to the other and back), he gains **4 out of 4 marks**.

In part (b), Tom has approached this by focusing mainly on one particular real-life situation of pressure/coercion, namely cults, and then briefly considering the role of education. Although this may seem a limited view, Tom discusses several strategies within these contexts; therefore, he does address the question requirement and in a fairly analytical way. The main weakness of this answer is the lack of research evidence: one study is mentioned, but without names or date or evaluation. Tom is awarded **10 out of 16 marks** (*ku* 5/8 *ae* 5/8) for this part, giving him an overall mark of **14 out of 20 marks**.

### Alice

(a) A situational factor is something that is not in your nature. If it is in your nature it would be an individual factor like you might be the kind of person who is more likely to conform. Other people can be situational factors. So if other people behave in a certain way you do the same, even if you don't agree. But if they are all agreeing strongly and nobody else is disagreeing, it could be that the environment acted as a situational factor. If you were in a situation which was unfamiliar to you, like becoming an aunt or uncle to a sister's new baby, you might not really know what to do but would conform to the social role of 'aunt' or 'uncle'.

(b) There are many different strategies for resisting social pressure or coercion: responsibility for own actions, moral reasoning and awareness of own values, disobedient models and so on. I will look at evidence for some of these.

Responsibility for own actions. In studies of obedience, such as Milgram's, many of the people who did not fully obey said when they were interviewed later, that the reason was they felt a sense of personal responsibility, such as Gretchen Brandt. Milgram said that those who did obey were in an agentic state because they saw themselves as just following orders. In a shock experiment Kipper and Har-Even (1984) found that participants would give weaker electric shocks to other people if they were given an increased sense of responsibility, compared to those who were told they had to be 'task-focused'. On the other hand a real-world study of German officers found that being given personal responsibility did not lead to lower obedience levels in an incident in Poland where Major Trapp allowed his troops to choose whether to obey orders to kill Jews or not.

Moral reasoning and awareness of own values. Kohlberg proposed a stage theory of the development of moral reasoning and found a link between the level of moral development and being able to resist the pressure to obey in Milgram's study. Kohlberg interviewed the participants and those who had not obeyed had more developed morals.

Disobedient models. One of Milgram's findings was that obedience levels dropped when there were disobedient peers. It would seem that the disobedience of others frees individuals to behave according to their own principles rather than experiencing social pressure. However the Polish incident mentioned above again contradicts this because, in that incident, some of the soldiers did choose to disobey but the others still went along.

In conclusion there is evidence for various strategies to resist social pressure: by taking responsibility for one's actions, by using a higher level of moral reasoning and by seeing other people refusing to obey orders. Some of these strategies are used in schools to train young people to resist bad influences like pressure to take drugs

**Examiner's comments**    Alice also gains **4 out of 4 marks** for part (a). She makes a good start with her distinction between situational and individual factors. She has focused more clearly than Tom on situational factors, although she might have applied appropriate terminology for the first of her two points: she could have referred to 'strength of agreement' or 'size of majority' or 'social support'. The second point is enhanced by her use of an example. In referring to social roles, she could also have supported her answer by mentioning Zimbardo *et al.*; however, it is an excellent answer even as it stands.

Alice has given an excellent answer to part (b), showing extensive use of evidence (unlike Tom!). It is not 'perfect': more examples from everyday life would be useful (in general, in questions on an applied aspect, like this one, relevance to people's everyday lives should be considered). Most of her research references show no date. However, her answer is well constructed; she has selected a manageable amount of material from her knowledge of the topic; concepts are clearly explained; she refers to appropriate research and gives analytical and evaluative points. She gains **14 out of 16 marks** (ku 7/8 ae 7/8), and has an overall mark of **18 out of 20 marks**.

## Question 2    Analyse the effects of 'autonomous' and 'agentic' behaviour on obedience. (ku 4  ae 2)

### Tom

Milgram distinguished between autonomous and agentic behaviour, and these are linked to feelings of personal responsibility. Autonomous behaviour is when a person follows their own conscience. They feel responsible for their behaviour and are governed by their morals. Agentic behaviour is when they feel they are the agent of someone else so the other person bears the sense of responsibility so they don't think they are accountable. Milgram suggested that when a person is in an agentic state they will mindlessly obey orders even if the orders are for destructive action. A person is in an agentic state when they perceive that someone else has more authority. Milgram claimed that the ones who obeyed in his study were more agentic and those who didn't were more autonomous. Various situational or dispositional factors may be the cause. For example if there are other disobedient people (situational) or if the person has strong moral principles (dispositional). Milgram illustrated this with interviews with people who refused to continue, such as Gretchen Brandt, because of their principles. In some conditions of Milgram's study people didn't obey as much e.g. when there were disobedient peers or they were face-to-face with their victim.

### Alice

Milgram studied obedience in a group of men. The men were told the experiment was about learning. They were asked to give electric shocks to a learner when he made a mistake. If they didn't want to go on the experimenter said they must or they would spoil the experiment. 65% went to the highest level of shocks demonstrating total obedience. Before the experiment took place people were asked what they thought people would do and predicted that no one would behave like this so one of the findings of this study is that people are much more obedient than we think they are. Milgram suggested that the reason people obey is because they become agents of the authority figure which is the agentic state rather than being in the more usual autonomous state where you act under your own orders.

Some real life studies have found people were highly obedient. For example Hofling's study of nurses found that almost all of the nurses obeyed the unknown doctor whereas what they were doing was totally against orders. On the other hand, another study of nurses (Rank and Jacobsen) found almost no obedience when the nurses were allowed to ask other nurses what they should do. .

**Examiner's comments**    Tom evidently has sound knowledge of the concepts of agentic and autonomous behaviour. However, his answer is not very well organised, and his points sometimes lack clarity of expression. Nevertheless, he distinguishes the two concepts, analyses their link with the notion of personal responsibility and explains their effect on obedience. He is somewhat 'fixated' on Milgram (and should have given research dates), but he does *interpret* this material thus making it relevant to the question. Tom achieves **5 out of 6 marks** (ku 3/4 ae 2/2).

In contrast, Alice falls into the trap of simply *describing* obedience research. She does briefly mention agentic and autonomous behaviour, but there is no depth to her explanation of these concepts and no analysis of their effect on obedience. Alice is clearly quite knowledgeable about obedience research, but she has failed to use her knowledge *effectively* to answer the question. She gets **2 out of 6 marks** (ku 2/4 ae 0/2).

S ocial psychology is the study of social behaviour, which occurs when two or more members of the same species interact. Social psychology is concerned with how people influence each other's behaviour (social influence) as well as how our thoughts influence our social behaviour (social cognition).

The study of social relationships concerns the factors that lead to the formation and maintenance of relationships, as well as to breakdown. Such relationships include friendships, associations between family members, romantic attachments and marriage – although research tends to focus on the last two.

| Chapter contents | Unit content for the topic 'Social relationships' | Comment |
|---|---|---|
| **Aspect 1: Theories of relationships** | | |
| Economic theories<br>    page 213<br>Evolutionary/sociobiological theories<br>    page 216<br>Stage theories of relationships<br>    page 219 | Theories of relationships:<br>• economic theories<br>• evolutionary/sociobiological theories<br>• the role of attachment<br>• matching hypothesis<br>• stage theories of relationships | *Our relationships with others have an enormous influence on our lives. This first Aspect deals with a range of theoretical explanations of relationships, with the emphasis on couple relationships. You should be able to explain why we engage in, and remain in relationships, according to **economic** theories, and **evolutionary** and **sociobiological** approaches. You will consider how the kind of **attachment** relationship(s) we had in early childhood may impact on our interactions with others in adult life. The role of attractiveness in starting a couple relationship is addressed by the **matching hypothesis**, and a different view of relationships is proposed in **stage theories**, tracing the development of relationships over the longer term.* |
| **Aspect 2: Relationship breakdown** | | |
| Explanations of relationship breakdown: factors<br>    page 221<br>Explanations of relationship breakdown: stages<br>    page 224<br>Benefits of relationships<br>    page 226 | Explanations of relationship breakdown:<br>• environmental, interpersonal and individual factors<br>• gender differences in benefits of relationships | *Unfortunately, many relationships do break down, so, in studying this Aspect, you will be able to analyse the many different factors involved. Couples split up because of reasons to do with their **environment**, their **interpersonal** behaviours, and/or their **individual personalities**. There is widespread, general agreement that a good couple relationship is beneficial, but you will consider evidence that the **sexes** do not **benefit equally**.* |
| **Aspect 3: Effects of divorce** | | |
| Effects of divorce on children<br>    page 228<br>Mitigating factors<br>    page 232 | Effects of divorce on children:<br>• self-esteem<br>• aggression<br>• mental health<br>Mitigating factors, including<br>• lack of conflict during break-up<br>• continued relationships with both parents | *Traditionally it has been believed that divorce or separation of parents will invariably have detrimental consequences for their children. Here, consideration of research evidence will help you to get a clearer picture of the effects of parental relationship breakdown, and to see that a negative outcome for children is by no means inevitable. Characteristics such as **self-esteem**, **aggression** and **mental health** have been studied in children following parental separation; however, you should be able to explain how **factors** such as **lack of parental conflict**, and the opportunity to **continue** seeing both parents, can reduce or **mitigate** harmful effects on children.* |

**234** Sample questions with students' answers and examiner's comments

# Aspect 1:   Theories of relationships

Psychologists' theories and studies of social relationships have largely focused on romantic relationships between men and women in Western cultures. Perhaps this reflects the fact that this 'partner' relationship is the one that we think most about. We spend lots of *time* involved in other relationships – with friends, with family, with teachers and so on – but we don't discuss or worry about these relationships in the same way. Over the next few pages we will consider theories which focus on the formation of romantic relationships.

## Economic theories

We start with **economic theories** of relationships which emphasise that commitment to a relationship is dependent on the profitability of the relationship.

*explanation*

### Social exchange theory

**Social exchange theory** (Thibaut and Kelley, 1959) acknowledges that the formation of relationships is not a one-way process, but involves an interaction between the two partners, each with their own needs and expectations.

*Profit and loss*
At the centre of this theory is the assumption that all social behaviour is a series of exchanges; individuals attempt to maximise their rewards and minimise their costs. In our society, people exchange resources with the expectation (or at least the hope) that they will earn a *profit*; i.e. that rewards will exceed the costs incurred. Rewards that we may receive from a relationship include being cared for, companionship and even sex. Costs may include effort, financial investment and time wasted (i.e. missed opportunities with others because of being in that particular relationship). Rewards minus costs equal the outcome (a profit or a loss). Social exchange theory, in line with other economic theories of human behaviour, stresses that commitment to a relationship is dependent on the profitability of this outcome.

*Comparison level*
In order to judge whether one person offers something better or worse than we might expect from another, Thibaut and Kelley (1959) proposed that we develop a *comparison level*, a standard against which all our relationships are judged. Our comparison level (CL) is a product of our experiences in other relationships together with our general views of what we might expect from this particular exchange. If we judge that the potential profit in a new relationship exceeds our CL, the relationship will be judged as worthwhile, and the other person is seen as attractive as a partner. If the final result is negative (profit is less than our CL), we will be dissatisfied with the relationship and the other person is thus perceived as less attractive.

A related concept is the *comparison level for alternatives*, where the person weighs up a potential increase in rewards from a different partner, less any costs associated with ending the current relationship. A new relationship can take the place of the current one if its profit level is significantly higher.

*Stages in the development of a relationship*
Thibaut and Kelley believed that there were four stages in the development of a relationship:

1. *Sampling*. People consider the potential costs and rewards of a new relationship and compare it with other relationships available at the time.

2. *Bargaining*. As the relationship develops, partners give and receive rewards which tests whether a deeper relationship is worthwhile.

3. *Commitment*. As predictability increases in the relationship, each partner knows how to elicit rewards from the other, and costs are lowered.

4. *Institutionalisation*. Norms are developed within the relationship, which establishes the patterns of rewards and costs for each partner.

## evaluation

### Profit and loss

The notion of exchange has been used to explain why some women stay in abusive relationships. Rusbult and Martz (1995) argue that when investments are high (e.g. children) and alternatives are low (e.g. nowhere else to live, no money) this would be a profit situation and a woman would remain in a relationship.

However, Aronson (1999) argues that simply making comparisons between profit and loss is not realistic. He believes that it is *increases* in reward that are crucial rather than just constant rewards.

### Comparison level

Support can be found by looking at how people in a relationship deal with potential alternatives; one way of dealing with such potential alternatives is to reduce them as a means of protecting the relationship. Simpson *et al.* (1990) asked participants to rate members of the opposite sex in terms of attractiveness; those participants who were involved in a relationship gave lower ratings. However, social exchange theory does not explain why some people leave relationships despite having no alternative nor does it suggest how great the disparity in CL has to be to become unsatisfactory.

### Strengths

The theory is relevant to many different kinds of relationship: friends, work colleagues, children and lovers. It also can be used to explain individual differences – both those between individuals and within individuals. Different individuals perceive profits and losses differently and therefore what is acceptable for one person is not acceptable for another. Differences within an individual may occur over time because alternatives change and this changes the person's comparison level.

### Limitations

On the other hand, the theory has been criticised for focusing too much on the individual's perspective and ignoring the social aspects of a relationship, such as how partners talk with each other and interpret shared events (Duck and Sants, 1983). The main criticism, however, focuses on the selfish nature of the theory. Are people only motivated to maintain relationships out of hedonistic (selfish) concerns? It is possible that such principles only apply in *individualist* cultures, if at all. In addition, the subjective nature of rewards and costs makes it possible to justify almost any behaviour in terms of positive cost–benefit outcome. Finally, social exchange theory has been criticised for ignoring an essential component of relationships: fairness in exchange rather than seeking a profit. Equity theory (see below) was developed to extend social exchange theory to take this into account.

The social exchange home page: oak.cats. ohiou.edu/~al891396/exchange.htm

### KEY TERMS

**Equity theory:** This predicts that people select relationships where cost–reward balance is fair. Equity is not the same as equality: one partner may have more rewards than the other but only if they also have more costs.

## explanation

## Equity theory

### Inequity and distress

In social exchange theory, we learned that all social behaviour is a series of exchanges, with individuals attempting to maximise their rewards and minimise their costs. **Equity theory** (Walster *et al.*, 1978) is an extension of that underlying belief, with its central assumption that people strive to achieve fairness in their relationships and feel distressed if they perceive unfairness (Messick and Cook, 1983). Where equity theory departs from social exchange theory is the view that *any* kind of inequity has the potential to create distress. People who give a great deal in a relationship and get little in return would perceive inequity and would, therefore, be dissatisfied in the relationship. However, the same is true of those who *receive* a great deal and give little in return. This is also an inequitable relationship, with the same consequence for both partners – dissatisfaction. As you might imagine, the greater the perceived inequity, the greater is the dissatisfaction.

### Ratio of inputs and outputs

An important point to bear in mind when considering this theory is that *equity* does not necessarily mean *equality*: it is possible for each partner to contribute (and receive) very different amounts and for the relationship still to be equitable. What is considered 'fair' in a relationship (in terms of input and output) is largely a subjective opinion for each partner. Thus, although one partner perceives themselves as putting in less than the other, the relationship will still be judged fair if they get less out of the relationship (relative to the other person). This is explained in

**Equitable and inequitable relationships**

A receives 12 units of reward from 10 units of effort.

B receives 120 units of reward from 100 units of effort.

**Outcome for A&B is 1.2 units profit = equitable relationship.**

A receives 12 units of reward from 10 units of effort.

B receives 100 units of reward from 120 units of effort.

**Outcome for A is 1.2 units profit, and B is 0.83 units profit = inequitable relationship.**

terms of a person's perceived ratio of inputs and outputs, a subjective assessment of the relative inputs of each partner relative to the outcomes for that partner. Deciding whether a relationship is equitable, therefore, involves some fairly complicated mathematics. An equitable relationship should, according to the theory, be one where one partner's benefits divided by their costs equals their partner's benefits divided by their costs. If we perceive inequality in our relationship, then we are motivated to restore it. This can be achieved in several different ways; for example, we may change the amount we input into the relationship or we may change our perceptions of relative inputs and outputs in order to restore the appearance of equity.

## evaluation

### Over- and under-benefit
The principle of fairness or equity means that both partners should feel equally uneasy if they are either under- or over-benefited. However, it is difficult to see why getting less rather than more should feel the same. Research supports this. For example, Hatfield *et al.* (1979) found that under-benefited newlyweds expressed the lowest level of satisfaction with their marriage; the over-benefited came next, and those who perceived an equitable relationship had the highest level of satisfaction.

### Equity in long-term relationships
Exchange and equity become less of an issue in long-term relationships. Clark and Mills (1979) suggest that short-term relationships are based on principles of 'exchange', whereas longer-term relationships are governed more by a desire to respond to one's partner's needs. These are called communal relationships; there is still some concern with equity, but partners tend to believe that things will balance out in the long run.

### Limitations
Equity theory, like social exchange theory, has been criticised for its mechanistic, 'economic' approach to relationships. People may not be rational decision-makers when it comes to relationships but, instead, are often influenced by strong emotions. Moghaddam (1998) suggests that such 'economic' theories only apply to Western relationships and even then only to certain short-term relationships among individuals with high mobility (i.e. students – which isn't surprising since many of the studies have involved student participants).

### Recent research
In the past, psychologists have focused on producing theories to explain relationships, such as equity theory which suggests that maintenance is related to rather complicated calculations and reassessments. More recently, research has shifted from such *quantitative* considerations to a more *qualitative* analysis of what is actually going on in these relationships, as is the case with research on roles and relationships. This latter approach may provide us with a richer understanding of the dynamics of relationships.

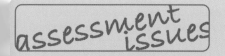

assessment issues

## Describe the main features of *one* economic theory of relationships. (*ku 6 ae 0*)

This is the kind of straightforward question that often produces a sigh of relief, with the immediate thought, 'I know this. I can do this question!' It's great to feel confident, as long as you don't get *complacent*. Even with this kind of question, there are things to think about that will help you maximise your marks. For a start, there are no *ae* marks, so your focus should be on descriptive rather than evaluation material. Secondly, it's sensible to start with a definition of economic theories. Thirdly, you are asked to write about only one theory, so it would be a waste of time to write about a second one – although, if there were *ae* marks available, you could use a second theory as a means of evaluation.

You would be likely to choose social exchange theory or equity theory for your answer – either way, make sure you give *solid* information like terminology of concepts (e.g. minimising costs, comparison level, etc.), and theorists' names (and dates). If you don't, your answer runs the risk of sounding like no more than common sense.

In our current Western culture, people talk a great deal about relationships, both in our everyday conversations and in the media – and we all have 'theories' about how to find a suitable partner, whether we want commitment, whether women and men want the same things, why couples split up, etc. So throughout your study of relationships, make a special effort to sound like a psychologist, rather than the man (or woman) down the pub!

**Evolutionary theory:** This is based on Darwin's principle of natural selection – the more that a genetically determined behaviour promotes successful reproduction, the more likely it is to be passed on to the next generation; such traits are 'naturally selected'.

**Sociobiological theory:** This offers an explanation of social behaviour in terms of evolutionary theory.

**Matching hypothesis:** This predicts that individuals seek partners who are equally socially desirable, in terms of characteristics such as physical attractiveness, personality and resources.

# Evolutionary/sociobiological theories

Both **evolutionary theory** and **sociobiological theory** explain behaviour in terms of adaptiveness – behaviours are perpetuated if they maximise an individual's survival and reproduction. In this section we consider two explanations that are related to adaptiveness: (1) evolutionary/sociobiological theory and the importance of differential reproductive investments by males and females and (2) the influence of early attachment on later mate choices.

One of the implications of evolutionary theory is that physical attractiveness 'advertises' an individual's fertility and therefore males in particular seek physically attractive mates to ensure their reproductive success. In contrast, the **matching hypothesis** suggests that we seek partners whose physical attractiveness matches our own rather than those who are most physically attractive. We will have a look at the evidence related to this hypothesis on page 218.

## explanation

### Evolutionary/sociobiological theory

Evolutionary psychologists dealing with mate-choice claim that men and women originally faced quite different *adaptive* problems in our ancestral environment (the *environment of evolutionary adaptation*, or *EEA*), and that as a result, they evolved differently. These adaptive mechanisms are still active today, unconsciously guiding the mate-choice of men and women.

*Different reproductive investment*
Human females invest a great deal in their offspring, being pregnant for nine months (with considerable health risks for themselves), providing intensive care for the child, and being dependent on external support and resources while doing so. As a consequence of this heavy parental investment, women can have relatively few offspring over their lifetime. It is therefore imperative that a female should look for a partner who is willing and able to provide resources for her and her offspring.

Red cheeks, rosy full lips and glossy hair are all signs of youth and reproductive fitness.

On the other hand, the investment of men in the reproductive stakes can be very low. The reproductive capacity of a male during his lifetime is virtually infinite (provided that he is able to obtain enough women who are willing to reproduce with him!) Rather than quality, therefore, we might expect males to be more concerned with *quantity* of mates, keeping the individual contributions to each relationship low. Although we probably know people we think fit this description, most males do exercise a certain degree of careful choice. The male should, for example, be sure that his partners are fertile and that he is unlikely to be 'cuckolded' (tricked into raising another man's child as his own). Men, therefore, will look for cues that signify fertility and sexual faithfulness in their partners.

*Evolutionarily significant characteristics*
What then, are the characteristics that provide the necessary cues for males and females i.e. the traits that make them attractive to the opposite sex? Men seek signs of reproductive value which are related to age and healthiness, and indicated by a women's physical appearance (e.g. smooth skin, white teeth, good muscle tone).

In contrast, a woman should be attracted to males who have characteristics that indicate social and economic advantages (which represent possession, or potential to possess, valuable resources). Research has also tended to find that women prefer men who are humorous and 'kind' (presumably indicating their willingness to share these resources).

Both partners are also interested in evidence of good genetic quality in order to ensure offspring who will survive. Youthfulness can be an indicator of robust genes as can a healthy complexion and athletic build. Symmetry is another cue because it requires robust genes to be maintained. This may explain why symmetry is so important in attractiveness.

## evaluation

*Research support*
We expect men to look for cues that signify fertility, which is what was found in personal ads in US newspapers: 42% of males sought a youthful mate compared with 25% of females; 44% of males sought a physically attractive partner compared with 22% of females (Waynforth and

Dunbar, 1995). This study also found that women tended to emphasise their attractiveness whereas men emphasised their economic status and earning power, as predicted by evolutionary theory.

Different reproductive investment means that we might also expect men to be more concerned with sexual faithfulness than women because a man does not want to be tricked into raising another man's child as his own. Buss *et al.* (1992) found that men showed greater physiological distress than women (as measured by GSR) when asked to imagine scenes of sexual infidelity. In both instances women were more distressed by emotional unfaithfulness.

Finally, we would expect male and female preferences to be similar all over the world if such preferences are inherited. Buss (1989) surveyed over 10,000 people in 37 countries and found that, in general, men preferred women who were younger than themselves, and women preferred men who were older than themselves.

*Limitations*
On the other hand, there are significant cultural differences in what counts as attractive. For example, fashions in clothing and body decoration vary enormously across cultures and across different historical periods. What is fashionable one year may no longer be fashionable in subsequent years. It is likely that both factors – evolutionary pressure and social influences – determine attraction in any cultural group.

All evolutionary explanations can be subjected to a common set of criticisms. First of all, such explanations are *post hoc* (after the fact), offered to account for the continuance of observed behaviours. A second criticism is that human behaviour may be different from non-human animal behaviour. For instance, our behaviour is considerably more controlled by conscious, cognitive factors and therefore we might suppose that interpersonal attraction is less governed by evolutionary pressures than in non-human animals.

## explanation

## The role of attachment

At the beginning of this book we looked at *attachment theory*, in particular at Bowlby's (1969) account of attachment as an adaptive process (see page 5). He proposed that attachment promotes survival and reproduction because strong attachment means that an infant is more likely to be well cared for when young and defenceless. In addition, attachments form the basis for later social relationships: they provide a template for social relationships and this promotes survival and reproduction.

*The continuity hypothesis*
Bowlby (1969) suggested that the way caregivers treat their infants determines their personality types in later life. Babies who develop confidence generally have mothers who are reliable in their responses to the infant's needs. Mothers who are slow to respond to their baby's needs produce children who are generally anxious. Mothers who are cold and unresponsive to their baby tend to produce children who are somewhat distant and detached. From these observations, Ainsworth (1967) produced three distinct *styles* of attachment: *secure*, *insecure-resistant* and *insecure-avoidant*. According to Bowlby, later relationships are likely to be a continuation of these attachment styles because the mother's behaviour creates an **internal working model** of relationships which leads the infant to expect the same in later relationships.

## evaluation

*The continuity hypothesis*
On page 6, research evidence that supported the *continuity hypothesis* was described; for example, the study by Hazan and Shaver (1987) suggests that adults who were securely attached as infants went on to have more positive experiences in their adult romantic relationships whereas *insecure-ambivalent* types worried that their partners didn't really love them and *insecure-avoidant* lovers typically feared intimacy. The Minnesota longitudinal study, found that the securely attached infants were rated highest for social competence, were less isolated and more popular (Sroufe *et al.*, 1999).

*Limitations*

On the other hand, the *temperament hypothesis* (see page 6) suggests that continuity is not due to early attachment experiences but rather to innate predispositions to be warm and friendly or difficult and socially awkward.

A further limitation is that most continuity studies (e.g. Hazan and Shaver) rely on retrospective classification – asking adults questions about their early lives in order to assess infant attachment. Such recollections are likely to be flawed; however, longitudinal studies support the findings. For example, McCarthy (1999) studied women whose attachment types were recorded in infancy. Those who had been classified in infancy as *avoidant* had the greatest difficulty in romantic relationships and those who had been classified as *resistant* had the poorest friendships. Women who were securely attached as infants had the most successful romantic relationships and friendships. This supports the view that attachment type predicts relationships in adult life.

**explanation**

## Matching hypothesis

Evolutionary theory would lead us to expect that everyone would seek the same physical features in their partner – those features that indicate good genetic quality. However, this may not necessarily be the case. If we all were only attracted to the most physically attractive individuals then it would be very difficult to find a mate because everyone would be competing for a select group. This may explain why the *matching hypothesis* operates. Walster *et al.* (1966) suggest that we are attracted to those individuals that closely *match* our perceptions of our own level of attractiveness. Although we may desire physically attractive individuals as potential partners, one's 'realistic' social choices must be a compromise.

In fact, Walster *et al.* proposed that social choices are not simply based on physical attractiveness but rather on a range of socially desirable traits such as personality and possessing good material assets as well as physical attractiveness. The matching hypothesis has been explained within *social exchange theory* (see page 213). At the centre of this theory is the assumption that all social behaviour is a series of exchanges; individuals attempt to maximise their rewards and minimise their costs.

The matching hypothesis has two specific predictions:

1. The more socially desirable a person is, the more socially desirable they would expect their partner to be.
2. Couples who are matched are more likely to have a happy and enduring relationship.

**evaluation**

*Research evidence*

Walster *et al.* (1966) conducted the 'computer dance study' (see Star Study on the next page) which did not provide support for the matching hypothesis; however, subsequent more realistic studies (e.g. Walster and Walster, 1969) did. 'Fait accompli' studies (studies that look at similarity in real-life couples) have also supported the matching hypothesis. For example, Murstein (1972) found that real-life couples were rated as being more similar in terms of physical attractiveness than randomly paired couples. Price and Vandenberg (1980) provided cross-cultural support; they studied married couples in America and Sweden and found similarity on many different variables, including physical similarity and social and behavioural variables. They also found evidence that similarity is due to initial choice rather than to the fact that partners may become more similar over time.

The focus of research on the matching hypothesis, and interpersonal attraction, is on romantic relationships but it has also been found that matching occurs in same-sex friendships with friends tending to pick people like themselves (Cash and Derlega, 1978).

*Limitations*

Huston (1973) argued that 'matching' was not done for balance, as social exchange theory would predict, but because of fear of rejection by someone more attractive. He found that when participants had no reason to fear rejection they did choose the most physically attractive person.

The matching hypothesis explanation assumes that potential partners have a relatively free choice, so it is less applicable where choice is reduced, for example in cultures where arranged marriages are customary.

# Investigating theories of relationships: The computer dance study

(WALSTER *ET AL.*, 1966)

## Aims

To see whether an individual will choose a partner of approximately the same social desirability and, after going out on a date with this person, will express greatest liking for a partner of approximately the same social desirability.

## Method and procedure

A 'computer dance' was set up during freshers week at an American University. When students purchased their tickets they were (a) rated by a panel of four older students in terms of physical attractiveness and (b) asked to fill in a questionnaire about themselves, ostensibly to match them with a similar date for the dance; in fact, matching was done randomly.

Two days later, each student was assigned a date for the dance. In total, 332 couples were involved. During the dance the students were asked to rate their dates. After the dance (four to six months later), all students were contacted and asked if they had continued to see their dates.

## Results

The overriding factor in whether the dates liked each other was physical attractiveness rather than matching; in other words, students rated their partners more highly if they were physically attractive and the degree of similarity between partners (as measured by the questionnaire) showed no relation to liking. Physical attractiveness was also the main factor in whether an individual continued dating their partner.

## Conclusion

The findings appear to support the claims of evolutionary theory rather than the matching hypothesis.

## Evaluation

*Sample bias*

The participants in this study were students who are less likely to be interested in long-term relationships and thus their criteria might not reflect those that operate in other relationships.

*Ecological validity*

How realistic was this study? In real life people usually have some choice about whom they date. In another study (Walster and Walster, 1969), participants were given some choice (in terms of physical attractiveness) and allowed to meet beforehand. In this case, matching was apparent.

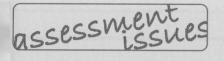

*assessment issues*

**Evaluate the matching hypothesis as an explanation of relationship formation. (ku 2 ae 4)**

Questions that ask you only to 'evaluate' may have a few marks for knowledge and understanding, as is the case here. So, your strategy should be to briefly outline the features of the matching hypothesis explanation, before considering evaluation points in some detail. The *findings* of the Walster *et al.* (1966) study would be a good choice of material for showing evaluation, but don't get caught up in describing the *procedure*. Also, this should not be the *only* evidence you use; it did not support the matching hypothesis so, ideally, you should mention the later studies which *did*. You can also gain *ae* marks here by evaluating the concept itself in its theoretical context, for example how it relates to social exchange theory.

**Stage theories:** These describe the development of any behaviour in terms of a fixed sequence of qualitatively different, discrete stages.

*Thibaut and Kelley's social exchange theory included four stages of the development of relationships so you could include it here.*

# Stage theories of relationships

So far we have looked at economic theories and evolutionary/sociobiological theories of social relationships. In the final section of this Aspect we will consider **stage theories** which, as the name suggests, describe the development of relationships in terms of a series of stages. One assumption of stage theories in psychology is that each stage is a prerequisite for the stage that follows. A second assumption is that each stage is qualitatively different in some way rather than just being more of the previous stage. Related to this is the assumption that, rather than gradually changing, we typically make sudden shifts to a new plateau of understanding and behaviour.

explanation

## ABCDE model

Levinger (1980) proposed that all relationships (both friendly and romantic ones) go through five stages as the relationship matures. At each stage, there are positive factors that promote the development of the relationship (e.g. frequent contact) and negative factors that act in reverse (e.g. infrequent contact). The stages are:

**A** *Acquaintance/initial attraction*. When we meet new people we often feel initial attraction, based on physical attractiveness and similarity.

**B** *Build up*. We become closer and more interdependent as each person reveals more about their private selves.

**C** *Consolidation/continuation*. The relationship becomes a life-long commitment. Longer-term pledges are made such as marriage.

**D** *Deterioration and decline*. In some cases the relationship may deteriorate. This may be due to a variety of factors such as lack of effort or rewards, the availability of alternatives, lack of proximity. These are examined in detail in Aspect 2 of this chapter.

**E** *Ending*. The relationship ends when partners agree to separate or one leaves.

Levinger portrays relationships as being dynamic and nonlinear; they are dependent on the inputs of both partners at any one time, each constantly affecting and being affected by the other. For example, one partner might react more negatively because she fears her partner has become bored with the relationship; her negativity leads her partner to behave more coolly thus confirming her initial suspicions and so causing her to become even more negative.

evaluation

Stage theories are often criticised for being more descriptive than explanatory. They describe *what* happens rather than *why* it happens. Theories which focus on 'why' attempt to explain *why* partners are initially attracted (e.g. sociobiological theory) and *why* some relationships continue whereas others don't (e.g. equity theory). Dindia and Baxter (1987) focused on the *strategies* that couples use to maintain their relationship (see page 222); this is an approach which may ultimately have more useful applications than stage theories (e.g. advising couples about how to repair unsatisfactory relationships).

Stage theories are also criticised for the lack of evidence for a fixed series of stages in social relationships. Brehm (1992) suggests that it is better to talk about 'phases' which take place at different times for different people.

explanation

## Stimulus-value-role theory (SVR)

Bernard Murstein (1976, 1987) proposed a stage theory to describe how we select our friends and also our romantic partners. At each stage, individuals may be filtered out:

- *Stimulus* stage. Physical attributes are important; we assess the other person in terms of physical attributes. In general, we are attracted to people of a similar age, appearance and ethnicity.

- *Value* stage. Values become more important. We compare our values with those of a potential friend/partner and only continue the relationship if their values are sufficiently compatible.

- *Role* stage. Roles are shared out in an effort to build a relationship, for example one person takes on the role of the dominant partner or the social secretary while the other takes on the opposite roles. Role distribution works best if roles are complementary.

evaluation

*Strengths*
Unlike the distinctly sequential nature of Levinger's ABCDE model, Murstein's theory emphasises factors rather than stages. Each factor may assume particular importance at different times in a relationship but all have an influence throughout the relationship.

*Roles in relationships*

The importance of roles has been studied by Duck (1999). Duck suggests that, to sustain a relationship successfully, both partners must observe various relational rules that apply to their respective roles within the relationship, such as 'husband' or 'wife'. The existence of socially approved roles and our success in enacting those roles play an important part in maintaining and preserving the relationship. Once such an arrangement has been worked out, it strengthens the relationship, providing common experiences to talk about and common problems to resolve.

There is evidence that some roles are innately programmed. For example, Taylor *et al.* (2000) suggested that women have evolved 'tend and befriend' behaviours, at least at times of stress (see page 64). This would lead them in general to take a more nurturing role in a relationship. In parallel, men have evolved a 'fight or flight' stress response to deal with threatening situations, so they would naturally take the protector role in preference to a nurturant role.

*assessment issues*

(a) **Discuss evolutionary/sociobiological explanations of social relationships, referring to research evidence in your answer. (*ku 8 ae 4*)**

(b) **Analyse the possible effects of childhood attachment on social relationships in later life. (*ku 4 ae 4*)**

As you know, any essay answer must be well organised. This is a two-part essay question (essay questions can be in either one or two parts), so much of the organisation is already done for you, but it is still helpful to draw up a plan of your content within each part. In part (a), the *ae* element can be addressed by interpreting research evidence in relation to the claims made by the theory, as well as theoretical limitations of the evolutionary approach. Comparison with other explanations, such as the matching hypothesis or stage theories, would be another useful means of showing evaluation.

In a two-part essay like this the parts are usually closely related. In this question, a clever move (worthy of *ae* marks!) is to relate your part (b) content to part (a). For example, you might explain that childhood attachment, as well as being adaptive in infancy (in terms of getting basic needs satisfied), may also be considered adaptive in terms of greater likelihood of successful relationships later in life. This would be one way to show *analysis*, as demanded by the question, and indeed this area lends itself to in-depth analysis, taking into account factors such as *adaptiveness, quality of attachment, temperament, continuity*, etc.

# Aspect 2:  Relationship breakdown

## Explanations of relationship breakdown: factors

Some relationships flourish, some survive in name alone and some fail completely. Early research in the area of relationship breakdown tended to focus almost exclusively on the *statistics* of relationship breakdown rather than the *processes*. More recently, psychologists have begun to look at the factors that might explain why some relationships break down. These can be considered in terms of environmental, interpersonal and individual factors.

## Environmental factors

Relationships may break down because of factors outside the relationship, i.e. in the physical or social environment.

### Distance

One factor that has been shown to contribute to the *formation* of relationships is proximity. For example, Festinger *et al.* (1950) found that students who had dormitory rooms that others had to pass by more frequently were more likely to have friends. The more you see people, the more likely it is for a relationship to develop. The converse is also true. There are clearly some circumstances where relationships become strained simply because partners cannot

Saying goodbye as her partner leaves on a year's tour of duty

maintain close contact. Going away to university, for example, places a great strain on existing relationships and is often responsible for their breakdown (Shaver *et al.*, 1985). Whilst long-term romantic relationships *should* be strong enough to survive the pressures of decreased daily contact, it is evident that for many this isn't the case.

However, some relationships do survive reduced proximity. Long-distance romantic relationships (LDRR) and long-distance friendships (LDF) are perhaps more common than we think. One study found that 70% of students sampled had experienced at least one LDRR and that 90% said that they had experienced one LDF (Rohlfing, 1998). The fact that in our mobile society people do have to move and do become separated from family, friends and/or partner means that it is useful to understand the management strategies that people use. For example, Holt and Stone (1988) found that there was little decrease in relationship satisfaction as long as lovers were able to reunite regularly.

### Work stress
In Chapter 3, when looking at the SRRS scale (page 68), we saw that various aspects of relationships (e.g. getting divorced or married) may cause increased stress. The converse is also true – stress, particularly stress at work, may cause difficulty in relationships and contribute to their breakdown.

### Social support
An important factor in the experience of stress is the extent of social support. For example, Kamarck *et al.* (1990, see Chapter 3, page 62) showed that the presence of friends reduces stress. Thus the negative effects of work stress can be lessened by having a good network of friends.

Social support also has an impact on the breakdown of relationships because one of the key ways to deal with problems in a relationship is to talk about them. Duck (1999) included the effects of social support in his stage theory (see page 224). Other people may act as arbitrators and try to help save the relationship, or may side with one partner supporting their decision to end the relationship.

## Interpersonal factors
Relationship breakdown may be explained in terms of the interactions between partners.

### Boredom
According to social exchange theory (see page 213), people look for rewards in their relationships, one of which is 'stimulation'. We would expect, therefore, that lack of stimulation would be a reason why relationships break down. There is evidence (e.g. Baxter, 1994) that lack of stimulation (i.e. boredom or a belief that the relationship isn't going anywhere) is often quoted when breaking off a relationship. People expect relationships to change and develop, and when they do not this is seen as sufficient justification to end the relationship or begin a new one (i.e. have an affair).

### Maintenance and repair strategies
A healthy relationship requires constant maintenance. Dindia and Baxter (1987) examined the strategies used by 50 married couples and how these influenced marital satisfaction. They reported 49 different strategies ranging from the fairly trivial (e.g. talking about each other's day) through to strategies such as compliments and gifts. The lack of such strategies contributes to relationship breakdown. The researchers also found that couples had repair strategies for dealing with situations when the relationship got into trouble, although these were fewer than the strategies available for maintenance.

### Rule violation
Argyle and Henderson's (1984) research on friendship 'rules' have provided insight into those aspects of rule violation that are particularly relevant to friendship breakdown. They asked individuals to think of a specific friendship that had lapsed for reasons that might be attributed to the relationship itself (rather than other factors such as moving away). Argyle and Henderson then asked their participants to rate the extent to which any failure to keep friendship rules had contributed to the breakdown of that relationship. The rule violations found to be most critical included jealousy, lack of tolerance for a third-party relationship, disclosing confidences, not volunteering help when needed, and criticising the person publicly.

## Individual factors

Characteristics or behaviours of individual partners may explain the breakdown of a relationship.

### Predisposing personal factors

Duck (1981) proposed that there are some factors which are present at the start of a relationship which make it more vulnerable to breakdown, such as the emotional instability of one of the partners or disgusting personal habits. In addition to such predisposing personal factors, Duck added a second category of 'precipitating factors' which would act as the trigger to breakdown. These precipitating factors are situational rather than dispositional, such as deception, boredom, relocation, or conflict. This links back to some of the environmental factors described earlier.

### Factors associated with instability

Duck (1992) also suggested that there are certain factors that create instability in a romantic relationship and may ultimately cause breakdown; for example difference in age, difference in demographic background (race, religion), partners who come from lower socio-economic classes and partners whose parents divorced or had a large number of sexual partners.

### Lack of skills

Some people find relationships difficult because they lack the interpersonal skills to make the relationship mutually satisfying. Individuals lacking social skills may be poor conversationalists; they may be poor at indicating their interest in other people and are likely to be generally unrewarding in their interactions with others (Duck, 1991). The lack of social skills therefore means that others perceive them as not being interested in relating, so a relationship tends to break down before it really gets going.

---

**evaluation**

### Evaluation of factors that lead to relationship breakdown

The factors listed in this section are the converse of factors related to initial attraction: for example, proximity and stimulation all lead to attraction; the lack of these leads to relationship breakdown. Felmlee (1995), in her 'theory of fatal attraction', suggested that the opposite was true – it is the same factors that led to initial attraction that ultimately spell disaster. For example, a partner's lively behaviour may initially have been attractive but eventually becomes annoying.

*Cultural differences*
The factors identified in this section may only apply to certain groups of people. Non-Western relationships may be formed differently (e.g. arranged marriages) and it is therefore likely that different pressures will function in relationship breakdown. For example, in an arranged marriage entire families and communities are involved and commitment is an important feature in relationship maintenance. If a couple moves into a different culture, the influence of the community and their commitment may be threatened, leading to relationship breakdown.

Individual factors are less likely to matter in non-Western relationships where there is greater emphasis on community values. Moghaddam *et al.* (1993) contrasted Western relationships with non-Western ones, saying that the former are likely to be ***individualist*** (seeking individual gratification), voluntary and temporary whereas the latter are ***collectivist*** (attention to group responsibilities), obligatory and permanent. Thus we would expect social networks to play a greater role in non-Western relationships.

*Gender differences*
There are also gender differences in the reasons for relationship breakdown. Women are more likely to stress unhappiness and incompatibility as reasons for breakdown, whereas men are particularly upset by 'sexual witholding' (Brehm and Kassin, 1996). Argyle and Henderson found that women identified lack of emotional support as a critical factor in breakdown, whereas men thought that absence of fun was more important.

Women have more desire to stay friends after a relationship has broken up, whereas men want to 'cut their losses and move on' (Akert, 1998).

**Analyse the effects that environmental factors may have on the breakdown of relationships. (*ku* 3 *ae* 3)**

First, choose your factors: decide which ones to use and how many. You could write about the effects of distance between partners, work stress, social support, or even culture. Two or three factors would be sensible, for a six-mark question. Your choice should be based on the extent to which you feel you can show *analysis,* as required in the question. For example, if you write about long-distance relationships, can you explain that the *distance* factor in an established relationship works in a converse way to initial attraction processes, where *proximity* is important? Or, if you state that in some *cultures* arranged marriages are common, can you explain exactly *how* this may affect relationship breakdown? How might *work stress and social support interact* in relationship problems? These would all be sound analytical points. And when you're making these points, don't forget to slip in researchers' name and dates wherever relevant!

# Explanations of relationship breakdown: stages

Earlier in this chapter we looked at stage theories that describe the *development* of relationships; psychologists have also described characteristic stages in the *undoing* of relationships. We will look at one such stage theory plus one Star Study of relationship breakdown.

*explanation*

## Duck's stage theory

Duck's theory (Duck, 1999) sees the breakdown of relationships as going through several different phases. This model takes account of the fact that partners frequently feel uneasy about a relationship *before* they even talk to their partner about it, that relationships exist within a more complicated social matrix, and that individuals are motivated to look back on the breakdown of their relationship with some feelings of justification for their actions. Each of the four phases proposed by the model has an associated repair strategy:

1. *Intrapsychic phase* – dissatisfaction with partner. During this phase, a person may begin to reflect on the deficiencies of their current relationship, perhaps in terms of the costs and benefits associated with it. At this stage there may be little outward show of dissatisfaction, and perhaps a determination to 'put things right'. Beyond a certain point, however, these deficiencies will prompt the dissatisfied person to begin the process of communicating their feelings to the partner, although this will be indirect at first (e.g. through hints, or through expression to a third party). *Repair strategy* – re-establish liking for partner.

2. *Dyadic phase* – confrontation with partner. After a partner has decided that the problems with their relationship need airing, it is time for confrontation with the other person. This phase is characterised by argument (with both sides probably disagreeing about responsibility for the current state of affairs) and some consideration of how things might be put right. At this stage, there is still the possibility that the relationship might be repaired. *Repair strategy* – express conflict, clear the air and reformulate rules for the future relationship.

3. *Social phase* – publication of relationship distress. Up to this point, partners might have kept their dissatisfaction fairly private, but it now spills over to a network of friends and family. These may take sides, offer advice and support, and may help in mending any disputes. Such social support may even speed the partners towards breakdown through revelations about one of the partners. Social networks serve another important role, however they may offer support after the break-up has occurred. *Repair strategy* – outsiders can take a hand.

4. *Grave-dressing phase* – getting over it all and tidying up. Having left a relationship, partners attempt to justify their actions. This process is important as each partner must present themselves to others as being trustworthy and loyal, key attributes for future relationships. Each strives to construct their 'story' of the failed relationship that does not paint their role in unfavourable terms. Whilst part of this process is undoubtedly face saving concerning its failure, it also helps the person justify their original commitment to the relationship (e.g. 'He used to be so considerate and thoughtful, but then he started to take me for granted'). *Repair strategy* – decide on a mutually acceptable version of events; salvage friendship.

*evaluation*

*Strengths*

The model has the advantage of showing that breakdown is not just a sudden step but a process. A particular strength of this model is that it includes repair strategies which are appropriate to different stages –Duck suggested what could be done at each stage to repair the relationship; these strategies could be applied, for example, to marriage guidance.

*Limitations*

It does not explain *why* relationships break down, it just describes the steps. In contrast, the factors for relationship breakdown (see pages 221–223) offer insights into the process and can also be applied to relationships other than romantic ones.

Furthermore, Duck's approach does not include the *experience* of breaking up, something which Akert (1998) looked at in a study of students' experience of breaking up. He found that the more both partners are involved in decisions that have to be made, the fewer physical symptoms they experienced, such as appetite loss and sleeplessness.

## star**STUDY**

# Investigating relationship breakdown: Boston couples study

(**H**ILL *ET AL.*, 1976)

### Aims

To study and be able to describe the breaking-up process in dating couples: its precipitating factors, its timing and its aftermath.

### Method and procedure

This was a longitudinal study conducted over two years. At the start, 231 dating couples were recruited from colleges in the Boston area and asked individually to answer a questionnaire. The couples had been dating for a median period of eight months; very few were engaged.

After 2 years, 103 of the couples had broken up; 18 of these couples were interviewed in depth about the break-up.

### Results

In terms of the *factors* that might predict break-ups, it was found that couples were less likely to break up if they were more closely matched in terms of age, educational plans, intelligence, physical attractiveness, and especially social attitudes and values. Break-ups were more common in couples where there was unequal commitment.

In terms of the *process* of breaking up, the study found that the timing of break-ups was related to the school calendar probably because it provided an easier formula for breaking up (e.g. breaking up during the Christmas holiday). The desire to break up was seldom mutual; women were somewhat more likely to be the ones to precipitate the break-up.

### Conclusion

The findings provide support for a number of explanations. For example, the close matching of couples who remained together supports the matching hypothesis; the association between unequal commitments and break-ups supports social exchange theory.

In terms of the process of breaking up, the study showed the importance of having a special formula or rituals to facilitate the ending of a brief relationship without unduly hurting the other person's feelings (such as saying 'I'll see you next term' rather than 'I don't like you any more').

### Evaluation

*Restricted perspective*

The findings of this study are only relevant to romantic involvements where there is little commitment and cannot be applied to relationships such as marriage or long-term relationships where an important commitment has been made.

*Qualitative data*

The size of the sample and the use of in-depth interviews mean that a substantial amount of data was collected about how people think and feel (**qualitative data**). The advantage of this is that it provides many useful insights. The disadvantage is that it is difficult to summarise the findings neatly.

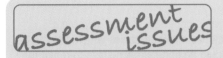

**Describe *one* explanation of relationship breakdown. (*ku 6 ae 0*)**

You have studied several different *kinds* of explanations of relationship breakdown, so for this question you could choose to write about sets of factors, such as environmental factors, interpersonal factors, individual factors – which all try to explain the *origins* and *processes* of breakdown. Or you could choose to write about a stage theory, describing a sequence of relationship deterioration. Duck's stage theory would be suitable; Duck's terminology is challenging but maybe you enjoy a terminological challenge! Or you could use a stage theory that applies to the whole 'lifespan' of a relationship, i.e. Levinger's ABCDE model (1980), but this may not be such a wise choice as only the last two of the five stages are relevant to breakdown.

## Benefits of relationships

In this final section of Aspect 2 we look at the benefits of relationships and focus particularly on the gender differences in these benefits. Evolutionary theory predicts that there are gender differences in what men and women seek in relationships, but research has shown other important gender differences in association with relationships.

### Research into the benefits of relationships

#### Married versus single

Research has found very striking and significant effects from being married. Cochrane (1988) analysed the data from the Mental Health Enquiry for England for 1981 (see graph). Single people were found to be three times more likely than married people – and widowed people four times more likely – to be admitted to a mental hospital in any one year. Such admissions include serious mental illness, such as schizophrenia, but also more 'commonplace' problems, such as anxiety disorders or depression.

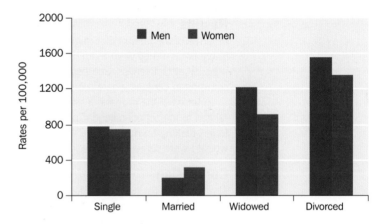

Similar results have been found for physical health. For example, people who are divorced or widowed have a particularly high risk of dying prematurely (Johnson *et al.*, 2000). These results are widespread across the world.

#### Explanations

Why is marriage good for people? Wilson and Oswald (2005) reviewed relevant research and produced the following reasons:

- *Financial* – married couples gain financially.
- *Protective* – marriage brings emotional support, which reduces stress (see Chapter 3, e.g. Kamarck *et al.*, 1990).
- *Guardian* – marriage reduces stress, which reduces risky behaviours (e.g. smoking, less sleep), which brings health benefits (Wickrama *et al.*, 1997).
- *Selection* – individuals who are mentally/physically healthier are more likely to be selected as partners. Thus health may be a cause rather than an effect of marriage.

Wilson and Oswald concluded that research evidence lends most support to the protective explanation; however, the others have been found to be significant too.

# Gender differences

### Gender differences in mental health

A common conclusion from the research on the benefits of marriage is that men do better from being married than women. For example, Cochrane (1988) found that married women are much more likely to be admitted to mental hospital than married men, although married women are still less likely to be admitted to mental hospital than single women. So marriage is clearly protective of mental health for all genders but, amongst the married, men are protected far more than are women.

Similar results were produced in a meta-analysis of a large number of American studies; Haring-Hidore *et al.* (1985) found that subjective well-being was highest in married participants but this was most especially true for men.

### Gender differences in physical health

In terms of longevity, Lillard and Waite (1995) found that married men have significantly lower mortality risk than single men; the difference is greater than between married and single women. Hibbard and Pope (1993) found that marriage *quality* affects mortality risks for women but not men; i.e. low-quality marriages give women less protection than if in a high-quality marriage.

### Explanation

Why do men get more benefit from being married than women? One possibility is that men get more 'protection' from marriage than women; i.e. they gain more emotional support. Women have more developed social networks than men outside their marriage and already gain support from these (Shumaker and Hill, 1991). This would also explain why males suffer more than women when widowed or divorced.

A second possibility is that marriage leads men to cut back on risky behaviours (such as smoking and drinking), whereas this is less true for women – the guardian explanation.

It is also possible that the selection effect might be stronger for men than women because men have to take the lead in courtship and proposing marriage, so only the mentally healthiest men get married.

Men stand to gain more from marriage than women – in terms of mental and physical health, although both are better off than people who are single, widowed or divorced. Blanchflower and Oswald (2004) estimate that the effect of marriage on mental well-being is equivalent to having an extra $100,000 a year!

*assessment issues*

**Discuss the claim that females and males do not benefit equally from relationships. (ku 3 ae 3)**

Having read the material on the last few pages, you'll be familiar with the phenomenon that females seem to derive less benefit from relationships than men. How should you 'discuss the claim'? A sensible approach would be to start by stating some research evidence of gender differences, i.e. evidence of differences in mental and physical health between men and women, single and married. This will get you *ku* marks. For the *ae* marks, you could then point out that, although this evidence that gender differences exist is strong, the *reasons* for these differences are by no means certain. You might go on to consider the various explanations that have been proposed. In this way, you will have 'discussed the claim'.

## Aspect 3: Effects of divorce

### Effects of divorce on children

In 2004, the number of divorces granted in the UK increased by 0.2% to 167,116: of these, 53% involved at least one child under the age of 16. Children whose parents separate are likely to show a range of negative outcomes, some of which can be extremely long-lasting. Research suggests that these negative outcomes can begin long before divorce and may continue long after. In particular, conflict and poor parent–child relationships are among the major risk factors linked to long-term problems for children. In this section, we look at research into the effects of divorce on children and in the next section examine some of the mitigating factors that help to minimise its impact on future outcomes.

### Effects on self-esteem

Research has produced inconsistent results regarding the relationships between divorce and the self-esteem of children and adolescents.

#### Negative effects

Some research has found significant differences between the self-esteem of children of divorced families and those from intact families (i.e. where parents had not divorced). In a survey of adolescents aged 13 to 18, Bynum and Durm (1996) found that those from intact families scored significantly higher on measures of self-esteem than adolescents from divorced families. Beer (1989) conducted a study that also indicated that self-esteem among children aged 10–12 was significantly influenced by divorce. A more recent study carried out in Norway (see Star Study on the next page) found that, although adolescents generally show an increase in self-esteem between the ages of 14 and 18, this increase is significantly less for children from divorced families and particularly so for girls from divorced families.

#### Counter evidence

Other research has found no significant difference in the self-esteem of children of divorced families compared with that of children of intact families. For example, Durm *et al.* (1997) studied 108 students aged 15 to 19, and, although they found evidence of a difference in self-esteem between boys and girls (girls had significantly lower self-esteem than boys), there was no significant difference in the self-esteem scores of students from divorced and intact families.

---

*evaluation*

Evaluation of research on self-esteem

One way of reconciling the seemingly contradictory results of research in this area is to consider the role of *individual differences*. One important individual difference appears to be the age of the child at the time of parental separation. Very young children are more likely to respond to the break-up with increased fearfulness, behavioural regression (behaving like a younger child) and worry about abandonment, whereas older children may be more anxious and blameful, and feel overwhelmed by a sense of helplessness (Wallerstein, 1983). Girls appear to cope better with divorce, which might be explained by the fact that mothers are most often the custodial parent.

However, some studies appear to contradict the conventional view that divorce has more negative impacts on boys than on girls. One meta-analysis did find more negative impact on boys than on girls, but only with respect to certain measures, most notably social relationships and cooperativeness. In other areas, such as academic attachment, boys appeared to suffer no more detrimental consequences than did girls (Amato and Keith, 1991). A key factor appears to be the degree of support available for the child post-divorce. There is a good deal of evidence demonstrating the value of support for good post-divorce adjustment for adults (e.g. Chiraboga *et al.*, 1979) but rather surprisingly, increased support for *parents* appears to relate to both the *child's* post-divorce adjustment and the quality of the parent–child relationship (Dunst, 2000).

## star**STUDY**

# Investigating the effects of divorce: Adolescents with a childhood experience of parental divorce

**(STØRKSEN *ET AL.*, 2005)**

## Aims

The study investigated three main research questions:
1. Is the development of psychological adjustment and well-being of adolescents of divorce different compared with the development of other adolescents?
2. Does gender interact with divorce in affecting this development?
3. Does the absence of a biological parent account for some of the effects of divorce on adolescent development?

## Method

This was a prospective study carried out using data from the Nord-Trøndelag Health study in Norway. Data for this study were collected between the years 1995–1997 (time 1, T1), and again between the years 2000–2001 (T2).

As part of this study, adolescents were asked the question 'Have your parents separated or divorced?' Those who answered *yes* at T1 and T2 made up the 'divorce' group (number of adolescents (n) = 413), and those who answered *no* made up the 'no-divorce' group (n = 1758). The ratio of boys to girls was similar in both groups. Each adolescent was assessed at T1 and T2 for anxiety and depression, subjective well-being, self-esteem, and level of school functioning.

## Results

In relation to the original aims:
1. The general trend for all adolescents was more adjustment problems at T2 and a slight increase in self-esteem over the same period. However, for the divorce group, the increase in adjustment problems was more pronounced, and the increase in self-esteem smaller compared with the no-divorce group.
2. The boys in the divorce group had a significant increase in school problems compared with the no-divorce group, but girls showed a significant negative change on *all* variables compared with the no-divorce group.
3. Absence of the father was more important in affecting relative change in psychological adjustment among boys than among girls, with boys in 'father-absent' families more likely to develop distress than girls.

## Conclusion

1. The findings indicate that the development of psychological distress and adjustment problems during adolescence differs between those with a childhood experience of divorce and those with no such experience.
2. The gender differences evident in adolescents in the divorce group suggest that negative outcomes following divorce are more pronounced in girls rather than boys.
3. Results suggest that boys are in special need of daily contact with a father figure during adolescence, whereas for girls, the development of a close relationship with the father is not dependent on the father's residence.

## Evaluation

### Cultural bias

As the study was conducted in Norway the results may not apply to other cultural groups. For example, they may not apply in **collectivist** societies where the wider family provides greater support. Other cultural differences may influence the results; for example, people may have different attitudes towards divorce in other countries/cultures and this would affect the experience of children involved in divorce.

### Historical bias

We might also consider historical bias. Amato (2001) suggests that patterns are changing in the way divorce is experienced. This means we should always be cautious about generalising from any study as attitudes are constantly changing.

## Effects on aggression

### General findings

A number of researchers have found that children of divorce are more aggressive than children whose parents stayed married. For example, Emery (1988) found that this was particularly the case for boys. Other studies (e.g. Lester, 1993) have found that murder and suicide rates are higher for divorced children than for children from intact families. In a meta-analysis conducted in the 1990s, Amato (2001) reported that, compared with children of continuously married parents, children with divorced parents had more conduct problems and poorer psychological adjustment generally. However, despite the fact that these findings are statistically significant, the effect sizes are rather small indicating that the impact of divorce on aggression appears to have little practical importance.

### Research on very young children

Very few of the studies in Amato's (2001) meta-analysis involved very young children (those of preschool age). Clark-Stewart et al. (2000), however, carried out an extensive study of the effects of divorce on very young children. Researchers selected children from three distinct groups: (a) children from single, never married families; (b) children whose parents separated/divorced before the child was three years old; and (c) children from intact, married families. The children were assessed on a number of variables, including conduct and behaviour problems at 15, 24 and 36 months. Children from the group who had experienced parental divorce prior to age three scored significantly lower on most measures (including behaviour problems) than did children from intact families. However, when the researchers controlled for variables such as family income, level of parental education and maternal depressive symptoms, these negative outcomes disappeared. As a result, the researchers concluded that it is not divorce itself that has the greatest influence on the outcomes for the child, but rather the variables that frequently accompany divorce.

### Are the effects getting better or worse?

In the early 1990s, a meta-analysis of the effects of divorce (Amato and Keith, 1991) reported that the negative effects of divorce on aggression and delinquency had diminished from the 1950s to the 1980s. Amato (2001) suggested that this trend was due to the decreased social stigma surrounding divorce and the increased availability and effectiveness of child-centred support in the 1980s. However, Amato warned that this trend appears to be reversing with a more recent meta-analysis reporting an increase in negative outcomes for children who experience parental divorce. Why would this be the case? One possible cause for this new trend may be an increase in the number of low-discord marriages which end in divorce. Amato suggests that, in such divorces, the unexpectedness of divorce creates additional trauma for the child.

## Effects on mental health

### The detrimental effects of parental divorce

The breakdown of a marriage is typically very stressful for parents *and* children, with most researchers agreeing that divorce and separation produces acute emotional and psychological disturbance for most parents and children. For example, Beer (1989) found that children from divorced homes scored significantly higher on the Children's Depression Inventory than children from intact families. A major study in the US found that 40% of the children studied were still depressed 5 years after the divorce (Wallerstein and Kelly, 1980). In adulthood, only 60% of them were married, compared with 80% from intact families (Wallerstein et al., 2000). However, a meta-analysis of over 200 research studies concluded that children's stress arising from parental separation usually fades over time (Rodgers and Pryor, 1998), although overall there was a greater probability of poor outcomes for children from separated families. More recent studies, and studies with more sophisticated methodology, tend to report fewer mental health differences between children of these two groups than did earlier studies (e.g. Kelly, 2000). Most divorced children fall within the average range of adjustment, and even those effects that persist into adulthood seem eventually to disappear. Although adolescents from divorced families are more at risk than children from intact families, by the age of 33 they are indistinguishable from children from never-divorced families (Chase-Lansdale et al., 1995).

Judith Wallerstein

### Conflicting views

Two major longitudinal studies into the effects of divorce on children have produced conflicting results. The first, a 25-year US study, was begun in the early 1970s and the long-term findings were published in 2000 (Wallerstein and Blakeslee, 2000). The other study – also carried out in the US – followed more than 2500 children over three decades (Hetherington and Kelly, 2002). Wallerstein and Hetherington came to very different conclusions about the long-term effect of divorce on children, particularly on their mental health. Wallerstein concluded that a significant number of children had permanent emotional scars that lingered through adolescence and well into adulthood. These included depression, fear of failure, fear of commitment, and fear of following their parents' path. In contrast, Hetherington's research found that, although a significant number (25%) of children from divorced families did suffer mental health problems (compared with only 10% of children from intact families), the great majority showed very little long-term damage and were functioning well. One interesting finding was that some girls developed *increased* competence and strength as a result of the divorce.

---

*evaluation*

### Evaluation of effects of divorce

Who is right? The two studies had very different methodologies. Wallerstein's study used only a small sample of children who were intensively interviewed for thousands of hours over several decades. In contrast, Hetherington studied the records of several thousand children and based her conclusions on a statistical analysis of these records, rather than on the results of subjective interviews. Does that make one approach better than the other? No, rather the very different approaches of the two studies complement each other, offering a different perspective on the same problem. The children studied in Wallerstein's research were, however, predominantly white, upper middle class and well educated, making it risky to assume that her findings apply equally to other groups.

A major limitation of both these studies, and many similar studies of divorce, is that they fail to address the question of whether the emotional damage observed was a consequence of the divorce itself, or the conflict that had caused the divorce. Sun (2001) addressed this question in a longitudinal study of nearly 800 children, which was designed to see if the negative outcomes related to parental divorce were more associated with the divorce itself or with pre-divorce issues. Each child was assessed on a variety of variables pre-divorce and again when they were adolescents in an attempt to understand if post-divorce outcomes could be attributable to parental conflict that occurs before the divorce. The results of this study showed that *pre*-divorce variables (e.g. increased family conflict), tended to lead to poor student outcomes (e.g. weaker self-esteem, and increased adjustment problems) even before the divorce occurred. Divorce may be a positive outcome because it reduces the incidence of face-to-face confrontations between parents (and the associated emotional stress for the child) and limits any further damage to the emotional well-being of the child.

---

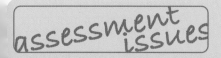

**Discuss the findings of *one* research study relating to the effects of parental break-up on children. (*ku 4 ae 2*)**

For this single research study question, the Størksen *et al.* (2005) research (see the Star Study, page 229) would be a good choice. As always, check first for the *skills* requirement – in this case, the term *discuss* involves both descriptive and analytical/evaluative skills. Secondly, check for the *content* required – here you are asked only about the *findings*. This key word could so easily be overlooked unless you read the question *very* carefully. The focus of your answer would therefore be on describing the *results* (for the *ku* marks) and interpreting these to draw *conclusions* (for the *ae* marks).

### Parental Alienation Syndrome

*What is it?* Gardner (1985) has described cases of intense rejection of a parent by children after divorce which he referred to as 'parental alienation syndrome' (PAS). PAS originates with the systematic vilification by one parent of the other parent with the intent of alienating the child from the other parent. Gardner describes children with PAS as 'obsessed with hatred of a parent'.

*Why does it occur?* A parent experiencing divorce is grieving and experiences a significant degree of loss, including loss of intimacy and loss of economic stability; this is compounded by a depressed mood and poor self-concept. This leads to feelings of helplessness, which may convert to anger and externalisation of these negative feelings. By manipulating the child's feelings towards the other parent, the illusion of an increased sense of control is created, thereby decreasing feelings of helplessness.

*How common is it?* Research on the effects of divorce rarely mentions children who reject one parent following marital separation. In an analysis of 16 case studies that met Gardner's criteria for PAS, Dunne and Hedrick (1994) found that the syndrome can occur regardless of the length of the relationship prior to separation and that it may occur immediately following separation, or not until many years after the divorce. PAS can occur in very young children or in older children who have previously enjoyed a lengthy and positive relationship with the alienated parent.

*Parenting magazines and websites often give advice to parents on how to reduce the potentially harmful effects of parental conflict on their children. For example, the BBC website on Parenting suggests ways of avoiding rows, making rows less destructive, and explaining to children what's happening in arguments.*

See www.bbc.co.uk/parenting/family_matters/you_row.shtml

## Mitigating factors

Although research is far from conclusive on the matter, there is evidence that some circumstances make the experience of divorce worse for children, and some make it better. Key factors that contribute to healthy adjustment after parental separation include appropriate parenting, access to the non-residential parent, and low parental conflict. When parents show high levels of conflict during and after divorce, adjustment is more difficult for their children. When parents show better emotional adjustment after the divorce, so do the children. Research is fairly inconclusive about the importance of children's ongoing relationship with their non-residential parent (most usually the father), with most large-scale studies finding no relationship between frequency of the access parent's visits and child adjustment. However, a number of studies have reported positive outcomes for children in cooperative families where non-residential fathers are actively involved with their children.

## Lack of conflict during break-up

### Effects of conflict

As we have already seen, conflict prior to divorce can be a key factor in children's adjustment. Rodgers and Pryor (1998) established that family conflict before, during and after parental separation was stressful for children, who may respond by becoming anxious, aggressive or withdrawn. A number of research studies have shown that conflict among parents during and after the separation process increases the risk of negative psychological and behavioural outcomes for children. This risk increases when violence between parents is involved and rises even higher when the children themselves are physically abused as a result of the conflict (Johnston, 1994).

### Direct and indirect effects

Research suggests that marital conflict may have both direct and indirect effects on children (Kelly, 1993). High levels of marital conflict may *directly* influence the child through the modelling (social learning) process. When children see their parents dealing with emotional distress through anger and aggression, they are more likely to incorporate these responses into their own behavioural repertoire.

Marital conflict may also have *indirect* effects on children's adjustment because of changes in the parent–child relationship. Research has shown that high levels of marital conflict are associated with less warm and empathic relationships between parent and child (Belsky *et al.*, 1991) and that continued parental conflict after divorce may interfere with parents' ability to be responsive to the needs of their children. This may make existing problems worse or even create new problems for children. Tscham *et al.* (1990) found that mothers reporting higher levels of post-separation conflict with their spouses were more rejecting with their children and also tended to use their children more for both emotional support and the expression of conflict (see Note on *Parental Alienation Syndrome*).

### Reducing conflict

A great deal of research has focused on the effects of parental conflict on the children of divorce. Much of this has shown that parental conflict does have harmful effects on children, but in particular it appears to be the manner in which this conflict is resolved that most affects the outcomes for the child.

High levels of discord between parents tends to leave children feeling 'caught in the middle' (e.g. they may have to carry messages or may be asked intrusive questions about the other parent), and this feeling has been found to relate to adjustment (Buchanan *et al.*, 1991). High levels of conflict do not always lead to negative outcomes unless a child feels caught up in it by one or both parents. A longitudinal study by Maccoby *et al.* (1990) found that in the second year after divorce, 60% of children were not experiencing post-divorce conflict between their parents, either because their parents had disengaged from each other or were capable of cooperative communication with each other.

What is clear, however, is that experiencing good relationships with both parents as well as an absence of continuing conflict is 'generally conducive to the most positive outcome for the children involved' (Smith *et al.*, 2003). Divorce is nearly always a painful time for all concerned, particularly for children, but at least, by reducing the post-separation conflict, the negative outcomes can be minimised for the child.

## Continued relationships with both parents

A number of studies have found that non-residential mothers and their children manage to maintain contact more successfully than do non-residential fathers and their children. Maccoby *et al.* (1993) found that over a three-year period, children living with their mothers saw their fathers less and less often, whereas for children living with their fathers, the number of times they visited their mother increased over the same period.

### Educational outcomes

A meta-analysis of British studies concluded that, although continuing contact with the non-residential parent may benefit children's adjustment, there is no simple relationship between developmental outcomes and frequency of contact (Rodgers and Pryor, 1998). The ongoing involvement of non-residential parents with their children does, however, appear to be consistently linked to academic achievement. McLanahan (1999) found that children's school performance declined less when fathers were involved with their schoolwork after separation. Children from divorced families were also less likely to gain a university degree, in part because parental aspirations appear to decrease for adolescents in divorced families compared with adolescents in never-divorced families. In a US study, divorced fathers were often unwilling to fund their children's post-school education, especially if they had remarried and had children in the new relationship (Wallerstein and Lewis, 1998).

### Emotional adjustment

When a non-residential parent (usually the father) has frequent contact, there is minimal conflict and children tend to fare well; however, when there is conflict, frequent visits are related to poorer adjustment of children (Hetherington and Kelly, 2002). Maccoby and Mnookin (1992) found that adolescent emotional adjustment (e.g. absence of depression and low levels of deviant behaviours) is influenced by many factors including a feeling of closeness to the residential parent and low-conflict co-parenting relationships. An Israeli study (Kaffman *et al.*, 1989) found that about two-thirds of a sample of kibbutz children whose parents had divorced but maintained a high degree of cooperation reached a satisfactory emotional level of adjustment by the second year after divorce. Although this outcome was in part influenced by children simply getting used to their new status, it was also positively influenced by the continuous physical proximity of the non-residential parent and the neutralisation of parenting issues as subjects for dispute.

*Psychological research does not offer any simple answers to the question of the effects of divorce. You might enhance your own understanding of the issues by considering what advice you would give to mothers and fathers about how best to help their children through divorce.*

## assessment issues

**Discuss factors that may mitigate the possible harmful effects of parental break-up on children. (*ku* 4 *ae* 4)**

Unlike some other questions asking you to 'discuss factors …' in this one you are *not* spoilt for choice – which makes your task easier. The factors you could write about are *lack of conflict* and *continued relationships with both parents,* as discussed above. One possible source of uncertainty in the question is the word 'mitigate'; although this is not a specialist psychological term, it is uncommon in everyday conversations. However, it features in the Topic content for this Aspect and is therefore likely to be used in exam questions.

*In this section we show you student answers to possible exam questions plus examiner's comments on these answers. Remember that in the actual exam (and NABs) your questions for this Topic will always add up to 20 marks. The question may be one essay worth 20 marks or a number of smaller questions (such as those shown below) which add up to 20 marks.*

**Question 1**   Describe and analyse the role of environmental, interpersonal and individual factors in relationship breakdown. (*ku* 10 *ae* 4)

### Tom

One example of an environmental factor is distance. When a couple has to spend some time apart this may cause their relationship to break down. However it isn't true that separation always leads to relationship breakdown. For example, Rohfling did a study of students and found that 90% said they had had one long distance relationship. However this may not be typical of people generally because students are often living a long way from home and so often have to have such relationships.

Another environmental factor is work stress. Work stress may cause difficulties in relationships or it may be the other way round, that people who are having difficulties in their relationships then feel more stressed at work. Social support may be one way to break this vicious cycle and in itself is another environmental factor. In Duck's stage theory of relationship breakdown he suggested that there is a social phase when friends may help mend problems in a relationship.

Interpersonal factors include boredom and rule violation. One partner may feel bored and that leads to relationship breakdown. Felmlee's theory of relationship breakdown suggested that it is often the things which first attracted you to a person which ultimately cease to be interesting (or become annoying) and this is what causes relationships to breakdown. Argyle and Henderson did research into rule violation. This study was good because it investigated friendships rather than romantic relationships. Argyle and Henderson found that the most important rule violations included jealousy, breaking confidences and criticising the person publicly.

Individual factors are characteristics of your partner which may lead to breakdown. Duck suggested that individuals may start a relationship with certain characteristics (predisposing factors) which make it likely that the relationship won't last. For example one partner may be emotionally unstable or might have some disgusting habits. Other individual factors include partners who are quite different in age or religion or interests. If you come from a family where your parents divorced it is also more likely that your relationship might breakdown.

**Examiner's comments**    Tom's answer is focused on the question and provides a full answer. It is well organised, although it would be useful to provide a brief introduction, to put the topic in context. He shows analysis in the way he presents contradictory evidence, relates factors to an overall theory of relationship breakdown, refers to interaction between factors, and questions the direction of effects between stress and relationship difficulties. An excellent answer that deserves full marks: **14 out of 14 marks** (*ku* 10/10 *ae* 4/4).

### Alice

Duck proposed a stage theory of relationship breakdown which included environmental, interpersonal and individual factors. There were four stages. The first stage is the intrapsychic phase. This is a time when individual factors are important. You might feel dissatisfied with your partner or bored with them. All of these factors are what would lead the relationship to breakdown. In this phase the repair strategy is to try to start liking the person again.

The second stage is the dyadic phase where you confront your partner. You may be having arguments with your partner and if these are not resolved the relationship will go on breaking down. At this stage the repair strategy would be to clear the air and work out some new strategies with your partner.

In the third stage partners start talking to friends about what's gone wrong and their friends may try to help repair the relationship, which is the repair strategy. Friends are an important source of help because it is good to think through what you're doing and talk about it. Friends also reduce stress (Kamarck).

One of the criticisms of this theory is that events may not happen in this order. Another criticism is that this theory is just a description, it doesn't really explain why relationships breakdown. One strength of the model is that repair strategies are suggested for each stage which could be useful in marriage guidance because it gives you something to focus on.

**Examiner's comments**    Alice has got off on the wrong foot: she has written about a theory of relationship breakdown and tried to 'shoehorn in' references to environmental, interpersonal and individual factors. Although it is fine to link factors to theory(ies), Alice's focus on a theory was not an effective strategy and her last paragraph is irrelevant. She does get some *ku* marks for describing certain environmental, interpersonal and individual factors, even if not by name (such as talking to friends/social support = environmental factor). She even gets 1 *ae* mark for *analysing* how some factors are related to stages of break-up. However, overall she could have had many more marks through selecting more appropriate material to answer the question set. She gets **5 out of 14 marks** (*ku* 4/10 *ae* 1/4).

**Question 2**    Describe and evaluate *two* economic theories of relationships. (*ku 6 ae 4*)

### Tom

There are two main economic theories of relationships: social exchange theory (Thibaut and Kelley) and equity theory (Walster et al.). Both suggest that people strive to have some kind of 'economic' balance in their relationships but social exchange theory is calculated in terms of a profit whereas equity theory suggests that people seek equity. In social exchange theory 'profit' is calculated by subtracting the costs from the rewards. In equity theory it is more complex. One partner might give a little and get a little whereas the other partner gives a lot and receives a lot. There is equity in this, whereas if the second partner actually doesn't receive very much then the relationship is inequitable and doomed to failure. And the same would be true if both partners received the same amount but one partner gave more than the other.

Both theories have been criticised because they suggest that people go round calculating what they have. The theories don't really suggest that people are adding things up but they are unconsciously aware of the differences in gains and losses. Nevertheless it still sounds like they are behaving rationally. This ignores the fact that people often have strong emotions and one of the prime things in a relationship might be physical attraction which isn't a reward or a loss. Another criticism by Clark and Mills is that such economic theories may be relevant to short-term relationships but long-term relationships are governed by other factors. They call such relationships 'communal' where there is less concern with exchange or equity. Most of the research done on relationships has been done with students who perhaps are more focused on short-term relationships and therefore this makes it seem as if people in general behave in this way.

**Examiner's comments**    Tom's answer is slightly disorganised. In the first paragraph he jumps from one theory to another, rather than dealing with social exchange theory then equity theory more systematically. His explanations of both theories are rather lacking in clarity, for example, he should stress that it is the individual's *perceived* inputs and outputs that are important, and that these are *relative* to the partner's. However, he does cover several key features of both theories. He has not distinguished between the two theories in his criticisms, but this is acceptable as the points he makes do apply to both. Tom is awarded **8 out of 10 marks** (*ku 4/6 ae 4/4*).

### Alice

One example of an economic theory of relationships is the social exchange theory by Thibaut and Kelley (1959). They proposed that relationships are based on estimates of profit and loss by partners, which is why it is an economic theory. People seek to maximise their rewards and minimise their costs. Overall they wish to be in profit which means that the rewards should be more than the losses. 'Rewards' include all sorts of things such as being cared for by your partner, companionship, cooking meals etc. 'Costs' include the effort you have to make to maintain the relationship, expenses, unpleasant habits and missed opportunities because of being with your partner. People will not remain committed to a relationship unless they are in profit. In order to determine whether we are better or worse off we have a 'comparison level' so we can

compare what we have with what we might expect to have. The relationship is OK if the potential profit exceeds the comparison level. We also have a comparison level for alternatives – if the potential rewards from an alternative relationship exceed current profit then we might end the current relationship.

One criticism of this theory is that it suggests that people make such calculations and suggests that people are basically selfish, only in a relationship to get what they can from it. Another criticism is that it ignores the interactions between two people and focuses on the individual's perspective. On the positive side it can be used to explain all sorts of different relationships, not just romantic ones, and also explains why people may change their views of a relationship over time – because the profits/losses have changed. It also explains why people stay in abusive relationships

**Examiner's comments**    The problem with Alice's answer is that she has described only *one* theory, social exchange, whereas the question asks for *two*. So Alice can access only half of the marks on offer. Her description and evaluation of the one theory are very detailed and accurate, so she would achieve **5 out of 10 marks** (*ku 3/6 ae 2/4*).

# Topic: Atypical behaviour – definitions and origins

Individual differences are those aspects of each of us that distinguish us from others, such as personality and intelligence. Each of us also differs in the extent to which we are 'normal'. For the most part deviation from normal is not a problem, but in some circumstances it is.

Atypical behaviour refers to behaviour that is not usual or typical and may be psychologically unhealthy. Psychologists prefer to use the term 'atypical' rather than 'abnormal' because of the negative perceptions that go with the term 'abnormal'. Atypical behaviours are not necessarily undesirable: individuals who have Down's syndrome or who are gifted display 'atypical' behaviours but these may be viewed positively.

| Chapter contents | Unit content for the Topic 'Atypical behaviour – definitions and origins' | Comment |
|---|---|---|
| **Aspect 1: Definitions of atypical/abnormal behaviour** | | |
| Definition 1: statistical infrequency<br>    page 237<br>Definition 2: deviation from social norms<br>    page 239<br>Definition 3: failure to function adequately<br>    page 240<br>Definition 4: deviation from ideal mental health<br>    page 241 | Range of definitions of atypical/abnormal behaviour | *In everyday conversations, people often have quite varied views on what, exactly, 'normal' or 'abnormal' behaviour is and on what constitutes 'mental health' or 'mental illness'. Psychologists talk in terms of 'atypical' behaviour, or 'psychological disorder', but find it hard to agree on a single definition of such terms. Behaviour may be considered 'atypical' if it is* **statistically infrequent**, *or if it goes against* **social norms;** *someone who is unable to cope with ordinary everyday life (i.e.* **'fails to function adequately'**), *or who does not show* **'ideal mental health'**, *may also be regarded as 'atypical' or 'abnormal'. However, each of these definitions has strengths and shortcomings, so you should be able to evaluate them.* |
| **Aspect 2: Approaches to explaining disorder** | | |
| The medical model<br>    page 243<br>The cognitive approach<br>    page 245<br>The behaviourist approach<br>    page 246 | Range of approaches to explaining disorder, including:<br>• the medical model<br>• cognitive approach<br>• behaviourist approach<br>• psychoanalytic approach<br>• humanistic approach | *Just as psychologists and psychiatrists may not agree on how to* **define** *atypical behaviour, they also have different views on how disorder arises. Here, you will study* **five approaches** *to explaining disorder: the* **medical model, cognitive, behaviourist, psychoanalytic** *and* **humanistic** *approaches. You should be able to compare and evaluate the explanations put forward in these approaches.* |
| **Aspect 3: Aetiology of depression, schizophrenia and phobias** | | |
| Depression<br>    page 251<br>Schizophrenia<br>    page 254<br>Phobias<br>    page 255 | Aetiology of specific common disorders:<br>• depression<br>• schizophrenia<br>• phobias | *The aetiology of a disorder is an explanation of how it originated. You will not be surprised to learn that various explanations have been proposed for* **depression, schizophrenia** *and* **phobia**. *As well as becoming familiar with the characteristics of these disorders, you will study several explanations of each, which are often based on the* **approaches** *that you studied in the previous Aspect.* |

| Chapter contents | Unit content for the Topic 'Atypical behaviour – definitions and origins' | Comment |
|---|---|---|
| **Aspect 4: Classification systems** | | |
| A description of ICD and DSM page 257<br>Reliability and validity of classification systems page 259 | • structure, reliability and validity of current ICD and DSM systems<br>• gender, ethnic and cultural biases in diagnosis | *Disorders are named and organised into* **classification systems,** *in much the same way that physical illnesses are categorised, according to symptoms. The classification is then used, mainly by psychiatrists, to* **diagnose** *disorders (and, thereafter, to decide on appropriate treatment). In this Aspect, you will learn about the* **structure** *of such classification systems and will see why it is important that these systems are* **reliable** *and* **valid.** **Biases** *that may arise in diagnosis, due to* **gender, ethnicity** *or* **culture,** *are also examined.* |
| **263    Sample questions with students' answers and examiner's comments** | | |

You'll notice that there are fewer Star Studies in this chapter than some other chapters. This is because the various Aspects of these Individual Differences Topics are closely related to each other, so the Star Studies that we provide are relevant to more than one Aspect. Of course, as with all the other Topics, this chapter provides a range of research evidence relevant to each Aspect.

# Aspect 1: Definitions of atypical/abnormal behaviour

**Atypical or abnormal:** A psychological condition or behaviour that departs from the norm or is harmful and distressing to the individual or those around them. Atypical/abnormal behaviours are usually those that violate society's ideas of what is an appropriate level of functioning.

One of the most difficult tasks for those working within the field of atypical psychology is to *define* abnormality. The definition of what constitutes **atypical** or **abnormal** behaviour has undergone dramatic transformations through history. The way in which our ancestors dealt with the problem of abnormal behaviour (e.g. exorcism, the burning of witches, trepanning, etc.) reflected the very different beliefs that they held about the nature and cause of abnormal behaviour. Although we have moved on in our understanding of what constitutes normal and abnormal behaviour (and therefore who requires treatment), the *definition* of abnormality itself inevitably remains a judgment. In this section, we consider some of the attempts to define this most elusive concept. As will become evident, no one single definition is adequate on its own.

## Definition 1: statistical infrequency

Probably the most obvious way to define abnormality is in terms of statistical frequency and infrequency. How do we know what is statistically frequent or 'normal'? Researchers and government agencies collect statistics to tell us. Such statistics tell us things like what age is most typical for women (and men) to have their first baby, the average shoe size for 10-year-old children, how many hours a night most people sleep, what kinds of things people typically dream about and so on.

These statistics can be used to define the 'norm' for any group of people. A norm is something that is usual or regular or typical. If we can define what is most common or normal, then we also have an idea of what is not common, i.e. abnormal or atypical. For example, it is not the norm to have your first baby when you are over 40 or under 20. It is also not the norm to feel that your behaviour is controlled by aliens (a symptom of schizophrenia).

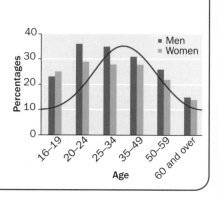

### note

**Normal distribution**

A normal distribution is what you get if you plot the frequency of any randomly determined events. For example, if you plot shoe sizes of all the women you know or if you plot the life of the light bulbs in your house you should get a normal distribution. This graph shows the percentage of adults in different age groups who smoke cigarettes. This is not a *true* normal distribution as it is not symmetrical, a symmetrical line is drawn in red.

What is interesting is that if you draw a graph of most aspects of human behaviour you get a normal distribution – this is illustrated by a symmetrical bell-shaped curve similar to the one shown in red on the graph. In a normal distribution, most people (the 'normals') are in the central group, clustered around the mean, and fewer people (the 'abnormals') are at either extreme.

---

*evaluation*

## Statistical infrequency definition

*Strengths*

In some situations it is appropriate to use a statistical criterion to define abnormality. For example, mental retardation is a category of mental illness in the DSM classification scheme (see page 257) and is defined in terms of the normal distribution using the concept of **standard deviation** to establish a cut-off point for abnormality – people who are two standard deviations below the mean (i.e. have an IQ of 70 or lower) are considered to be mentally retarded.

*Limitations*
*Is all abnormal behaviour undesirable?*
The main objection to the statistical infrequency approach is that many abnormal behaviours are actually desirable. For example, very few people have an IQ (a measure of intelligence) over 150 yet we would not want to suggest that this is an undesirable characteristic. Equally, there are some *normal* (statistically common) behaviours that are *undesirable*. For example, depression is relatively common yet it is undesirable. In order to identify behaviours that need treatment we need to have a means of identifying those behaviours that are infrequent *and* undesirable.

*Where do we place the cut-off point?*
If abnormality is defined in terms of statistical infrequency, one has to decide where to separate normality from abnormality. For example, we might look at shoe size and designate normality as anyone whose shoe size falls within the range of 80% of the population. The other 20% are abnormal. Or would a division of 85% and 15% be better? The cut-off point is an arbitrary decision.

*Cultural relativism*
How do we cope with the fact that behaviours differ from one culture to the next? Behaviours that are statistically infrequent in one culture may be statistically more frequent in another. For example, one of the symptoms of schizophrenia is claiming to hear voices. However, this is an experience regarded as normal and even desirable in some cultures. In some cultures, the 'shaman' is a revered religious figure with the ability to speak to spirits.

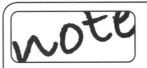

**What is meant by cultural relativism?**

Each of the definitions of abnormality presented here is in fact subject to the influence of *culture*. What is abnormal (i.e. norm violating) in one society may be perfectly normal (i.e. norm consistent) in another. The behaviour itself hasn't changed, but the society has. By which culture's standards, therefore, do we judge behaviour to be atypical or abnormal? The definitions are inevitably relative to a particular culture's standards. This is **cultural relativism**.

In addition, within a single society such as the UK, there are many *subcultures* or other subgroups that may also have different norms for acceptable behaviour or which differ in their experience of mental disorders. However, any deviation from the norms of the dominant culture is seen as indicative of an underlying pathology or 'illness'.

KEY TERMS

**Cultural relativism:** The view that behaviour cannot be judged properly unless it is viewed in the context of the culture in which it originates.

Abnormal according to what criteria?

# Definition 2: deviation from social norms

The statistical infrequency model uses the idea of deviation from a norm. This second way to define abnormality also uses the concept of deviation but this time not in a statistical sense. This time, deviation is in the sense of deviant behaviour – behaviour which is considered anti-social or undesirable. In any society, there are social norms – standards of acceptable behaviour, morals and attitudes that are set by the social group. For example, people who are rude or surly are behaving, in our society, in a socially deviant way (if not, perhaps, in an *abnormal* or *atypical* way).

Social standards also govern what is acceptable in sexual behaviour. In the past, homosexuality was classified as deviant behaviour. Currently the DSM classification scheme (see page 258) contains a category called 'sexual and gender identity disorders' which includes paedophilia and voyeurism. Such behaviours are socially deviant.

*evaluation*

## Evaluation of the deviation from social norms definition

*Strengths*
This model does distinguish between desirable and undesirable behaviour, a feature which was absent from the statistical infrequency model. Also, as the social deviancy model takes into account the possibly damaging effect that behaviour has on others, it is therefore in the interests of the greater good of society.

*Limitations*
Susceptible to abuse.

The main difficulty with the concept of deviation from social norms is that social acceptability varies as times change. What is socially acceptable now was not socially acceptable 50 years ago. For example, today homosexuality is acceptable but in the past it was included under sexual and gender identity disorders. In Russia 50 years ago, anyone who disagreed with the state was regarded as insane and placed in a mental institution. If we define abnormality in terms of deviation from social norms, we allow diagnoses that are made purely in terms of prevailing social morals and attitudes. Szasz (1974) claimed that mental illness was simply a means of social control, a way to exclude non-conformists from society.

*Cultural relativism*
Attempting to define abnormality in terms of social norms is obviously bound by culture because social norms are defined by the culture. **Classification systems**, such as **DSM** and **ICD** (see page 257), are almost entirely based on the social norms of the dominant culture in the West (white and middle class). Using one set of criteria for different cultural (and subcultural) groups results, as we shall see, in differential diagnosis rates.

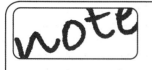

### Thomas Szasz

Dr Thomas Stephen Szasz (born in 1920) has written a number of radical and highly influential books criticising the way that mental illness is regarded by our Western society. In The Myth of Mental Illness (1960), he argued that mental illnesses are not the same as physical illnesses yet we try to treat them as such. Szasz suggested that the concept of mental illness merely obscures the difficulties that people face. A belief in the idea of mental illness is, he argues, no more sophisticated than the belief previously held by people that witches and devils were responsible for problems in social living. His arguments are considered on pages 244 and 262.

---

*assessment issues*

### Explain and evaluate *two* definitions of atypical behaviour. (*ku 4 ae 4*)

You have a choice of subject matter in this question, so make the most of it! Naturally, you'll choose the two definitions about which you have the greatest knowledge (for the *ku* marks) and, in particular, about which you can give substantial *evaluation* points (for the *ae* marks). So far we have looked at two definitions – there are two more to come.

What exactly are examiners looking for? They don't tell you the answers (not surprisingly!), but they *do* tell you quite precisely what skills they want to see in your answer: you can find this in the *Marking Instructions* on the SQA website (www.sqa.org. uk – Psychology pages). In the section entitled *Generic Requirements*, you'll find detailed descriptions of the kinds of performance that will achieve a grade A, grade B, etc., and these requirements are standard, from year to year, regardless of the actual questions. Use the Generic Requirements when writing practice answers to past exam question for revision – read them *before you start* your practice answers, then judge your efforts against each bullet point of the grade A description: have you demonstrated 'accurate, relevant and detailed psychological knowledge' and 'evidence of thorough understanding'? Is your response 'coherent and logically structured'? Have you 'provided appropriate examples'? and so on. Read the grade D and NA (No Award) descriptions too – these tell you what your answer should NOT be like!

## Definition 3: failure to function adequately

The first two definitions of abnormality focus on comparing behaviour with some kind of standard to determine normality. An alternative approach is to consider normality from the *individual's* point of view. Abnormality can then be judged in terms of not being able to cope with the demands of everyday living. For example, if you are feeling depressed this is acceptable as long as you can continue to go to work, eat meals, wash your clothes, and generally go about your day-to-day life. As soon as depression interferes with such things, the individual might label their own behaviour 'abnormal' and would wish to seek treatment.

So 'failure to function adequately' refers to the individual's ability (or inability) to cope with day-to-day living. This definition encompasses bizarre behaviour and/or behaviours that distress an individual or others.

---

*evaluation*

### Failure to function adequately definition

*Strengths*
This model of abnormality recognises the subjective experience of the individual. It also means that abnormality is relatively easy to judge objectively because one can list behaviours (such as 'able to dress self', 'can prepare meals') and thus determine when treatment is required.

*Limitations:* who judges?
In order to determine 'failure to function adequately' someone needs to decide if this is, in fact, the case. It may be the individual who makes this decision (they may be aware that

they are not managing day-to-day life) or it may be someone else. Sometimes, an individual may be quite content with the situation and/or simply unaware that they are not coping; it is others who are uncomfortable and judge the behaviour as abnormal. For example, many people with schizophrenia do not feel that there is a problem, although their erratic behaviour is distressing to others and may even be dangerous, as in the case of someone like Peter Sutcliffe, the Yorkshire Ripper. The question is, who has the right to make the judgment about whether a person is failing to cope adequately.

*Cultural relativism*
Definitions of adequate functioning are related to cultural ideas of how one's life should be lived. The failure-to-function criteria are likely to result in differential diagnoses when applied to people from different cultures because the standard of one culture is being used to measure another. This may explain why lower-class and non-white patients are more often diagnosed with mental disorders – because their lifestyles are non-traditional and this may lead to a judgement of failing to function adequately.

# Definition 4: deviation from ideal mental health

Marie Jahoda (1958) pointed out that we define physical illness in part by looking at the *absence* of signs of physical health. Physical health is indicated by having correct body temperature, normal skin colour, normal blood pressure, and so on. Why not do the same for mental illness? Jahoda conducted a review of what others had written about positive mental health and identified six categories that were commonly referred to:

- self-attitudes – having high self-esteem and a strong sense of identity
- personal growth and **self-actualisation** – the extent to which an individual develops their full capabilities
- integration –such as being able to cope with stressful situations
- autonomy – being independent and self-regulating
- having an accurate perception of reality
- mastery of the environment – including the ability to love, function at work and in interpersonal relations, adjust to new situations and solve problems (as if!).

This model proposes that the absence of these criteria indicates abnormality and therefore a potential mental disorder.

*evaluation*

## The deviation from ideal mental health definition

*Strengths*
The deviation from mental health model is a positive approach to the definition of abnormality; it focuses on what is considered desirable rather than what is undesirable.

*Limitations*
*Who can achieve these criteria?*
According to these criteria most of us are abnormal in some way and possibly mentally disordered. Jahoda presented the criteria as ideal, and they certainly represent an idealised state of mental health. We also have to ask how many criteria have to be lacking before a person would be judged as abnormal.

*Cultural relativism*
Many if not most of the criteria of the ideal mental health model are culture-bound. If we apply these criteria to people from non-Western or even non-middle-class social groups we find a higher incidence of abnormality. For example, the criterion of self-actualisation is relevant to members of **individualist** cultures but not **collectivist** cultures, where individuals strive for the greater good of the community rather than more self-centred goals.

### Case study: school phobia

Robert was an underweight eight-year-old who had always been reluctant to go to school. Every school night, the boy ate little and even that was brought up later. He became more and more anxious as the evening wore on. When he couldn't get to sleep he would cry, and his mother would come and tell him stories.

In the morning, Robert got up early and paced up and down or sat in a corner occasionally rushing to the toilet to be sick. When it was time to go to school, he had to be pushed out of the house, although often his tears and complaints of feeling unwell led his mother to relent and allow him to stay home.

If he did go to school, there was some solace in the fact that his mother would visit the school at play time bringing some milk and cookies. She came because that was part of the 'deal' about going to school but also because she would otherwise worry about Robert.

Surprisingly, Robert got on quite well with the other children and was well liked, despite crying on the way to school and often acting like a baby. He was good at athletics and quite bright. He did not like being away from home for anything – he did not go to play at friends' houses. But it wasn't just being away from home that caused the problem; Robert was simply terrified of school.

(Adapted from Oltmanns *et al.*, 1999)

### Is Robert's behaviour abnormal? How does it fit our definitions?

*Statistical infrequency*: Such school phobia is statistically rare. Most children go to school happily; some go to school unhappily but do not experience any of Robert's physical symptoms, or his sense of terror. This suggests that his behaviour is abnormal when compared with the norms for his age group.

*Deviation from social norms*: Robert is able to cope with social relations, so he is not deviant in that respect. His unwillingness to travel beyond his immediate environment is a deviation from social norms and undesirable for normal development.

*Failure to function adequately*: Robert's phobia clearly prevents him from attending school, which is a part of day-to-day life. However, his behaviour may *appear* to be dysfunctional in one sense but may serve another function – to prevent separation between him and his mother.

*Deviation from ideal mental health*: Robert's behaviour demonstrates a lack of most of the criteria for ideal mental health, such as poor self-esteem, being unable to cope with stressful situations, lack of autonomy and lack of environmental mastery. It is likely that his behaviour, if it continued, would prevent personal growth.

*DSM*: School phobia is not listed as a category in the DSM but is discussed as an aspect of separation anxiety disorder (an excessive anxiety about being away from home lasting for more than a month).

The therapist identified the key issue as being Robert's anxious nature. Robert received lots of love from his mother but worried that this would cease if he stopped being good. When he started school, he immediately was thrown into a new fear of not succeeding. The anxiety of school coupled with the anxiety of being separated from his mother led to Robert's intense phobia. In the next section, on models of abnormality, we will look at further explanations of Robert's behaviour.

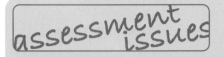

### Common theme: cross-cultural comparison

In answering questions on various Aspects of this Topic, you may well consider whether a definition, or an approach or a classification, applies universally *across all cultures* or only within one particular culture, i.e. is *culturally relative*. Cross-cultural comparison of psychological processes and behaviours is a *common theme* in psychology. Many theories and research studies can be criticised for neglecting cultural differences both between and within countries/societies and between different historical periods in the same society. Critics have often accused psychologists of *ethnocentrism*, i.e. believing that explanations based on their own (usually Western) culture apply universally. (Ethnocentrism literally means to be centred on one's own culture and see things only from that viewpoint.) Whenever you make these kinds of points about cross-cultural issues, in this and other areas of psychology, you are showing skills of both analysis and evaluation (and gaining *ae* marks, where available).

Cultural issues arise again in the last Aspect of this Topic, where you will study cultural (and other) biases in diagnosis of disorder (see page 261). In this applied Aspect, cultural bias has *ethical* implications, as individuals may suffer because of it.

# Aspect 2: Approaches to explaining disorder

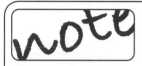

### The biological approach in psychology

In Chapter 3 we explored the physiological approach to explaining stress. This involved a consideration of how bodily systems can be used to explain the causes and effects of stress. The biological approach encompasses more than physiology. It includes genetic explanations of behaviour as well.

*Definitions* of abnormality are concerned with identifying what behaviours or symptoms are abnormal. Now we turn to *explaining* how these abnormal behaviours might have come about, using different approaches in psychology to explain the onset of abnormality (atypical behaviour). There are five main approaches in psychology: biological (medical), cognitive, behaviourist, psychoanalytic and humanistic. Each of these is called an 'approach', meaning that it represents a way to explain behaviour. An 'approach' is a bit like being a pessimist or an optimist. A pessimist sees a glass with some liquid in it as half empty whereas an optimist sees it as half full. Such characteristic views of the world are an 'approach' (sometimes called a 'perspective' or view of the world). A biological psychologist explains behaviour in terms of biological factors whereas a cognitive psychologist uses explanations based on an individual's mental processes. Each approach makes certain *assumptions* about the nature of human behaviour.

## The medical model

The medical model represents the views of mainstream *psychiatry*. All behaviour is seen as rooted in underlying biological processes in the body. Any abnormality must, therefore, have specific causes that lie in some bodily malfunction or in genetic factors. Cure is only possible by removing the root cause and returning the body to its 'normal' level of functioning. As this is similar to the diagnosis of *physical* disease by the medical profession, this psychological model is also referred to as the *medical* model of abnormality and mental disorders are represented as mental *illnesses*. Because of its emphasis on *scientific* investigation and understanding, the biological model is the most widely respected approach to abnormality. However, its representation of mental disorders as 'disease' states equivalent to physical illnesses also makes it one of the most controversial.

### Assumption 1: abnormality is caused by physical factors
The biological (medical) model assumes that all mental disorders are related to some change in the body. Mental disorders are like physical disorders; i.e. they are illnesses. Such changes or illnesses may be caused by one of four possible factors: genes, biochemical substances, neuroanatomy and/or micro-organisms.

### Assumption 2: abnormality is inherited
The genetic view is that mental illness is programmed in an individual's genetic material, which is passed from parent to child. One way of investigating this possibility is through the use of twin studies. For example, pairs of identical twins are compared – if one twin has a disorder, then the question is whether the other twin has it as well. This provides us with a **concordance rate**. There are low concordance rates for some mental disorders (e.g. phobias) but quite high concordance rates for others (e.g. schizophrenia, see Aspect 3).

### Assumption 3: certain genes lead to abnormal biochemistry and/or abnormal neuroanatomy
Genes tell the body how to function. They determine, for example, the production of **hormones** and **neurotransmitters**. In the module on stress, we mentioned the hormone *adrenaline*. High levels of adrenaline are associated with increased arousal whereas low levels have been found in depressed individuals. Genes also determine the structure of the brain (neuroanatomy). Some research has indicated that people with schizophrenia have larger cavities (ventricles) in their brains than is normal.

**KEY TERMS**

**Concordance rate:** The extent to which two individuals share similar characteristics.

**Neurotransmitter:** Biochemical substances that carry signals between neurons (nerve cells) in the brain and nervous system.

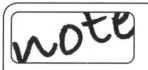

A *psychiatrist* is a person who trained as a doctor and then studied psychiatry. Such doctors tend to adhere to the medical model. A *clinical psychologist* is a person who is trained to diagnose and treat mental disorders but is not a medical doctor. The two terms 'psychiatrist' and 'psychologist' are often confused.

*evaluation*

## Evaluation of the medical model

*Cause or effect?*
It is not clear whether abnormal biochemistry/neuroanatomy is a cause of abnormal behaviour, or whether it is in fact a consequence.

*Inconclusive evidence*
Concordance rates are never 100% (see Star Study on page 253). It is likely that, in the case of certain disorders, individuals inherit susceptibility for the disorder but the disorder only develops if the individual is exposed to stressful life conditions. This is called the **diathesis-stress model** ('diathesis' means a constitutional disposition).

*Humane or inhumane?*
Historically, the emergence of the medical model in the eighteenth century led to more humane treatment for mental patients. Until then, mental illness was blamed on demonic possession or on evil in the individual. The medical model offered a different source of blame – the illness, which was potentially treatable. This became a more humane approach to mental illness.

*Mental disorders are not the same as physical diseases*
Thomas Szasz (2000) asserts that mental functions are not reducible to brain functions and that mental diseases are not brain diseases, in fact not diseases at all. Szasz makes the distinction between diseases of the brain (such as epilepsy) and diseases of the mind (such as an irrational belief that one's body is already dead) and states that the two are not equally 'illnesses'. To Szasz, such irrational beliefs cannot be explained by means of physical defects or diseases and cannot therefore be called illnesses in the same way as we would call epilepsy a physical illness.

On the other hand, physical and mental illnesses have many things in common. Both have fuzzy boundaries and are culturally defined. The distinction between them is misleading because there is much that is 'physical' in mental disorders and much that is 'mental' in physical disorders.

**KEY TERMS**

**Diathesis-stress model:** A belief that, in the case of certain disorders, individuals inherit susceptibility for the disorder (*diathesis*) which develops only if the individual is exposed to intolerable conditions (*stress*).

As touch, taste, sight, smell and hearing boarded the chartered flight to Havana, Professor Fitzherbert knew in his heart that he had lost more than good friends. In fact, he had finally lost his senses.

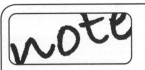

### note

*Using the medical model to explain Robert's school phobia*
From the perspective of the medical model, Robert's separation anxiety may be partly caused by a predisposition to be anxious. He may be anxious by nature and even have inherited a tendency to develop phobias. There is evidence that certain personality traits and mental disorders are inherited. It may be that these innate tendencies, coupled with certain life experiences (e.g. maternal overprotection), could explain his separation anxiety disorder and school phobia.

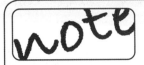

### note

*Psychological versus biological approaches*
We started Aspect 2 with the medical model, which is a *biological approach* to abnormality, stressing the importance of organic (i.e. bodily) processes in behaviour, and which therefore sees abnormal behaviour as being caused by either anatomical or biochemical problems in the brain. We will now look at psychological approaches to abnormality – the cognitive, behaviourist, psychoanalytic and humanistic approaches. *Psychological approaches* focus more on the psychological dimensions of behaviour (e.g. the way a person thinks, feels or acts). As with the definitions covered earlier, none of the approaches offers a *complete* explanation of abnormality, and none can explain the entire spectrum of abnormal behaviour.

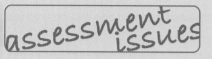

**Describe and evaluate the medical model as an explanation of mental disorder. (ku 12 ae 8)**

In this topic you are studying five approaches to disorder, and this kind of question could be asked about any of them, in the exam or NABs. You shouldn't find it difficult to show knowledge and understanding (*ku*) of the medical/biological model (assuming that you've done your revision!). It is important to recognise that you have several sources of relevant material for this question: there's the description of the medical model itself in Aspect 2 of this chapter and you'll find further information on biological explanations in Aspect 3, in relation to the origins of three specific disorders (on pages 251–257). You can also use evaluation material from both of these sources (for the *ae* marks). What's more, you can draw on your knowledge of the *other* approaches discussed in both Aspects to make *comparisons* with the medical model, thus demonstrating further *ae* skills. For example, the cognitive approach contradicts the medical model's *determinism* in claiming that the causes of disorder are within the individual's control. So, for some questions, especially those with a relatively high mark allocation, it is important to cast your net widely for relevant material.

# The cognitive approach

Cognitive psychologists explain abnormality in terms of irrational and negative thinking. The problem is the way an individual is thinking – if you change the thinking, the problem will disappear.

## Assumption 1: abnormality is caused by faulty thinking

The cognitive approach assumes that thinking, expectations and attitudes (i.e. cognitions) direct behaviour. Mental illness is the result of faulty and irrational thinking which prevents the individual from behaving adaptively. The issue is not the problem itself but the way you *think* about it. Examples of faulty thinking include maladaptive beliefs about oneself (e.g. thinking that there are perfect solutions to everything) and upsetting thoughts (fleeting images that go through one's mind without conscious control). Such thoughts can lead one to failure and depression.

## Assumption 2: the individual is in control

Many approaches to abnormality (such as the medical model, and the behaviourist and psychoanalytic approaches covered on pages 246 to 249) take the view that an individual's behaviour is controlled by forces outside of their own control – physiological, genetic, unconscious or environmental factors. We use the word *determinism* to describe this. In contrast the cognitive approach portrays the individual as being in control because the individual controls their own thoughts. According to this approach, abnormality occurs when this control is 'faulty' in some way.

*Faulty cognitions may be a product of learning (behavioural approach) or they may be innate (biological approach).*

## note

### *The cognitive approach in psychology*

The second chapter of this book was an example of the cognitive approach in psychology – applied to the study of human memory. Cognitive psychology focuses on internal mental processes and on how thinking shapes our behaviour. Much of contemporary psychology is concerned with human *cognition*, for example how people perceive, reason and judge the world around them.

## evaluation | Evaluation of the cognitive approach

*Faulty thinking may be the effect rather than the cause of a mental disorder*
It is not clear which comes first. Do thoughts and beliefs really cause disturbance, or does mental disorder lead to faulty thinking? It may be that, for example, a depressed individual develops a negative way of thinking *because* of their depression rather than the other way around.

*Blames the patient not situational factors*
The cognitive approach suggests that it is the patient who is responsible. This may lead one to overlook situational factors, for example not considering how life events or family problems

may have contributed to the mental disorder. The disorder is simply in the patient's mind and recovery lies in changing that, rather than the individual's environment. It also may be unethical to 'blame the patient' in this way.

*Therapeutic success*

The success of cognitive therapies such as stress inoculation training (see page 73) lends support to the claim that many forms of abnormal behaviour are indeed the result of disordered thinking. A meta-analysis of 475 studies looking at the success of various psychological therapies found that cognitive therapies were the most effective form of treatment for a range of mental illnesses (Smith *et al.*, 1980).

### *Using the cognitive model to explain Robert's school phobia*

The cognitive view would be that Robert's phobia was a result of his placing undue emphasis on negative events in his environment and holding irrational assumptions about his abilities to cope. An example of his irrational assumptions was his view that his mother's and teacher's approval was paramount. These 'faulty thoughts' prevented him from changing his behaviour.

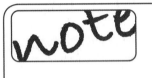

### *What is an 'assumption'?*

Each of these approaches or models is based on a set of assumptions. An assumption is a belief or view that is held prior to proof. For many people religious beliefs are *assumptions* – they do not require proof. An assumption is something that is taken as being true and then used as the basis for further action. Therefore, a psychologist who is a behaviourist will *assume* that certain things are true, whereas a psychoanalytic psychologist will have their own set of beliefs concerning the cause of a particular thought, feeling or behaviour.

## The behaviourist approach

Behaviourists believe that our actions are determined largely by the experiences that we have in life, rather than by any underlying pathology or unconscious forces. Abnormality is seen as the development of behaviour patterns that are considered maladaptive for the individual, established through **classical** and **operant conditioning** or through observational learning. Most learned behaviours are adaptive, helping people to lead happy and productive lives, but maladaptive (and therefore undesirable) behaviours can be acquired in the same way.

### Assumption 1: abnormal behaviours are learned through conditioning

All behaviour is learned through experience. Abnormal behaviour is no different from normal behaviour. We can use the principles of classical and operant conditioning to explain all behaviour (see pages 3–4).

According to the principle of classical conditioning, a psychological disorder develops when an experience (neutral stimulus) produces an extremely unpleasant response such as fear (conditioned response) so that the situation will be avoided at all costs in the future.

According to the principle of operant conditioning, a psychological disorder develops when a maladaptive behaviour is rewarded. This means that such behaviours may be functional for the individual, at least at the time they are learned. For example, if a person finds that he gets increasingly more attention when behaving in a wild and erratic fashion, this behaviour will be repeated.

### Assumption 2: only behaviour is important

Behaviourists believe that we need only concern ourselves with what can be observed – the mind is an unnecessary concept (a direct contrast to the cognitive, psychoanalytic and humanistic views of abnormality). Therefore, there are no such things as *mental* illnesses.

### Assumption 3: the same laws apply to human and non-human animal behaviour

According to the principles of evolution, all animals are formed from the same basic stimulus–response units. This means that it is reasonable to conduct research on non-human animals, like rats and pigeons, and make generalisations to human behaviour.

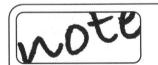

### The behaviourist approach in psychology

*Learning theory* (conditioning) is the bedrock of the behaviourist approach. According to behaviourism, which was first formulated around the start of the twentieth century, we are born as a blank slate, on which experience writes. A later development was *social learning theory*, introduced by Albert Bandura in the 1960s. He pointed out that much of what we learn is the consequence of observation, indirect rewards/punishments and modelling.

*evaluation* | **The behaviourist approach**

*Scientific and testable*
The simplicity of the approach makes it easy to conduct research to test how association and rewards affect behaviour. Experimental studies (such as Watson and Rayner's study of Little Albert, see page 257) have shown how abnormal behaviours can be learned, giving support to the approach.

*Can't account for all human behaviour*
There is no doubt that learning theory can account for some aspects of normal and abnormal behaviour. For example, some individuals develop a phobia of dogs after being bitten (classical conditioning). However, much of human behaviour is more complex than this, as we saw in our study of stress. The way we *think* about things also affects our experiences. Behaviourism disregards thoughts and emotions and so is not a complete explanation of human behaviour.

*Symptoms and not the cause*
Part of the success of this approach comes from the effectiveness of behavioural therapies in treating the symptoms of abnormal behaviour (in Chapter 11 we look at cognitive-behavioural therapies which combine elements of both cognitive and behavioural approaches). However, these do not work with all disorders, suggesting that the symptoms are only the tip of the iceberg. If you remove the symptoms, the cause still remains, and the symptoms will simply resurface, possibly in another form (called *symptom substitution*).

**Using the behavioural model to explain Robert's school phobia**

The behavioural model accounts for Robert's phobia by suggesting that it developed as a result of classical conditioning, as outlined in the account of Little Albert (page 256). School became associated with anxiety, and therefore Robert found that avoidance of the feared object (school) reduced his anxiety. Continued absence served to reduce further the fear and was thus reinforcing. Robert also received a kind of reward for staying away from school – he continued to enjoy his mother's company. In addition, when he did go to school, she visited him. This meant that his phobic behaviour was rewarded.

*The psychoanalytic approach is sometimes referred to as the 'psychodynamic' approach because it is particularly concerned with the dynamics of personality – the factors that drive individuals to behave as they do.*

**KEY TERMS**

**Id:** The irrational, primitive part of personality. It is present at birth, demands immediate satisfaction and is ruled by the *pleasure principle* – an innate drive to seek immediate satisfaction.

**Ego:** The conscious, rational part of the personality. It develops by the end of the infant's first year, as a child interacts with the constraints of reality and thus is governed by the *reality principle*. There are inevitable conflicts with the id.

**Superego:** This develops between the ages of three and six, and embodies our conscience and sense of right and wrong.

**Ego defences:** Unconscious methods, such as repression and displacement, which help the ego deal with feelings of anxiety and thus 'defend' the ego.

# The psychoanalytic approach

Sigmund Freud was the first to challenge the medical model, claiming that mental disorders are caused by psychological rather than physical factors. The essence of the psychoanalytic approach is that much of our behaviour is motivated (driven) by underlying psychological conflicts of which we are largely unaware (i.e. *unconscious* forces). The result is that behaviour can often be explained in terms of deeper, hidden meanings. Psychoanalytic theorists focus mostly on past experiences, notably early parent–child relationships, because they believe that the majority of psychological conflicts are rooted in these relationships.

### Assumption 1: mental disorder results from psychological rather than physical causes
Freud believed that the origins of mental disorders lie in the *unresolved conflicts* of *childhood* which are *unconscious*. Mental illnesses are not the outcome of physical disorder.

### Assumption 2: unresolved conflicts cause mental disorder
Conflicts between the **id**, **ego** and **superego** create anxiety. (NB These three 'personality structures' are not intended to be real things but to represent aspects of self and motivation.) The ego protects itself with various defence mechanisms (**ego defences**). These defences can be the cause of disturbed behaviour. For example, **repression** is the blocking of unpleasant thoughts and placing them in the unconscious. Another defence mechanism is *displacement* (see Little Hans on page 280).

The ego must satisfy the conflicting demands of the id and superego.

**Assumption 3: early experiences cause mental disorder**

In childhood, the ego is not developed enough to deal with traumas and such traumas are therefore repressed. For example, a child may experience the death of a parent early in life and repress associated feelings. Later in life other losses may cause the individual to re-experience the earlier loss, and previously unexpressed anger about the loss is directed inwards towards the self, causing depression.

**Assumption 4: unconscious motivations cause mental disorder**

Freud proposed that the unconscious consists of information that is either very hard or almost impossible to bring into conscious awareness. However, it still exerts a powerful motivating effect on behaviour but one which cannot be controlled until brought into conscious awareness.

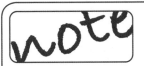

### *The psychoanalytic approach in psychology*

In Chapters 1 and 2 we looked briefly at the psychoanalytic approach – when considering Freud's explanation of attachment and also his explanation for forgetting (repression). A psychoanalytic psychologist explains behaviour in terms of early experience and hidden meanings.

*evaluation* | ## The psychoanalytic approach

*Very influential*

Freud's theory was the first attempt to explain mental illness in psychological terms. It has had an enormous influence on our understanding of normal and abnormal behaviour as well as on literature and the world in general. Much of this understanding has been absorbed into our culture so we are not aware of it.

*Too much emphasis on sex*

Freud was perhaps over concerned with physical (sexual) factors and made little reference to the influence of society (social factors) on development. This may be a reflection of the times during which he lived – when there was much repression of sexual feelings.

*Poor research evidence*

Freud based his theory on his observations of behaviour – but these were largely of middle-class Viennese women suffering from mental disorders. So it is a major leap to apply generalisations derived from this sample to the normal development of children nowadays. Freud's study of Little Hans was his only case history of a child (see pages 280–281), although he did also make careful observations of his own children's development.

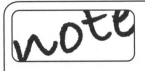

### *Using the psychoanalytic model to explain Robert's school phobia*

According to the psychoanalytic view, Robert may have had a fear of failing and this created anxiety. In order to cope with this anxiety, Robert's feelings about school were repressed and he dealt with this by avoiding the object that created the fear – school. The phobia is the ego's way of not confronting the repressed problem. In addition to this phobia Robert also suffered from separation anxiety which may have developed out of an insecure attachment with his mother. Such insecurity leads a child to feel anxious when separated and the associated anxiety would have been repressed. The method of coping would be to avoid separation. The implications of this are important – simply to try to get Robert to school (dealing with symptoms) would not overcome the real causes, and his anxieties would remain.

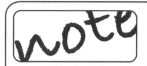

### Case study: Anna O.

Anna O. suffered severe paralysis on her right side as well as nausea and difficulty drinking (Freud, 1910). Freud demonstrated that these physical symptoms actually had a psychological cause. During discussions with her, it became apparent that she developed a fear of drinking when a dog that she hated drank from her glass, and her other symptoms originated when she was caring for her sick father. Anna could not express her anxiety about his illness but did express it later, during psychoanalysis. As soon as she had the opportunity to make these unconscious thoughts conscious, her paralysis disappeared.

## The humanistic approach

Carl Rogers (1959) was the 'founder' of counselling, an example of a humanistic approach to treating mental disorder. Humanistic approaches are a reflection of modern-day society in the same way that both psychoanalysis and behaviourism were in their time. Humanistic psychologists reject behaviourist and psychodynamic perspectives as being reductionist and determinist. They portray individuals as being in control rather than being controlled by external forces. They also feel that other perspectives do not take account of a key element in behaviour – the sense of being the one who is having the experience. The emphasis of the humanistic approach is on the unique qualities of each individual and their capacity to be self-determining and responsible.

### Assumption 1: each individual is unique
What matters is each person's subjective view rather than some objective reality. Humanistic psychologists take a *person-centred* approach and define 'reality' in terms of the individual's perspective rather than the therapist's perspective.

### Assumption 2: human nature is positive and inherently good
Each person strives for growth and **self-actualisation**, an individual's innate tendency to move towards autonomy (i.e. self-determination). Jahoda (1958) included self-actualisation in her list of criteria for mental health (see page 241).

### Assumption 3: personal responsibility
Rogers proposed that taking responsibility for oneself is the route to healthy self-development. As long as an individual remains controlled by other people or other things, they cannot take responsibility for their behaviour and therefore cannot begin to change it. If an individual describes their behaviour in terms of what is 'me' (their self-concept) and what is not 'me', then the 'not me' behaviours remain beyond personal control. For example, if they say, 'I lied but that isn't like me' then they are not 'owning' the lying behaviour and cannot control it. Such attitudes create a sense of discord which leads to maladjustment. Only when an individual takes self-responsibility (self-determination) and admits all behaviours into their self-concept is personal growth possible, resulting in psychological health.

### Assumption 4: Unconditional and conditional love
Personal responsibility and self-actualisation are only possible if an individual has a healthy self-concept and a strong sense of **self-esteem**. This is achieved through **unconditional positive regard** from significant others, which frees an individual from striving for social approval and enables them to construct a healthy self-concept, be able to make choices (self-determination) and seek self-actualisation. Rogers suggested that *conditional love* leads to maladjustment because the self and **ideal self** are in conflict and self-esteem is low.

---

**KEY TERMS**

**Self-esteem:** The feelings that a person has about themselves.

**Unconditional positive regard:** Providing affection and respect without any conditions attached.

**Ideal self:** The person you would like to be.

---

### The humanistic approach in psychology

In the 1950s, a number of psychologists felt that the traditional approaches of behaviourism and psychoanalysis were too deterministic and overlooked the role of free will in human behaviour. A new movement, humanistic psychology, was created as a third force in psychology. *Humanistic psychology* is derived from the wider principles of humanism, a system of belief that explains the world in terms of human rather than divine causes and which emphasises the personal worth of each individual.

*evaluation*

## Evaluation of the humanistic approach

*Culturally relative*
The concept of self-actualisation (and the humanistic approach generally) may be culturally relative. People in **collectivist** societies do not, in general, strive to maximise their own potential but instead strive to maximise the group potential.

*Offers a contrasting approach*
The humanistic approach does offer a counterpoint to other theories of personality and represents a third force in psychology. With the exception of the cognitive approach, all other approaches are *determinist*, whereas the humanistic approach emphasises the importance of free will and personal responsibility. The validity of this approach may be supported by evidence related to the experience of stress. Research shows that the harmful effects of stress are reduced if a person feels more in control. For example, Kim *et al.* (1997) found that children who felt in control showed fewer signs of stress when parents divorced.

*Usefulness*
Client-centred therapy and counselling have become a huge 'industry' underpinning self-help groups and telephone help lines.

### note

**Using the humanistic model to explain Robert's school phobia**
A humanistic psychologist would suggest that Robert may have experienced conditional love from his mother which led to an unrealistic ideal self. His inability to become that 'ideal self' led to conflict which was expressed as a phobia about going to school. This particular phobia might occur because he wanted to stay near his mother in his constant striving to obtain her approval and love. Conditional love is also related to low self-esteem and a lack of a sense of personal control – the phobia might be a way to make him feel that he had some control over his life.

### assessment issues

**Common theme: nature–nurture interaction**

The five approaches to disorder encompassed by this Aspect reflect the main broad perspectives in psychology in general. In other chapters too, you will encounter (or have already encountered) explanations from some of these perspectives (e.g. in Early Socialisation and in Stress). One feature which often distinguishes these approaches is their varying emphasis on nature and nurture – a *common theme* in psychology. In the NABs and exam, you could be asked questions on various approaches and various disorders. One way of analysing different approaches is to *compare* their assumptions regarding innate (nature) and environmental (nurture) factors in disorder. The medical model strongly emphasises biological (including genetic) factors, whereas, to varying degrees, the psychological approaches (cognitive, behaviourist, psychoanalytic and humanistic) place greater importance on environmental influences and their *interaction* with innate influences. The **diathesis-stress model** is a good theoretical example of such interaction.

# Aspect 3: Aetiology of depression, schizophrenia and phobias

*The symptoms of a disorder are referred to as* clinical characteristics. *These symptoms are listed in the manuals used to diagnose mental illness – DSM and ICD (see page 257).*

*Depression is classed as a* mood disorder. *Most people with a mood disorder suffer only from depression (therefore they have* unipolar disorder*) whereas others experience states of mania that alternate with their depression (hence* bipolar disorder*). We have focused on explanations of unipolar disorder (also called 'major depression'). For the sake of simplicity, we refer to this as 'depression'.*

We will now consider explanations of the causes of three common disorders. Several alternative explanations are given for each disorder, drawn from the five approaches discussed in Aspect 2.

## Depression
### What is depression?

Depression is a low emotional state characterised by significant levels of sadness, lack of energy and self-worth, and feelings of guilt (Comer, 2003). Depression ranks first among the top 10 causes of worldwide disability.

The formal diagnosis of depression requires the presence of:

- *sad, depressed mood* – as indicated either by subjective report (feeling sad or empty) or by observation made by others (e.g. appears tearful)
- *loss of interest and pleasure in usual activities* – as indicated either by subjective account or by observation made by others

plus at least three symptoms from the following list: difficulties in sleeping (although some patients desire to sleep all the time); shift in activity level; becoming either lethargic or agitated; poor appetite and weight loss, or increased appetite and weight gain; loss of energy and great fatigue; negative self-concept, feelings of worthlessness and guilt; difficulty in concentrating; recurrent thoughts of death or suicide.

The symptoms must cause significant distress or impairment in general functioning, and not be better accounted for by bereavement (the loss of a loved one). For a diagnosis of depression to be given, these symptoms should be present all or most of the time and should persist for longer than two weeks.

### The aetiology of depression

#### The biological (medical) approach

One possible explanation of the **aetiology** of depression is that depression is inherited. Twin studies illustrate this (see Star Study on page 253) as do family studies and adoption studies. Family studies select people who already have depression (the **probands**), and examine whether other members of their family have been or might be diagnosed with depression. Research has tended to find that around 20% of such relatives have depression compared with a figure of around 10% for the population at large (Harrington *et al.*, 1993). Wender *et al.* (1986) studied the biological relatives of adopted people who had been hospitalised for severe depression. They found a much higher incidence of severe depression in the biological relatives of the depressed group than in the biological relatives of a non-depressed control group. A second biological explanation is that neurotransmitters (such as noradrenaline and serotonin) function abnormally in depressed individuals. For example, *noradrenaline* levels were found to be low in depressed individuals (Bunney and Davis, 1965). Cerebrospinal fluid in depressed patients contains reduced amounts of a major *serotonin* by-product, signifying reduced levels of serotonin in the brain itself (McNeal and Cimbolic, 1986).

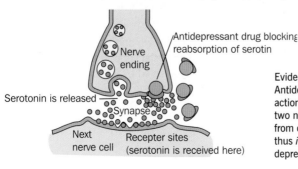

Evidence for the link between serotonin and depression: Antidepressant drugs such as Prozac (fluoxetine) affect the action of serotonin at the nerve endings. The gap between two nerves is called a 'synapse'. When serotonin is released from one nerve, Prozac blocks its re-absorption by this nerve thus *increasing* serotonin activity at the synapse and *reducing* depressive symptoms.

Explanations in terms of neurotransmitters do not necessarily show that such biochemicals *cause* depression; altered levels might be an *effect* of the psychological state. A further issue concerns evidence from the use of antidepressants. It takes several weeks for the effects of antidepressants to be detected despite the fact that serotonin levels are raised immediately. This suggests that serotonin is not a direct cause of depression.

## The cognitive approach

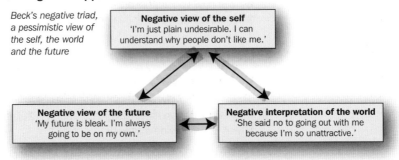

*Beck's negative triad, a pessimistic view of the self, the world and the future*

**Negative view of the self**
'I'm just plain undesirable. I can understand why people don't like me.'

**Negative view of the future**
'My future is bleak. I'm always going to be on my own.'

**Negative interpretation of the world**
'She said no to going out with me because I'm so unattractive.'

One of the best known examples of the cognitive approach is Aaron Beck's explanation of depression. Beck (1976) believed that depressed individuals feel as they do because their thinking is biased towards negative interpretations of the world acquired during childhood. The cause may be a variety of factors, including parental and/or peer rejection, criticisms by teachers, or depressive attitudes of parents. These negative **schemas** (e.g. expecting to fail) are activated whenever the person encounters a new situation (e.g. an examination) that resembles the original conditions (e.g. parental ridicule) in which these schemas were learned. Negative schemas and cognitive biases maintain what Beck calls the *negative triad*, a pessimistic view of the self, the world (not being able to cope with the demands of the environment) and the future.

The theory has led to a successful cognitive therapy and is supported by research that bears out many of Beck's predictions. For example, Hammen and Krantz (1976) found that depressed women made more logical errors when asked to interpret written material than did non-depressed participants. Bates *et al.* (1999) found that depressed participants who were given negative thought-like statements (e.g. 'I'll never complete this work') became more and more depressed.

*explanation*

## The sociocultural approach

Taking the **sociocultural approach**, Brown and Harris (1978) showed that episodes of depression were almost always preceded by a major life event. After studying depressed women in Camberwell, London, Brown and Harris concluded that two circumstances appeared to increase a person's vulnerability to life events. The first of these was the presence of long-term difficulties, such as being in a longstanding difficult relationship. The second was the existence of vulnerability factors, such as having 3 or more children under the age of 14 years, not working outside the home, or the lack of a close, confiding relationship.

Life events may act as triggers in individuals who have a genetic vulnerability for a disorder. Kendler *et al.* (1995) found that the highest levels of depression were found in women who were exposed to recent negative life events (such as an assault or serious marital problems) *and* were most genetically at risk for depression (i.e. the identical co-twin of a woman diagnosed with depression).

One criticism of the research by Brown and Harris is that the sample comprised only women and, since women rely more on social support than men (Frydenberg and Lewis, 1993), they are more likely to be adversely affected by its absence.

> **KEY TERMS**
>
> **Sociocultural approach:** Psychological explanations that stress the role of social and family relationships.

# Investigating aetiology: A biological explanation of depression

(MᴄGᴜꜰꜰɪɴ *ET AL.*, 1996)

## Aims

This study used twins to investigate the contribution of genes and shared family environment to unipolar depression. The basis of twin studies is that identical (or monozygotic, MZ) twins are naturally occurring clones of each other, having all of their genes in common. On the other hand, fraternal (or dizygotic, DZ) twins share just half of their genes. If we assume that the environment shared by twins is roughly the same for both types of twin, then any greater similarity between identical pairs than between fraternal pairs shows the action of genes.

## Method and procedure

The study involved 177 probands with unipolar depression. A proband, in this case, is an individual diagnosed with depression who has a twin as yet undiagnosed with any conditions. The probands were found via the Maudsley Hospital Twin Register (London, England). The twins were assessed genetically to determine whether they were MZ or DZ twins; 68 were MZ twins and 109 were DZ. Both twins were assessed by a psychiatrist for symptoms of depression.

## Results

**Concordance** was 46% in identical and 20% in fraternal twins, a highly significant difference.

## Conclusion

The evidence provides strong support for a genetic component in unipolar depression and suggests that even when individuals are living together it is their genes and not the shared family environment that is creating the illness.

## Evaluation

*Importance of environmental factors*

While genetic relatedness clearly increases the risk of depression, the concordance figures are not very high, even for identical twins, indicating that other factors contribute to the onset of the disorder. The ***diathesis-stress model*** is likely to offer the best explanation.

*Comorbidity*

The low genetic concordance rates for depression may be explained in terms of **comorbidity**. It may be that people inherit a vulnerability for a wider range of disorders, so a twin may not develop depression but may develop a related disorder; genes may predispose individuals to a range of disorders rather than one particular disorder. If this were the case we would expect to see higher concordance when looking at a range of disorders in related individuals. There is some research support for this. For example, Kendler *et al.* (1992) found a higher incidence of mental disorder when looking at depression *and* generalised anxiety disorder in twins rather than depression alone, and concluded that depression and generalised anxiety disorder were influenced by the same genetic factors. This suggests that some disorders, such as depression, are caused by genes that underlie a number of different disorders. The actual symptoms (and disorder) that develop could be related to environmental triggers (the *diathesis-stress model*).

---

**KEY TERMS**

**Comorbidity:** When two or more mental illnesses occur together and perhaps have some common cause.

---

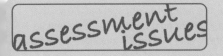

assessment issues

**Discuss the origins of depression, according to *one* approach to disorder. Refer to research evidence in your answer. (*ku* 6 *ae* 4)**

Whichever approach you choose, you can draw on your knowledge of the approach itself, *and* how that approach explains the *specific* disorder of depression. For example, if you decide to write about the *biological (medical model)* approach, you can use information from pages 243–244 and pages 251–252. As you have to 'discuss' the origins, your analysis of the biological approach could include *comparison* with alternative approach(es). For example, you could make a comparison with the *cognitive* approach, in which case you can refer to studies relevant to that approach too, such as Hammen and Krantz (1976) or Bates *et al.* (1999). In order to evaluate the origins of depression, you can highlight the strengths and weaknesses of your explanation(s) and can refer to criticisms of any evidence you use (e.g. McGuffin *et al.*). If you do refer to evidence in this way, don't just state the results (that will get you some *ku* marks); to show *ae* skills you must *interpret* the evidence in relation to the proposed theory or concept.

Movies on mental illness for psychology students. See: home.epix. net/~tcannon1/psychopathmovies/all. html, and Mental Help.net's review of films for teaching about schizophrenia – mentalhelp.net/poc/view_doc. php?type=news&id=37081

# Schizophrenia
## What is schizophrenia?

Schizophrenia is characterised by a profound disruption of thought and emotion, which affects a person's language, perception, affect, and even sense of self. The symptoms of schizophrenia are typically divided into *positive* and *negative* symptoms. Positive symptoms are those that appear to reflect an excess or distortion of normal functions. Negative symptoms are those that appear to reflect a diminution or loss of normal functions, which often persist during periods of low (or absent) positive symptoms.

Positive symptoms include *delusions*, *hallucinations* (e.g. hearing voices, seeing lights, feeling bugs crawling under the skin), *experiences of being controlled* (e.g. by aliens or radio implants) and *disordered thinking* (e.g. feeling that thoughts have been withdrawn from the mind).

Negative symptoms include *affective flattening* (reduction in the range and intensity of emotional expression), *alogia* (poverty of speech), and *avolition* (difficulty in engaging in goal-directed behaviour).

## The aetiology of schizophrenia

### The biological (medical) approach

According to this approach, schizophrenia is either inherited and/or caused by some biological abnormality. Inheritance evidence comes from family, twin and adoption studies. For example, Gottesman (1991) showed that schizophrenia is more common among biological relatives of a person with schizophrenia, and that the closer the degree of genetic relatedness, the greater the risk (see graph).

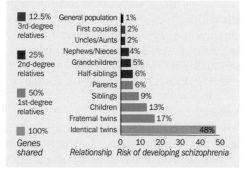

Evidence for biological abnormalities comes from studies of neurotransmitters (such as dopamine) and brain structure. The *dopamine hypothesis* proposes that dopamine levels are excessively high in people with schizophrenia. Dopamine plays a key role in guiding attention, so high levels may well lead to the problems of attention, perception and thought found in those with schizophrenia (Comer, 2003).

Using brain-imaging techniques, researchers have discovered that many people with schizophrenia have enlarged brain ventricles, the cavities in the brain that contain nutrients for the brain. On average, the ventricles of a person with schizophrenia are about 15% bigger than normal (Torrey, 2002).

The dopamine hypothesis is supported by evidence for the action of antipsychotic drugs that block dopamine production at nerve endings and reduce attentional deficits found in people with schizophrenia. However, antipsychotic drugs are only effective for the positive symptoms of the disorder. This means that, at best, excessive dopamine can only explain *some* types of schizophrenia. Also people with schizophrenia are not the only ones who respond to antipsychotic medication. This suggests that dopamine abnormalities are not specifically related to symptoms of schizophrenia but may be a generic symptom of all disorders.

### The behaviourist approach

Behaviourists have attempted to explain the symptoms of schizophrenia as being the consequences of faulty learning (e.g. Liberman, 1982). If a child receives little or no social reinforcement early on in life (e.g. because of parental disinterest), then instead of focusing on social stimuli in the normal way, they will attend to inappropriate and irrelevant environmental cues (e.g. the sound of a word rather than its meaning or the brightness of light in a room). As a result, their verbal and other behavioural responses will eventually appear somewhat bizarre. Those who observe the child's behaviour will either avoid it or respond erratically. This will reinforce the bizarre behaviours, and, eventually, the child will deteriorate into a schizophrenic state.

The validity of behavioural explanations has some support from the success of behavioural therapies used with patients with schizophrenia. For example, social skills training techniques have been used to help them acquire useful social skills (e.g. Scott and Dixon, 1995). The fact that such programmes can be successful in reintegrating people with schizophrenia back into the community suggests that these are skills that they failed to learn in the first place.

**The humanistic approach**
Double bind theory (Bateson et al., 1956) suggests that children who frequently receive contradictory messages from their parents are more likely to develop schizophrenia. For example, if a mother tells her son that she loves him yet at the same time turns her head away in disgust, the child receives two conflicting messages about their relationship on different communicative levels, one of affection on the verbal level, and one of animosity on the non-verbal level. Bateson et al. argued that the child's ability to respond to the mother is incapacitated by such contradictions because one message effectively invalidates the other. Prolonged exposure to such interactions prevents the development of an internally coherent construction of reality and, in the long run, this manifests itself as typically schizophrenic symptoms, such as flattened affect, delusions and hallucinations, and incoherent thinking and speaking.

There is some evidence to support this particular account of how family relationships may lead to schizophrenia. Berger (1965) found that people with schizophrenia reported a higher recall of double bind statements by their mothers than people without schizophrenia. However, this evidence may not be reliable as patients' recall may be affected by their schizophrenia. Other studies are less supportive. Liem (1974) measured patterns of parental communication in families with a child with schizophrenia and found no difference when the patterns were compared with those of normal families. Hall and Levin (1980) analysed data from a number of previous studies and found no difference between families with and without a member with schizophrenia in the degree to which verbal and non-verbal communication were in agreement.

# Phobias
## What are phobias?

*All of the explanations presented in this Aspect can be evaluated in the ways suggested in Aspect 2 where we gave general evaluations of each approach.*

A fear becomes a phobia when it interferes with normal functioning. A phobic disorder involves extreme persistent and irrational fear together with lack of control, which is strongly out of proportion to the danger.

Three categories of phobias are distinguished by DSM-IV:

- *Agoraphobia*. Fear of open spaces or public places: about 50% of all people clinically diagnosed with a phobia are suffering from agoraphobia with panic disorder. In most cases, the panic disorder starts first; fear of having another attack leads to agoraphobia because the individual feels insecure about being in public due to the panic disorder.

- *Social phobias*. The person exhibits extreme concern about their own behaviour and the reactions of others, for example, fears about talking or eating in public.

- *Specific phobias*. Specific phobias, such as zoophobias (fear of animals), fear of water, heights, etc., generally have little impact on overall quality of life.

## The aetiology of phobias
### The biological (medical) approach
One explanation is that phobias are inherited. Torgersen (1983) compared 32 identical twins with 53 fraternal adult same-sexed twins, where one twin (the **proband**) had a diagnosed disorder. Anxiety disorders with panic attacks were five times more frequent among the identical twins than in the fraternal twins.

A second biological explanation is that people with a phobia have some biological difference, which may or may not be inherited: for example, they might have generally higher levels of physiological arousal which makes them more sensitive to their external environment. Such higher arousal levels may not be inherited.

There is a third, rather different biological explanation – *biological preparedness*. Seligman (1971) proposed that people have an innate predisposition to develop certain 'ancient' fears because these things posed a real threat to our ancestors, for example snakes, heights, storms, darkness, strangers, separation and leaving the home range.

Kendler *et al*. (1992) concluded that specific phobias have a relatively small genetic component whereas agoraphobia appears to be more related to genetic vulnerability. Both involve additional exposure to negative environmental influences (the *diathesis-stress model*).

Biological preparedness can explain the fact that some phobias are more common than others, such as snakes rather than slugs, tigers rather than motor cars (even though cars pose a real threat today). However, this concept may apply to everyday fears rather than to clinical phobias.

### The behaviourist approach

Mowrer (1947) proposed the *two-process theory* that learning phobias involves classical plus operant conditioning. Classical conditioning is described in the case study of Little Albert (see next page); fear is an unconditioned response to certain things such as a loud noise (unconditioned stimulus). If noise is associated with a conditioned stimulus such as a furry rabbit, then eventually the rabbit too may elicit a fear response. In a second stage, operant conditioning occurs. The avoidance of the phobic stimulus reduces fear and is thus reinforcing (**negative reinforcement**). In future, then, a person can avoid the fear associated with an object or situation by avoiding it completely.

Social learning theory can also be used to explain the acquisition of phobias – we model our behaviour on others. If we observe some people (especially parents or important others) avoiding certain objects, we may imitate this if it appears to be rewarding.

Some phobias may be learned in this way but it doesn't explain why, for example, many people who are bitten by dogs don't go on to develop phobias about dogs (DiNardo *et al*., 1988), so learning theory is unlikely to be a total explanation of mental disorder. In addition, we should point out that people don't tend to develop fear of some objects (such as electrical sockets), which suggests that we are biologically 'prepared' to fear certain things which may have *once* been dangerous (see above).

On the other hand, the success of behavioural therapies suggests that behaviour can be 'unlearned', supporting the claim that it has been acquired through such learning in the first place.

### The psychoanalytic approach

Freud (1909) suggested that phobias arise when a person experiences anxieties and unconsciously deals with them through repression. Feelings that are repressed are expressed elsewhere, in this case by attaching the anxiety to other objects or people. Thus a phobia develops. If the original conflict is resolved, the phobia will disappear. This is illustrated in the case study of Little Hans (see page 280).

One problem with Freudian explanations generally is that they lack *falsifiability*, i.e. it is impossible either to prove or disprove them. Ideally, we should be able to test any explanation to see if it is valid. As it stands, we cannot be sure that, for example, Hans' phobia was due to repressed anxieties or whether, alternatively, it was the result of classical conditioning – the accident with a horse made him experience fear which then became associated with horses.

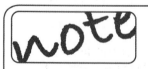

### Little Albert

John B. Watson and Rosalie Rayner (1920) sought to provide experimental evidence that emotion could be learned through classical conditioning (mentioned on page 3). They worked with an 11-month-old boy called 'Little Albert' (not to be confused with Little Hans!). They first tested Albert's responses to white, fluffy objects: a white rat, a rabbit, and white cotton wool. He initially showed no fear response to these.

Next they set about creating a conditioned response to these previously neutral objects. To do this they used a steel bar that was four feet long. When Albert reached out for the rat they struck the bar with a hammer behind his head to startle him. They repeated this three times and then repeated the procedure a week later. After this, whenever they showed the rat to Albert, he began to cry. Watson and Rayner had created a fear response in Little Albert using classical conditioning.

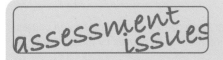

**Describe and evaluate the behaviourist approach to explaining the causes of phobias. (*ku 6 ae 4*)**

Why do teachers tell students (again and again!) 'Read the question VERY CAREFULLY'? Surely this is obvious? Well yes, but many students still lose many marks through failing to follow this obviously sensible advice. How can you avoid this pitfall? Take a close look at this question, and break it down into its component parts. First, what it's *about*: (1) the behaviourist approach, (2) phobias and, in particular, (3) the causes of phobias. Then, what you have to *do*: (1) describe and (2) evaluate.

Once you have identified each component in turn like this, you can start to put your knowledge of these together to construct your answer. Some teachers call this *deconstructing* or *dissecting* a question. By using this systematic strategy, you are far less likely to include irrelevant material (e.g. explaining causes of disorders other than phobias) or forget to evaluate. Deconstructing a question in this way is a good basis for creating a *plan* of your answer before you start.

# Aspect 4:  Classification systems

## What are classification systems?

**Classification scheme:** A set of diagnostic criteria that allows a diagnosis to be made. There are classification schemes for physical and mental disorders (as well as for other things).

**DSM:** The classification system produced by the American Psychiatric Association and predominantly used in the US and Canada.

**ICD:** A classification system produced by the World Health Organisation which includes physical as well as mental diseases. This is used worldwide.

The medical approach to understanding mental illness assumes that psychological disorders are the same as physical illnesses – they are disease states that have a common cluster of symptoms. A condition can be diagnosed by identifying presenting symptoms and matching these to possible illnesses. For example, if you have an itchy rash, small red spots that develop into blisters and a temperature, it is likely that you have chicken pox. In the same way, a psychiatrist would diagnose depression if a patient displayed the clinical characteristics listed on page 251. The main reason for doing this is to provide appropriate treatments. **Classification schemes** are also important for conducting research on the causes of specific disorders.

The first classification scheme for mental illnesses was developed by Emil Kraepelin (1856–1926). Today, there are two main classification schemes in use – **DSM** and **ICD**. Such systems are under constant revision and are given numbers. The versions in current use are DSM-IV-TR and ICD-10, reflecting their revision number. Recent revisions have aimed to make DSM and ICD more similar. These classification systems are described on the next page, followed by an evaluation in terms of their **reliability** and **validity**.

## A description of ICD and DSM

A comparison of ICD and DSM

| | ICD-10 (1992) | DSM-IV (1994) DSM-IV-TR (2000) |
|---|---|---|
| **Full title** | International Statistical Classification of Diseases and Related Health Problems | Diagnostic and Statistical Manual of Mental Disorders |
| **Designed** | For *statistical* data collection about physical and psychological diseases | As a *diagnostic* tool, to identify clusters of symptoms and match them to clinical characteristics of mental disorders |
| **Basis of classification scheme** | Some recognition of possible causes, e.g. organic disorders are one category | No assumption is made about causes, categories are entirely descriptive |

## ICD-10

ICD lists 11 major categories of mental disorder. Within these categories, information on causes (aetiology) is included. This is to satisfy the desire for information on causes by those treating or researching illnesses. The categories are:

- organic disorders (e.g. Alzheimer's)
- schizophrenia, schizotypal and delusional disorders
- mental and behaviour disorders due to psychoactive substance use
- mood (affective) disorders
- neurotic disorders (e.g. phobias), stress-related and somatoform disorders
- behavioural and emotional disorders of childhood and adolescence (e.g. attention deficit disorder)
- disorders of psychological development (e.g. autism)
- mental retardation
- disorders of adult personality (e.g. gender disorders, gambling)
- behavioural syndromes associated with physiological disturbances and physical factors (e.g. eating and sleep disorders)
- unspecified mental disorder.

*You do not need to memorise the whole list of categories – just remember a few to use as examples.*

## DSM-IV-TR

The disorders identified in DSM are defined by descriptive and observable symptoms rather than by those features that are believed to cause each disorder. DSM is a multi-axial system; i.e. there are five separate criteria or axes. Each patient is evaluated on each of the five axes below:

Axis 1: *Clinical disorder diagnosed*. This includes all major disorders, for example eating disorders, schizophrenia, depression, phobias, and dissociative disorders.

Axis 2: *Personality disorders and mental retardation*. A patient may have long-term patterns of impaired functioning, e.g. antisocial personality disorder.

Axis 3: *General medical conditions*. These are conditions (e.g. diabetes or Alzheimer's) that might explain mentally disordered behaviour.

Axis 4: *Psychosocial and environmental problems*. Any significant stressful events in the last 12 months are taken into consideration.

*DSM has 16 categories of mental illness which are listed in Axis 1 (compared with 11 in ICD).*

Axis 5: *Global assessment of functioning* (GAF) on a 100-point scale. This assesses the person's ability to cope with the demands of everyday life.

The use of axes 4 and 5 is not compulsory; they refer more to the social functioning of a patient.

### An example of using DSM-IV

Mark is a 56-year-old machine operator. His supervisor noted that Mark had become frequently absent from work, had difficulty getting along with others and often had a strong odour of alcohol on his breath after his lunch break. Although Mark had been a heavy drinker for 30 years, his consumption had increased after his wife had divorced him six months ago. She claimed she could no longer tolerate his drinking, extreme jealousy, and unwarranted suspicions concerning her marital fidelity. Co-workers avoided Mark because he was a cold, unemotional person who distrusted others.

During interviews with the therapist, Mark revealed very little about himself. He blamed others for his drinking problems: if his wife had been faithful or if others were not out to get him, he would drink less. Mark appeared to overreact to any perceived criticisms of himself.

*The evaluation*: Mark's heavy use of alcohol, which interfered with his functioning, resulted in an alcohol abuse diagnosis on Axis I. Mark also exhibited a personality disorder, which was diagnosed as paranoid personality on Axis 2 because of his suspiciousness, hypervigilance, and other behaviours. Cirrhosis of the liver was noted on Axis 3. The clinical psychologist noted Mark's divorce and difficulties in his job on Axis 4. Mark was given 54 on the Global Assessment of Functioning scale (GAF), used in Axis 5 to rate his current level of functioning, mainly because he was experiencing difficulty at work and in his social relationships.

(Adapted from Sue *et al.*, 1994, p.124)

# Reliability and validity of classification systems

The major issue with classification schemes is 'how meaningful are they?' If a diagnosis varies each time a classification system is used then the system can be said to lack **reliability**. If a classification category doesn't represent something real and discrete (i.e. there should not be 'fuzzy' boundaries between one disorder and another disorder), and the diagnosis does not lead to a specific therapy, then it can be said to lack **validity**. In this section we will consider ways to assess the reliability and validity of classification schemes. We first consider a landmark study by Rosenhan that challenged the reliability, validity and usefulness of classification and diagnosis.

**starSTUDY**

## Investigating classification systems: Being sane in insane places

(ROSENHAN, 1973)

# Study 1

## Aims
'If sanity and insanity exist, how shall we know them?' Rosenhan was interested in the question of whether the diagnosis of insanity is based on characteristics of patients themselves or whether it is based on the context in which a patient is seen.

## Method and procedure
Rosenhan arranged for 'pseudopatients' (people who were actually 'normal') to seek admission to various mental hospitals in the US. There were eight adults involved (including Rosenhan himself). They each contacted a hospital and asked for an appointment at which they reported that they were hearing voices. Apart from the voices, all their other self-descriptions were true and normal. Once admitted, they were told by Rosenhan to follow the ward routine and keep notes about their environment. The only way they would be released would be to be judged as recovered so they tried to behave as normally as possible.

## Results
All pseudopatients were admitted and all bar one were diagnosed as schizophrenic. The length of hospitalisation varied from 7 to 52 days, with an average of 19 days. When they were discharged, it was with a diagnosis of 'schizophrenia in remission' (i.e. symptoms not present at the moment).

## Conclusion
As the pseudopatients were never detected, this study suggests that the psychiatric diagnosis of 'abnormality' has less to do with the patient and more to do with the (insane) environment in which they are found. The failure to detect sanity may be because doctors have a stronger bias towards calling a healthy person sick than a sick person healthy.

# Study 2

## Aims
To see if the tendency toward diagnosing the sane as insane could be reversed.

## Method and procedure
Staff in one psychiatric hospital were informed of the results of the first study and told that at some time during the next three months, one or more pseudopatients would seek admission to the hospital. Each member of staff was asked to rate all patients who sought admission using a 10-point scale where 1 reflected high confidence that the patient was a pseudopatient.

## Results
Over the 3 months, 193 patients were admitted for treatment. None of them was actually a pseudopatient, but 41 were judged to be pseudopatients by at least 1 staff member, and 23 were suspected by at least 1 psychiatrist.

## Conclusion
This second part of the study suggests that psychiatric diagnoses are unreliable.

## Evaluation
*Ecological validity*
To what extent can we generalise these findings to the real world? One problem is that, in the real world, psychiatrists wouldn't expect that someone might be pretending and they would

therefore assume that anyone seeking admission must have a good reason to do so. This would explain their willingness to commit a patient on flimsy evidence and challenges the conclusion that 'real-life' diagnosis is unreliable.

*Lack of objectivity*

This study could be described as a **participant observation**. This is not a highly objective method because observations are influenced by the fact that the observers are also part of the study. Rosenhan was interested in the interactions between staff and patients, but the record kept by pseudopatients may be unreliable because they were being treated as patients and this may have affected their views on the behaviour of the psychiatric staff.

# Reliability

If a classification system is reliable, a diagnosis based on the system should be the same (consistent) when repeated. This can be demonstrated by *inter-rater reliability* – comparing the diagnoses made by two or more *clinicians* (psychologists or psychiatrists) when independently assessing a patient. If the system is reliable, they should agree. It can also be assessed using **test–retest reliability** – the same clinician assesses the same information at different times. These forms of reliability can be measured quantitatively and expressed as a **correlation coefficient**.

## ICD

Early versions of ICD were regarded as unreliable, but ICD-10 (the most recent version) is claimed to show good reliability. However, Nilsson *et al.* (2000) still reported low inter-rater reliability (just under 60% agreement between clinicians, or a correlation of +0.60).

## DSM

Early studies of DSM found low inter-rater reliability (e.g. Spitzer and Fleiss, 1974) and low test–retest reliability (e.g. Beck, 1962). Much of this unreliability was attributed to lack of clarity over which symptoms belonged to which categories. DSM-IV is probably more reliable than ICD-10 because of greater symptom specificity. Recent revisions of DSM have claimed to improve symptom specificity and reliability; for example, Cunningham-Williams *et al.* (2006) found good reliability for pathological gambling disorder.

# Validity

Validity concerns whether a person has been given the 'right' diagnosis, i.e. the diagnosis is of their 'real' condition; and that classificatory systems measure what they claim to measure. This can be established in different ways; a few are described below.

## Aetiological validity

The disorder should have the same cause in all patients who have the disorder. As we saw on page 254, there may be different kinds of schizophrenia and therefore the current classification lacks validity.

## Descriptive validity

Patients in different diagnostic categories should differ from each other; i.e. their symptoms should be different. This tends to be poor: for example Eysenck (1997) reports that patients with an anxiety disorder are also frequently diagnosed with one or more other anxiety disorders.

Descriptive validity is reduced by *comorbidity* – patients often have two or more disorders, e.g. a patient with anorexia often also has symptoms of depression.

## Predictive validity

Predictive validity concerns the extent to which a diagnosis leads to a predictable course of a disease. Lahey *et al.* (2006) compared predictive validity for ICD and DSM in the diagnosis of attention disorders in young children. The study compared the ICD category of hyperkinetic disorder (HKD) with the DSM category of attention deficit/hyperactivity disorder (ADHD). All children who met the ICD criteria for HKD met the DSM criteria for ADHD but only 26% of those diagnosed as ADHD met the criteria for HKD. Six years later all of the ADHD children displayed more social and academic impairment than a control group but the same was not true of the ICD children, suggesting higher predictive validity for DSM.

Predictive validity can also be demonstrated by the success of therapies; in other words, if a diagnosis of depression leads to its successful treatment then this confirms that the original diagnosis was correct. The problem is that psychological disorders do not, in general, have specific causes and all therapies assume a specific cause. Therefore, their lack of success may be due to this rather than to the diagnosis. It is also difficult to assess the success of therapies because of the range of factors that affect success (such as individual differences in drug susceptibility).

## Gender, cultural and ethnic biases

### Gender bias

There are significant differences in the rates of diagnosis for men and women for certain disorders. For example, women are more likely to be diagnosed with depression and specific phobias whereas men are more likely to be diagnosed with alcohol abuse or anti-social conduct (Robins *et al.*, 1984). Some of these differences may be real but they may also be due to biased diagnoses. Flanagan and Blashfield (2003) found that the same description of an individual was likely to be rated as histrionic if the individual was female. Worrell and Remer (1992) suggested that bias may be due to traditional sex stereotypes which mean, for instance, that clinicians are more likely to interpret women's behaviours as hysterical or submissive.

### Cultural bias

Cultural bias may be shown in the way classification schemes are constructed. In Aspect 1 of this chapter we looked at the problem of *cultural relativity* – definitions of abnormality tend to be rooted in cultural beliefs and vary between cultures and within the same culture at different historical times. In the past, homosexuality was included as a disorder in the classification systems but changing cultural attitudes led this to alter. Currently, there are many so-called 'culture-bound syndromes' which are not fully represented in classification schemes. (These include *koro*, an anxiety disorder found almost exclusively in Asia which is based on the fear that a person's penis or labia will retract into their body.) This means that classification schemes are inevitably culturally biased.

Cultural bias may also be shown in the way that classification schemes are used to diagnose mental illness. This may apply to *ethnic* groups (see below) or to *social class* groups. For example, people of lower social classes are much more likely to receive a diagnosis of schizophrenia (Barlow and Durand, 1995). Such a bias may be due to a real difference (e.g. the more stressful life circumstances of people in poverty may make them more vulnerable to mental illness, the *social causation hypothesis*) or because clinicians have biased perceptions of lower-class individuals.

### Ethnic bias

Another example of cultural bias is the bias against particular ethnic groups (cultural groups who share a common ancestry). Members of ethnic groups may be identified as ill when they exhibit behaviours that are normal within their own culture (e.g. hearing voices). Cochrane and Sashidharan (1995) report that black African-Caribbean immigrants in the UK are up to seven times more likely than white people to receive a diagnosis of schizophrenia. This high incidence of mental illness could be explained in terms of stress (immigrants experience greater stress than natives, e.g. because of prejudice); however, the fact that Asians are diagnosed at about the same rate as whites suggests that high African-Caribbean diagnosis rates are due to specific cultural biases. This view is further supported by Blake (1973) who found that, when clinicians were given a case study, they were more likely to diagnose schizophrenia if the individual was described as African-American.

Research studies suggest that some individuals are more likely to be diagnosed as mentally ill than others. For example, women are more likely to be diagnosed than men and black African-Caribbean immigrants are more likely to be diagnosed as schizophrenic than white people. Are such differences real or are they due to prejudices?

*evaluation*

## The reliability and validity of classification systems

*Strengths of ICD and DSM*

Classification systems are useful. They enable clinicians to communicate effectively, to provide appropriate therapies that have some degree of success, to predict the future course of the disorder, and to conduct research in psychological illnesses.

Both ICD and DSM are continually updated, so reliability and validity are always improving.

*Limitations of ICD and DSM*
*Labelling*
Providing a label for a collection of symptoms creates an illusion of causation and cure. Classification of mental illness is regarded by some as a 'pseudoscience' – a technique parading as a scientific process. The particular problem with labelling mental illness is that such labels tend to be global and enduring, and possibly self-fulfilling – a person becomes a 'schizophrenic' rather than an 'individual with schizophrenia'.

*Is mental classification any worse than physical classification?*
Symptoms of mental illness are often subjective, unlike the symptoms of physical illness which can be diagnosed using objective medical tests. However, Falek and Moser (1975) found that inter-doctor reliability when diagnosing physical disorders such as tonsillitis (without using laboratory tests) was no better than for schizophrenia.

*Alternative classification schemes*
ICD and DSM are not the only classification schemes. Other classification schemes are in use in other countries. For example, the Chinese Classification of Mental Disorders (CCMD-III) contains 10 categories fairly similar to those in ICD, but there are also culturally distinctive categories and it does exclude behaviours not found in China, such as pathological gambling.

ICD and DSM describe disease states with a unique set of symptoms and causes. Goldfried and Davison (1976) developed a classification system related to the behaviourist approach which focuses on behaviours only. Following the study described on page 259, Rosenhan recommended that one solution to the problem of unreliable diagnosis would be to rely more on behavioural symptoms and less on labels.

Finally, DSM and ICD are *nomothetic* systems, based on generalisations about people. Some clinicians use a more *idiographic* approach where each patient is treated as a unique case. This approach makes it hard to develop an understanding of the causes of mental disorder but Szasz (1960), in his book *The Myth of Mental Illness*, argued that this is not necessary in order to treat mental illness. It is sufficient to regard these disorders as 'problems in living'.

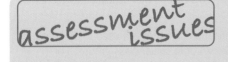
assessment issues

**Explain what is meant by "validity" of a classification system, and assess the validity of the ICD and the DSM classification systems. (*ku* 4 *ae* 4)**

Clearly this is a question of two halves. The marks are split equally between knowledge/understanding skills (*ku*) for the *explain* part, and analysis/evaluation skills (*ae*) for the *assess* part. Validity, and its close associate, reliability, are quite abstract concepts. The fact that they have some similar features and are often inextricably linked doesn't make it any easier to explain them! There is no quick fix to coping with the challenge of learning and writing about these concepts. But if you spend time learning and testing yourself on the *terminology* and writing *practice answers*, you'll be halfway there. To make the task more manageable, try dividing the question above into its two parts and answer each one separately. Then do the same again, substituting *reliability* for *validity*!

*In this section we show you student answers to possible exam questions plus examiner's comments on these answers. Remember that in the actual exam (and NABs) your questions for this Topic will always add up to 20 marks. The question may be one essay worth 20 marks or a number of smaller questions (such as those shown below) which add up to 20 marks.*

**Question 1**    Consider how cultural bias may arise, in the diagnosis of psychological disorder. (*ku* 3 *ae* 3)

### Tom

One way to diagnose psychological disorders is the social norms model. According to this model abnormality is defined as deviating from social norms. Social norms are standards that any society has about what counts as acceptable behaviour. To be rude or bullying is antisocial behaviour and not normal.

This approach to diagnosis is culturally biased because abnormality is defined by what the society thinks is 'right'. In some societies it might be regarded as OK to behave aggressively but if those people came to this country they might be diagnosed as mentally ill.

There are other ways to define abnormality e.g. in terms of what is usual behaviour for people in that culture. This is a statistical norm. This is again culturally relative because some behaviours are statistically normal in one culture but not another. For example having hallucinations is normal in some cultures. In this country if you said you were having hallucinations you might be diagnosed as mentally ill.

### Alice

There are two classification schemes that are used – the ICD and the DSM (currently revisions 10 and IV respectively). These schemes are culture-biased because the symptoms that are included are those that are shown by Western people. The classification schemes used to include homosexuality as a mental disorder but as our culture's attitudes towards homosexuality have changed, this has now been left out. There are also some disorders which are called 'culture-bound'. These are disorders that appear in one culture but not another, such as koro, which is not in our classification scheme and would not be diagnosed here but it is a recognised syndrome in some parts of the world.

Cultural bias may also be shown in the way that people from lower social classes are more likely to be diagnosed as mentally ill. It is possible that this happens because people from lower social classes are more likely to be mentally ill because they have more stressful lives. In which case this is not a cultural bias but a reality. On the other hand it may be because clinicians have biased perceptions of lower class people and more readily label them as mentally ill.

Ethnic groups are also biased against in diagnosis. In one study it was found that African-Caribbeans were seven times more likely to be diagnosed with schizophrenia as white people.

**Examiner's comments**    Tom has made a poor decision in tackling the question in terms of definitions, rather than focusing on diagnosis, as specified in the question. Perhaps he spotted the term 'cultural bias' and missed the word 'diagnosis'. The most useful material to use here is the information on classification systems. Unfortunately Tom has not mentioned these, but he gains some marks for his relevant examples of behaviours and his analysis of cultural relativity in relation to these, i.e. that they might be seen as normal in one culture but diagnosed as abnormal in another. He gains **3 out of 6 marks** (*ku* 2/3 *ae* 1/3).

Alice has gone straight to the point by stating that the classification systems, ICD and DSM, are used for the purposes of diagnosis of psychological disorder – so she has accurately identified the main point of the question right away, and addressed it. She then criticises the systems as culturally biased. Her criticism would be more meaningful if she had first provided a little detail on the structure of the systems, to put her evaluative points into context. Although she gives appropriate examples of disorders that are subject to cultural bias, she has not organised them well, as she starts by identifying *Western* culture, then gives an example of variation in classification over *time* within a culture (homosexuality), then goes back to an example that contrasts Western with other cultures (koro). She refers to evidence, but gives no names or dates. In spite of these faults, overall she provides enough evidence of understanding to merit full marks: **6 out of 6 marks** (*ku* 3/3 *ae* 3/3).

**Question 2**    Describe the cognitive approach to explaining the causes of depression, and compare it with *one* other explanation of this disorder. (*ku* 6 *ae* 4)

### Tom

The cognitive approach to abnormality suggests that it is the way that a person thinks which is the problem. People who have psychological disorders think in a faulty way which means that any treatment should focus on changing the way that you think about your problem. Cognitive therapy has been used for people who are depressed. In fact there are a number of different therapies that all believe that depression occurs because you have a depressive way of looking at the world. Beck's theory is one example. He said there was a depressive triad.

One of the limitations of this model is that it really only works for people who

can think and talk about their disorder. A good point is that cognitive therapies can be relatively quick and they can lead you to cope better in the future because you develop strategies for dealing with problems.

You can compare this approach with the humanistic view which says that people get depressed because they have not had proper love in childhood so they have low self-esteem. They are desperate to be liked. Upsetting life events like marital problems or having no close friend can cause depression (Brown and Harris 1978). The humanistic approach is quite similar to the cognitive approach as it also claims childhood experiences make you think or feel in negative ways about yourself. Both approaches are not as deterministic as others.

*Examiner's comments*    Tom evidently has a basic understanding of the two approaches he has written about. One feature that stands out from his answer is the lack of appropriate terminology (e.g. he could use 'high need for social approval' instead of 'desperate to be liked'; 'unconditional love' instead of 'proper love'). Another improvement would have been to give examples of negative thoughts for the cognitive approach. He has also become side-tracked into writing about therapies: material on therapies *can* be used appropriately in this kind of question, as long as it is pointed out that success in therapy can be interpreted as support for the explanation of *origins* of disorder. However, Tom has not done this. Nevertheless, he has addressed the question, including attempts to *compare* the two approaches, as required (for *ae* marks). He gains **5 out of 10 marks** (*ku* 3/6 *ae* 2/4).

## Alice

Beck (1976) explained depression using the cognitive approach. He suggested that depressed people acquire a negative view of the world when they are children. They learn this from people around them such as their parents and teachers. It might be that these other people were very critical or they may have had a depressive style of thinking themselves. Beck suggests that depressed people have a negative triad – a negative view of the world, themselves and the future. Their inbuilt expectation of failure is aroused every time they meet a new situation that resembles their earlier experiences of failure.

You can compare this with the medical model which seeks to explain depression in terms of there being something physically wrong with you. One explanation is that it is an imbalance of the neurotransmitters serotonin and noradrenaline. The evidence for this is that depressed people have lower levels of both of these than normal people and also that drugs which increase levels of serotonin are effective in treating depression. Another biological explanation is that depression is something you inherit, which could be linked to neurotransmitters because what you would inherit would be low levels of the neurotransmitters. Evidence comes from twin studies which show that identical twins are more likely to both experience depression than fraternal twins (McGuffin et al., 1996).

One criticism of the medical model is that low levels of neurotransmitters may not actually cause depression but may be a side effect of being depressed. Psychological states can create changes in neurotransmitters which could then be treated by antidepressants. Another criticism is that it can't be the whole explanation because concordance rates between identical twins are never 100%. The diathesis-stress model probably offers the best explanation, which is that some people are born with a predisposition to become clinically depressed but they only get depressed if there are certain stressors in their life which could include having negative experiences in childhood.

*Examiner's comments*    Alice has provided good descriptions of both the cognitive and medical models in relation to depression. Again, some examples would enhance the material on the cognitive approach. On the other hand, she has explained concepts clearly and referred to evidence for both approaches, so she gains all 6 *ku* marks. Alice gives a detailed evaluation of the medical model in her second and third paragraphs, but she seems to have forgotten that the focus here should be to *compare* the two approaches. Alice achieves **8 out of 10 marks** (*ku* 6/6 *ae* 2/4).

## Question 3    Describe and evaluate *one* definition of atypical behaviour. (*ku* 2 *ae* 2)

### Tom

One definition is the statistical model. This model suggests that anything is abnormal if it occurs infrequently in the population. Measles and depression are abnormal because they don't occur often.

The problem with this definition is that some things that are abnormal are actually desirable, such as being a genius, whereas some things which are abnormal, according to this definition, are not desirable, such as divorce. Another problem is that this definition is culturally biased because the norms from one society may then be used to evaluate what is normal or abnormal in another society. For example hearing voices might be statistically uncommon in the UK and thus a sign of abnormality whereas it is common in some other cultures and shouldn't be a sign of abnormality.

### Alice

One way to define atypical behaviour is 'failure to function adequately'. This definition states that atypical behaviour is behaviour that makes it difficult for an individual to cope with the pressures and tasks of day-to-day living. This definition explains atypical behaviour from the individual's perspective instead of using some external standard. Just because you don't behave the same way as someone else may make you unusual but shouldn't necessarily be a cause for concern. Whereas treatment is required if a condition makes it difficult for a person to function normally.

The important strength of this definition is that it deals with atypical behaviour from the patient's view. However this has a down side because someone may feel they are coping fine and don't need any help but might be a threat to society. There is also the question of who judges whether a person is coping.

*Examiner's comments*    Tom's *evaluation* material is sound, so he gains both *ae* marks. However, his description of the statistical infrequency definition is weak (maybe he thought it was too obvious to bother writing very much); this is a pity as he appears to be knowledgeable on the topic. Still, he gets **3 out of 4 marks** (*ku* 1/2 *ae* 2/2).

Alice's answer has some weaknesses: an example of inability to cope with day-to-day living would have been useful, and she could have expanded the point that she hints at briefly in her last sentence to make it clearer. However, overall her explanations are sound, so she gains the full **4 marks** (*ku* 2/2 *ae* 2/2).

Individual differences are those aspects of each of us that distinguish us from others, such as personality and intelligence. Each of us also differs in the extent to which we are 'normal'. For the most part, deviation from normal is not a problem, but in some circumstances it is.

Atypical behaviour refers to behaviour that is not usual or typical and may be psychologically unhealthy. Psychologists prefer to use the term 'atypical' rather than 'abnormal' because of the negative perceptions that go with the term 'abnormal'. Therapies are methods of treatment; the term 'psychotherapy' is used to refer to treatments which employ psychological rather than physical techniques. Physical or 'somatic' therapies are also used to treat psychological disorders, using methods similar to those used in treating physical disorders.

| Chapter contents | Unit content for the topic 'Atypical behaviour – therapies' | Comment |
|---|---|---|
| **Aspect 1: Therapeutic approaches** | | |
| Somatic therapies page 266 Psychological approaches page 269 | • Somatic therapies based on the medical model <br> • Psychological approaches, including: <br> –cognitive-behavioural therapies <br> –behaviourist therapies <br> –psychoanalytic therapies <br> –humanistic therapies | *People with mental disorder may be treated in a variety of ways, depending on the approach(es) adopted by the practitioner (whether psychologist or psychiatrist, therapist or counsellor). Here you will study a range of therapeutic approaches, including* **somatic** *(physical) treatments such as drugs, and* **psychological** *treatments from* **cognitive-behavioural, behaviourist, psychoanalytic** *and* **humanistic** *approaches. You should be able to compare and evaluate these approaches.* |
| **Aspect 2: Therapeutic approaches in specific disorders** | | |
| Treating depression page 275 Treating schizophrenia page 277 Treating phobias page 279 | Therapeutic approaches in specific common disorders: <br> • depression, <br> • schizophrenia, <br> • phobias | *Treatment of a person with a mental health problem will also depend on the* **specific disorder** *that has been diagnosed, although certain therapies may adopt a similar approach across a range of disorders. In this Aspect, you will examine the kinds of* **therapeutic approaches** *deemed suitable for each of three* **specific disorders** *in turn:* **depression, schizophrenia** *and* **phobia.** |
| **Aspect 3: Care of people with mental health problems** | | |
| Institutional and community care page 281 Attitudes to mental illness page 285 | • Care of people with mental health problems in institutions or in the community <br> • Htistorical perspective <br> • Attitudes of the general public towards people with mental health problems. | *In society in general, understanding of the concepts of 'mental health' and 'mental illness' has varied greatly over time, and so have ideas about the best way to* **care for people with mental health problems**. *In the recent past, in the UK, large psychiatric hospitals were the norm; however currently* **care in the community** *is favoured. You will learn that, historically, individuals were often dealt with in* **cruel and inhumane ways**, *and a stigma still persists to some extent, in the form of* **negative attitudes on the part of the public.** |

288    Sample questions with students' answers and examiner's comments

You'll notice that there are fewer Star Studies in this chapter than some other chapters. This is because the various aspects of these Individual Differences Topics are closely related to each other, so the Star Studies that we provide are relevant to more than one Aspect. Of course, as with all the other Topics, this chapter provides a range of research evidence relevant to each Aspect.

# Aspect 1:  Therapeutic approaches

*The symptoms of schizophrenia are typically divided into* positive *and* negative symptoms. See page 254 for further details.

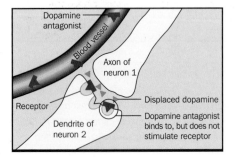

# Somatic therapies

**Somatic therapies** are related to the biological approach to atypical behaviour, which sees all behaviour as caused by underlying physiological processes in the body: 'somatic' means 'of the body'. The obvious implication is that cure is only possible by removing the root cause and returning the body to its 'normal' level of functioning. Thus, somatic therapies target physiological process such as the functioning of **neurotransmitters**, **hormones** and parts of the brain. Because of its similarity to the diagnosis of *physical* disease, the approach is also referred to as the **medical model** of abnormality, and mental disorders are represented as mental *illnesses*. You can read more about the medical model on page 243.

The three main examples of somatic therapies are **chemotherapy** (drugs), **electroconvulsive therapy** (ECT) and **psychosurgery**.

## Chemotherapy

A quarter of all the medication prescribed in Britain consists of psychiatric (psychoactive) drugs – drugs which modify the working of the brain and affect mood and behaviour (www.sane.org.uk). It was the discovery in the 1950s of antipsychotic drugs which made it possible to discharge thousands of people from mental hospitals to lead near-normal lives. For the first time, the outlook for sufferers with mental illness began to look brighter.

### Antipsychotic drugs

Antipsychotic drugs are used to treat *psychotic* illnesses – severe mental illnesses, such as schizophrenia. '*Typical*' (or *conventional*) antipsychotics (such as *chlorpromazine*) are used primarily to combat the positive symptoms of schizophrenia, such as hallucinations and thought disturbances. Abnormally high levels of the neurotransmitter dopamine are associated with schizophrenia (see page 254) and may be the reason for the characteristic thought disturbances. The antipsychotic drugs work as dopamine *antagonists* in that they bind to but do not stimulate dopamine receptors (particularly the D2 receptors), thus blocking the action of the neurotransmitter (see diagram below).

The *atypical* antipsychotic drugs (such as *clozapine*) may have beneficial effects on both positive and negative symptoms. They act on the dopamine system and the *serotonin* system, by only temporarily occupying the D2 receptors and then rapidly separating to allow normal dopamine transmission. This may explain why such atypical antipsychotics have lower levels of side effects (such as *tardive dyskinesia* – involuntary movements of the mouth and tongue) compared with conventional antipsychotics.

### Anti-anxiety drugs

The drugs most commonly used to treat anxiety are the *benzodiazepines* (BZs) and beta-blockers. Benzodiazepines work by depressing the part of the brain (the *reticular activating system*) that regulates how active the brain is. They do this by increasing the action of a substance called gamma-amino-butyric acid (GABA), a chemical involved in slowing down the transmission of nerve signals in the brain.

*Beta-blockers* reduce the effect of adrenaline (produced when we are anxious) by causing arteries to widen thereby slowing the action of the heart and decreasing its force of contraction, leading to a fall in blood pressure and thus reducing the physical symptoms of anxiety.

Antidepressant drugs are discussed on page 275, and strengths and limitations of antipsychotic drugs are presented on page 277.

### The mechanics of drug therapy

Before drugs can work, they have to enter the bloodstream and travel to the brain which is protected from substances in the blood by the *blood–brain barrier*. The amount of drug that actually arrives at the brain depends on the extent to which it is absorbed, excreted or converted into inactive substances before it has been able to penetrate this barrier. When taken by mouth, drugs are absorbed by the gut and pass into the liver. This breaks down and destroys much of the active ingredients of the drug so that less is available to cross the blood–brain barrier. If the drug is injected, it enters directly into the bloodstream bypassing the liver. This means that smaller doses can achieve a given effect when the drug is injected than when it is taken by mouth.

*evaluation*

## Chemotherapy

*Strengths*

Research evidence indicates that chemotherapies do work, which is a good reason to use them! For example, one report found that relapse rates were lower when schizophrenics used antipsychotic medicines than when using a *placebo* (a substitute pill with no physiological effects) (WHO, 2001). However they do not *always* work, which may be due to the fact that mental disorders (such as depression and schizophrenia) are not simply due to biological causes.

One of the great appeals of using chemotherapy is that it requires little effort from the user; considerably less than for therapies such as **psychoanalysis.** In reality, however, many clinicians advocate a mixture of chemotherapy and some form of psychotherapy (Comer, 2002).

*Limitations*

The success of drugs may be psychological rather than pharmacological – patients' belief in their efficacy may explain their value. Kirsch *et al.* (2002) reviewed 38 studies of antidepressants and found that patients who were given placebos fared almost as well as those getting real drugs. However, other reviews have found rather stronger effects for the real drugs. For example, Mulrow *et al.* (2000) compared the use of tricyclics (antidepressants) and placebos in 28 studies and found a success rate of 35% for placebos and 60% for tricyclics.

Drugs only offer temporary alleviation of symptoms. As soon as the patient stops taking drugs the effectiveness ceases. It may be preferable in the long term to seek a treatment that addresses the problem itself rather than one that deals only with the symptoms.

All chemotherapies have side effects which vary from individual to individual, such as constipation, low blood pressure and blurred vision. The problem of side effects is one of the main reasons why chemotherapies fail – because patients stop taking their medications.

*Biological treatments, and the underlying explanations, are determinist. They suggest that an individual has no control over their recovery – recovery is achieved by external forces. Lack of control in itself can be stressful.*

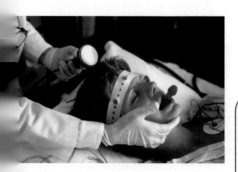

## Electroconvulsive therapy

ECT is generally used in severely depressed patients. The National Institute for Clinical Excellence (2003) suggests that ECT should only be used in cases where all other treatments have failed or when the condition is considered to be potentially life threatening because of suicide risk. The procedure involves passing a small electric current (approximately 0.6 amps), lasting about half a second, through two scalp electrodes to create a seizure lasting up to one minute, which affects the entire brain. In unilateral ECT, one electrode is placed above the temple of the non-dominant side of the brain, and a second in the middle of the forehead. The patient is anaesthetised and given a nerve-blocking agent to prevent their muscles contracting during the treatment and causing fractures. ECT is usually given 3 times a week, with the patient requiring between 3 and 15 treatments.

### Explaining how ECT works

One possibility is that ECT works on noradrenaline levels in the brain. Low levels of noradrenaline are one biological explanation of depression (see page 251); ECT may decrease the amount of noradrenaline produced by neurons thus 'tricking' them into producing more because they sense less (Sapolsky, 2000).

Alternatively, it may be that ECT seizures cause a shift in the body's hormonal system, and it is this which causes a decrease in the symptoms of depression.

*evaluation*

**Sectioning**

*The Mental Health Act 1983 and Mental Health (Care and Treatment) (Scotland) Act 2003 govern the admission of people to psychiatric hospital against their will, their rights while detained, discharge from hospital, and aftercare. The Act is divided into Sections which is why the term 'sectioned' is used to mean being compulsorily admitted to hospital.*

ECT

ECT is a quick, easy solution when compared with drugs and psychotherapy, and it may be the only alternative when patients fail to respond to other forms of treatment.

In most textbooks, ECT is reported as being very successful for the treatment of severe depression. For example, Comer (2002) states that 60–70% of ECT patients improve after treatment. However, Sackheim *et al.* (2001) found that 84% of the patients they studied relapsed within 6 months of having ECT, and Lowinger and Dobie (1969) reported that improvement rates as high as 80% can be expected with placebo treatment alone.

Critics question the use of a method that has yet to be explained (see note at bottom of page 267). Abrams (1997) says that it is akin to arguing that if you thump the TV and get a picture this is a recommendation to keep doing it. Breggin (1997) argues that reported improvement may simply be the 'artificial euphoria' that often follows any brain trauma, and that the mechanism of ECT is simply the brain damage that it produces. Another issue is the potential side effects, such as impaired memory, cardiovascular changes and headaches (Datto, 2000). Finally, there are ethical considerations; a worrying number of patients are given ECT without consenting to it. One report considered patients *sectioned* under the Mental Health Act, finding that 59% had not consented to ECT (Department of Health, 1999).

# Psychosurgery

*Prefrontal lobotomy* is one example of psychosurgery. It involves selective destruction of nerve fibres in the frontal lobe of the brain (an area which is involved in impulse control and mood regulation) and its purpose is to alleviate some of the severe symptoms of mental illness. In the 1940s, when such operations were first performed, the techniques were fairly crude, as shown in the diagram. Today neurosurgeons use computer-based stereotactic imaging to locate precise points within the brain and sever connections.

*evaluation*

Psychosurgery

There is no doubt that early practices of psychosurgery were both inappropriate and ineffective. Lobotomies had a fatality rate of up to 6% and a range of severe physical side effects such as brain seizures and lack of emotional responsiveness (Comer, 2002). Modern psychosurgery is a different matter. The most significant side effect is still irreversible damage to the brain which is claimed to impair mental functioning. However, Cohen *et al.* (1999) studied 12 patients who underwent a cingulotomy (another form of psychosurgery) and found only mild impairments of focused and sustained attention after 1 year. In a general review of research, Cosgrove and Raugh (2001) report that cingulotomy was effective in 56% of patients with obsessive-compulsive disorder (OCD) and 65% of patients with major affective disorder. However, currently in the US only about 25 patients per year are treated and the number is even smaller in the UK, thus the numbers of patients studied are very small.

A possible alternative to psychosurgery is deep brain stimulation where surgeons thread wires through the skull. No tissue is destroyed. The wires, which remain embedded in the brain, are connected to a battery pack implanted in the chest. The batteries produce an adjustable, high-frequency current that interrupts the brain circuitry involved in, for example, OCD. If it doesn't work, it can always be turned off. Gabriels *et al.* (2003) found that out of four OCD patients, three experienced relief of their symptoms when the electrical current was on.

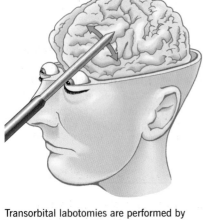

Transorbital labotomies are performed by inserting a sharp instrument into the train through the eye socket. This is rotated to cut the white matter tracts to and from the prefrontal lobes.

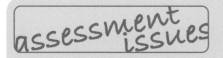

**Describe and evaluate *one* type of somatic therapy for mental disorder. (*ku 3 ae 3*)**

Every time you answer a question, whether in NABs or exam, you must 'answer the question set' – your teachers have probably been saying this to you for as long as you can remember! Why do they go on about it? Because in exams students very often do *not* answer the question set; rather they answer the question they *think* they have read (maybe due to bias in perception), or the question they *wish* had been set (maybe due to denial or other Freudian defence mechanism!). Whatever the reason, marks will be low, and the greater the number of marks available, the more marks can be lost through such a basic error. Avoid this potential disaster by getting into the habit of stripping the question down to its component parts; i.e. 'deconstruct' the question. In this question for example, the key part to start focusing on is '*one* type of therapy' (for mental disorder). Next, notice that this must be a *somatic* therapy. Having decided which somatic therapy to write about, note the 'command' words: you must '*describe*' and '*evaluate*'. As you plan and write your answer, keep checking that you are indeed 'answering the question set' – have you addressed all the elements that you identified?

*All the psychological therapies discussed here are derived from psychological approaches which were described in Chapter 10.*

Dr Albert Ellis

# Psychological approaches

Psychological approaches to abnormality focus more on the psychological dimensions of human behaviour (e.g. the way a person thinks, feels, or acts) than the biological/medical approach does, and psychological approaches base their interpretation of abnormal behaviour on problems in these areas.

## Cognitive-behavioural therapy

**Cognitive-behavioural therapy (CBT)** is derived from the cognitive approach to abnormality (see page 245). Such therapies combine cognitive therapy with behavioural techniques which focus on behaviour alone (see **Behaviourist therapies**, below), and it is argued that the combination works better than either of the two techniques on their own (Kendall and Hammen, 1998). Cognitive-behavioural therapy (CBT) involves identifying maladaptive *thinking* and then developing coping strategies (i.e. *behavioural* change).

You may have already studied one example of CBT – stress inoculation therapy (SIT). This is discussed on page 73 along with a Star Study that has investigated the cognitive-behavioural approach to therapy for psychological disorder. We will now look at two other forms of CBT.

### Rational-emotive behaviour therapy (REBT)
REBT, developed by Albert Ellis (1957), is based on the idea that individuals frequently develop self-defeating habits because of faulty beliefs about themselves and the world around them. Ellis used the ABC model to express this relationship:

A   *Activating events* are things that happen in a person's life (e.g. getting dumped by a girlfriend/boyfriend).
B   *Beliefs* are explanations of the event. They may be rational and tolerable (e.g. 'I guess I deserved it, but I'll get over it') or irrational and self-defeating ('She must really want to hurt me; I'm such an idiot).
C   *Consequences* may be productive or unproductive, depending on the beliefs that we have about the activating event.

REBT helps the client understand irrational *beliefs* and the *consequences* of thinking in this way, and helps them substitute more effective problem-solving methods. Because it is not the activating events that cause unproductive consequences, REBT focuses on the self-defeating beliefs that accompany them. The patient is encouraged to *dispute* these beliefs in the following ways:

- *logical disputing* – self-defeating beliefs do not follow logically from the information available (e.g. 'Does thinking this way make sense?')

- *empirical disputing* – self-defeating beliefs may not be consistent with reality (e.g. 'Where is the proof that this belief is accurate?')

- *pragmatic disputing* – emphasises the lack of usefulness of self-defeating beliefs (e.g. 'How is this belief likely to help me?').

Effective disputing changes self-defeating beliefs into more rational beliefs. The individual can move from catastrophising ('I have really let my family down – I am a complete loser') to more rational interpretations of events ('I may have failed but, if I work harder, next time I'll nail it'). This in turn helps them to feel better, and eventually become more self-accepting.

### Modelling

One CBT technique that uses a more behavioural emphasis is *participant modelling*, where the therapist models certain target behaviour which the client then imitates. Underpinning this application is the idea of observational learning, from Bandura's social learning theory (Bandura, 1969, see page 173). In one example, a woman with a phobia of snakes watched the therapist handle a snake without fear; gradually, she became able to handle it herself by copying the therapist (Bandura, 1971). Modelling is also used in stress-inoculation therapy.

*evaluation*

## Cognitive-behavioural therapies

*General comments on CBTs*

Studies that compare different therapies tend to group cognitive-behavioural therapies (CBTs) together, reporting that these jointly have the highest overall success rate compared with other psychotherapies (David and Avellino, 2003). However, Wampold *et al.* (2002) suggest that this may be because non-bona fide treatments (i.e. those with no theoretical framework) are included in the comparison therapies; when they are excluded from analysis CBT is not superior to these other therapies. Research on the use of CBTs with schizophrenia is described on page 278.

CBTs are cost-effective because they are relatively short term, and they are popular because they don't involve searching for deep meanings. In comparison with therapies that focus on behaviour alone (i.e. behaviourist therapies, below), a further strength of CBT is that it treats causes rather than just symptoms, providing help now and in the future.

*REBT*

Ellis (1957) claimed a 90% success rate for REBT, taking an average of 27 sessions to complete treatment. Smith and Glass (1977), in a *meta-analysis* of 475 studies of psychotherapies, cited REBT as having the second highest average success rate among 10 forms of psychotherapy (second to systematic desensitisation).

On the negative side, REBT is regarded as one of the most aggressive CBTs (Rosenhan and Seligman, 1989) and, in addition, it is judgemental. These aspects of the therapy raise ethical concerns.

## Behaviourist therapies

Behaviourist therapies are derived from the behaviourist approach to abnormality (see page 246). They have a number of characteristics that distinguish them from other types of therapeutic approach (Sternberg, 1995).

- They are deliberately *short term*, typically requiring only a relatively small number of sessions.

- They target the *symptoms* rather than the underlying problem, on the grounds that the original causes of a maladaptive behaviour may have little to do with the factors that are currently maintaining it.

- They are intentionally *directive*; it is the therapist who formulates a treatment plan.

We will look at examples of two behaviourist therapies, the first based on **classical conditioning** and the second based on **operant conditioning**. (See pages 3 and 4 for more on classical and operant conditioning.)

### Systematic desensitisation (SD)

An individual might learn that their feared stimulus is not so fearful after all – if only they could re-experience the feared stimulus, but the anxiety that it creates blocks such recovery, because the person always avoids the stimulus, to reduce anxiety. SD overcomes this by introducing the feared stimulus *gradually*. The therapy is based on the principle of *counterconditioning*; the two responses (relaxation and fear) are incompatible so the fear is eventually dispelled.

SD typically involves the following steps. First, patients are taught how to relax their muscles completely. The therapist and patient would then together construct a desensitisation hierarchy, which is a series of imagined scenes, each one causing a little more anxiety than the previous one. The patient gradually works their way through their desensitisation hierarchy, visualising each anxiety-evoking event while engaging in the competing relaxation response (the relaxed state is incompatible with anxiety). Once the patient has mastered one step in the hierarchy (i.e. they can remain relaxed while imagining it), they are ready to move onto the next, continuing in this way until they have eventually mastered the feared situation that caused them to seek help in the first place. The new conditioned response to the previously feared object is now relaxation.

*evaluation* | **Systematic desensitisation**

Research has found that SD is successful for a range of anxiety disorders. For example, about 75% of patients with phobias respond to SD (McGrath *et al.*, 1990). However, spontaneous recovery from phobias has been found to be as high as 50–60% at 1 year (McMorran *et al.*, 2001), which means that SD may in fact contribute little. See page 279 for a further discussion of the use of SD with phobias.

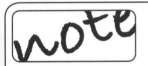

### Primary and secondary reinforcers

The tokens received by patients are reinforcing (see pages 3–4) – they increase the probability that a person will repeat the rewarded behaviour. Tokens are an example of a *secondary reinforcer* – things that have no intrinsic value to an organism but take on rewarding properties when paired with a *primary reinforcer* such as food. Money is the classic example of a secondary reinforcer.

### Token economy (TE)

Patients in psychiatric institutions are given tokens (such as poker chips) for socially constructive behaviour (such as personal hygiene, or being friendly to other patients), but tokens are withheld when unwanted behaviours are exhibited. The tokens are worth nothing in themselves but can be exchanged for desirable items and activities. There are six main steps in a token economy programme:

1. *Target behaviour identified* – i.e. desirable behaviours must be defined (for reward/reinforcement), as well as any undesirable behaviour (for punishment).
2. *Nature of token identified* – i.e. choose something with no intrinsic value (e.g. a poker chip) but not something (such as money) which already has reinforcing properties.
3. *Reinforcers (rewards) identified* – desired items such as sweets, cigarettes, trips to the pub, etc.
4. *Schedule of reinforcement determined* – in the beginning, it is necessary to reinforce every instance of the desired behaviour (continuous reinforcement). As time progresses, partial reinforcement schedules are more effective in maintaining the desired behaviour.
5. *Exchange rate determined* – i.e. the desired items or events must be 'priced'. A chocolate bar may be 5 tokens whereas a trip to the pub might be 20 tokens.
6. *Location and time of day* in which the tokens are exchanged is determined.

*evaluation* | **Token economy**

In the 1970s, a particularly widespread use of token economies was to help treat long-term psychiatric patients who were being prepared for transfer into the community. Paul and Lentz (1977) found that, after 4 years, 98% of schizophrenic patients treated under a token economy system had been discharged from their institution compared with 71% treated in any other kind of program.

Token economies are used in other institutional settings, such as residential schools. Neumark (1998) studied a scheme used in a residential school for children with severe emotional or behavioural difficulties; children previously described as unteachable or hyperactive were, after therapy, able to sit down and read quietly, and increased their reading age by up to three years in the first year at the school.

Most studies, however, do not indicate whether desirable behaviours continue when tokens stop or if the learning that takes place in an institutional setting generalises to other settings. Furthermore, the method is expensive and time consuming: it requires intensive training and concentrated effort to be maintained. Simpler operant conditioning techniques may be just as effective and easier.

Token economies raise *ethical* concerns because they are manipulative. Withholding privileges and basic rights (such as access to food and freedom of movement, which are withheld from patients and only granted as a reward if 'earned') has been ruled unethical by US courts (Emmelkamp, 1994).

'But who has won?' This question the Dodo could not answer without a great deal of thought. At last the Dodo said, '*Everybody has won, and all must have prizes.*' (*Alice's Adventures in Wonderland*.)

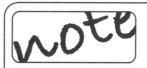

### The Dodo bird effect

Rosenzweig (1936) proposed that there were so many common factors in various different psychotherapies that only small differences would be found when comparing different ones. The commonalities include being able to talk to a sympathetic person, which may enhance self-esteem, and having an opportunity to express one's thoughts (Sloane *et al.*, 1975). Luborsky *et al.* (1975, 2002) reviewed over 100 different studies that compared different therapies and found that there were only small differences.

Such small differences may occur because of difficulties in comparing treatments (Howard *et al.*, 1997). It is also the case that interaction effects between patient qualities and treatment types may reduce effects. For example, an introvert personality may do better using one kind of therapy than an extrovert; when treatments were chosen to match patients' personality, larger effects were reported (Blatt and Ford, 1994).

**KEY TERMS**

**Psychoanalysis:** The therapy based on the view that mental illnesses are caused by unconscious factors; treatment seeks to make the unconscious conscious and thus enable the patient to deal with their anxieties.

*Freud introduced the notion that mental illness may have a psychological cause and thus also introduced the idea that treatment should be psychological. In this sense, psychoanalysis was a trailblazer for all psychotherapies.*

*Humanistic and cognitive therapists prefer to use the word 'client' instead of 'patient' to reflect the role of the therapist as advisor or facilitator rather than director.*

## Psychoanalysis

Reverse psychology

Freud developed his techniques through working with his own patients and used their successful outcomes as proof that his approach worked. Anna O. (above) was one of his earliest cases (see description on page 249). In fact, however, she did not recover fully and spent time later in institutions (Guttmann, 2001).

The essence of the psychoanalytic approach (see page 247) is that much of our behaviour is motivated (driven) by underlying psychological desires and conflicts of which we are largely unaware (i.e. *unconscious* forces). The focus of psychoanalysis, therefore, is not treatment of the 'presenting problem' (the symptom that caused the person to seek help) but the removal of underlying conflicts that the person has repressed into their unconscious mind.

The therapist (or analyst) achieves this by means of various techniques. In *free association*, the patient expresses thoughts exactly as they occur, so that areas of conflict are brought into consciousness. The therapist helps interpret these for the patient, who corrects, rejects, and adds further thoughts and feelings. Patients may initially offer resistance to the therapist's interpretations (e.g. changing the subject to avoid a painful discussion), or they may display *transference,* where they recreate feelings and conflicts (e.g. with parents) and transfer these towards the therapist. Therapists also use *dream interpretation* as a means of accessing the unconscious by looking beyond the *manifest content* (the actual content) of the dream to its *latent content* (what it means or represents in terms of unconscious feelings).

Psychoanalytic therapists focus mostly on past experiences, notably early parent–child relationships because they believe that the majority of psychological conflicts are rooted in these relationships. Psychoanalysis is not a brief form of therapy. Patients tend to meet up with the therapist four or five times a week. Together the patient and therapist examine the same issues over and over again, sometimes over a period of years, in an attempt to gain greater clarity concerning the causes of the patient's neurotic behaviour.

## *evaluation* — Evaluation of psychoanalysis

In the meta-analysis by Smith and Glass (1977) cited earlier, psychoanalysis was found to be effective but not as effective as cognitive-behavioural therapies and almost equal to placebo treatments. Such meta-analyses are problematic because they lump studies together which may not, in reality, be using the same method. Many factors determine the likelihood of success, including the nature of the therapy, therapist, patient and illness.

Even if the therapy were effective it is only appropriate for certain mental illnesses (where patients have insight into their condition) and certain groups of people (those who are articulate and have the time and money for such treatments). The term 'YAVIS' has been used to describe such patients – young, attractive, verbal, intelligent and successful. An additional issue is that psychoanalysis assumes that a patient can reliably recall early memories that have been repressed, yet there is little evidence to support this (Loftus, 1995).

**KEY TERMS**

**Humanistic therapy:** Concentrates on the present and aims to enable a person to make full use of their personal capacities, leading to *self-actualisation*.

## Humanistic therapies

The humanistic approach (see page 249) emphasises the importance of the client's perspective, thus **humanistic therapies** are often described as 'client-centred'. They are also 'non-directive' because humanistic psychologists emphasise the importance of self-determination; the client should control the course of therapy and should also take responsibility for their own life rather than being controlled.

### Client-centred therapy – counselling

Carl Rogers (1951) founded client-centred therapy which grew into the widespread counselling movement. His basic belief was that each individual had the capacity to be 'self-righting' if given the right circumstances. To do this the therapist must show:

- *unconditional positive regard* – accepting the client unconditionally and non-judgementally to allow the client to freely explore their feelings
- *empathy* – accurately understanding what the client is feeling from their perspective
- *congruence* – the counsellor must be authentic and genuine, not an aloof professional but someone who displays genuine warmth.

The therapist reflects the client's feelings back to them in an uncritical way so that the client can deal with their own feelings. This enables the client to become self-accepting and thus able to control all aspects of self. Rogers said that as long as a client can say 'I don't know why I do it' or 'I'm just not myself when I do those things' they have not fully accepted themselves.

Psychological adjustment occurs when all experiences can be assimilated into a consistent concept of self.

There is nothing unique about the counselling relationship; the same features are present in all good relationships and thus many friendships provide the same therapeutic process – enabling an individual to develop and grow in their own way.

---

**evaluation** | **Counselling**

Rogers' practice and philosophy can be felt everywhere. The principles of counselling have been adopted in a wide variety of self-help groups (such as Alcoholics Anonymous) as well as in marriage guidance and bereavement counselling, and by the Samaritans and so on. Many professionals, such as doctors and teachers, have also adopted the principles of counselling as a means of communicating with clients. In fact, the same principles may operate in many other therapies and explain their effectiveness; for example, when a doctor is prescribing drugs for depression an amount of counselling may take place.

Research has shown that counselling has often been more effective than direct methods in treating a range of problems. For example, Lawrence (1971) found that backward readers improved more when given counselling alone rather than counselling plus help with their reading or help with reading alone.

Like psychoanalysis, the method is not appropriate for serious mental disorders where an individual does not have insight into their condition. It is also not appropriate for certain types of personality, such as people who do not wish to explore themselves but prefer to be directed about what to do (see, for example, the **authoritarian personality** on page 150).

One of the problems with counselling is that success depends on the skills of individual counsellors and it has proved difficult to identify exactly what makes for a good counsellor (Beutler *et al.*, 1994).

---

*This therapy grew in part out of the Gestalt movement in psychology, named after the German word for 'organised whole'.*

## Gestalt therapy

Fritz Perls *et al.* (1951) formulated this *present-centred* approach, which is focused on the client's responses in the here and now. Past experiences are still relevant because they may be causing difficulties, for example due to repression. The Gestalt therapist operates in a more dynamic and active manner than that of a client-centred counsellor, although they avoid interpreting and evaluating a client's behaviour as this can block immediate experience and provoke defensiveness.

*Awareness* is a key concept because Perls felt that psychological disorder was the result of a loss of contact with reality. A client is encouraged to become aware of their own feelings and behaviours and thus gain insights which will enable self-healing. Therapy may involve 'experiments' in awareness focusing; and clients are encouraged to notice their physical and emotional responses; they might, for example, be asked to give the selected physical areas a 'voice'.

Techniques include role-playing, experiments, homework, dream analysis and the 'empty chair' – the therapist may ask the client to imagine holding a conversation with someone or something imagined to be in the empty chair, such as the client's father or a teacher, which stimulates their thinking, allowing them to explore their feelings and possibly repressed emotions.

---

**evaluation** | **Gestalt therapy**

Some critics see Gestalt therapy as overly invasive because it seeks to confront and even frustrate clients, which may raise ethical issues relating to psychological harm. However, clients do take responsibility for their participation in the therapy, so when something **cathartic** happens it is with their permission.

Like client-centred counselling, Gestalt therapy is only appropriate for certain individuals. Very little research has been done on its effectiveness because Gestalt therapists believe that personal experiences and self-awareness cannot be measured objectively (Greenberg *et al.*, 1998).

## assessment issues

**Compare and contrast behaviourist and humanistic therapies in the treatment of atypical behaviour. (*ku* 12 *ae* 8)**

Essay questions like this one demand a high level of skills, both in planning and actually writing the essay. Such skills take time and effort to develop. An important way that you can improve your skills is by practising writing essays for homework and revision (e.g. using past papers) and making the most of feedback on these from your teacher. When approaching a NAB, prelim or the exam itself, look back at the feedback you received on previous assessments. You can even assess your efforts yourself, by using information from the SQA course documents (www.sqa.org.uk, consult the Psychology pages). Find the *Marking Instructions* for either the Specimen exam question paper or for the most recent actual exam paper, and turn to the *Generic Requirements* section near the start; these are standard requirements, giving descriptions of the kind of answers that would merit a grade A, grade B, and so on (such as 'accurate, relevant and detailed psychological knowledge', 'evidence of thorough understanding', 'coherent and logically structured', etc.). Which grade description best describes *your* performance? Aim to produce work that fits the grade A description, of course!

# Aspect 2: Therapeutic approaches in specific disorders

We now consider therapies for three common disorders. Several alternative therapies are given for each disorder, drawn from the five approaches discussed in Aspect 1. In principle, *any* therapeutic approach may be applied to *any* disorder, but in practice each specific disorder is treated in the main by a limited range of therapies – those whose effectiveness has been demonstrated for that disorder. You should also bear in mind that psychiatrists, psychologists and therapists attempt to treat the person, rather than the disorder, and that many of their clients have a diagnosis of more than one disorder (termed '**comorbidity**').

## Treating depression

*Symptoms and explanations of depression are discussed on pages 251–253.*

The main treatments used for depression are somatic therapies (antidepressants and ECT) and cognitive-behavioural therapy, although other forms of psychotherapy are commonly used, such as counselling (see page 273).

### Somatic treatments

#### Chemotherapy: antidepressants

Depression is thought to be due to insufficient amounts of the neurotransmitters *serotonin* and *adrenaline* being produced in the nerve endings (see diagram on page 251).

Depression has traditionally been treated by two major classes of antidepressant drug: the *monoamine oxidase (MAO) inhibitors* and the *tricyclics*. Although MAO inhibitors help about half of the depressed patients who take them (Thase *et al.*, 1995), they can create serious medical problems because MAO is necessary to break down the chemical *tyramine* in the liver. If tyramine is not broken down, it can accumulate and may even cause death.

*note*

### Prozac for pets?

A 1996 article in the magazine *Dogs Today* described how *Prozac* had been used with dogs such as Jannie, a shadow-chasing pointer treated for obsessive-compulsive disorder (Neville, 1996). Similarly, Hart *et al.* (2005) describe how SSRIs such as Prozac can be successful in the treatment of cats stressed out by events such as moving home. These cats respond to their stress by excessive urine marking, but the administration of SSRIs over an eight-week period was found to significantly reduce this behaviour.

Mike's Abyssinian cat 'Sasha' was prescribed Prozac following the stress of their last house move – owner and cat are now doing fine!

The *tricyclic* antidepressants block the mechanism that re-absorbs both serotonin and adrenaline into the pre-synaptic cell after it has fired. As a result, more of these neurotransmitters are left in the synapse, prolonging their activity and making transmission of the next impulse easier. Research suggests that tricyclics appear to be relatively ineffective in the treatment of depression. In a review of studies carried out between 1986 and 1994, Sommers-Flanagan and Sommers-Flanagan (1996) concluded that tricyclics are no more effective than a placebo even in studies designed to maximise the effects of the antidepressants.

More recently, depression has been treated by *selective serotonin re-uptake inhibitors* (SSRIs). SSRIs work in much the same way as the tricyclics but, instead of blocking the re-uptake of different neurotransmitters, they block mainly serotonin (or 5-HT) and so increase the quantity available to activate neighbouring brain cells. Drugs that selectively block the re-uptake of noradrenaline (also called norepinephrine) only (i.e. *selective norepinephrine re-uptake inhibitors*) are also now available.

A meta-analysis of 49 studies (Joffe *et al.*, 1996) showed that the therapeutic effects of SSRIs were significantly larger than using a placebo alone, although there was no significant increase in the therapeutic effectiveness of SSRIs compared with the earlier tricyclic antidepressants. However, the studies were restricted only to those published in the English language in MEDLINE (an online search facility).

### ECT

As we saw on page 267, ECT is generally reported as being very successful for the treatment of severe depression. An audit of ECT in Scotland between 1996 and 1999 reported that 75% of people with depressive illness showed a definite improvement after ECT. Despite this however, its use has declined steadily over the last 50 years. One reason for this decline is the concern over potential side effects (such as memory loss) as well as the frightening nature of the procedure itself (Comer, 2004). Another reason is the therapeutic success enjoyed by antidepressant drugs. Even so, ECT is still used routinely and remains, for some, a cause for concern. One report estimated that 59% of patients sectioned and given ECT did not consent to the treatment (Department of Health, 1999).

## Cognitive-behavioural therapy (CBT)

Psychological treatments of depression can help the depressed individual in several ways. For example, supportive counselling can ease the pain of depression as well as the feelings of hopelessness that accompany the depressive state. CBT helps the individual to change the negative thinking, unrealistic expectations, and overly critical self-evaluations that both produce and sustain the depressive state (see page 252). CBT helps the individual recognise which issues in their life are critical, and which are relatively minor, and helps them construct a more positive view of themselves and of life generally. Therapy may also require changing those stressful aspects of an individual's life that contribute to their depression. This may involve better ways of dealing with stress or interpersonal therapy to deal with relationship difficulties.

## Case study of depression

Tony was 41 years old and a successful owner of his own double glazing company. He was married and was a loving father to his three children. Tony had recently heard of the death from cancer of a close childhood friend and, although saddened by the news, had not thought too much more about it. In the months that followed, however, he began to develop a preoccupation with his own health, becoming convinced that he too might have cancer. Although Tony was reassured by his doctor that he was fit and healthy, these morbid feelings would not go away, and he began to worry how his family would survive if he were to die suddenly. He found himself unable to sleep at night, and could no longer concentrate at work, nor enjoy time spent with his wife and children. He was frequently weepy and was unable to concentrate, spending most of his time simply moping around the house. He decided to pay another visit to the doctor.

This time, his doctor diagnosed Tony's symptoms as depression and decided to start him on a course of antidepressants. The doctor told him that about 60% of people with depression respond favourably to antidepressants, and so this treatment should relieve some of the worst symptoms. Although his mood did improve, Tony did not like the side effects that he was experiencing. As the months passed, he did not feel that he was making the progress he should be, and the low moods returned.

## note

### Antidepressants versus cognitive-behavioural therapy

DeRubeis *et al.* (2005) compared the efficacy of antidepressant medications versus CBT in the treatment of moderate to severe depression: 240 outpatients were given either 16 weeks of antidepressant medication, 16 weeks of CBT, or 8 weeks of a placebo pill. Results indicated an advantage for each of the active treatments over the placebo. The researchers concluded that CBT could be as effective as drug treatment for the treatment of moderate to severe major depression, although they did caution that its effectiveness may depend on a high level of therapist experience or expertise. One limitation of drug treatments, however, is that patients with depression are often overwhelmed by problems in their lives that drugs simply cannot solve. CBT has the advantage that it teaches people skills that help them to cope with such problems.

This time Tony's doctor referred him to a psychologist who would arrange some cognitive psychotherapy which might prove more suitable for Tony. After meeting Tony for the first time, the psychologist agreed that he met the DSM-IV criteria for major depressive order, as he exhibited a low depressed mood, had sleeping difficulties and had lost interest in everyday activities. The psychologist believed that the cause of Tony's depression was his style of thinking, in particular an irrational belief that, because his friend had died of cancer, he too would develop the same illness. The major goal of the cognitive therapy would be to change Tony's negative bias and negative style of interpretation and so remove the source of his depression. Over the following months, Tony attended regular therapy sessions as well as continuing to take a low dose of antidepressants. Gradually he reported that his depression was easing, and he now saw problems in his life as challenges rather than something that would overwhelm him.

## assessment issues

**Describe and evaluate *one* type of therapy that may be used to treat someone suffering depression. (ku 4 ae 4)**

Choose 'your' therapy, making sure that it's one that you can evaluate as well as describe, and that it is an appropriate one for depression. Your choice might be broad or narrow: for example, you might decide to write about the cognitive-behavioural approach to treating depression; alternatively, you might focus more narrowly on, say, Beck's use of CBT for depression. To demonstrate knowledge and understanding (for the *ku* marks), simply describe your chosen therapy. For the *ae* marks, it would naturally be sensible to cite evidence of *effectiveness* of this therapy; another useful source of *ae* material would be *comparison* of your chosen therapy with other treatment(s) for depression. There may also be ethical concerns, such as the very directive nature of some forms of CBT (e.g. REBT). In other words, there is an abundance of analytical/evaluative material whichever therapy you pick. And don't forget that in this case, although the focus is on therapy for one specific disorder, i.e. Aspect 2 of the Topic, you can draw on material (descriptive and evaluative) from Aspect 1 as well.

*Symptoms and explanations of schizophrenia are discussed on pages 254–255.*

# Treating schizophrenia

Schizophrenia, like depression, is largely treated through the use of chemotherapy (drugs) although cognitive-behavioural therapies are important too. In Aspect 1 we also looked at the use of Token Economies, a form of behaviourist therapy (see page 271) which can be used with schizophrenic patients.

## Chemotherapy: antipsychotics

As we saw on page 266, antipsychotics can be split into two types; 'typical' (or conventional) and 'atypical' antipsychotics. Both typical and atypical antipsychotics work by altering the level of neurotransmitters in the brain, mainly the neurotransmitter dopamine, although atypical antipsychotics such as *clozapine* affect both dopamine and other neurotransmitters such as serotonin. Antipsychotic drugs help the person with schizophrenia in a number of ways. They may reduce the hallucinations and delusions, and can help the person interact more normally with others. As a result of taking antipsychotic medication, a person with schizophrenia may behave more socially and as a result become less isolated.

### Effectiveness of antipsychotics

Davis *et al.* (1989) summarised over 100 studies comparing conventional antipsychotics and placebo in the treatment of schizophrenia. They concluded that the antipsychotic drug was significantly more effective than the placebo in the vast majority of studies. Overall, approximately three-quarters of patients treated with conventional antipsychotics were much improved after six weeks compared with less than one-quarter of patients treated with a placebo only. Evidence from a large number of studies suggests that the use of conventional antipsychotic drugs significantly reduces the risk of relapse of the positive symptoms of schizophrenia (Davis *et al.*, 1993).

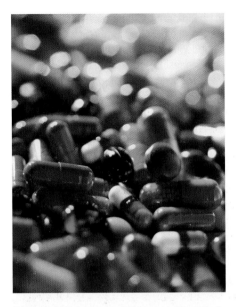

Antipsychotic drugs can help reduce the risk of symptoms of schizophrenia, but they can cause serious side effects.

The newer atypical antipsychotics are claimed to help a higher proportion of patients, although not all studies have confirmed this. Davis *et al.* (2003) carried out a meta-analysis of 124 studies and reported that not all found improved effectiveness for the atypical drugs compared with more conventional drugs. In the CATIE study by Lieberman *et al.*, first published in 2005, and involving more than 1400 patients, a conventional antipsychotic drug, *perphenazine*, was found to be just as effective as the newer (and more expensive) atypical drugs and no more likely to cause neuorological side effects.

### The downside of antipsychotics

One of the most unfortunate side effects of conventional antipsychotic drugs such as *chlorpromazine* is that as well as reducing psychotic symptoms they can also produce *extrapyramidal effects*. These are disturbances in the areas of the brain that control movement, and include Parkinsonian symptoms, where patients develop movement disorders (such as muscle tremors and muscle rigidity) typical of patients with Parkinson's disease. About half of the patients taking conventional antipsychotic medication experience such symptoms. Such symptoms appear to be a consequence of the reduction of dopamine activity in the *substantia nigra*, a part of the brain that coordinates movement and posture. Despite the reduced risk of extrapyramidal effects with the newer 'atypical' antipsychotics, they too have their problems. People taking clozapine, for example, have a 1% risk of developing *agranulocytosis*, a potentially life-threatening drop in the number of white blood cells.

## Cognitive-behavioural therapy

Cognitive-behavioural therapy focuses on the link between what you think about yourself or a situation (the cognitive part) and how this in turn affects the way you act (the behaviour part). The aim of CBT is to help a person find more realistic and appropriate ways of coping with the problems in their life. The use of CBT in the treatment of schizophrenia has become increasingly common in the UK over the past 10 years. CBT helps people with schizophrenia identify the negative thoughts that drive their emotions, and modify the hallucinations and delusions that make up the *positive symptoms* (see page 254) of this disorder. Techniques range from the questioning of delusional content to work on dysfunctional beliefs about the self (e.g. 'I am evil and damaged' or 'I am special and unique'). Homework exercises allow patients to make sense of their distressing experiences and to see the positive effects of more rational responding and coping strategies. CBT helps the patient to understand why they appear to have changed so much, and to see the point of taking medication and attending treatment sessions. As a result, advocates of CBT have claimed that its use has led to reductions in relapse and subsequent re-hospitalisation of patients suffering from schizophrenia.

### Does it work?

Tarrier *et al.* (1998) investigated whether cognitive-behavioural therapy (CBT) resulted in a significant improvement in positive symptoms for patients with chronic schizophrenia. Researchers randomly allocated patients to one of three conditions: intensive CBT with routine care, supportive counselling and routine care, or routine care alone. After three months, researchers found significant improvements in the severity and number of positive symptoms in those treated with CBT, with those treated with supportive counselling showing a smaller and non-significant improvement in symptoms, and those with routine care alone showing very little, if any, improvement.

Studies such as Tarrier *et al.*'s suggest an important therapeutic role for CBT in the treatment of schizophrenia, but this conclusion may not be as clear cut as it appears. First, the improvements for the group receiving supportive counselling were midway between the groups receiving CBT and those receiving routine care alone, yet did not differ significantly from either. This is important given that CBT is likely to be substantially more expensive than supportive counselling. Also significant is the fact that one-quarter of those receiving CBT dropped out or refused follow-up, while this figure was only one-eighth for those receiving supportive counselling. A most damning indictment of CBT comes from Turkington and McKenna (2003) who, in a review of studies testing the effectiveness of CBT in the treatment of schizophrenia, conclude that 'If CBT were a drug, these studies would have been sufficient to consign it to history'.

> ## note
>
> ### *Common theme: alternative explanations*
>
> Throughout the Higher psychology course, you'll notice that whatever the Topic, there is usually more than one explanation for behaviours and mental processes. Many exam and NABs questions expect you to provide *alternative explanations* of psychological processes, and in these cases there may well be *ae* marks available for analysis and evaluation. Often this means that you should describe different *theories* or *models*, e.g. of memory (see Chapter 2). Or, different *approaches* may be required, for example, psychoanalytic and behaviourist explanations of infant attachment (Chapter 1), or cognitive and humanistic explanations of the origins of disorder (Chapter 10). In the current Topic, you may get the opportunity to discuss alternative explanations of how therapies *work*: from your reading of Aspects 1 and 2 you can see that certain treatments appear to be effective, but that psychologists' views are divided on the precise processes that may be involved. For example, if you are analysing/evaluating ECT, a somatic therapy, you could consider the different explanations about exactly how it may 'work', whether by altering the activity of neurotransmitters, or by causing brain damage, etc. Whatever the topic, by showing your awareness of alternative explanations, you will be demonstrating skills of analysis and evaluation.

*Symptoms and explanations of phobias (social and specific) are discussed on pages 255–257.*

# Treating phobias

Phobias tend to be treated with psychological rather than somatic therapies, reflecting the reduced role of biological factors in such disorders. Anti-anxiety drugs may be used along with psychotherapy to reduce feelings of anxiety but often relaxation techniques alone are used.

## Cognitive-behavioural therapy

The treatment of choice for most social phobias (such as agoraphobia – fear of open spaces) is cognitive-behavioural therapy within a group setting (cognitive behavioural *group* therapy or CBGT). This treatment involves behavioural and cognitive elements. The behavioural component is similar to systematic desensitisation, a behaviourist therapy which is described on page 271. In CBGT, the group engages in simulated exposures to feared situations through role-plays – an individual is first exposed to their least feared social situations, and then as they feel able to conquer these relatively minor situations, they move up on their hierarchy of feared situations, ending with the thing they fear the most (such as eating in public). If they begin to feel anxious during a simulated situation, they are taught to use a variety of relaxation techniques to reduce the anxiety. Through these 'covert' simulations (using imagination rather than the real thing), people with social phobias are gradually able to conquer their fears in a safe and supportive environment. Group members may also be given 'homework' assignments where they are required to face their feared situations in real life (*in vivo* exposure).

A key aspect of this technique is the cognitive therapy that also takes place. The therapist educates patients about how they can replace the irrational beliefs that lead to anxiety with more realistic and rational beliefs. During the simulation scenarios, group members challenge each other's irrational beliefs, giving the individual the opportunity for cognitive restructuring. CBGT, therefore, is a balancing act between exposure and periods of cognitive restructuring.

### Does it work?

Beck *et al.* (1994) found CBT to be more effective than supportive therapy, relaxation and drugs in the treatment of panic disorder and agoraphobia. The long-term effects of CBT have also been shown to be superior to other techniques (Clark *et al.*, 1994). Systematic desensitisation (SD) has been demonstrated to be an effective treatment for both specific and social phobias. For example, Capafóns *et al.* (1998) found that covert desensitisation techniques were effective in the treatment of fear of flying. What is clear, however, from a number of studies, is that *in vivo* desensitisation tends to be more effective than *covert* desensitisation.

Some psychologists are more cautious about the effectiveness of CBT/CBGT and SD. Klein *et al.* (1983) compared SD with supportive psychotherapy for patients with a social phobia

'OK, maybe I shouldn't have skipped a few steps back there …'

(agoraphobia) or with a specific phobia. They found no difference in effectiveness (those receiving supportive psychotherapy had also done well), suggesting that the 'active ingredient' in SD or CBT may simply be the generation of hopeful expectancies that their phobia can be overcome.

## Psychoanalysis

According to the psychoanalytic view, phobias are a defence against anxiety produced by repressed impulses or conflicts. This anxiety is transferred to an object or situation which then becomes the phobic stimulus. A phobia, therefore, is a symbolic expression of these repressed feelings, such as sexual or aggressive impulses. The individual must avoid the phobic object or situation so that they do not have to deal with these repressed impulses. The aim of psychoanalytic treatments is to uncover the repressed conflicts, analyse what they mean to the patient and substitute more realistic appraisals for those that are based on the limited understanding of childhood. Psychoanalysts believe that when an individual fully understands the meaning and origin of these repressed feelings, the fear will disappear or at least will become manageable.

### Does it work?

Unfortunately, psychoanalysis has tended to prove disappointing in the treatment of phobias. Although patients usually find the therapy helpful in decreasing general anxiety as well as in identifying feelings and thoughts associated with phobic avoidance, the phobic symptoms often remain. There are, however, some studies which demonstrate the beneficial effects of psychoanalysis in the treatment of phobias. For example, Knijnik *et al.* (2004) found that a variation of psychoanalysis (psychodynamic group treatment, or PGT) was superior to a placebo control group in a 12-week randomised trial. Its most famous application, however, must be the case of Little Hans (see Star Study below).

## starSTUDY
# Investigating therapeutic approaches: Little Hans
(FREUD, 1909)

### Aims

Hans's father recorded the details of this case study. He was very interested in psychoanalysis and used it to analyse his son's early development. Freud's aim in publishing this case study was to provide support for his theory of personality development. Freud believed that when boys are aged three to five they go through the phallic stage, during which their libido is focused on their genitals. At this time, little boys would experience the Oedipus conflict – desire for their mother and jealousy towards their father, leading to feelings of guilt which would be repressed. Resolution occurs when the boy identifies with his father.

Freud also used the case study to support his explanation of and treatment for phobias. Phobias may develop at any time of life as a means of dealing with repressed feelings. Psychoanalysis aims to make the unconscious conscious thus enabling the individual to accept their feelings.

### Method and procedure

The participant in this case study was a boy called Little Hans who was aged between three to five during the period of the study. Hans's father recorded events and conversations with Hans and these reports regularly to Freud. Both Freud and the father offered interpretations of Hans's behaviour based on the principles of psychoanalysis, i.e. offering Hans explanations of his thoughts and fantasies so that Hans could come to understand them himself.

### Results

The case study revealed that Hans had sexual fantasies about his mother and saw his father as a rival. He also felt jealous of his younger sister because her birth meant less contact for him with his mother. All of these feelings led Hans to experience feelings of conflict and anxiety. Hans developed a phobia of horses pulling a laden cart. This phobia gradually receded as Hans came to accept his real fears and identify with his father.

### Conclusion

Freud suggested that Hans's fear of horses developed for several reasons. First, Hans once heard a man saying to a child, 'Don't put your finger to the white horse or it'll bite you'. Hans also once asked his mother if she would like to put her finger on his penis. His mother told him this would not be proper. Hans projected one source of anxiety onto another – he became afraid of being bitten by a white horse whereas he was really scared that his mother would leave him.

Secondly, Hans saw a horse with a laden cart fall down and thought that the horse was dead. The horse symbolised his wish that his father (big whiskers and glasses like blinkers) would die, and the laden cart symbolised his mother pregnant with his sister, and when it fell over this was like giving birth. Therefore, the laden cart symbolised his dying father and his mother giving birth – both events that filled him with anxiety.

Freud claimed that this provided support for his theory of psychosexual development, and evidence for his explanation of the origins of disordered behaviour.

### Evaluation

*Case studies*

The 'uniqueness' of a case makes it difficult to generalise to all other people. On the other hand, case studies provide psychologists with rich detail and allow them to study unusual behaviours such as phobias.

*Interviews*

Interviews enable us to find out what people are thinking, which you can't do if you just observe their behaviour; for example, Hans could tell us his dreams etc. On the negative side, interviews may not produce information that is valid or reliable. Hans may not have told the truth, but instead provided the answers that he thought his father wanted to hear. Moreover, his father may have asked questions in a way which 'led' Hans to provide the answers he wanted. Freud believed that, even if a response is triggered by suggestion, it is not arbitrary. In any case, Hans did sometimes disagree with his father's suggestions, and there were benefits of the close relationship (more intimate details would be revealed).

## assessment issues

**Describe *one* therapeutic approach that may be used to help a person suffering from a phobia. (*ku* 4 *ae* 0)**

This is a straightforward four-mark question. As it requires only *ku* skills, try to resist the temptation to write evaluative points, however much you know about the pros and cons of systematic desensitisation (or whichever therapeutic approach you choose). You may not necessarily be penalised for doing so, but the worry is that you may neglect the 'knowledge and understanding' content, which should be quite detailed. In some questions, such as this one, you may be able to exploit your knowledge of links between different Topics. For example, if you wrote about psychoanalytic therapy, perhaps giving the example of Little Hans, you could draw on your knowledge of the psychoanalytic view of Early Socialisation (Chapter 1). If you demonstrate your awareness of such links you are showing the skill of *integration,* which examiners see as a sign of 'deep' understanding.

# Aspect 3: Care of people with mental health problems

KEY TERMS

**Institutional care:** Caring for the mentally ill in a psychiatric unit within a hospital as distinct from outpatient care or care within the community.

**Community-based care:** An attempt to 'normalise' the mentally ill by treating them at home or within their own community. This allows individuals to live as normal a life as possible rather than the regimented life of a psychiatric hospital.

## Institutional and community care

Individuals with severe mental illnesses used to be locked away in asylums or mental hospitals. Today in the UK, psychiatric care may involve a period of hospital stay and occasionally a period of enforced detention (**institutional care**). Most psychiatric care, however, takes place in the community (**community-based care**).

## Institutional care

A psychiatric hospital is an institution (or unit in a general hospital) that specialises in the treatment of people with serious mental illnesses such as schizophrenia. Although there are many different types of psychiatric institution, most have certain common characteristics

*The ways in which people with mental health problems are cared for varies within the same culture over time (historical changes) and also varies between cultures.*

Further information about the Mental Health (Care and Treatment) (Scotland) Act 2003 can be found at www.scotland. gov.ukpublications/2003/11/18547/29201

(e.g. for particularly vulnerable patients, there are frequently elaborate procedures to prevent suicide). They attempt to reduce the amount of sensory stimulation that patients receive and try to provide as normal an environment for patients as possible. In the UK, people with mental illnesses receive psychiatric care in hospital only for as long as is considered necessary. The dominant form of treatment is medication, although some hospitals also provide 'talking treatments' such as counselling, group therapy or some form of occupational therapy. Although most psychiatric wards are unlocked, some people are confined to locked wards because they are detained under the Mental Health Act.

### The Mental Health Act 1983 and Mental Health (Care and Treatment) (Scotland) Act 2003

Although some people are admitted for treatment voluntarily, others are compulsorily placed in hospital (i.e. they are 'sectioned') under the Mental Health Act. The term *'sectioning'* is used because the Act is divided into Sections (see page 268). Under recent Scottish legislation, a person may be admitted to hospital without their consent for a period of 72 hours (emergency detention). This occurs if a medical practitioner judges that their health, safety or welfare, or that of another person is at immediate risk. If there is no immediate risk, a 28-day detention order may be sought for psychiatric assessment. If, at the end of this time, the medical recommendation is for a further stay, the person can be detained for treatment for a further six months.

### Secure units and special hospitals

Some people who have mental health problems become caught up in the criminal justice system and may be admitted to a regional secure unit direct from the courts or from prison under the Mental Health Act. Others with a major mental disorder who are considered to pose a serious threat to others may be admitted to a high-security special hospital such as the State Hospital in Lanarkshire (Carstairs) or Broadmoor in England.

*evaluation*

## Institutional care

### Patient appreciation of institutional care

Biancosino *et al.* (2004) assessed patients' opinions on the perceived benefit of treatment received while they were hospitalised in a residential facility. Although all forms of therapy were considered helpful by most of those sampled, the 'therapy' with the highest score was 'talking to a doctor' and the least-valued item was 'group activities'. Treatments that allowed interactions with the outside world were also well received.

### The 'myth of mental illness'

Critics of the medical model, such as Thomas Szasz (1960) and R.D. Laing (1967), argued that people with mental illnesses have a 'fake disease' and the scientific categories imposed by mental health professionals are actually used as a form of social control. The term 'mental illness' is a euphemism for behaviours that are disapproved of, with hospitalisation as a way of forcing 'treatment' on these individuals to punish them and make them conform. Szasz claimed that nobody should be deprived of their liberty unless they have committed a criminal offence; therefore, depriving someone of their liberty 'for their own good' (e.g. under the Mental Health Act) is immoral.

### Institutional racism in psychiatry

We discussed institutional racism in Chapter 6 (see pages 147 and 161–162). Sashidharan (2001) claims that psychiatry, like policing and the criminal justice system, militates against the interests of black people in this country. Although it is argued by some that black people are overrepresented in psychiatric care because they experience higher rates of mental illness, others argue that it is a consequence of psychiatry being used as a form of social control. Elsewhere, Lay *et al.* (2005) found that, in Switzerland, immigrant groups experienced higher rates of compulsory hospital admission and were more likely to be admitted with a lower severity of mental illness.

### Limited access to talking therapies

In a recent report, the Healthcare Commission (2005) claimed that psychiatric treatment in the UK still placed too much emphasis on drug treatments and not enough on 'talking therapies' such as counselling and psychotherapy. This is despite strong evidence that a combination of drugs and psychological treatments can provide real benefits.

For an insight into life in a high-security special hospital, visit www.tsh.scot.nhs.uk/
Read the remarkable story of a Uist crofter and artist who spent 50 years in an Inverness psychiatric hospital: bjp.rcpsych.org/cgi/content/full/181/6/0

## Community-based care

Care in the community as we know it today gained its main impetus in the 1960s, an era which saw a major change in attitude towards the treatment of the mentally ill and an increased focus on patients' rights. It represented a movement away from the isolation of the mentally ill in old Victorian asylums towards their integration into the community. By the early 1990s, many large psychiatric hospitals had closed down completely. The aim was to 'normalise' the mentally ill, removing the stigma of mental illness and so allow individuals to live as normal a life as possible.

### Who provides care in the community?

Various bodies provide care for those with mental health problems, usually working in partnership. Although systems differ somewhat between Scotland, Wales and England, an individual may receive care not just from health services, but also from social services and voluntary agencies such as Mind. A range of professionals may be involved, including psychiatrists, psychologists, social workers, community psychiatric nurses and occupational therapists, making up Community Mental Health Teams (CMHTs). CMHTs usually support people with more serious mental disorders such as schizophrenia and bipolar disorder (manic depression). In Scotland, services are coordinated by Mental Health Officers (MHOs) appointed by local authorities. MHO responsibilities were extended under the Mental Health (Care and Treatment) (Scotland) Act 2003.

### Community care services

The aim of these services is to provide individuals with mental health problems with the kind of help and care that enables them to continue living in their own home or in supported accommodation. This includes day care centres, which provide recreation, therapy and rehabilitation. Befriending schemes can ease feelings of loneliness and isolation, as support and friendship are given on a one-to-one basis by specially trained volunteers. Voluntary organisations often provide an advocacy service, whereby an experienced worker will accompany a client at appointments and meetings in order to help them to communicate their needs and views, for example in relation to treatment, welfare benefits, housing and vocational training. Self-help groups may also be available.

### Hostels and therapeutic communities

Hostels are short-term shared housing facilities which help individuals to gain greater independence as well as supporting them with their mental health problems. A special form of hostel is the *therapeutic community* where residents have regular house meetings with a live-in therapist or counsellor.

---

*evaluation* | Community-based care

Research evaluating the effectiveness of community-based care has tended to support the claim that home treatment is as effective as hospital-based care and is more acceptable to both clients and their relatives. For example, Arvidsson and Ericson (2005) carried out a follow-up study to assess the impact of the 1995 Swedish reform in mental health, which placed greater emphasis on community-based care. They found that the number of days of inpatient care for persons given a diagnosis of schizophrenia was drastically reduced, demonstrating that community care was an effective form of treatment.

Community-based care also has its critics. Singh (1994) argues that living in the community is not inherently therapeutic, particularly as people first became ill while living 'in the community'. He claims that many people with mental health problems experience profound loneliness and alienation within their communities and may experience deep-rooted prejudice against them. Many people who are most at need of mental health support (e.g. drug users and the homeless) have never been institutionalised and are receiving inadequate care from the community. This may in part be due to the difficult management problems posed by such individuals, but may also be a product of the fact that they deny having a mental illness, and/or scare stories about the abusive nature of psychiatry. As a result, many people most in need of care are also most alienated from it.

The nature of community care varies between cultures, and the Western model of institutionalisation versus community care is not universal. For example, in Pakistan, when a mentally ill person is admitted to hospital, a family member stays with them, adopting an important role in providing care (e.g. food, personal care and companionship) (Karim *et al.*,

For some people, care in the community is less of a reality.

2004). The Mental Health (Care and Treatment) (Scotland) Act 2003 places a legal duty on local authorities to promote the well-being and social development of people with a mental disorder who are not in hospital. This represents a change in approach to the care of mentally ill people, emphasising factors in the community which promote positive mental health and those which prevent mental ill-health.

star**STUDY**

# Investigating institutional care: Community-based care versus hospital care

**(MUIJEN *ET AL.*, 1992)**

## Aims
To compare the effectiveness of care within an individual's own community with standard hospital care for patients with a serious mental illness.

## Method and procedure
One hundred and eighty-nine patients aged between 18 and 64 living in London were randomly allocated to either receiving psychiatric care within their own homes or receiving care as day patients within a hospital. After three months, approximately two-thirds of each group were evaluated, with effectiveness of care assessed using a number of outcome measures, such as psychiatric diagnosis, social functioning and patients' (and relatives') satisfaction.

## Results
For the three-month period of evaluation, required hospital stay was significantly less in the home care group compared with the hospital care group (median stay 6 days compared with 53 days for the hospital care group). Both groups showed improvements in clinical and social functioning. Improvements were slightly greater in the home care group.

On a global adjustment scale, home care patients improved by 26.8 points, and the hospital care group by 21.6 points.

## Conclusion
The findings suggest that home-based care does offer some advantages over hospital-based care, both for patients and their relatives.

The fact that a much smaller number of patients dropped out of the home care programme suggests that it is more appreciated by patients than is standard hospital care.

## Evaluation

### Application
This study demonstrates a major advantage of community-based care, in that it eases the pressure on much needed beds by providing more than adequate levels of care for patients who can be supported out of hospital.

### Lack of objectivity
Critics of community-based care argue that studies such as this should not be accepted at face value, suggesting that researchers may not have been objective in their evaluations as they stand to gain most from the success of community-based approaches.

This was the scene in Bedlam, the common name for the mental hospital called Bethlem, as depicted by Hogarth (1735).

Many websites provide interesting anecdotes about the treatment of mental illness through the ages, for example www.usyd.edu.au/hps/course2003/3010.html and bms.brown.edu/HistoryofPsychiatry/hop.html

## note

### A potted history of the treatment of mental illness

- *The Greeks and Romans*. There is evidence that the mentally ill were treated with compassion by the ancient Greeks and Romans, with 'treatment' usually in the form of music, sedation or even opium.
- *The Middle Ages*. From the fall of the Roman Empire in the fifth century AD until the fifteenth century, the mentally ill were less humanely treated, with most subjected to fairly brutal treatment or simply left to roam the streets.
- *The seventeenth century*. In the UK, nothing much changed until the first mental hospital (the Bethlem Royal Hospital, see picture on page 284) opened in London. However, the mentally ill were still regarded more with curiosity than compassion, and for a small price the public could wander through the wards to observe the 'patients' for their own amusement.
- *The nineteenth century*. The number of people incarcerated in mental hospitals under the lunacy laws increased steadily during the nineteenth century in Victorian Britain. Owing to advances in medicine, mental illness was regarded with greater understanding and more humanely treated.
- *The twentieth century*. Despite the advent of the National Health Service in the UK in the 1940s, the legal rights of mental health patients remained largely unchanged. In 1959, however, under the Mental Health Act, mental health professionals gained control from magistrates over who should receive mental health care. The 1960s saw a move away from the institutional approach of the Victorian asylums towards treatment within the community.

## assessment issues

**Describe different types of care that may be provided for people with mental health problems. (ku 4 ae 0)**

This is another straightforward question, requiring only *ku* skills. If you've done your revision, it should present no problem. But beware complacency! Think carefully about which area(s) of your knowledge you need to use. Possibly the main risk in this question lies in the four-letter word 'care'. You could easily launch yourself into a couple of paragraphs on *therapies* rather than *care* – and gain zero marks. One way to avoid this hazard (in any Topic) is to ensure that you are thoroughly familiar with the way in which each Topic is organised in the Unit content: you should know the titles of the Aspects, and what material is contained in each Aspect. If you organise your file of course notes according to these Aspects, you're less likely to go wrong. In this question, you should recognise straight away that you are being asked about the third Aspect of the Topic, 'Care of people with mental health problems'.

On the other hand, there are also occasions when you may need to 'import' material across different Aspects of the Topic: for example, you might be asked a question on humanistic methods of treating depression. In order to do this, you would need to adapt the more general material in Aspect 1 on humanistic therapies to discuss treatment of depression (covered in Aspect 2). Once again, you'll be able to spot this if you are crystal clear about how the content (and your own notes) is structured.

> *There is a strong negative halo associated with the mentally ill. They are considered, unselectively, as being 'all things bad'. The average man generalises to the point of considering the mentally ill as dirty, unintelligent, insincere and worthless.*
>
> (Nunnally, 1961)

## Attitudes to mental illness

The experience of being mentally ill is profoundly affected by the attitudes held by others about mental illness.

## Perceptions of mental illness

The quotation is the conclusion from a six-year study carried out in the 1950s. Have things changed in the intervening years? Research still suggests that mentally ill people are perceived negatively, and that subsequent behaviour towards such individuals is also negative. Attitudes towards the mentally ill can be summarised under the following headings (Segal, 1978).

The film *A Beautiful Mind* tells the story of Nobel Prize-winning mathematician John Nash who battled schizophrenia for much of his life.

For movies about mental illness, see home.epix.net/~tcannon1/psychopathmovies/all.html and mentalhelp.net/poc/view_doc.php?type=news&id=37081

### Range of behaviour

The public regards a broader range of behaviours as representing mental illness than was previously the case. This is partly due to the portrayal of mental illness in films such as *A Beautiful Mind* (about a man with schizophrenia) and *As Good as it Gets* (about a man with obsessive-compulsive disorder). However, public perceptions of the 'seriousness' of a mental disorder tend to rely more on perceived dangerousness than on any other factor.

### Labelling

The media and other sources (such as research) tend to reinforce the negative connotation of the label of 'mental illness' and so increase the likelihood that the person displaying that behaviour will experience social isolation. Critics of this view argue that, because labelling results in receiving much needed support, it provides significant benefits for the person labelled mentally ill. Rosenfield (1997) found that the stigma associated with the label of mental illness and the services received were both significantly associated with quality of life, but in opposite ways. The stigma associated with mental illness lowered the person's quality of life, whereas the services received raised it.

### Social distance

Media reports may increase the public's desire to avoid mentally ill individuals. Angermeyer and Matschinger (1996) found that there was a marked increase in desired social distance from mentally ill people immediately following highly publicised violent attacks by individuals with severe mental illnesses. Angermeyer *et al.* (2003) found that beliefs about the *cause* of an individual's mental illness also had an impact on people's desire for social distance. Those who blamed the individual for their illness expressed a stronger desire for social distance.

### Attitudes and actions

Social psychology tells us that attitudes do not necessarily predict behaviour towards the attitudinal object. Is this the case with the mentally ill? Early research suggested that individuals with mental illness tend to experience more discrimination than other members of society. More recently, a survey carried out by the National Schizophrenia Fellowship (Scotland) in 2001 found that 41% of people with mental health problems living in Scottish communities had experienced harassment, compared with 15% of the general public. A 2001 study carried out by the Department for Work and Pensions found that only 37% of employers said that they would take on people with mental illness, compared with the 62% who would employ physically disabled people.

## Research on attitudes to mental illness

### Tolerance for mental illness

Research has typically shown that members of the public hold relatively intolerant attitudes towards the mentally ill. A number of misconceptions exist about mental illness and about people who have mental illnesses. Research (e.g. Nieradzik and Cochrane, 1985) has shown that the larger the number of negative misconceptions about mental illness, the greater the intolerance. Several 'myths' are common within these misconceptions, including the belief that individuals are responsible in some way for their mental illness, or that their inability to overcome their illness is due to their lack of willpower (Furnham and Henley, 1988). Intolerance is also based on the belief that individuals with disorders such as schizophrenia are dangerous or violent (Wahl, 1992).

### Misconceptions about mental illness

A fundamental factor in these misconceptions is the lack of understanding in many people as to what constitutes a mental illness. Wolffe *et al.* (1996) found that 21% of people surveyed could not name *any* type of mental illness, and a further 19% could name only one. Over three-quarters of respondents thought that they could tell if somebody was mentally ill, citing odd behaviour (73%) as the method of distinction. The vast majority of respondents in this survey cited environment stresses as the major cause of mental illness, with genetic and physiological causes trailing far behind.

### Representations of mental illness in the media

A substantial number of studies have demonstrated the media's power to influence public perception including our understanding of mental illness. A large-scale Australian review of research in this area (Francis *et al.*, 2001) concluded that media representations of mental illness promote negative images and stereotypes – in particular, the false connection between mental illness and violence. Recent research in the UK suggests that the British press may be guilty of misguiding the public and promoting distorted views of mental illness (Morgan, 2006). This study found that the press consistently gave disproportionate and sensationalised coverage to psychotic illnesses such as schizophrenia, often linking them to serious crime. Not only does this lead to damaging misconceptions of psychotic conditions, but it also affects understanding of the more common neurotic illnesses.

A report by the mental health charity, Mind, claimed that negative media coverage had a direct and harmful impact on the lives of people with mental illness. Mind (2000) surveyed 515 people suffering from a range of disorders. Half said that the media coverage had a negative effect on their own mental health, and 34% said that this led directly to an increase in their depression and anxiety.

### Changing attitudes

In 2002 and 2004, national surveys of attitudes to mental health were conducted in Scotland. Results indicated 'some positive shifts' in attitudes over that period (Braunholtz *et al.*, 2004). Furthermore, it was found that people who were aware of the anti-stigma publicity campaigns 'see me' and 'Choose Life' were more likely to have positive views. This suggests that it may be possible to reduce negative perceptions of mental health problems by harnessing the power of the media.

For information on the campaigns 'see me' and 'Choose Life' see www. seemescotland.org and www.chooselife. net/web/site/home/Home.asp.

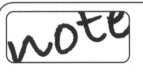

**Campaigns**

The 'see me' and 'Choose Life' projects form part of Scotland's national strategy for improving mental health. 'Choose Life' is a national 10-year plan aimed at reducing suicides in Scotland by 20% by 2013. It focuses on action planning at local level, so each area of Scotland has a Choose Life Coordinator.

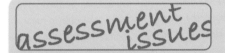

**Common theme: cultural influences on behaviour**

In many areas of psychology, explanations of behaviours and mental processes address cultural influences. For example, cross-cultural comparisons are made in parenting practices, and in most social psychology topics (such as conformity and obedience). In the study of atypical behaviour, cultural bias is found in the ways that 'abnormality' is defined, and in the ways that people with mental health problems are diagnosed and treated. It's important to remember that 'cultural differences' exist not just between countries and communities, but also between different points in *time*, even in the same society. As we have seen, forms of care offered to people with mental health problems are strongly affected by prevailing public attitudes, which can and do vary greatly (over time and place). In assessments, whenever you demonstrate awareness of relevant cultural influences you are likely to gain credit, whether this is explicitly demanded in the question or not. Ask yourself 'Is this behaviour universal?'

## Chapter: Atypical behaviour – therapies                    Exam questions and answers

*In this section we show you student answers to possible exam questions plus examiner's comments on these answers. Remember that in the actual exam (and NABs) your questions for this Topic will always add up to 20 marks. The question may be one essay worth 20 marks or a number of smaller questions (such as those shown below) which add up to 20 marks.*

### Question 1    What is meant by 'care in the community'? (*ku 3  ae 0*)

| Tom | Alice |
| --- | --- |
| The phrase 'care in the community' refers to the idea that some mental patients are cared for in the community, by doctors and nurses and psychiatrists. They may live in a flat where they are visited regularly to see if they are getting on OK. | The invention of psychoactive drugs has meant that mental patients with more severe mental disorders don't have to be locked up in mental institutions but instead can live in the normal community where community health teams supervise their care. There are day centres which provide recreation and rehabilitation which is important so they don't feel lonely and isolated. There are also hostels where they are supervised but can learn to be more independent. Therapy is available in the hostels and day centres. |

**Examiner's comments**    Very little useful material is given by Tom. He gains no marks: **0 out of 3 marks** (*ku* 0/3  *ae* 0/0).

Alice starts well by describing community care in relation to institutional care. The latter part of her answer is fairly sound but needs a little more substance: she should explain more clearly that people may live either at home or in supported accommodation. It would also be helpful to indicate the kinds of professionals that make up the community mental health teams, and/or the agencies that provide services. Alice gains **2 out of 3 marks** (*ku* 2/3  *ae* 0/0).

### Question 2    Compare *two* types of therapy that may be used to help a phobic client. (*ku 6  ae 4*)

#### Tom

Phobic clients might be helped by systematic desensitisation (SD). In this therapy the client is asked to list a series of things that are progressively more fearful. They are also taught how to relax. Then the therapist takes them through the stages, each time ensuring that the client relaxes and copes with his/her fear. Eventually they get to the top of the hierarchy which might be holding a spider or being in a room full of birds or standing in an open space. This means they have overcome their phobia.

Studies have shown that SD is very effective with phobias. McGrath et al. (1990) showed that about 75% of patients respond to the therapy and a study by Meichenbaum showed that it also helped them to overcome other, non-treated phobias. On the other hand many phobias disappear by themselves over time. Also if the phobia is caused by some underlying problem you don't really treat this and so the phobia may come back. But Behaviourists would say there may not be an underlying problem, for example a phobia might be learned through classical conditioning and therefore treatments don't need to address an underlying problem.

A different way of coping with phobias might be to use drugs, like anti-anxiety drugs. Beta-blockers reduce levels of adrenaline which makes you feel anxious so the drug makes you feel less anxious. If you feel less anxious you may be able to rationalise the fear or it might be useful to use this with another therapy, like a cognitive therapy because you can cope better once the anxiety is reduced. Comer recommends that this is the most effective way to treat psychological disorders – by mixing chemotherapy with another therapy.

The advantage of using drugs is they are quick and easy whereas psychotherapies take quite a bit of time and also effort. The disadvantage is that there may be side effects.

**Examiner's comments**    Tom's answer shows several strengths. The descriptions of his chosen therapies are sound, if a little lacking in detail; he refers briefly to research evidence and shows analytical skill in presenting not just a criticism of SD (that the underlying problem is not treated) but also the behaviourists' counter-argument in defence of their approach. His answer would be enhanced by setting his therapies in their theoretical contexts (i.e. the behaviourist approach and medical model). It would also be enhanced by using appropriate terminology: for example, he might have referred to SD's basis in classical conditioning, and the principle of 'incompatible responses'. He has explained 'symptom substitution' but failed to use that term. In the last paragraph Tom has made an attempt at 'comparing' the therapies, as required in the question. He has *contrasted* the two in terms of differences in time and effort invested, but he could also have elaborated on *similarities*, such as the failure to tackle any underlying problem, which is relevant to both (not just SD). For this answer he gains **8 out of 10 marks** (*ku* 5/6  *ae* 3/4).

### Alice

Two ways that could be used would be stress inoculation training and psychoanalysis. Stress inoculation training is good because it enables you to deal with similar problems in the future. It involves a series of steps to help you deal with stress and phobia is a stress-related disorder. The steps are first to conceptualise the problem, then to acquire skills that help cope with stress, such as relaxation and time management. In the final stage people are told to try their new skills out in different situations through imagining or role play.

Psychoanalysis might also be good for serious phobias. Psychoanalysis involves making unconscious thoughts conscious; things may have been repressed in early childhood because they caused anxiety, like in the case of Little Hans. Repressed thoughts are held in the unconscious and might give rise to phobias. Psychoanalysis involves free association where a patient talks about whatever comes into their head and therefore they may eventually get into the unconscious stuff. In the case of Little Hans he talked to his father and Freud about his thoughts and expressed them also in talking about his dreams. His father offered interpretations of his thoughts so he could realise what he was really bothered about and thus he overcame his phobia of horses.

**Examiner's comments**    In using SIT as one of her chosen therapies, Alice has adopted a sound strategy of borrowing relevant material from another topic of the course (stress) to apply to this question and thus shows integration of her knowledge. She has given a good description of the stages of SIT and psychoanalytic therapy. Unfortunately, she has not responded at all to the 'compare' requirement of the question: she has not mentioned any similarities or differences between the therapies and has provided little in the way of analytical or evaluative content. She is awarded **6 out of 10 marks** (ku 5/6 ae 1/4).

**Question 3**    Describe the cognitive-behavioural approach to therapy. (ku 6 ae 0)

### Tom

The essence of the cognitive-behavioural approach to treating psychological disorders is that the problem lies in the way you think about things rather than being a separate problem. If you can change the way you think then this will result in a cure. This has currently become the most popular approach to treatment especially for less serious illnesses such as depression or stress-related disorders. The therapist gets the patient or client to describe their problem and to reconceptualise it as a problem that can be solved. The therapist then helps the client develop skills to help deal with the problem. Finally the client practises the new skills. The important thing is that this whole process gives the client some skills that can be used any time a problem exists.

**Examiner's comments**    Tom shows some grasp of the basic principles of the cognitive-behavioural approach to therapy, and has made a good start by outlining the cognitive explanation of disorder. However, his answer is sketchy; he might have pointed out more clearly that the approach draws on techniques from both the cognitive and behavioural approaches and that CBT aims to change both thought processes and behaviours. One or more specific therapies could have been briefly described, along with their proponents, such as Ellis or Beck. This is a mediocre answer; it may be that Tom's knowledge is actually limited, due to inadequate revision, or it may be that he has the necessary knowledge but has failed to tailor it to the question. He gets **3 out of 6 marks** (ku 3/6 ae 0/0).

### Alice

The cognitive-behavioural approach to therapy is based on the cognitive view of disorder and aims to change behaviour by means of changing thinking patterns. In the cognitive approach someone who has a psychological problem has developed faulty beliefs about themselves and the world around them. The purpose of therapy is to help the client identify and challenge these beliefs. Albert Ellis' rational-emotive behavioural therapy (REBT) is a good example of a cognitive-behavioural therapy. He developed this in the 1950s and 60s though he is still practising now. He called his model the ABC model. A is activating events, B are beliefs and C are consequences. REBT encourages people to start disputing their negative beliefs about themselves, and this means that future consequences will be better. The disputing may be logical, empirical or pragmatic. Such a therapy requires quite a lot of active involvement from the client and also might be regarded as unethical because the challenges may be quite negative. Other forms of CBT include Beck's approach and Meichenbaum's SIT, in which clients are given 'homework' tasks. These techniques are based on similar principles to Ellis' approach.

**Examiner's comments**    Alice's answer shows more substantial knowledge than Tom's. She sets her answer in context by outlining the CBT approach to therapy and linking it to the cognitive view of disorder. In describing only one specific type of CBT (REBT), she seems to have overlooked the fact that the question asks about the CBT *approach*; however, she resolves this problem to some extent in her last sentence. As in Tom's case, it would have been useful to provide some examples of the kinds of beliefs and behaviours that can be changed. Perhaps Alice has not noticed that there are no *ae* marks for this question, as she has given evaluative material in her penultimate sentence. She gains **5 out of 6 marks** (ku 5/6 ae 0/0).

ndividual differences are those aspects of each of us that distinguish us from others, such as personality and intelligence. Each of us also differs in the extent to which we are 'normal'.

Intelligence is a key individual difference. It eludes easy definition because there are many different aspects to intelligent behaviour. One way to define it is in terms of learning and thinking, but we might also regard someone as 'intelligent' if they can cope with other challenging tasks such as climbing Mount Everest or managing a successful company.

The various Aspects of these Individual Differences Topics are closely related to each other, so the Star Studies that we provide are relevant to more than one Aspect. Of course, as with all the other Topics, this chapter provides a range of research evidence relevant to each Aspect.

| Chapter contents | Unit content for the Topic 'Intelligence' | Comment |
|---|---|---|
| **Aspect 1: Intelligence and IQ** | | |
| Theories of intelligence page 291<br>The nature of IQ page 295 | • Nature of intelligence, and the intelligence/IQ distinction<br>• Measurement of IQ<br>• Theoretical views of intelligence, including:<br>  –factor theories<br>  –information-processing approach | *Many attempts have been made at defining 'Intelligence'. In this Aspect, we consider various **definitions**, as well as the **difference between intelligence and IQ** (intelligence quotient), which is often overlooked. The study of intelligence has mainly been concerned with identifying and explaining **individual differences**, so ways of **measuring IQ** are described. You will then examine **factor theories** of intelligence, which see intelligence as comprising a range of different kinds of abilities, and the **information-processing approach**, which describes intelligence in terms of the cognitive processes that we use to deal with information.* |
| **Aspect 2: Nature–nurture debate in intelligence** | | |
| Genetic factors in intelligence page 298<br>Environmental factors in intelligence page 302<br>Interactionist approaches page 304 | Nature–nurture debate in intelligence:<br>• genetic relatedness and IQ<br>• twins and adoption studies<br>• effects of early deprivation and environmental enrichment<br>• interactionist approaches | *'**Nature**' and '**nurture**' influences have been hotly debated in the study of intelligence, probably more so than in any other area of psychology. In this Aspect we take a critical look at various types of relevant evidence: you should be able to assess the importance of **genetic relatedness in IQ**, according to studies of **twins** and **adopted children**. Studies of children who have suffered **deprivation**, or have received **environmental enrichment**, also help us to understand what factors may account for individual differences in intelligence. You should be able to interpret such evidence from an **interactionist** perspective.* |
| **Aspect 3: Uses of IQ testing** | | |
| IQ testing in education and employment page 306<br>Cultural bias in IQ testing page 310 | Uses of IQ testing:<br>• educational selection<br>• recruitment in employment and military organisations<br>• effect of cultural biases on validity/reliability of IQ tests | ***IQ tests** are used in various settings in everyday life. Although less commonly than in the past, many UK **schools** still select pupils using IQ tests. IQ tests have long been used by **employers**, such as the police, civil service, and **military organisations**, in their recruitment procedures. You may be familiar with IQ testing as a form of popular entertainment, as seen in the BBC's Test the Nation series. However, as the use of IQ tests can have serious consequences for individuals, it is important that they are **valid** and **reliable**; one threat to validity and reliability arises from potential **cultural biases**.* |

# Aspect 1: Intelligence and IQ

## Theories of intelligence
### What is intelligence?

'Intelligence' is a word we use all the time, but could you define it? Psychologists have difficulty agreeing on a definition. In general, when we say someone is intelligent we are referring to mental abilities such as their ability to reason, to solve problems, to think abstractly, to learn and so on. Intelligence is also an adaptive trait – particularly among our ancestors because individuals who were more intelligent were more likely to survive and reproduce.

There are three main questions related to intelligence:

1  *What is it?* Do people have just one general intelligence or are there separate forms of intelligence such as being good at maths but not good at languages? Such questions are addressed by theories of intelligence which we will consider shortly.
2  *Can intelligence be reliably measured?* We measure intelligence using IQ tests, but how meaningful are such tests? We will consider this issue on pages 295–299 and again in Aspect 3 when we look at the uses of IQ tests and the question of cultural bias.
3  *Is intelligence inherited?* Or do life experiences shape your intelligence? The nature–nurture question is examined in Aspect 2.

Do you think cats are more intelligent than dogs? How could you decide? What makes one animal more intelligent than another or one person more intelligent than another?

*explanation*    ### Factor theories

One approach to answering the question 'What is intelligence?' has been to use a method called **factor analysis** to find out what factors or abilities underlie high intelligence scores. Imagine that you give various mental tests to a large group of people. We then correlate the scores of each test with the scores of every other test in turn, producing a **correlation coefficient** (see page 115) for each pair of tests. If there is a strong correlation between any two tests this suggests that they share an intervening variable or common factor.

*Spearman's two-factor theory*
Charles Spearman (1904) invented statistical tests of correlation and also invented factor analysis. Using his new tests he found that children's scores on a range of mental tests were positively correlated, which led him to suggest that there is one general mental ability which underlies all cognitive performance. He called this the *g* factor. He suggested that there are also specific factors (called *s* factors). Differences between individuals are largely due to the *g* factor, but the *s* factor explains why each person is not uniformly competent at all tasks.

*Later factor models*
A range of other theories have been developed from Spearman's original, all using factor analysis to identify components. For example, Thurstone (1938) found that there was not a single factor underlying all test results; instead, he identified seven distinct *primary mental abilities* (*PMAs*): spatial ability, perceptual speed, numerical reasoning, verbal meaning, word fluency, memory, and inductive reasoning (generating rules from a set of observations). Thurstone regarded *g* as an average of these PMAs. The PMAs are independent and not correlated; thus *g* will vary depending on which mental tests are used and which PMAs they tap.

Vernon (1950) also used factor analysis and proposed a hierarchical model which had a set of *group factors* between *g* and *s* factors; *g* is what all tests measure, *major group factors* are what some tests measure, *minor group factors* are what particular tests measure, and *specific* factors are what particular tests measure on specific occasions. Because Vernon's theory accounted for a general factor and group factors, it was seen as reconciling Spearman's two-factor theory (which doesn't have group factors) and Thurstone's multiple-factor theory (which doesn't have a general factor).

*Cattell's fluid and crystallised intelligence*
Cattell (1963) conducted his own factor analysis of mental tests and concluded that *g* could be divided into *fluid intelligence* (*gf*), which is basically abstract reasoning and innate, and *crystallised intelligence* (*gc*), which encompasses knowledge that comes from experience. Examples of *gc* include vocabulary, the ability to see similarities between objects and situations, and general information. Examples of *gf* include solving puzzles, classifying figures into categories and changing problem-solving strategies easily with each new problem.

*evaluation*

*Factor analysis*
The strength of the factor analysis approach is that one can produce objective statistical facts, or at least so it appears. In fact, the factors that are identified are not 'real' – they are just arbitrary categories. Often, when the same data are analysed using a different method of factor analysis or by a different person, different factors emerge. So it seems that the approach is actually relatively subjective despite objective appearance.

Another criticism of the approach is that many of the theories are based on rather restricted samples. For example, in the main, Spearman and Vernon tested schoolchildren; the data from such a sample may have shown less evidence of crystallised intelligence.

A third criticism is that all the factor theories assume that a large component of intelligence is inherited and thus should be apparent at an early age. We will look at the evidence for and against innate intelligence in Aspect 2 of this chapter.

*Research evidence*
Despite such criticisms, the concept of *g* is alive and well. Recent neurophysiological research (Duncan *et al.*, 2000) provides some strong support (see Star Study below).

## starSTUDY

# Investigating intelligence: A neural basis for *g*
**(DUNCAN ET AL., 2000)**

### Aims
There are two opposing explanations for factor theories of intelligence: (1) that there is one general factor (*g*) that contributes significantly to all cognitive activity and (2) that there are various component factors or information-processing functions. It is not possible when using factor analysis to distinguish between these two explanations because an apparent general factor may in fact be several independent information-processing functions that underlie most mental abilities. However, it may be possible to distinguish between the explanations by comparing the pattern of neural activity displayed when people are engaged in different kinds of mental tasks. The aim of this study was to see if a discrete area of the brain becomes active during IQ tests, or whether neural activity is spread over a wide area.

### Method and procedure
In this study, 13 human volunteers completed 3 types of general intelligence test (spatial, verbal, and perceptual-motor) while brain activity was assessed using *PET scanning* – radioactive glucose is injected into the body and taken up by active areas of the brain because they need glucose for energy. This enables researchers to see what parts of the brain are active while participants are engaged in different tasks. The three types of test were adapted from standard tests and selected because their correlations with *g* were high. For each task, there was a corresponding low *g* control test based on similar materials but having no problem-solving element.

### Results
The researchers found that, despite the diverse task content of the three types of test, the lateral prefrontal cortex of one or both hemispheres became particularly activated in each case when participants were engaged on the high *g* tests but not the control tests.

## Conclusion

These results suggest that the lateral prefrontal cortex contains the 'seat' of general intelligence and this underlies major mental activities rather than there being a range of different locations each for individual information-processing functions. In other words, the study identified a neural basis for *g*.

## Evaluation

*Correlation not cause*
Sternberg (2000) has criticised the conclusions of this study because the results merely show that prefrontal lobe activity is *associated* with certain aspects of intellectual functioning but this does not demonstrate a causal relationship.

*Further research*
It is possible that further research using more advanced brain investigation techniques will pinpoint specialised regions within the general area of the prefrontal cortex, and these regions could be related to specific information-processing functions.

---

*explanation*

## Information-processing approach

An information-processing theory is essentially one which uses concepts drawn from computer technology – input, output, storage, programmes, routines, and so on. Such theories view cognitive activity as the taking in, processing and outputting of information. Information-processing theories assume that one person is more intelligent than another because they can process information more efficiently. The goal of information-processing theories is to determine what people do when they have to deal with complex problems – what **metacognitive** skills or strategies they use.

*Case's information-processing theory*
Robbie Case (1992) suggested that greater efficiency in information-processing ability occurs as children become able to use their *mental space* more effectively. Mental space (or M space) is a concept rather similar to 'working memory' (see page 36). It describes that area of the brain where information is stored during processing. There is a limit to the amount of information that can be held in M space at any one time. However, the amount of data that can be processed increases with age because of the following factors:

- *Brain maturation*, especially changes in the myelin sheath (a fatty protective layer around the nerves which increases), leads to faster neural transmission rates.

- *Strategies* become more automatic with practice and so need less conscious attention, thus freeing M space for other work. Once strategies are sufficiently automatic, they can become 'central conceptual structures', allowing children to think about their experience in more advanced ways and to develop more efficient ways to solve problems – in effect to move to a new stage of development.

- *Metacognitive skills* (thinking about thinking) are especially important for efficient use of M space, for example being aware of what words you do or do not understand when reading something, monitoring your own progress when tackling a mental task, consciously trying different ways of solving a problem, etc.

*Sternberg's triarchic theory*
Robert Sternberg (1988) incorporated information-processing into a broader theory of intelligence. He argued that traditional theories look at only one aspect of intelligence whereas he felt that intelligence comprises three factors or 'subtheories' of intelligence:

- *Componential* (analytical) subtheory, the individual's internal world. This view is that intelligence comprises mental components such as reasoning ability. One of the most fundamental components is the set of metacognitive processes that control the strategies and tactics used in intelligent behaviour. This is the information-processing aspect of triarchic theory and it is the aspect of intelligence usually tested by intelligence tests.

### KEY TERMS

**Metacognitive.** These skills are higher-order skills which give us control over thinking or cognitive tasks, such as how to approach a learning task, knowing how to evaluate your performance, monitoring comprehension, etc.

- *Contextual* (practical) subtheory, the individual's external world. This view is that intelligence is useful to the extent that it is applied in a real world context. It is about how a person uses their intelligence in everyday life – in their work, relationships, etc. It is about intelligence helping us to adapt to changing conditions, a kind of streetwise knowledge. Some people are particularly good at, for example, knowing the right time to ask for promotion, or knowing how to manipulate others for their own good, or working out the cheapest or quickest way to get from A to B using public transport.

- *Experiential* (creative) subtheory, an individual's past experiences link the internal and external world. This view is that intelligence mediates between the mental components you have and the demands of your environment. Intelligence is about formulating new ideas from previously unrelated information based on past experience. This is the creative aspect of intelligence.

According to Sternberg, a complete explanation of intelligence must entail all of these three subtheories. Conventional notions of intelligence miss this important interaction between components, context and experience.

## evaluation

*Information processing versus factor theories*
The strength of the information-processing approach is that it addresses the problem of *how* people actually solve complex problems, whereas the factorial approach traditionally has offered a *description* of the human intellect. A further contrast between the two approaches is that the information-processing approach portrays intelligence as consisting of many different mental processes whereas some (but not all) factor analysis models see intelligence as a unitary mental process (*g*), although even *g* theorists recognise a variety of component skills such as speed of processing, capacity of working memory, ability to sustain attention, etc.

*Evaluation of Case's theory*
This theory lends itself to research investigations. For example, Chi (1978) tested participants' recall for pieces on a chess board; one group comprised children who were relative experts at chess whereas a second group was made up of adults who were novices at the game. Research typically finds that people's recall ability (for example recalling digits after hearing them once) improves with age. In Chi's study, however, it was the children who could recall more. This finding is attributed to their experience with chess pieces which meant that certain combinations were automatic 'central conceptual structures' and led to the ability to process more information.

There are also interesting applications of this theory. For example, it can be used to measure intelligence; the emphasis on strategies means development can be measured in terms of the number of items an individual can recall. The theory can also be applied to education, by, for example, training students in metacognitive skills.

*Evaluation of Sternberg's theory*
The strengths of this theory are in its breadth and its attempt to link internal mental abilities to external use of intelligence. It also attempts to link theories of intelligence (in the domain of individual differences psychology) with the domain of cognitive psychology.

The theory has interesting applications. It suggests that intelligence can be enhanced through training programmes which provide links between the training and real-world behaviour. Such programmes provide explicit instruction in strategies for coping with novel tasks/situations, i.e. creative and practical thinking. Sternberg and Grigorenko (2004) report that such programmes have led to improved school performance.

Probably the main criticism is that the theory offers a framework rather than a detailed account of the processes and structures involved in intelligence. For example, it is not clear how the three subtheories relate to each other. In addition, Gottfredson (2003) claims that there is no clear evidence that 'practical intelligence' is anything different from skills that are already measured. She also claims, in contrast to Sternberg, that it has not proved to be a useful construct.

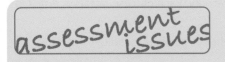

## The nature of IQ

### What is meant by IQ?

**KEY TERMS**

**IQ:** A numerical score representing a person's intelligence based on their score on a test of intelligence.

There is a *distinction between intelligence and IQ*. The letters **IQ** stand for 'intelligence quotient'. The term 'quotient' is used because the score derived from an intelligence test used to be calculated by dividing test score (i.e. mental age) by chronological age (you may recall that a quotient is what you get when you divide one number by another). It was multiplied by 100 to remove fractions.

More recent IQ test scores are not determined by the quotient method. They use *norms* to work out a persons' IQ based on their score and age. We will explain this further when discussing standardisation.

Try an intelligence test yourself at www.bbc.co.uk/testthenation/ or www.intelligencetest.com or www.queendom.com

**The distinction between intelligence and IQ**

The concept of intelligence is concerned with the theory of what underlies intelligent behaviour. IQ is a score that represents an individual's intelligence. Such scores make it appear as if intelligence is a real 'thing' whereas inevitably test scores represent a test designer's concept of intelligence and the abilities through which intelligence is measured.

**Items from a test of verbal intelligence**

1. Which of the following five is least like the other four? Celery, lettuce, onion, grape, asparagus
2. What would be the next number in this series?
   15 ... 12 ... 13 ... 10 ... 11 ... 8 ... ?
3. Gina is faster than Jan, and Nora is slower than Gina. Which of the following statements would be most accurate?
   a) Nora is faster than Jan.
   b) Nora is slower than Jan.
   c) Nora is as fast as Jan.
   d) It is impossible to tell whether Jan or Nora is faster.

Source:
http://www.queendom.com/cgi-bin/tests/transfer.cgi

## Measurement of IQ

You may have taken an intelligence test during the course of your school life even though you were not aware that it was a test of your intelligence. Broadly speaking, such tests come in two forms: tests of verbal intelligence and tests of non-verbal (performance) intelligence, as illustrated here and on page 312 (Raven matrices).

Tests of non-verbal intelligence assess performance on tasks that require minimal verbal materials, i.e. use few words. Such tests enable more accurate assessment of individuals who have problems with verbal materials such as those who are deaf, or have limited English, or have communication disorders. This doesn't mean that there are two *kinds* of intelligence but that there are two routes to assessing intelligence. The existence of separate verbal and non-verbal IQ scores also means that it is possible to detect students who are underperforming – they do well on the non-verbal scales but not on verbal scales because the verbal scale relies more on experience/learning rather than innate abilities.

One of the best known IQ tests is the Stanford-Binet test which is administered individually. The fifth edition (2003) tests five factors: fluid reasoning, knowledge, quantitative reasoning, visual-spatial processing, and working memory. Each of these factors is tested in the two separate domains, verbal and non-verbal.

Some IQ tests are designed to be given individually, whereas others (e.g. the British Ability scales) are designed to be given to groups of people.

### Other tests of intelligence

There are many other tests of thinking, such as tests of creativity. Such tests might include questions like 'How many uses can you think of for a paper clip?' There are also tests of animal intelligence, illustrated by the Birdbrain of Britain.

### *Psychometrics*

IQ tests are 'psychometric tests' – tests that measure psychological abilities. Such tests consist of a set of tasks that can be given to an individual or to a group of people and produce a score that can be represented as a number or category.

Some tests measure qualities other than intelligence, for example personality, attitudes, mood, aptitudes for particular jobs, and so on.

Psychometric tests generally produce **quantitative data** (see page 102) although there are some tests, such as the Rorschach Personality test which produces **qualitative data**.

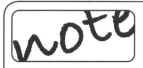

### *Birdbrain of Britain*

Brooks-King and Hurrell (1958) devised tests of bird intelligence and showed that some bird species are more intelligent than others. One test used a perspex device with holes which enabled peanuts to be suspended on matchsticks. If a bird removed the right matchsticks, the peanut would fall to the bottom so that it could be eaten. Blue tits and coal tits were the only species that could solve this test which involved up to five rows of matchsticks.

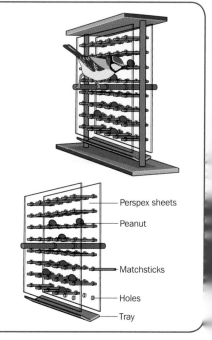

*We covered the concepts of* **validity** *and* **reliability** *in Chapter 4 (see page 112).*

## Construction of IQ tests

### Item selection

How does one go about constructing a test of intelligence? The 'test designer' has beliefs about what constitutes intelligent behaviour and sets about devising test items which appear to test such behaviour. It is important that items on the test should be drawn from common, shared cultural experiences thus giving each candidate equal opportunity to provide suitable answers.

Once the test items have been selected, the IQ test must be standardised and be shown to have high **reliability** and **validity**. All IQ test manuals provide this information as well as instructions about administration.

### Standardisation

In order to understand what a person's test score *means* we need to compare one person's score with those from many other people of the same age who have done the same test. This is the process of **standardisation**. It demonstrates whether an individual's score is average, above average or very above average, etc.

The process involves giving the test to a large, representative sample of people and establishing the *norms* for each age group, for example finding out the mean score and spread of scores for each age group. The raw scores are converted to a standard scale where the mean mark is given a score of 100. On the test, the actual mean mark might be 34 but this is now converted to 100. Next the standard deviation for all the scores is calculated. The standard deviation is a measure of the spread of data around the mean. It is assumed that IQ scores have a *normal distribution* (as shown in the graph), which means that the number of people scoring between one standard deviation above and one standard deviation below the mean will be 68% of the population who take the test; 95% of all scores fall between two standard deviations above and below the mean. The standard deviation for IQ tests is usually 15 so a test score which is one standard deviation below the mean is converted to a score of 85 and a score one standard deviation above the mean is converted to a score of 115. Scores in between are calculated on a pro-rata basis.

### Normal distribution

A normal distribution the bell-shaped distribution of scores that is obtained when you plot a set of randomly determined events. For example, if you measured the life of 1000 light bulbs and plotted them on a graph you should obtain a normal distribution. Most of the 'lives' will cluster around the mean (let's say this is 7 months) – if it is a true normal distribution, 68% will be within one standard deviation of the mean (which might be 2 months either side of 7). Very, very few bulbs will last 1 month or 13 months. (See also 'Normal distribution' on page 238).

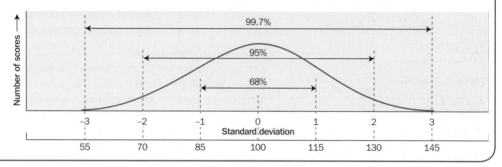

### Reliability

There are two kinds of **reliability**: external and internal. *External reliability* concerns consistency over time. If an IQ test is measuring innate potential then a person's score should not change much over time. Therefore, we would expect that, if the same person is tested on several occasions, the test should produce the same score (**test–retest** reliability, see page 112). In order to assess test–retest reliability tests are divided into two halves (A and B); form A is given on the first occasion and form B is given a few weeks or months later.

Reliability can also be assessed for internal consistency (*internal reliability*). This can be done by giving the test to a group of people and then dividing the test items into two arbitrary groups and correlating the scores on both halves (called **split-half method**). Most well-known intelligence tests have fairly good reliability, for example +0.85. Items that do not correlate well with the overall score are excluded.

### Validity

A test is valid if it measures what it claims to measure. There are several ways of establishing validity. One way is called **criterion validity** where test scores are correlated with some other measure (or criterion) of intelligent behaviour such as educational success. If this is current behaviour, it is called **concurrent validity** and if it is future behaviour it is called **predictive validity**. Typically, such correlations are high although not perfect (between +0.40 and +0.60).

*evaluation*

### IQ tests

*Quantitative data*

IQ tests produce *quantitative data* which are straightforward to analyse. The problem with such numerical data is that they oversimplify an extremely complex ability. (The issue of quantitative versus qualitative measurement is discussed on page 112.) In fairness, most IQ tests produce more than one score, for example separate scores for different skills or subtests.

*Reification*

The term 'reify' is used to describe situations where something which is abstract (such as intelligence) is turned into something tangible (such as IQ). Inevitably, people then see IQ as based on a real thing and forget that it is speculative; IQ scores are based on one particular view of what intelligence is and thus their validity can be challenged. They may well test what the test designer intended to test (the definition of validity) – but is that intelligence? We can use tests to estimate a psychological quality like intelligence but we cannot obtain a valid measure unless we can define the quality precisely and ensure that our measurement techniques match the definition.

Traditional tests also tend to have a narrow view of intelligence, equating it with reasoning ability and ignoring other aspects of intelligence such as musical intelligence or creativity or Sternberg's componential and experiential aspects of intelligence. It can be argued that a score on an IQ test just shows how good you are at taking IQ tests.

*Cultural bias*
Early versions of the Stanford-Binet test were standardised on white children only and therefore a black child's IQ score was really a measure of how well they performed on a white standard. The wider problem of cultural bias is discussed in Aspect 3 of this chapter.

*Innate versus acquired ability*
Many people assume that the score you receive on an IQ test reflects an innate ability or potential. However, tests can't measure innate potential because you cannot test intelligence directly but can only test the abilities through which intelligence is measured.

*Group versus individual tests*
Conducting individual IQ tests is very time consuming and prone to bias because the tester may encourage some testees more than others and thus enhance their performance unfairly. In some cases, however, this kind of help is important to ensure that an individual is relaxed and their true abilities are demonstrated. On the other hand, group tests are much easier to conduct; they have a higher level of control and can be easily marked as the questions used in such tests usually have one correct answer.

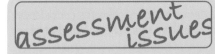

**Explain what is meant by "intelligence" *and* "IQ".** *(ku 4 ae 0)*

This is a straightforward definition question, or two-definition question to be precise. When answering *any* question, one of the first things to do is to *locate* it: the Topic itself is obvious (in this case 'Intelligence'), but you need to identify in your own mind which particular *Aspect* or part of an Aspect the question focuses on. After all, every Topic you study contains a large amount of material, so for every question that you answer you must be selective in the material you use. Here, although intelligence and IQ are referred to throughout the Intelligence chapter, the most relevant part for this question is of course the first Aspect of the chapter, where both of these key terms are defined. Don't be tempted to write everything you know about these concepts! Keep the size of your answer in proportion to the number of marks available.

# Aspect 2: Nature–nurture debate in intelligence

## KEY TERMS

**Nature:** Favoured by *nativists* or *hereditarians*, in whose view nature does not simply refer to abilities present at birth but to any ability determined by genes, including those that appear during development as a result of maturation (such as talking).

**Nurture:** Favoured by the *empiricists*, whose view is that everything is learned through interactions with the environment (the physical and social world), which may be more widely referred to as 'experience'.

**Nature–nurture debate:** The debate over the relative influence of nature and nurture on any particular behaviour.

Where does your intelligence come from? Is it a trait that you get from your parents' genes or is it a product of the type of environment in which you were raised? The answer to this question is obviously that *both* genes (**nature**) and environment (**nurture**) contribute. Nevertheless researchers have been keen to establish the relative contributions of each to intelligence: the **nature–nurture** debate.

## Genetic factors in intelligence
### What are genetic factors?

Genes are the mechanism by which some psychological and physical characteristics are passed from one generation to the next. Each child receives half of their genes from their mother and half from their father.

### Studies of genetic relatedness
#### Family studies
Bouchard and McGue (1981) conducted a meta-analysis on the results of over 100 studies on the heritability of IQ. They found that the closer the genetic link, the higher the correlation between IQs. For example, siblings reared together had a correlation of +0.45 whereas for half-siblings (genetic link weaker) the correlation was +0.35.

**Twin studies**

The study by Bouchard and McGue (1981) included data from twin studies. Identical (monozygotic – MZ) twins share 100% of their genes while fraternal (non-identical, dizygotic – DZ) twins share just 50% of their genes. If heredity is the main influence on intelligence, identical twins should be more similar than fraternal twins because they share more of their genes. Occasionally, researchers get the chance to study identical twins that have been raised apart. Any resemblance is then more likely to be a product of genetic factors (which are shared) than environmental factors (which are different).

Bouchard and McGue found that even when identical twins are raised apart their IQs still correlate quite highly (+0.72). This degree of resemblance, although not as high as for identical twins raised together (+0.86), was higher than the figure for fraternal twins raised together (see table). This suggests that our genes do contribute to our intelligence level, and that this contribution is possibly stronger than the contribution played by environmental factors.

| Type of relationship | Number of | | Mean correlation coefficient |
| --- | --- | --- | --- |
| | Separate studies | Pairs of relatives | |
| Identical twins raised together | 34 | 4672 | +0.86 |
| Identical twins raised apart | 3 | 65 | +0.72 |
| Same-sex fraternal twins raised together | 29 | 3670 | +0.62 |
| Opposite-sex fraternal twins raised together | 18 | 1592 | +0.57 |

Source: Bouchard and McGue (1981)

Thomas Bouchard has also been a key figure in an ongoing twin study, the Minnesota Study of Twins Reared Apart which began in 1979 and has followed 100 pairs of identical and fraternal twins separated in infancy. The results of this research suggest that about 70% of the IQ differences found are associated with genetic variation (Bouchard et al., 1990). Interestingly, the researchers concluded that these differences in IQ are mainly due to the *indirect* influence of people's genes on their intellectual development; i.e. a person's genes influence their environment and this leads to IQ differences (see page 301).

Other twin studies generally support these findings. For example, the Swedish Adoption/Twin Study of Ageing (SATSA) found that identical twins had the same IQ correlations (+0.79) whether they were reared together or apart. This study found that about 80% of the variance in IQ is inherited (Pedersen et al., 1992).

evaluation

Studies of genetic relatedness

*Twin studies*

Twin studies are natural or quasi-experiments (there is no random allocation to groups and no direct manipulation of the independent variable), which means that they do not demonstrate a causal relationship. Twin studies only show that there is a strong *relationship* between genes and IQ. This relationship may be due to *indirect* genetic influences (as outlined below) as well as to direct ones.

The data from twin studies show the importance of genetic factors but also provide support for environmental factors. Even when individuals share identical genes, their intelligence is not identical. This means that some other factors must be contributing to the development of their intellect. This may be the child's environment, but even when identical twins share the same environment the correlation in their IQs is not 100%. This is because of the **non-shared environment**. Two people in the same home do not have the same experiences – different chance experiences, different friends, etc. all create unique experiences for each individual. The assumption that people living together experience the same environment was mistakenly made by early researchers.

*Genetic determinism*

Berlucchi (1999) argues that the brain is so complex that genetic effects are not predictable; if *you* started out again you would not develop in the same way! The presumption that genes have straightforward effects is simplistic.

## Adoption studies

Adoption studies assess hereditary influences on intelligence by examining the resemblance between adopted children and their biological and adoptive parents/siblings. Within such studies, it is assumed that any similarities between an adopted child and their biological parent are due only to genetic effects and that any similarities between an adopted child and their adoptive parent are purely environmental.

One study, the Texas Adoption Project, has followed over 500 adopted children and their biological mothers and their adopted families: Loehlin *et al*. (1989) reported that at age 8 the children had an IQ correlation of +0.25 with their biological mother (genetic link) and +0.15 with their adoptive mother (environmental link). The IQ correlation between unrelated siblings was +0.26 at 8 years of age. At age 18, all correlations with adopted relatives were almost zero. This suggests that in *early childhood* it is environmental factors that mostly influence IQ development: adopted siblings and parents share no genetic factors but do share environmental influences. In *late adolescence* it seems that environmental factors no longer have *any* influence. This *increasing* heritability seems puzzling but can be explained in terms of a kind of gene–environment interaction, which Scarr and McCartney (1983) call niche picking (see page 301).

**starSTUDY**

## Investigating the nature–nurture debate in intelligence: The Colorado Adoption Project

(PLOMIN *ET AL*., 1997)

### Aims

The Colorado Adoption Project (CAP) is an ongoing longitudinal study that aims to study the genetic and environmental influences on traits such as intelligence, personality and behaviour. It started in 1976.

### Procedure and method

The researchers contacted birth mothers (and where possible fathers) of babies who had been adopted in their first month of life. There has also been a control group of non-adopted children and their families; 442 families are still involved in the study. Assessments have included face-to-face interviews as well as interviews over the phone, and psychological testing of both parents and children.

### Results

The findings related to IQ are shown in the graph below. At the beginning of the study, correlations between children and their biological parents were marginally higher than with adoptive parents. By the time the children reached adolescence, they increasingly resembled their *biological* parents in terms of cognitive abilities.

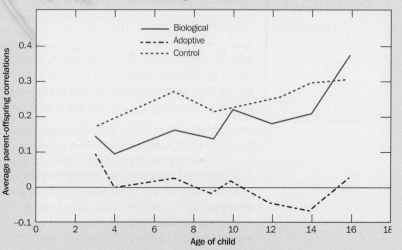

## Conclusion

The results show that the adopted children become increasingly like their biological parents and less like their adoptive parents as they get older. These results suggest that parent–offspring resemblance for general cognitive ability is due in the long term to genetic factors and that the family environment created by adopted parents does not contribute significantly to the adult IQ of their adopted children.

## Evaluation

*Extensive data*

The size and duration of this project and the wealth of measures used to study the children and their families has produced a sizeable database from which to draw conclusions. This is a *positive* criticism of this study.

*Validity of IQ tests*

On the negative side, IQ tests may not be a valid means of assessing intelligence (see criticisms elsewhere in this chapter) which, if true, means that the data on IQ are meaningless.

*Arthur Jensen (1969) argued that there are significant differences in the IQ scores of white and black Americans and that this is mainly due to inherited differences. See page 311 for further discussion.*

# Direct and indirect genetic effects

## Direct effects

The studies examined so far in this Aspect are related to *direct* genetic effects – the view that children inherit specific genes from their parents which 'cause' high or low IQ. Research has been trying to isolate the specific genes that might be involved. For example, Plomin and colleagues (Chorney *et al.*, 1998) studied 50 gifted children in the US whose SAT (Scholastic Aptitude Test) scores were equivalent to an IQ score of 160 or higher, comparing their DNA with children of average IQ. They found that a particular variant of one specific gene (insulin-like growth factor 2, or IGF2R for short) on Chromosome 6 was twice as common in the sample of children with ultra-high IQs as it was in those with average IQs. This gene has at least seven different *alleles* (alternative forms of the same gene), and two of these alleles were more common in the high IQ children. In particular, Allele 5 was more common in extremely high-IQ groups (46% had at least one IGF2R Allele 5) than in the average-IQ group (only 23% had at least one Allele 5). Although these findings may not seem that impressive, they do show clear differences between individuals with higher and average intelligence.

## Indirect genetic influences

It is important to recognise that genes can also influence behaviour *indirectly* in a number of ways. For example, parents' genes influence aspects of parents' behaviour which then influence their children. An intelligent parent is likely to be better educated and thus have more books at home. The parents' genes lead to an environment that is more intellectually stimulating. Thus a child's IQ is enhanced indirectly and passively by genetic factors.

Indirect effects can also explain the findings from adoption studies that as children grow up they become more similar to their genetic relatives. This is because they seek out experiences and environments that suit their genes – **niche picking** – your genes select your environment (e.g. liking for books) and then the environment shapes you.

We will discuss 'gene–environment' interactions further on page 304.

### KEY TERMS

**Niche picking:** The tendency to actively seek environments that suit our inherited tendencies.

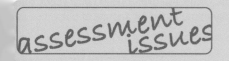

**Describe and evaluate findings from twin studies that suggest there are genetic influences on IQ. (ku 3 ae 3)**

Although the mark allocation is only six marks, this is a relatively complex question, so take a few moments to break it down. The focus here is on *twin studies*, and specifically, what they tell us about *genetic influences on IQ*. So, hopefully, you can bring to mind two or more examples of relevant twin studies (such as Bouchard and McGue, and Pedersen *et al.*). Next, what do you have to *do* with this material? *Describe* and *evaluate*. Having identified all the elements of the question in this way, you should be able to systematically address each of them in turn, without getting side-tracked from what's relevant, and without forgetting essential bits. This tactic is sometimes called *deconstructing* or *dissecting* a question.

Environmental factors such as clean air, a good diet and physical exercise, can have an effect on a person's IQ.

# Environmental factors in intelligence

## What are environmental factors?

Environmental factors include any influences outside the individual – this includes physical influences, such as good diet and clean air, and social influences, such as parents, teachers, peers and books. A belief in the importance of environmental factors in the development of intelligence leads to the view that human intelligence is relatively malleable and to the development of intervention programmes designed to boost the scholastic achievement of children who would otherwise be limited by low IQ. Many environmental factors have been identified as affecting intelligence, such as early deprivation, and, more recently, researchers have investigated the possible link between diet and IQ. It appears, as we might always have believed, that we are what we eat!

## Effects of early deprivation

In the 1930s, psychologists in an American orphanage considered the possibility that the children's poor mental and emotional development was not a product of their biological inheritance, but a result of their institutionalisation and the associated lack of mother love. In order to test this, they transferred 13 of the most seriously retarded infants (average age 19 months) to an institution for adult mentally retarded women. Each infant became attached to one particular, mildly retarded woman who acted as a mother substitute for the child. The subsequent development of these children was compared with that of a control group of similar children who had remained in the orphanage, receiving no individual attention. In the group with the mother substitutes, IQ levels *increased* by an average of 32 points over the next 4 years, whereas the control group lost an average of 21 IQ points over the same period (Skeels and Dye, 1939. This study was also mentioned on page 17).

In a follow-up study carried out 27 years later, this difference between the two sets of children was still evident. Those in the experimental group had graduated from high school and were self-supporting, whereas those in the control group had progressed no further than the third grade, and remained institutionalised for life (Skeels, 1966). This study challenged the belief – widespread at that time – that IQ was fixed for life.

The effects of attachment on intellectual development can be explained in several ways, which are discussed in Chapter 1. First of all, attachment provides a child with a secure base so that they feel able to explore the environment more freely even when their mother figure is not present. The more a child explores, the more they learn. Secondly, attachment reduces stress whereas deprivation is associated with anxiety. This has been shown in research: for example, one study of Romanian children found higher levels of the stress hormone cortisol on weekdays when the children were in a badly run day care centre, than on weekends when they were home with their parents (Carlson *et al*., 1995). The importance of this is that stress hormones, such as cortisol, slow mental growth.

## Environmental enrichment

### Intervention programmes

The Perry Preschool Project (Schweinhart *et al*., 1993) studied 123 African American children who were born in poverty and were at high risk of failing in school. From 1962–1967, when the children were between three and four, they were randomly divided into a preschool group, who received a high-quality programme, and a comparison group, who received no preschool programme. The compensatory education programme involved a half-day every week of active learning with the preschoolers plus a weekly 90-minute home visit over a period of 2 years. The researchers found positive effects for the preschool programme group on a range of outcomes as shown in the table on the next page.

| Major findings of the Perry Preschool Project | | |
| --- | --- | --- |
| Category | Preschool | No preschool |
| Mean IQ at age 5 | 95 | 83 |
| Age 15 achievement test | 122.2 | 94.5 |
| High school graduation | 67% | 49% |
| % of years spent in special education | 16% | 28% |
| Post-secondary education | 38% | 51% |
| Arrested or detained | 31% | 51% |
| Receiving welfare at age 19 | 18% | 32% |

The findings of this study have been supported by a number of other intervention projects, such as the American Operation Headstart begun in the 1960s. Thousands of children from disadvantaged homes were involved in preschool programmes to boost their cognitive performance before they started school. It was argued that such children lacked some of the early benefits enjoyed by more middle-class children in terms of, for example, health care and intellectual stimulation, and that they were therefore disadvantaged even before they started school. Such disadvantages usually get worse and perpetuate a cycle of failure. In general, Headstart children showed IQ gains of about 10 points in the first year at school in comparison with control groups, but this usually disappeared (Zigler and Styfco, 1993). However, as with the Perry Preschool findings, long-term effects have been observed, such as participants being more likely to obtain a high school certificate.

The Carolina Abecedarian Project (Ramey and Campbell, 1984) had a similar outcome. This project focused on mothers with low IQs and their infants; a special day care programme was run from infancy and extra medical attention was given. By school age, the children had higher IQs than a control group but IQs declined soon thereafter.

This common outcome of rather minimal effects from intervention programmes may be because other environmental factors overwhelm the comparatively small influence of the schooling.

### Improved living conditions and the Flynn effect
Wheeler (1942) studied a rural US community over a 10-year period and found that as living conditions improved (new roads, new schools, better living conditions) children's IQ scores increased by 11 points.

In fact, IQs all over the world have been increasing. This is called the *Flynn effect* after James Flynn who has been studying IQ scores from many countries for the last 60 years. Since 1940, IQ scores have been increasing by about 3 points per decade; Dutch gains between 1952 and 1982 were 20 IQ points, and Israeli gains were similar (Flynn, 1987). There are three possible explanations. First, it could be that human intelligence is evolving, but such a rapid development cannot be explained in terms of genetic change. Secondly, it could be that people are getting better at doing IQ tests because, for example, we are more used to doing timed activities and are more familiar with visually based technologies. This would mean that IQ is not actually changing. Or thirdly, it could be that environmental factors (such as diet, better living conditions, more information available on the Internet, etc.) are enabling individuals to reach the maximum level of their *reaction range* (see page 305).

### Diet
There is increasing evidence that dietary interventions can affect measured intelligence. Schoenthaler and Bier (1999) carried out studies in schools and other institutions in England, Scotland, Wales, and Belgium. In each of these studies, children who received vitamin-mineral supplements performed better, in tests of their non-verbal IQ, than those who simply received a placebo.

The researchers also found that the standard deviation (measuring the spread of scores) for IQ change was consistently larger in each experimental group compared with its control group. This was presumably because the few children in each group who were most poorly nourished were showing large changes as a result of the supplements. This research suggests that

The evidence shows that environmental factors may be at least as important as genetic factors. But Bouchard *et al.* (1990) argue that, even if genetic factors are stronger, this does not detract from the need to provide children with a good-quality environment (parenting, education, etc.).

poor diet may lead to impaired intelligence and that vitamin-mineral supplementation 'may restore the cognitive abilities of these children by raising low blood nutrient concentrations' (Schoenthaler and Bier, 1999). They note, however, that such supplementation does not appear to improve the IQs of adequately nourished children.

### Home environment

Certain features of a child's home culture have been shown to relate positively or negatively with intellectual development. Bradley *et al.* (1989) used the HOME inventory and found that the IQs of children with low HOME scores declined by 10–20 points between age 1 and 3, whereas the opposite was true of children with high HOME scores. The most significant positive influences on IQ were parental involvement, provision of age-appropriate play materials and opportunities for daily stimulation (Bradley *et al.*, 1989). The importance of stimulation is illustrated in a study by Greenough *et al.* (1987) who found that rats reared in an enriched environment had larger brains than those raised in an impoverished environment; the former had more connections between the neurons in their brain and were smarter.

**assessment issues**

**Discuss evidence of the effects of environmental enrichment on children's IQ. (ku 4  ae 4)**

There are many and varied examples of evidence for the effects of environmental enrichment on children's IQ. You will no doubt describe and evaluate evidence of the effects of a stimulating home environment, of attachment, diet, education and living conditions, etc. Interpretation of such findings often involves quite subtle points, so try to demonstrate your understanding of these. For example, the effects of lack of attachment on IQ were well known but it is only in recent times that researchers such as Carlson *et al.* (1995) discovered a mechanism for this effect, i.e. that the anxiety of deprivation leads to over-production of cortisol (a stress hormone) which in turn impairs mental development. If you have read the Early Socialisation chapter (or when you do so), you'll recognise the strong link between the 'deprivation' Aspect of that Topic and this current Aspect of the Intelligence Topic. Thinking about these links helps to deepen your understanding by *integrating* your knowledge of different areas of psychology.

## Interactionist approaches

At one time, nature and nurture were seen as largely independent and additive factors; however, a more contemporary view is that the two processes do not just interact but are inextricably entwined. It is no longer really a debate at all but a new understanding of how genes work.

### Nature affects nurture

We have already reviewed some gene–environment interactions, such as the concept of niche picking (see page 301). These illustrate how our genes influence the environment.

### Nurture affects nature

One would think that the structure of the brain, like all aspects of your biological system, is programmed by your genes. However, there are many research studies that show that experience has a profound effect on the development of the brain. For example, Pascual-Leone *et al.* (1995) found not only that the region of the brain that controls finger movement increased in size over the course of only five days in participants required to play a finger exercise on the piano daily *but also* a similar effect occurred when participants merely imagined doing the exercises. Studies with non-human animals have observed the way that neurons shrink and grow in response to changing environmental conditions (e.g. when exposed to light and dark) (Edwards and Cline, 1999).

*"Genes do not just write the script; they also play the parts" (Ridley, 2003), and they play the parts according to the direction of the environment.*

### Nature via nurture

Ridley (2003) suggests that the description of gene–environment interactions does not go far enough in expressing the relationship between nature and nurture. It isn't just nature that is affected by experience but genes themselves are affected by nurture. For example, one study looked at a gene called RSG4. The activity of this gene was found to be low in people with schizophrenia. It was lowered further when individuals experienced acute stress (Mirnics *et al.*, 2001). In other words, experience changed the way the *gene* behaved.

### Interaction makes adaptive sense

The interdependence of nature and nurture makes adaptive sense – hardwired systems, such as areas of the brain for memory and language, are necessary because without genes for these systems it would not be possible to learn and recall. But a flexible system that responds to the environment ensures that each individual makes maximum use of its innate qualities. In order to do this, it is the environment that turns genes on and off.

## Nature and nurture interacting

It is not always easy or possible to disentangle nature and nurture. One example of the complexity of the nature–nurture interaction is seen in *transgenerational* effects – apparently inherited factors that skip a generation. For example, pregnant women in Holland during the Second World War gave birth to normal-sized infants despite being near starvation (an environmental influence) yet their grandchildren were very small. Such effects are now explained in terms of *epigenetic* material – non-genetic material that is transmitted across generations which may regulate the activity of genes and which is caused by environmental changes (Reik *et al.*, 1993).

The classic example of blended nature and nurture is phenylketonuria (PKU), an inherited disorder that prevents the protein phenylalanine from being metabolised, resulting in brain damage. However, if the condition is detected at birth, an infant can be given a diet devoid of phenylalanine and thus brain damage is averted. If prevention can be achieved through environmental manipulation, is this condition due to nature or nurture?

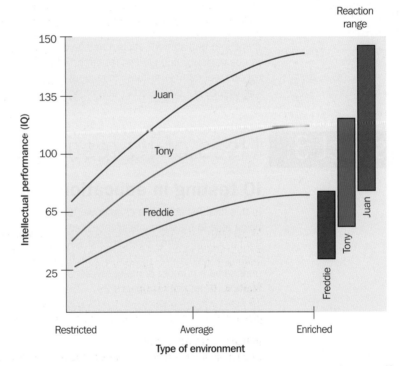

One view of the development of intelligence is that we are born with a **reaction range** (Gottesman, 1963). Our genes predispose us to a certain IQ range but the actual range that develops depends on experience. This illustrates another way in which nature and nurture interact.

## Interdependence

There are many views of the relationship between nature and nurture that illustrate the interdependence between them, such as the concept of reaction range which is illustrated on the left. A further example of this interdependence is shown in some recent IQ research by Turkheimer *et al.* (2003). They examined IQ scores from over 350 children from both poor and better-off families and found a very important difference. In children from poor backgrounds, almost all the variability in IQ was accounted for by their *shared environment* and none was related to genetic factors (heritability was +0.10). In the richer families, the opposite was true (heritability was +0.72). This research emphasises the extent to which nature and nurture are interdependent. In situations where the environment is supportive, the environmental component is minimised and the influence of genes is maximised – variability is mainly due to genetic influences. In situations where the environment is unsupportive, the opposite occurs – variability is mainly due to environmental factors (see the picture on page 312). This is a critical point when considering IQ research. Apparent genetic effects may be an artefact of research if a study has only looked at children from well-off families.

### Shared and non-shared environment

On page 299 we referred to the 'non-shared environment'. Traditionally, IQ research has looked at genetics versus environment and presumed that people brought up in the same home shared the same environment. However, more recently it has been recognised that this is not so. What was once regarded as 'the environment' breaks down into surroundings that are *shared* with peers and siblings (such as parents or number of books in the home) and those that are *non-shared* (such as particular friends or the age of the child when their parents divorced – a younger child might be more affected than a sibling who was older at the time). Some aspects of this non-shared environment are actively selected (or 'picked') by an individual and, most importantly, it is your genes that influence the kind of things that you prefer (niche picking). This means that trying to separate effects into nature or nurture doesn't work so simply.

*assessment issues*

### Common theme: nature–nurture interaction

As you read the different chapters in this book, you'll notice that the concepts of *nature* and *nurture* crop up in various places. It's clear that these concepts, and in particular the *interaction* between them, represent a *common underlying theme* in psychology. Relative contributions of genetic and environmental factors are relevant to our understanding of a whole range of psychological processes and behaviours, but nowhere has this issue been researched more thoroughly than in the study of intelligence and IQ. It is an issue that has far-reaching social and political implications beyond the scope of this book, in relation to education policy, crime and punishment, racism and so on. It is a dynamic issue that is affected by developments in neuroscience and genetic research. The section above (pages 304–306) provides a detailed overview of nature–nurture interaction; many of the concepts addressed here apply not just to intelligence but also to other psychological processes that you are studying.

## Aspect 3: Uses of IQ testing

### IQ testing in education and employment

In this final Aspect of the chapter we turn to the question of usefulness. The whole point of being able to measure intelligence is to do something with it. The first IQ test was developed by the Frenchman Alfred Binet around 1900. His principal goal was to produce a test which would identify students who needed special help in coping with the school curriculum. This test has undergone a number of major revisions but continues today as one of the major IQ tests, the Stanford-Binet test (see pages 297–298).

The second major development in IQ testing can be related to military organisations. At the start of the First World War, Robert Yerkes persuaded the US Army to allow him to develop IQ tests that would identify the ablest army recruits. Yerkes's tests were used with nearly two million recruits and, after the war, enquiries flooded in from schools and businesses that recognised the potential value of such tests for ranking and streaming students and employees. In this section, we will look at a few examples of such uses. One thing is clear – there are those who believe in the predictive power (and thus usefulness) of IQ tests and those who regard IQ tests as flawed, biased, and political tools of oppression.

### IQ testing in education

From Binet's time onwards, one of the main uses of IQ tests has been to identify students who require special education, including identifying the more able.

#### Identifying students with higher ability

The 11-plus test still exists in parts of the UK as a means of selecting which students should go on to grammar schools. The origin of these tests lies in the work of Sir Cyril Burt who believed that intelligence was largely inherited. In 1926 Burt began advocating for a national testing program that would identify the brighter students. Since he believed that intelligence is fixed by the age of 11, he suggested that all UK students should be tested at this age and then permanently segregated into grammar, secondary modern or technical education. He felt that such a system would establish a meritocracy; i.e. advantage should go to those who deserved it (because they had ability) rather than those who are born into it (because of wealth

"... then we have the intelligence test. If we find any you're out."

© www.cartoonstock.com

or pushy parents). The 11-plus would give economically disadvantaged children educational opportunities that they would not otherwise receive.

The 'meritocracy' argument was revived more recently by the hereditarians Herrnstein and Murray (1994) who argued in their book *The Bell Curve* that we waste valuable resources trying to educate everyone in the same way. From the viewpoint of society, they suggested, it would be better to use IQ scores as a means of determining what education is appropriate for each individual and allow the most able to rise to positions of power.

### Diagnosis of learning disabilities

The assessment of learning disabilities usually relies on administering *individual* tests; one of the best known of these is the Wechsler Intelligence Scale for Children; another is the Stanford-Binet test. Specific problems such as dyslexia are diagnosed using IQ tests – individuals may be classified as dyslexic if their reading skills are below what would be expected from their IQ scores. One issue in using IQ tests with people who have learning disabilities is that it is important to use tests that have been designed for the particular ability range; if the test used is aimed at those with average or high abilities, it will not discriminate well between those of low ability.

### Streaming

It is a common practice in schools to place students in ability-related 'sets' for certain subjects such as maths and English. Schools may use an IQ test to aid this process.

---

*evaluation*

## IQ testing in education

*Meritocracy*

The debate is extremely emotional and sensitive and political. The hereditarians' view is adopted by the political right wing which believes that IQ differences are inherited and that enrichment programmes are largely a waste of time. The evidence reviewed in Aspect 2 can be used to assess their claims.

*Validity and reliability of IQ tests*

The use of IQ tests presumes that they are measuring some 'real' quality; however, evidence related to the inherent *cultural bias* in such tests challenges this. The US courts (*Larry P* v. *Riles*, 1984) ruled that IQ tests could not be used to determine special education placement because they were designed and standardised on an all-white population and were thus culturally biased. Their use would lead to an imbalance of minority students in special needs categories. Cultural bias is discussed further on page 310.

Another issue, related to the validity of IQ tests, is their predictive ability. The correlation between IQ scores and grades is about +0.50, a strong correlation (APA Task Force, 1995). However, the APA Task Force points out that correlations of this magnitude account for only about 25% of the overall variance. This means that successful school learning depends on many characteristics other than intelligence, such as persistence, interest in school and willingness to study.

Research suggests that IQ tests have poor reliability: for example, Smith (1991) claims that IQ scores may vary by as much as 15 points from one test to another. In one study, 99 school psychologists independently scored an individual IQ test from the same records and came up with IQs ranging from 63 to 117 for the same hypothetical person (Sattler, 1982).

It seems that the objective and scientific nature of IQ tests is an illusion. However, is there any better alternative? IQ tests are cheap and established, and thus they continue to be used. Sternberg and colleagues (Bundy *et al.* 2001) concluded that 'conventional tests of intelligence can be useful but only if they are interpreted very carefully, taking into account the factors that can affect them, and in conjunction with other measures'.

*Labelling*

Another issue related to the use of IQ tests is their effect on subsequent performance. A classic study by Rosenthal and Jacobsen (1966) showed how teacher expectations affect pupil performance. In this study, students in a primary school were all given an IQ test and the teachers were given a report identifying some students as 'academic bloomers', i.e. students who had the potential to do better at school than they were currently doing (the 'bloomers' were randomly selected). When the students were retested a year later, many of the supposed 'bloomers' showed significant IQ gains.

The significance of this finding is that once an individual has been labelled as 'high IQ' or 'low IQ' they and others will have expectations about their future performance and these expectations may affect subsequent performance, a self-fulfilling prophecy. It might be that high correlations between IQ score and subsequent achievement could be explained in terms of this 'prophecy'.

## IQ testing in employment

### Recruitment in employment

Many companies use IQ tests to assess the potential ability of future employees or for internal promotions. These tests are also used by the civil service and the military. The rationale is that general intelligence level underpins our performance on any task. According to Gottfredson (2002), $g$ is the best single predictor of job performance. The APA Task Force (1995) concluded that IQ test performance accounts for some 29% of the variance in job performance. Hunter and Hunter (1984) pooled validity across a number of studies and found that IQ tests had a much higher predictive ability for success (+0.54) than any other measure, such as experience (+0.18) or interview (+0.14).

### Aptitude tests

Recruitment agencies tend to use aptitude and achievement tests more than straightforward IQ tests when assessing future employees. Aptitude tests were introduced early on when psychologists realised that employers and military organisations need more specific information than is given by an IQ score. In fact such 'aptitude tests', as opposed to IQ tests, are often preferred by UK employers, for example tests that look at abilities to use words/numbers/tools, learn new things, etc. Many employers (e.g. Fire service, Police, Society of Electricians) have developed their own aptitude tests.

In 1971, The US Supreme Court (*Griggs* v. *Duke Power Co.*) ruled that IQ tests could not be used as the controlling factor in selecting employees if the test was not directly relevant to the job or if the use of the test would discriminate unfairly by race (see section on cultural bias on page 310). It is permissible, however, to use tests of specific aptitudes, i.e. a test which fairly measures an applicant's ability to perform a particular job or class of jobs.

### The military

The US military uses its own aptitude-based test (see Star Study below). In the UK, the Army uses the British Army Recruitment Battery (BARB) as an entrance test to assess applicants' ability (a 'battery' is a set of tests). The Air Force and Navy also use a set of tests that assess reasoning, language, numeracy and mechanical comprehension.

## star**STUDY**

## Investigating the use of IQ testing: Predicting training success

(REE AND EARLES, 1991)

### Aims

To investigate whether $g$ can predict job performance as well as any aptitude tests.

### Method and procedure

The participants were 78,041 American Air Force enlistees recruited during the years 1984–1988. They were tested with the Armed Services Vocational Aptitude Battery (ASVAB) and completed both their basic military training and a job training course. They were mainly white (80%) and male (83%) and high school graduates (99%).

The ASVAB is a multiple-aptitude test composed of 10 subtests: general science, arithmetic reasoning, word knowledge, paragraph comprehension, numerical operations, coding speed, auto and shop information, mathematics knowledge, mechanical comprehension and electronics information. Factor analysis was used to calculate the $g$ component of the test results as well as the $s$ factors which contributed to performance on the subtests.

### Results

It was found that job training grades could be predicted by $g$ alone; $s$ factors added little to this prediction; i.e. there was a high correlation between the $g$ score of an individual and their subsequent success on the job training course.

## Conclusion
The results suggest that intelligence alone (*g*) can be used for job selection and has good *predictive validity*.

## Evaluation
*Cultural bias*

This study only demonstrates that *g* has predictive validity if used with the white American population for which the tests were designed. It does not demonstrate that intelligence tests that measure *g* can predict subsequent performance for groups of people that the tests were not designed for.

*Contrasting results*

Other studies have not found as much predictive power for IQ tests in relation to job performance: for example, jobs that are less *g* loaded may correlate less well (see Evaluation of using IQ tests in employment).

---

## note

### IQ tests and the death penalty

In 1992, the US Supreme Court ruled that people with mental retardation cannot be executed. Mental retardation is partly determined by using an IQ test – a score below 70 is regarded as a sign of retardation. A diagnosis of mental retardation is also determined with reference to the individual's coping skills and must be diagnosed prior to age 18. A jury decides on the diagnosis. The use of IQ tests, even in conjunction with other evidence, is worrying given the problems with validity and reliability. Furthermore, Ceci *et al*. (2003) point out that the rise in IQ scores over recent decades (the *Flynn effect* – see page 303) means that individuals who might have scored below 70 and been classified as mentally retarded may now be achieving higher scores and thus no longer be classified as mentally retarded. This has implications for the sentencing of convicted criminals who are on the borderline of being mentally retarded, especially in states which retain the death penalty.

---

## evaluation

### Evaluation of IQ testing in employment

*Does IQ predict job performance?*

The study by Ree and Earles (1991, see Star Study above) suggests that IQ tests can predict job performance. However, Sternberg (see page 294) argues that traditional IQ tests fail to measure the kind of skills that would be relevant to job performance, such as creativity and practical knowledge. In addition, there is some variation in terms of how much a job is *g* loaded. Jobs that require greater cognitive complexity correlate more highly with *g*. However, in some cases negative correlations have been found between IQ and job performance. For example, amongst salesmen there was a negative correlation of −0.27 between IQ score and sales per hour, and amongst bankers there was a zero correlation between the IQ score and on-the-job competency (Hunter and Hunter, 1984).

*Aptitude tests*

Some people argue that *g* underlies all of these aptitude tests and thus an IQ test is equally effective as using an aptitude test. It is also possible to use subtest scores on an IQ test to provide information about specific aptitudes, for example verbal reasoning or numeracy. On the other hand, such subtest scores tend to lack reliability because they are based on a small set of test items.

**Describe and evaluate the use of IQ testing in educational selection.** (*ku 4 ae 4*)

Once again we have a question featuring the IQ concept (see Assessment Issue on page 000). And once again you need to locate the relevant material for your response: this question is not a theoretical one about what IQ or intelligence is but is about the practical uses of IQ tests in people's lives (Aspect 3 rather than Aspect 1). If you read the question carefully, you'll see that the wording is very similar to the words of the Unit content listed at the start of the chapter. By becoming thoroughly familiar with the wording of the Unit content, you'll find that the words used in NABs and exam questions will generally appear familiar to you too. A good way of developing this familiarity is to organise your own file of course notes according to the headings and subheadings of the chapter (which generally follow the Unit content), and use these to organise your revision aids as well.

A further point in relation to this question, and other questions on applied Aspects, is that you may be able to draw upon examples from media reports: educational selection is a political 'hot topic' so look out for relevant news items and documentaries.

Read about IQ testing on the BBC website: www.bbc.co.uk/science/hottopics/intelligence/q.shtml

**KEY TERMS**

**Cultural bias:** The tendency to judge all people in terms of one's own cultural assumptions.

# Cultural bias in IQ testing
## What is cultural bias?

The term 'culture' refers to the rules, customs and so on which bind together a group of people. This encompasses different racial or ethnic groups and different subcultures (lower versus middle class, men and women). One of the features of IQ tests is that they are based on the assumption that there is an innate ability which can be measured. If intelligence is not innate then IQ tests must be measuring the result of our life experiences and social background. Even if intelligence is innate, one cannot test intelligence directly but can only test the abilities through which intelligence is expressed, i.e. life experiences. This means that test items are inevitably shaped or biased by a particular culture – the culture in which the test was designed.

## Cultural bias

### Ethnic bias

The US Army tests were amongst the first IQ tests used. There were two forms of the test: the Army Alpha was designed for literate recruits and the Army Beta for illiterates. In the end there were so many recruits to be tested that many illiterates were given the Army Alpha. Examples from both tests are shown on the next page. It is no surprise that recent European immigrants, with little knowledge of the English language or customs, did very poorly on the test as did black recruits who were mainly illiterate. The immediate effect of this was that such recruits were not ranked above ordinary privates. However, the more lasting effect was that the statistics culled from this testing were used to argue 'scientifically' that immigration from southern and eastern Europe to the US should be halted because the people were intellectually inferior and interbreeding would lead to a decline in American intelligence. This had a significant impact on Jewish immigration to the US in the Second World War because most of the Jews who needed to escape from the advancing German army were from southeast Europe, and the American quotas were full (Gould, 1981).

**note**

*The Mismeasure of Man*

In his book the *Mismeasure of Man*, Gould (1981) described the use of IQ tests as 'scientific racism'. He commented that 'the abstraction of intelligence as a single entity, its location in the brain, its quantification as one number for each individual, and the use of these numbers to rank people in a single series of worthiness, invariably [leads to the finding] that oppressed and disadvantaged groups – races, classes or sexes – are innately inferior and deserve their status' (pp. 24–25).

### Examples from the Alpha test

- *Analogies*, such as 'Washington is to Adams as first is to …?' [Answer: second, because Washington was the first US president and Adams was the second].
- *Filling in the next number in a sequence*, such as 'What number comes next: 1, 3, 6, 10?' [Answer: 15].

Multiple choice:

- 'Crisco is a: patent medicine, disinfectant, tooth paste, food product?' [Answer: food product].
- 'Christy Mathewson is famous as a: writer, artist, baseball player, comedian?' [Answer: baseball].

### Examples from the Beta test

There were seven parts containing pictures and symbols. One part (examples pictured below) required recruits to spot what was missing in each picture. In case you were wondering, a rivet is missing from the knife in picture 10 and the ball is missing from the man's right hand in picture 15. The rest are obvious!

The **BITCH IQ test** was devised by Williams (1972) to illustrate the absurdity of certain IQ test items. Some example items are:

- 'Alley apple' is (a) brick, (b) piece of fruit, (c) dog, (d) horse?
- CPT means a standard of (a) time, (b) tune, (c) tale, (d) twist?

*Answers are (a) each time.*

### Racial bias

In 1969, American psychologist Arthur Jensen published a controversial article in which he presented an explanation for the differing IQ scores between black and white Americans. The mean for blacks was 85 whereas for whites it was 100. He suggested that this 15-point difference was predominantly a product of genetic factors and maintained that compensatory programs would not make any difference to this differential (Jensen, 1998).

Various alternative explanations have been given for the 15-point IQ difference, notably that it is based on the erroneous assumption that IQ tests are measuring a real factor whereas in reality all IQ tests are rooted in cultural assumptions. Williams (1972) devised the BITCH IQ test to illustrate this point (see left).

A second argument is that it is an erroneous assumption that IQ scores are equivalent when they are taken from samples raised in different environments; in such a case, IQ score differences are not due to genetic factors but to environmental factors. This is illustrated on the next page. This is a form of cultural bias because it has been assumed that environmental/cultural differences do not have an effect. The research by Turkheimer *et al.* (see page 305) also suggests that when environmental conditions are poor, environment plays a bigger role in determining IQ.

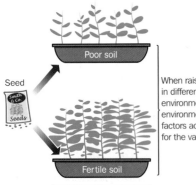

When raised in the same environment, genetic factors account for the differences

Jensen reported that the IQs of black American children are 15 points lower than those of white American children – but such comparisons make no sense because the two groups come from two different kinds of environment and this is the source of their IQ difference.

## Culture fair tests

Tests of verbal intelligence are inevitably related to acquired knowledge because you are using language which is learned. This is generally regarded as reasonable since higher intelligence is positively related to greater knowledge. However, as we have seen, problems arise when using tests with different cultural groups and IQ tests are inevitably used in this way. For example, tests designed by white, middle-class Americans are used with lower-class Americans and many immigrant American groups.

Tests of non-verbal intelligence are more 'culture fair' than those of verbal IQ because they do not rely on acquired knowledge. The Raven Matrices Test is an example of a non-verbal test (see below). However, even non-verbal tests are related to experience – on the Raven Matrices test you will do better if you have practised this kind of task.

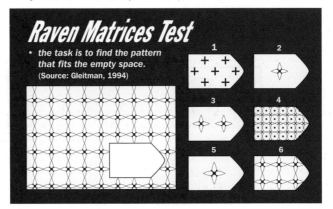

In addition, non-verbal tests make cultural assumptions about what we mean by intelligence. For example, abstract reasoning is a Western view of intelligence and even the idea of doing a pencil-and-paper test is alien to some cultural groups. Consider the following study – Serpell (1979) compared the performance of Zambian and British schoolchildren on tests that required them to make models out of wire and reproduce drawings (plus do two other pattern-reproduction tasks). The Zambian children performed better with wire; the British children performed better in drawing. This highlights the dangers of using such tasks as measures of intelligence (symbolic and representational thought, in particular) – we are erroneously assuming that, because the tasks are visual/pictorial and language-free, they are 'culture free'.

In addition, even if you could design a culture-fair test, some cultural groups are less motivated to do well on IQ tests and this leads to lower scores. For example, Zigler *et al.* (1973) found that lower-class children improved their test performance by 10 points if they had a play session with the tester before doing a test so as to decrease anxiety, whereas middle-class children only gained 3 points.

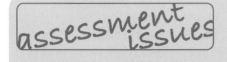

### Common theme: cross-cultural issues and cultural bias

As you'll know from reading this chapter, IQ testing was developed within European and American cultures during the 20th century. Early researchers often claimed (or simply assumed) that the tests and the underpinning theories they had produced could be applied universally. They failed to recognise that the IQ tests were specific to the culture that produced them, and as a result validity was weak and standardisation processes were inadequate. This kind of cultural bias is a *common underlying theme* in psychology. It arises from shortcomings in research methodologies and flaws in theory as a result. In the case of IQ testing in particular, cultural bias has led to harmful effects in terms of disadvantaging certain cultural groups, and worse, providing 'justification' for such treatment; this is a serious ethical concern. Whenever you write about cross-cultural issues or cultural bias, such material offers an abundance of analytical and evaluation points.

Chapter: Intelligence

*In this section we show you student answers to possible exam questions plus examiner's comments on these answers. Remember that in the actual exam (and NABs) your questions for this Topic will always add up to 20 marks. The question may be one essay worth 20 marks or a number of smaller questions (such as those shown below) which add up to 20 marks.*

## Question 1    What do psychologists mean by 'cultural bias' in IQ testing? (ku 4 ae 0)

### Tom

'Cultural bias' refers to the fact that IQ tests are written by a person who uses his own ideas about what intelligence is and these ideas are likely to be affected by his cultural views. Therefore the test is suitable for people within that culture, but not for people from other cultures. It is also the case that any IQ test has to test acquired knowledge rather than being able to tap into the hypothetical ability of intelligence. The items that are used to test intelligence are related to what people in that culture happen to know.

### Alice

Cultural bias can be defined as the tendency to judge all people in terms of your own cultural assumptions. When applied to IQ testing it is producing IQ tests which are based on a particular culture's view of intelligence.

*Examiner's comments*    Tom's answer shows that he has some understanding of 'cultural bias', but his answer is expressed in rather woolly everyday language, and would be enhanced by more precise explanation and appropriate terminology. For example, he could have referred to the way that cultural bias threatens the validity of IQ tests, and explained more clearly why this is the case (e.g. by describing the role of standardisation using particular populations). He gains **3 out of 4 marks** (ku 3/4 ae 0/0).

Alice starts off quite well with a sound definition of the concept 'cultural bias'. However, she should have expanded on what this means in the context of IQ testing (referring to validity, standardisation, etc.). As it stands, her second sentence adds little to what she has already said. Alice gains **1 out of 4 marks** (ku 1/4 ae 0/0).

## Question 2    Analyse the extent to which environmental enrichment may help deprived children 'catch up' in terms of IQ development. (ku 4 ae 4)

### Tom

There have been various enrichment programmes to help children from deprived backgrounds to improve their IQ so when they start school they are not at a disadvantage. One such programme was called 'Headstart'. This was started in the US in the 1960s and involved extra time in nursery schools. At first the children showed quite significant gains in IQ, about 10 points, but these disappeared within a few years (Zigler and Styfco, 1993). The Perry Preschool Project was similar but involved home visits as well. The study involved two groups of disadvantaged children – one group had the enrichment programme and the other did not.

There were again initial gains in IQ and also at age 15 the enriched group did better on an achievement test. When they followed these groups up later they found that those who had the intervention were less likely to have been arrested or to be on welfare in early adulthood. It's not surprising that IQ gains are not long lasting because there are so many factors that influence IQ, but it does show that enrichment programmes have some benefit.

However the fact that IQ does not remain boosted does suggest that genetic factors may be important. Perhaps the most likely explanation is the reaction range – that we are each born with a potential range for our IQ, like we have for our height, and the level we reach within this range depends on life experiences.

*Examiner's comments*    Tom has evidently revised this area quite thoroughly, however his reading of the question has been less thorough. First, it would have been useful to start by briefly describing the kinds of deprivation that may adversely affect children's IQ – this would provide a context for his explanation of enrichment processes. Secondly, Tom's interpretation of 'environmental enrichment' is rather narrow; he has addressed only intervention programmes (i.e. compensatory education). Tom does attempt analysis in the last paragraph in terms of nature–nurture interaction; however, this is rather limited. He achieves **5 out of 8 marks** (ku 3/4 ae 2/4).

### Alice

There are various ways to enrich the environment of children. One way that has been investigated by psychologists is in terms of diet. In one study (Schoenthaler and Bier, 1999) one group of children were given vitamin supplements and it was found that their non-verbal IQs became higher than a group who had no supplements. The children didn't know they were receiving mineral supplements so the improvement was not due

to expectations – expectations are another kind of environmental factor. In a study by Rosenthal and Jacobsen they showed that IQs increased when teachers had expectations that certain students would do better. In this study the teachers were told that some students were currently underachieving as shown by an IQ test. By the end of the year these students were actually better.

One of the interesting things in the study on diet was that the effects were greatest for the students who were most poorly nourished but had less effect on those who were adequately nourished. Diet is linked to the Flynn effect which is the fact that IQs around the world are constantly increasing. This can only be due to such things as improved diet and greater exposure to knowledge through the TV and Internet.

**Examiner's comments**   Alice also shows some understanding of these concepts; however, it is simply not substantial enough for an eight-mark question. Also, like Tom, she has adopted too narrow a focus, this time on diet. She does gain some credit for her reference to 'expectations' as a kind of environmental enrichment, although the Rosenthal and Jacobsen study is not the most obvious choice of material. Nevertheless, she shows quite good analysis skills in her interpretation of research findings. Alice gains **4 out of 8 marks** (*ku* 2/4 *ae* 2/4).

## Question 3   Discuss the information-processing approach to explaining intelligence. (*ku* 6 *ae* 4)

### Tom

Case presented an information-processing theory. He suggested that intelligence develops as the nervous system matures so that information can be passed around the brain more quickly. Also information-processing improves because children learn to use cognitive skills more automatically making their processing more efficient. Your mental space (M space – which is a bit like working memory) can only hold a limited amount at any time. If you learn metacognitive skills (thinking about thinking) then this means you can use less M space for the same tasks because you do it more efficiently. Children, as they develop, also learn conceptual mental structures which enable them to think more efficiently.

One study that supports this was done by Chi (1978). He compared young experienced chess players with older novice ones and found that the younger ones could remember moves on a chess board better whereas the older ones could recall lists of digits better. The children's better skills were presumably because they had learned mental structures for storing information about chess moves which meant they were more efficient with such tasks.

Case's ideas about information-processing have been used to measure intelligence e.g. by testing how many digits you can recall or other metacognitive skills as a way of assessing your intelligence.

Another example of the information-processing approach is Sternberg's triarchic theory which combines some of Case's ideas with two other subtheories of intelligence. Sternberg felt that all other theorists ignored the importance of using your intelligence practically and how experience combines with innate mental processes.

**Examiner's comments**   Tom gives a clear account of Case's theory, including explanation of its key concepts and supporting evidence. But the question asks about 'the information-processing approach', not about a particular theory, so a better strategy would be to describe the main principles of the information-processing approach first, then go on to deal with one or both of the theories covered in the text. The command of the question is to 'discuss', requiring both *ku* and *ae* skills. However, Tom has shown only limited analysis/evaluation. For example, in stating that Case's theory can be used to measure intelligence, he should have emphasised that this practical application represents a strength of the theory/approach. He gains **6 out of 10 marks** (*ku* 4/6 *ae* 2/4).

### Alice

The information-processing approach to intelligence focuses on the idea that mental processes are like a computer. Perhaps the best known information-processing theory is Sternberg's. He called it a triarchic theory because he said there were three 'theories' or subtheories of intelligence. The first part is the information processing bit. He called this the componential 'theory' i.e. the mental components in your mind such as reasoning ability and metacognitive skills. Metacognitive skills are skills that you learn to think about thinking such as being able to study effectively. These components are what makes a person intelligent. The other two subtheories are contextual and experiential. Contextual is your ability to use your intelligence in the real world and solve practical problems. Experiential is the extent to which you can use your experience and solve new problems combining both componential and contextual intelligence.

One of the good things about this theory is that it has a broad view of intelligence and doesn't just limit it to hypothetical mental abilities but considers how intelligence is used and develops all as part of what we mean by 'intelligence'. Sternberg has also used this theory to develop training programmes so that people can maximise their intellectual abilities in the real world. The main criticism has been that the theory is not that clear, for example it's not clear how the subtheories relate to each other.

You can contrast this approach with the factor analysis approach. Factor theories identify certain factors which underlie intelligent behaviour. Spearman claimed that there was one general factor (g) that was responsible for all intelligent behaviour and this was innate. There are also specific factors which explain why people are better at some things than others. The factor approach was popular in the early half of the 20th century but information processing is more popular now.

**Examiner's comments**   Alice provides a good introduction to the information-processing approach, making it clear that she is doing what the question asks. She has then focused on one particular theory, giving detailed material on Sternberg. However, it would have been sensible to mention at least one other theory. Her last two paragraphs show fairly competent skills of both analysis and evaluation, including an attempted comparison with factor approaches in intelligence, but she could have enhanced this material by supporting her points with evidence. Sometimes she does not express ideas very clearly. For example, although she describes some key principles of the factor analysis approach, she does not explain exactly *how* this contrasts with the information-processing approach. Alice is awarded **8 out of 10 marks** (*ku* 5/6 *ae* 3/4).

# References

Abbey, A. (1982) Sex differences in attributions for friendly behaviour: Do males misperceive females' friendliness? *Journal of Personality and Social Psychology*, **42**, 830–838.

Abernethy, E.M. (1940) The effect of changed environmental conditions upon the results of college examinations. *Journal of Psychology*, **10**, 293–301.

Aboud, F. and Doyle, A. (1993) The early development of ethnic identity and attitudes. In: *Ethnic Identity: Formation and Transmission among Hispanics and other Minorities* (ed. Bernal, M. and Knight, G). State University of New York Press, Albany, NY.

Aboud, F. and Doyle, A. (1996) Does talk of race foster prejudice or tolerance in children? *Canadian Journal of Behavioural Science*, **28**(3), 161–170.

Abrams, R. (1997) *Electroconvulsive Therapy*, 3rd edn. Oxford University Press, New York.

Adler, U.B. (2003) Karate and mental health: can the practice of martial art reduce aggressive tendencies? Unpublished PhD dissertation. Pace University.

Adorno, T.W., Frenkel-Brunswik, E., Levinson, D.J. and Sanford, R.N. (1950) *The Authoritarian Personality*. Harper, New York.

Aguero, J.E., Bloch, L., and Byrne, D. (1984) The relationships among sexual beliefs, attitudes, experience, and homophobia. *Journal of Homosexuality*, **10**, 95–107.

Ainsworth, M.D.S. (1967) *Infancy in Uganda: Child Care and the Growth of Love*. Johns Hopkins University Press, Baltimore.

Ainsworth, M.D.S. and Bell, S.M. (1970) Attachment, exploration and separation: illustrated by the behaviour of two-year-olds in a Strange Situation. *Child Development*, **41**, 49–65.

Ainsworth, M.D.S., Blehar, M.C., Waters, E. and Wall, S. (1978) *Patterns of Attachment: A Psychological Study of the Strange Situation*. Lawrence Erlbaum, Hillsdale, NJ.

Akert, R. (1998) Terminating romantic relationships: the role of personal responsibility and gender. Unpublished manuscript, Wellesley College.

Allport, G.W. (1968) The historical background of modern psychology. In: *Handbook of Social Psychology*, 2nd edn, Vol 1 (ed. Lindzey, G. and Aronson, E). Addison-Wesley, Reading, MA, pp. 1–80.

Altmeyer, B. (1998) The other 'authoritarian personality'. In: *Advances in Experimental Social Psychology*, Vol. 30 (ed. Zanna, M.P.) Academic Press, San Diego, pp. 47–92.

Amato, P.R. (2001) Children of divorce in the 1990s: an update of the Amato and Keith (1991) meta-analysis. *Journal of Family Psychology*, **15**(3), 355–370.

Amato, P.R. and Keith, B. (1991) Parental divorce and the well-being of children: a meta-analysis. *Psychological Bulletin*, **110**, 26–46.

Andersen, S.M. and Zimbardo, P.G. (1984) On resisting social influence. *Cultic Studies Journal*, **1**(2), 196–219.

Anderson, C.A. (1987) Temperature and aggression: effects on quarterly, yearly and city rates of violent and nonviolent crime. *Journal of Personality and Social Psychology*, **46**, 91–97.

Andreeva, G. (1984) Cognitive processes in developing groups. In: *Directions in Soviet Social Psychology* (ed. Strickland, L.H.). Springer, New York, pp. 67–82.

Angermeyer M.C. and Matschinger, H. (1996) The effect of violent attacks by schizophrenic persons on the attitude of the public towards the mentally ill. *Social Science and Medicine*, **43**(12), 1721–1728.

Angermeyer, M.C., Beck, M. and Matschinger, H. (2003) Determinants of the public's preference for social distance from people with schizophrenia. *Canadian Journal of Psychiatry*, **48**, 663–668.

APA Task Force (1995) *Stalking the Wild Taboo*. www.lrainc.com/swtaboo/taboos/apa_01.html (accessed July 2006).

Araragi, C. (1983) The effect of the Jigsaw learning method on children's academic performance and learning attitude. *Japanese Journal of Educational Psychology*, **31**, 102–112.

Arendt, H. (1963) *Eichmann in Jerusalem. A Report on the Banality of Evil*. The Viking Press, New York.

Argyle, M., and Henderson, M. (1984) The rules of friendship. *Journal of Social and Personal Relationships*, **1**, 211–237.

Aronson, E. (1999) *The Social Animal*, 8th edn. Worth Publishers, New York.

Aronson, E. and Bridgeman, D. (1979) Jigsaw groups and the desegregated classroom: in pursuit of common goals. *Personality and Social Psychology Bulletin*, **5**, 438–446.

Aronson, E., Blaney, N., Stephan, C., Sikes, J. and Snapp, M. (1978) *The Jigsaw Classroom*. Sage Publications, Beverly Hills, CA.

Arvidsson, H. and Ericson, B.G. (2005) The development of psychiatric care after the mental health care reform in Sweden. A case register study. *Nordic Journal of Psychiatry*, **59**, 186–192.

Asch, S.E. (1955) Opinions and social pressure. *Scientific American*, **193,** 31–35.

Atkinson, R.C. and Raugh, M.R. (1975). An application of the mnemonic keyword method to the acquisition of a Russian vocabulary. *Journal of Experimental Psychology: Human Learning and Memory*, **104**, 126–133.

Atkinson, R.C. and Shiffrin, R.M. (1968) Human memory: a proposed system and its control processes. In: *The Psychology of Learning and Motivation*. Vol. 2 (ed. Spence, K.W. and Spence, J.T.). Academic Press, London.

Aunola K., Nurmi, J-E., Onatsu-Arvilommi, T. and Pulkkinen, L. (1999) The role of parents' self-esteem, mastery-orientation and social background in their parenting styles. *Scandinavian Journal of Psychology*, **40**(4), 307–317.

Austin, E., and Johnson, K. (1997) Effects of general and alcohol-specific media literacy training on children's decision making about alcohol. *Journal of Health Communication*, **2**, 17–42.

Baddeley, A.D. (1966) The influence of acoustic and semantic similarity on long term memory for word sequences. *Quarterly Journal of Experimental Psychology*, **18**, 302–309.

Baddeley, A.D. (1990) *Human Memory: Theory and Practice*. Allyn and Bacon, Boston, MA.

Baddeley, A.D. and Hitch, G.J. (1974) Working memory. In: *The Psychology of Learning and Motivation*, Vol. 8 (ed. Bower, G.H.). Academic Press, London.

Baddeley, A.D. and Hitch, G.J. (1977) Recency re-examined. In: *Attention and Performance* (ed. Dornic, S.). Erlbaum, New Jersey.

Baddeley, A.D. and Longman, D.J.A. (1978) The influence of length and frequency of training sessions on the rate of learning type. *Ergonomics*, **21**, 627–635.

Baddeley, A.D., Thomson, N. and Buchanan, M. (1975a) Word length and the structure of short-term memory. *Journal of Verbal Learning and Verbal Behavior*, **14**, 575–589.

Baddeley, A.D., Grant, S., Wright, E. and Thomson, N. (1975b) Imagery and visual working memory. In: *Attention and Performance*, Vol. 5, (ed. Rabbitt, P.M.A. and Dornic, S.). Academic Press, London.

Bahrick, H.P., Bahrick, P.O. and Wittinger, R.P. (1975) Fifty years of memory for names and faces: a cross-sectional approach. *Journal of Experimental Psychology: General*, **104**, 54–75.

Bandura, A. (1962) Social learning through imitation. *Nebraska Symposium on Motivation*, **10**, 211–269.

Bandura, A. (1965) Influences of models' reinforcement contingencies on the acquisition of initiative responses. *Journal of Personality and Social Psychology*, **1**, 589–593.

Bandura, A. (1969) *Principles of Behavior Modification.* Holt, Rinehart & Winston, New York.

Bandura, A. (1971) *Social Learning Theory.* General Learning Press, Morristown, NJ.

Bandura, A. (1986) *Social Foundations of Thought and Action: A Social Cognitive Theory.* Prentice-Hall, Englewood Cliffs, NJ.

Bandura, A. (2002) Selective moral disengagement in the exercise of moral agency. *Journal of Moral Education,* **31**(2) 101–119.

Bandura, A. and Ribes-Inesta, E. (1976) *Analysis of Delinquency and Aggression.* Lawrence Erlbaum Associates, NJ.

Bandura, A. and Walters, R.H. (1963) *Social Learning and Personality Development.* Holt, Rinehart and Winston, New York.

Bandura, A., Ross, D. and Ross, S.A. (1961) Transmission of aggression through imitation of aggressive models. *Journal of Abnormal and Social* Psychology, **63**, 575–582.

Bandura, A., Ross, D. and Ross, S.A. (1963) Transmission of aggression through imitation of aggressive models. *Journal of Abnormal and Social Psychology,* **66**, 3–11.

Barlow, D.H. and Durand, V.M. (1995) *Abnormal Psychology: An Integrative Approach.* Brooks/Cole Publishing Company, Pacific Grove.

Baron, R.A. (1976). The reduction of human aggression: a field study of the influence of incompatible reactions. *Journal of Applied Social Psychology,* **6**, 260–274.

Baron, R.A. and Bell, P.A. (1976) Aggression and heat: the influence of ambient temperature, negative affect, and a cooling drink on physical aggression. *Journal of Personality and Social Psychology,* **33**, 245–255.

Baron, R.A. and Richardson, D.R. (1994) *Human Aggression,* 2nd edn. Plenum, New York.

Bates, G.W., Thompson, J.C. and Flanagan, C. (1999) The effectiveness of individual versus group induction of depressed mood. *Journal of Psychology,* **133**(3), 245–252.

Bateson, G., Jackson, D., Haley, J. and Weakland, J. (1956) Toward a theory of schizophrenia. *Behavioural Science,* **1**, 251–64.

Baumrind, D. (1964) Some thoughts on ethics of research: after reading Milgram's behavioural study of obedience. *American Psychologist,* **19**, 421–423.

Baumrind, D. (1991) Parenting styles and adolescent development. In: *Encyclopedia of Adolescence* (ed. Lerner, R.M., Petersen, A.C. and Brooks-Gunn, J.). Garland, New York, pp. 746–758.

Baxter, L.A. (1994) A dialogic approach to relational maintenance. In: *Communication and Relational Maintenance* (ed. Canary, D. and Stafford, L.). Academic Press, New York.

Beardsley, T. (1997) The machinery of thought. *Scientific American,* August: 58–63.

Beck, A. (1962). Reliability of psychiatric diagnoses I: a critique of systematic studies. *American Journal of Psychiatry,* **119**, 210–216.

Beck, A.T. (1976) *Cognitive Therapy and Emotional Disorders.* International Universities Press, New York.

Beck, J.G., Stanley, M.A., Baldwin, L.E., Deagle, E.A. and Averill, P.M. (1994) Comparison of cognitive therapy and relaxation training for panic disorder. *Journal of Consulting and Clinical Psychology,* **62**, 818–826.

Beer, J. (1989) Relationship of divorce to self-concept, self-esteem, and grade point average of fifth and sixth grade school children. *Psychological Reports,* **65**, 1379–1383.

Belmont Report (1978) *The Belmont Report: Ethical Principles and Guidelines for the Protection of Human Subjects of Research.* The National Commission for the Protection of Human Subjects of Biomedical and Behavioural Research, Department of Health, Education and Welfare Publication No (OS) 78-0012. US Government Printing Office, Washington, DC.

Belsky, J. (1984) The determinants of parenting: a process model. *Child Development,* **55**, 83–96.

Belsky, J. and Rovine, M. (1987) Temperament and attachment security in the Strange Situation: a rapprochement. *Child Development,* **58**, 787–795.

Belsky, J., Youngblade, L., Rovine, M. and Volling, B. (1991) Patterns of marital change and parent-child interaction. *Journal of Marriage and the Family,* **53**, 487–498.

Belson, W. (1978) *Television Violence and the Adolescent Boy.* Teakfield, Franborough.

Benokraitis, N.V. and Feagin, J.R. (1999) *Modern Sexism: Blatant, Subtle, and Covert Discrimination,* 2nd edn. Prentice-Hall, Englewood Cliffs, NJ.

Berger, A. (1965) A test of the double-bind hypothesis of schizophrenia. *Family Process,* **4**, 198–205.

Berkowitz, L. (1978) Whatever happened to the frustration aggression hypothesis? *American Behavioral Scientist,* **21**(5), 691–708.

Berlucchi, G. (1999) The myth of the clonable brain. In: *Mind Myths: Exploring Popular Assumptions about the Mind and Brain* (ed. Sala, S.D.). Wiley, Chichester.

Bermond, B., Mos, J., Meelis, W., van der Poel, A.M. and Kruk, M.R. (1982) Aggression induced by stimulation of the hypothalamus: effects of androgens. *Pharmacology, Biochemistry and Behaviour,* **16**(1), 41–45.

Bettencourt, B.A. and Miller, N. (1996) Gender differences in aggression as a function of provocation: a meta-analysis. *Psychological Bulletin,* **119**, 422–447.

Beutler, L.E., Machad, P.P.P. and Allstetter Neufeldt, S. (1994) Therapist values. In: *Handbook of Psychotherapy and Behaviour Change,* 4th edn (ed. Bergin, A.E. and Garfield, S.L.). Wiley, New York, pp. 229–269.

Bhui, K., Stansfeld, S., McKenzie, K., Karlsen, S., Nazroo, J. and Weich, S. (2005) Racial/ethnic discrimination and common mental disorders among workers: findings from the EMPIRIC study of ethnic minority groups in the United Kingdom. *American Journal of Public Health,* **95**(3), 496–501.

Biaggio, M.K. (1987) A survey of psychologists' perspectives on catharsis. *Journal of Psychology,* **121**, 243–248.

Biancosino, B., Barbui, C., Pera, V., Osti, M., Rocchi, D., Marmai, L. and Grassi, L. (2004) Patient opinions on the benefits of treatment programs in residential psychiatric care. *Canadian Journal of Psychiatry,* **49**(9), 613–620.

Bickman, L. (1974) Clothes make the person. *Psychology Today,* **8**(4), 48–51.

Bierhoff, H. (2002) *Prosocial Behaviour.* Psychology Press, Hove, Sussex.

Bjørkqvist, K., Üsterman, K. and Lagerspetz, K.M.J. (1992) The development of direct and indirect aggressive strategies in males and females. In: *Of Mice and Women: Aspects of Female Aggression* (ed. Bjørkqvist, K. and Niemelä, P.). Academic Press, San Diego, CA.

Blake, W. (1973) The influence of race on diagnosis. *Smith College Studies in Social Work,* **43**, 184–192.

Blanchflower, D.G. and Oswald, A.J. (2004) Well-being over time in Britain and the USA. *Journal of Public Economics,* **88**, 1359–1386.

Blatt, S.J. and Ford, R. (1994) *Therapeutic Change: An Object Relations Perspective.* New York, Plenum.

BMRB survey (2004) Committee on Standards in Public Life: *Survey of Public Attitudes towards Conduct in Public Life.* BMRB Socia Research, London.

Bouchard, T.J. and McGue, M. (1981) Familial studies of intelligence: a review. *Science,* **212**, 1055–1059.

Bouchard, T.J., Jr., Lykken, D.T., McGue, M., Segal, N.L. and Tellegen, A. (1990) Sources of human psychological differences: the Minnesota study of twins reared apart. *Science,* **250**, 223–228.

Bousfield, W.A. (1953) The occurrence of clustering in the recall of randomly arranged associates. *Journal of General Psychology,* **49**, 229–240.

Bower, G.H. (1972). Mental imagery and associative learning. In: *Cognition in Learning and Memory* (ed. Gregg, L.W.). Wiley, New York.

Bower, G.H. and Springston, F. (1970) Pauses as recording points in a letter series. *Journal of Experimental* Psychology, **83**, 421–430.

Bower, G.H., Clark, M., Lesgold, A. and Winzenz, D. (1969) Hierarchical retrieval schemes, in recall of categorised word lists, *Journal of Verbal Learning and Verbal Behaviour,* **8**, 323–343.

Bower, T.G.R. (1981) Cognitive development. In: *Child Development 0–5* (ed. Roberts, M. and Tamburrini, J.). Holmes McDougall, Edinburgh.

Bowlby, J. (1944) Forty-four juvenile thieves: their characters and their home life. *International Journal of Psychoanalysis*, **25**, 1–57, 207–228.

Bowlby, J. (1951) *Maternal Care and Mental Health*. World Health Organisation, Geneva.

Bowlby, J. (1953) *Child Care and the Growth of Love*. Penguin, Harmondsworth.

Bowlby, J. (1969) *Attachment and Loss*: Vol. 1, *Attachment*. Hogarth, London.

Bowlby, J., Ainsworth, M., Boston, M. and Rosenbluth, D. (1956) The effects of mother-child separation: a follow-up study. *British Journal of Medical Psychology*, **29**, 211.

Bradley, B.P. and Baddeley, A.D. (1990) Emotional factors in forgetting. *Psychological Medicine*, **20**, 351–355.

Bradley, L.A. (1995) Chronic benign pain. In: *Behaviour and Medicine*, 2nd edn (ed. Wedding, D.). Mosby-Year Book, St. Louis, MO.

Bradley, R.H., Caldwell, B.M. and Rock, S.L. (1988) Home environment and school performance: a ten-year follow-up and examination of three models of environmental action. *Child Development*, **59**, 852–67.

Brady, J.V. (1958) Ulcers in executive monkeys. *Scientific American*, **199**, 95–100.

Brandimote, M.A., Hitch, G.J. and Bishop, D.V.M. (1992) Influence of short-term memory codes on visual processing: evidence from image transformation tasks. *Journal of Experimental Psychology: Learning, Memory and Cognition*, **18**, 157–165.

Braunholtz, S., Davidson, S. and King, S. (2004) *Well? What do you think? The Second National Scottish Survey of Public Attitudes to Mental Health, Mental Well-being and Mental Health Problems*. The Stationery Office, Edinburgh.

Breggin, P. (1997). *Brain-disabling Treatments in Psychiatry*. Springer, New York.

Brehm, S. (1992) *Intimate Relationships*. McGraw-Hill, New York.

Brehm, S.S. and Kassin, S.M. (1996) *Social Psychology*, 3rd edn. Houghton Mifflin, Boston.

Brenner, V., Nicholson, B. C. and Fox, R. A. (1999) Evaluation of a community-based parenting program with the parents of young children. *Early Child Development and Care*, **148**, 1–9.

Breuer, J. and Freud, S. (1893–1895) *Studies on Hysteria*. Standard Edition, 2. Hogarth Press, London.

Brewer, M.B. (1979). Ingroup bias in the minimal intergroup situation: a cognitive motivational analysis. *Psychological Bulletin*, **86**, 307–324.

British Psychological Society (2000). *Code of Conduct, Ethical Principles* and *Guidelines*. BPS, Leicester.

Bronzaft, A.L. (1997) Noise: issues for environmental and health policy. In: *Environmental Issues for the 21st Century* (ed. Thompson, P.J.). Peter Lang Publishing, New York.

Brooks-King, M. and Hurrell., H.G. (1958) Intelligence tests with tits. *British Birds*, **51**(12), 514–524.

Brown, R. (1995) *Prejudice: It's Social Psychology*. Blackwell, Oxford.

Brown, G.W. and Birley, J.L.T. (1968) Crises and life events and the onset of schizophrenia. *Journal of Health and Social Behaviour*. **9**, 203–14.

Brown, G.W. and Harris, T.O. (1978) *Social Origins of Depression: A Study of Psychiatric Disorder in Women*. Tavistock Publications, London.

Browne, K. and Pennell, A. (2000) The influence of film and video on young people and violence. In: *Violent Children and Adolescents: Asking the Question Why* (ed. Boswell, G.). Whurr Publishers, London.

Browning, C. (1992) *Ordinary Men: Reserve Police Battalion 101 and the Final Solution in Poland*. HarperCollins, New York.

Buchanan, C., Maccoby, E. and Dornbusch, E. (1991) Caught between parents: adolescents' experience in divorced homes. Child Development, **62**, 1008–1029.

Bundy, D.A., Grigorenko, E.L. and Sternberg, R.J. (2001) The predictive value of IQ, *Merrill-Palmer Quarterly*, **47**(1), 1–41.

Bunney, W.E., and Davis, J.M. (1965) Norepinephrine in depressive reactions: a review. *Archives of General Psychiatry*, **13**, 483–494.

Burger, J.M. and Cooper, H.M. (1979) The desirability of control. *Motivation and Emotion*, **3**, 381–393.

Burnstein, E. and Worchel, P. (1962) Arbitrariness of frustration and its consequences for aggression in a social situation. *Journal of Personality*, **30**, 528–540.

Bushman, B.J., Baumeister, R.F. and Stack, A.D. (1999) Catharsis, aggression, and persuasive influence: self-fulfilling or self-defeating prophecies? *Journal of Personality and Social Psychology*, **76**, 367–376.

Buss, D.M. (1989) Sex differences in human mate preferences: evolutionary hypothesis tested in 37 cultures. *Behavioural and Brain Sciences*, **12**, 1–49.

Buss, D.M., Larsen, R.J., Westen, D., and Semmelroth, J. (1992) Sex differences in jealousy: evolution, physiology and psychology. *Psychological Science*, **3**, 251–255.

Buzan, T. (1993) *The Mind Map Book*. BBC, London.

Bynum, M.K., and Durm, M.W. (1996) Children of divorce and its effect on their self-esteem. *Psychological Reports*, **79**, 447–450.

Cairns E. and Hewstone M. (2002) Northern Ireland: the impact of peacemaking in Northern Ireland on intergroup behaviour. In: *Peace Education: The Concept, Principles and Practices around the World* (ed. Salomom, G. and Neov Mahmah, B.). Lawrence Erlbaum Associates, NJ.

Cairns, E., Hewstone, M., Hamberger, J., Niens, U. and Voci, A. (2006) The contact hypothesis, forgiveness, and peace psychology in identity-based conflicts: Northern Ireland. *Journal of Social Issues*, **62**(1), 99–120.

Calhoun, J.B. (1962) Population density and social pathology. *Scientific American*, February, 206.

Campbell, A. (2002) *A Mind of her Own: The Evolutionary Psychology of Women*. Oxford University Press, Oxford.

Capafóns, J.I,, Sosa, C.D. and Avero, P. (1998) Systematic desensitization in the treatment of fear of flying. *Psychology in Spain*, **2**(1), 11–16.

Carlson, M., Dragomir, C., and Earls, F. (1995) Effects of social deprivation on cortisol regulation in institutionalized Romanian infants. *Society of Neuroscience Abstracts*, **21**, 524.

Carroll, D. (1992) *Health Psychology: Stress, Behaviour and Disease*. The Falmer Press, London.

Carvel, J. (2004) Race training for all mental health staff. *The Guardian*, 27 April.

Case, R. (1992) Neo-Piagetian theories of intellectual development. In: *Piaget's Theory: Prospects and Possibilities* (ed. Beilin, H. and Pufal, P.B.). Erlbaum, Hillsdale, New Jersey.

Cash, T.F. and Derlega, V.J. (1978) The matching hypothesis: physical attractiveness among same-sexed friends. *Personality and Social Psychology Bulletin*, **4**, 240–243.

Caspi, A., McClay, J., Moffitt, T.E., Mill, J., Martin, J., Craig, I.W., Taylor, A. and Poulton, R. (2002) Role of genotype in the cycle of violence in maltreated children. *Science*, **297**(Aug), 851–854.

Cattell, R.B. (1963) Theory of fluid and crystallised intelligence: a critical experiment. *Journal of Educational Psychology*, **54**, 1–22.

Ceci, S. J., Scullin, M. H. and Kanaya, T. (2003) The difficulty of basing death penalty eligibility on IQ cut-off scores for mental retardation. *Ethics and Behavior*, **13**(1), 11–17.

Chamberlin, R.W. (1978) Relationships between child-rearing styles and child behavior over time. *American Journal of Diseases of Children*, **132**(2), 155–60.

Chang, M.J. (2002) The impact of an undergraduate diversity course requirement on students' racial views and attitudes. *Journal of General Education*, **51**(1), 1–42.

Charlton, T., Gunter, B. and Hannan, A. (eds.) (2000) *Broadcast Television Effects in a Remote Community*. Lawrence Erlbaum, Hillsdale, NJ.

Chase-Lansdale, P.L., Cherlin, A.J. and Kiernan, K.E. (1995) The long-term effects of parental divorce on the mental health of young adults: a developmental perspective. *Child Development*, **66**(6), 1614–1634.

Chi, M.T. (1978) Knowledge structures and memory development. In: *Child Thinking: What Develops?* (ed. Siegle, R.S.). Erlbaum, Hillsdale, NJ.

Chiraboga, D.A., Coho, A., Stein, J.A. and Roberts, J. (1979) Divorce, stress and social supports: a study in helpseeking behavior. *Journal of Divorce*, **3**, 121–135.

Chorney, M.J., Chorney, K., Seese, N., Owen, M.J., Daniels, J., McGuffin, P., Thompson, L. A., Detterman, D. K., Benbow, C., Lubinski, D., Eley, T. and Plomin, R. (1998) A qualitative trait locus associated with cognitive ability in children. *Psychological Science*, **9**(3), 159–166.

Clark, D.M., Salkovskis, P.M., Hackman, A., Middleton, H., Anastasiades, P. and Gelder, M. (1994) A comparison of cognitive therapy, applied relaxation and imipramine in the treatment of panic disorder. *British Journal of Psychiatry*, **164**, 759–769.

Clark, Mm and Mills, J. (1979) Interpersonal attraction in exchange and communal relationships. *Journal of Personality and Social Psychology*, **37**, 12–24.

Clark, R.D. III (1994) A few parallels between group polarisation and minority influence. In: *Minority Influence* (ed. Moscovici, S, Mucchi-Faina , A. and Maass, A.). Nelson Hall, Chicago.

Clarke-Stewart, K.A., Vandell, D.L., McCartney, K. and Owen, M.T. (2000) Effects of parental separation and divorce on very young children. *Journal of Family Psychology*, **14**(2), 304–326.

Clifford, B.R., Gunter, B. and McAleer, J. (1995) *Program Evaluation, Comprehension and Impact*. Erlbaum, Hillsdale, NJ.

Coates, B., Pusser, H.E. and Goodman, I. (1976) The influence of 'Sesame Street' and 'Mister Rogers' Neighbourhood' on children's social behavior in the preschool. *Child Development*, **47**, 138–144.

Cochrane, R. (1977) Mental illness in immigrants to England and Wales: an analysis of mental hospital admissions, 1971. *Social Psychiatry*, **12**, 25–35.

Cochrane, R. (1988) Marriage, separation and divorce. In: *Handbook of Life Stress, Cognition and Health* (ed. Fisher, S. and Reason, J.). J. Wiley and Sons, New York.

Cochrane, R. and Sashidharan, S.P. (1995) Mental health and ethnic minorities: a review of the literature and implications for services. Paper presented to the Birmingham and Northern Health Trust.

Cohen, C.E. (1981) Person categories and social perception: testing some boundaries of the processing effects of prior knowledge. *Journal of Personality and Social Psychology*, **40**, 441–452.

Cohen , L.E. and Felson, M. (1979) Social change and crime rate trends: a routine activity approach. *American Sociological Review*, **44**, 588–608.

Cohen, R.A., Kaplan, R.F., Moser, D.J., Jenkins, M.A. and Wilkinson, H. (1999) Impairments of attention after cingulotomy. *Neurology*, **53**(4), 819–824.

Cohen, S., Tyrrell, D.A.J. and Smith, A.P. (1993) Negative life events, perceived stress, negative affect, and susceptibility to the common cold. *Journal of Personality and Social Psychology*, **64**, 131–140.

Comer, R.J. (2002) *Fundamentals of Abnormal Psychology*, 3rd edn. Worth, New York.

Comer, R.J. (2003) *Abnormal Psychology*, 6th edn. Worth, New York.

Comer, R.J. (2004) *Fundamentals of Abnormal Psychology*, 5th edn. Worth, New York.

Commission for Social Care Inspection (CSCI) (2006) *National Report: Living Well in Later Life*. www.healthcarecommission.org.uk/contentdisplay.cfm?cit_id=449&widCall1=customWidgets.content_view_1&search_string=living%20well&usecache=false (accessed August 2006).

Coolican, H. (1996) *Introduction to Research Methods and Statistics in Psychology*. Hodder & Stoughton, London.

Cook, H.B.K. (1992) Matrifocality and female aggression in Margeriteço society. In: *Of Mice and Women: Aspects of Female Aggression* (ed. Bjørkqvist, K. and Niemelä, P.). Academic Press, San Diego, CA.

Cooper, C.L., Sadri, G., Allison, T. and Reynolds P. (1992) Stress counselling in the Post Office. *Counselling Psychology Quarterly*, **3**, 3–11.

Cosgrove, G.R. and Rauch, S.L. (2001) *Psychosurgery*. neurosurgery.mgh.harvard.edu/functional/Psychosurgery2001.htm.

Cowan, K. and Valentine, G. (2006). *Tuned Out: The BBC's Portrayal of Lesbian and Gay People*. Stonewall.org (accessed July 2006).

Cox, J.C. (1993) Traditional Asian martial arts training. a review. *Quest*, 45, 366–388.

Cox, T. (1978) *Stress*. Macmillan Press, London.

Cox, T. (1993) *Stress Research and Stress Management: Putting Theory to Work*. HSE Contract Research Report, No 61. HMSO, London.

Craik, F.I.M. and Lockhart, R.S. (1972) Levels of processing: a framework for memory research. *Journal of Verbal Learning and Verbal Behavior*, **11**, 671–684.

Craik, F.I.M. and Tulving, E. (1975) Depth of processing and the retention of words in episodic memory. *Journal of Experimental Psychology*, **104**, 268–294.

Craik, F.I.M. and Watkins, M.J. (1973) The role of rehearsal in short-term memory. *Journal of Verbal Learning and Verbal Behaviour*, **12**, 599–607.

Cuddy, A.J.C., and Fiske, S.T. (2002) Doddering, but dear: process, content, and function in stereotyping of older persons. In: *Ageism: Stereotyping and Prejudice against Older Persons* (ed. Nelson, T.). MIT Press, Cambridge, MA, pp. 3–26.

Cuddy, A.J.C., Norton, M.I. and Fiske, S.T. (2005) This old stereotype: the pervasiveness and persistence of the elderly stereotype. *Journal of Social Issues*, **61**(2), 267–285.

Cumberbatch, G. (2001) Interview on www.videostandards.org.uk/video_violence.htm. (accessed January 2003).

Cumberbatch, G., Gauntlett, S., Richards, M. and Littlejohns, V. (2001) *Top 10 TV: Ethnic Minority Group Representation on Popular Television.* Report for the Commission for Racial Equality. London.

Cunningham-Williams, R.M., Krygiel, J. and Books, S.J. (2006) Racial/ethnic differences in the reliability of DSM-IV Pathological Gambling Disorder. *Society for Social Work and Research*. 14 January, at sswr.confex.com/sswr/2006/techprogram/P4719.HTM (accessed June 2006).

Datto, C.J. (2000) Side effects of electroconvulsive therapy. *Depression and Anxiety*, **12**(3), 130–134.

David, D. and Avellino, M. (2003) A synopsis of rational-emotive behaviour therapy (REBT): Basic/fundamental and applied research. www.rebt.org/synopsis.htm (accessed August 2003).

Davis, J.M., Barter, J.T. and Kane, J.M. (1989) Antipsychotic drugs. In: *Comprehensive Textbook of Psychiatry,* Vol. 5. (ed. Kaplan, H.I. and Sadock, B.J.). Williams & Wilkins, Baltimore, MD, pp. 1591–1626.

Davis, J.M., Chen, N. and Glick, I.D. (2003) A meta-analysis of the efficacy of second-generation antipsychotics. *Archives of General Psychiatry*, **60**, 553–564.

Davis, J.M., Janicak, P.G., Singla, A. and Sharma, R.P. (1993) Maintenance antipsychotic medication. In: *Antipsychotic Drugs and Their Side-Effects* (ed. Barnes, T.R.E.). Academic Press, York, pp. 183–203.

DeLongis, A., Coyne, J.C., Dakof, G., Folkman, S. and Lazarus, R.S. (1982) The impact of daily hassles, uplifts and major life events to health status. *Health Psychology*, **1**, 119–136.

DeLongis, A., Folkman, S. and Lazarus, R.S. (1988) The impact of daily stress on health and mood: psychological and social resources as mediators. *Journal of Personality and Social Psychology*, **54**, 486–495.

Department for Work and Pensions (2001) *Recruiting Benefit Claimants: Qualitative Research with Employers in ONE Pilot Areas*. Research Series Paper No 150, prepared by Bunt, K., Shury, J. and Vivian, D. DWP, London.

Department of Health (1999) *Electro-convulsive Therapy: Survey Covering the Period from January 1999 to March 1999, England*. Statistical Bulletin 1999/22.

DeRubeis, R.J., Hollon, S.D., Amsterdam, J.D., Shelton, R.C., Young, P.R., Salomon, R.M., O'Reardon, J.P., Lovett, M.L., Gladis, M.M., Brown, L.L. and Gallop, R. (2005) Cognitive therapy vs medications in the treatment of moderate to severe depression. *Archives of General Psychiatry*. **62**, 409–416.

Deutsch, M., and Collins, M.E. (1951) *Interracial Housing*. University of Minnesota Press, Minneapolis, MN.

Deutsch, M. and Gerard, H.B. (1955). A study of normative and informational influence upon individual judgement. *Journal of Abnormal and Social Psychology*, **51**, 629–636.

Devine, P.G. (1989) Stereotypes and prejudice: their automatic and controlled components. *Journal of Personality and Social Psychology*, **56**, 5–18.

Diab, L.N. (1970) A study of intragroup and intergroup relations among experimentally produced small groups. *Genetic Psychology Monograph*, **82**, 49–82.

Dill, K.E. and Dill, J.C. (1998) Video game violence: a review of the literature. *Aggression and Violent Behavior*, **3**(4), 407–428.

DiNardo, P.A., Guzy, L.T., Jenkins, J.A., Bak, R.M., Tomasi, S.F. and Copland, M. (1988) Etiology and maintenance of dog fears. *Behaviour Research and Therapy*, **26**, 241–244.

Dindia, K. and Baxter, L.A. (1987) Maintenance and repair strategies in marital relationships. *Journal of Social and Personal Relationships*, **4**, 143–58.

Dollard, J., and Miller, N.E. (1950) *Personality and Psychotherapy*. McGraw-Hill, New York.

Dollard, J., Doob, L.W., Miller, N.E., Mowrer, O.H. and Sears, R.R. (1939) *Frustration and Aggression*. Yale University Press, New Haven, CT.

Donnerstein, E. and Wilson, D.W. (1976) The effects of noise and perceived control upon ongoing and subsequent aggression. *Journal of Personality and Social Psychology*, **34**, 774–781.

Dovidio, J.F., Brigham, J.C., Johnson, B.T. and Gaertner, S.L. (1996) Stereotyping, prejudice and discrimination: another look. In: *Stereotypes and Stereotyping* (ed. Macrae, C.N., Stangor, C. and Hewstone, M.). Guildford Press, New York, pp. 276–319.

Drabman, R.S. and Thomas, M.H. (1974) Does media violence increase children's toleration of real-life aggression? *Developmental Psychology*, **19**(3), 418–421.

Duck, S.W. (1981) Toward a research map for the study of relationship breakdown. In: Personal Relationships, Vol. 3, *Personal Relationships in Disorder* (ed. Duck, S. and Gilmour, R.). Academic Press, London.

Duck, S.W. (1991) *Friends for Life*. Harvester-Wheatsheaf, Hemel Hempstead.

Duck, S.W. (1992) *Human Relationships*, 2nd edn. Sage Publications, London.

Duck, S. (1999) *Relating to Others*, 2nd edn. Open University Press, Buckingham.

Duck, S.W. and Sants, H.K.A. (1983) On the origin of the specious: are personal relationships really interpersonal states? *Journal of Social and Clinical Psychology*, **1**, 27–41.

Duncan, J., Seitz, R.J., Kolodny, J., Bor, D., Herzog, H., Ahmed, A., Newell, F.N. and Emslie, H. (2000) A neural basis for general intelligence. *Science*, **289**, 457–459.

Dunne, J. and Hedrick, M. (1994) The parental alienation syndrome: an analysis of sixteen selected cases. *Journal of Divorce and Remarriage*, **21**, 21–38.

Dunst, C.J. (2000) Revising 'rethinking early intervention.' *Topics in Early Childhood Special Education*, **20**(2), 95.

Durm, M.W., Giddens, A. and Blandenship, M. (1997) Parental marital status and self-esteem of boys and girls. *Psychological Reports*, **81**, 125–126.

Dylan, B. (1985) *Biograph*. Sony.

Eagly, A.H. (1978) Sex differences in influenceability. *Psychological Bulletin*, **85**, 86–116.

Eagly, A.H. and Carli, L. (1981) Sex of researchers and sex-typed communications as determinants of sex differences in influenceability: a meta-analysis of social influence studies. *Psychological Bulletin*, **90**, 1–20.

Edwards, J.A. and Cline, H.T. (1999) Light-induced calcium influx into retinal axons is regulated by presynaptic nicotinic acetylcholine receptor activity in vivo. *The Journal of Neurophysiology*, **81**(2), 895–907.

Ekman, P. and Friesen, W.V. (1978) *Manual for the Facial Action Coding System*. Consulting Psychology Press. Palo Alto, CA.

Elliott, J., Golenbock, S.A. and Talmadge, W. (2001) *The Angry Eye*. Guidance Associates, Mount Kisco, NY.

Elliott, J., Golenbock, S.A., Robins, P. and Talmadge, W. (2003) *The Stolen Eye*. Annamax Media Pty Ltd and Angry Eye Productions LLC. See www.newsreel.org/nav/title.asp?tc=CN0143.

Ellis, A. (1957) *How to Live with a 'Neurotic'*. Wilshire Books, Hollywood, CA.

Ellis, N. and Beaton, A. (1993) Factors affecting the learning of foreign language vocabulary: imagery keyword mediators and phonological short-term memory. *Quarterly Journal of Experimental Psychology*, **46**(A), 533–558.

Emery, R.E. (1988) *Marriage, Divorce, and Children's Adjustment*. Sage Publication, Newbury Park, CA, pp. 50–54.

Emmelkamp, P.M. (1994) Behaviour therapy with adults. In: *Handbook of Psychotherapy and Behaviour Change*, 4th edn (ed. Bergin, A.E. and Garfield, S.L.). Wiley, New York.

Endler, N.S. and Parker, J.D.A. (1990). Multidimensional assessment of coping: a critical evaluation. *Journal of Personality and Social Psychology*, **58**, 844–854.

Equal Opportunities Commission (2006) Consultation response: Low Pay Commission, extending the national minimum wage to 16 and 17 year old. www.eoc.org.uk/default.aspx?page=15614 (accessed August 2006).

Eron, L.D. (1993) No doubt about it, media violence affects behavior. *Media and Values*, **64**, 14.

Eron, L. D. and Huesmann, L. R. (1986) The role of television in the development of prosocial and antisocial behaviour. In: *Development of Antisocial and Prosocial Behavior* (ed. Olweus, D., Block, J. and Radke-Yarrow, M.). Academic Press, New York, pp. 285–314.

Evans, G., Bullinger, M. and Hygger, S. (1998) The effects of chronic exposure to aircraft noise. *Psychological Science*, **9**(1), 75–77.

Evans, P., Bristow, M., Hucklebridge, F., Clow, A. and Pang, F.-Y. (1994) Stress, arousal, cortisol and secretory immunoglobulin A in students undergoing assessment. *British Journal of Clinical Psychology*, **33**, 575–6.

Evans, P. Clow, A. and Hucklebridge, F. (1997) Stress and the immune system. *The Psychologist*, **10**(7), 303–307.

Eysenck, M.W. (1994). *Individual Differences: Normal and Abnormal*. Psychology Press, Hove, UK.

Eysenck, M.W. (1997) *Anxiety and Cognition: A Unified Theory*. Psychology Press, Hove, Sussex.

Eysenck, M.W. (1998) *Psychology: An Integrated Approach*. Longman, Harlow, Essex.

Eysenck, M.W. (2001) *Psychology for A2 level*. Psychology Press, Hove, Sussex.

Falek, A. and Moser, H.M. (1975) Classification in schizophrenia. *Archive of General Psychiatry*, **32**, 59–67.

Farah, M.J., Peronnet, F., Gonon, M.A. and Giard, M.H. (1988) Electrophysiological evidence for a shared representational medium for visual images and visual percepts. *Journal of Experimental Psychology: General*, **117**, 248–257.

Farrand, R., Hussain, F. and Hennessy, E. (2002) The efficacy of the 'mind map' study technique. *Medical Education*, **36**(5), 426–431.

Feindler, E.L., Marriot, S.A. and Iwata, M. (1984) Group anger control for junior high school delinquents. *Cognitive Therapy and Research*, **8**(3), 299–311.

Felmlee, D.H. (1995) Fatal attractions: affection and disaffection in intimate relationships. *Journal of Social and Personal Relationships*, **12**, 295–311.

Festinger, L., Schachter, S., and Back, K. (1950) *Social Pressures in Informal Groups: A Study of a Housing Community*. Harper, New York.

Festinger, L., Riecken, H.W. and Schachter, S. (1956) *When Prophecy Fails.* University of Minnesota Press, Minneapolis.

Fiske, S.T., Cuddy, A.J.C., Glick, P.S. and Xu, J. (2002) A model of (often mixed) stereotype content: competence and warmth respectively follow from perceived status and competition. *Journal of Personality and Social Psychology*, **82**, 878–902.

Flanagan, E.H. and Blashfield, R.K. (2003) Gender bias in the diagnosis of personality disorders: the roles of base rates and social stereotypes. *Journal of Personality Disorders*, **17**, 431–446.

Fleshner, M. (2000) Exercise and neuroendocrine regulation of antibody production: protective effect of physical activity on stress-induced suppression of the specific antibody response. *International Journal of Sports Medicine*, **21**, 14–15.

Floody, O.R. (1968) Hormones and aggression in female animals. In: *Hormones and Aggressive Behaviour* (ed. Suare, B.B.). Plenum Press, New York.

Flynn, J.R. (1987) Massive IQ gains in 14 nations: What IQ tests really measure. *Psychological Bulletin*, **101**, 171–191.

Fontaine, P. (1998) Modern racism in Canada. Donald Gow Memorial Lecture, 1998. School of Policy Studies, Queen's University, Ontario, Canada.

Fowles, J. (1999) *The Case for Television Violence.* Sage, Thousand Oaks, CA.

Fox, N. (1977) Attachment of Kibbutz infants to mother and metapelet. *Child Development*, **48**, 1228–1239.

Francis, C., Pirkis, J., Dunt, D., and Blood, R. W. (2001) *Mental Health and Illness in the Media: A Review of the Literature.* Mental Health and Special Programs Branch, Department of Health and Aging, Australia, Canberra.

Frank, R.A., Kromelow, S., Helford, M.C. and Harding, C. (2005) Primary caregiving father families: do they differ in division of child care and housework? www.slowlane.com/research/FAMJOU.html (accessed January 2006).

Frankenhauser, M. (1983) The sympathetic-adrenal and pituitary-adrenal response to challenge: comparison between the sexes. In: *Biobehavioural Biases in Coronary Heart Disease* (ed. Dembroski, T.M., Schmidt, T.H. and Blumchen, G.). Karger, Basel.

Freedman, J. (2002) *Media Violence and its Effect on Aggression: Assessing the Scientific Evidence.* University of Toronto Press, Toronto.

Freud, S. (1909) Analysis of phobia in a five-year-old boy. In: *The Complete Psychological Works: The Standard Edition*, Vol. 10 (ed. and trans. Strachey, J., 1976). Norton, New York.

Freud, S. (1910) The origin and development of psychoanalysis. *American Journal of Psychology*, **21**, 181–218.

Freud, S. (1924) The loss of reality in neurosis and psychosis. In: *Sigmund Freud's Collected Papers*, Vol. 2. Hogarth Press, London, pp. 272–282.

Freud, S. (1930) Civilization and Its Discontents. In: *The Standard Edition of the Complete Psychological Works of Sigmund Freud*, Vol. 21 (ed. Strachey, J.). The Hogarth Press, London.

Friedman, L.A. and Kimball, A.W. (1986) Coronary heart disease mortality and alcohol consumption in Framington. *American Journal of Epidemiology*, **124**, 481–489.

Friedman, M. (1996) *Type A Behavior: Its Diagnosis and Treatment.* Plenum Press (Kluwer Academic Press), New York.

Friedman, M. and Rosenman, R.H. (1974) *Type A Behaviour and Your Heart.* Knopf, New York.

Frodi, A.M., Lamb, M., Leavitt, L. and Donovan, W. (1978) Fathers' and mothers' responses to infant smiles and cries. *Infant Behavior and Development*, **1**, 187–198.

Frydenberg, E., and Lewis, R. (1993) Boys play sport and girls turn to others: age, gender and ethnicity as determinants of coping. *Journal of Adolescence*, **16**, 253–266.

Fujinaga, T., Kasuga, T., Uchida, N. and Saiga, H. (1990) Long-term follow-up study of children developmentally retarded by early environmental deprivation. *Genetic, Social and General Psychology Monographs*, **116**, 37–104.

Furnham, A. (2002) *Growing Up With Advertising*: Social Affairs Unit, London.

Furnham, A., and Henley, S. (1988) Lay beliefs about overcoming psychological problems. *Journal of Social and Clinical Psychology*, **6**, 423–438.

Gabriels, L., Cosyns, P., Nuttin, B., Demeulemeester, H. and Gybels, J. (2003) Deep brain stimulation for treatment-refractory obsessive-compulsive disorder: psychopathological and neuropsychological outcome in three cases. *Acta Psychiatra Scandinavia*, **107**, 275–282.

Gadow, K.D. and Sprafkin, J. (1989) Field experiments of television violence. *Pediatrics*, **83**, 399–405.

Gamson, W.A., Fireman, B. and Rytina, S. (1982) *Encounters with Unjust Authority.* Dorsey Press, Homewood, IL.

Gardner, R.A. (1985) Recent trends in divorce and custody litigation. *Academy Forum*, **29**(2), 3–7.

Garland, J. and Rowe, M. (1996) Racism and anti-racism in English football. In: *Racism and Xenophobia in European Football* (eds. Merkel, U. and Tokorski, W.). Meyer & Meyer, Aachen.

Gauntlett, D. (1998) Ten things wrong with the 'effects model'. In: *Approaches to Audiences – A Reader* (ed. Dickinson, R., Harindranath, R. and Linné, O.). Arnold, London.

Geen, R. and Berkowitz, L. (1967) Some conditions facilitating the occurrence of aggression after the observation of violence. *Journal of Personality*, **35**, 666–676.

Geen, R.G. and O'Neal, E.C. (1969) Activation of cue-elicited aggression on general arousal. *Journal of Personality and Social Psychology*, **11**, 289–292.

Geen, R.G. and Quanty, M.B. (1977) The catharsis of aggression: an evaluation of a hypothesis. In: *Advances in Experimental Social Psychology* (ed. Berkowitz, L.), **10**, 1–37. Academic Press, New York.

Geiger, B. (1996) *Fathers as Primary Caregivers.* Greenwood, Westport, CT.

Gentile, D.A., Lynch, P.J., Ruh Linder, J. and Walsh, D.A. (2004) The effects of violent video game habits on adolescent hostility, aggressive behaviors and school performance. *Journal of Adolescence*, **27**, 5–22.

Glanzer, M. and Cunitz, A.R. (1966) Two storage mechanisms in free recall. *Journal of Verbal Learning and Verbal Behavior*, **5**, 351–360.

Glass, D.C., Singer, J.E. and Friedman, L.W. (1969) Psychic cost of adaptation to an environmental stressor. *Journal of Personality and Social Psychology*, **12**, 200–210.

Goldfarb, W. (1943) The effects of early institutional care on adolescent personality. *Journal of Experimental Education*, **12**, 106–129.

Goldfried, M.R. and Davison, G.C. (1975) *Clinical Behavior Therapy.* Holt, Rinehart & Winston, New York.

Goldhagen, D. (1996) *Hitler's Willing Executioners: Ordinary Germans and the Holocaust.* Knopf, New York.

Goodwin, D.W., Powell, B., Bremer, D., Hoine, H. and Stern, J. (1969) Alcohol and recall: state-dependent effects in man. *Science*, **163**, 1358–1360.

Gottesman, I.I. (1963) Heritability of personality: a demonstration. *Psychological Monographs*, **77** (Whole no. 572).

Gottesman, I.I. (1991) *Schizophrenia Genesis: The Origins of Madness.* W.H. Freeman, New York.

Gottfredson, L.S. (2002) Where and why g matters: not a mystery. *Human Performance*, **15**(1/2), 25–46.

Gottfredson, L.S. (2003) On Sternberg's 'Reply to Gottfredson'. *Intelligence*, **31**, 415–424.

Gould, S.J. (1981) *The Mismeasure of Man.* Penguin, Harmondsworth, Middlesex.

Greenberg, L.S., Watson, J.C. and Lietaer, G. (eds) (1998) *Handbook of Experiential Psychotherapy.* Guildford Press, New York.

Greenfield, P.M. (1984) *Mind and Media: The Effect of Television, Video Games and Computers.* Fontana, Aylesbury.

Greenough, W.T., Black, J.E. and Wallace, C.S. (1987) Experience and brain development. *Child Development*, **58**, 539–559.

Grossmann, K.E. and Grossmann, K. (1991) Attachment quality as an organizer of emotional and behavioural responses in a longitudinal perspective. In: *Attachment Across the Life Cycle* (ed. Parkes, C.M., Stevenson-Hinde, J. and Marris, P.). Tavistock/Routledge, London.

Gu, P. (2003) Vocabulary learning in a second language: person, task, context and strategies. *Teaching English as a Second or Foreign Language*, **7**(2). www-writing. berkeley.edu/TESL-EJ/ej26/a4.html (accessed November 2005).

Guttmann, M.G. (2001) *The Enigma of Anna O*. Moyer Bell, Wickford, RI.

Haeger, G. (1993) Social and temporal comparisons in a European context. MSc thesis, University of Kent.

Hagell, A. and Newburn, T. (1994) *Young Offenders and the Media*. Batsford, London.

Hall, J.A. and Levin, S. (1980) Affect and verbal-nonverbal discrepancy in schizophrenic and non-schizophrenic family communication. *British Journal of Psychiatry*, **137**, 78–92.

Hammen, C.L. and Krantz, S. (1976) Effect of success and failure on depressive cognitions. *Journal of Abnormal Psychology*, **85**(8), 577–588.

Hansard Society (2005) *Enhancing Engagement*. www.hansardsociety.org. uk/node/view/310. (accessed July 2006).

Hansen, W.B., and Graham, J.W. (1991) Preventing alcohol, marijuana, and cigarette use among adolescents: peer pressure resistance training versus establishing conservative norms. *Preventive Medicine*, **20**, 414–430.

Haring-Hidore, M., Stock, W.A., Okun, M.A. and Witter, R.A. (1985) Marital status and subjective wellbeing: a research synthesis. *Journal of Marriage and the Family*, **47**, 947–953.

Harlow, H.F. (1959) Love in infant monkeys. *Scientific American*, **200**(6), 68–74.

Harrington, R.C., Fudge, H., Rutter, M.L., Bredenkamp, D., Groothues, C. and Pridham, J. (1993) Child and adult depression: a test of continuities with data from a family study. *British Journal of Psychiatry*, **162**, 627–633.

Hart, B.L., Cliff, K.D., Tynes, V.V. and Bergman, L. (2005) Control of urine marking by use of long-term treatment with fluoxetine or clomipramine in cats. *Journal of the American Veterinary Medical Association* **226**(3), 378–382.

Hastrup, J.L., Light, K.C. and Obrist, P.A. (1980) Relationship of cardiovascular stress response to parental history of hypertension and to sex differences. *Psychophysiology*, **17**, 317–318.

Hatfield, E., Utne, M.K., and Traupmann, J. (1979) Equity theory and intimate relationships. In: *Exchange Theory in Developing Relationships* (ed. Burges, R.L. and Husto, T.L.). Academic Press, New York.

Hazan, C. and Shaver, P.R. (1987) Romantic love conceptualised as an attachment process. *Journal of Personality and Social Psychology*, **52**, 511–524.

Healey, J., Gill, M. and McHugh, D. (2005) *MPs and Politics in Our Time*. Dod's Parliamentary Communications, London.

Healthcare Commission (2005) *Mental Health Patient Survey*. See www. healthcarecommission.org.uk/ nationalfindings/surveys/patientsurveys. cfm?widCall1=customWidgets.content_view_ 1&cit_id=493.

Hearold, S. (1986) A synthesis of 1043 effects of television on social behaviour. In: *Public Communication and Behaviour*, Vol. 1 (ed. Comstock, G.). Academic Press, Orlando, FL.

Heermann, J.A., Jones, L.C. and Wikoff, R.L. (1994) Measurement of parent behavior during interactions with their infants. *Infant Behavior and Development*, **17**, 311–321.

Hegarty, P. (2002) 'It's not a choice, it's the way we're built.' Symbolic beliefs about sexual orientation in the US and Britain. *Journal of Community and Applied Social Psychology*, **12**, 153–166.

Herrnstein, R.J. and Murray, C.A. (1994) *The Bell Curve: Intelligence and Class Structure in American Life*. New York, Free Press.

Hetherington, E. M. and Kelly, J. (2002) *For Better or Worse*. Norton, New York.

Hewstone, M. (2003) Intergroup contact: Panacea for prejudice? *The Psychologist*, **16**(7), 352–355.

Hibbard, J.H. and Pope, C.R. (1993) The quality of social roles as predictors of morbidity and mortality. *Social Science and Medicine*, **36**, 217–225.

Hill, C.T., Rubin, Z. and Peplau, L.A. (1976) Break-ups before marriage: the end of 103 affairs. *Journal of Social Issues*, **32**(1), 147–167.

Himmelweit, H.T., Oppenheim, A.N. and Vince, P. (1958) *Television and the Child: An Empirical Study into the Efects of Television on the Young*. Oxford University Press, London.

Hinde, R.A., Spencer-Booth, Y. and Bruce, M. 1966. Effects of 6-day maternal deprivation on rhesus monkey infants. *Nature*, **210**, 1021–1023.

Hitch, G. and Baddeley, A.D. (1976) Verbal reasoning and working memory. *Quarterly Journal of Experimental Psychology*, **28**, 603–621.

Hodges, J. and Tizard, B. (1989) Social and family relationships of ex-institutional adolescents. *Journal of Child Psychology and Psychiatry*, **30**, 77–97.

Hoffman, M.L. (1970) Moral development. In: *Carmichael's Manual of Child Psychology*, Vol. 2. (ed. Mussen, P.H.). Wiley, New York.

Hofling, K.C., Brontzman, E., Dalrymple, S., Graves, N. and Pierce, C.M. (1966) An experimental study in the nurse–physician relationship. *Journal of Mental and Nervous Disorders*, **43**, 171–178.

Hogan, D.E. and Mallott, M. (2005) Changing racial prejudice through diversity education. *Journal of College Student Development*, **46**(2), 115–125.

Hogg, M.A. and Vaughan, G.M. (2002). *Social Psychology*, 3rd edn. Prentice Hall, London.

Holmes, T. H. and Rahe, R. H. (1967) The social readjustment rating scale. *Journal of Psychosomatic Research*, **11**, 213–218.

Holt, P.A. and Stone, G.L. (1988) Needs, coping strategies and coping outcomes associated with long-distance relationships. *Journal of College Student Development*, **29**, 136–141.

Hornberger, R. H. (1959) The differential reduction of aggressive responses as a function of interpolated activities. *American Psychologist*, **14**, 354.

Hornsey, M.J., Spears, R., Cremers, I. and Hogg, M.A. (2003). Relations between high and low power groups: the importance of legitimacy. *Personality and Social Psychology Bulletin*, **29**, 216–227.

Horwitz, A.V. and White, H.R. (1998) The relationship of cohabitation and mental health: a study of a young adult cohort. *Journal of Marriage and the Family*, **60**, 505–514.

Howard, K.I., Krause, MS., Saunders, S.M. and Kopta, S.M. (1997). Trials and tribulations in the meta-analysis of treatment differences: comment on Wampold et al. (1997). *Psychological Bulletin*, **122**, 221–225.

Huesmann, L.R., Eron, L.D., Klein, R., Brice, P., and Fisher, P. (1983) Mitigating the imitation of aggressive behaviors by changing children's attitudes about media violence. *Journal of Personality and Social Psychology*, **44**, 899–910.

Huesmann, L.R. and Bachrach, R.S. (1988) Differential effects of television violence in kibbutz and city children. In: *Television and its Audience: International Research* (ed. Patterson, R. and Drummond, P.). BFI Publishing, London, pp. 154–176.

Huesmann, L. R. and Moise, J. (1996) Media violence: a demonstrated public health threat to children. *The Harvard Mental Health Letter*, June.

Huesmann, L.R., Moise-Titus, J., Podolski, C. and Eron, L.D. (2003) Longitudinal relations between children's exposure to TV violence and their aggressive and violent behavior in young adulthood: 1977–1992. *Developmental Psychology*, **39**(2), 201–221.

Hunter, J.E. and Hunter, R.F. (1984). Validity and utility of alternate predictors of job performance. *Psychological Bulletin*, **96**(1), 72–98.

Huston, T. L. (1973) Ambiguity of acceptance, social desirability and dating choice. *Journal of Experimental Psychology*, **9**, 32–42.

Hutchings, J. and Lane, E. (2006) Reaching those who need it most. *The Psychologist*, **19**(8), 480–483.

Hyman, H.H. and Sheatsley, P.B. (1954) The Authoritarian Personality? A Methodological Critique. In: *Studies in the Method and Scope of the Authoritarian Personality* (ed. Christie, R. and Jahoda, M.). Free Press, Glencoe, IL.

Ironson, G., Friedman, A., Klimas, N., Antoni, M., Fletcher, M.A., LaPerriere, A., Simoneau, J. and Schneiderman, N. (1994) Distress, denial and low adherence to behavioral interventions predict faster disease progression in gay men infected with Human Immunodeficiency Virus. *International Journal of Behavioral Medicine*, **1**, 90–105.

Jacobs, J. (1887) Experiments in prehension, *Mind*, **12**, 75–79.

Jacobs, P.A., Brunton, M. and Melville, M.M. (1965) Aggressive behaviour, mental abnormality and XXY male. *Nature*, **208**, 1351–1352.

Jahoda, M. (1958) *Current Concepts of Positive Mental Health*. Basic Books, New York.

Jeavons, S. and Sevastos, P. (2003) A matched cohort study of career progression: glass ceiling effect or gender inequality? *Australian Journal of Psychology Supplement*, **55**, 130.

Jenness, A. (1932) The role of discussion in changing opinion regarding matter of fact. *Journal of Abnormal and Social Psychology*, **27**, 279–296.

Jensen, A.R. (1969) How much can we boost IQ and scholastic achievement? *Harvard Educational Review*, **39**, 1–123.

Jensen, A.R. (1998) *The g Factor: The Science of Mental Ability*. Praeger, Westport, CT.

Joffe, R., Sokolov, S. and Streiner, D. (1996) Antidepressant treatment of depression: a meta-analysis. *Canadian Journal of Psychiatry*, **41**, 613–616.

Johansson, G., Aronsson, G. and Lindstrom, B.O. (1978) Social psychological and neuroendocrine reactions in highly mechanised work. *Ergonomics*, **21**, 583–599.

Johnson, J.G., Cohen, P., Smailes, E.M., Kasen, S. and Brook, J.S. (2002) Television viewing and aggressive behaviour during adolescence and adulthood. *Science*, **295**, 2468–2471.

Johnson, N.J., Backlund, E., Sorlie, P.D. and Loveless, C.A. (2000) Marital status and mortality: The National Longitudinal Mortality Study. *Annals of Epidemiology*, **10**, 224–238.

Johnston, J.R. (1994) High conflict divorce. *The Future of Children*, **4**, 164–182.

Jones, D.N., Pickett, J., Oates, M.R. and Barbor, P. (1987) *Understanding Child Abuse*, 2nd edn. Macmillan, London.

Josephson, W.L. (1987) Television violence and children's aggression: testing the priming, social script, and disinhibition predictions. *Journal of Personality and Social Psychology*, **53**, 882–890.

Jost, A. (1897). Die assoziationsfestigkeit in iher abhängigkeit von der verteilung der wiederholungen. *Zeitschrift für Psychologie*, **14**, 436–472.

Kaffman, M., Elizur, E., Shoham, S. and Gilead-Roelofs, N. (1989) Divorce in the kibbutz: determinants of breakup. *Journal of Divorce*, **11**(3), 189–211.

Kagan, J. (1984) *The Nature of the Child*. Basic Books, New York.

Kalmuss, D. (1984) The intergenerational transmission of marital aggression. *Journal of Marriage and the Family*, **46**(1), 11–19.

Kamarck, T.W., Manuck, S.B. and Jennings, J.R. (1990) Social support reduces cardiovascular reactivity to psychological challenge: a laboratory model. *Psychosomatic Medicine*, **52**, 42–58.

Karim, S., Saeed, K. Rana, M.H., Mubbashar, M.H. and Jenkins, R. (2004) Pakistan mental health country profile. *International Review of Psychiatry*, **16**, 83–92.

Karon, B.P. and Widener, A. J. (1997) Repressed memories and World War II: Lest we forget! *Professional Psychology: Research and Practice*, **28**(4), 338–340.

Kelly, J. (2000) Children's adjustment in conflicted marriage and divorce: a decade review of research. *Journal of the American Academy of Child and Adolescent Psychiatry*, **39**(8), 963–973.

Kelman, H. (1958) Compliance, identification and internalisation: three processes of attitude change. *Journal of Conflict Resolution*, **2**, 51–60.

Kelman, H.C. (1973) Violence without moral restraint: reflections on the dehumanization of victims and victimizers. *Journal of Social Issues*, **29**(4), 25–61.

Kendall, P.C. and Hammen, C. (1998) *Abnormal Psychology*, 2nd edn. Houghton Mifflin, Boston.

Kendler, K.S., Heath, A., Neale, M., Kessler, R. and Eaves, L. (1992) A population-based twin study of alcoholism in women. *Journal of the American Medical Association*, **268**(14), 1877–1882.

Kendler, K.S. Kessler, R.C., Walters, E.E., MacLean, C., Neale, M.C., Heath, A.C. and Eaves, L.J. (1995) Stressful life events, genetic liability, and onset of an episode of major depression in women. *American Journal of Psychiatry*, **152**, 833–842.

Kenrick, D.T. and MacFarlane, S.W. (1986) Ambient temperature and horn honking: a field study of the heat/aggression relationship. *Environment and Behaviour*, **18**, 179–191.

Kiecolt-Glaser, J.K., Garner, W., Speicher, C.E., Penn, G.M., Holliday, J. and Glaser, R. (1984) Psychosocial modifiers of immunocompetence in medical students. *Psychosomatic Medicine*, **46**, 7–14.

Kilham, W. and Mann, L. (1974) Level of destructive obedience as a function of transmitter and expectant roles in the Milgram obedience paradigm. *Journal of Personality and Social Psychology*, **29**, 696–702.

Kilpatrick, S.M. (2005) Peer review of 'Relations between social support and physical health' by Corey M. Clark. www.personalityresearch.org/papers/clark.html (accessed December 2005).

Kim, H.K. and McKenry, P.C. (1998) Social networks and support: a comparison of African Americans, Asian Americans, Caucasians, and Hispanics. *Journal of Comparative Family Studies*, **29**, 313–336.

Kim, L.S., Sandler, I.N. and Tein, J.Y. (1997) Locus of control as a stress moderator and mediator in children of divorce. *Journal of Abnormal Child Psychology*, **25**(2), 145–155.

Kipper, D.A. and Har-Even, D. (1984) Role-playing techniques: the differential effect of behavior simulation interventions on the readiness to inflict pain. *Journal of Clinical Psychology*, **40**, 936–941.

Kirsch, I., Moore, T.J., Scoboria, A. and Nicholls, S.S. (2002) The emperor's new drugs: an analysis of antidepressant medication data submitted to the U.S. Food and Drug Administration. Prevention and Treatment 5: Article 23. Available at journals.apa.org/prevention/volume5/pre0050023a.html.

Klein, D.F., Zitrin, C.M., Woerner, M.G. and Ross, D.C. (1983) Treatment of phobias. II. Behavior therapy and supportive psychotherapy: are there any specific ingredients? *Archives of General Psychiatry*, **40**(2), 139–145.

Knijnik, D.Z., Kapczinski, F, Chachamovich, E., Margis, R. and Eizirik, C.L. (2004) Psychodynamic group treatment for generalized social phobia. *Revista Brasileira de Psiquatria*, **26**(2), 77–81.

Kobasa, S.C. (1979) Personality and resistance to illness. *American Journal of Community Psychology*, **7**, 413–423.

Kohlberg, L. (1969) Stage and sequence: the cognitive-developmental approach to socialisation. In: *Handbook of Socialisation Theory and Practice* (ed. Goslin, D.A.). Rand McNally, Skokie, IL.

Koluchová, J. (1976) The further development of twins after severe and prolonged deprivation: a second report. *Journal of Child Psychology and Psychiatry*, **17**, 181–188.

Koluchová, J. (1991) Severely deprived twins after 22 years observation. *Studia Psychologica*, **33**, 23–28.

Kulik, J.A. and Brown, R. (1979) Frustration, attribution of blame, and aggression. *Journal of Experimental Social Psychology*, **15**, 183–194.

Lahey, B.B., Pelham, W.E., Chronis, A., Massetti, G., Kipp, H., Ehrhardt, A. and Lee, S.S. (2006) Predictive validity of ICD-10 hyperkinetic disorder relative to DSM-IV attention-deficit/hyperactivity disorder among younger children. *Journal of Child Psychology and Psychiatry*, **47**(5), 472–479.

Laing, R.D. (1967) *The Politics of Experience and the Bird of Paradise*. Penguin, Harmondsworth.

Lalancette, M.F. and Standing, L.G. (1990). Asch fails again. *Social Behaviour and Personality*, **18**(1), 7–12.

Lamb, M.E. (1981) The development of father-infant relationships. In: *The Role of the Father in Child Development* (ed. Lamb, M.E.). Wiley, New York.

Lamb, M.E. (1997) Fathers and child development: an introductory overview and guide. In: *The Role of the Father in Child Development*, 3rd edn (ed. Lamb, M.E.). John Wiley and Sons, Inc., New York, pp. 1–18.

Lamb, M.E. and Roopnarine, J. L. (1979) Peer influences on sex-role development in preschoolers. *Child Development*, **50**, 1219–1222.

Lancet editorial (2003) A victory for affirmative action. *The Lancet*, **362**(9377), 1.

Larsen, K.S. (1974) Conformity and the Asch experiment. *Journal of Social Psychology*, **94**, 303–304.

Larson, J.D. (1992) Anger and aggression management techniques through the *Think First* curriculum. *Journal of Offender Rehabilitation*, **18**, 101–117.

Lashley, K. (1931). Mass action in cerebral function. *Science*, **73**, 245–254.

Lawrence, D. (1971) The effects of counselling on retarded readers. *Educational Research*, **13**, 119–24.

Lay, B., Lauber, C. and Rössler, W. (2005) Are immigrants at a disadvantage in psychiatric in-patient care? *Acta Psychiatrica Scandinavica*, **111**(5), 358–366.

Lazarus, R.S. (1999) *Stress and Emotion: A New Synthesis*. Free Association Books, London.

Lazarus, R.S. and Folkman, S. (1984) *Stress, Appraisal and Coping*. Springer, New York.

Lee, L. (1984) Sequences in separation: a framework for investigating endings of the personal (romantic) relationship. *Journal of Social and Personal Relationships*, **1**, 49–74.

Lemyre, L. and Smith, P.M. (1985) Intergroup discrimination and self-esteem in the minimal group paradigm. *Journal of Personality and Social Psychology*, **49**, 660–670.

Lester, D. (1993) Time-series versus regional correlates of rates of personal violence. *Death Studies*, **17**(6), 529–534.

Levi, P. (1989) *The Drowned and the Sacred*. Abacus, London.

Levinger, G. (1980). Toward the analysis of close relationships. *Journal of Experimental Social Psychology*, **16**, 510–544.

Lewis, C. (2002) Should parenting be taught? *The Psychologist*, **15**(10), 510–512.

Lieberman, J.A. et al. (2005) Effectiveness of antipsychotic drugs in patients with chronic schizophrenia, *New England Journal of Medicine*, **353**(12), 1209–1223.

Liberman, R.P. (1982) Assessment of social skills. *Schizophrenia Bulletin*, **8**(1), 82–84.

Liem, J. (1974) Effects of verbal communications of parents and children: a comparison of normal and schizophrenic families. *Journal of Consulting and Clinical Psychology*, **42**, 438–450.

Lillard, L.A. and Waite L.J. (1995) Til death do us part: marital disruption and mortality. *American Journal of Sociology*, **100**, 1131–1156.

Linn, R. (2001) Conscience at war: on the relationship between moral psychology and moral resistance. *Journal of Peace Psychology*, **7940**, 337–355.

Linn, R. and Gilligan, C. (1990) One action, two moral orientations: the tension between justice and care voices in Israeli selective conscientious objectors. *New Ideas in Psychology*, **8**. 189–204.

Liss, M.B. and Reinhardt, L.C. (1979) Behavioural and attitudinal responses to pro-social programs. Paper presented at the meeting for the Society for Research in Child Development, San Franciso, CA.

Livingstone, S. (2001) Media effects research: complex answers to complex questions. *Psychology Review*, **7**(3), 28–31.

Lochman, J.E. (1992) Cognitive-behavioural intervention with aggressive boys: three-year follow-up and preventive effects. *Journal of Consulting and Clinical Psychology*, **60**(3), 426–432.

Loehlin, J.C., Horn, J.M. and Willerman, L. (1989) Modeling IQ change: evidence from the Texas Adoption Project. *Child Development*, **60**, 893–904.

Loftus, E. (1995) Remembering dangerously. *The Skeptical Inquirer*, **19**(2), 20–29.

Lorenz, K.Z. (1966) *On Aggression*. Harcourt, Brace and World, New York.

Lowinger, P. and Dobie, S.A. (1969) Study of placebo response rates. *Archives of General Psychiatry*, **20**, 84–88.

Luborsky, L., Singer, B. and Luborsky, L. (1975) Comparative studies of psychotherapies. *Archives of General Psychiatry*, **32**, 995–1008.

Luborsky, L., Rosenthal, R., Diguer, L., Andrusyna, T.P., Berman, J.S., Levitt, J.T., Seligman, D.A. and Krause, E.D. (2002) The Dodo bird verdict is alive and well – mostly. *Clinical Psychology: Science and Practice*, **9**(1), 2–12.

Maccoby, E., Depner, C. and Mnookin, R. (1990) Co-parenting in the second year after divorce. *Journal of Marriage and the Family*, **52**, 141–155.

Maccoby, E. E. and Mnookin, R. H. (1992) *Dividing the Child: Social and Legal Dilemmas of Custody*. Harvard University Press, Cambridge, MA.

Maccoby, E. E., Buchanan, C. M., Mnookin, R. H. and Dornbusch, S. M. (1993) Postdivorce roles of mothers and fathers in the lives of their children. *Journal of Family Psychology*, **7**(1), 24–38.

Macintyre, S. and Homel, R. (1997) Danger on the dance floor: a study of interior design, crowding and aggression in nightclubs. In: *Policing for Prevention: Reducing Crime, Public Intoxication, and Injury*. Crime Prevention Studies, Vol. 7 (ed. Homel, R.) Criminal Justice Press, New York.

MacPherson, W. (1999) *The Stephen Lawrence Inquiry. Report of an Inquiry by Sir Willam MacPherson of Cluny*. Stationery Office, London.

Maddi, S.R. (1987) Hardiness training at Illinois Bell Telephone. In: *Health Promotion Evaluation* (ed. Opatz, J.P.). National Wellness Institute, Stevens Point, WI.

Main, M. and Weston, D.R. (1981) The quality of the toddler's relationship to mother and father: related to conflict behaviour and the readiness to establish new relationships. *Child Development*, **52**, 932–940.

Malathi, A. and Damodaran, A. (1999) Stress due to exams in medical students – role of yoga. *Indian Journal of Physiological Pharmacology*, **43**(2), 218–224.

Mandel, D.R. (1998) The obedience alibi: Milgram's account of the Holocaust reconsidered. *Analyse und Kritik: Zeitschrift für Sozialwissenschaften*, **20**, 74–94.

Mandler, G. (1967) Organisation and memory. In: *The Psychology of Learning and Motivation: Advances in Research and Theory*, Vol. 1 (ed. Spence, K.W. and Spence, J.T.). Academic Press, London.

Marmot, M., Bosma, H., Hemingway, H., Brunner, E. and Stansfield, S. (1997) Contribution of job control and other risk factors to social variation in health disease incidence. *The Lancet*, **350**, 235–239.

Martin, R.A. and Lefcourt, H.M. (1983) Sense of humor as a moderator of the relation between stressors and moods. *Journal of Personality and Social Psychology*, **45**(6), 1313–1324.

Matthews, K.A., Glass, D.C., Rosenman, R.H. and Bortner, R.W. (1977) Competitive drive, pattern A, and coronary heart disease: a further analysis of some data from the Western Collaborative Group Study. *Journal of Chronic Diseases*, **30**, 489–498.

Maurer D. and Maurer C. (1989) *The World of the Newborn*. Viking, London.

Mays, V.M and Cochran, S.D. (2001) Mental health correlates of perceived discrimination among lesbian, gay and bisexual adults in the United States. *American Journal of Public Health*, **91**, 1869–1876.

McCarthy, G. (1999) Attachment style and adult love relationships and friendships: A study of a group of women at risk of experiencing relationship difficulties. *British Journal of Medical Psychology*, **72**, 305–321.

McDonald, P.J., and Wooten, S.A. (1988) The influence of incompatible responses on the reduction of aggression: an alternative explanation. *Journal of Social Psychology*, **128**(3), 401–406.

McFarland, S.G. and Adelson, S. (1996) An omnibus study of personality, values and prejudices. Paper presented at the Annual Convention of the International Society for Political Psychology. Vancouver, British Columbia.

McGrath, T., Tsui, E., Humphries, S. and Yule, W. (1990) Successful treatment of a noise phobia in a nine-year-old girl with systematic desensitization in vivo. *Educational Psychology*, **10**, 79–83.

McGuffin, P., Katz, R., Rutherford, J. and Watkins S. (1996) The heritability of DSM-IV unipolar depression: a hospital based twin register study. *Archives of General Psychiatry*, **53**, 129–136.

McLanahan, S.S. (1999) Father absence and children's welfare. In: *Coping With Divorce, Single Parenting, and Remarriage: A Risk and Resiliency Perspective* (ed. Hetherington, E.M.). Erlbaum, Mahwah, NJ.

McMorran, J., Crowther, D.C., McMorran, S., Prince, C., YoungMin, S., Pleat, J. and Wacogne, I. (2001) *General Practice Notebook: A UK Medical Encyclopedia*. www.gpnotebook.co.uk/simplepage. cfm?ID=1328873547 (accessed Oct 2006).

McNeal, E.T. and Cimbolic, P. (1986) Antidepressants and biochemical theories of depression. *Psychological Bulletin*, **99**(3), 361–374.

Mead, M. (1935) *Sex and Temperament in Three Primitive Societies*. Morrow, New York.

Mead, M. (1949) *Male and Female*. Morrow, New York.

Mednick, B., Gabrill, W. and Hutchings, B. (1984) Genetic influences in criminal convictions. Evidence from an adoption cohort. *Science*, **244**, 981–984.

Meichenbaum, D. (1977) *Cognitive-behaviour Modification: An Integrative Approach*. Plenum Press, New York.

Meichenbaum, D. (1985) *Stress Inoculation Training*. Pergamon, New York.

Melhuish, E., Belsky, J. and Leyland, A. (2005) *Early Impacts of Sure Start Local Programmes on Children and Families. Report of the Cross-sectional Study of 9 and 36 Months old Children and their Families.* HMSO, London.

Merkle, R.C. (1988) How many bytes in human memory? *Foresight Update*, **4**. Article can be found at www.merkle.com/humanMemory.html (accessed October 2006).

Merkel, U. and Tokarski, W. (eds) (1996) *Racism and Xenophobia in European Football*. Meyer and Meyer, Aachen.

Messick, D.M. and Cook, K.S. (eds) (1983) *Equity Theory: Psychological and Sociological Perspectives*. Praeger, New York.

Middlemist, D.R., Knowles, E.S. and Matter, C.F. (1976) Personal space invasions in the lavatory: suggestive evidence for arousal. *Journal of Personality and Social Psychology*, **33**, 541–546.

Miles, C. and Hardman, E. (1998) State-dependent memory produced by aerobic exercise. *Ergonomics*, **41**(1), 20–28.

Milgram, S. (1963) Behavioural study of obedience. *Journal of Abnormal and Social Psychology*, **67**, 371–378.

Milgram, S. (1974) *Obedience to Authority: An Experimental View*. Harper and Row, New York.

Miller, G.A. (1956) The magic number seven, plus or minus two: some limits on our capacity for processing information. *Psychological Review*, **63**, 81–93.

Miller, N. and Davidson-Podgorny, G. (1987) Theoretical models of intergroup relations and the use of cooperative teams as an intervention for desegregated settings. *Review of Personality and Social Psychology*, **9**, 41–67.

Miller, N. and DiCara, L. (1967) Instrumental learning of heart rate changes in curarised rats: shaping and specificity to discriminative stimulus. *Journal of Comparative and Physiological Psychology*, **63**, 12–19.

Mind (2000) *Counting the Cost.* Mind, London.

Mirnics, K., Middleton, F.A., Lewis, D.A. and Levitt, P. (2001) Analysis of complex brain disorders with gene expression microarrays: schizophrenia as a disease of the synapse. *Trends in Neurosciences*, **24**, 479–486.

Moghaddam, F.M. (1998) *Social Psychology: Exploring Universals Across Cultures*. W.H. Freeman and Co, New York.

Moghaddam, F.M., Taylor, D.M. and Wright, S.C. (1993) *Social Psychology in Cross-cultural Perspective*. W.H. Freeman, New York.

Morgan, K. (2006) *The Public Face of Mental Illness*. University of Leicester, Leicester.

MORI poll (2005) www.mori.com/polls/2005/bma.shtml (accessed July 2006).

Morris, J.N., Heady, J.A., Raffle, P.A.B., Roberts, C.G. and Parks, J.W. (1953) Coronary heart-disease and physical activity of work. *Lancet*, **ii**, 1053–7, 1111–20.

Morris, T., Greer, S., Pettingale, R.W. and Watson, M. (1981) Patterns of expression of anger and their psychological correlates in women with breast cancer, *Journal of Psychosomatic Research*, **25**, 111–117.

Moscovici, S. (1976) *Social Influence and Social Change*. Academic Press, London.

Moscovici, S. (1980). Toward a theory of conversion behaviour. In: *Advances in Experimental Social Psychology*, Vol. 13 (ed. Berkowitz, L.). Academic Press, New York.

Moscovici, S. and Nemeth, C. (1974) Social influence II: minority influence. In: *Social Psychology: Classic and Contemporary Integrations* (ed. Nemeth, C.). Rand McNally, Chicago.

Moscovici, S., Lage, E. and Naffrenchoux, M. (1969) Influence of a consistent minority on the responses of a majority in a colour perception task. *Sociometry*, **32**, 365–380.

Mowrer, O.H. (1947) On the dual nature of learning: a re-interpretation of 'conditioning' and 'problem-solving'. *Harvard Educational Review*, **17**, 102–148.

Muigen, M., Marks, J., Connoly, I. and Audini, B. (1992) Home-based care and standard hospital care for patients with severe mental illness: a randomised controlled trial. *BMJ*, **304**, 749–754.

Mulrow, C.D., Williams, J.W., Chiquette, E., Aguilar, C., Hitchcock-Noel, P., Lee, S., Cornell, J., and Stamm, K. (2000) Efficacy of newer medications for treating depression in primary care patients. *American Journal of Medicine*, **108**(1), 54–64.

Mumford, D.B., Whitehouse, A.M. and Plattes, M. (1991) Sociocultural correlates of eating disorders among Asian schoolgirls in Bradford. *British Journal of Psychiatry*, **158**, 222–228.

Mummendey, A., Simon, B., Dietze, C., Grunert, M., Haeger, G., Kessler, S., Lettben, S. and Schaferhoof, S. (1992) Categorization is not enough: intergroup discrimination in negative outcome allocation. *Journal of Experimental Social Psychology*, **28**, 125–44.

Murstein, B.I. (1972) Physical attractiveness and marital choice. *Journal of Personality and Social Psychology*, **22**, 8–12.

Murstein, B.I. (1976) *Who Will Marry Whom? Theories and Research in Marital Choice.* Springer, New York.

Murstein, B.I. (1987) A clarification and extension of the SVR theory of dyadic parting. *Journal of Marriage and the Family*, **49**, 929–933.

Myers, D.G. and Spencer, S.J. (2003) *Social Psychology: Canadian Edition.* McGraw-Hill Ryerson, Toronto.

Myers, L.B. and Brewin, C.R. (1994) Recall of early experiences and the repressive coping style. *Journal of Abnormal Psychology*, **103**, 288–292.

Nathanson A.I. and Cantor, J. (2000) Reducing the aggression-promoting effect of violent cartoons by increasing children's fictional involvement with the victim. *Journal of Broadcasting and Electronic Media*, **44**, 125–142.

National Family and Parenting Institute (2001) *Putting Families First: Priorities for a New Government.* NFPI, London.

National Institute for Clinical Excellence (2003) *ECT – Electroconvulsive therapy*. No 59. www.nice.org.uk/cat.asp?c=68305.

National Schizophrenia Fellowship Scotland (2001) *Give Us a Break:* Exploring harassment of people with mental health problems, Edinburgh.

National Television Violence Study (1994–1997) *National Television Violence Study Executive Summary*. Sage, Thousand Oaks, CA.

Nemeth, C. (1995) Dissent as driving cognition, attitudes and judgements. *Social Cognition*, **13**, 273–291.

Nemeth, C., Swedlund, M., and Kanki, G. (1974) Patterning of the minority's responses and their influence on the majority. *European Journal of Social Psychology*, **4**, 53–64.

Nemeth, C.J. and Brilmayer, A.G. (1987) Negotiation versus influence. *European Journal of Social Psychology*, **17**, 45–56.

Neumark, V. (1998) A token of our appreciation, *Times Educational Supplement*, 30 October.

Neville, P. (1996) Should your dog be on Prozac? *Dogs Today*, July, 36.

Nieradzil, K. and Cochrane, R. (1985) Public attitudes towards mental health illness – the effects of behaviour, roles and psychiatric labels. *International Journal of Social Psychiatry*, **31**(1), 23–33.

Nilsson, G., Petersson, H., Åhlfeldt, H. and Strender, L-E. (2000) Evaluation of three Swedish ICD-10 Primary Care Versions: Reliability and ease of use in diagnostic coding. *Methods of Information in Medicine*, **39**, 325–331.

Noble, G. (1975) *Children in Front of the Small Screen*. Constable, London.

Nuckolls, K.B., Cassel, J. and Kaplan, B.H. (1972). Psychological assets, life crisis and the prognosis of pregnancy. *American Journal of Epidemiology*, **95**, 431–441.

Nunnally, J.C. (1961) *Popular Conceptions of Mental Health: Their Development and Change*. Holt, Rinehart & Winston, New York.

Oltmanns, T.F., Neale, J.M. and Davison, G.C. (1999) *Case Studies in Abnormal Psychology*. John Wiley and Sons, New York.

Paik, H. and Comstock, G. (1994) The effects of television violence on anti-social behaviour: a meta-analysis. *Communication Research*, **21**, 516–546.

Paivio, A. (1971). *Imagery and Verbal Processes*. Holt, Rinehart and Winston, New York.

Palmer, S. and Strickland, L. (1995) *Stress Management: A Quick Guide*. Daniels Publishing, Cambridge.

Papez, J.W. (1937) Proposed mechanism of emotion. *Archives of Neurology and Pathology*, **38**, 725–743.

Parkes, K.R. and Sparkes, T.J. (1998) Organizational interventions to reduce work stress: are they effective? *A review of literature*. HSE books, Sudbury.

Pascual-Leone, A., Nguyet, D., Cohen, L.G., Brasil-Neto, J.P., Cammarota, A. and Hallett, M. (1995) Modulation of muscle responses evoked by transcranial magnetic stimulation during the acquisition of new fine motor skills. *Journal of Neurophysiology*, **74**(3), 1037–45.

Patterson, J., Mockford, C. and Stewart-Brown, S. (2005) Parents' perceptions of the value of the Webster-Stratton Parenting Programme: a qualitative study of a general practice based initiative. *Child Care, Health & Development*, **31**(1), 53–64.

Paul, G.L., and Lentz, R.J. (1977). *Psychosocial Treatment of Chronic Mental Patients: Milieu versus Social Learning Programs*. Harvard University Press, Cambridge, MA.

Payne, K.B. (2001) Prejudice and perception: the role of automatic and controlled processes in misperceiving a weapon. *Journal of Personality and Social Psychology*, **81**, 181–192.

Pedersen, N.L., Plomin, R., Nesselroade, J.R. and McClearn, G.E. (1992) A quantitative genetic analysis of cognitive abilities during the second half of the life span. *Psychological Science*, **3**, 347–353.

Perez, J., Papastamou, S. and Mugny, G. (1995) Zeitgeist and minority influence – where is the causality? A comment on Clark (1990) *European Journal of Social Psychology*, **25**, 703–710.

Perls, F.S., Hefferline, R.F. and Goodman, P. (1951) *Gestalt Therapy. Excitement and Growth in the Human Personality*. Penguin Books, Harmondsworth.

Perrin, S. and Spencer, C. (1980). The Asch effect: a child of its time. *Bulletin of the British Psychological Society*, **33**, 405–406.

Peterson, L.R. and Peterson, M.J. (1959) Short-term retention of individual verbal items. *Journal of Experimental Psychology*, **58**, 193–198.

Pettigrew, T.F. (1997) Generalised intergroup contact effects on prejudice. *Personality and Social Psychology Bulletin*, **23**, 173–185.

Pettigrew, T. F. (1998) Intergroup contact: theory, research and new perspectives. *Annual Review of Psychology*, **49**, 65–85.

Pettigrew, T.F. and Tropp, L.R. (2000) Does intergroup contact reduce prejudice? Recent meta-analytic findings. In: *Reducing Prejudice and Discrimination: The Claremont Symposium of Applied Social Psychology* (ed. Oskamp, S.). Lawrence Erlbaum, Mahwah, NJ, 93–114.

Phillips, D.P. (1986) Natural experiments on the effects of mass media violence on fatal aggression: strengths and weaknesses of a new approach. In *Advances in Experimental Social Psychology*, Vol. 19. (ed. Berkowitz, L.) Academic Press, New York.

Phillips, T. (2005) Speech given to the Manchester Council for Community Relations, 22 September. www.cre.gov.uk/Default.aspx.LocID-0hgnew07s.RefLocID-0hg00900c002.Lang-EN.htm (accessed August 2006).

Piliavin, I.M., Rodin, J. and Piliavin, J.A. (1969) Good Samaritanism: an underground phenomenon? *Journal of Personality and Social Psychology*, **13**, 289–299.

Pittinsky, T.L. (2006) *Allophilia*. www.ksg.harvard.edu/leadership/research/projects/allophilia/ (accessed October 2006).

Plomin, R., Fulker, D.W., Corley, R. and DeFries, J.C. (1997) Nature, nurture and cognitive development from 1–16 years: a parent-offspring adoption study. *Psychological Science*, **8**, 442–427.

Power, T.G., Kobayashi-Winata, H. and Kelley, M.L. (1992). Childrearing patterns in Japan and the United States: a cluster analytic study. *International Journal of Behavioral Development*, **15**(2), 185–205.

Price, R. and Vandenberg, S. (1980) Spouse similarity in American and Swedish couples. *Behavioural Genetics*, **10**, 59–71.

Quinton, D., Rutter, M. and Liddle, C. (1985) Institutional rearing, parenting difficulties, and marital support. *Annual Progress in Child Psychiatry and Child Development*, 173–206.

Rahe, R.H., Mahan, J. and Arthur, R. (1970) Prediction of near-future health-change from subjects' preceding life changes. *Journal of Psychosomatic Research*, **14**, 401–406.

Ramey, C.T. and Campbell, F.A. (1984) Preventive education for high-risk children: cognitive consequences of the Carolina Abecedarian Project. *American Journal of Mental Deficiency*, **88**(5), 515–523.

Rank, S.G. and Jacobsen, C.K. (1977) Hospital nurses' compliance with medication overdose orders: a failure to replicate. *Journal of Health and Social Behaviour*, **18**, 188–193.

Ree, M.J. and Earles, J.A. (1991) Predicting training success: not much more than *g*. *Personnel Psychology*, **44**, 321–331.

Reeve, J. (2006) The three styles of parenting. From www.lifespan.org/services/childhealth/parenting/styles.htm (accessed July 2006).

Reik, W., Romer, I., Barton, S.C., Surani, M.A., Howlett, S.K. and Klose, J. (1993) Adult phenotype in the mouse can be affected by epigenetic events in the early embryo. *Development*, **119**(3), 933–942.

Reitman, J.S. (1974) Without surreptitious rehearsal, information in short-term memory decays. *Journal of Verbal Learning and Verbal Behaviour*, **13**, 365–377.

Reynolds, K., Turner, J.C., Haslam, S.A. and Ryan, M. (2001) The role of personality and group factors in explaining prejudice. *Journal of Experimental Social Psychology*, **37**, 427–434.

Rich, M., Woods, E.R., Goodman, E., Emans, S.J. and DuRant, R.H. (1998) Aggressors or victims: gender and race in music video violence. *Pediatrics*, **101**(4), 669–674.

Richman, C.L., Kenton, L., Helfst, C., and Gaggar, N. (2004) The probability of intervention: gender x 'isms' effects. *Social Behavior and Personality*, **32**, 295–302.

Ridley, M. (2003) *Nature via Nurture*. Fourth Estate, London.

Riley, V. (1981) Psychoneuroendocrine influence on immuno-competence and neoplasia. *Science*, **212**, 1100–1109.

Robertson, J., and Bowlby, J. (1952) Responses of young children to separation from their mothers. *Courier Centre International de l'Enfance*, **2**, 131–142.

Robertson, J. and Robertson, J. (1967–73) *Young Children in Brief Separation*. Film Series. Concord Video and Film Council. New York University Film Library.

Robins, L.N., Helzer, J.E., Weissman, M.M., Orvaschel, H., Gruenberg, E., Burke, J.D. Jr and Regier, D.A. (1984) Lifetime prevalence of specific psychiatric disorders in three sites. *Archives of General Psychiatry*, **41**, 949–958 .

Rodgers, B. and Pryor, J. (1998) *Divorce and Separation: The Outcomes for Children*. Foundations No. 6108.

Roethlisberger, F.J., and Dickson, W.J. (1939) *Management and the Worker: An Account of a Research Program Conducted by the Western Electric Company, Chicago*. Harvard University Press, Cambridge, MA.

Rogers, C.R. (1951) *Client-centred Therapy: Its Current Practices, Implications and Theory.* Houghton-Mifflin, Boston.

Rogers, C.R. (1959) A theory of therapy, personality and interpersonal relationships, as developed in the client-centred framework. In: *Psychology: A Study of Science*, Vol. 3 (ed. Koch, S.). McGraw Hill, New York.

Rohlfing, M.E. (1998) 'Doesn't anyone stay in one place anymore?' An exploration of the understudied phenomenon of long-distance relationships. In: *Understanding Relationship Processes*, Vol. 6, *Understudied Relationships: Off the Beaten Track* (ed. Wood, J.T. and Duck, S.W.). Sage, Thousand Oaks, CA.

Rosenfield, S. (1997) Labeling mental illness: the effects of received services and perceived stigma on life satisfaction. *American Sociological Review*, **62**, 660–672.

Rosenhan, D.L. (1970) The natural socialisation of altruistic autonomy. In: *Altruism and Helping Behaviour* (ed. Macaulay, J.L. and Berkowitz, L.). Academic Press, New York.

Rosenhan, D.L. (1973) On being sane in insane places. *Science*, **179**, 250–258.

Rosenhan, D.L., and Seligman, M.E.P. (1989) *Abnormal Psychology*, 2nd edn. Norton, New York.

Rosenthal, R. (1966). *Experimenter Effects in Behavioural Research*. Appleton-Century-Crofts, New York.

Rosenthal, R. and Fode, K.L. (1963) The effect of experimenter bias on the performance of the albino rat. *Behavioural Science*, **8**(3), 183–189.

Rosenthal, R. and Jacobsen, L. (1966) Teacher expectations. *Psychological Reports*, **19**, 115–118.

Rosenzweig, S. (1936) Some implicit common factors in diverse methods of psychotherapy. *American Journal of Orthopsychiatry*, **6**, 412–415.

Rotter, J.B. (1966) Generalised expectancies for internal versus external control of reinforcement. *Psychological Monographs*, **30**(1), 1–26.

Rowe, D.C. (1990). As the twig is bent? The myth of child-rearing influences on personality development. *Journal of Counseling and Development*, **68**(6), 606–612.

Rummel, N., Levin, J.R. and Woodward, M.M. (2003) Do pictorial mnemonic text-learning aids give students something worth writing about? *Journal of Educational Psychology*, **95**(2), 327.

Rusbult, C.E., and Martz, J.M. (1995) Remaining in an abusive relationship: an investment model analysis of nonvoluntary commitment. *Personality and Social Psychology Bulletin*, **21**, 558–571.

Russek, H.I. and Zohman, B.L. (1958) Relative significance of heredity, diet and occupational stress in CHD of young adults. *American Journal of Medical Sciences*, **235**, 266–275.

Rutter, M. (1972, 1st edn; 1981, 2nd edn) *Maternal Deprivation Reassessed.* Harmondsworth, Penguin, Middlesex.

Rutter, M. and the ERA Study Team. (1998) Developmental catch-up and deficit following adoption after severe early privation. *Journal of Child Psychology and Psychiatry*, **39**, 465–476.

Ryback, R. S. (1969) The use of the goldfish as a model for alcohol amnesia in man. *Quarterly Journal of Studies on Alcohol*, **30**, 877–882.

Rymer, R. (1993) *Genie: Escape from a Silent Childhood.* Michael Joseph, London.

Sacher, W. (1993). Jugendgefährdung durch Video- und Computerspiele? [Is there a danger to youth from video and computer games?] *Zeitschrift für Pädagogik*, **39**, 313–333.

Sackheim, H.A., Haskett, R.F., Mulsant, B.H., Thase, M.E., Mann, J.J., Pettinati, H.M., Greenberg, R.M., Crowe, R.R., Cooper, T.B. and Prudic, J. (2001) Continuation pharmacotherapy in the prevention of relapse following electroconvulsive therapy: a randomized controlled trial. *JAMA: Journal of the American Medical Association*, **285**:1299–1307.

Sapolsky, R.M. (2000) *Why Zebras Don't Get Ulcers: An Updated Guide to Stress, Stress-Related Disease, and Coping.* W.H. Freeman and Company, New York.

Sashidharan, S, P. (2001) Institutional racism in British psychiatry. *Psychological Bulletin*, **25**, 244–247.

Sattler, J. (1982) *Assessment of Children's Intelligences and Special Abilities*. Allyn and Bacon, Boston.

Savin, H.B. (1973) Professors and psychological researchers: conflicting values in conflicting roles. *Cognition*, **2**, 147–149.

Scarr, S. (1992) Developmental theories for the 1990s: development and individual differences. *Child Development*, **63**, 1–19.

Scarr, S. and McCartney, K. (1983) How people make their own environments: a theory of genotype-environment effects. *Child Development*, **54**, 424–435.

Schachter, D.L. (1996). *Searching for Memory: The Brain, the Mind, and the Past*. Basic Books, New York.

Schachter, S. (1951) Deviation, rejection and communication, *Journal of Abnormal and Social Psychology*, **46**, 190–207.

Schaefer, C., Coyne, J.C. and Lazarus, R.S. (1981) The health-related functions of social support. *Journal of Behavioral Medicine*, **4**(4), 381–406.

Schaffer, H.R. and Emerson, P.E. (1964) The development of social attachments in infancy. *Monographs of the Society for Research in Child Development*, **29**(3), serial no. 94.

Schell, F.J., Allolio, B. and Schonecke, O.W. (1994) Physiological and psychological effects of Hatha-Yoga exercise in healthy women. *International Journal of Psychonomics*, **41**(1–4), 46–52.

Schellenberg, E.G. (2004). Music lessons enhance IQ. *Psychological Science*, **15**, 511–514.

Schmitt, R.C. (1967) Differential mortality in Honolulu before 1900. *Hawaii Medical Journal*, **26**(6), 537–542.

Schoenthaler, S.J. and Bier, I.D. (1999) Vitamin-mineral intake and intelligence: a macrolevel analysis of randomized controlled trials. *Journal of Alternative and Complementary Medicine*, **5**(2), 125–134.

Schunk, D. H. (1983) Reward contingencies and the development of children's skills and self-efficacy. *Journal of Educational Psychology*, **75**, 511–518.

Schweinhart, L.J., Barnes, H.V. and Weikart, D.P. (1993) Significant benefits: the High/Scope Perry Preschool Study through age 27. *Monographs of the High/Scope Educational Research Foundation*, **10**, High/Scope Press, Ypsilanti, MI.

Scott, J.E. and Dixon, L.B. (1995) Psychological interventions for schizophrenia. *Schizophrenia Bulletin*, **21**(4), 621–630.

Scott, S. (2006) Improving children's lives, preventing criminality: Where next? *The Psychologist*, **19**(8), 484–487.

Scottish Executive (2005) Anti-racism Wave 4: Post-Campaign Evaluation Summary. www.scotland.gov.uk/Publications/2005/06/2895508/55101 (accessed August 2006).

Scoville, W.B. and Milner, B. (1957). Loss of recent memory after bilateral hippocampal lesions. *Journal of Neurology, Neurosurgery, and Psychiatry*, **20**, 11–21.

Sebrechts, M.M., Marsh, R.L. and Seaman, J.G. (1989) Secondary memory and very rapid forgetting. *Memory and Cognition*, **17**, 693–700.

Segal, S.P. (1978) Attitudes toward the mentally ill: a review. *Social Work*, **23**(3), 211–217.

Seligman, M.E.P. (1971) Phobias and preparedness. *Behaviour Therapy*, **2**, 307–320.

Selye, H. (1936) A syndrome produced by diverse nocuous agents. *Nature*, **138**, 32.

Selye, H. (1950) *Stress*. Acta Inc Med Publ., Montreal.

Serpell, R. (1979) How specific are perceptual skills? A cross-cultural study of pattern recognition. *British Journal of Psychology*, **70**, 365–380.

Shallice, T. (1967) Temporal summation and absolute brightness threshold. *British Journal of Mathematical and Statistical Psychology*, **20**, 129–162.

Shapiro, D. (2006) Self-reproach and personal responsibility. *Psychiatry*, **69**(1), 21–25.

Shaver, P.R., Furman, W. and Buhrmester, D. (1985) Transition to college: network changes, social skills and loneliness. In: *Understanding Personal Relationships* (ed. Duck, S.W. and Perlman, D.). Sage, London.

Sheridan, C.L. and Radmacher, S.A. (1992) *Health Psychology*. John Wiley and Sons, New York.

Sherif, M. (1935) A study of some factors in perception. *Archives of Psychology*, **27**, no. 187.

Sherif, M., Harvey, O.J., White, B.J., Hood, W.R. and Sherif, C.W. (1954) *Experimental Study of Positive and Negative Intergroup Attitudes between Experimentally Produced Groups. Robbers' Cave Study.* University of Oklahoma Press, Norman.

Shils, E. (1954) Authoritarianism, 'Right' and 'Left'. In: *Studies in the Method and Scope of the Authoritarian Personality* (ed. Christie, R. and Jahoda, M.). Free Press, Glencoe, IL.

Shumaker, S.A. and D.R. Hill (1991) Gender differences in social support and physical health. *Health Psychology*, **10**, 102–111.

Simon, H.A. (1974) How big is a chunk? *Science*, **183**, 482–488.

Simpson, J.A., Gangestad, S., and Lerma, M. (1990) Perception of physical attractiveness: mechanisms involved in the maintenance of romantic relationships. *Journal of Personality and Social Psychology*, **59**, 1192–1201.

Simpson, K. (2001) The role of testosterone in aggression. *McGill Journal of Medicine*, **6**, 32–40.

Singh, S.P. (1994) Community environment is stressful. *British Medical Journal: Letters*, **308**, 1235–1237.

Skarnulis, L. (2004) www.medicinenet. com/script/main/art.asp?articlekey=52360 (accessed December 2005).

Skeels, H. (1966) Adult status of children with contrasting early life experiences: a follow-up study. *Monographs of Society for Research of Child Development*, **31**(3), whole issue.

Skeels, H. and Dye, H.B. (1939) A study of the effects of differential stimulation on mentally retarded children. *Proceedings and Addresses of the American Association on Mental Deficiency*, **44**,114–136.

Skodak, M. and Skeels, H. (1949) A final follow-up study of 100 adopted children. *Journal of Genetic Psychology*, **75**, 85–125.

Slater, M.D., Henry, K.L., Swaim, R.C. and Anderson, L.L. (2003) Violent media content and aggressiveness in adolescents: a downward spiral model. *Communication Research*, **30**(6), 713–736.

Sloane, R.B., Staples, F.R., Cristol, A.H., Yorkston, N.J. and Whipple, K. (1975) *Short-term Analytically Oriented Psychotherapy vs Behaviour Therapy.* Harvard University Press, Cambridge, MA.

Small, M.F. (1998) *Our Babies, Ourselves: How Biology and Culture Shape the Way We Parent.* Random House, New York.

Smith, C.R. (1991) *Learning Disabilities: The Interaction of Learner, Task and Setting.* Allyn and Bacon, Boston.

Smith, J.C. and Glass, G.V. (1977) Meta-analysis of psychotherapy outcome studies. *American Psychologist*, **32**(9), 752–760.

Smith, J.C., Glass, G.V. and Miller, T.I. (1980) *The Benefits of Psychotherapy.* Johns Hopkins University Press, Baltimore.

Smith, L. (2005) Too few black and Asian faces at the top. *The Guardian*, 17 November.

Smith, P. and Bond, M.H. (1993) *Social Psychology across Cultures: Analysis and perspectives.* Harvester Wheatsheaf, New York.

Smith, P.K., Cowie, H. and Blades, M. (2003) *Understanding Children's Development*, 4th edn. Basil Blackwell, Oxford.

Snowman, J., Krebs, E.W. and Lockhart, L. (1980) Improving recall of information from prose in high-risk students through learning strategy training. *Journal of Instructional Psychology*, 7(1), 35–40.

Sommers-Flanagan, J. and Sommers-Flanagan, R. (1996) Efficacy of antidepressant medication on depressed youth: what psychologists should know. *Professional Psychology: Research and Practice*, **27**, 145–153.

Sonstroem, R.J. (1984). Exercise and self-esteem. *Exercise and Sports Sciences Review*, **12**, 123–155.

Spearman, C. (1904) General intelligence, objectively determined and measured. *American Journal of Psychology*, **15**, 201–293.

Sperling. G. (1960) The information available in brief visual presentations, *Psychological Monographs*, **74**(Whole no. 498), 1–29.

Spitz, R.A. and Wolf, K.M. (1946) Anaclitic depression. *Psychoanalytic Study of the Child*, **2**, 313–342.

Spitzer, R., and Fleiss, J. (1974). A re-analysis of the reliability of psychiatric diagnosis. *British Journal of Psychiatry*, **125**, 341–347.

Squire, L.R., Ojemann, J.G., Miezin, F.M., Petersen, S.E., Videen, T.O., and Raichle, M.E. (1992) Activation of the hippocampus in normal humans: a functional anatomical study of memory. *Proceedings of the National Academy of Science*, **89**, 1837–1841.

Sroufe, L.A., Carlson, E.A., Levy, A.K., and Egeland, B. (1999) Implications of attachment theory for developmental psychopathology. *Development and Psychopathology*, **11**, 1–13.

Stalder, D.R. (2005) Learning and motivational benefits of acronym use in Introductory Psychology. *Teaching of Psychology*, **32**(4), 222–228.

Sternberg, R.J. (1988) *The Triarchic Mind: A New Theory of Intelligence.* Viking Press, New York.

Sternberg, R.J. (1995). *In Search of the Human Mind*. Harcourt Brace, Fort Worth, TX.

Sternberg, R.J. (2000) The holey grail of general intelligence. *Science*, **289**(5478), 399–401.

Sternberg, R.J. and Grigorenko, E.L. (2004) Successful intelligence in the classroom. *Theory into Practice*, **43**(4), 274–280.

Sue, D., Sue, D. and Sue, S. (1994) *Understanding Abnormal Behaviour*, 4th edn. Houghton Mifflin Co., Boston.

Sutton, C., Utting, D. and Farrington, D. (2004) *Early Origins of Anti-social Behaviour: Support from the Start. Working with Young Children and their Families to Reduce the Risks of Cime and Anti-social Behaviour.* Research Report 524. Department for Education and Skills, London.

Steele, C.M. and Aronson, J. (1995) Stereotype threat and the intellectual test performance of African Americans. *Journal of Personality and Social Psychology*, **69**, 797–811.

Stephan, W.G. (1978) School desegregation: an evaluation of predictions made in Brown v. Board of Education. *Psychological Bulletin*, **85**, 217–238.

Størksen, I., Røysamb, E., Moum, T. and Tambs, K. (2005) Adolescents with a childhood experience of parental divorce: a longitudinal study of mental health and adjustment. *Journal of Adolescence*, **28**, 725–739.

Sun, Y. (2001). Family environment and adolescents' well-being before and after parents' marital disruption: a longitudinal analysis. *Journal of Marriage and Family*, **63**, 697–713.

Surgeon General's Scientific Advisory Committee on Television and Social Behaviour (1972) *Television and Growing Up: The Impact of Televised Violence.* US Government Printing Office, Washington, DC.

Swim, J.K., Hyers, L.L., Cohen, L.L., and Ferguson, M.J. (2001) Everyday sexism: evidence for its incidence, nature, and psychological impact from three daily diary studies. *Journal of Social Issues*, **57**, 31–54.

Symanski, D.M. (2005) Heterosexism and sexism as correlates of psychological distress in lesbians. *Journal of Counselling and Development*, **83**, 355–360.

Szasz, T.S. (1960) *The Myth of Mental Illness.* Paladin, London.

Szasz, T.S. (1974) *Ideology and Insanity.* Penguin, Harmondsworth, Middlesex.

Szasz, T.S. (2000) Mental disorders are not diseases. *USA Today Magazine.* January, p. 165

Tache, J., Selye, H. and Day, S. (1979). *Cancer, Stress, and Death.* Plenum Press, New York.

Tajfel, H. (1970) Experiments in intergroup discrimination. *Scientific American*, **223**, 96–105.

Tajfel, H. and Turner, J.C. (1979) An integrative theory of intergroup conflict. In: *The Social Psychology of Intergroup Relations* (ed. Austin, W.G. and Worchel, S.). Brooks/Cole, Monterey, CA, pp. 33–47.

Takahashi, K. (1990) Are the key assumptions of the 'strange situation' universal? *Human Development*, **33**, 23–30.

Tarrier, N., Yusupoff, L., Kinney, C., McCarthy, E., Gledhill, A., Haddock, G. and Morris, J. (1998) Ramdomised controlled trial of intensive cognitive behaviour therapy for patients with chronic schizophrenia. *British Medical Journal*, **317**, 303–307.

Taylor, S.E., Klein, L.C., Lewis, B.P., Grunewald, T.L., Gurung, R.A.R. and Updegraff, J.A. (2000) Biobehavioral responses to stress in females: tend-and-befriend, not fight-or-flight. *Psychological Review*, **107**(3), 411–429.

Temoshok, L. (1987) Personality, coping style, emotions, and cancer: towards an integrative model. *Cancer Surveys*, **6**, 545–567 (supplement).

Thase M.E., Trivedi M.H. and Rush A.J. (1995) MAOIs in the contemporary treatment of depression. *Neuropsychopharmacology*, **12**(3),185–219.

Theilgaard, A. 1984. A psychological study of the personalities of XYY and XXY men. *Acta Psychiatrica Scandinavica* (suppl.) **315**, 1–133.

Thibaut, J.W., and Kelley, H.H. (1959) *The Social Psychology of Groups*. Wiley, New York.

Thomson, D.V. and Tulving, E. (1970). Associative encoding and retrieval: weak and strong cues. *Journal of Experimental Psychology*, **86**, 255–262.

Thurstone, L.L. (1938) Primary mental abilities. *Psychometric Monographs, no.***1**.

Tinbergen, N. (1951) *The Study of Instinct*. Clarendon Press, Oxford.

Torgersen, S. (1983) Genetic factors in anxiety disorders. *Archives of General Psychiatry*, **40**, 1085–1089.

Torrey, E.F. (2002) Studies of individuals never treated with antipsychotic medications: a review. *Schizophrenia Research*, **58**(2–3), 101–115.

Triseliotis, J. (1984) Identity and security in adoption and long-term fostering. *Early Child Development and Care*, **15**(2–3), 149–170.

Trivers, R.L. (1972) Parental investment and sexual selection. In: *Sexual Selection and the Descent of Man* (ed. Campbell, B.). Aldine, Chicago.

Trojano, L. and Grossi, D. (1995) Phonological and lexical coding in verbal short-term memory and learning. *Brain and Cognition*, **21**, 336–54.

Tronick, E.Z., Morelli, G.A. and Ivey, P.K. (1992) The Efe forager infant and toddler's pattern of social relationships: multiple and simultaneous. *Developmental Psychology*, **28**, 568–577.

Tscham, J., Johnston, J., Kline, M., and Wallerstein, J. (1990) Conflict, loss, change and parent-child relationships: predicting children's adjustment during divorce. *Journal of Divorce*, **13**(4), 1–22.

TUC (2000a) *Black and Excluded*. TUC Publications, London.

TUC (2000b) *Qualifying for Racism*. TUC Publications, London.

Tulving, E. (1968) Theoretical issues in free recall. In: *Verbal Behaviour and General Behaviour Theory* (ed. Dixon, T. and D. Horton, D.). Prentice-Hall, Englewood Cliffs, N.J.

Tulving, E. and Psotka, J. (1971) Retroactive inhibition in free recall: inaccessibility of information available in the memory store. *Journal of Experimental Psychology*, **87**, 1–8.

Turkheimer, E., Haley, A., Waldron, M., D'Onofrio, B. and Gottesman, I.I. (2003) Socioeconomic status modifies heritability of IQ in young children. *Psychological Science*, **14**, 623–628.

Turkington, D. and McKenna, P. J. (2003) Is cognitive–behavioural therapy a worthwhile treatment for psychosis? *British Journal of Psychiatry*, **182**, 477–479.

Tyerman, A. and Spencer, C. (1983) A critical test of the Sherifs' Robbers' Cave experiments: intergroup competition and cooperation between groups of well-acquainted individuals. *Small Group Behavior*, **14**, 515–531.

Underwood, J. (1957) Interference and forgetting. *Psychological Review*, **64**, 49–60.

Van Avermaet, E. (1996) Social influence in small groups. In: *Introduction to Social Psychology: A European Perspective* (ed. Hewstone, M. Stroebe, W. and Stephenson, G.M.). Blackwell Publishers, Cambridge, MA.

Van IJzendoorn, M.H. and Kroonenberg, P.M. (1988) Cross-cultural patterns of attachment: a meta-analysis of the Strange Situation. *Child Development*, **59**, 147–156.

Veitch, R. and Griffitt, W. (1976) Good news, bad news: affective and interpersonal effects. *Journal of Applied Social Psychology*, **6**, 69–75.

Vernon, P.E. (1950) *The Structure of Human Abilities*. Methuen, London.

Vollebergh, W. (1991) *The Limits of Tolerance*. Rijksuniversiteit te Utrecht, Utrecht.

Waganaar, W.A. and Groeneweg, J. (1990) The memory of concentration camp survivors. *Applied Cognitive Psychology*, **4**, 77–87.

Wahl, O. F. (1992) Mass media images of mental illness: a review of the literature. *Journal of Community Psychology*, **20**, 343–352.

Walker, I. and Crogan, M. (1998) Academic performance, prejudice and the Jigsaw classroom: new pieces to the puzzle. *Journal of Community and Applied Social Psychology*, **8**, 381–393.

Wallerstein, J. (1983) Children of divorce: the psychological tasks of the child. *American Journal of Orthopsychiatry*, **53**, 230–243.

Wallerstein, J. L., and Blakeslee, S. (2000) The *Unexpected Legacy of Divorce: A 25-Year Landmark Study*. Hyperion, New York.

Wallerstein, J.S., and Kelly, J.B. (1980) *Surviving the Breakup: How Children and Parents Cope with Divorce*. Basic Books, New York.

Wallerstein, J.S. and Lewis, J. (1998) The long-term impact of divorce on children: a first report from a 25-year study. *Family and Conciliation Courts Review*, **36**, 368–383.

Walster, E.H. and Walster, G.W. (1969) The matching hypothesis. *Journal of Personality and Social Psychology*, 6, 248–253.

Walster, E., Aronson, V., Abrahams, D., and Rottman, L. (1966) The importance of physical attractiveness in dating behaviour.

Walster, E., Walster, G.W., and Berscheid, E. (1978) *Equity: Theory and Research*. Allyn and Bacon, Boston.

Walster, E., Aronson, V., Abrahams, D. and Rottmann, L. (1966) Importance of physical attractivenss in dating behaviour. *Journal of Personality and Social Psychology*, **4**, 508–516.

Wampold, B.E., Minami, T., Baskin, T.W. and Tierney, S.C. (2002) A meta-(re) analysis of the effects of cognitive therapy versus 'other therapies' for depression. *Journal of Affective Disorders*, **68**, 159–165.

Watson, J.B., and Rayner, R. (1920) Conditioned emotional reactions. *Journal of Experimental Psychology*, **3**, 1–14.

Waugh, N.C. and Norman, D. (1965) Primary memory. *Psychological Review*, **72**, 89–104.

Waynforth, D., and Dunbar, R.I.M. (1995) Conditional mate choice strategies in humans: evidence from 'lonely hearts' advertisements. *Behaviour*, **132**, 755–779.

Weg, R.B. (1983) Changing physiology of ageing. In: *Ageing: Scientific Perspectives and Social Issues*, 2nd edn (ed. Woodruff, D.S. and Birren, J.E.). Brooks/Cole, Monterey.

Weick, K. E., Gilfillian, D. P. and Keith, T. A. (1973) The effect of composer credibility on orchestra performance. *Sociometry*, **36**, 435–462.

Weiss, L. H. and Schwarz, J.C. (1996) The relationship between parenting types and older adolescents' personality, academic achievement, adjustment, and substance use. *Child Development*, **67**(5), 2101–2114.

Wender, P., Kety, H., Rosenthal, D., Schulsinger, F., Orthmann, J. and Lunde, I. (1986) Psychiatric disturbance in the biological and adoptive families of adopted individuals with affective disorder. *Archives of General Psychiatry*, **43**, 923–929.

Wheeler, L.R. (1942) A comparative study of the intelligence of East Tennessee mountain children. *Journal of Educational Psychology*, **33**, 321–334.

White, D.W. and Woolett, A. (1992) *Families: A Context for Development*. Falmer, London.

WHO (World Health Report) (2001) *Mental Health: New Understanding, New Hope*. World Health Organization, Geneva.

Wickrama, K.A.S., Lorenz, F.O., Conger, R.D. and Elder, G.H. Jr (1997) Marital quality and physical illness: a latent growth curve analysis. *Journal of Marriage and the Family*, **59**, 143–155.

Widdowson, E.M. (1951) Mental contentment and physical growth. *Lancet*, **1**, 1316–1318.

Wiebe, D.J. (1991) Hardiness and stress modification: a test of proposed mechanisms. *Journal of Personality and Social Psychology*, **64**, 491–499.

Williams, L.M. (1994) Recall of childhood tauma: a prospective study of women's memories of childhood abuse. *Journal of Consulting and Clinical Psychology*, **62**, 1167–1176.

Williams, R.L. (1972) *The BITCH Test (Black Intelligence Test of Cultural Homogeneity)*. Washington University, St. Louis, MI.

Williams, T.M. (ed.) (1986) *The Impact of Television: A National Experiment in Three Communities*. Academic Press, New York.

Williams, T.P. and Sogon, S. (1984) Group composition and conforming behaviour in Japanese students. *Japanese Psychological Research*, **26**, 231–234.

Wilson, C.M. and Oswald, A.J. (2005) How does marriage affect physical and psychological health? A survey of the longitudinal evidence. www2.warwick. ac.uk/fac/soc/economics/staff/faculty/oswald/healthlong2005.pdf. (accessed June 2006).

Wolff, G., Pathare, S., Craig, T. and Leff, J. (1996) Community knowledge of mental illness and reaction to mentally ill people. *British Journal of Psychiatry*, **168**, 191–198.

Worrell, J. and Remer, P. (1992) *Feminist Perspectives in Therapy*. Chichester, Hants: Wiley.

YouGov (2002) *Municipal Journal*, 4 July.

Zebrowitz, L.A. and Montepare, J.M. (2000) Too young, too old: stigmatizing adolescents and the elderly. In: *Stigma* (ed. Heatherton, T., Kleck, R., Hull, J.G. and Hebl, M.). Guilford Publications, NY, pp. 334–373.

Zigler, E. and Styfco, S.J. (1993) Using research and theory to justify and inform Head Start expansion. *Social Policy Report, Society for Research in Child Development*, **7**, 1–21.

Zigler, E.F., Abelson, W.D. and Seitz, V. (1973) Motivational factors in the performance of economically disadvantaged children on the Peabody Picture Vocabulary test. *Child Development*, **44**, 294–303.

Zillmann, D. (1971) Excitation transfer in communication-mediated aggressive behavior. *Journal of Experimental Social Psychology*, **7**, 419–434.

Zillmann, D. (1979) *Hostility and Aggression*. Erlbaum, Hillsdale, NJ.

Zillmann, D. (1988) Cognition-excitation interdepencies in aggressive behaviour. *Aggressive Behaviour*, **14**, 51–64.

Zimbardo, P.G. (1969) The human choice: individuation, reason and order versus deindividuation, impulse and chaos. *Nebraska Symposium on Motivation*, **17**, 237–307.

Zimbardo, P.G., Banks, P.G., Haney, C. and Jaffe, D. (1973) Pirandellian prison: the mind is a formidable jailor. *New York Times Magazine*, 8 April, 38–60.

# Index